signing

HOW TO SPEAK WITH YOUR HANDS

hooked on the memory of u
- neil diamond

signing

HOW TO SPEAK WITH YOUR HANDS

Revised Edition

ELAINE COSTELLO
Illustrated by Lois A. Lehman

BANTAM BOOKS
TORONTO • NEW YORK • LONDON • SYDNEY • AUCKLAND

SIGNING: HOW TO SPEAK WITH YOUR HANDS

A Bantam Book / September 1995
19 printings in previous edition through 1994

Illustrated by Lois A. Lehman
Cover and chapter pages designed by Jerry Pfeifer.

For information address: Bantam Books.

Library of Congress Cataloging-in-Publication Data

Costello, Elaine.
Signing : how to speak with your hands / Elaine Costello ; illustrated by Lois A. Lehman. — Rev. ed.
p. cm.
Includes bibliographical references and index.
ISBN 0-553-37539-3
1. Sign Language. I. Title.
HV2474.C67 1995
419—dc20 *94-46156*
CIP

Published simultaneously in the United States and Canada

Bantam Books are published by Bantam Books, a division of Bantam Doubleday Dell Publishing Group, Inc. Its trademark, consisting of the words "Bantam Books" and the portrayal of a rooster, is Registered in U.S. Patent and Trademark Office and in other countries. Marca Registrada. Bantam Books, 1540 Broadway, New York, New York 10036.

PRINTED IN THE UNITED STATES OF AMERICA

SEM 10 9 8 7 6 5 4 3

contents

acknowledgments

Deep appreciation is due to many people who helped bring this book to completion. Foremost is Gabriel Fontana, who had faith in my ability to do it and applauded as each milestone in the book's completion was passed. He made available the staff and facilities of Fontana Lithograph, Inc. and lent many personal hours in processing photographs, organizing sections, and generally lending support and assistance.

Without the talent of the illustrator, Lois Lehman, this book would not have been completed. She gave the book credibility and beauty at the same time through her incredible skill.

The critical molding provided by consultants has insured the book's accuracy. Gerald Buisson and Margaret Buisson reviewed early illustrations and assisted in developing the sign descriptions. Harry Hoemann and Larry Berke provided the final reviews to assure that all aspects of the book were linguistically sound.

This book might well be considered a family project since it took precedence over other aspects of family life while it was being developed. My daughters, Jennifer, Maria, and Laura, cleaned house, cooked meals, and otherwise provided for themselves when Mom was engrossed in writing. They typed rough drafts, sorted illustrations, developed photographs, and even moved the typewriter and boxes of resource materials along on family vacations.

The sign models illustrated in this book provided much more than their likenesses. They served the dual role of posing for endless photographs and of providing consultation in determining the most representative signs to use. Their names are listed below in grateful recognition.

Sign Models

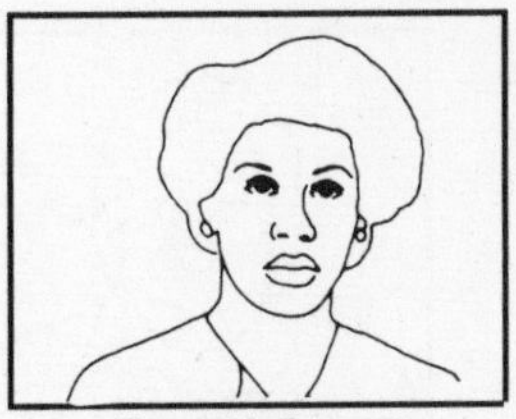

Karen M. Barnes

John S. Borum, Jr.

Clifford P. Bruffey

Ruth A. Bruffey

Cheryl K. Bruffey

Joshua Bruffey

Alan Cheifetz

Ellryne T. Coles

D'Anne Cummings

Pat Cunningham

Lee W. Ethridge

Mary Beth Ethridge

Mary Helen Figueroa

Jeri L. Gamble

Theodora Ing

Gary M. Jackson

Vera Jackson

Cathy L. Kruger

Bob H. Lenderman

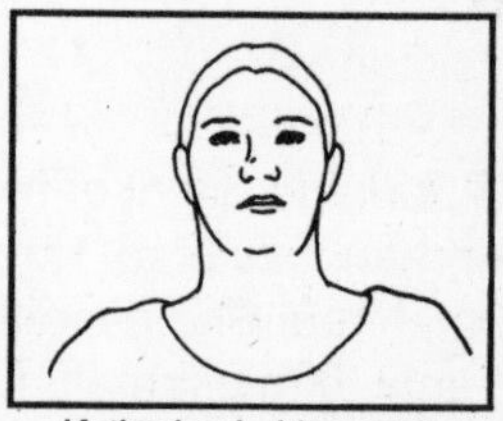
Katherine L. Lipscomb

Bennett H. Meyers

Gladys Z. Miller

Ralph R. Miller, Sr.

Ramesh Mirchandani

Frank W. Post

Cynthia Schaeffer

Kathy Seymour

Melinda J. Smith

introduction

In recent years sign language has shown an amazing growth in popularity. Thousands of individuals of all ages are discovering that the study of sign language can be a fascinating and rewarding adventure. *Signing: How to Speak With Your Hands* is designed to assist you in learning this vibrant, expressive language that is used by Deaf people throughout North America.

This book makes sign language study easier in many ways. It presents manageable amounts of new sign vocabulary within logical topical groupings. The illustrations are large and clear, presenting the full upper torso of the body so that the new signer can accurately duplicate the sign. Even though it is difficult to isolate any sign from its context, Lois Lehman has achieved a rare degree of accuracy in rendering each sign the way it is most commonly performed.

At the beginning of each chapter, linguistic principles are described which will broaden the use of the sign vocabulary presented in the book. This information about the structure of sign language comes from recent research into its grammatical features. Incorporating these principles into your signing will help you master the language as it is used by Deaf people.

This book does not contain all of the signs available in sign language. These 1,300 basic signs will provide enough vocabulary to express a vast number of ideas when coupled with the linguistic principles that are included. To use sign language fluently, you will find it necessary to practice your new skills with other signers. The more you associate with Deaf people, the easier it will become for you to send and receive information through sign language.

Introduction to Deafness

In the United States it is estimated that 32 million people have hearing losses of varying degrees of severity. Of this number, approximately two million individuals have hearing losses severe enough to be considered deaf. That is, they cannot hear or understand either speech or most of the sounds in the everyday environment, even with the help of a hearing aid. This population is comprised both of persons who have been deaf since infancy and persons who lost their hearing later in life.

Some of the causes of deafness are heredity, illness, physical abnormalities, trauma to the skull or ear, certain heavy medications, and, most common, loss of hearing acuity due to age. Hearing losses that are caused by diseases or obstructions in the outer ear can sometimes be corrected by surgery or a hearing aid. Hearing losses that result from damage to the auditory nerve to the brain are usually not candidates for surgery, and hearing aids cannot repair the damage.

Problems in the use of the English language typically persist throughout a Deaf person's life. Those who lose their hearing in infancy or at birth usually do not benefit from language stimulation from their parents and siblings during the early years when language is acquired. However, by learning sign language, deaf children can acquire the language base that will assist in the acquisition of English as a second language. People who lose their hearing after acquiring English language skills have less of an academic handicap than those who are born deaf.

Deaf people are employed in almost every occupational field. They drive cars, get married, buy homes, and have children, much like everyone else. Because of communication factors, many Deaf people are more comfortable in association with other Deaf people. They tend to marry other Deaf people whom they have met at schools for the deaf or at Deaf clubs. Most Deaf couples have hearing children who learn sign language early in life to communicate with their parents. Deaf people often have special electronics and telecommunication equipment in their homes. They may rely on Closed Captioning to watch television either by having a decoder or a television with a built-in decoder chip to reveal the captions. Electrical hook-ups may flash lights to indicate when the baby is crying, the doorbell is ringing, or the alarm clock is going off. Telecommunication devices that are modern versions of teletype equipment permit Deaf people to be in contact with other Deaf people through the telephone system. And every state now has relay systems whereby relay operators can bridge telephone gaps between Deaf people with telecommunication devices wishing to communicate with hearing people who do not have such devices.

When Deaf people have difficulty communicating with hearing people, they will often write notes to them. Some Deaf people are able to speechread, that is, to understand the mouth movements and facial expressions of a hearing person to comprehend what is said; but most Deaf people have limited speechreading skill, which is said to convey at best only about 50 percent of the communicated information. In education, medical, religious, or legal situations, when detailed information must be understood, Deaf people will often enlist the assistance of a certified sign language interpreter who will translate the spoken English information into sign language and then vocalize in English what the Deaf person signs.

What is Sign Language?

Sign language is a visual-gestural system of communication. It is the native language of Deaf people and was created by Deaf people for the purpose of communicating with each other. Within the Deaf community sign language is learned naturally as a first language from childhood. However, unlike most languages, sign language is more often passed on from child to child rather than from parent to child. This is because 90 percent of deaf children are born to hearing parents who do not know sign language. It has been shown that in isolated locations where there is no formal sign language, Deaf people will create their own visual-gestural language to communicate. Few hearing people master sign language fluency as well as a native user because for them, spoken languages are learned during the formative years of language acquisition, and sign language is learned as a second language with great effort. Hearing children whose parents are deaf learn sign language naturally and often become excellent interpreters.

The term *sign language* is used to describe all forms of manual communication. In this book, however, sign language will refer to American Sign Language, the language used by approximately one-half million Deaf people in the United States and Canada. Not all Deaf people use American Sign Language, but those who do share this common language bond are considered members of the *Deaf community*. The Deaf community, like other sub-cultures, is comprised of people who share common values, experiences, and, most importantly, a common language, which becomes their primary identifying feature. Members of the Deaf community, regardless of the severity of their hearing loss, must know and use American Sign Language in order to be included. Their language becomes the vehicle by which experiences are shared and passed on.

Not a lot is known of sign language use in the United States prior to 1815. It is known that quite a number of Deaf people lived in Martha's Vineyard, an island off the coast of Cape Cod where everyone, Deaf and hearing, spoke to each other using sign language. At that time, it was estimated that there were approximately 2,000 Deaf people in the United States. Certainly, as demonstrated by other isolated cultures, those Deaf people had established a sign language system for communicating with each other. Whether they developed it themselves or brought it from Europe is not known, but it is estimated that approximately 40 percent of American Sign Language as it is used today may be related to those early colonial signs.

In 1815, Thomas Hopkins Gallaudet went to Europe to study methods for instructing Deaf individuals. His first stop was England. There he was discouraged from learning the English methods because his instructors wanted him to stay for a long period of time to work with them; he had neither the time nor the money for an extended stay. During the time he was negotiating with the English experts, Gallaudet saw a demonstration by a visiting French lecturer, Abbé Sicard. He was so impressed by Sicard's method that he traveled to France to study with him. Gallaudet returned to the United States with a new-found knowledge of French signs and a Deaf Frenchman, Laurent Clerc, who became the first teacher of the Deaf in the United States. During his forty years of teaching, Clerc had great influence on shaping the language used by Deaf Americans. American Sign Language is heavily based on French Sign Language, with approximately 60 percent of present-day signs having their origins from the French.

American Sign Language is one of the most complete sign systems in the world. Most countries, however, have their own sign languages which have been refined and standardized with varying degrees of sophistication. A Deaf person traveling abroad would not immediately be able to converse with a Deaf person in another country without studying the sign language of that country as a foreign language, although communication barriers between different sign languages seem to be crossed more easily than those of spoken languages.

In an attempt to encourage international sign language communication, the World Federation of the Deaf is developing an international sign language called Gestuno. The lexicon of Gestuno consists of signs chosen by an international committee. The signs are not invented, but are selected from existing sign systems. Although Gestuno is intended for interpreting at international meetings, few Deaf or hearing people know it well. Also the number of signs presently available is so limited that a great many concepts cannot be expressed. It is doubtful that Gestuno will become a full-fledged language because of the absence of grammatical rules. Each signer is permitted to use the vocabulary of Gestuno within the syntax of his or her local language. Also, since it is not used by the Deaf community in any country, it will never be a living language, learned and passed on from generation to generation.

Hearing people frequently study the signs from American Sign Language without studying the grammar of the language, and then use the signs in the syntactical order of their own verbal language, English. This mixture of spoken and gestural language leads to the creation of "pidgin" language systems which have been formalized by some educators. Instead of signs representing concepts, as originally intended, signs are used to represent the meanings of English words. Using signs within an English syntax provides a visual way for Deaf children to learn English. Also, since this language (called "Manual English" or "Sign English") is easier for hearing people to acquire than American Sign Language, it provides a valuable communication link between hearing and Deaf people. Because Deaf people are familiar with the difficulty hearing people experience in trying to learn their language, they will try to accommodate by dropping many aspects of sign language's grammar and assuming the syntax of English themselves. This process is called *code-switching* and is the reason why Deaf people often begin a conversation by asking whether the other person is deaf or hearing so they will know whether to use American Sign Language or a pidgin form to facilitate communication if the person is hearing.

Parts of a Sign

Signs perform a function in sign language similar to the function of words in spoken languages. Just as words work together in various ways to make each word unique from other words, so also there are four units that comprise each sign to make each one unique. These four units or parts are its (1) handshape; (2) palm orientation; (3) movement; and (4) the locations where these occur. An omission or alteration of any one of the four parts may cause the sign to become a completely different sign.

In addition to these four parts that comprise the manual characteristics of a sign, there are non-manual characteristics as well. The non-manual characteristics include movements of the face, eyes, head, and body posture. As the hands execute a given sign, specific non-manual body behavior can simultaneously change the meaning or emphasis of that sign. Some simple examples of non-manual signals include the raising of an eyebrow to indicate a question and the shaking of the head to express a negative condition. A study of the linguistics of American Sign Language would reveal many more sophisticated uses of non-manual signals which can be incorporated into the meaning of a sign.

Terminology of Sign Language

Some of the terms used to refer to sign language need clarification in order to be used correctly. First, it is correct to say that you are learning *sign language* or learning *to sign* no matter what variety of sign language is meant. It is also all right to say that you are learning manual communication, but it is not as common. Generally, it is not acceptable to refer to sign language as hand signs or gestures, since these terms do not give sign language credit for being a true language. The lexicon within sign language is referred to as *signs*. If you are specifying the native language used by Deaf people in the Deaf community, use *American Sign Language* or its abbreviation *ASL*.

The translation of a sign is referred to linguistically as it *gloss*, or equivalent, in English. Often a gloss has several English words to explain the concept that the sign represents. For example, one sign formed by bringing both extended index fingers in an arc from the right shoulder to pointing forward, palms facing up, has a three-word English gloss: "up-until-now."

In educational settings, the terms *total communication, Sign English, Manual English, Contact Sign*, and *fingerspelling* are often used. "Total communication" is a philosophical declaration that it is the right of each Deaf individual to have access to information through any and all modes available. The possible modes are aural stimulation when there is residual hearing, speech-reading, written forms, gestures, facial expression, sign language, and fingerspelling. The philosophy states that neglecting to provide a deaf child with any of these avenues may prohibit the child from full language development.

"Sign English" (not to be confused with Signed English) is the use of signs from American Sign Language within an English syntactical order. It is the sign language form with which hearing people are most familiar. It is not recognized as a true language, but rather a pidgin language, a blending of two distinct languages, retaining some of the characteristics of each. Generally when using Sign English, a hearing person will speak while signing; much of the facial expression characteristic of American Sign Language is thus lost. In using Sign English, word endings, tense, articles, and plurality as we know them in English are not used. Because Sign English is not a true language, there are not established linguistic rules which govern it. It may take many forms leaning toward a heavy influence of either American Sign Language or of English, depending on the person using it. Its purpose is to facilitate communication between Deaf people and hearing people.

"Manual English" is a generic classification for various sign systems which have been invented to replicate English exactly through signs. Some of the most common Manual English systems include Signed English, Seeing Essential English (SEE I), Seeing Exact English (SEE II), and Linguistics of Visual English (LOVE). All of these systems function as a visual representation of the English language. Many of the signs borrowed from American Sign Language are modified by adding the fingerspelled handshape of the first letter of the English gloss. For example, the American Sign Language sign for the concepts "listen," "hear," "ear," and "sound" is the same; however, in Manual English, the sign would be produced with a "L" handshape for "listen," an "h" handshape for "hear," and so forth. In this way, the sign vocabulary is increased and further clarified.

Manual English is not considered a language, but rather an invented code. Each Manual English system has a code, or set of rules, by which it represents the vocabulary and structure of English. The major complaint about these systems is that they change the natural function of signs to represent concepts and force them to function like English words, often violating the intend of the original signs. Invented affixes, articles, and other devices are used to specify tense, plurality, and other inflectional variations. For example, in the Signed English system a movement of the "i" handshape, palm facing forward, from left to right at the end of a verb sign, meaning that it is the suffix "ing" added to the end of the verb sign, e.g., "walk" becomes "walking." Inventors of these systems refer to them as teaching tools to be used in instructional settings and at home to increase the deaf user's knowledge of English.

"Fingerspelling," or representing each letter of each word with a specific hand configuration, is the only system for making English utterances completely visible. It has, ideally, one-to-one equivalence for sequential alphabetical symbols as found in words. It can be produced rapidly enough to keep pace with normal speaking, but it involves a high degree of concentration for both the sender and the receiver. The primary objection to the method is that it depends highly on reading skills which are not normally acquired by a young child until past the formative period of language acquisition, when language is most easily acquired with ease as a natural language. On the positive side, few aspects of English grammar are forfeited. Fingerspelling more frequently is used as a supplement to other sign systems than as a method of its own. It is usually used for those concepts which have no formal sign existing in sign language. Learning to fingerspell is more difficult than learning to sign for most people, but it is worth learning first because it can greatly expand any signer's ability to communicate.

Learning to Sign

Sign language is a beautiful and expressive way of communicating. Many signs are natural gestures. Other signs are based on some characteristic of the sign's concept. For example, for the sign "cup," one hand represents a saucer and the other hand encircles the shape of a cup. The relationship between the sign and what it represents is called its "iconicity," and it is this iconicity that makes sign language easier to learn. Research into each sign's origin would probably reveal more signs are iconically based on French than is presently thought. Because such research has not been done to date, it is not possible to know the origins of many signs, though sometimes the origins are fairly easy to guess or are well known. For example, a charming nineteenth-century flavor is evident in the signs for "girl," where the thumb traces the outline of a bonnet string, and for "boy," where the fingers tip an imaginary cap. The signs for "gentleman" and "lady" include the thumb coming up and fluffing the ruffles worn on shirts and blouses in earlier days. Knowing these historical origins contributes to the fun of learning sign language.

The only way to become proficient at sign language is to use it, preferably with Deaf people. If this is not possible, you should practice with other hearing people. Most hearing people learning to sign will use the signs from American Sign Language combined with English syntax, matching each sign with an equivalent English word within the sentence. Sign language is not so very difficult to learn; in fact, a sign language student can probably express simple thoughts after only a few lessons. However, total proficiency in American Sign Language as used by native signers will probably take years and years of study and practice.

Deaf people are usually pleased at a hearing person's attempts at sign language communication. They are patient and willing to assist. They are cognizant that hearing people use signs within an English syntax, and because they are familiar with English, they will often slow down and use signs in English order, too. You should not be hesitant to try out your limited sign language skill; you will be delighted at the encouragement you will get from deaf people for your efforts.

Here are some suggestions to help you use sign language in a natural way. Remember that a good signer incorporates facial expression and body language into what is said. Use natural expressive gestures with your signing to be most effective. The normal signing space extends from the top of the head to the waist, extending laterally from shoulder to shoulder. Hold your hands comfortably at chest level when you are in between signs. Whether or not you are considered a good signer will be judged by a number of factors. Clarity and accuracy of producing the sign, smoothness, rhythm, and speed of production will all contribute to your skill. The only way that skill can be developed is through practice with other people. If you speak while signing, keep an even flow of speed between the vocal and manual languages.

How the Signs Were Selected for This Book

Twenty years ago, it was estimated that there were between 1,500 and 2,000 formal signs that comprised all of American Sign Language's lexicon. However, in the same way that spoken languages increase in vocabulary, sign language is a living, growing language. New signs have developed, some of which have been accepted by deaf people as part of their language, and some of which are used only by selected groups in selected environments. For example, new technology has created a need for signs to represent equipment and processes not dreamed of in earlier years. In a work environment, deaf employees may invent signs to facilitate their communication on the job. then in describing their jobs to friends at the local deaf club, the new signs might be used and picked up by a wider circle of the deaf community. As those people take the signs home and use them, and perhaps, use them as they travel, the signs may or may not become assimilated into the language.

the process of how new signs are developed demonstrates why sign language has variations. The variations include "home signs," that is those used within an individual family unit, local variations, as described above, and regional variations. the variations might well be thought of as dialects, not right or wrong, but simply different ways of saying the same thing—just as there are different regional pronunciation of English words like "tomato" and "aunt."

The signs displayed in this book are those which are basic to everyday conversations. Although some arbitrary decisions were made as to which variation of a sign was included, most decisions were based on how clearly the alternatives could be illustrated and which signs the sign models and artist preferred to use. It is logical that because the book was developed in Washington, D.C., many of the signs reflect usage in that area. As much as possible, specific regional signs were omitted; but, sometimes it is difficult to judge whether a sign has achieved national acceptance or not.

how to use this book

The signs in this book have been grouped by topics for two reasons. The topics comprise a manageable number of signs that might easily be learned by a student in a single sitting. Second, signs within a category often share certain aspects of forming them that will assist the learner in remembering them. If the book is to be used as a dictionary or a resource manual, the index in the back of the book will become an indispensable aid. The alphabetical listing of the English glosses in the index will give quick and easy access to any sign in the book.

At the beginning of each of the chapters in this book are grammatical notes closely associated with signs in that chapter. These notes will give the reader insight into many of the linguistic rules which govern American Sign Language. The notes are not meant to be definitive, but to provide basic information to help integrate the sign vocabulary into a living, expressive language as used by Deaf people.

Each of the 1,300 entries in this book has four parts: a sign illustration; English gloss(es); directions for forming the sign; and a "hint." Each part of the entry is intended to make the sign as clear as possible and to help the learner remember the sign vocabulary so that it can be recalled whenever desired.

Sign Illustrations

The most prominent part of each entry is the sign illustration itself. Since sign language is three-dimensional, depicting signs as a flat image on paper requires the use of arrows and explanations. The sign illustrations in this book use multiple images along with arrows to describe the sign formation and movement as accurately as possible.

In order to keep the drawings uncluttered, the numbers "1" and "2" indicate the sequence in which the parts of a compound sign are formed. A compound sign is much like a compound word—the putting together of two signs to form a sign with new lexical meaning. An example of a compound sign is the sign "lunch," which is made up of the signs "eat" and "noon."

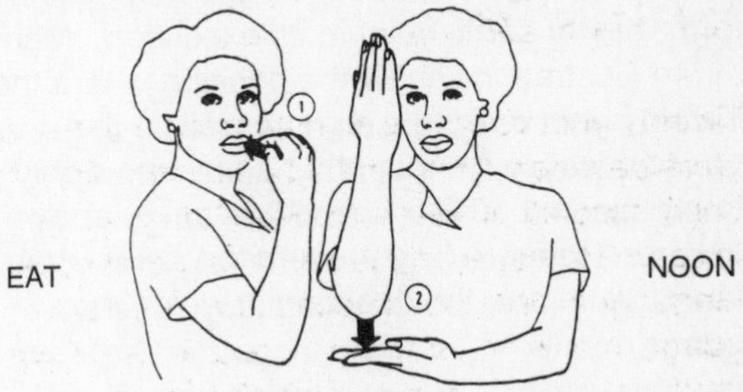

LUNCH

Generally, in this book, each part of a compound sign has the whole body of the signer drawn side-by-side and numbered to indicate that each part is a sign in and of itself.

The letters "a" and "b" are used in the illustrations to indicate a change of hand position or handshape in a sign. These letters are simply a device for showing the order in which the sign is formed. The second or subsequent hand positions are often shown in small circles to the left side of the main illustration. The sign for "mosquito" is an example of a sign made with a sequence of two handshapes and movements marked with "a" and "b."

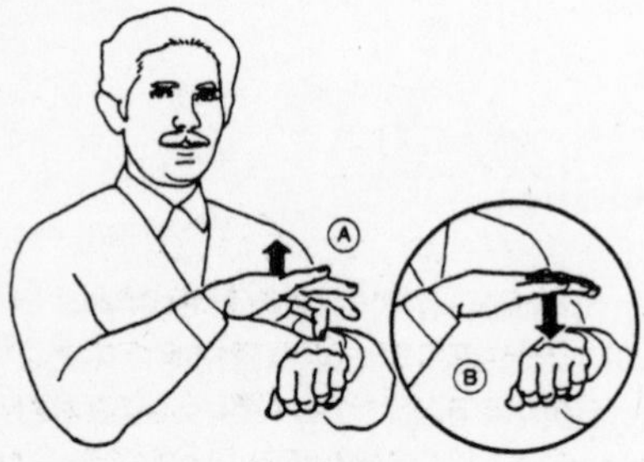

MOSQUITO

Most of the illustrations present the front view of the signer. This means that the illustrations are reversed from the way you would perform them yourself. For clarity's sake, some of the signs are drawn from a three-quarter view. All illustrations show a right-handed signer, and the descriptions are written for persons with a right-hand dominance. Left-handed signers should reverse the signs.

The illustrations represent a snapshot of sign formation at some point in its execution. Many of the illustrations show the position where the hands begin making a sign as well as the position where it ends; other signs show only the beginning position. In either case, arrows are used to more fully present the action that takes place and the direction in which the hands move.

English Glosses

Each entry is labeled with a boldface English word, or gloss, that most closely approximates the concept conveyed by the sign. In many cases, the sign may be used in various contexts to convey more than one English word, which are listed, too. These English words are not necessarily synonyms of each other, although they sometimes are. For example, the sign for "priest," in a different context may be used for "collar." And the sign for "box" is also the sign for "room," depending on the referent being discussed.

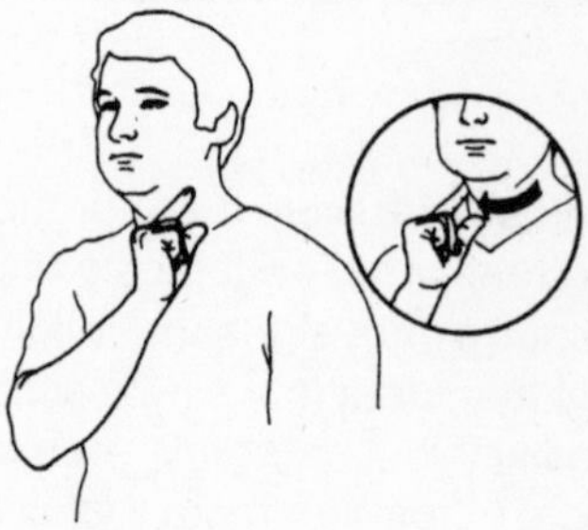

PRIEST or **COLLAR**

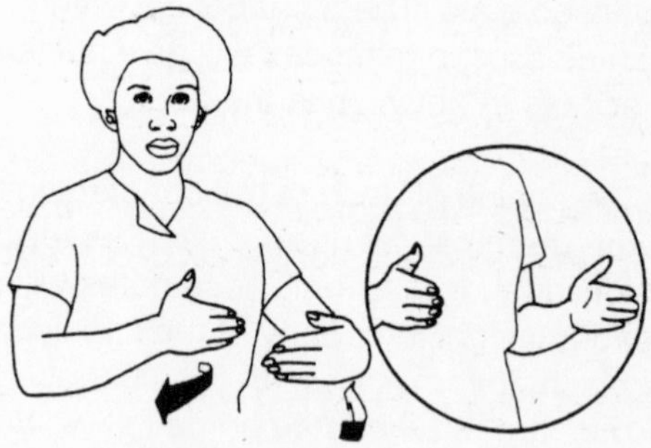

BOX or **ROOM**

Since signs represent concepts, you should be careful to choose the sign with the most similar meaning regardless of the English word. Your decision as to which sign to use should be based on what you are wanting to convey. For example, the English word "save" has several meanings. "Save" can mean "to rescue" and it can mean "to put away for future use," depending on thecontext. Although English has only one word for either use, sign language has a different sign for each context.

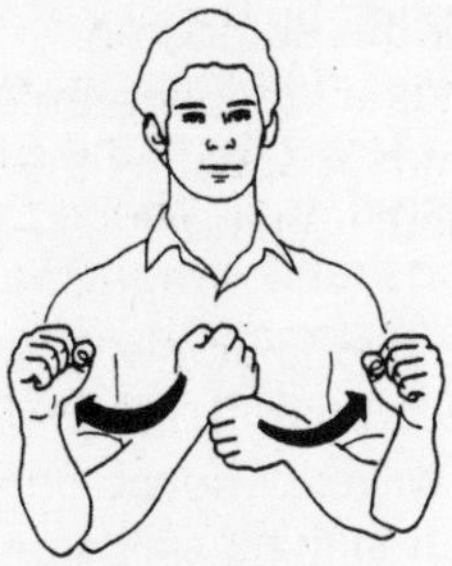

SAVE (rescue)

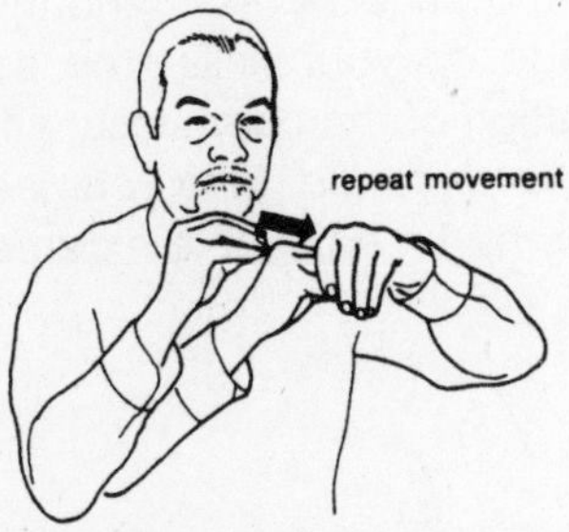

SAVE (put away for future use)

This book has deliberately avoided presenting the English gloss within a sample English sentence. Giving an English sentence may mislead the reader regarding the actual field of meaning intended by the sign. More correctly, the sign should be presented in a glossed American Sign Language sentence, but such a strategy would take more instruction than can be included in this introductory book of this size.

Written Explanations

The next part of each entry is the written explanation that is included to further clarify the sign production. The descriptions also specify whether the sign is to be produced with a single movement, or whether it is to be repeated, which is often the factor distinguishing two signs from one another. For example, the signs for "again"; and "often" are identical except that the movement is repeated to form "often."

RIGHT

REGULARLY

The written explanations describe all four aspects of sign production: hand shape, location, palm orientation, and movement. Most of the hand shapes are described in terms of the shape of a letter in the manual alphabet, e.g., "the right "k" hand." Some hand shapes are described as numbers, e.g., "opening into a "5" hand." Some hand shapes are unique and are described as follows:

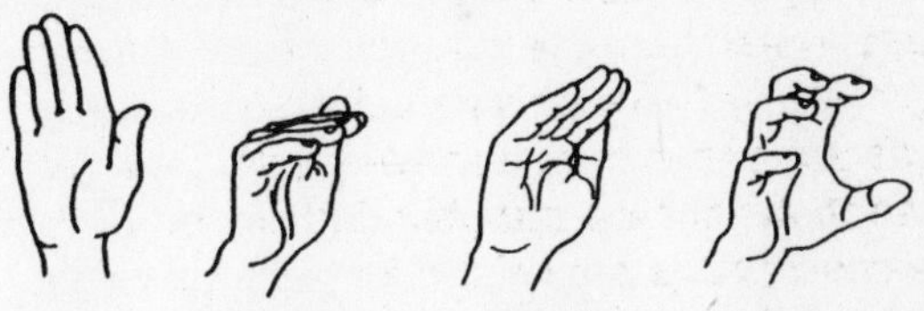

open **bent** **curved** **claw**

Hints

The final part of each entry is the "hint." The hints under the illustrations are simply that: mnemonic clues that will help the sign language learner in recalling the sign during the learning process. Some of the hints might reflect the sign's origin, but no attempt was made to research or explain the derivation of the sign.

Sometimes the hint refers the learner to the iconic nature of the sign by indicating what the sign's formation resembles (e.g., "ball": The shape of a ball). Iconicity is discussed more fully on page xiii of the Introduction. Sometimes the hint mentions the action that the sign is miming (e.g., "volleyball": Shows hitting a volleyball). For compound signs, the hint lists the signs that make up the new sign ("today": "now" + "day").

In the hints a reference is sometimes made to using the finger that often indicates signs of feeling. The reference means to use the bent middle finger to stroke as indicated. Examples of these signs are "feel," "pity," "sick," etc.

The hints may also refer to initialized sign, which is using the handshape of the first word of the English gloss. This is more fully explained on page 158.

Now It's Your Turn

Now you are ready to learn sign language, that wonderful, unique language that uses space and movement for the purpose of communication. It is a language that carried dignity and demands respect as the native language of the deaf community.

This book is dedicated to you who are willing to make the effort to learn to communicate with deaf people. You will experience considerable satisfaction as your signing skill grows. Use every opportunity to practice your skills with deaf people and observe first-hand the fullness of the language. As your skills grow so will your appreciation of the complexity and richness of the language. May your learning of sign language be an enjoyable experience.

glossary

American Sign Language—The language system created and used by Deaf people in North America. Known by its acronym, ASL, it has its roots in French Sign Language.

Americans with Disabilities Act (ADA)—A law passed on July 26, 1990, that guarantees full civil rights to over 43 million Americans with disabilities.

code-switching—Electing to use a particular sign language variety according to the signing ability of the conversant.

deaf—A hearing loss so severe that a person cannot hear or understand speech or sounds.

Deaf—People who are members of the Deaf community.

Deaf community—A cultural group of people who share a common language, values, attitudes, and experiences. Most members of the Deaf community have a hearing loss.

fingerspelling—The spelling out of words and sentences one letter at a time on the hands using the Manual Alphabet.

gloss—The translation of a sign into the English word or words that convey the same concept.

grammar—The structure and rules that govern a language.

hearing impaired—A generic term used to describe all levels of hearing loss from very mild losses to severe losses.

iconicity—The characteristic of some signs that it in some way resembles what it represents whether its appearance or what it does. Those signs that resemble what they represent are said to be "iconic" or "transparent."

inclusion—The provision for education of all students regardless of disability within the public school program by providing appropriate modifications to the instructional environment and program.

initialized sign—A sign that is executed using the handshape from the Manual Alphabet that corresponds to the first letter of the English word having a similar meaning.

interpreting—The changing of spoken languages into sign language; "reverse interpreting" is using spoken language to express what is said in sign language. "Transliteration" is also sometimes used to describe the translation process between oral and sign languages.

language—A system of arbitrary symbols and grammatical rules that are used for communication and to pass culture to future generations.

lexicon—The vocabulary of a language.

linguistics—The scientific study of a language, including its acquisition by children, its grammar, and how people use it.

mainstreaming—As mandated by Public Law 94-142, the free and appropriate education of disabled children in the public school program with other children, as identified in each child's Individualized Education Program (IEP).

Manual Alphabet—The representation of each letter of the written alphabet with distinct handshapes.

manual communication—The generic term used to refer to any form of signing, including sign language, Manual English, and fingerspelling. The most familiar Manual English systems are Signed English and Seeing Exact English (SEE).

Manual English—A generic term for the various sign systems which have been invented as a visual representation of the English language using signs.

native language—The first language of a person, usually learned through assimilation from infancy through interaction with parents.

pidgin language—A language variety that shares a combination of vocabulary and grammar of two distinct languages. A pidgin language usually develops naturally when two groups of people do not share a common language but desire to communicate with each other.

relay service—Also known as Dual Party Relay (DPR), this system, now available in every state allows Deaf people to call a telephone relay service using their Text Telephone where an operator will convey the message by voice. Likewise, it is used by people without a Text Telephone to relay voice message through an operator who conveys it by Text Telephone to the Deaf recipient.

sign—A unit of sign language that represents a concept. A sign is made with either one or both hands formed in distinctive handshapes. The sign also has a location, orientation, and movement which are peculiar to it.

Sign English—Also known as Contact Sign, the use of signs from American Sign Language within an English syntactic order. Sign English is a pidgin language which may take many forms, leaning toward a heavy influence of either American Sign Language or of English, depending on the person using it.

signer—The person using sign language.

text telephone (TT)—Also known as TTY and telecommunication device for the deaf (TDD), this instrument permits Deaf people to communicate by telephone by typing messages to one another.

Total Communication—The philosophy that each Deaf individual has the right to have access to information through any and all input modes, including aural stimulation, speechreading, written forms, gestures, facial expression, sign language, and fingerspelling.

variation—Differences in production, vocabulary, or grammar of a language due to factors such as geographic area, racial or ethnic influences, age, sex, and education.

selected readings

Baker-Shenk, C. and D. Cokely. 1980. *American Sign Language: A Teacher's Resource Text on Grammar and Culture.* Washington, D.C.: Gallaudet University Press.

Benderly, B. L. 1990. *Dancing Without Music: Deafness in America.* Washington, D.C.: Gallaudet University Press. Original edition, Garden City, N.Y.: Anchor Press/Doubleday, 1980.

Cohen, L. H. 1994. *Train Go Sorry: Inside a Deaf World.* Boston: Houghton Mifflin Company.

Gannon, J. 1981. *Deaf Heritage: A Narrative History of Deaf America.* Silver Spring, MD: National Association of the Deaf.

Jacobs, L. 1989. *A Deaf Adult Speaks Out.* 3d ed. Washington, D.C.: Gallaudet University Press.

Lane, H. 1992. *The Mask of Benevolence: Disabling the Deaf Community.* New York: Alfred A. Knopf.

Lane, H. 1984. *When the Mind Hears: A History of the Deaf.* New York: Random House.

Moores, D. F. 1987. *Educating the Deaf: Psychology, Principles, and Practices.* 3d ed. Boston: Houghton Mifflin Company.

Neisser, A. 1990. *The Other Side of Silence: Sign Language and the Deaf Community in America.* Washington, D.C.: Gallaudet University Press. Original edition, New York: Alfred A. Knopf, 1983.

Padden, C. and T. Humphries. 1988. *Deaf in America: Voices from a Culture.* Cambridge: Harvard University Press.

Preston, P. 1994. *Mother Father Deaf: Living between Sound and Silence.* Cambridge: Havard University Press.

Sacks, O. 1989. *Seeing Voices: A Journey into the World of the Deaf.* Berkeley: University of California Press.

Schein, J. D. 1989. *At Home Among Strangers.* Washington, D.C.: Gallaudet University Press.

Spradley, T., and J. Spradley. 1985. *Deaf Like Me.* Washington, D.C.: Gallaudet University Press. Original edition, New York: Random House, 1978.

Van Cleve, J. V., Ed. 1987. *Gallaudet Encyclopedia of Deaf People and Deafness.* New York: McGraw-Hill Book Company.

Van Cleve, J. V. and B. A. Crouch. 1989. *A Place of Their Own: Creating the Deaf Community in America.* Washington, D.C.: Gallaudet University Press.

Walker, L. A. 1986. *A Loss for Words: The Story of Deafness in a Family.* New York: Harper Collins.

Walker, L. A. 1994. *Hand, Heart, & Mind: The Story of the Education of America's Deaf People.* New York: Dial Books.

signing

HOW TO SPEAK WITH YOUR HANDS

one
THE BASICS

Common Phrases
Questions
Negatives
The Manual Alphabet

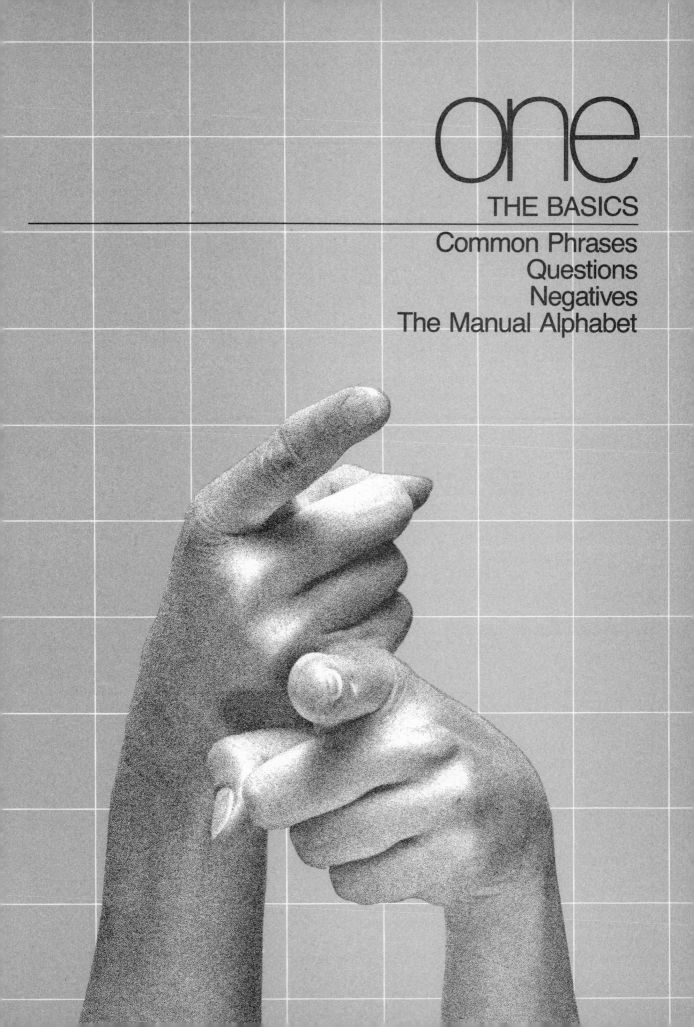

FINGERSPELLING

Fingerspelling is the spelling out of words and sentences one letter at a time on the hands using the manual alphabet. The manual alphabet has 26 distinct hand configurations to represent each letter of the alphabet. Combining them together in smooth succession makes it possible to express and receive ideas. Fingerspelling is used in sign language sentences as a supplement to express ideas for which there are no formal signs, such as proper names and technical terms. Fingerspelling is produced at a comfortable position in front of the side of the chest with the palm facing forward.

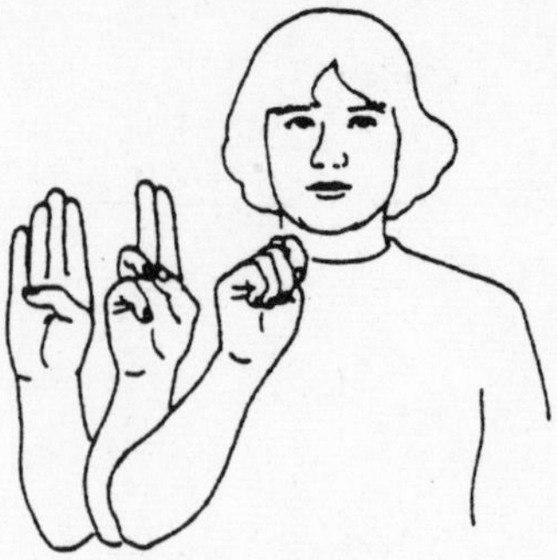

B—U—T tub
③ ② ①

QUESTIONS

Body language is an important part of asking a question. With a quizzical facial expression, lean forward while asking the question, and hold the last part of the sign a little longer than usual. A question mark may be added at the beginning or at the end of some questions.

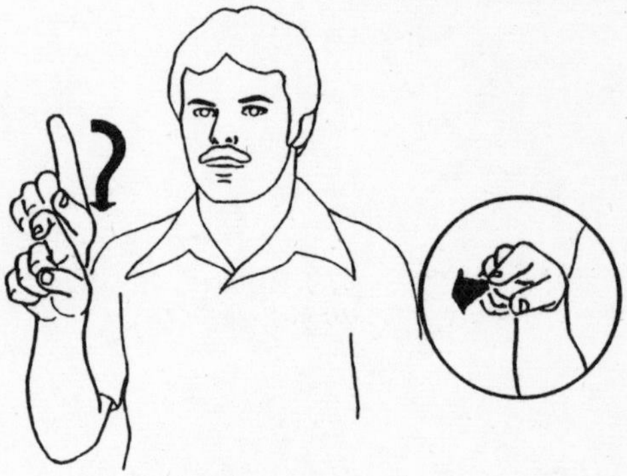

question

NEGATIVES

Some signs, such as "nothing" and "not," can be used to make a sentence negative. For example, "not" plus "honest" becomes "dishonest." Usually a negative sentence is accompanied by a side to side headshake. Other facial cues such as squeezing the eyebrows together, pinching the lips, and sucking the breath can further modify the negated sign to show sincerity, surprise, concern, anger, or other information.

Some signs become negative by a deliberate twisting outward of the wrist. Examples of these signs are "want," "like," and "know."

not + honest = dishonest

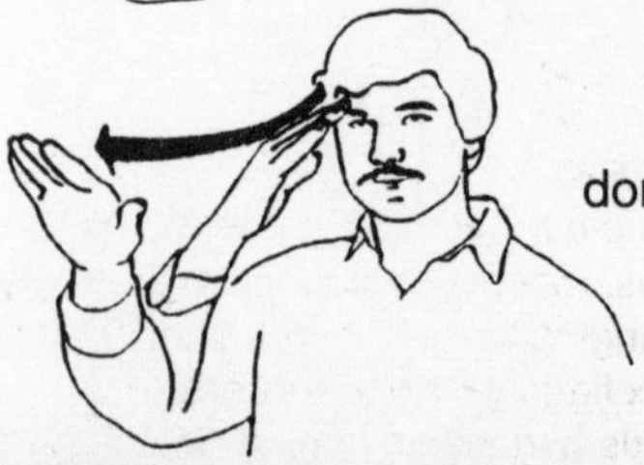

don't know

Common Phrases

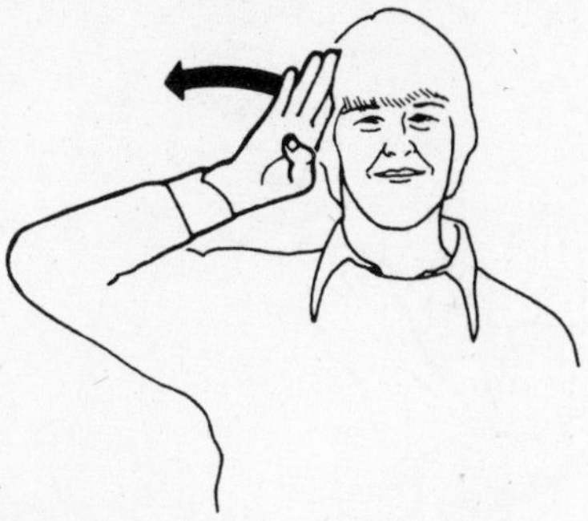

HELLO, HI
Beginning with the index finger of the right "b" hand at the right side of the head, palm facing forward and fingers pointing up, move the hand to the right with a deliberate movement.
Hint: Saluting a greeting.

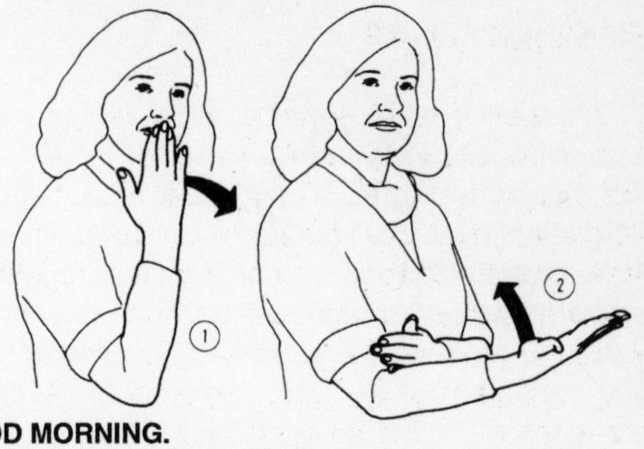

GOOD MORNING.
Move the fingers of the open right hand from the chin forward a short distance. Then, with the open left hand in the crook of the extended right arm, bring the right palm upward toward the face.
Hint: "Good" plus "morning."

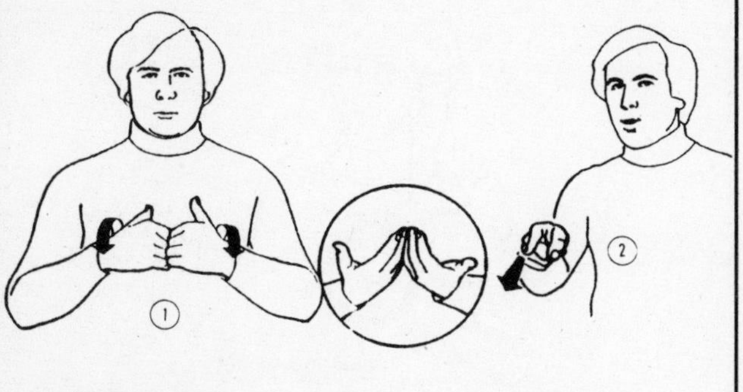

HOW ARE YOU?
With the knuckles of both bent hands touching each other and the fingers touching the chest, move the fingers up, ending with the palms facing up. Then point the extended right finger forward.
Hint: "How" plus "you." It is not necessary to sign "are."

I'M FINE.
Beginning with the thumb of the right "5" hand touching the chest, palm facing left, move the hand forward. Note: You may leave the thumb in place in the middle of the chest and wiggle all of the fingers to mean "super fine."
Hint: This sign is for "fine." It is not necessary to sign "I'm."

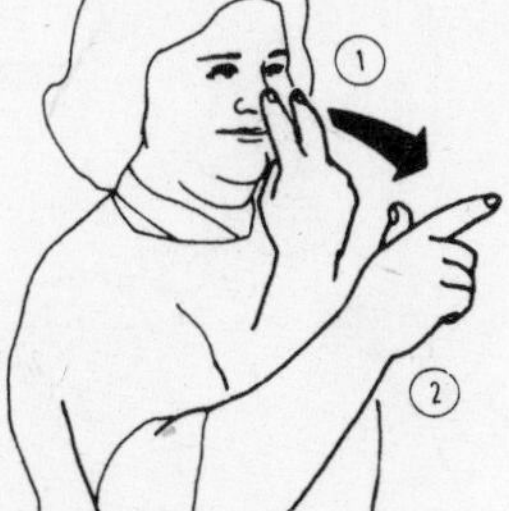

SEE YOU LATER.
Beginning with the fingers of the right "v" hand pointing toward the eyes, move the hand forward by twisting the wrist while changing to an "l" hand, ending with the extended index finger pointing forward.
Hint: "See" plus a modified form of "later." "You" is not necessary.

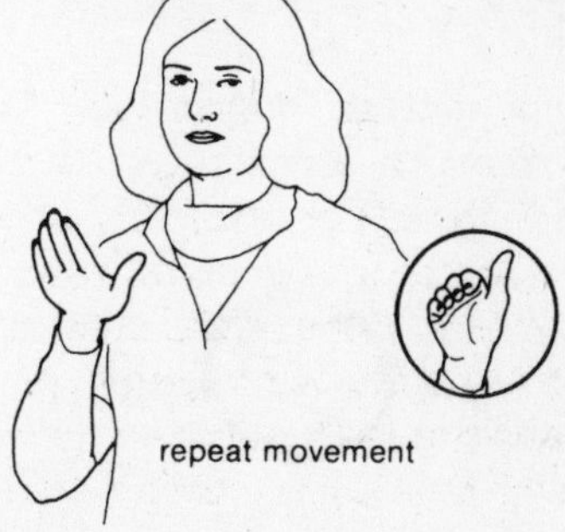

GOOD-BYE.
Holding the open right hand in front of the right shoulder, palm facing forward, bend the fingers up and down with a repeated movement.
Hint: Mime waving good-bye.

THANK YOU. YOU'RE WELCOME.
Bring the fingers of the open right hand forward from the mouth.
Hint: When meaning "You're welcome," it is almost like saying "Thank you for thanking me."

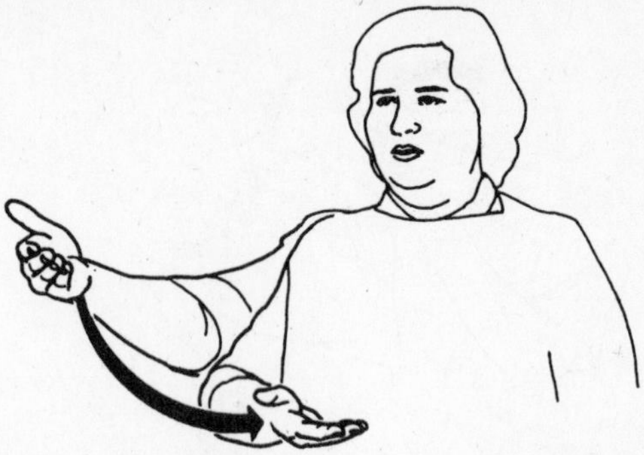

YOU'RE WELCOME.
Bring the curved right hand from in front of the right side of the body downward and in toward the waist, palm facing up.
Hint: This is the sign "welcome"; "you're" is not necessary.

EXCUSE ME. FORGIVE ME.
Brush the fingertips of the bent right hand from the heel to the fingers of the left palm with a repeated movement.
Hint: Brushing the mistake aside.

I'M SORRY.
Rub the palm side of the right "a" hand in a repeated circular movement on the chest.
Hint: Beating the heart in sorrow.

PLEASE
Rub the palm of the open right hand in a repeated circular movement on the chest.
Hint: Rubbing the heart with pleasure.

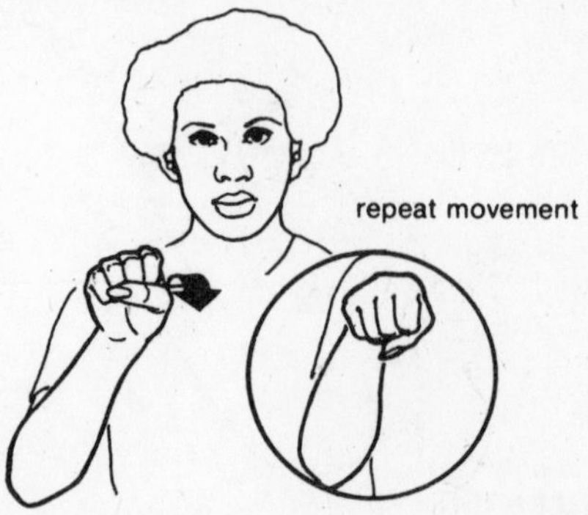

YES
Move the right "s" hand, palm facing forward, up and down by bending the wrist with a small repeated movement.
Hint: Nodding the head affirmatively.

I MADE A MISTAKE.
Tap the knuckles of the right "y" hand on the chin. Then point the extended right index finger to the middle of the chest.
Hint: "Wrong" plus "me." This sign is used almost as an apology for making a mistake.

THAT'S TRUE. REALLY.
Move the extended index finger, palm facing left and finger pointing up, from the lips forward in an arc with a deliberate movement. Note: This sign is often used for emphasis after a sentence.

I SEE. I UNDERSTAND.
Gently shake the right "y" hand, palm facing down, up and down with a small movement by bending the wrist. Note: This sign is often used as an indication of agreement with what the other person is saying.

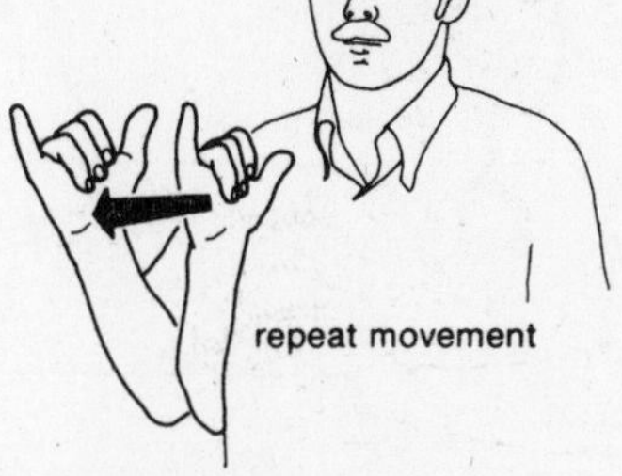

ME, TOO. I AGREE WITH YOU.
Move the right "y" hand, palm left, forward and back with a repeated movement from the chest by bending the elbow.
Hint: Move the sign for "same" between yourself and the person with whom you have the same opinion.

GOOD LUCK.
Move the thumb of the right "10" hand, palm facing left, forward with a short deliberate movement. Note: This sign is sometimes used as a good-bye greeting.

BE CAREFUL. TAKE CARE.
With a double movement, tap the little-finger side of the right "k" hand, palm left, on the index-finger side of the left "k" hand, palm right.

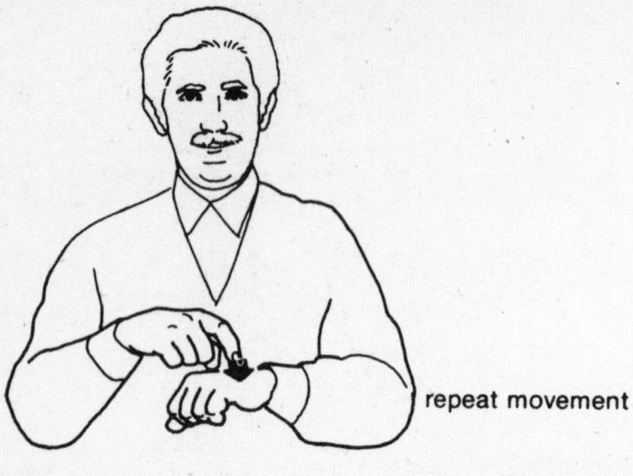

WHAT TIME IS IT?
With an inquisitive expression, tap the curved extended right index finger, palm facing down, to the back of the left wrist held in front of the chest.
Hint: This is a natural gesture for inquiring about the time.

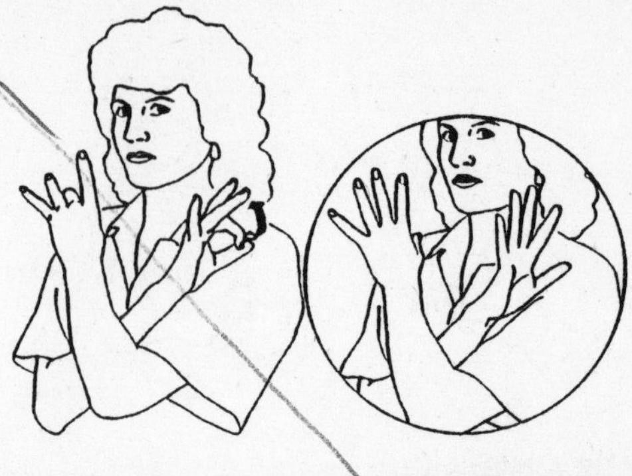

IT'S NOT MY FAULT. CAREFREE, IRRESPONSIBLE
With the fingers of both "8" hands touching the opposite shoulder, palms facing outward in opposite directions, flick the middle fingers open forming "5" hands.
Hint: Flicking responsibility from one's shoulders.

whats, going(spin index in circle) (R) hand on top@ L

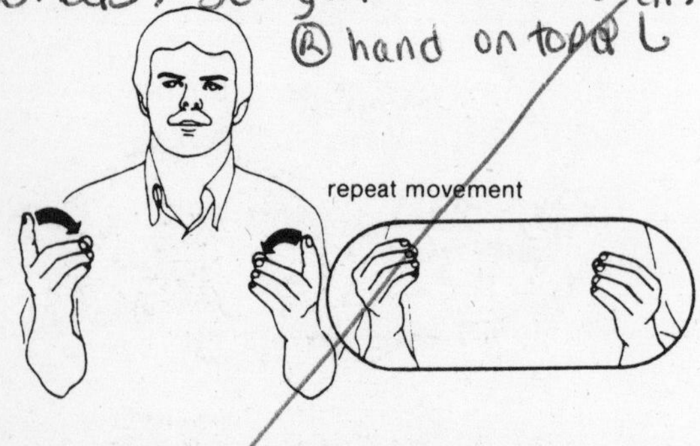

WHAT'S GOING ON? WHAT SHALL I DO?
Bring the extended index fingers of both "d" hands up and down with a repeated motion, palms facing the chest.
Hint: Rapidly fingerspell "d" "o." This can be translated as "do-do."

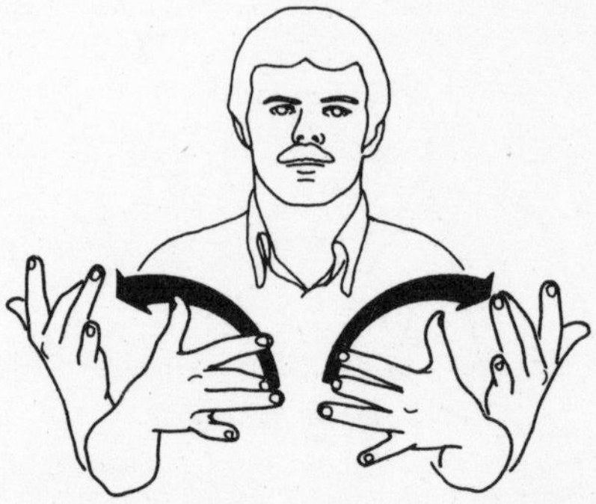

WHAT'S HAPPENING? WHAT'S UP? THRILL
Beginning with the bent middle fingers of both "5" hands touching the chest near each other, move the hands upward and outward toward the shoulders with a quick movement.

I LOVE YOU.
With the little finger, index finger, and thumb of the right hand extended, hold the right hand up in front of the chest, palm facing forward.
Hint: Informal sign made of the initials "i," "l," and "y."

I LOVE YOU.
Point the extended right index finger to the center of the chest, palm facing in. Cross the arms of both "a" hands at the wrists and lay them on the chest. Then point the extended right index finger forward.
Hint: "I" plus "love" plus "you."

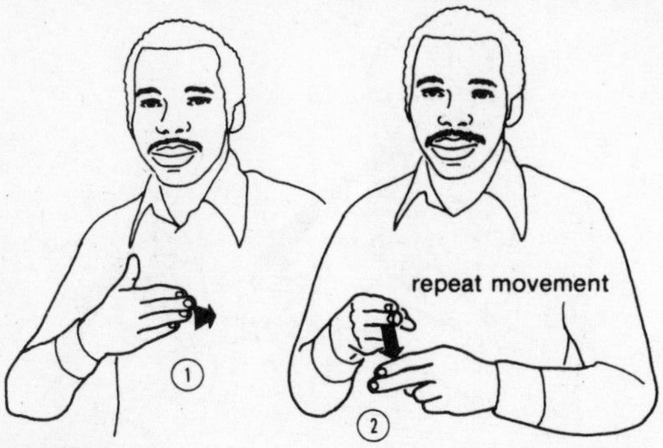

MY NAME IS ...
Place the palm of the open right hand on the center of the chest. Then with a double movement tap the middle-finger side of the right "h" fingers, palm facing left, on the index-finger side of the left "h" fingers, palm facing right.
Hint: "My" plus "name"; it is not necessary to sign "is." Follow by fingerspelling your name.

I DOUBT IT.
Beginning with the right "v" fingers pointing to the eyes, palm facing in, move the hand forward, bending the fingers as the hand moves.
Hint: Similar to "blind"; shows you are blind to the idea.

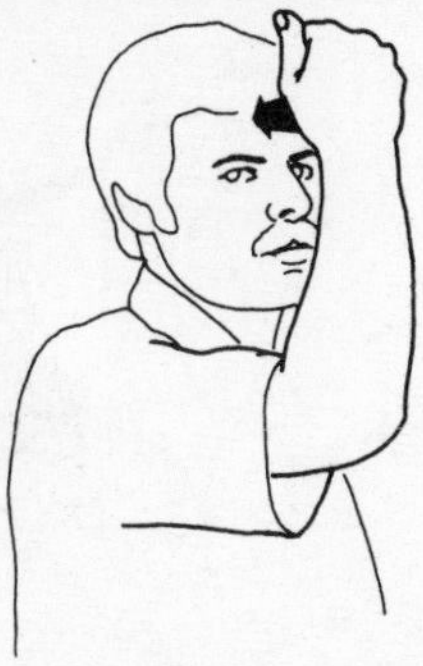

THAT'S DUMB.
Tap the palm side of the right "a" hand against the center of the forehead.
Hint: This sign should be used as a self-accusation when making a mistake.

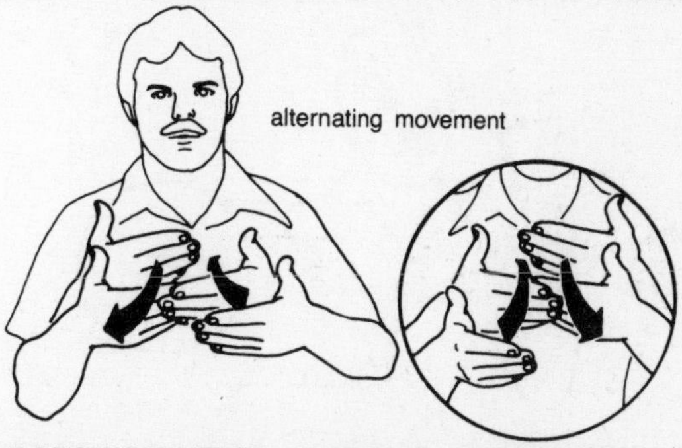

IT DOESN'T MATTER, HOWEVER, ALTHOUGH
With both open hands in front of the chest, palms facing in and fingers pointing toward each other and overlapping slightly, brush the fingers back and forward past each other in opposite directions bending the fingers out of the way as the hands move.
Hint: Shows that your opinion can be swayed either way.

POOR THING. THAT'S TOO BAD.
With the bent middle finger of the right "5" hand stroke the air toward the person or object being pitied with a double movement.
Hint: Sign "feel" in the air in sympathy for another person or thing.

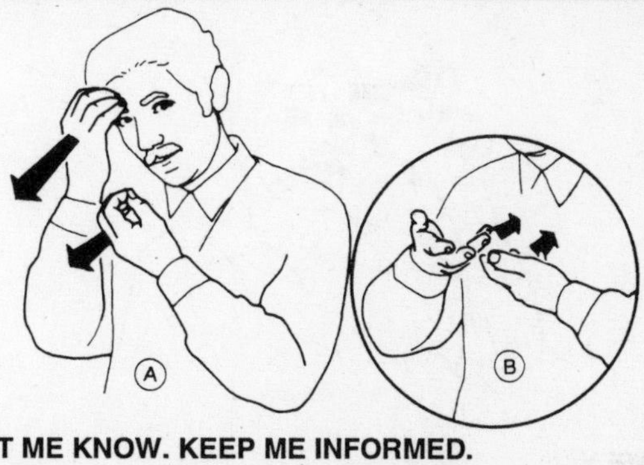

LET ME KNOW. KEEP ME INFORMED.
Beginning with the fingers of the right flattened "o" hand near the forehead and the left flattened "o" hand somewhat forward, move both hands down and in toward the chest while opening into "5" hands.
Hint: Shows a vagueness.

Questions

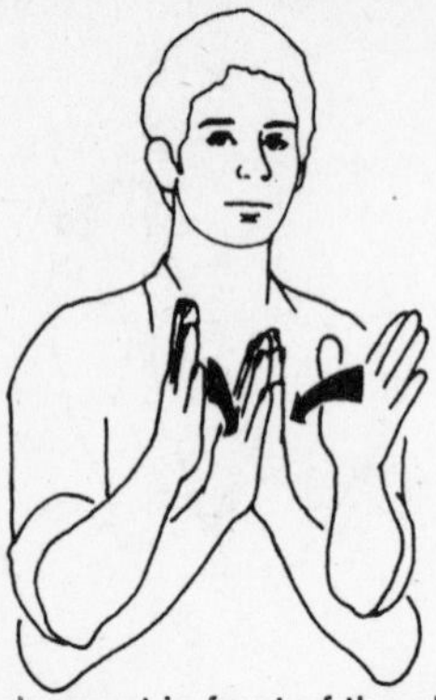

ASK
Beginning the hands apart in front of the chest, palms facing each other and fingers pointing up, bring the palms together while moving the hands in toward the chest.
Hint: Mime asking a question.

ANSWER, REPLY
Beginning with the right extended index finger pointing up in front of the lips and the left extended index finger pointing up somewhat forward, bring both hands forward simultaneously by bending the wrists, ending with the fingers pointing forward.
Hint: Words coming straight out of the mouth in reply.

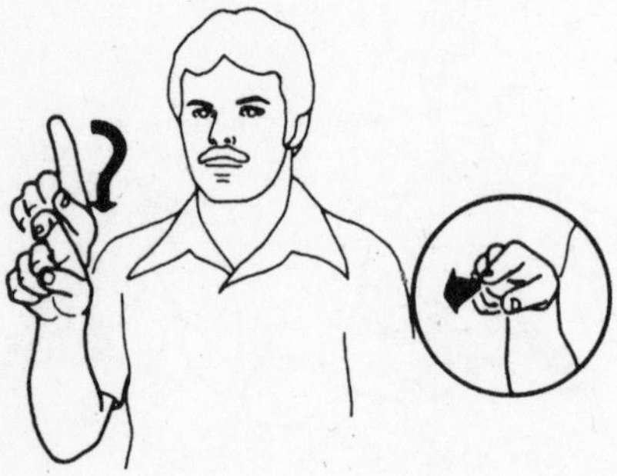

QUESTION
Move the extended right index finger from pointing up in front of the right shoulder, palm facing forward, down with a curved movement ending with the finger pointing forward.
Note: This sign is used before or after a question.
Hint: Traces the shape of a question mark in the air.

WHY?
Beginning with the fingers of the bent right hand touching the forehead, move the hand forward while changing to a "y" hand.
Hint: Taking a thought form the brain and presenting it for investigation.

FOR
Beginning the extended right index finger pointing to the right side of the forehead, twist the hand quickly outward, ending with the finger pointing forward.

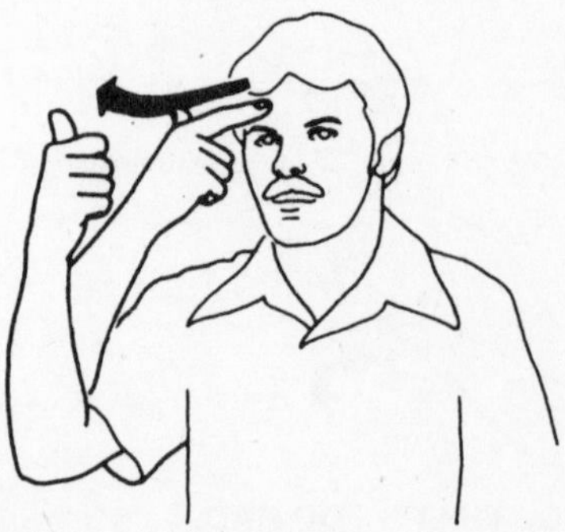

BECAUSE
Beginning with the index finger of the right "I" hand touching the forehead, palm facing back, move the hand outward to the right while changing to a "10" hand.

WHO?
With the extended right index finger make a small circle around the mouth.
Hint: The finger traces the shape of the mouth when saying "who."

HOW?
With the knuckles of both bent hands touching each other and the fingers touching the chest, move the fingers up, ending with the palms facing up.

WHICH?
Move both "10" hands, palms facing each other and thumbs pointing up, up and down in front of the chest with alternating movements.
Hint: The alternating movement indicates a sense of doubt.

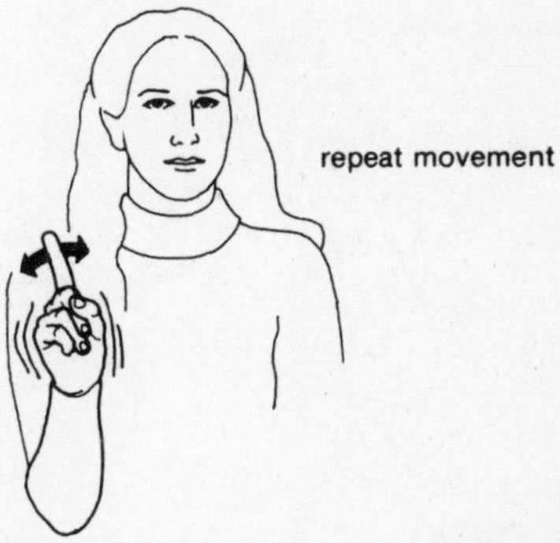

WHERE?
Shake the extended right index finger from side to side in front of the right shoulder, palm facing forward.
Hint: A natural sign when looking for something.

WHEN?
With the extended right index finger above the left extended index finger, palms facing each other, make a small circle with the right index finger and bring it straight down to touch the left index finger.

WHAT?
Brush the extended right index finger, palm facing left, downward across the open left palm held in front of the chest, palm facing right.

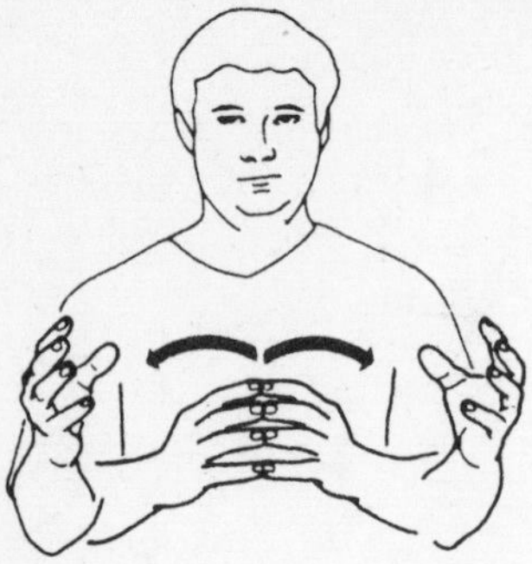

HOW MUCH?
Beginning with fingertips of both curved open hands touching in front of the chest, palms facing each other, move the hands outward to about shoulder width.
Hint: Hands encircle a vague quantity.

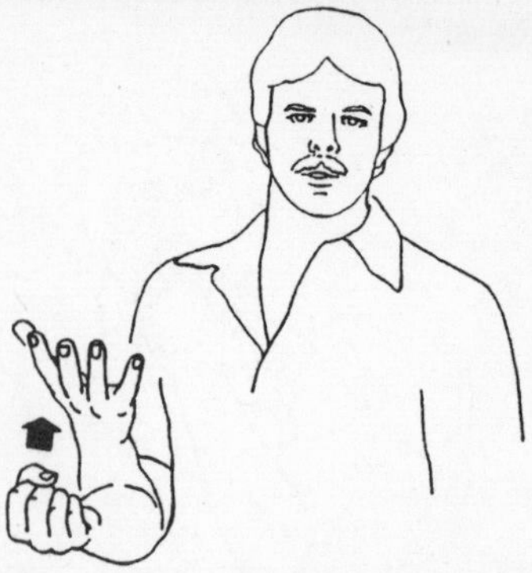

HOW MANY?
With the right "s" hand in front of the right side of the chest, palm facing up, flick the fingers upward with a quizzical look on the face. Note: This sign can be made with one hand or both hands.
Hint: Similar to the sign for "many," except made with a single movement.

WHAT FOR?
Beginning the extended right index finger pointing to the right side of the forehead, twist the hand quickly outward with short double movement, turning the finger to point forward each time.
Hint: "For-for."

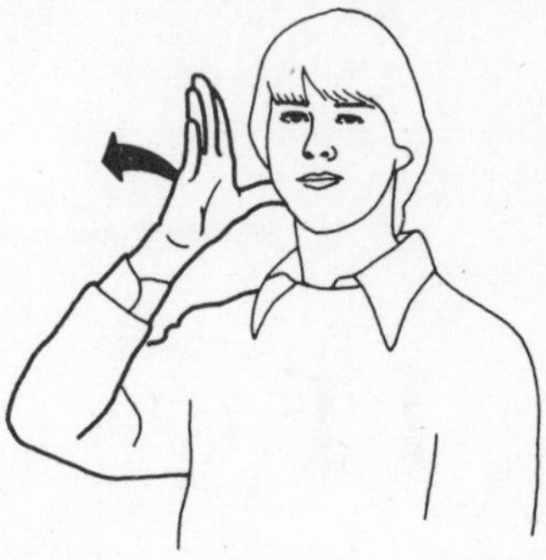

WILL? SHALL?
Bring the open right hand, palm facing left, forward from the right cheek.
Hint: The movement forward indicates the future.

HAVE? DID? FINISH, COMPLETE
Bring both "5" hands from in front of the chest, palms facing up, downward with a twist of the wrists, ending with the palms facing down.
Hint: This sign is used at the beginning or end of a sentence to find out if an action is finished or complete.

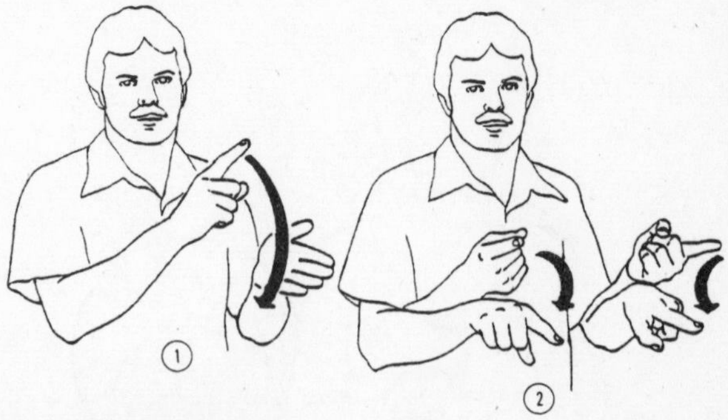

WHAT HAPPENED?
Brush the extended right index finger downward across the open left palm. Then beginning with both extended index fingers pointing forward in front of the chest, palms up, twist the wrists to turn the palms down.
Hint: "What" plus "happen."

Negatives

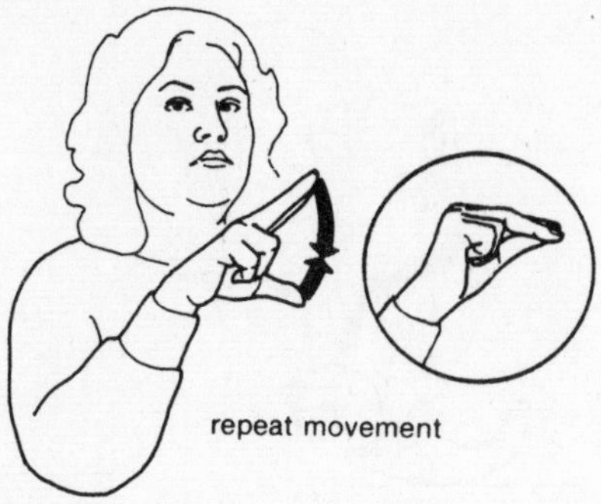

NO
Tap the extended index and middle fingers of the right hand to the right thumb with two quick movements.
Hint: The fingerspelled letters "n-o" produced quickly.

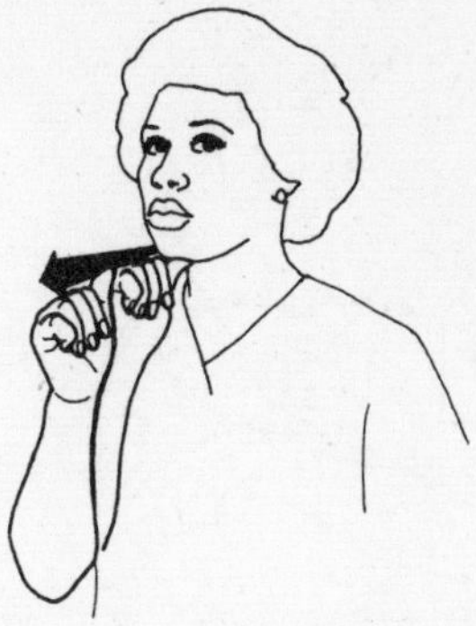

NOT, DON'T
Bring the thumb of the right "a" hand, palm left, forward from under the chin.

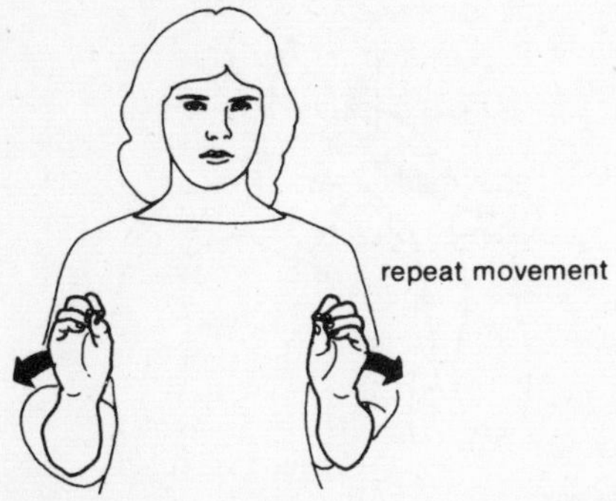

NONE, NO, NOBODY
Shake both "o" hands, palms facing forward, with a short repeated movement in front of each side of the chest.
Hint: Shaking something to show that it contains nothing.

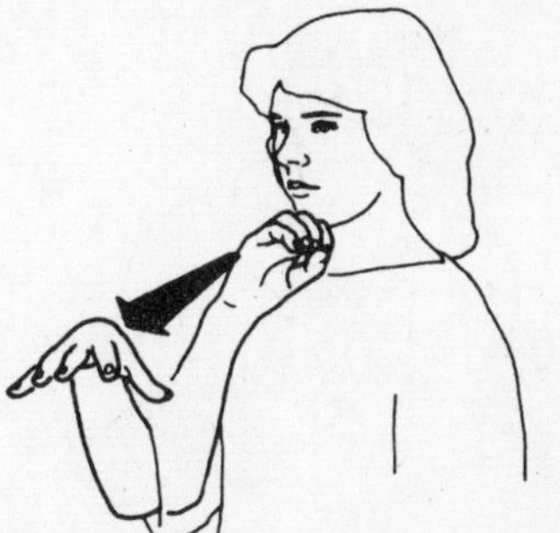

NOTHING
Bring the right "o" hand, palm left, from under the chin forward while opening the fingers into a "5" hand, palm facing down.
Hint: Throwing "zero" away from the body.

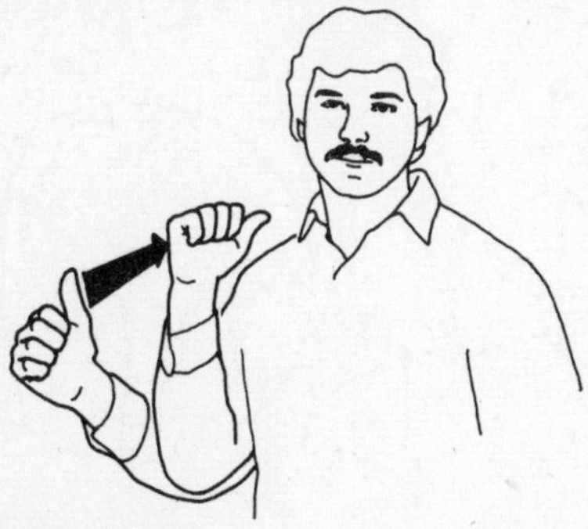

WON'T, REFUSE
Move the thumb of the right "10" hand back over the right shoulder with a deliberate movement, palm facing left.
Hint: Natural gesture for refusing something.

DON'T, DO NOT
Beginning with both open hands crossed at the wrists in front of the body, palms facing down, move the hands apart to in front of each side of the body with a deliberate movement.
Hint: Natural sign for "don't."

CAN'T, CANNOT, IMPOSSIBLE
Bring the extended right index finger down in front of the chest striking the extended left index finger as it passes.

NEVER
Bring the right "b" hand, palm facing left, from near the right cheek downward in a wavy movement to the lower chest.
Hint: The hand seems to clear the slate.

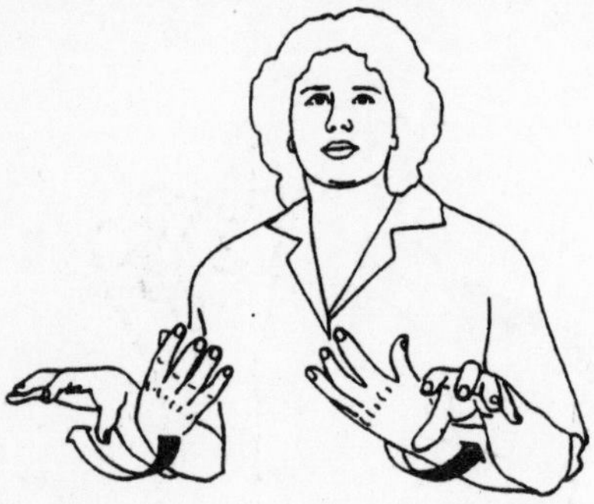

DON'T WANT
Beginning with both "claw" hands in front of the chest, palms facing up, twist the wrists sharply to turn the palms down.
Hint: "Want" plus the movement away that makes it become negative.

DON'T CARE
Move the extended right index finger forward from touching the nose, ending with the finger pointing forward.

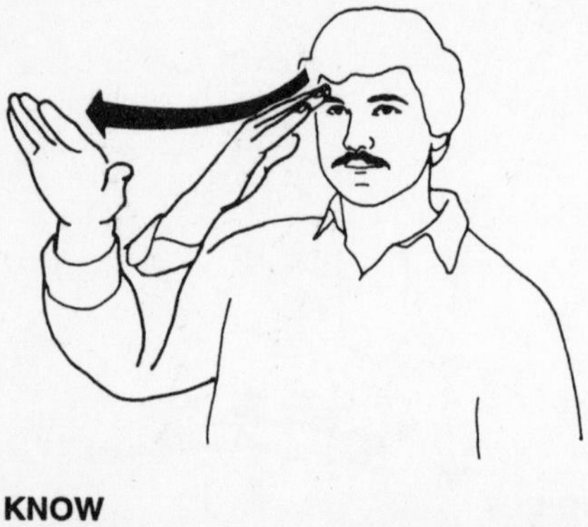

DON'T KNOW
Bring the fingertips of the open right hand, palm down, from touching the right side of the forehead, outward in an arc, ending with the fingers pointing forward.
Hint: "Know" plus the movement away that makes it become negative.

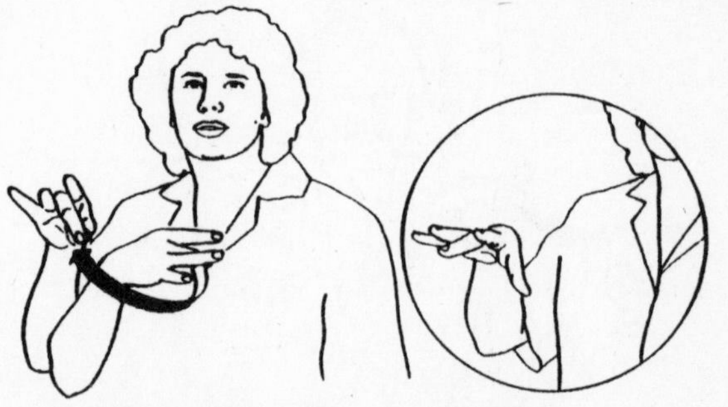

DON'T LIKE, DISLIKE
Beginning with the fingertips of the right "8" hand touching the chest, twist the hand sharply forward while opening to a "5" hand, palm facing down.
Hint: "Like" plus the movement away that makes it become negative.

The American Manual Alphabet

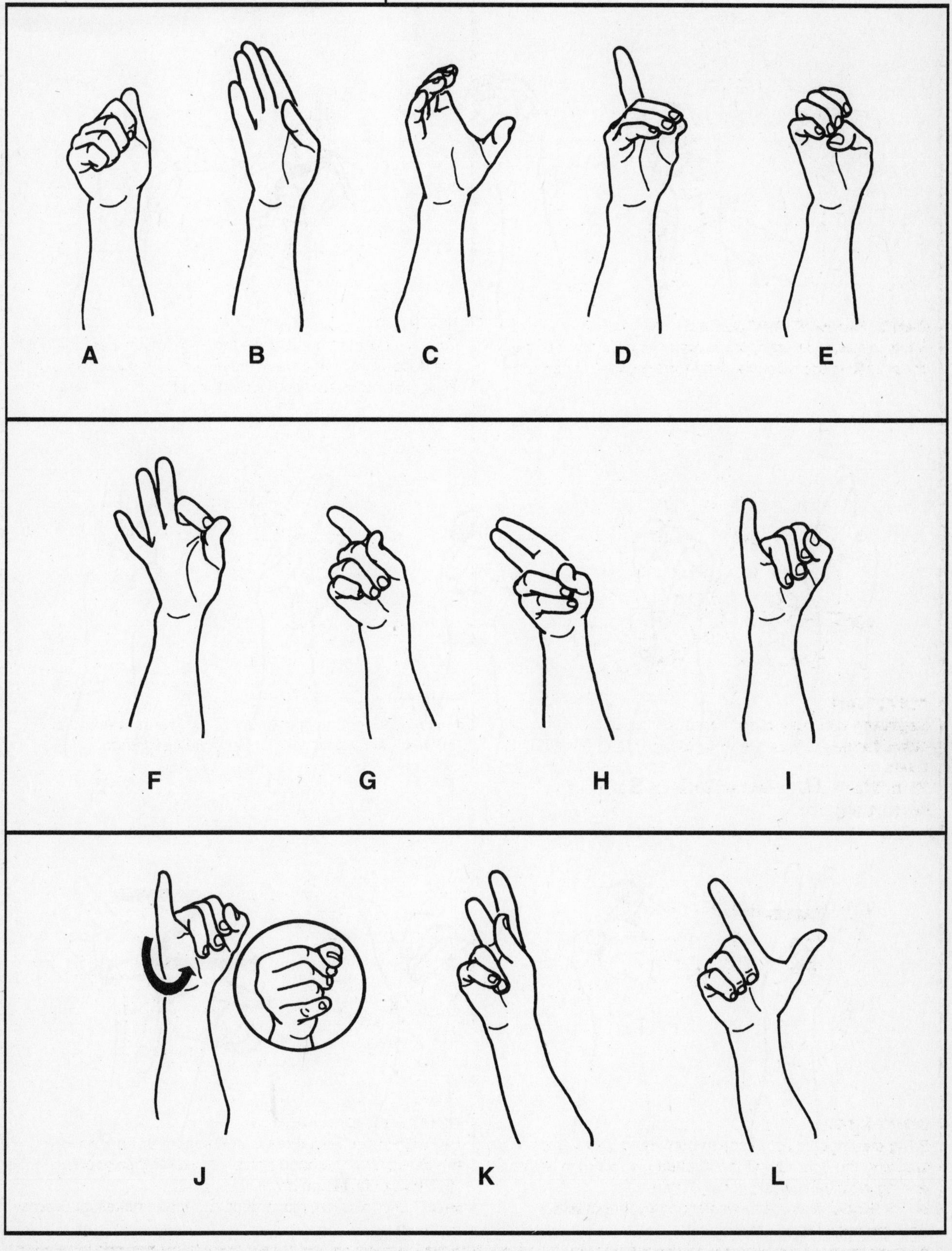

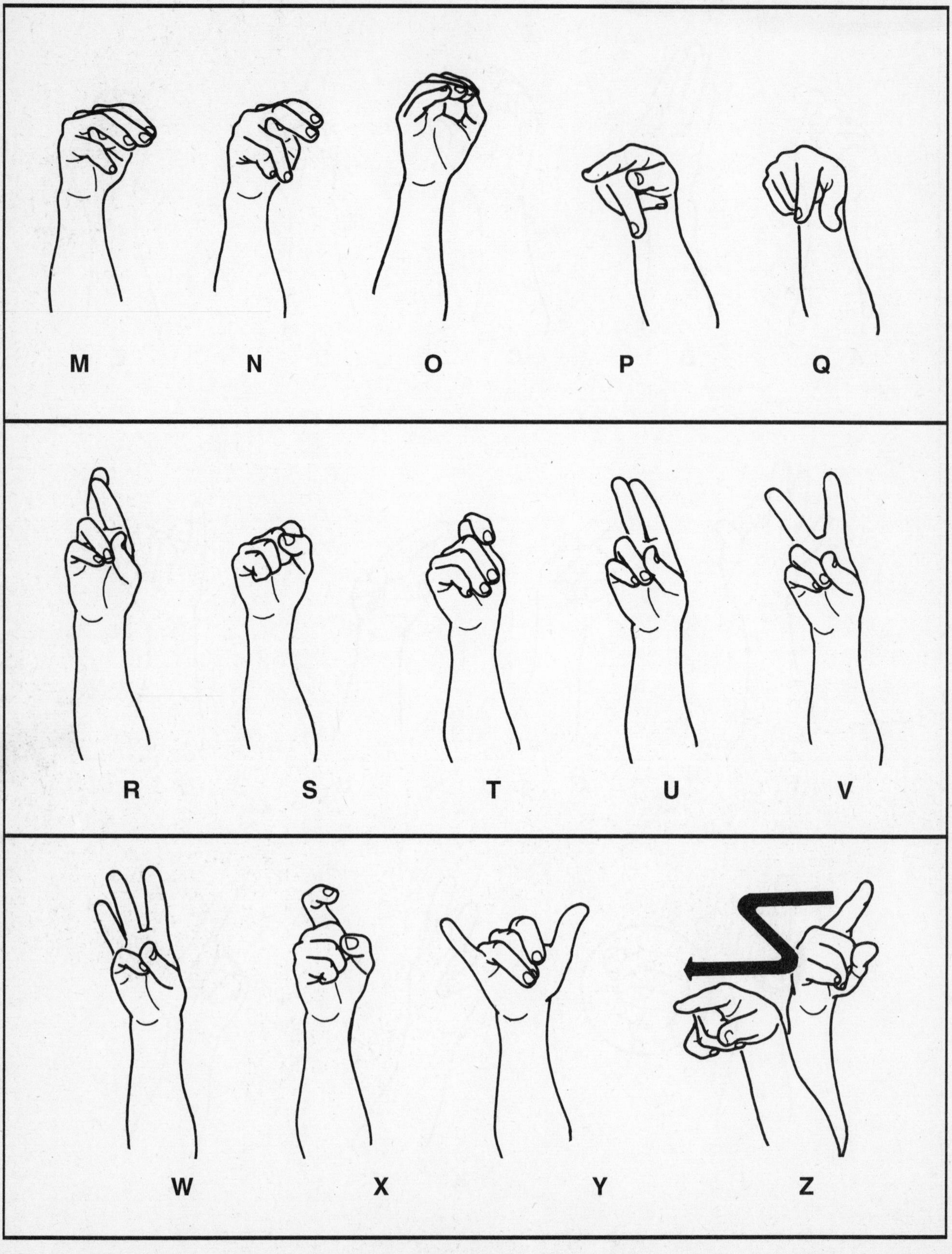
M
N
O
P
Q
R
S
T
U
V
W
X
Y
Z

two
THINGS

Around the House
Clothing
Animals

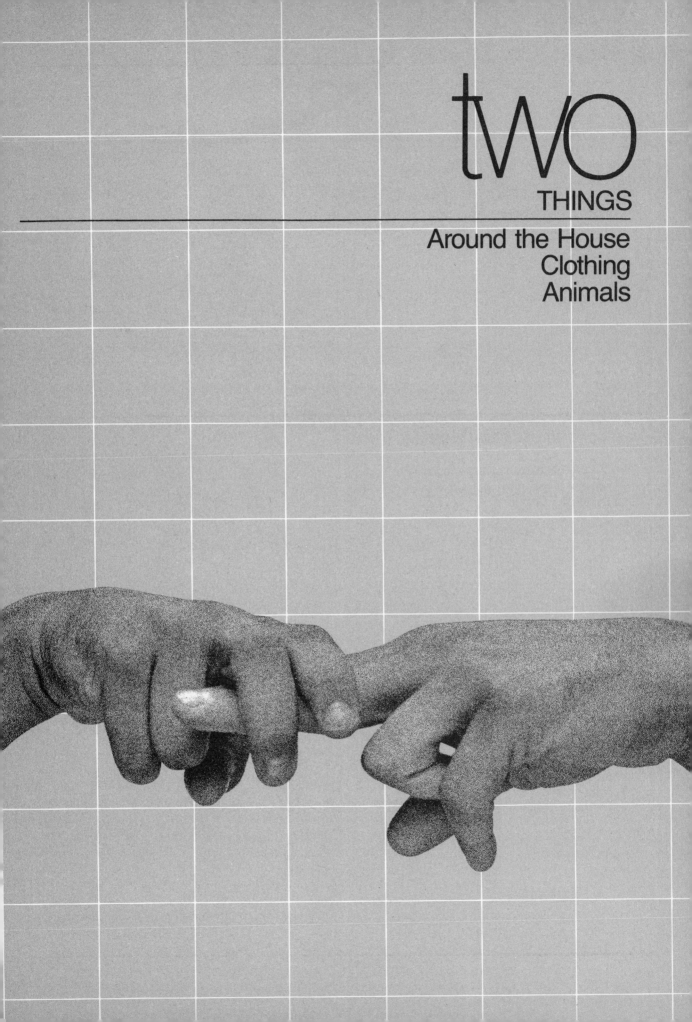

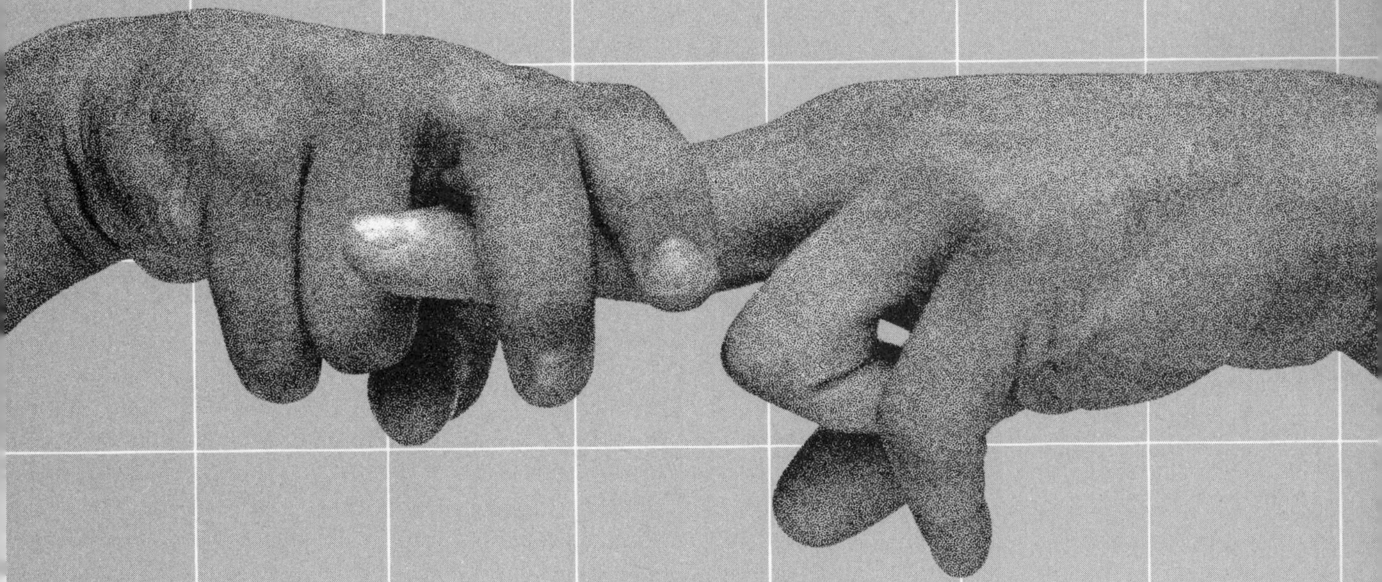

ONE WAY TO FORM PLURALS

Plurals may be formed by adding a sign to indicate quantity after the noun sign. Some examples of quantifiers that can be used include numbers or quantity signs such as "horde," "many," or "all."

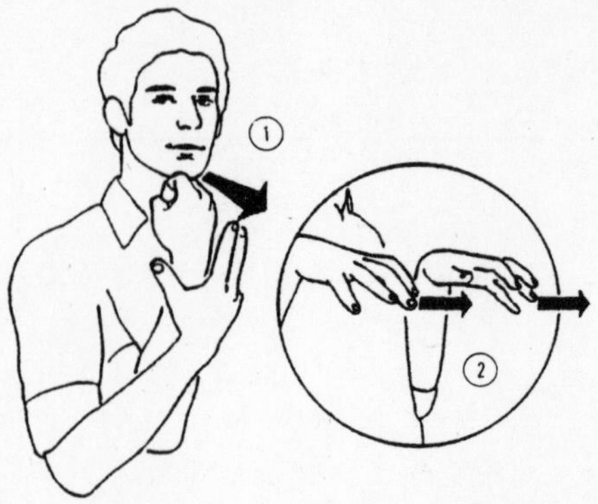

frog + horde = many frogs

A SECOND WAY TO FORM PLURALS

Plurals may be formed by signing the verb or noun sign several times, moving the hands sideways to a new location each time.

house—house—house = many houses

A THIRD WAY TO FORM PLURALS

Plurals may be formed by pointing the index finger at different locations where the noun sign is imagined to be, indicating that there are many objects.

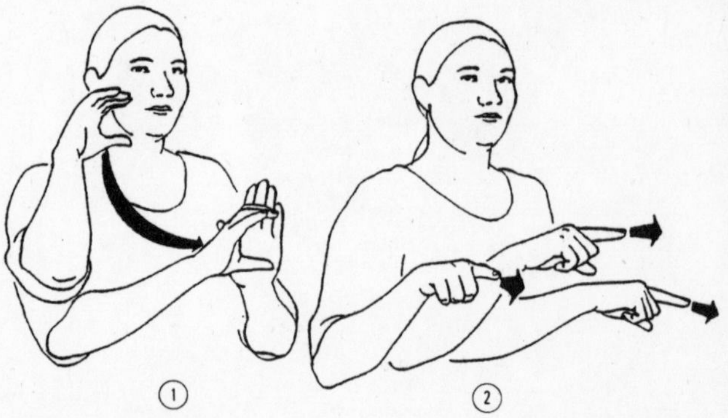

picture + there—there—there = many pictures

Around the House

HOME
With the right fingertips and thumb together, touch the lower cheek and then the upper cheek.
Hint: A modification of "eat" and "sleep" to show that a home is a place to eat and sleep.

HOUSE
Beginning with the index-finger sides of both "b" hands touching in front of the forehead, palms facing down, bring the hands down and outward at an angle to about shoulder width and then straight down, ending with the palms facing each other.
Hint: Shows the shape of a roof and walls of a house.

ROOF
Beginning with the fingertips of both "b" hands touching in front of the forehead, palms facing down, bring the hands down and outward at an angle a short distance.
Hint: Shows the shape of a roof.

no "R"

ROOM
Beginning with both "r" hands in front of the body, both palms facing in and left hand closer to the body than the right hand, straighten the wrists to move the hands to the sides, ending with the palms facing each other.
Hint: Initialized sign showing the walls of a room.

BASEMENT, CELLAR
Move the right "10" hand, thumb pointing up, in a small repeated circle under the open left hand, palm facing down.

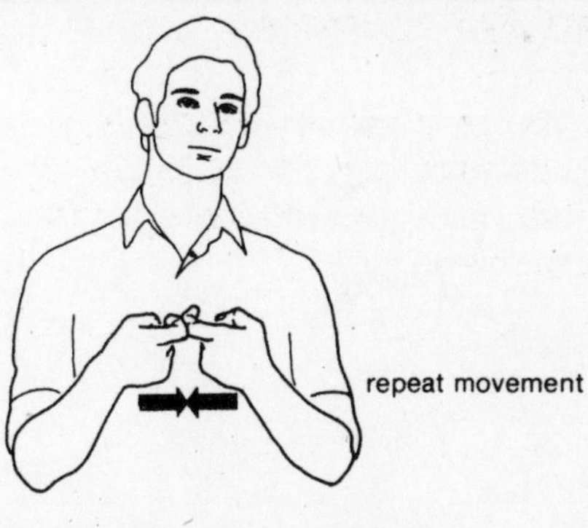

ELECTRICITY, ELECTRIC, BATTERY
Tap the bent knuckles of both "x" hands together with a repeated movement in front of the chest, palms facing in.
Hint: Represents an electrical charge.

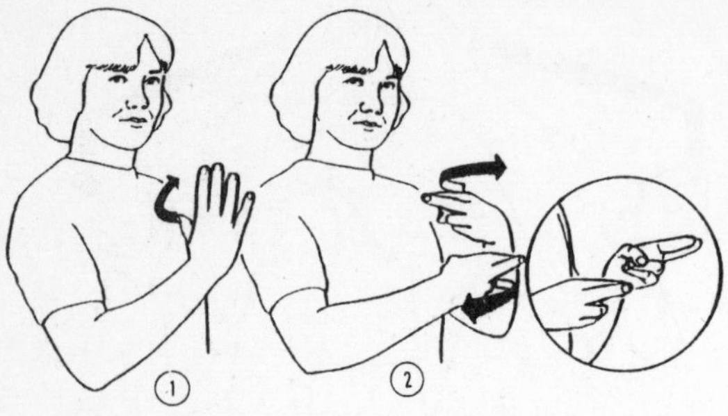

LIVING ROOM
Brush the thumb of the right "5" hand, palm facing left, upward on the chest. Then, beginning with both "r" hands in front of the body, both palms facing in and left hand closer to the body than the right hand, move the hands to the sides, ending with the palms facing each other.
Hint: "Fancy" plus "room."

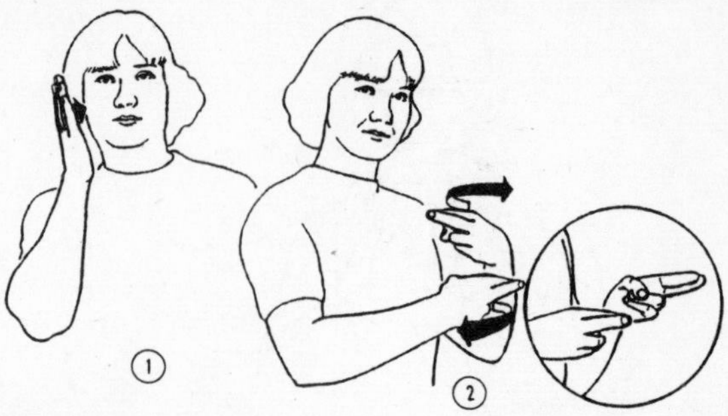

BEDROOM
Place the palm of the open right hand against the right cheek. Then, beginning with both "r" hands in front of the body, both palms facing in and left hand closer to the body than the right hand, move the hands to the sides, ending with the palms facing each other.
Hint: "Bed" plus "room."

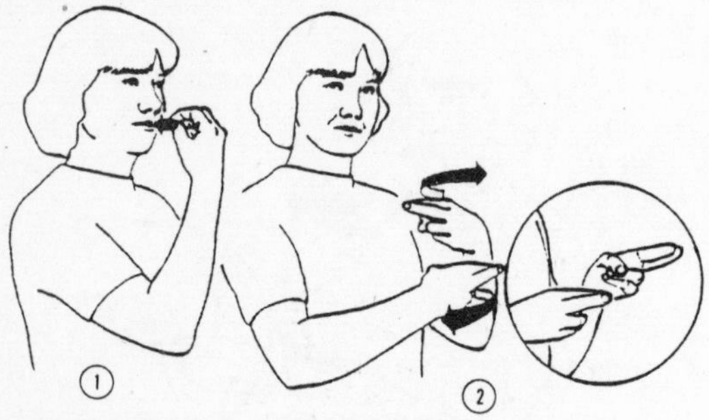

DINING ROOM
With the thumb pinched to the fingers, touch the lips with the fingertips of the right hand. Then, beginning with both "r" hands in front of the body, both palms facing in and left hand closer to the body than the right hand, move the hands to the sides, ending with the palms facing each other.
Hint: "Eat" plus "room."

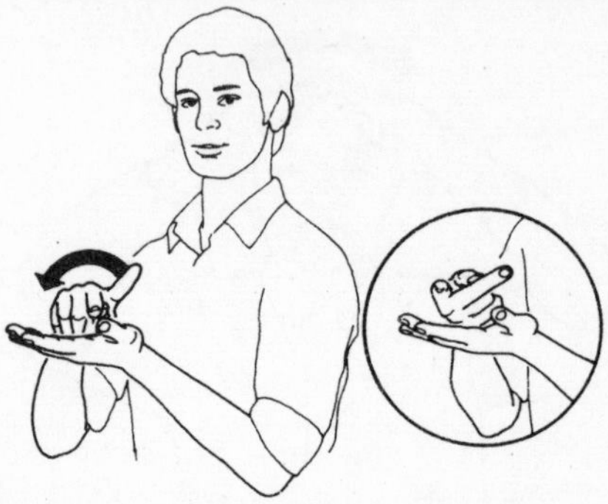

KITCHEN
Beginning with the palm side of the right "k" hand on the palm of the open left hand held in front of the chest flip the right hand over, ending with the palm facing up.
Hint: Initialized sign made similar to the sign for "cook."

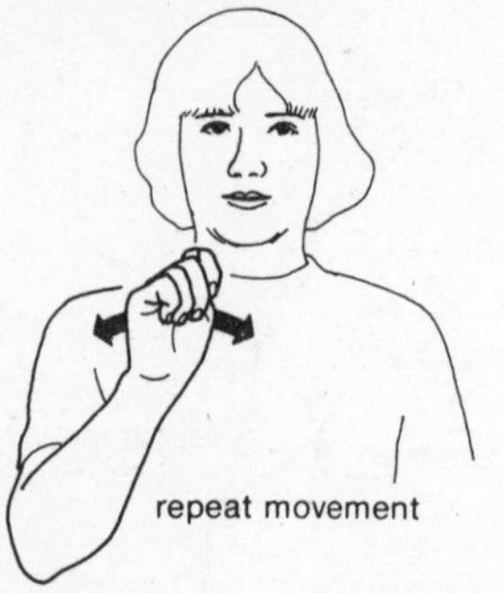

TOILET, BATHROOM
Shake the right "t" hand, palm facing forward, with a short repeated movement in front of the chest.
Hint: Initialized sign.

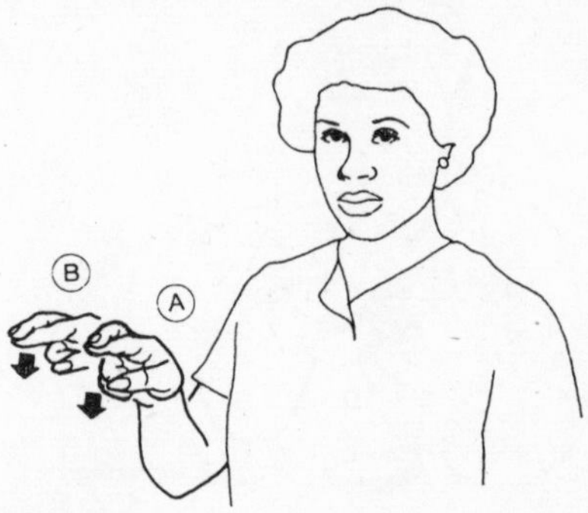

REST ROOM
Bounce the right "r" hand, palm facing down, downward in front of the right side of the body and then again to the right.
Hint: Abbreviation "r-r."

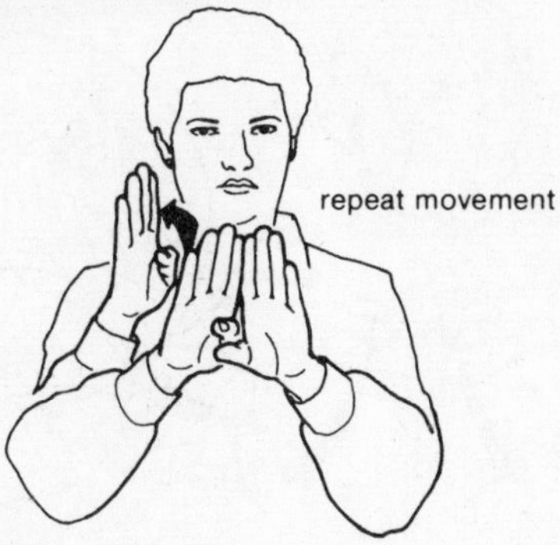

DOOR
With the index-finger sides of both "b" hands touching in front of the chest, palms forward, swing the right hand back turning the palm left with a double movement.
Hint: Opening and closing a door.

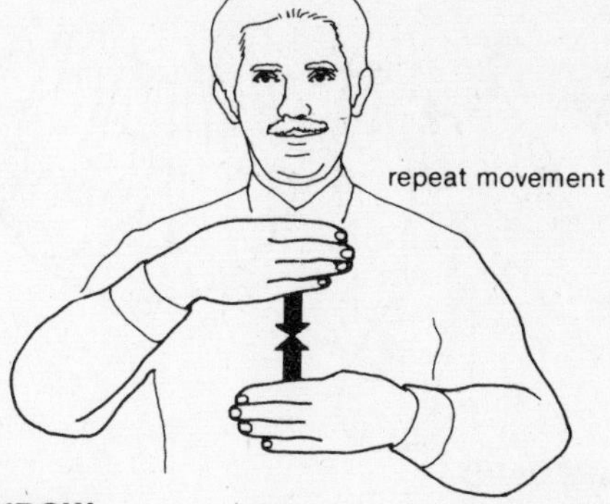

WINDOW
Beginning with the right "b" hand above the left "b" hand in front of the chest, both palms facing in, tap the little-finger side of the right hand and the index-finger side of the left hand together with a double movement.
Hint: Shows opening and closing a window.

just point up

CEILING
Beginning with the index-finger side of the right "b" hand touching the little-finger side of the left "b" hand over the head, both palms facing down, bring the right hand forward at the same level.
Hint: Shows the flat surface of the ceiling.

FLOOR
Beginning with the index-finger sides of both "b" hands touching in front of the body, both palms facing down, move the hands smoothly outward to in front of each side of the body.
Hint: Shows the flat surface of the floor.

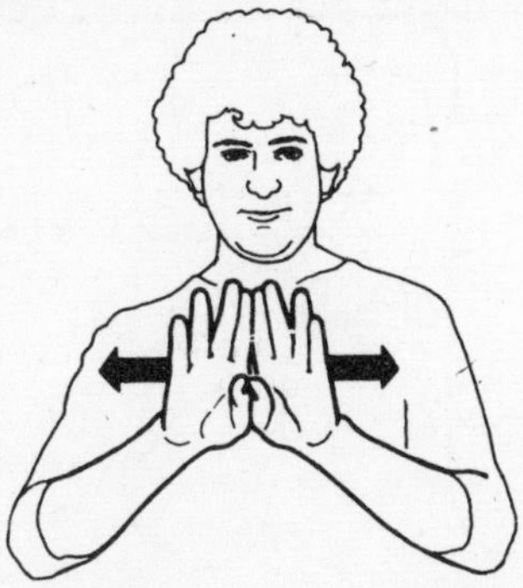

WALL
Beginning with the index-finger sides of both "b" hands touching in front of the body, both palms facing forward, move the hands smoothly outward to in front of each side of the body.
Hint: Shows the flat surface of the wall.

or peace sign wiggling fingers as good

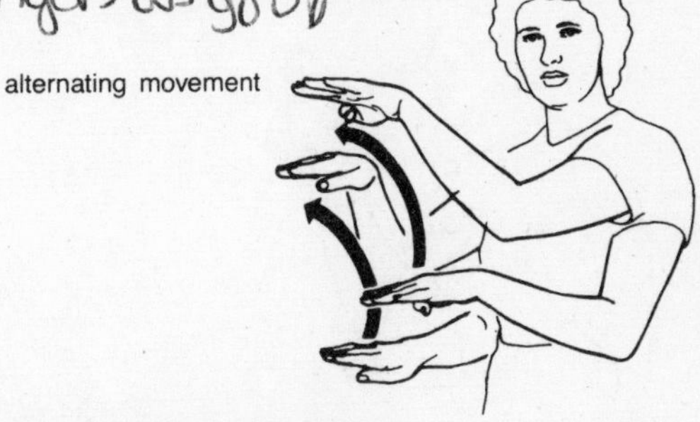

STAIRS, STEPS, STAIRWAY
Move both "b" hands, palms down, upward by alternatingly moving the hands over one another.
Hint: Shows climbing stairs.

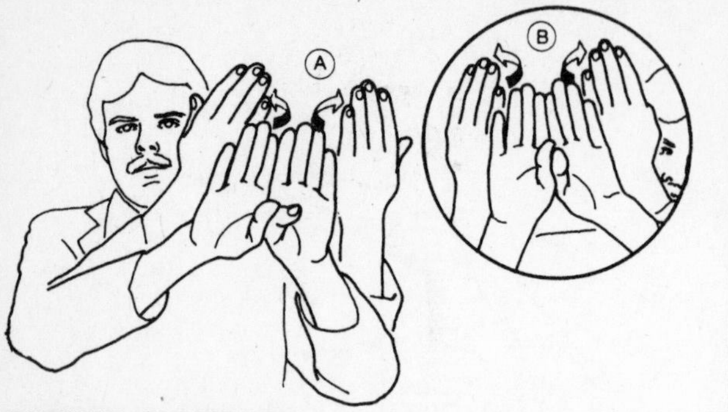

CABINET, CUPBOARD
With the index-finger sides of both "b" hands touching in front of the left side of the head, palms facing forward, swing both hands back turning the palms in toward the face. Repeat in front of the right side of the head.
Hint: Opening several doors at head level.

CLOSET
Brush the thumbs of both "5" hands, palms facing in, downward and outward on each side of the chest. Then, beginning with the index-finger sides of both "b" hands touching in front of the chest, palms forward, swing the right hand back turning the palm left.
Hint: "Clothes" + "door."

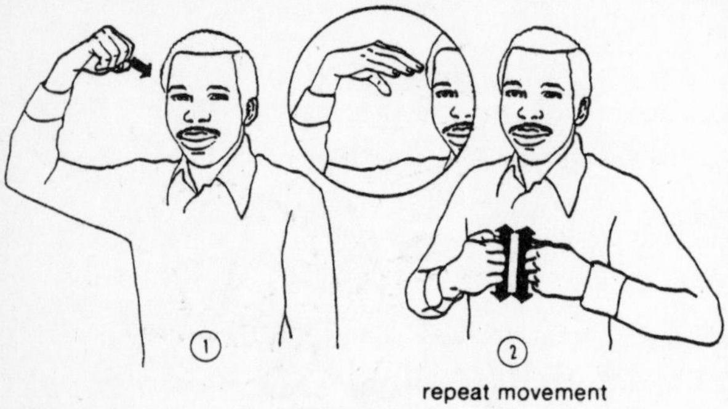

SHOWER
Beginning with the right "s" hand above the right side of the head, palm left, flick the fingers open into a "5" hand. Then rub the knuckles of both "a" hands, palms facing in, up and down on each side of the chest with a double movement.
Hint: Water coming from a shower head plus "bathe."

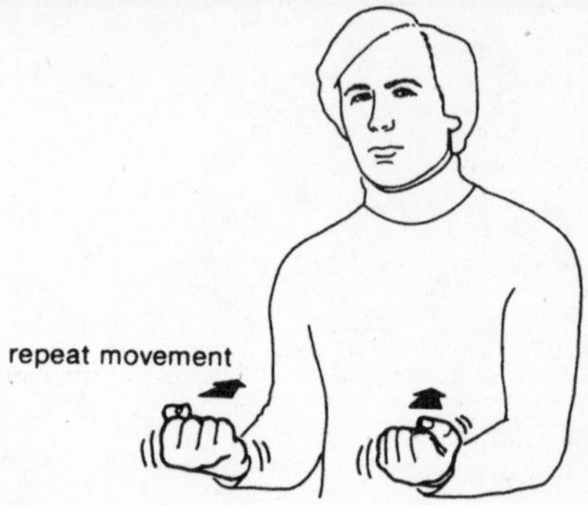

DRAWER
Beginning with both "s" hands in front of the each side of the body, palms facing up, pull the hands toward the body with a short double movement. Note: Both "c" hands could be used instead.
Hint: Pulling open a drawer.

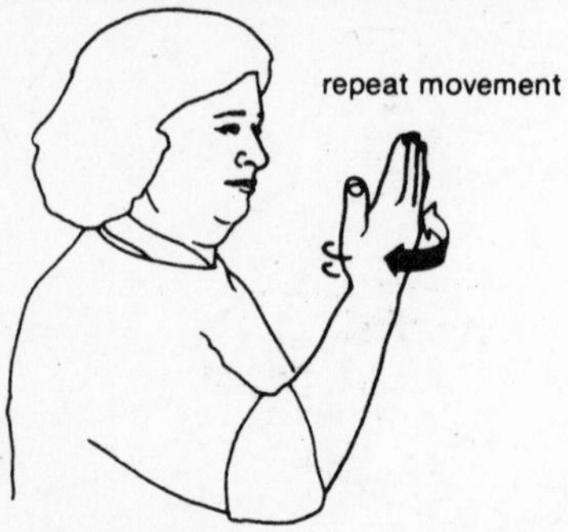

MIRROR, REFLECTION
With the fingers of the open right hand pointing up, twist the hand repeatedly with a small movement near the right side of the head.
Hint: Looking at a reflection in a mirror.

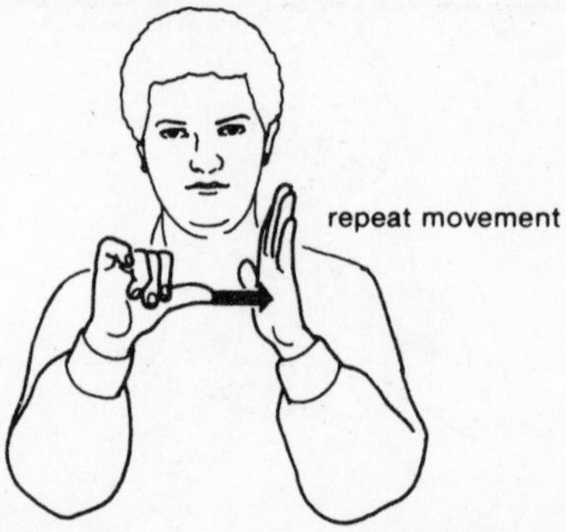

DOORBELL
Push the extended thumb of the right "10" hand, palm facing forward, with a double movement into the open left palm held up in front of the chest, palm facing right and fingers pointing up.
Hint: Ringing a doorbell by pushing on it.

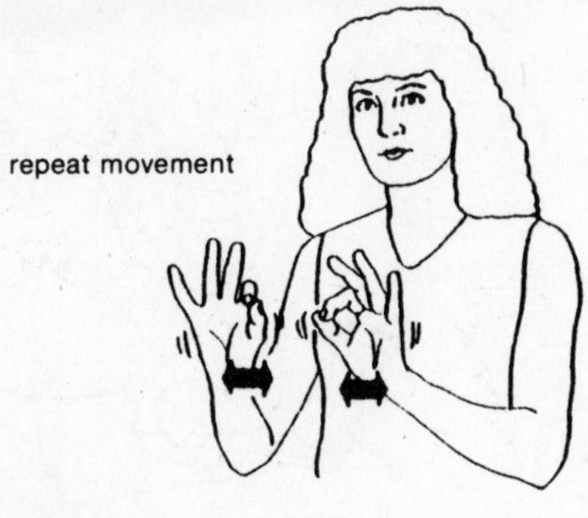

FURNITURE
With both "f" hands near each other in front of the chest, palms facing forward, shake the hands from side to side with a small repeated movement.
Hint: Initialized sign.

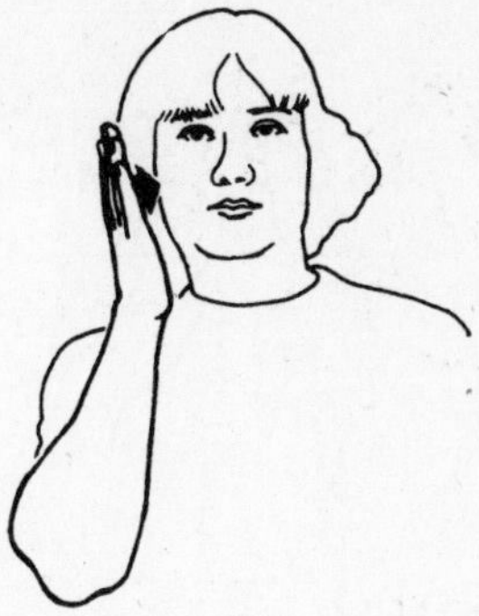

BED
Place the palm of the open right hand against the right cheek.
Hint: Laying one's head on a pillow.

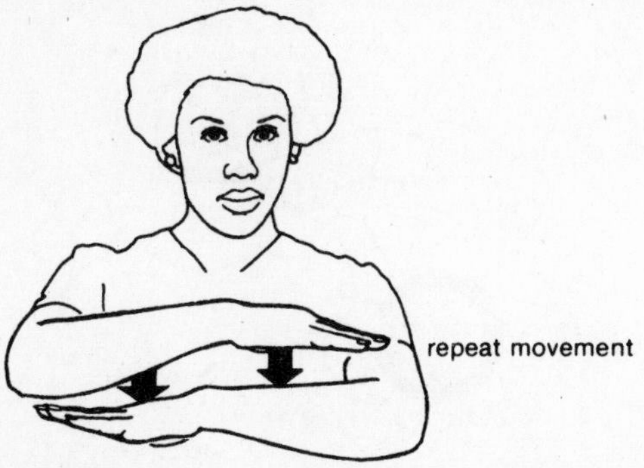

TABLE, DESK
Bring the bent right forearm and open hand, palm facing down with a short double movement, down on the top of the bent left arm and open hand held across the body, palm facing down.
Hint: Represents the top of a table or desk.

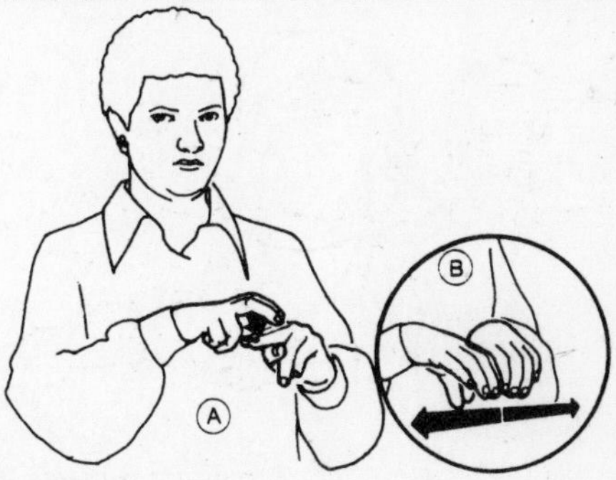

COUCH, SOFA
Place the right curved "u" fingers across the left "u" fingers, both palms facing down. Then beginning with the index-finger sides of both "c" hands together in front of the chest, both palms facing down, move the hands apart to in front of the sides of the body.
Hint: "Sit" plus indicating a long place to sit.

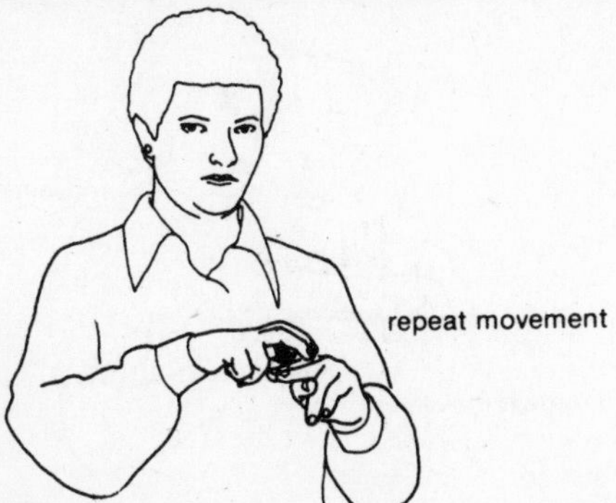

CHAIR, SEAT
With a double movement tap the curved right "u" fingers across the extended left "u" fingers, both palms facing down.
Hint: Legs hanging from the seat of a chair.

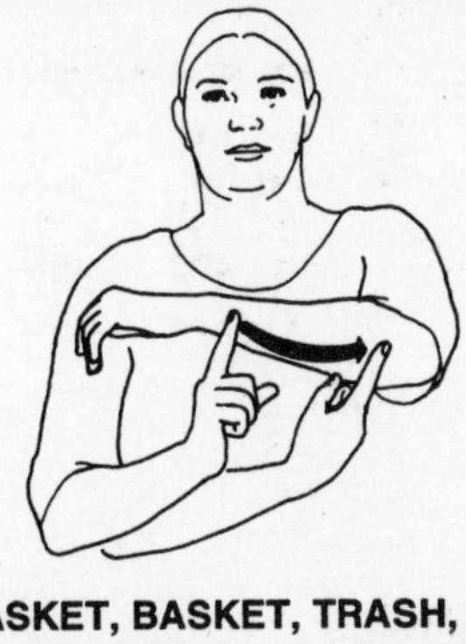

WASTEBASKET, BASKET, TRASH, GARBAGE
Touch the extended right index finger first to near the wrist and then near the elbow of the bent left arm held across the chest.
Hint: Carrying a basket on the arm.

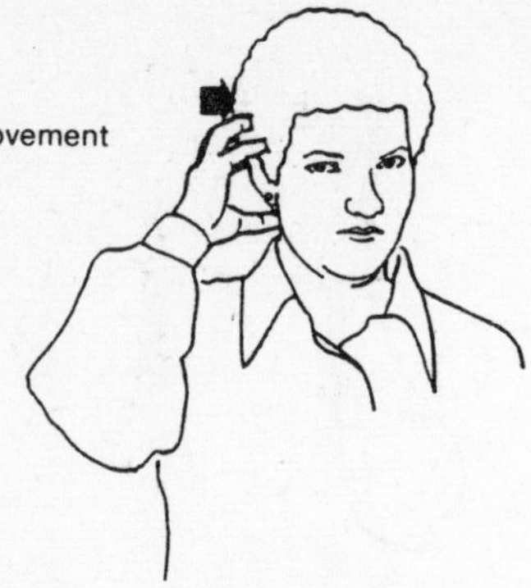

RADIO

Tap the fingertips of the right "claw" hand over the right ear with a double movement. Note: The sign can be made with both hands.

Hint: Headset for listening to the radio.

VACUUM CLEANER, VACUUM

With the right "5" hand dangling down from the wrist over the open left hand, palm facing up, move the right hand back and forth with a shaking movement over the left palm.

Hint: Action of a vacuum moving across carpet.

TELEPHONE, PHONE, CALL

Bring the knuckles of the right "y" hand to near the right ear.

Hint: Mime holding a telephone.

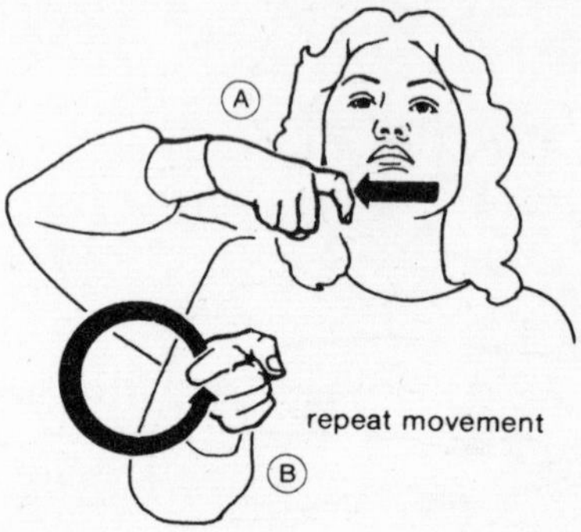

DRYER

Pull the index finger of the right "x" hand, palm facing down, from left to right across the chin. Then make a repeated circle in front of the body with the extended right index finger, palm facing left and finger pointing forward.

Hint: "Dry" plus the movement of clothes inside a dryer.

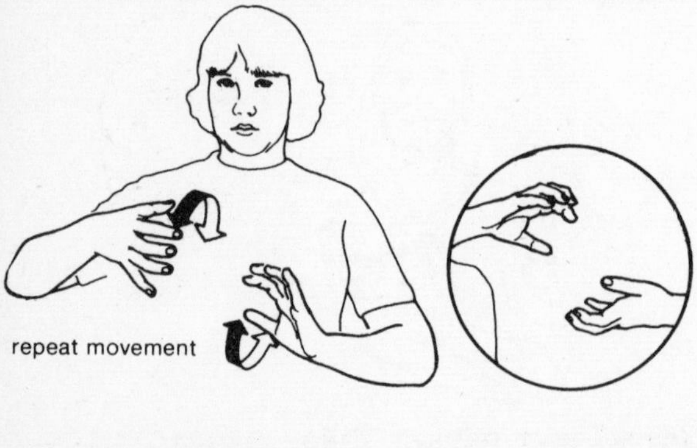

WASHING MACHINE

With the right "claw" hand above the left "claw" hand, palms facing each other, twist the wrists in opposite directions with a double movement.

Hint: The movement of a washing machine agitator.

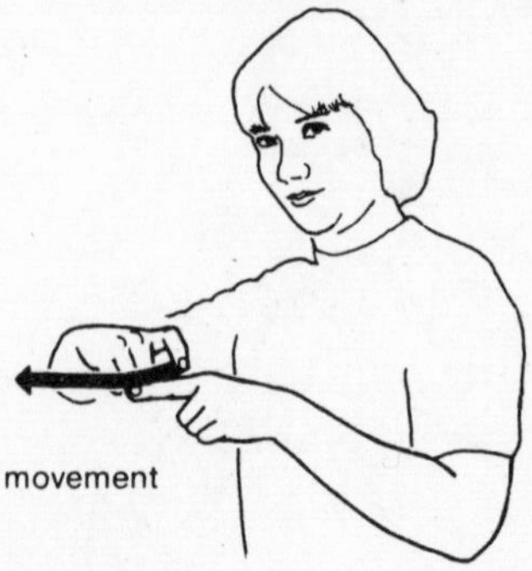

SEWING MACHINE

Move the index fingertip of the right "x" hand, palm facing down, with a repeated movement from the base to the fingertip of the extended left index finger, palm facing right.

Hint: Stitching along seam lines.

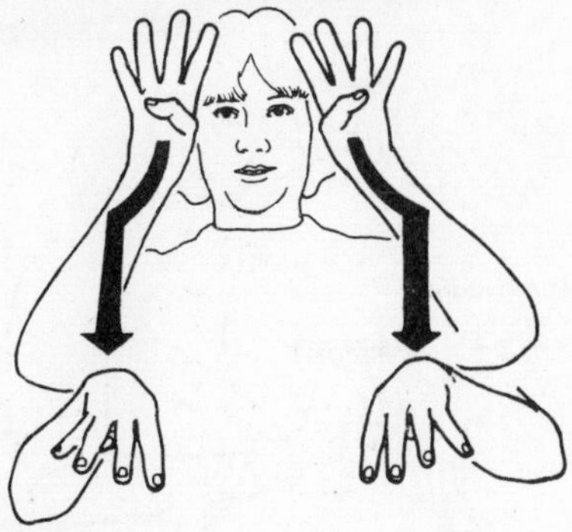

CURTAINS
Bring both "4" hands, palms facing forward, from near each side of the head down and apart to in front of each shoulder and then straight down, ending with the palms facing down.
Hint: Shows the shape of curtains pulled back.

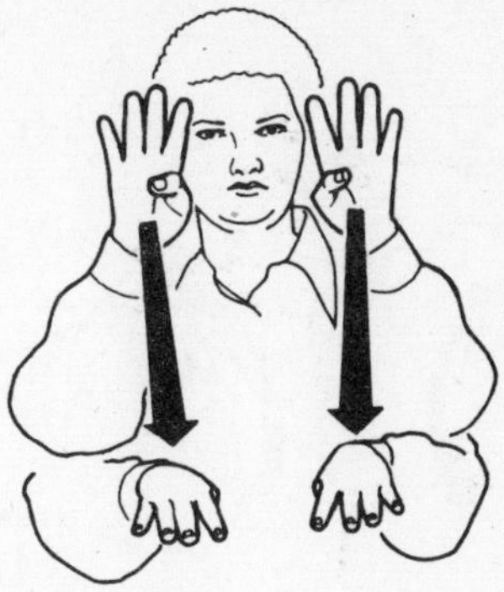

DRAPES
Bring both "4" hands, palms facing forward, from near each side of the head down to in front of the chest, ending with the palms facing down.
Hint: Shows the shape of hanging drape panels.

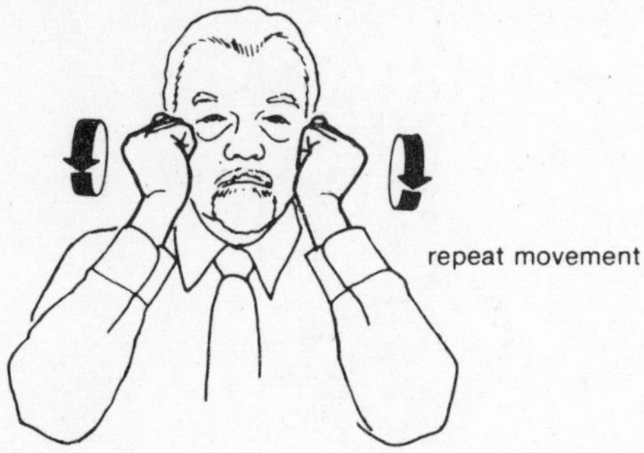

TOWEL
Rub the palm sides of both "a" hands in circular movements on the cheeks.
Hint: Drying with a towel.

BLANKET, SHEET, COVER
Bring both "b" hands, palms facing down, from in front of the chest up to the neck.
Hint: Covering with a blanket.

PICTURE, PHOTOGRAPH, PHOTO
Bring the right "c" hand, palm facing forward, downward from the right side of the face, ending with the thumb side of the right hand against the palm of the open left hand held in front of the chest.
Hint: Taking an image and recording it on paper.

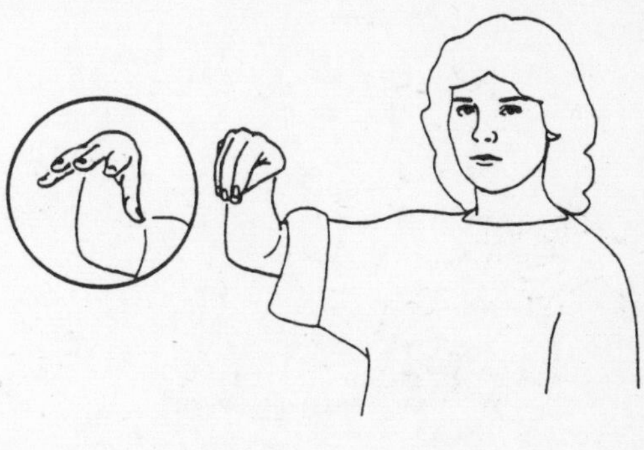

LAMP
With the right fingers and thumb pinched together in front of the right shoulder, palm facing down, open the fingers to a "5" hand, fingers dangling down.
Hint: Light coming down from under a lamp shade.

Clothing

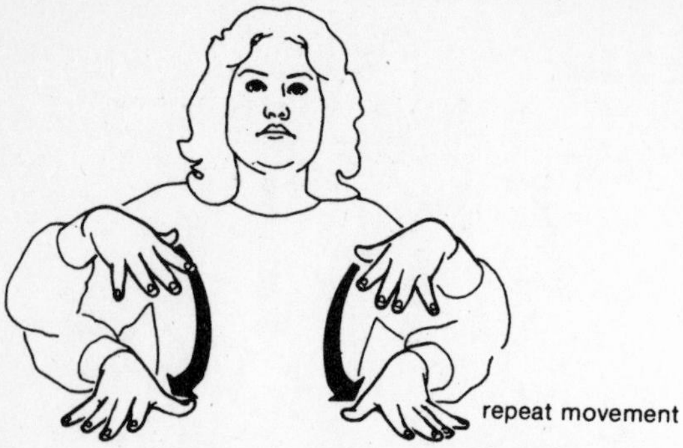

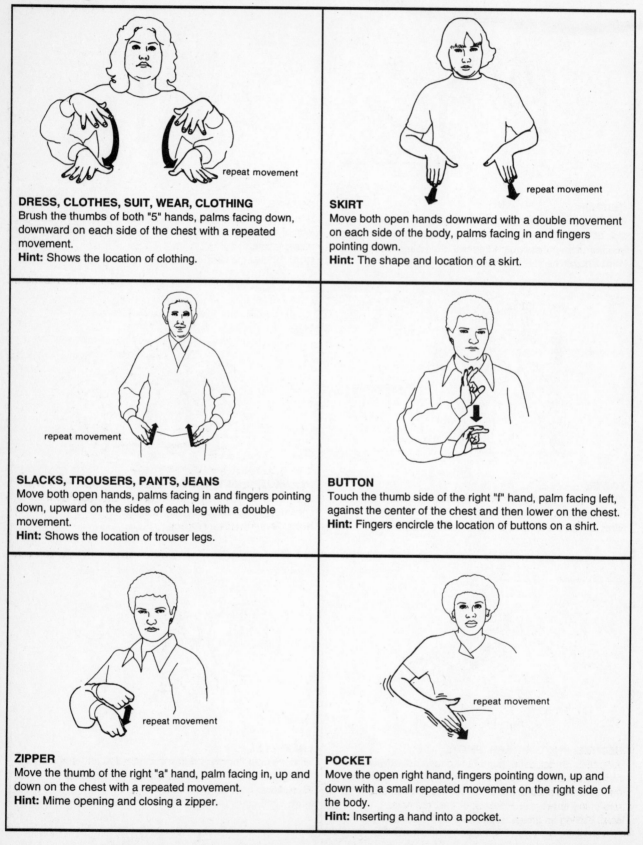

DRESS, CLOTHES, SUIT, WEAR, CLOTHING
Brush the thumbs of both "5" hands, palms facing down, downward on each side of the chest with a repeated movement.
Hint: Shows the location of clothing.

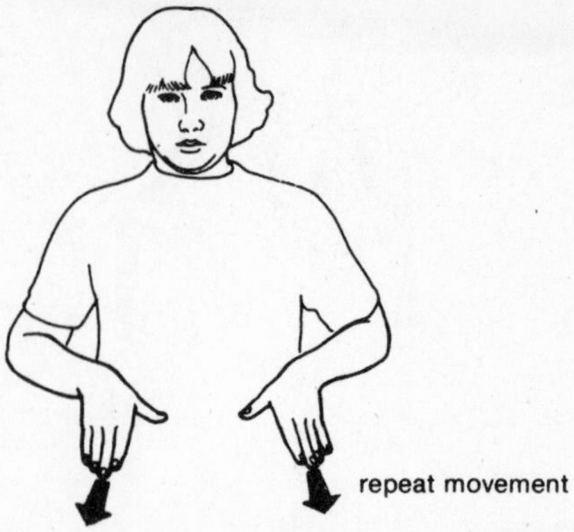

SKIRT
Move both open hands downward with a double movement on each side of the body, palms facing in and fingers pointing down.
Hint: The shape and location of a skirt.

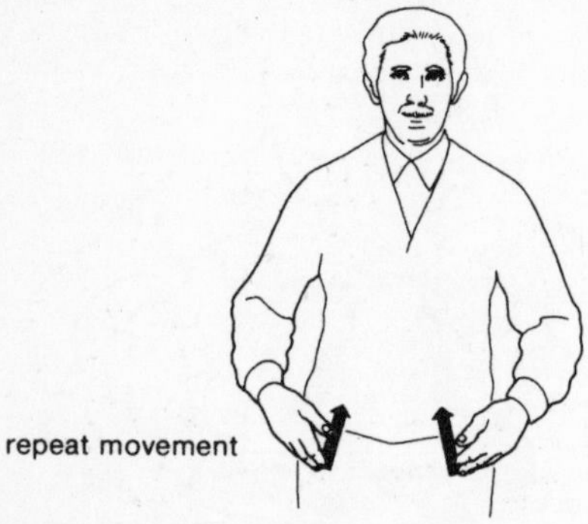

SLACKS, TROUSERS, PANTS, JEANS
Move both open hands, palms facing in and fingers pointing down, upward on the sides of each leg with a double movement.
Hint: Shows the location of trouser legs.

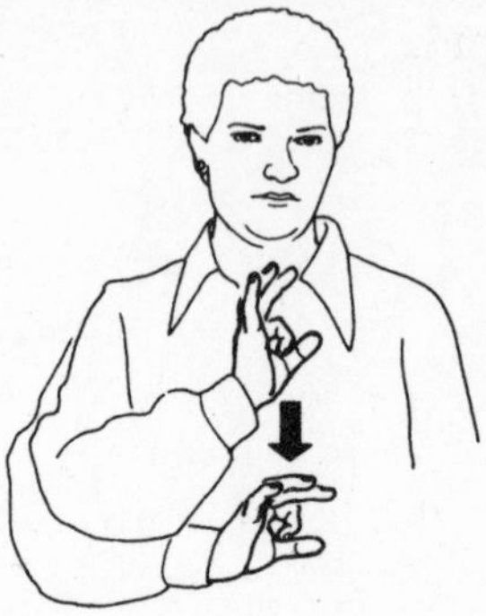

BUTTON
Touch the thumb side of the right "f" hand, palm facing left, against the center of the chest and then lower on the chest.
Hint: Fingers encircle the location of buttons on a shirt.

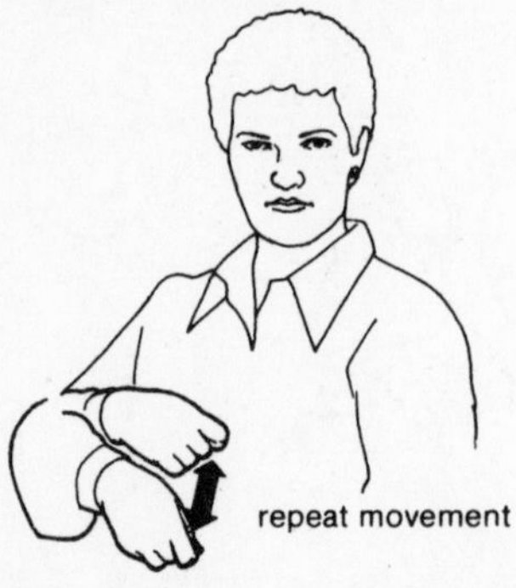

ZIPPER
Move the thumb of the right "a" hand, palm facing in, up and down on the chest with a repeated movement.
Hint: Mime opening and closing a zipper.

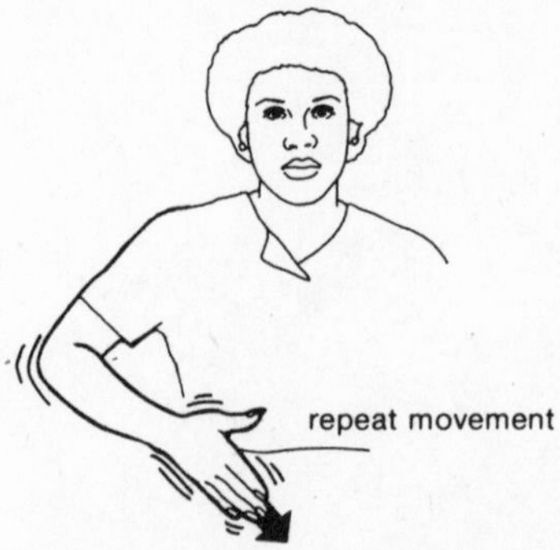

POCKET
Move the open right hand, fingers pointing down, up and down with a small repeated movement on the right side of the body.
Hint: Inserting a hand into a pocket.

SCARF
With the thumbs and index fingers of both "a" hands pinched together, move the hands down from each temple to near each other under the chin.
Hint: Shows tying a scarf under the chin.

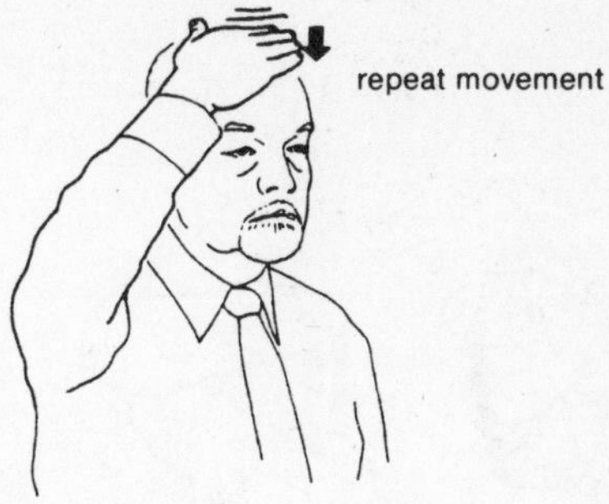

HAT
Pat the palm of the open right hand on top of the head with a repeated movement.
Hint: Shows the location a hat is worn.

BELT
Beginning with both "h" hand near the sides of the waist, palms facing each other, bring the hands around to touch the fingers in front of the body.
Hint: Fingers encircle the location where a belt is worn.

LUGGAGE, BAGGAGE, SUITCASE
With both elbows bent and extended, bring both "s" hands, palms facing each other, upwardwith a short repeated movement near each side of the body.
Hint: Shows holding luggage.

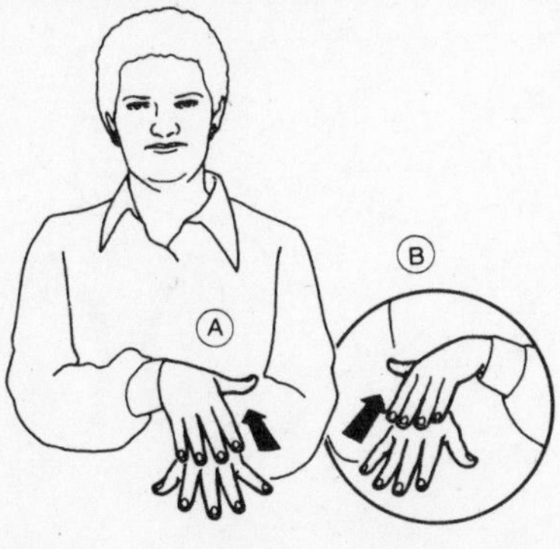

GLOVES
With both "5" hands in front of the body, palms facing down and fingers pointing forward, stroke the right fingers from the fingers over the back of the left hand toward the wrist and then the left over the back of the right hand.
Hint: Pulling on gloves.

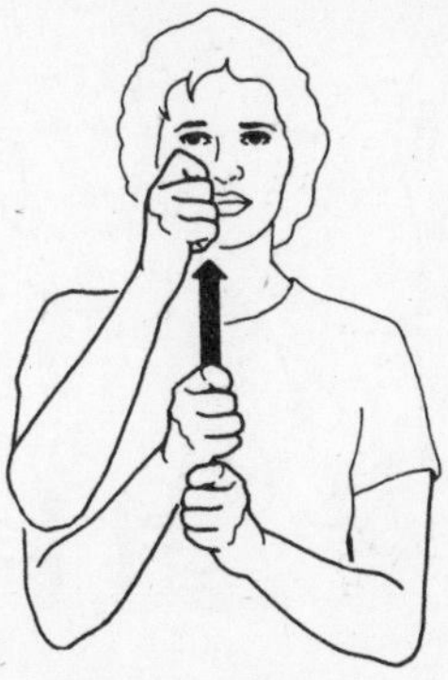

UMBRELLA
With the right "s" hand above the left "s" hand, both palms facing in, raise the right hand upward to face level.
Hint: Mime opening an umbrella.

SWEATER
Bring both "a" hands downward on each side of the chest to about waist level, palms facing in.
Hint: Mime pulling on a sweater.

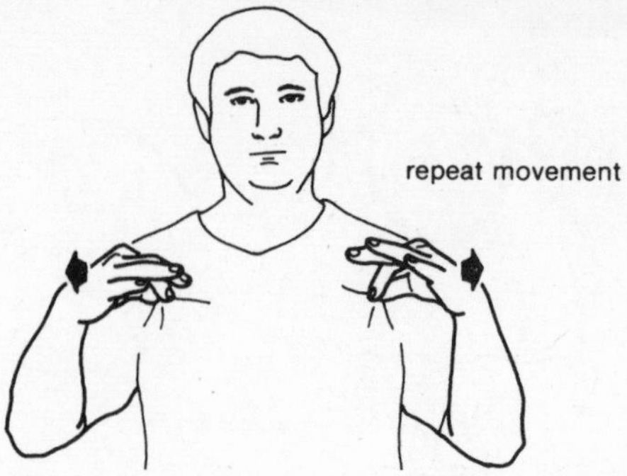

SHIRT
Pull forward with a short repeated movement on the clothes near each shoulder with the fingers of both "f" hands, palms facing in.
Hint: Shows the location of a shirt.

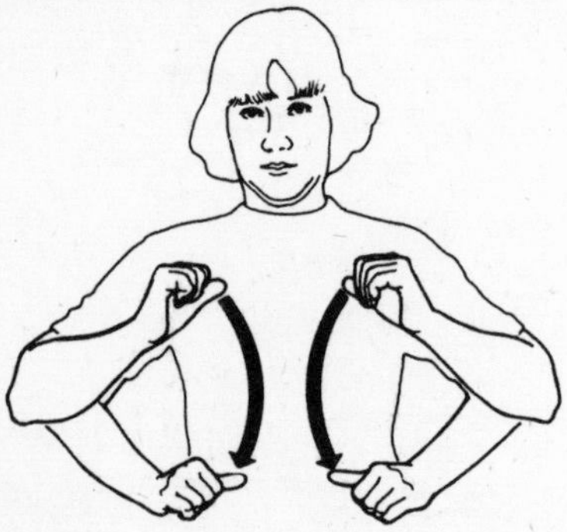

COAT, JACKET
Move both "a" hands, palms facing each other, downward in an arc from near the shoulders to each side of the waist.
Hint: The thumbs follow the lapels of a coat.

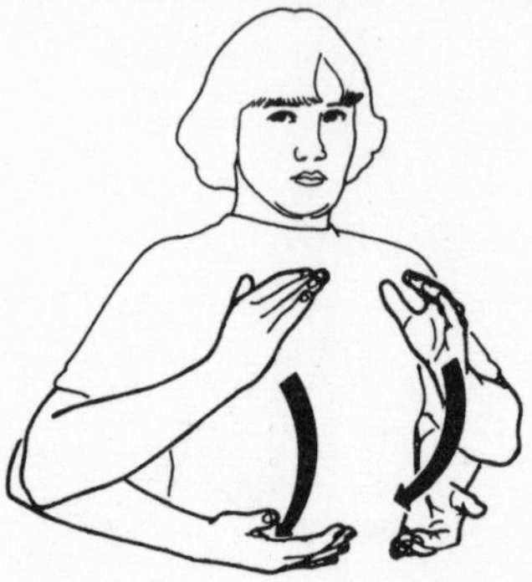

BLOUSE
Beginning with the thumb side of both curved hands near each shoulder, palms facing down, move the hands downward in an arc, ending with the palms facing up near the waist.
Hint: Shows the shape of a blouse.

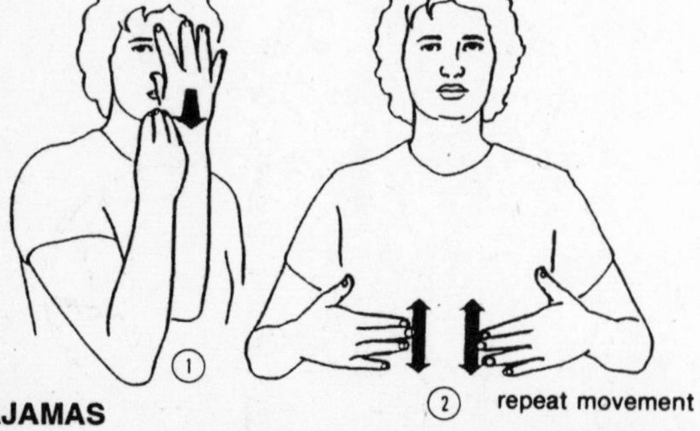

PAJAMAS
Beginning with the right "5" hand in front of the face, palm facing in, bring the hand forward while closing the fingers to the thumb. Then rub the fingers of both open hands, palms facing in and fingers pointing toward each other, up and down with a repeated movement on each side of the chest.
Hint: "Sleep" plus "clothes."

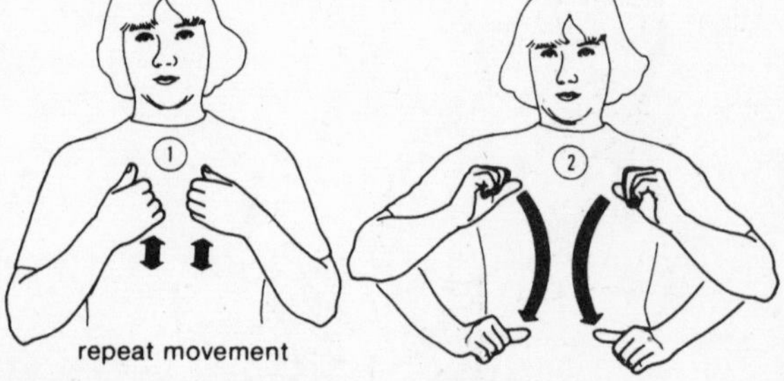

BATHROBE
Rub the palm sides of both "a" hands up and down on the chest with a repeated movement. Then move both "a" hands from near the shoulders, palms facing each other, downward in an arc to near the waist.
Hint: "Bath" plus "coat."

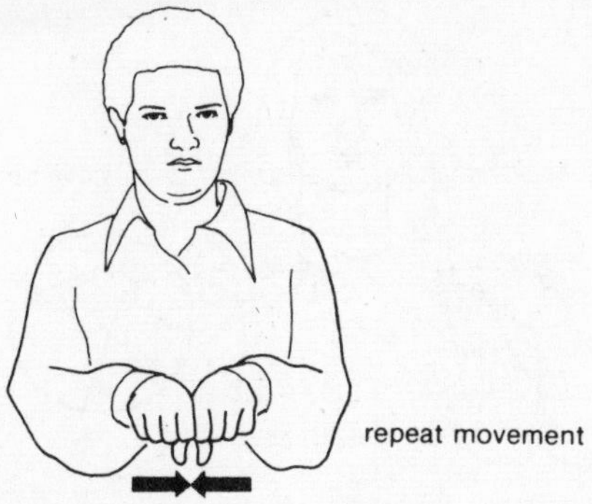

SHOES
Tap the thumb side of both"s" hands together with a double movement in front of the body, palms facing down.
Hint: Clicking the heels of shoes together.

extend L arm
® "b" tap arm

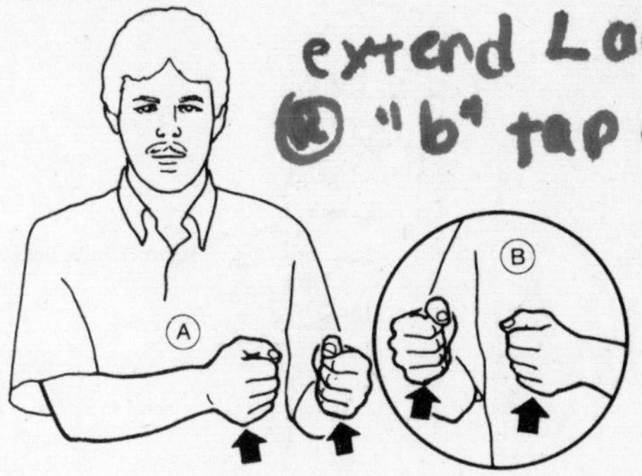

BOOTS
Pull both "s" hands, palms facing each other, upward with a short deliberate movement first in front of the left side of the body and then in front of the right side of the body.
Hint: Mime pulling on boots.

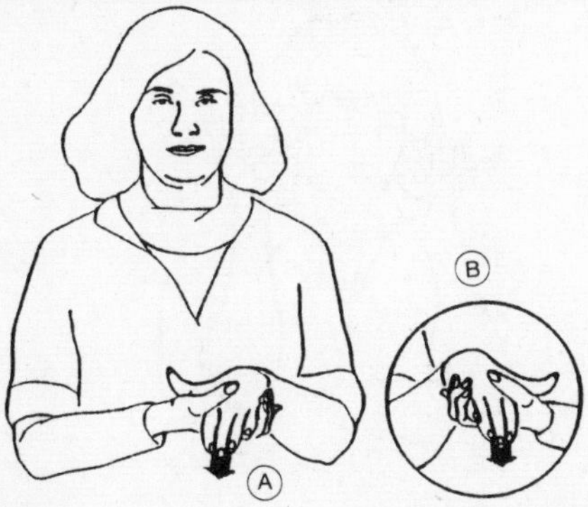

SLIPPERS
Slip the open right hand, palm facing down, between the thumb and index finger of the left "c" hand, palm facing up. Repeat the action by reversing the hands.
Hint: Shows slipping the foot into a slipper.

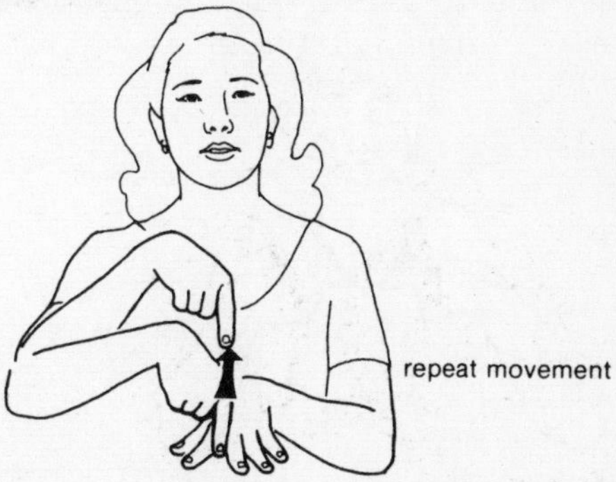

SANDALS
Beginning with the extended right index finger pointing down between the index and middle fingers of the left "5" hand held in front of the body, palm facing down, bring the right hand up and down with a double movement.

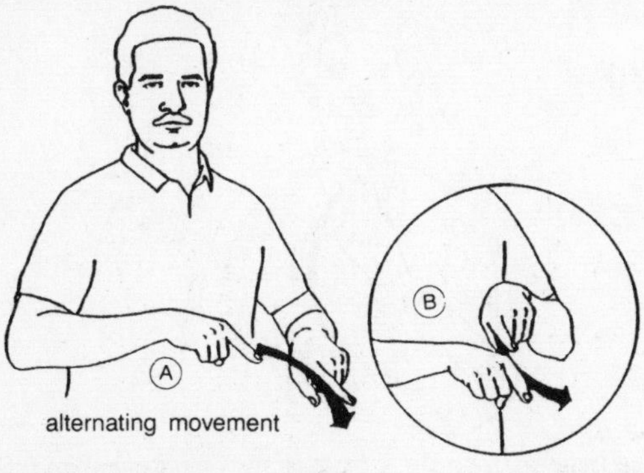

SOCKS, STOCKINGS, HOSE
Slide the thumb sides of both extended index fingers against each other with an alternating forward and back movement, palms facing down and fingers pointing forward.
Hint: The action of knitting needles when making socks.

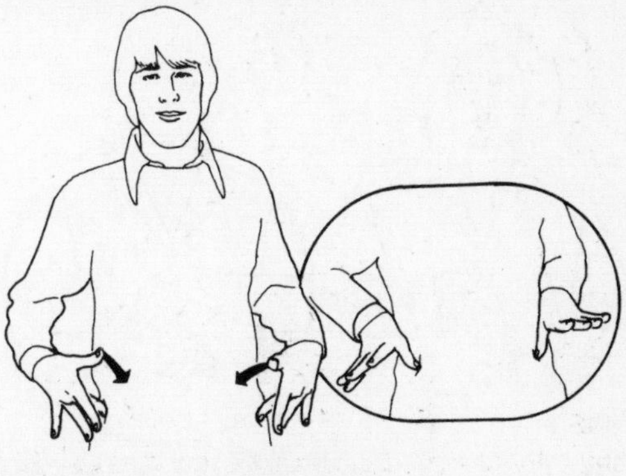

PANTIES, PANTS, UNDERWEAR
Touch the bent middle fingers and then the thumbs of both "5" hands on each side of the body below the waist.
Hint: Indicates the part of the body covered by panties.

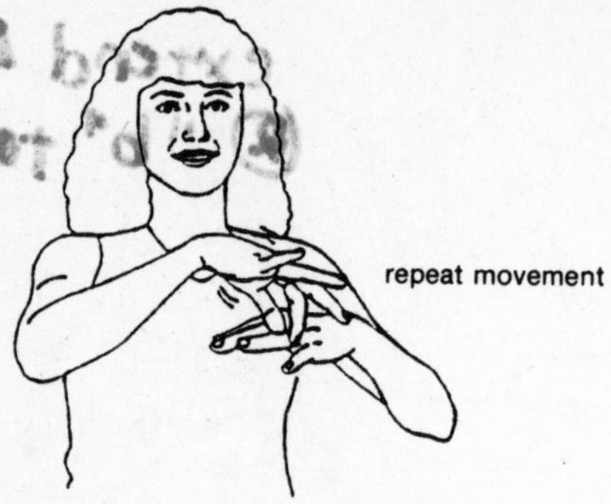

RING

With the left hand held in front of the chest, palm facing down, hold and shake the base of the left ring finger with the bent thumb and index finger of the right "5" hand.

Hint: Putting on an imaginary ring.

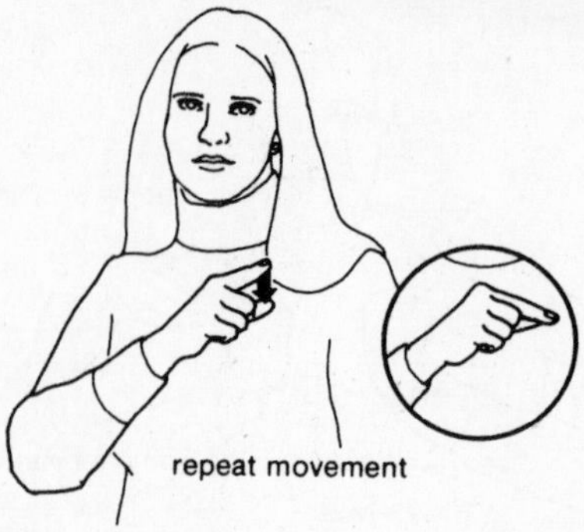

PIN, BROOCH

With the thumb side of the right "g" hand against the left side of the chest, palm facing left, open and close the index finger and thumb with a double movement.

Hint: Shows where a pin is worn.

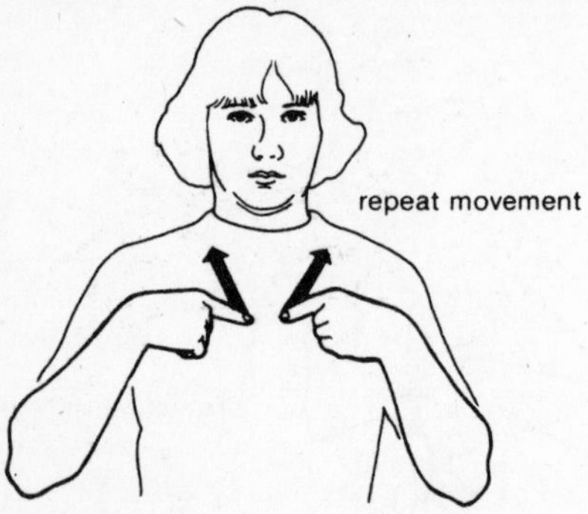

NECKLACE, BEADS

Beginning with both extended index fingers touching near each other on the chest, move the fingers upward toward the shoulders with a double movement.

Hint: The fingers outline the shape and location of a necklace.

EARRINGS

Touch each earlobe with the fingertips of both "f" hands, palms facing each other.

Hint: Location of earrings.

BRACELET

With the thumb and middle fingers of the right hand encircling the left wrist, twist the right hand forward with a double movement.

Hint: Shows the location of a bracelet on the arm.

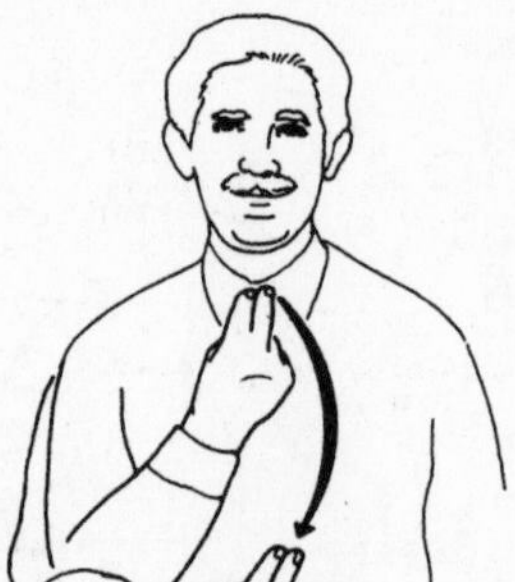

NECKTIE, TIE

Touch the fingertips of the right "u" hand, palm facing in, from just below the neck to the lower chest.

Hint: Location of where a tie is worn.

Animals

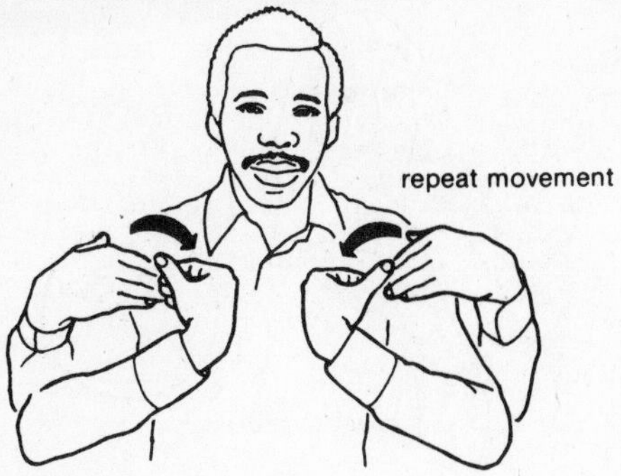

ANIMAL
Beginning with the fingertips of both bent hands on each side of chest, palms facing outward in opposite directions, roll the hands downward with a double movement while keeping the fingers in place.

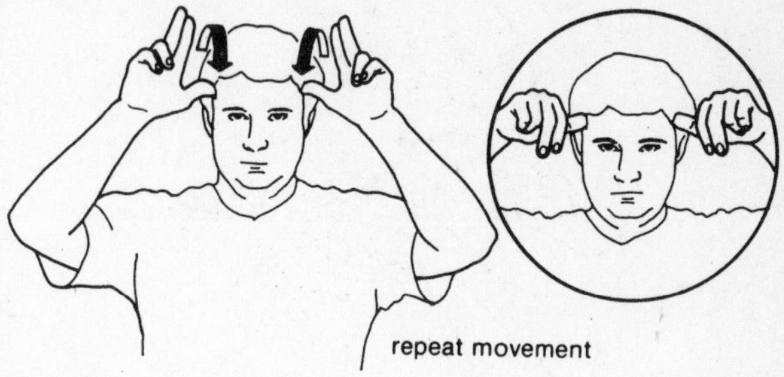

HORSE
With the extended thumbs of both "u" hands touching each side of the head, palms facing forward, bend the fingers up and down with a double movement.
Hint: Shows a horse's ears.

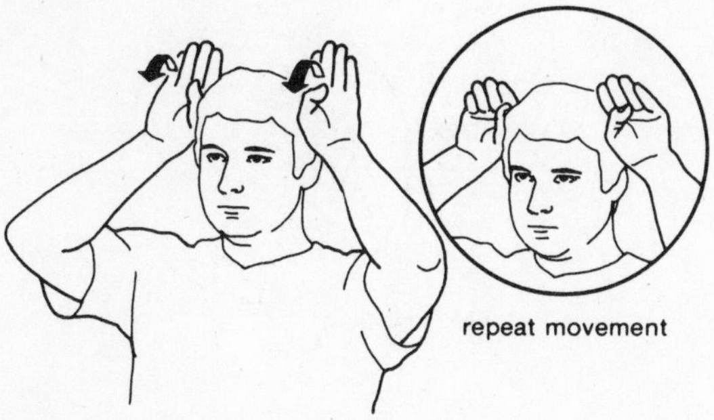

DONKEY, MULE
With the thumb side of both "b" hands touching each side of the head, palms facing forward, bend the fingers up and down with a double movement.
Hint: Shows the flapping of a donkey's ears.

COW, CATTLE
With the thumbs of both "y" hands touching each side of the head, palms facing forward, twist the wrists forward with a double movement.
Hint: Shows a cow's horns.

BULL, BISON
Beginning with the thumbs of both "y" hands touching each side of the head, palms facing forward, bring the hands upward and outward a short distance.
Hint: Shows a bull's horns.

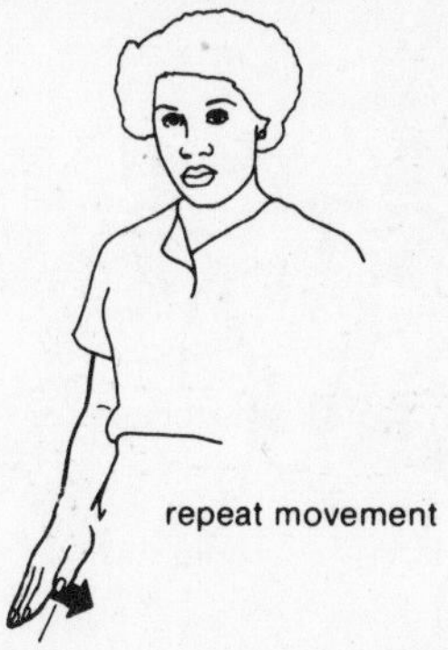

DOG
With a repeated movement pat the right thigh with the palm of the open right hand, fingers pointing down.
Hint: Patting the leg to get a dog's attention.

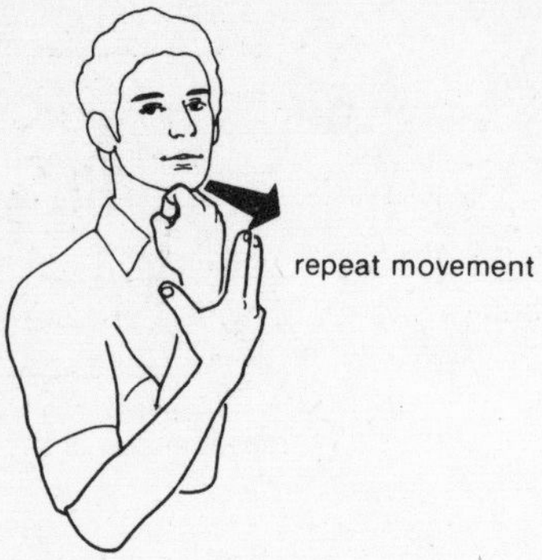

FROG
Beginning with the thumb holding down the right "u" fingers under the chin, move the hand forward with a double movement, flicking the "u" fingers upward each time.
Hint: Shows a frog's throat moving when croaking.

SNAKE, REPTILE, VIPER
Beginning with the index-finger side of the right bent "v" hand near the mouth, palm facing left, move the hand forward with a wavy movement.
Hint: Shows the fangs of a snake as it strikes.

TURKEY, THANKSGIVING
Move the right "g" hand from under the nose, palm facing left, downward to in front of the chin while turning the palm down, wiggling the fingers from side to side under the chin.
Hint: Follows the shape of a turkey's wattle.

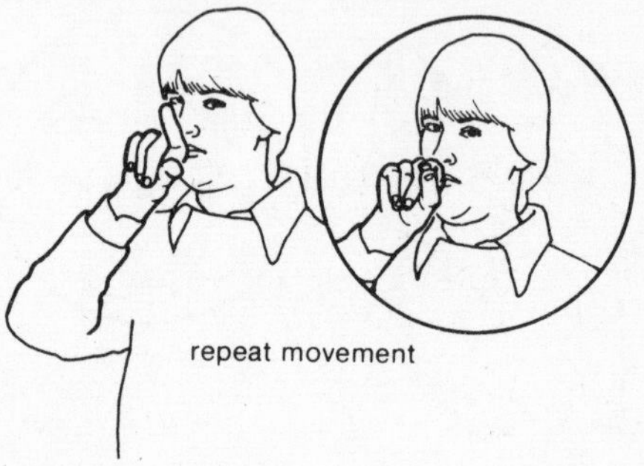

CHICKEN, BIRD, HEN
With the back of the right "g" hand at the mouth, palm facing forward, open and close the thumb and index finger with a double movement.
Hint: The movement of a duck's bill when it chirps or eats.

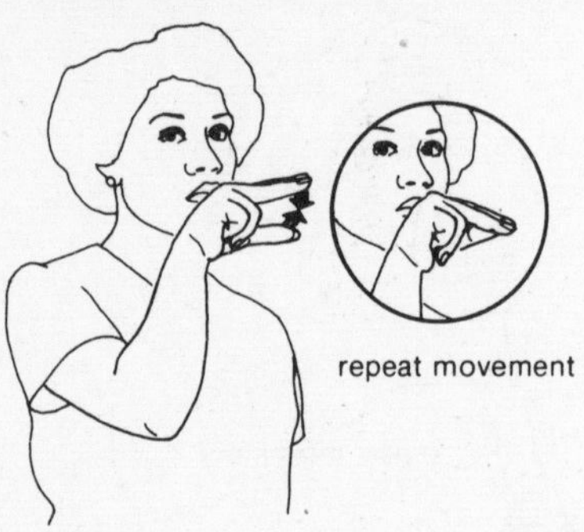

DUCK
With the back of the bent right hand at the mouth and the index finger, middle finger, and thumb extended, open and close the fingers to the thumb with a double movement.
Hint: Shows the movement of a duck's bill when quacking.

FISH
With the extended index left finger touching the wrist of the open right hand, palm facing left and fingers pointing forward, wave the right hand by bending the wrist with a double movement.
Hint: Shows a fish swimming through water.

LION
Move the right "claw" hand, palm facing down, from the forehead back over the head.
Hint: Shows a lion's mane.

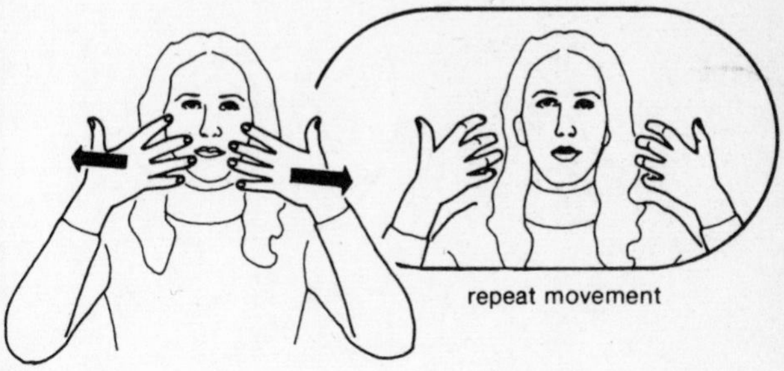

TIGER
Beginning with the fingertips of both "5" hands on each cheek, palms facing in and fingers pointing toward each other, pull the hands to the sides of the cheeks with a double movement while changing to "claw" hands each time.
Hint: Shows the puffy cheeks of a tiger.

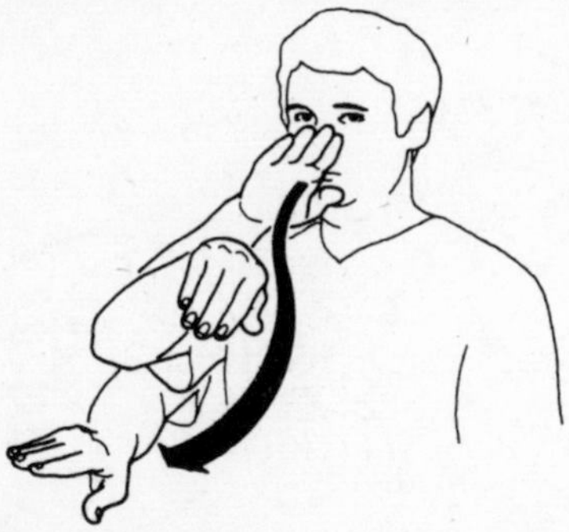

ELEPHANT
Beginning with the back of the open right hand in front of the nose, palm facing down and fingers pointing forward, move the hand downward and forward with a wavy movement.
Hint: Follows the shape of an elephant's trunk.

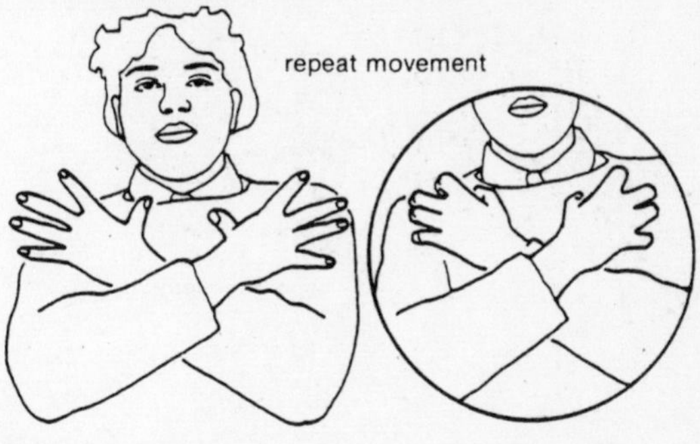

BEAR
Repeatedly scratch the upper chest near the opposite shoulder with both "5" hands crossed in front of the chest.
Hint: Shows a bear hug.

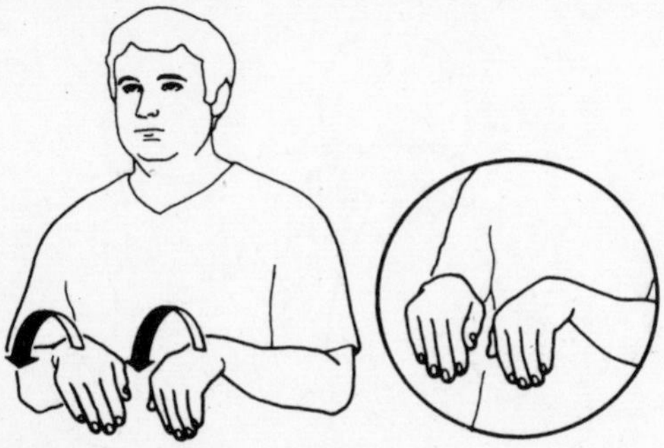

KANGAROO
Move both bent hands held side by side in front of the body, palms facing down, from near the chest forward in small arcs.
Hint: Follows the hopping movement of a kangaroo.

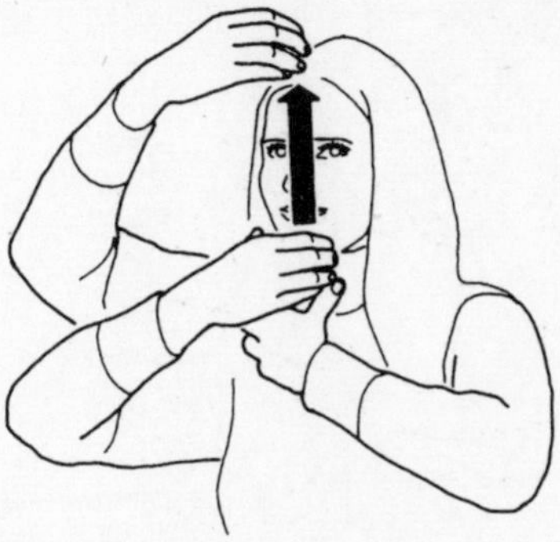

GIRAFFE
With the little-finger side of the right "c" hand on the index-finger side of the left "c" hand in front of the neck, both palms facing in, move the right hand upward in front of the face.

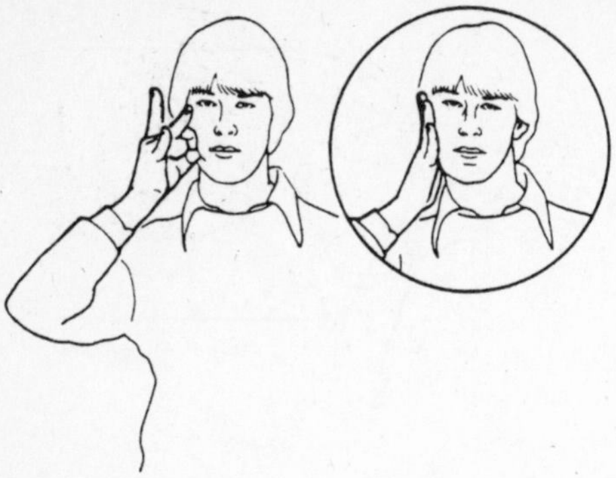

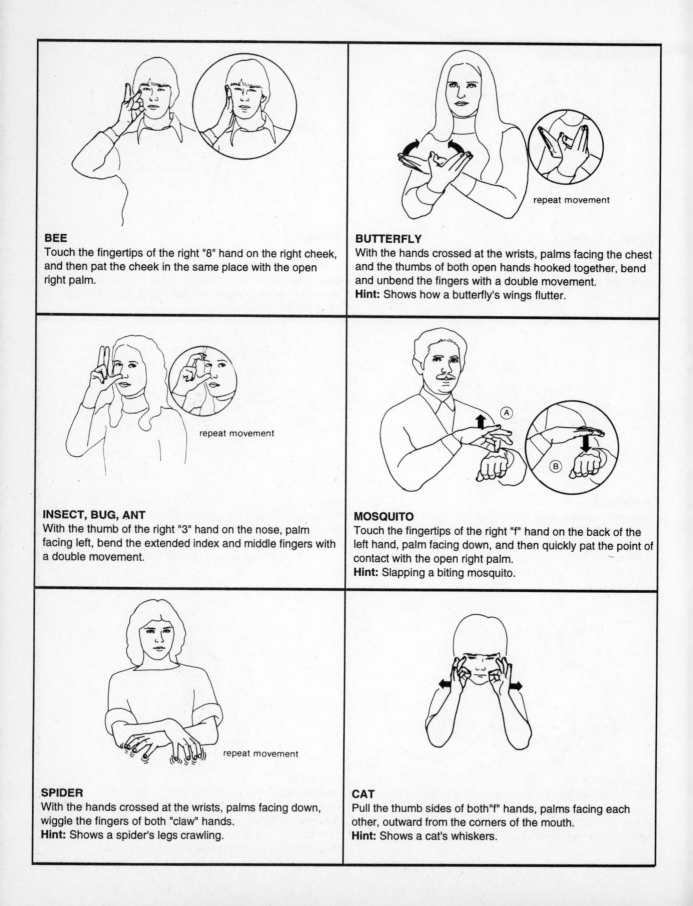

BEE
Touch the fingertips of the right "8" hand on the right cheek, and then pat the cheek in the same place with the open right palm.

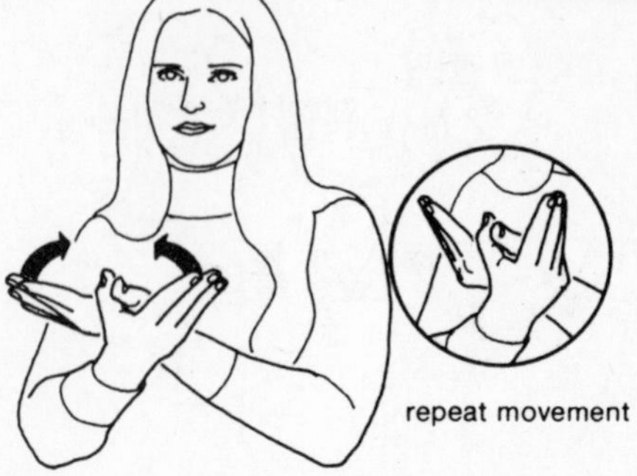

BUTTERFLY
With the hands crossed at the wrists, palms facing the chest and the thumbs of both open hands hooked together, bend and unbend the fingers with a double movement.
Hint: Shows how a butterfly's wings flutter.

INSECT, BUG, ANT
With the thumb of the right "3" hand on the nose, palm facing left, bend the extended index and middle fingers with a double movement.

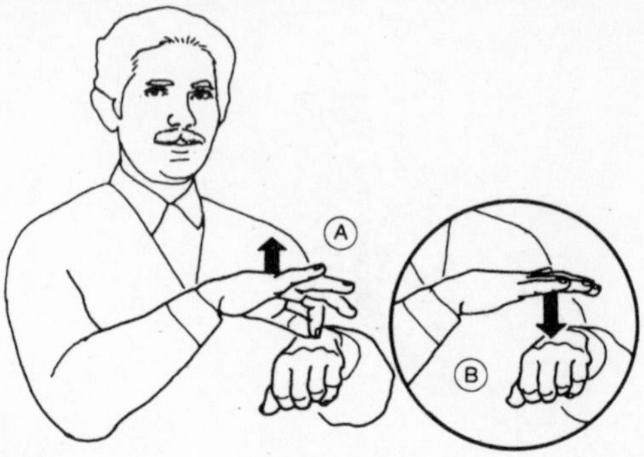

MOSQUITO
Touch the fingertips of the right "f" hand on the back of the left hand, palm facing down, and then quickly pat the point of contact with the open right palm.
Hint: Slapping a biting mosquito.

SPIDER
With the hands crossed at the wrists, palms facing down, wiggle the fingers of both "claw" hands.
Hint: Shows a spider's legs crawling.

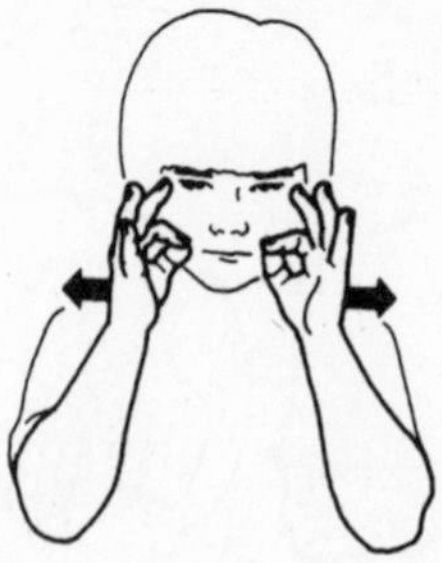

CAT
Pull the thumb sides of both"f" hands, palms facing each other, outward from the corners of the mouth.
Hint: Shows a cat's whiskers.

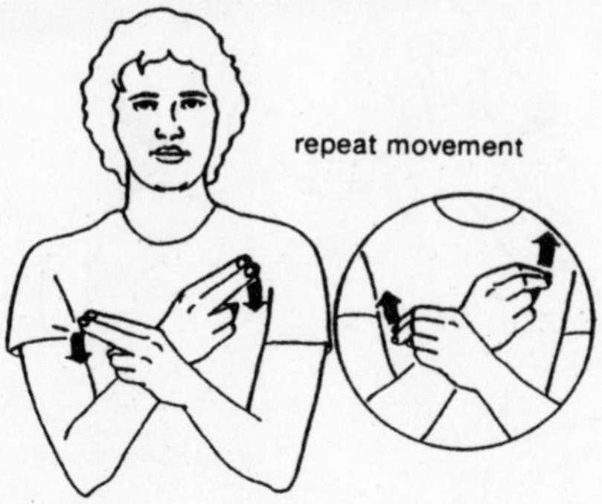

RABBIT, BUNNY, HARE
With both "u" hands crossed at the wrists, palms facing in, bend the fingers of both hands with a double movement.
Hint: Shows the movement of a rabbit's ears.

SKUNK
Move the thumb side of the right "k" hand, palm facing down, from the forehead back over the head, ending with the palm facing up.
Hint: Shows the stripe on a skunk's head.

MOUSE
Brush the extended right index finger, palm facing left, across the nose with a double movement .
Hint: Shows the twitching of a mouse's nose.

RAT
Brush the fingers of the right "r" hand, palm facing left, across the nose with a double movement.
Hint: Initialized sign showing the twitching of a rat's nose.

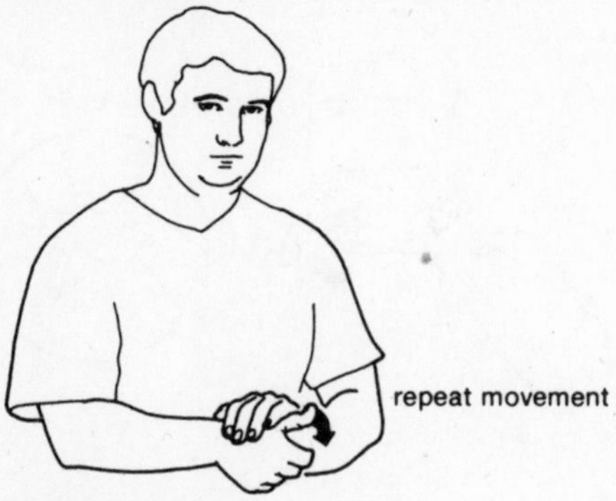

TURTLE, TORTOISE
With the left palm cupped over the right "a" hand, palm facing left, wiggle the right thumb.
Hint: A turtle head extending out from its shell.

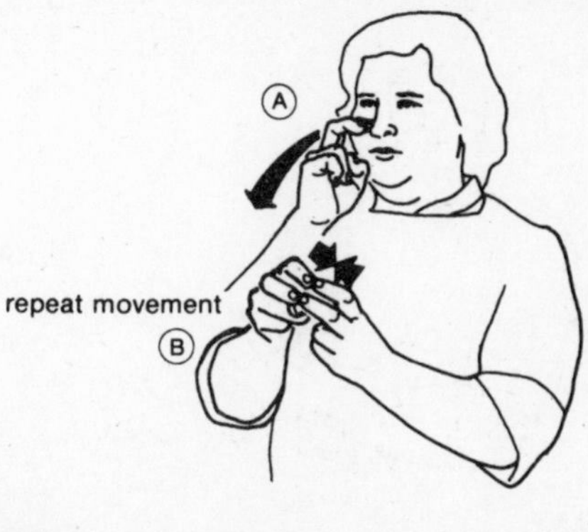

SQUIRREL
Move the right bent "v" hand from the nose, palm facing left, downward to repeatedly tap the fingertips of the left bent "v" hand held in front of the chest, palm facing right.
Hint: Shows a squirrel's paws in front of the chest.

FOX
With the thumb side of the right "f" hand encircling the nose, palm facing left, twist the hand to the left with a double movement.
Hint: Initialized sign showing the shape of a fox's nose.

MOOSE
Beginning with the thumbs of both "5" hands touching each side of the forehead, palms facing forward, move the hands upward and outward in small arcs.
Hint: Shows a moose's large antlers.

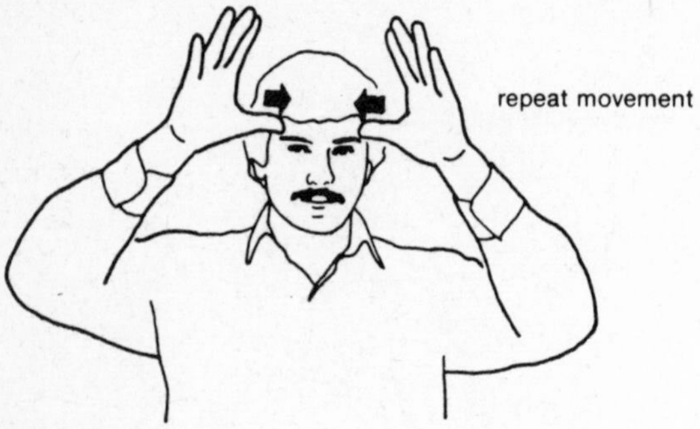

DEER, REINDEER
Tap the thumbs of both "5" hands on each side of the forehead with a double movement, palms facing forward.
Hint: Shows a deer's antlers.

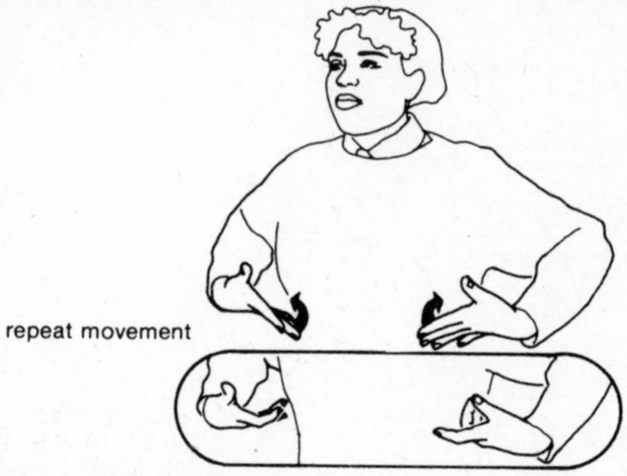

MONKEY, APE
Scratch upward on each side of the chest near the underarm with both "5" hands, palms facing up.
Hint: Mimes the scratching that is characteristic of monkeys.

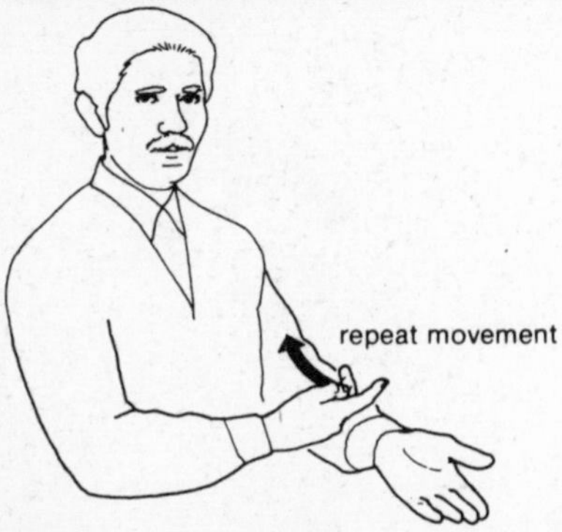

SHEEP, LAMB
Sweep the back of the right "k" hand, palm facing up, from the wrist toward the crook of the extended left arm with a double movement.
Hint: Shearing wool from sheep.

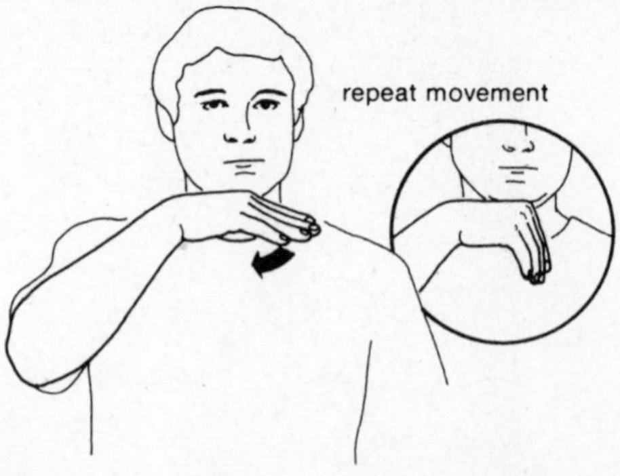

PIG, HOG
With the back of the open right hand under the chin, palm facing down, bend the fingers downward with a double movement.
Hint: Shows eating too much like a pig so you are full to the chin.

three

PEOPLE

Relationships
Careers
Other People
Pronouns

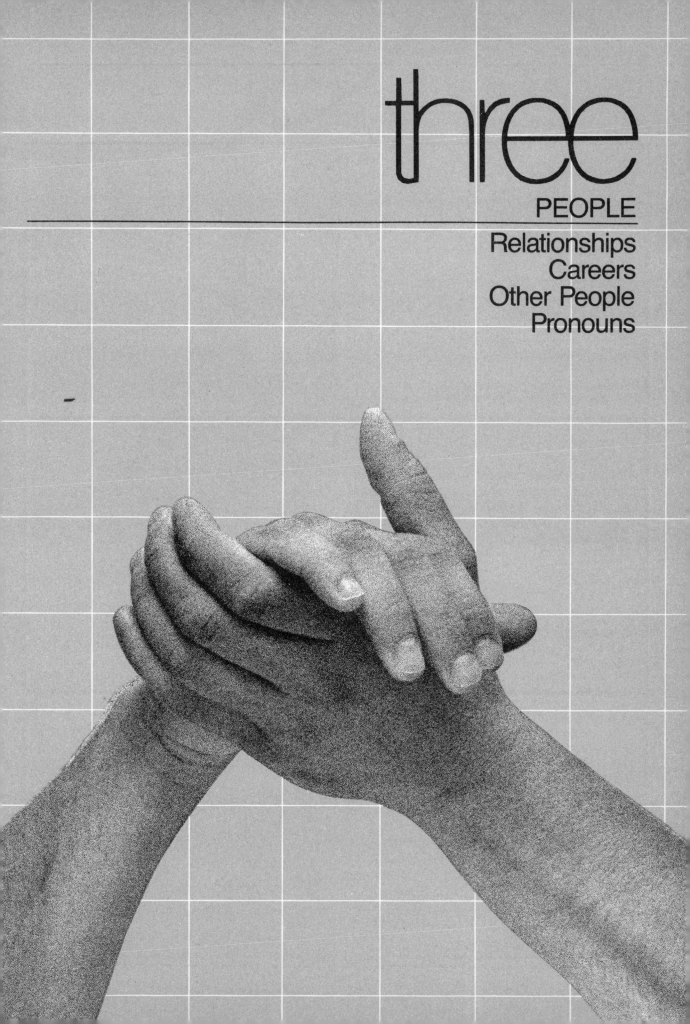

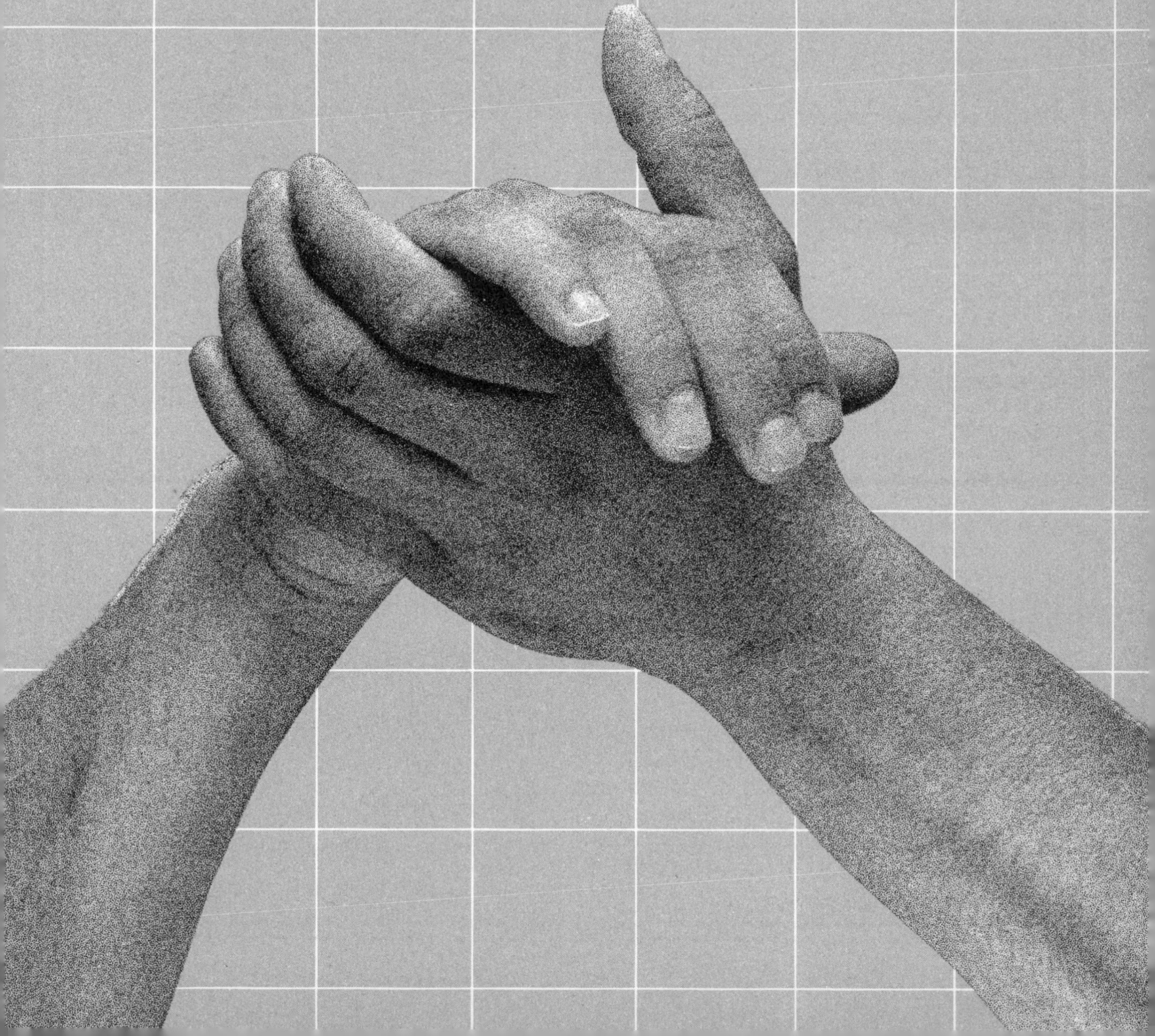

PRONOUNS

Pronouns are often indicated in sign language by establishing location where the person being discussed is imagined to be, and then pointing to that place each time the person is referred to. Using this method of establishing fixed locations for people, several people can be discussed during the same conversation by pointing to the location for each person.

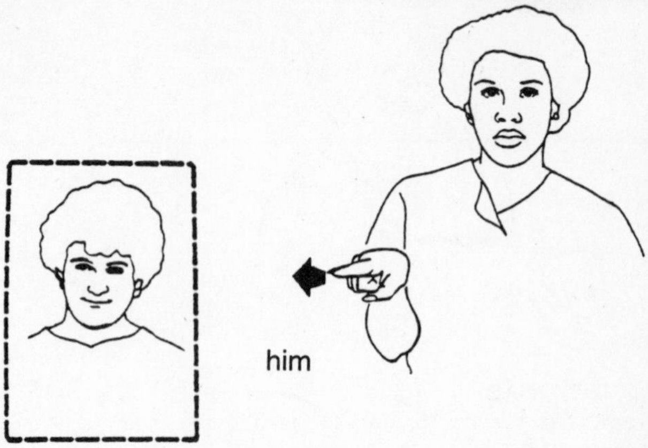

GENDER

The male or female gender is often incorporated into the sign by its location. Many male signs are made at the upper part of the head near the forehead. Many female signs are made near the lower cheek or chin.

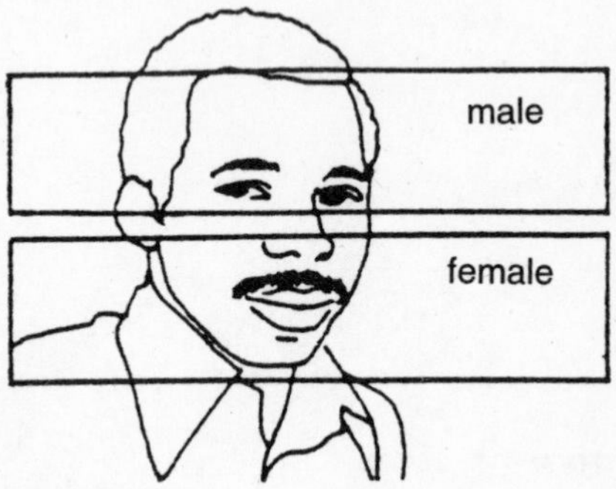

THE PERSON MARKER

Occupations and nationalities are often designated by adding an ending called a "person marker" after the sign. The marker is formed by bringing both flat hands, palms facing toward each other, down along the sides of the body. The sign is usually related to some aspect of what the person does. For example, "cook" or "chef" is formed by the verb sign "cook" plus "person marker" and "pilot" is the noun sign "airplane" plus "person marker." For nationalities, make the country's sign and follow with the person marker to designate that you are talking about a person from that country.

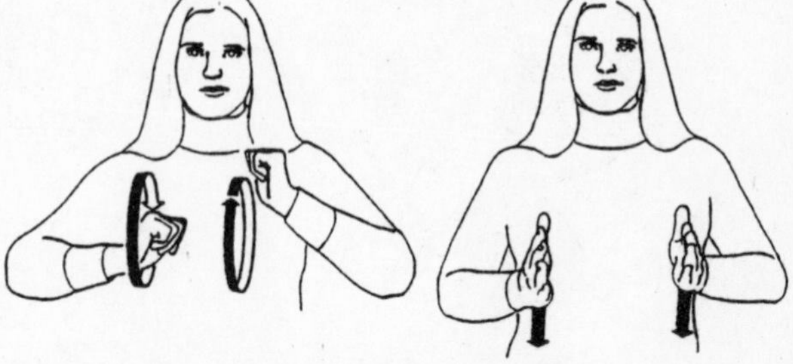

act + person marker = actress

Relationships

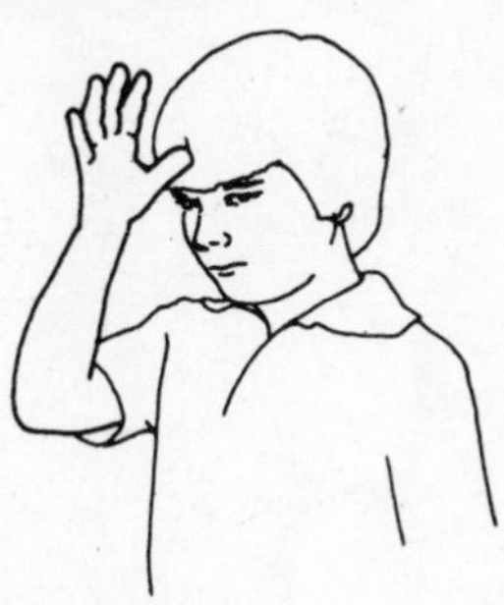

FATHER, DAD
Touch the thumb of the right "5" hand, palm facing left, to the center of the forehead. Optional: Wiggle the fingers while keeping the thumb in place.
Hint: Made in the male area of the head.

MOTHER, MOM
Touch the thumb of the right "5" hand, palm facing left, to the chin. Optional: Wiggle the fingers while keeping the thumb in place.
Hint: Made in the female area of the head.

GRANDFATHER, GRANDPA
Beginning with the thumb of the right open hand near the forehead, palm facing left, and the left open hand somewhat lower and forward, palm facing right, move the hands forward in double arcs.
Hint: The arcs indicate passing generations.

GRANDMOTHER, GRANDMA
Beginning with the thumb of the right open hand near the chin, palm facing left, and the left open hand somewhat lower and forward, palm facing right, move the hands forward in double arcs.
Hint: The arcs indicate passing generations.

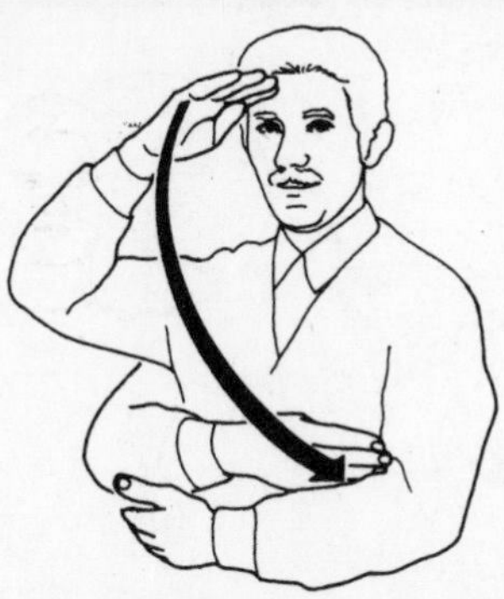

SON
Bring the right "b" hand smoothly down from the right side of the forehead, palm facing down, to the crook of the bent left arm held across the body, ending with both palms facing up.
Hint: Rocking a male child.

DAUGHTER
Bring the right "b" hand smoothly down from the right side of the chin, palm facing down, to the crook of the bent left arm held across the body, ending with both palms facing up.
Hint: Rocking a female child.

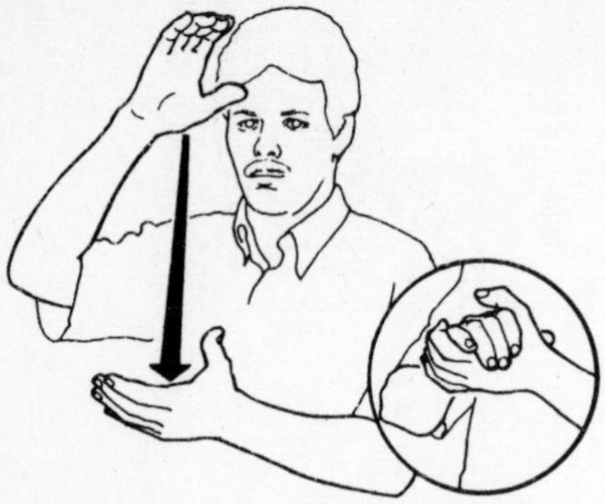

HUSBAND
Move the right "c" hand from near the right side of the forehead, palm facing left, smoothly down to clasp the curved left hand held in front of the body, palm facing up.
Hint: A form of "man" plus "marry"; a man who is married.

WIFE
Move the right "c" hand from near the right side of the chin, palm facing left, smoothly down to clasp the curved left hand held in front of the body, palm facing up.
Hint: A form of "woman" plus "marry"; a man who is married.

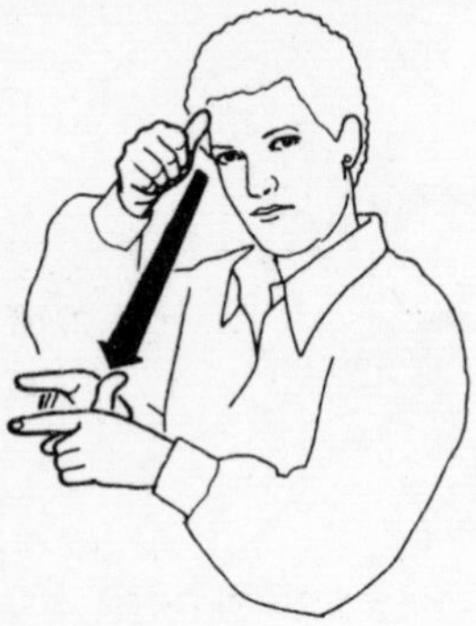

BROTHER
Bring the right "a" hand, palm facing left, from the right side of the forehead smoothly down while extending the index finger, ending with the little-finger side of the right hand on the index-finger side of the left hand, both index fingers pointing forward in front of the body.
Hint: "Male" plus a form of "same"; male in the same family.

SISTER
Bring the right "a" hand, palm facing left, from the right side of the chin smoothly down while extending the index finger, ending with the little-finger side of the right hand on the index-finger side of the left hand, both index fingers pointing forward in front of the body.
Hint: "Male" plus a form of "same"; male in the same family.

FAMILY
Beginning with the fingertips of both "f" hands touching in front of the chest, palms facing each other, move the hands in a circular movement forward until the little fingers meet.
Hint: Initialized sign formed similar to the sign for "class."

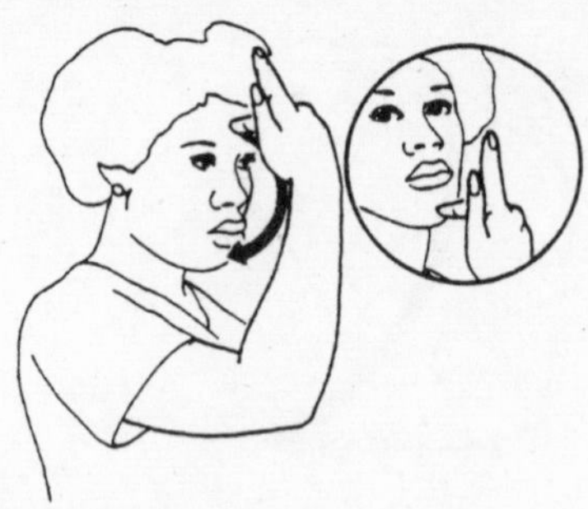

PARENTS
Touch the middle finger of the right "p" hand, palm facing in, first on the forehead and then on the chin.
Hint: Intitialized sign indicating the male and female areas of the head.

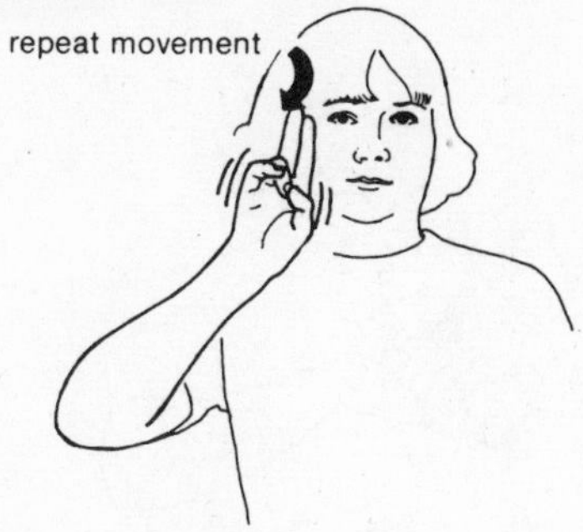

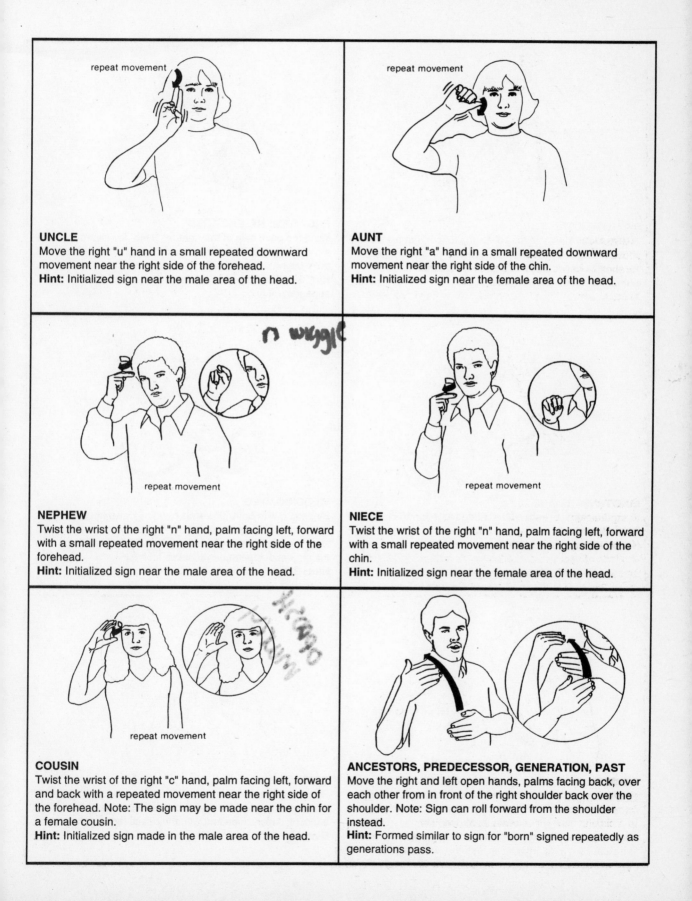

UNCLE
Move the right "u" hand in a small repeated downward movement near the right side of the forehead.
Hint: Initialized sign near the male area of the head.

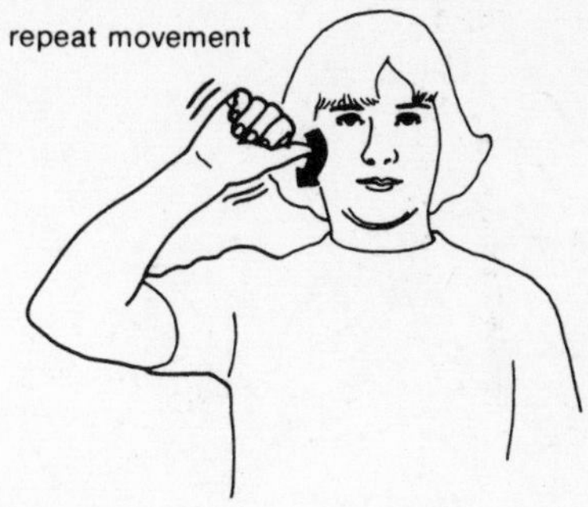

AUNT
Move the right "a" hand in a small repeated downward movement near the right side of the chin.
Hint: Initialized sign near the female area of the head.

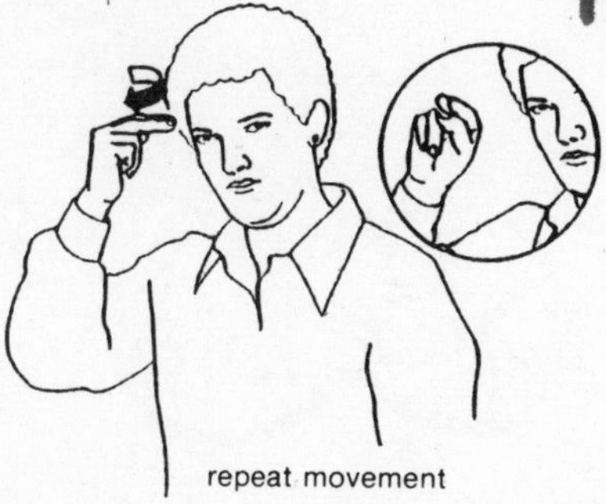

NEPHEW
Twist the wrist of the right "n" hand, palm facing left, forward with a small repeated movement near the right side of the forehead.
Hint: Initialized sign near the male area of the head.

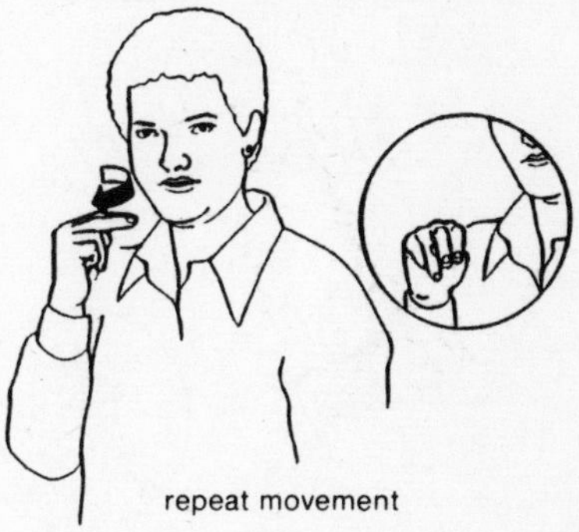

NIECE
Twist the wrist of the right "n" hand, palm facing left, forward with a small repeated movement near the right side of the chin.
Hint: Initialized sign near the female area of the head.

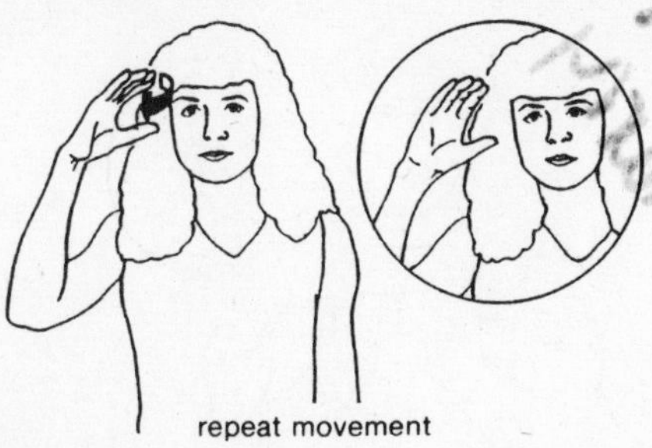

COUSIN
Twist the wrist of the right "c" hand, palm facing left, forward and back with a repeated movement near the right side of the forehead. Note: The sign may be made near the chin for a female cousin.
Hint: Initialized sign made in the male area of the head.

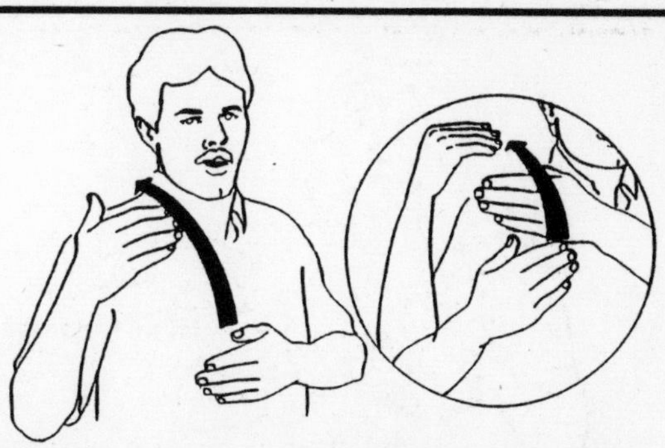

ANCESTORS, PREDECESSOR, GENERATION, PAST
Move the right and left open hands, palms facing back, over each other from in front of the right shoulder back over the shoulder. Note: Sign can roll forward from the shoulder instead.
Hint: Formed similar to sign for "born" signed repeatedly as generations pass.

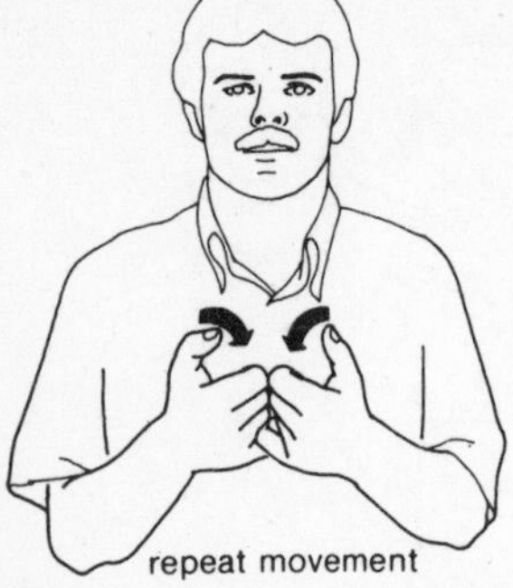

SWEETHEART

With the knuckles of both "10" hands together in front of the chest, palms facing in and little fingers interlocked, wiggle the thumbs downward with a double movement.

Hint: Two heads close together.

ENGAGEMENT, ENGAGED

Bring the palm side of the right "e" hand downward to touch the ring finger of the open left hand held in front of the chest, palm facing down.

Hint: Initialized sign indicating the location of an engagement ring.

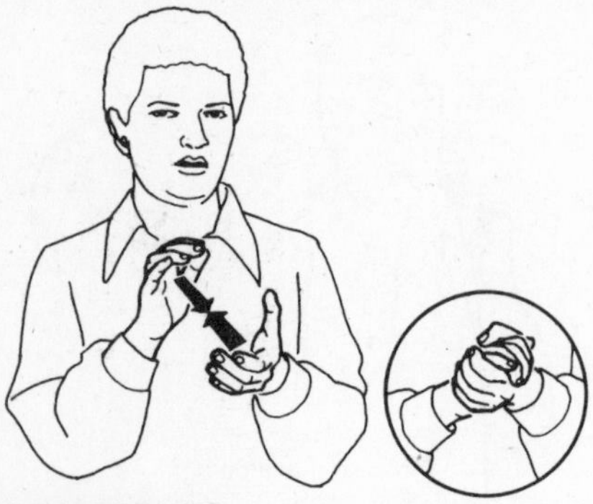

MARRY, MARRIAGE

Bring the palms of both curved hands together to clasp in front of the chest.

Hint: Joining of hands in marriage.

WEDDING, WED

Beginning with both "5" hands hanging down from bent wrists in front of each side of the chest, swing the fingers toward each other to grasp the fingers of the right hand with the fingers of the left hand, palms facing in.

Hint: Bringing the hands together during a wedding.

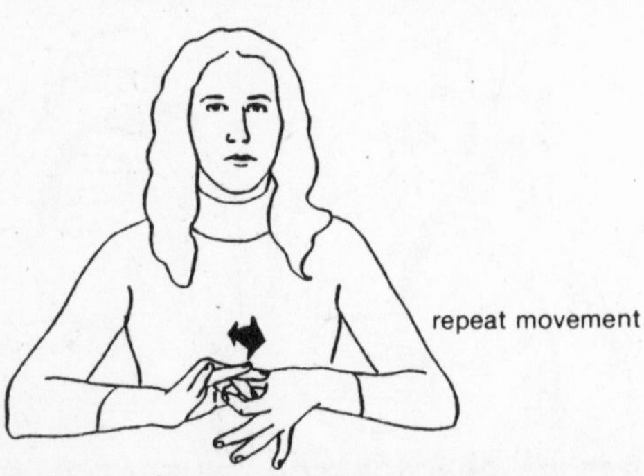

RELATIONSHIP, RELATE, BOND, CONNECTION

With the fingers of both "9" hands interlocked, right hand closer to the chest than the left hand, move the hands forward and back with a repeated movement.

Hint: Similar to the sign for "join" moving back and forward to indicate the relationship between the two things.

DIVORCE

Beginning with the fingers of both "d" hands touching in front of the chest, palms facing each other, twist the wrists suddenly forward, ending with the palms facing forward.

Hint: Initialized sign showing an abrupt parting.

Careers

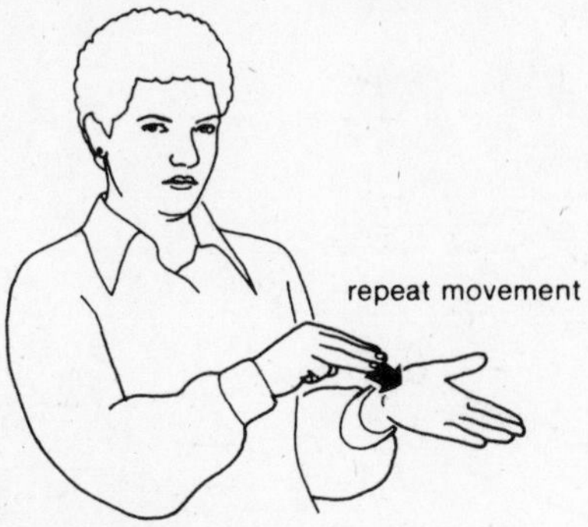

DOCTOR, MEDICAL
Tap the fingertips of the right "m" hand, palm facing down, on the wrist of the open left hand held in front of the chest, palm facing up.
Hint: Initialized sign showing where doctors touch to feel one's pulse.

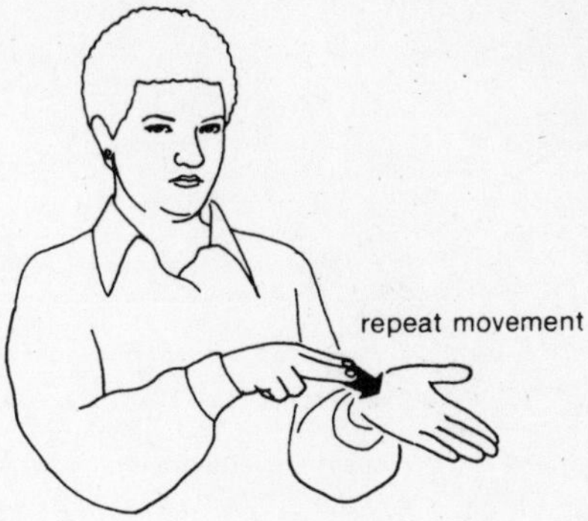

NURSE
Tap the fingertips of the right "n" hand, palm facing down, on the wrist of the open left hand held in front of the chest, palm facing up.
Hint: Initialized sign showing where nurses touch to feel one's pulse.

DENTIST
With a repeated movement tap the teeth with the fingertips of the right "d" hand, palm facing left.
Hint: Initialized sign showing where a dentist works on people.

PILOT
With the right thumb, index finger and little finger extended, move the right hand forward in front of the right shoulder. Then move both open hands downward along the sides of the body, palms facing each other.
Hint: "Fly" plus "person marker."

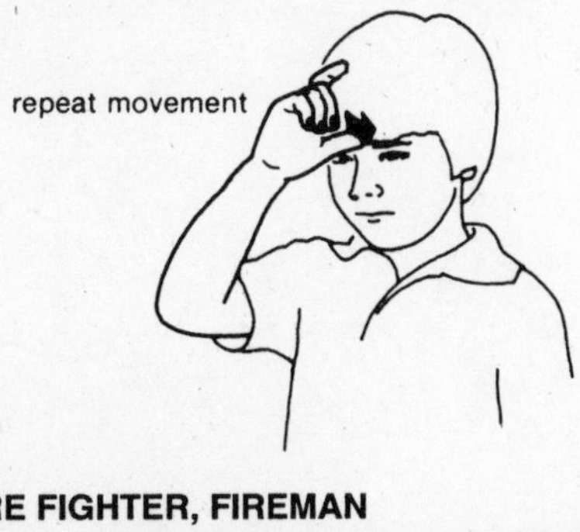

FIRE FIGHTER, FIREMAN
With the right thumb extended and index finger curved, tap the index-finger side of the right hand against the forehead with a double movement.
Hint: The fingers show the location of the insignia on a fire fighter's helmet.

LETTER CARRIER, MAILMAN
Bring the thumb of the right "10" hand, palm facing left, from the mouth downward to touch the thumb of the left "10" hand, palm facing right. Then move both open hands downward along the sides of the body, palms facing each other.
Hint: "Mail" plus "person marker."

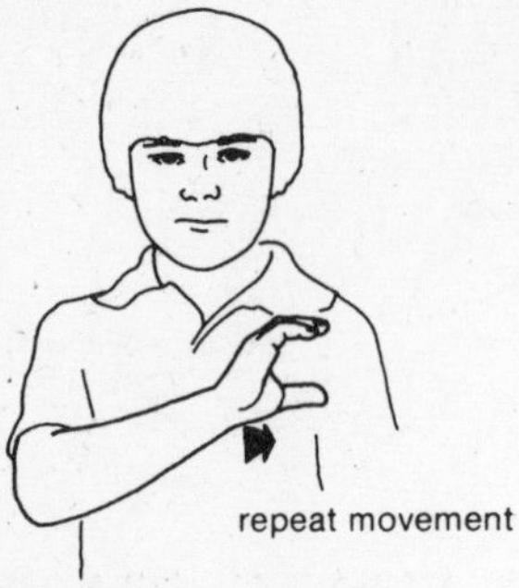

POLICE OFFICER, POLICE, COP
Tap the thumb side of the right "c" hand on the left side of the chest, palm facing left.
Hint: The hand encircles the location of a police badge.

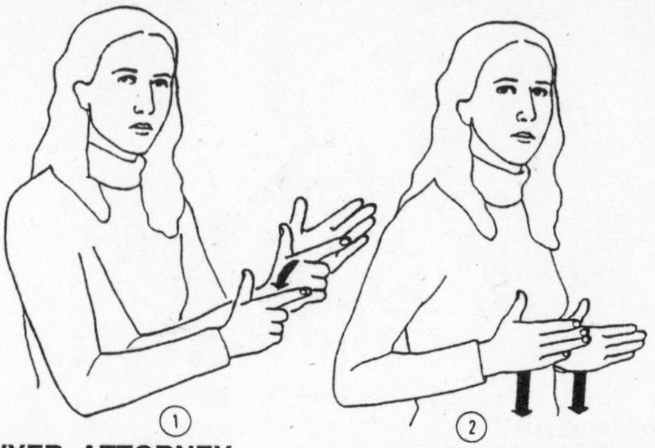

LAWYER, ATTORNEY
Touch the palm side of the right "l" hand first on the fingers and then on the heel of the open left palm held up in front of the chest. Then move both open hands downward along the sides of the body, palms facing each other.
Hint: "Law" plus "person marker."

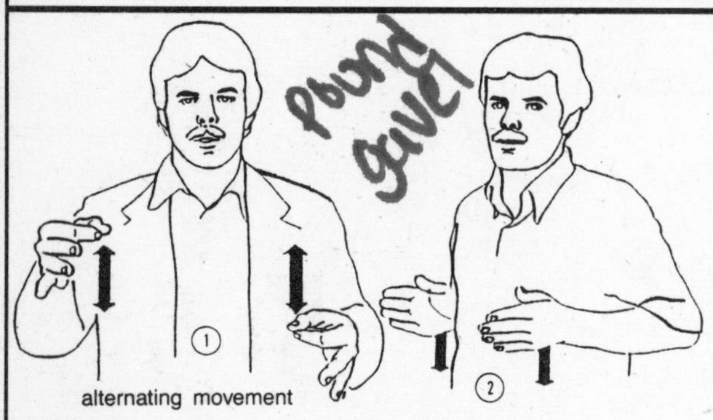

JUDGE
Move both "f" hands, palms facing each other, up and down with an alternating movement in front of each side of the chest. Then move both open hands downward along the sides of the body, palms facing each other.
Hint: Weighing on a balance plus "person marker."

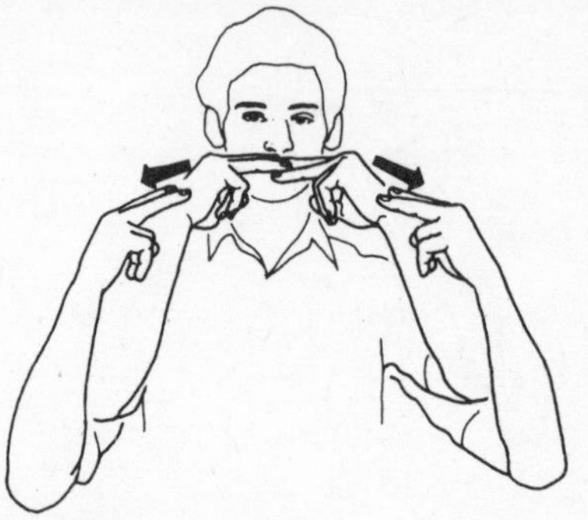

THIEF, ROBBER, BANDIT
Beginning with the fingers of both "h" hands touching under the nose, palms facing down, bring the hands apart to the sides of the face.
Hint: A mustachioed bandit.

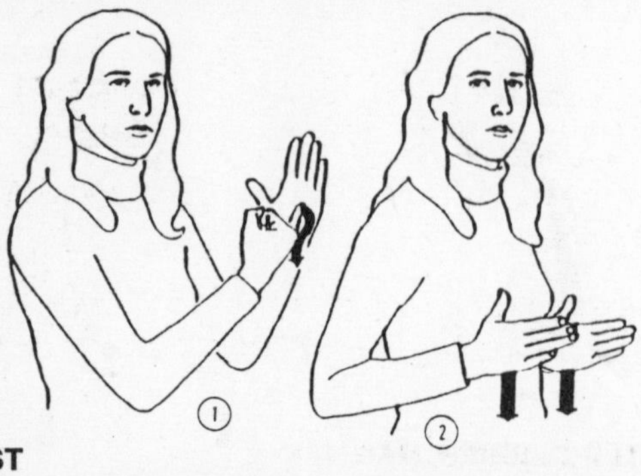

ARTIST
With the extended little finger of the right "i" hand draw a wavy line on the palm of the open left hand, palm facing right. Then move both open hands downward along the sides of the body, palms facing each other.
Hint: "Art" plus "person marker."

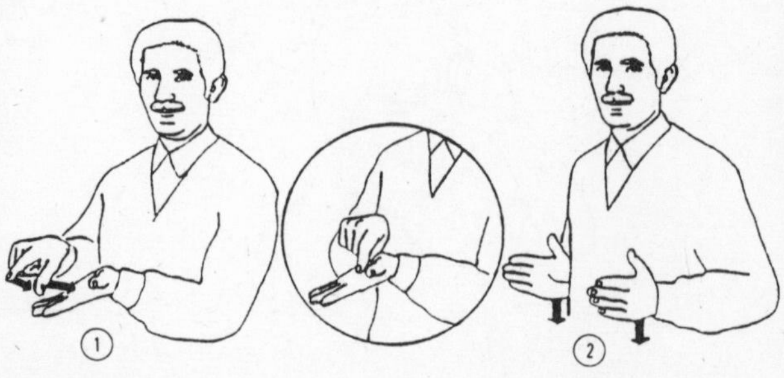

PRINTER
Bring the right "g" hand, palm facing down, from the fingers to the heel of the left open palm, closing the right index finger to the thumb as the hand moves. Then move both open hands downward along the sides of the body, palms facing each other.
Hint: "Print" plus "person marker."

SECRETARY
Bring the fingers of the right "h" hand from the right side of the mouth down to wipe across and off the palm of the open left hand held in front of the chest, palm facing up.
Hint: Recording words from the mouth on paper.

feale sign then Down both sides

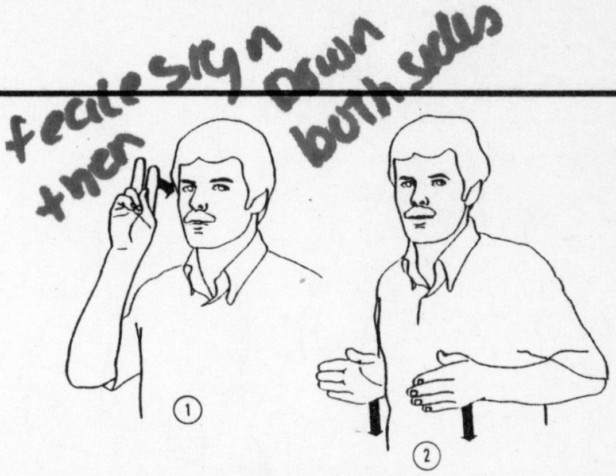

BARBER, BEAUTICIAN, HAIR DRESSER, HAIR STYLIST
While moving the right "v" hand back beside the right side of the head with a repeated movement, fingers pointing up and palm facing left, close the index finger and middle finger together repeatedly. Then move both open hands downward along the sides of the body, palms facing each other.
Hint: Mime cutting hair with scissors plus "person marker."

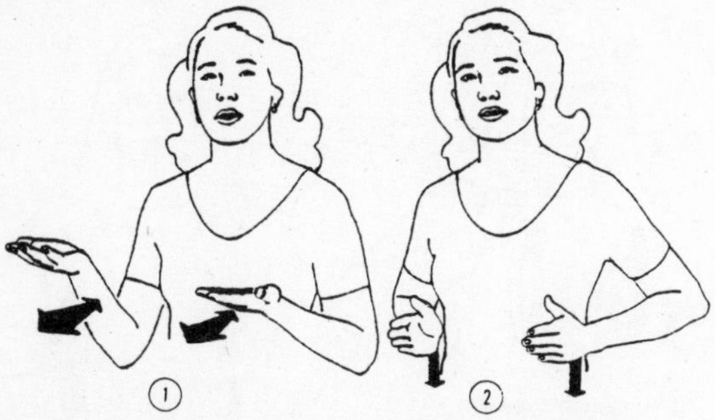

WAIT STAFF, WAITER, WAITRESS, SERVANT
Move both open hands, palms facing up, forward and back from the chest with an alternating double movement. Then move both open hands downward along the sides of the body, palms facing each other.
Hint: Carrying a tray while serving plus "person marker."

FARMER, AGRICULTURE, BUM, SLOPPY
Drag the thumb of the right "5" hand, palm facing left, from left to right across the chin. Then move both open hands downward along the sides of the body, palms facing each other.
Hint: "Farm" plus "person marker."

repeat movement

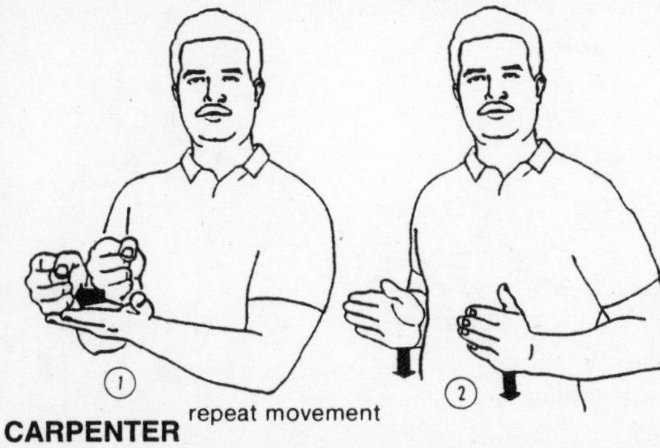

CARPENTER
Move the little-finger side of the right "s" hand, palm facing left, forward with a double movement across the palm of the left open hand. Then move both open hands downward along the sides of the body, palms facing each other.
Hint: Using a plane on a piece of wood plus "person marker."

repeat movement

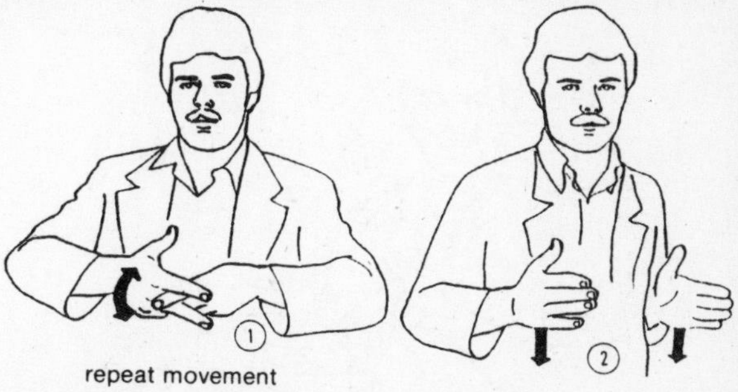

PLUMBER, MECHANIC
With the extended left index finger inserted between the index and middle fingers of the right "3" hand, twist the right hand up and down with a short repeated movement. Then move both open hands downward along the sides of the body, palms facing each other.
Hint: Twisting a wrench or a pipe plus "person marker."

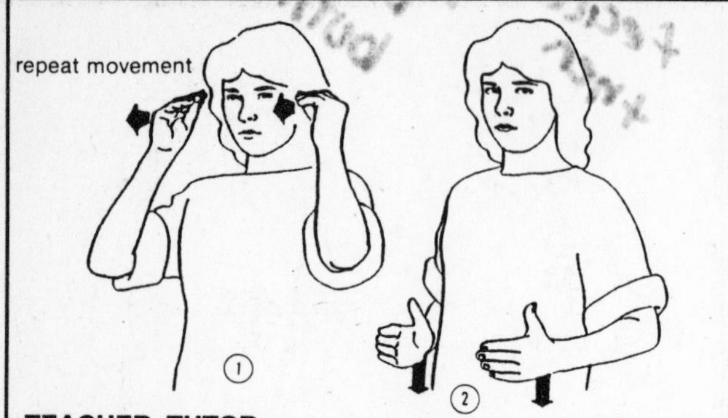

TEACHER, TUTOR
With the thumb touching the flattened fingers of each hand, palms facing down, move the hands forward with a short double movement in front of each side of the head. Then move both open hands downward along the sides of the body, palms facing each other.
Hint: "Teach" plus "person marker."

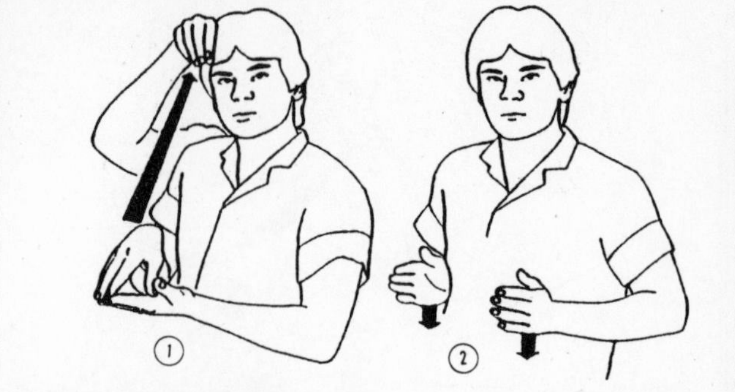

STUDENT, LEARNER
Beginning with the fingers of the right "5" hand touching the palm of the open left hand, palm facing up, bring the right hand up to the forehead while closing the fingers to the thumb as it moves. Then move both open hands downward along the sides of the body, palms facing each other.
Hint: "Learn" plus "person marker."

PRINCIPAL
Move the right "p" hand, palm facing down, in a large circle from the right side of the body, ending with the middle finger touching the back of the open left hand, palm facing down.
Hint: Initialized sign formed similar to "above" indicating that a principal is in a position above the students.

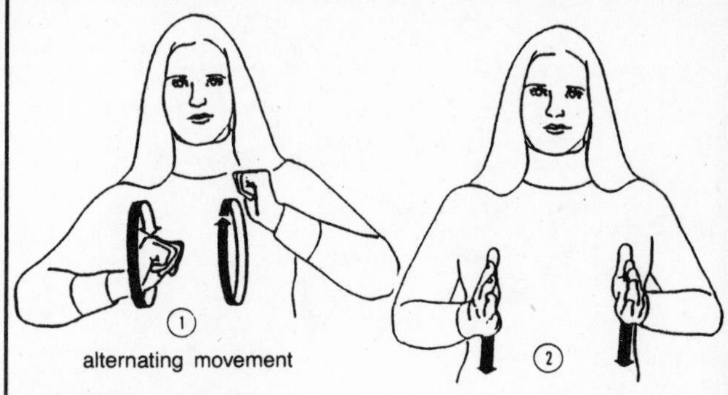

ACTOR, ACTRESS
Move the thumbs of both "a" hands, palms facing each other, in alternating circles downward on each side of the chest. Then move both open hands downward along the sides of the body, palms facing each other.
Hint: "Theater" plus "person marker."

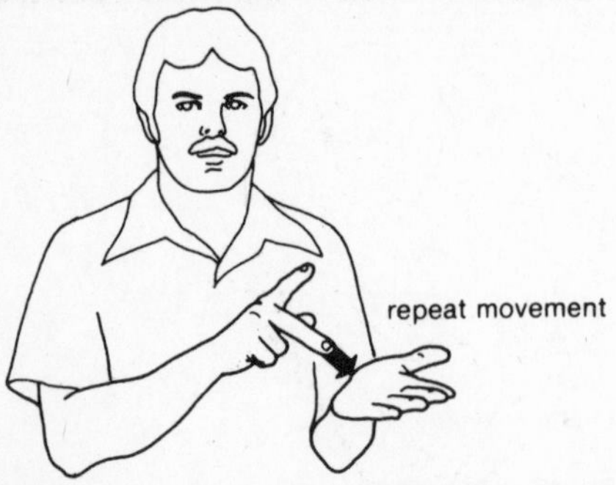

PSYCHIATRIST
Tap the middle finger of the right "p" hand, palm facing left, with a double movement on the wrist of the open left hand, palm facing up. Then move both open hands downward along the sides of the body, palms facing each other.
Hint: Initialized sign formed similar to "doctor."

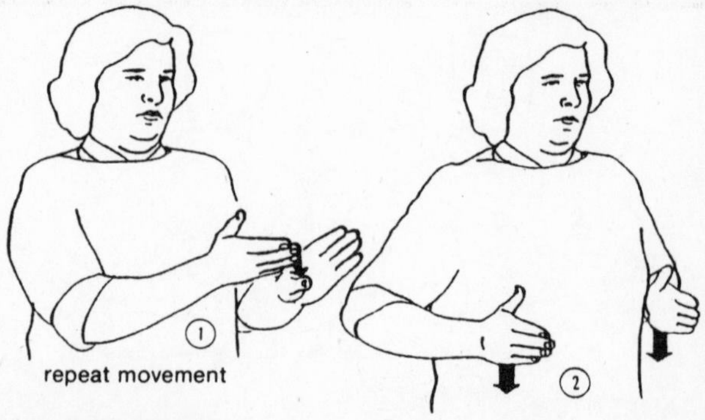

PSYCHOLOGIST
Tap the little-finger side of the open right hand, palm facing left, with a double movement in the crook between the index finger and thumb of the open left hand, palm facing right. Then move both open hands downward along the sides of the body, palms facing each other.

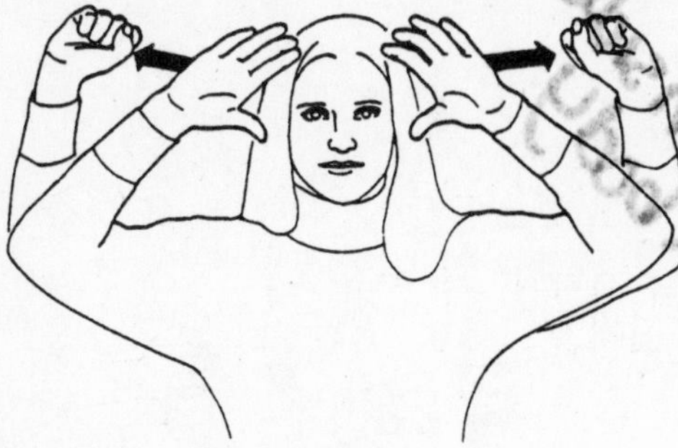

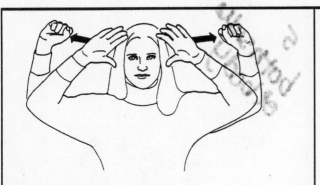

PRESIDENT, SUPERINTENDENT
Beginning with both curved hands near each side of the forehead, palms facing forward, bring the hands outward to each side while closing into "s" hands.
Hint: The hands follow the "horns of authority."

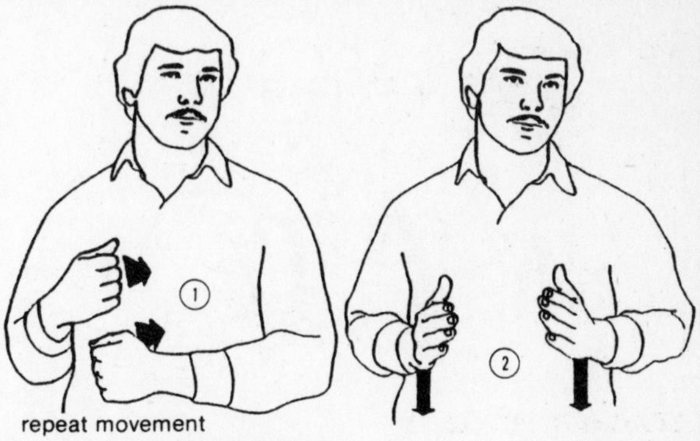

SOLDIER, ARMY, MILITARY
With on hand higher than the other, tap the palm sides of both "a" hands against the right side of the chest with a double movement. Then move both open hands downward along the sides of the body, palms facing each other.
Hint: Carrying a gun military style plus "person marker."

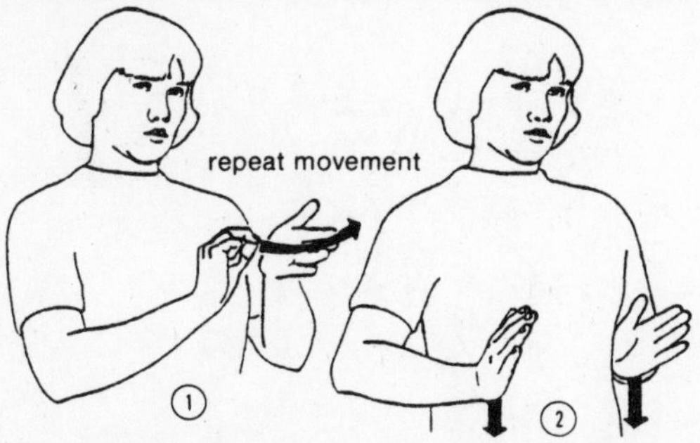

REPORTER, JOURNALIST, AUTHOR, WRITER
With the right thumb and index fingers pinched together, move the right hand across the open left palm from the heel to the fingers with a double movement. Then move both open hands downward along the sides of the body, palms facing each other.
Hint: "Write" plus "person marker."

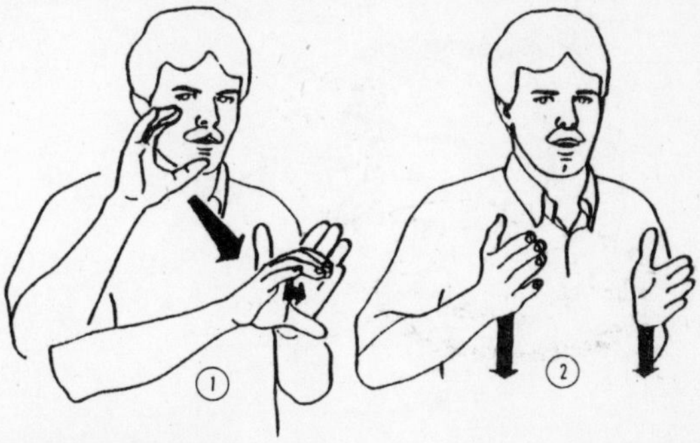

PHOTOGRAPHER
Bring the right "c" hand, palm facing forward, from the right side of the face downward, ending with the little-finger side of the right hand against the palm of the open left hand, palm facing right. Then move both open hands downward along the sides of the body, palms facing each other.
Hint: "Picture" plus "person marker."

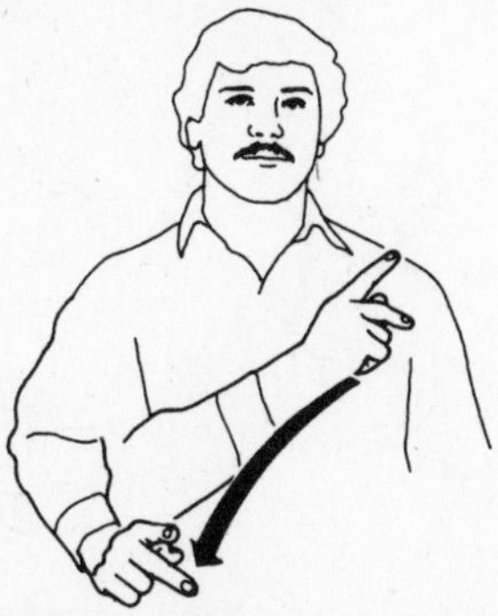

KING
Move the right "k" hand, palm facing in, from near the left shoulder down to the right hip.
Hint: Initialized sign showing the location of a royal sash.

QUEEN
Move the right "q" hand, palm facing in, from near the left shoulder down to the right hip.
Hint: Initialized sign showing the location of a royal sash.

Other People

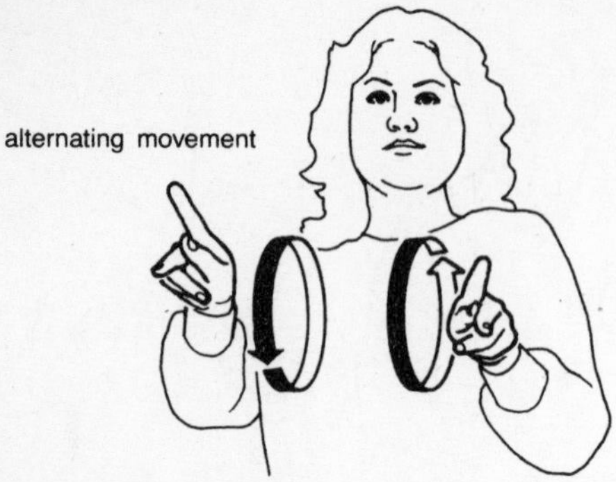

PEOPLE, MANKIND, FOLK, PUBLIC
Move both "p" hands, palms facing each other, forward in alternating circles in front of each side of the chest. Note: The circles may move back toward the chest instead.
Hint: Initialized sign; looks like people walking.

PERSON
Move both "p" hands downward along the sides of the body, palms facing each other.
Hint: Initialized sign following the contour of the body.

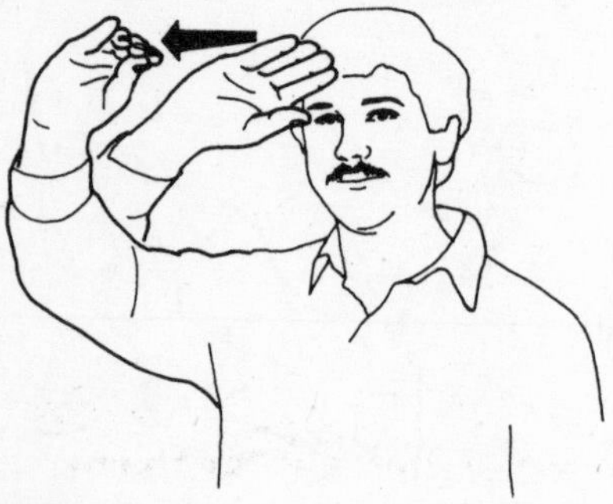

MAN, MALE
Beginning with the index-finger side of the curved right hand against the right side of the forehead, move the hand forward while closing the fingers to the thumb.
Hint: Tipping a man's hat.

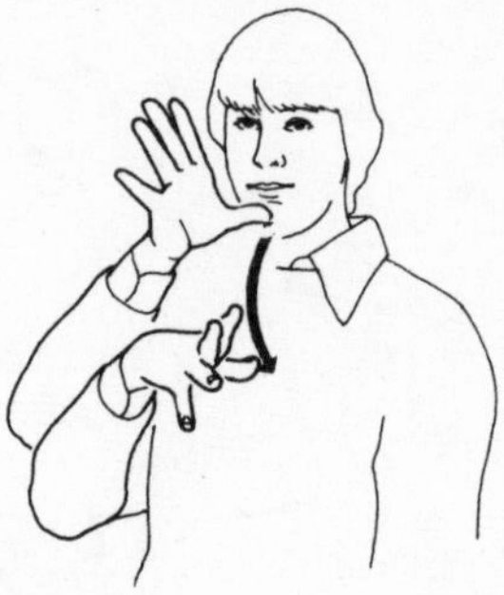

WOMAN, FEMALE
Touch the thumb of the right "5" hand, palm facing left, first to the chin and then to the chest.
Hint: A form of "mother" plus "fine" to indicate a woman with a fancy ruffle on her dress.

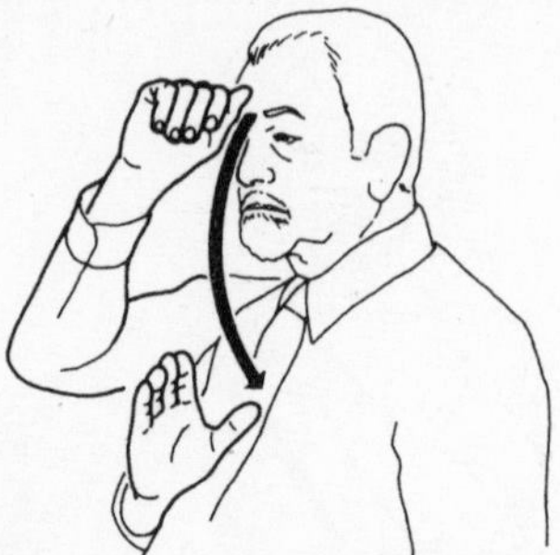

GENTLEMAN
Bring the thumb of the right "a" hand, palm facing left, from the forehead down while changing into an open hand, ending with the thumb of the open right hand touching the chest.
Hint: "Man" plus "fine."

LADY
Bring the thumb of the right "a" hand, palm facing left, from the chin down while changing into an open hand, ending with the thumb of the open right hand touching the chest.
Hint: "Woman" plus "fine."

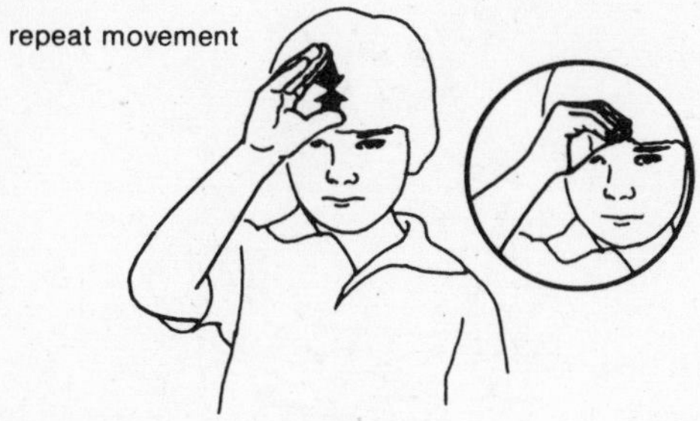

BOY
With the thumb side of the right flattened "c" hand against the forehead, palm facing left, close the fingers and thumb together with a double movement.
Hint: Tipping of a boy's hat.

GIRL
Pull the thumb of the right "a" hand, palm facing left, downward on the right side of the cheek with a short double movement.
Hint: Shows the location of a girl's bonnet strings.

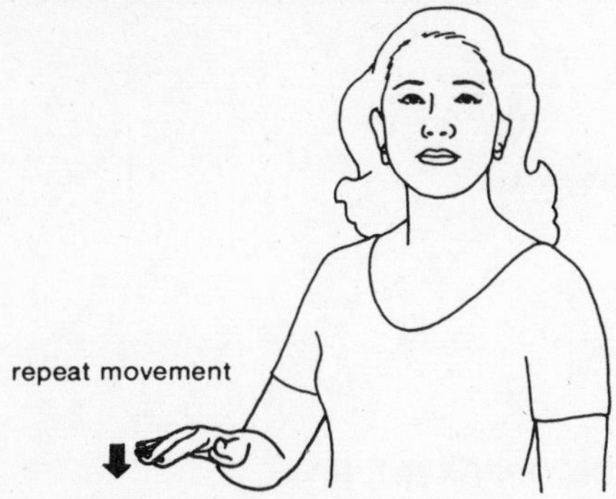

CHILD
Pat the open right hand downward with a short repeated movement near the right side of the body, palm facing down.
Hint: Patting a child on the head.

CHILDREN
Beginning with the index-finger sides of both open hands together in front of the chest, palms facing down, move the hands apart to each side in a series of small arcs.
Hint: Patting several children on the head.

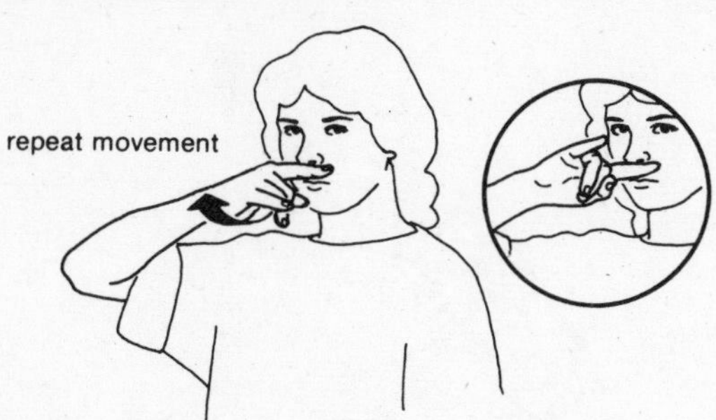

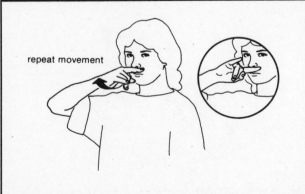

KID
With the index and little fingers of the right hand extended under the nose, palm facing down, twist the right hand up and down with a small repeated movement.
Hint: Wiping a child's nose.

TWINS
Touch the thumb side of the right "t" hand, palm facing left, to the right side of the chin and then the left side of the chin.
Hint: Initialized sign.

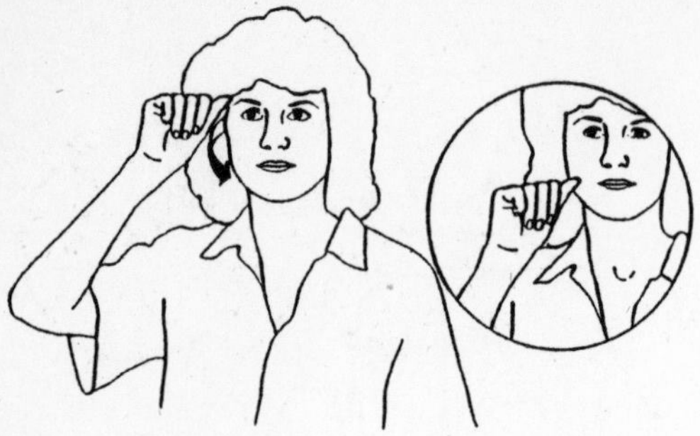

ADULT
Touch the thumb of the right "a" hand, palm facing forward, first to the right temple and then to near the right side of the chin.
Hint: Initialized sign touching the male and then the female portion of the head.

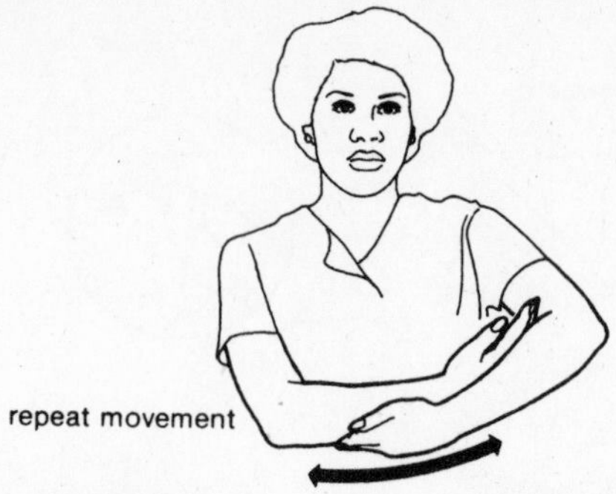

BABY, INFANT
With the back of the open right hand, palm facing up, laying across the bent left arm held across the chest, cradling the right arm in the open left hand and rocking back and forth with a repeated movement.
Hint: Rocking a baby.

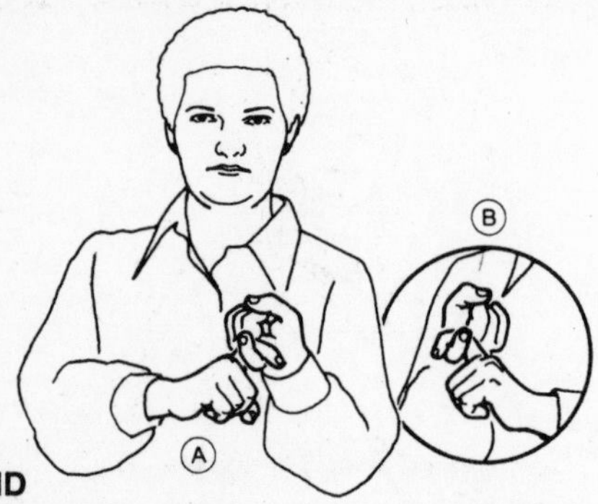

FRIEND
Hook the right bent index finger, palm facing down, on the left bent index finger held in front of the chest, palm facing up. Turn the hands over to reverse the positions.
Hint: A close relationship.

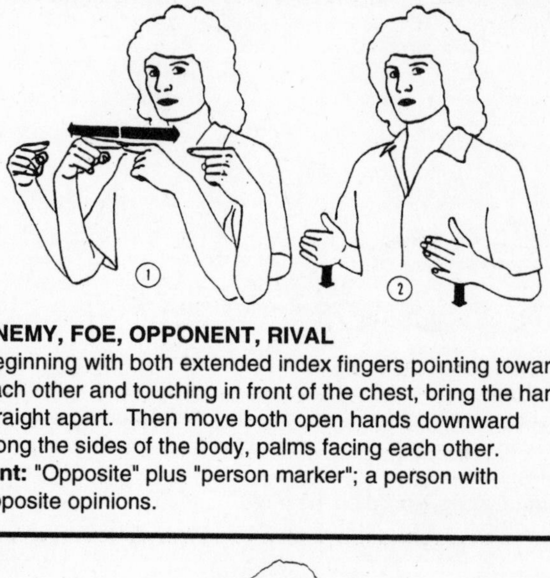

ENEMY, FOE, OPPONENT, RIVAL
Beginning with both extended index fingers pointing toward each other and touching in front of the chest, bring the hands straight apart. Then move both open hands downward along the sides of the body, palms facing each other.
Hint: "Opposite" plus "person marker"; a person with opposite opinions.

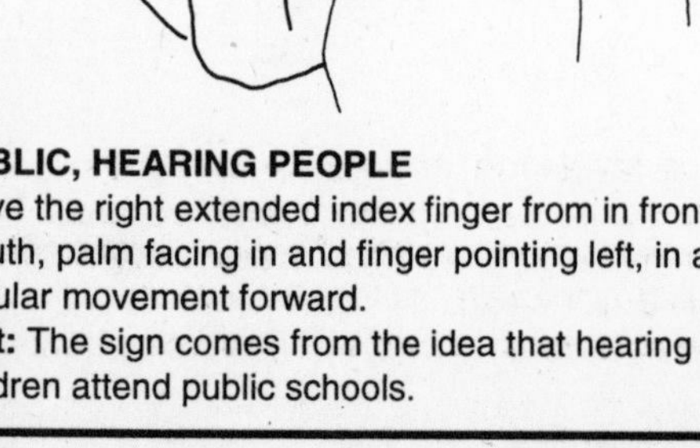

PUBLIC, HEARING PEOPLE
Move the right extended index finger from in front of the mouth, palm facing in and finger pointing left, in a repeated circular movement forward.
Hint: The sign comes from the idea that hearing (speaking) children attend public schools.

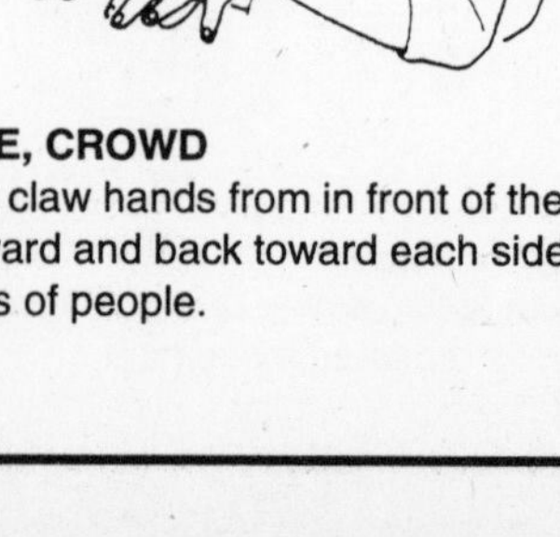

AUDIENCE, CROWD
Move both claw hands from in front of the body, palms facing down, upward and back toward each side of the chest.
Hint: Rows of people.

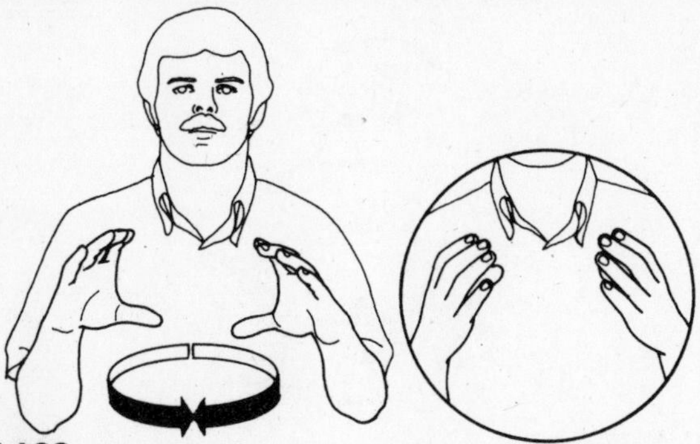

CLASS
Beginning with both "c" hands in front of each side of the chest, palms facing forward, move the hands outward in a circle until the little fingers come near each other, ending with the palms facing in.
Hint: Initialized sign encompassing a class or collection of things or people.

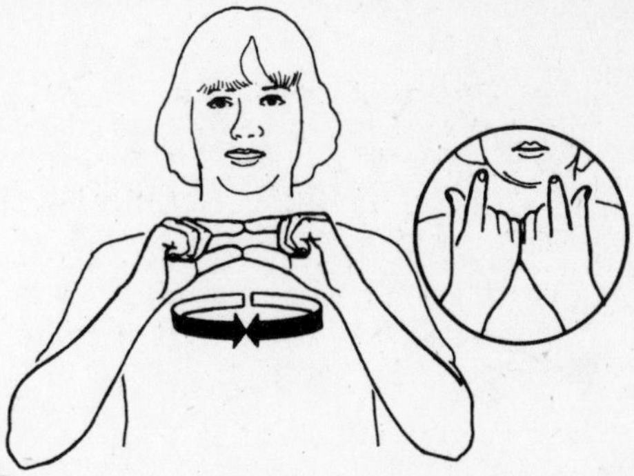

GROUP
Beginning with the extended fingers of both "g" hands touching in front of the chest, palms facing each other, move the hands outward in a circle until the little fingers come together, ending with the palms facing in.
Hint: Initialized sign formed similar to the sign for "class."

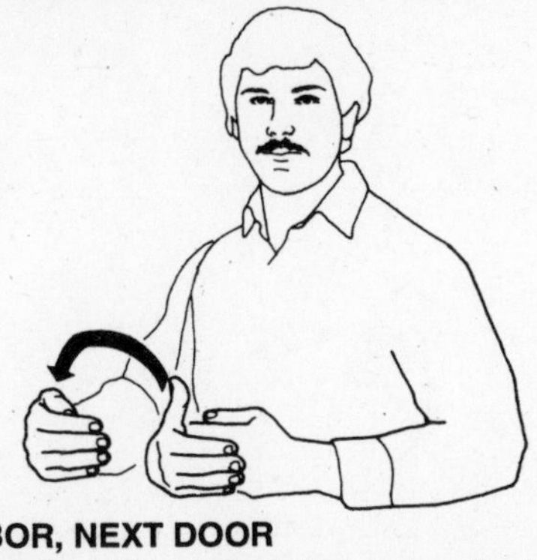

NEIGHBOR, NEXT DOOR
With the palm of the open right hand on the back of the open left hand in front of the body, both palms facing in and fingers pointing in opposite directions, move the right hand forward in an arc.
Hint: The next place.

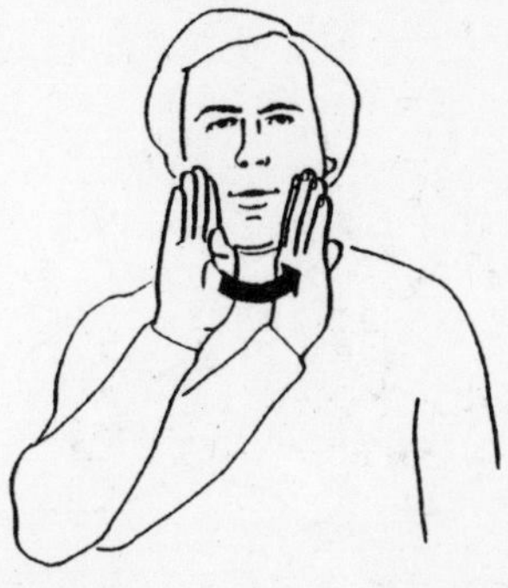

BACHELOR
Move the right "b" hand, palm facing left and fingers pointing up, from touching the right side of the chin to touching the left side of the chin.
Hint: Initialized sign.

INDIVIDUAL
Move both "i" hands, palms facing each other, downward in front of each side of the body.
Hint: Initialized sign formed similar to the sign for "person."

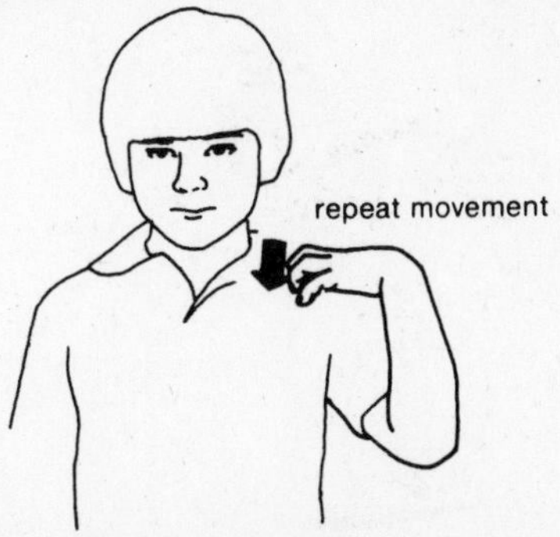

CAPTAIN, CHIEF, BOSS, CHAIRMAN, OFFICER
Tap the fingers of the left "claw" hand with a repeated movement on the top of the left shoulder. Note: The other hand may be used instead.
Hint: Shows the position of insignia on an officer's shoulder.

Pronouns

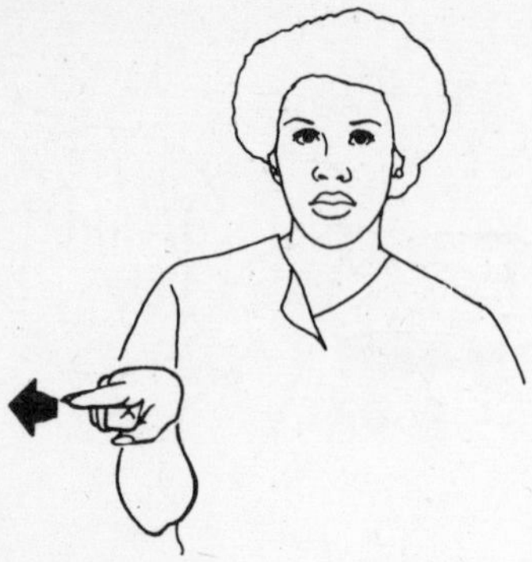

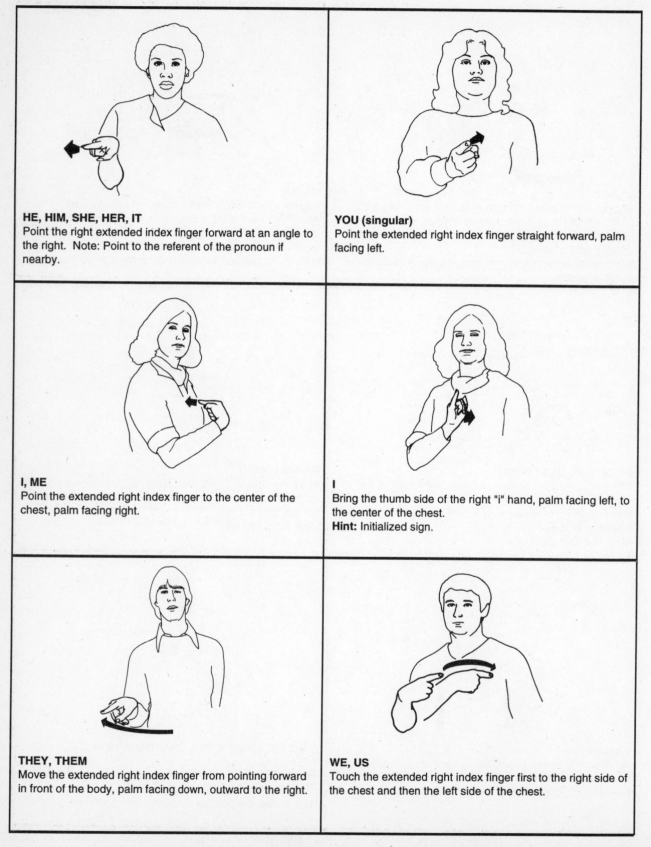

HE, HIM, SHE, HER, IT
Point the right extended index finger forward at an angle to the right. Note: Point to the referent of the pronoun if nearby.

YOU (singular)
Point the extended right index finger straight forward, palm facing left.

I, ME
Point the extended right index finger to the center of the chest, palm facing right.

I
Bring the thumb side of the right "i" hand, palm facing left, to the center of the chest.
Hint: Initialized sign.

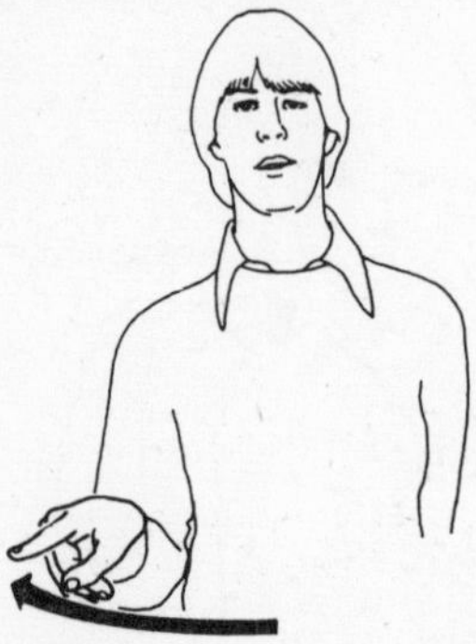

THEY, THEM
Move the extended right index finger from pointing forward in front of the body, palm facing down, outward to the right.

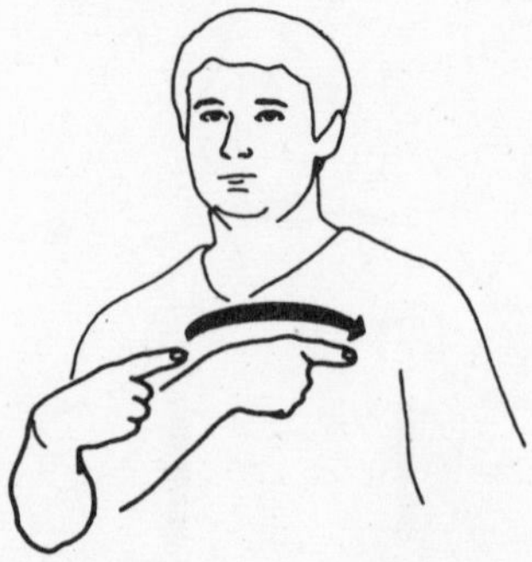

WE, US
Touch the extended right index finger first to the right side of the chest and then the left side of the chest.

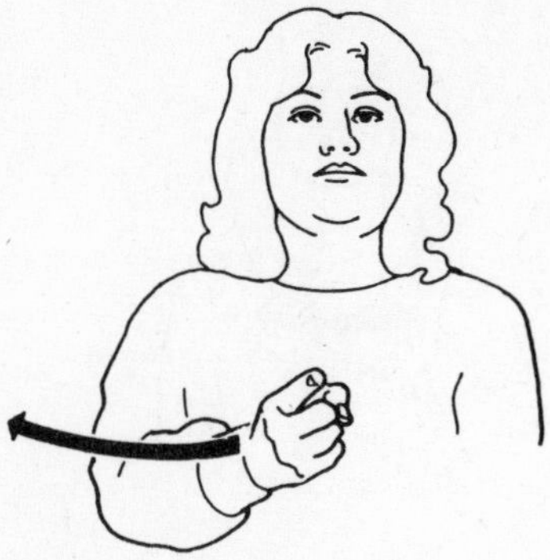

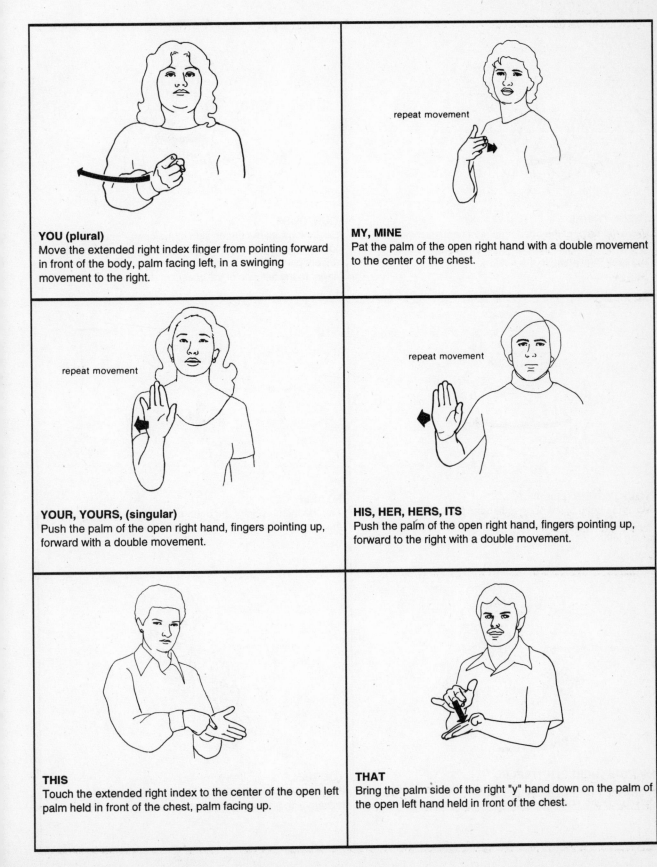

YOU (plural)
Move the extended right index finger from pointing forward in front of the body, palm facing left, in a swinging movement to the right.

MY, MINE
Pat the palm of the open right hand with a double movement to the center of the chest.

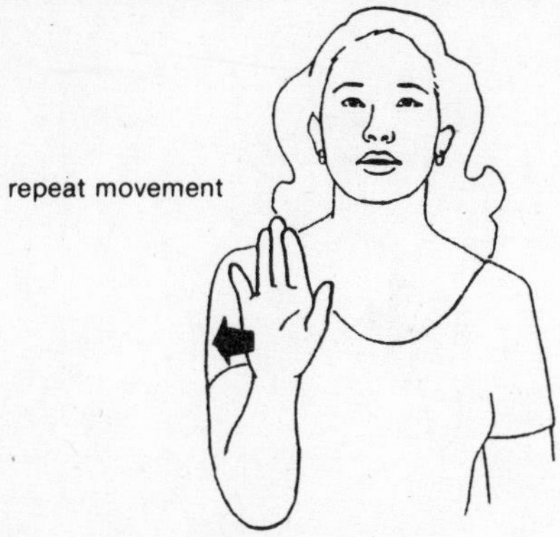

YOUR, YOURS, (singular)
Push the palm of the open right hand, fingers pointing up, forward with a double movement.

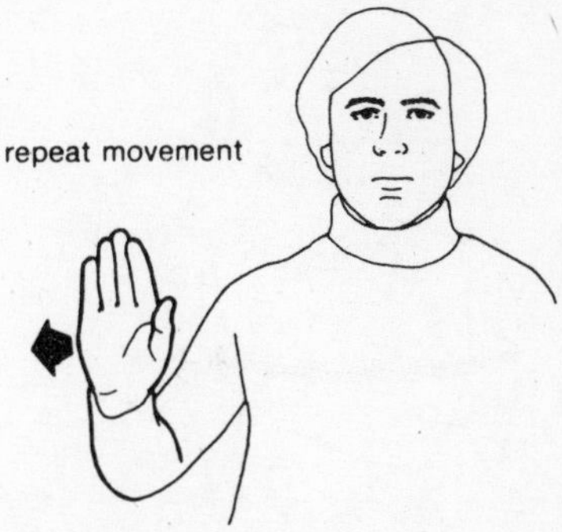

HIS, HER, HERS, ITS
Push the palm of the open right hand, fingers pointing up, forward to the right with a double movement.

THIS
Touch the extended right index to the center of the open left palm held in front of the chest, palm facing up.

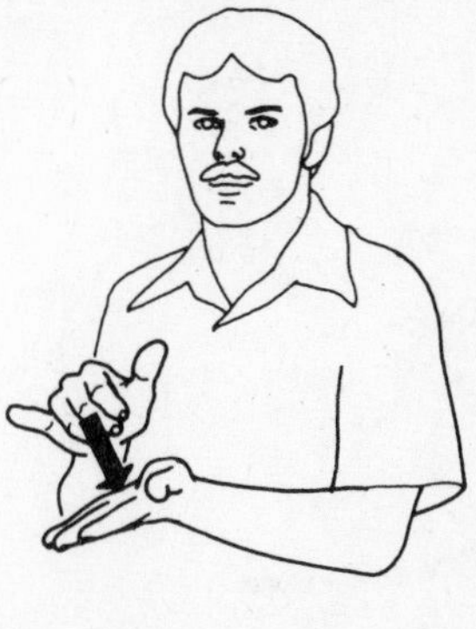

THAT
Bring the palm side of the right "y" hand down on the palm of the open left hand held in front of the chest.

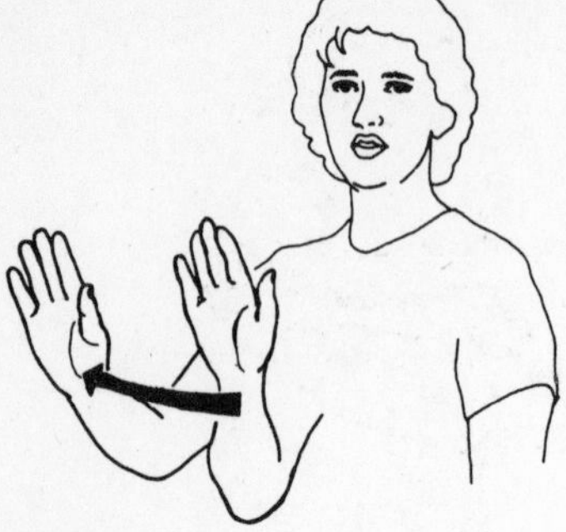

THEIR, THEIRS
Move the palm of the open right right hand from pointing forward in front of the body, fingers pointing up, in a swinging movement to the right.

OUR, OURS
Beginning with the thumb side of the open right hand touching the right side of the chest, palm facing left and fingers pointing up, move the hand to touch the right little finger to the left side of the chest.

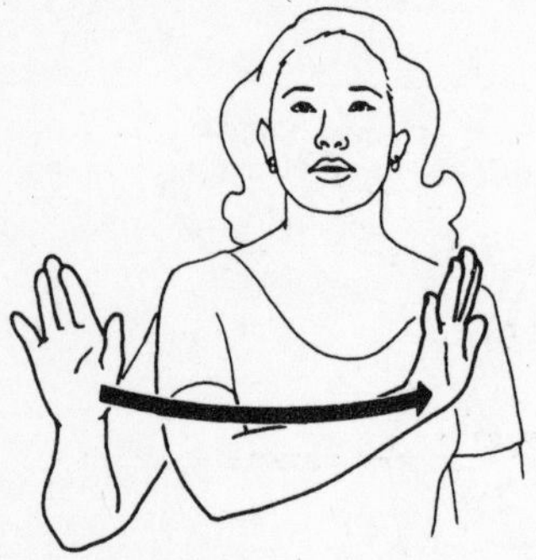

YOUR, YOURS (plural)
Move the palm of the open right hand from pointing forward in front of the right side of the body in a swinging movement to the left.

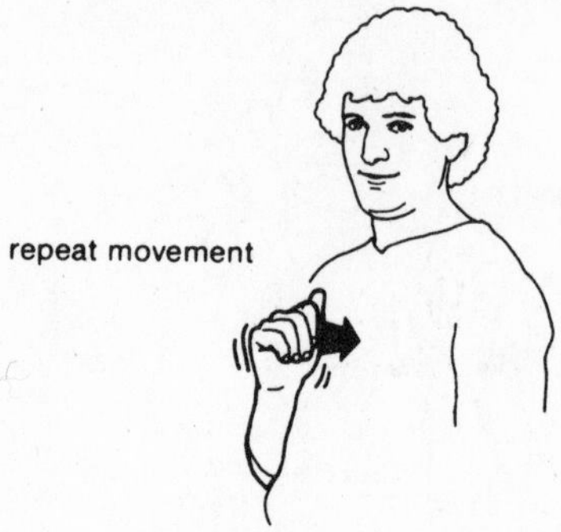

MYSELF
Tap the thumb side of the right "a" hand, palm facing left, to the center of the chest with a double movement.

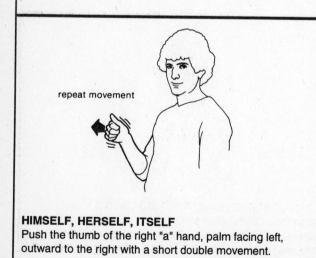

HIMSELF, HERSELF, ITSELF
Push the thumb of the right "a" hand, palm facing left, outward to the right with a short double movement.

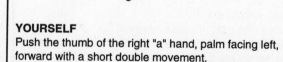

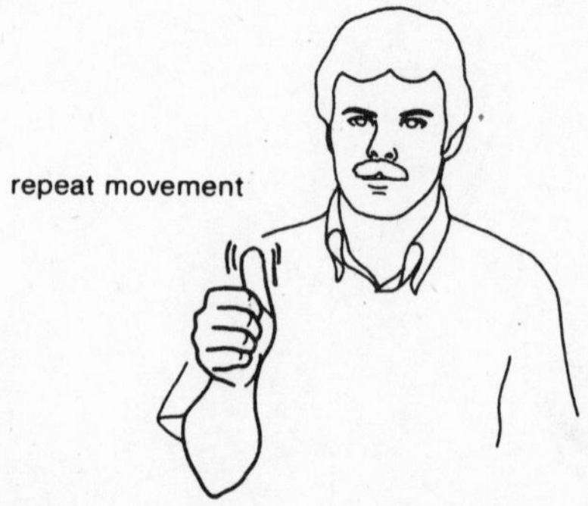

YOURSELF
Push the thumb of the right "a" hand, palm facing left, forward with a short double movement.

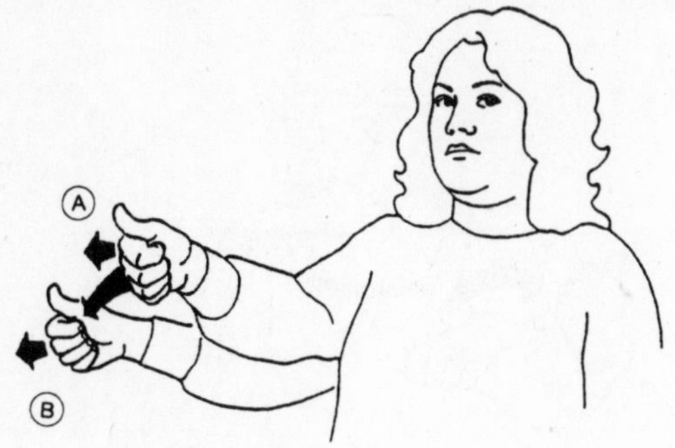

THEMSELVES
Push the thumb of the right "a" hand, palm facing left, forward to the right and then again farther to the right.

OURSELVES
Touch the thumb side of the right "a" hand first to the right side of the chest and then the left side of the chest.

YOURSELVES
Move the right "a" hand, palm facing left, from pointing forward in front of the body in a swinging movement outward to the right.

SOMEONE, SOMEBODY, SOMETHING
With the extended right index finger pointing upward in front of the right side of the chest, palm facing forward, make a small circle in the air with the whole arm.
Hint: The finger symbolizes an unknown person you are trying to identify.

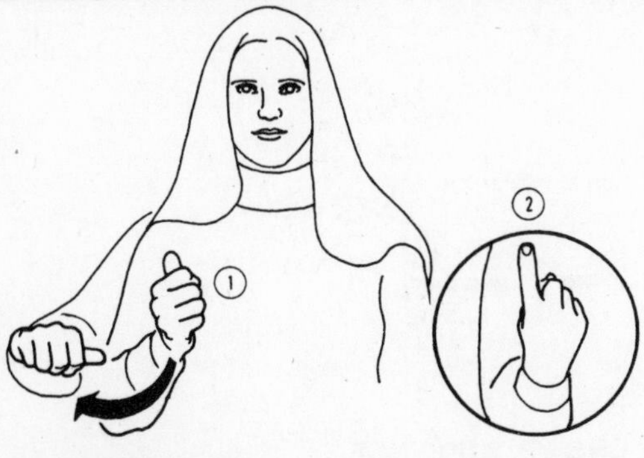

ANYONE, ANYBODY
Starting with the right "a" hand in front of the body, palm facing left, twist the wrist down, ending with the palm facing down. Then extend the right index finger upward in front of the right shoulder, palm facing in.
Hint: "Any" plus "one."

EACH OTHER, ONE ANOTHER, SOCIALIZE
Move the extended thumb of the right "10" hand, palm facing forward and thumb pointing down, in a circle over the extended thumb of the left "10" hand, palm facing right and thumb pointing up.
Hint: Symbolizes intermingling with one another.

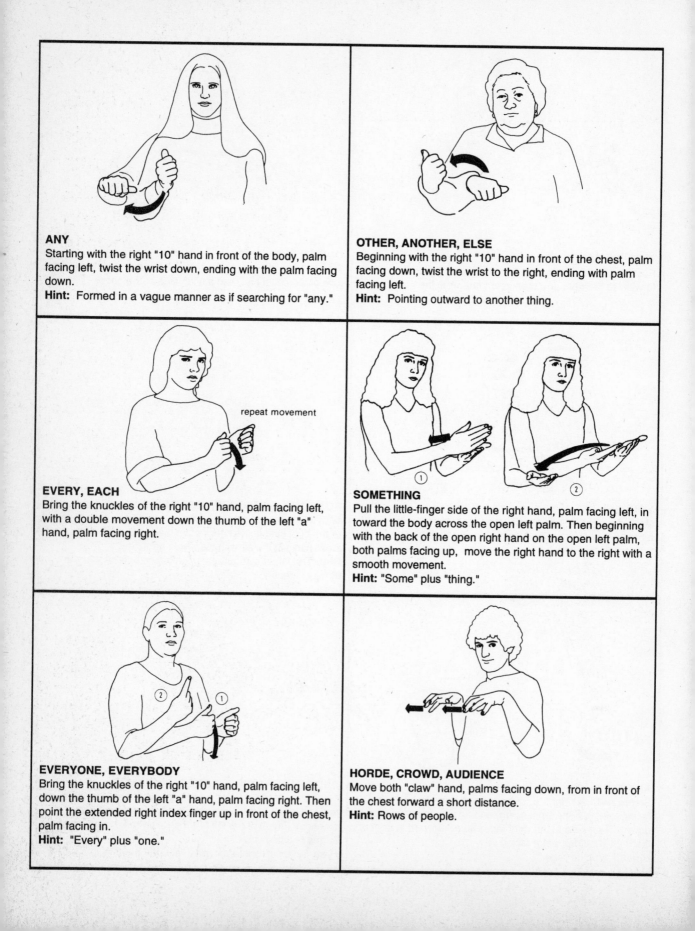

ANY
Starting with the right "10" hand in front of the body, palm facing left, twist the wrist down, ending with the palm facing down.
Hint: Formed in a vague manner as if searching for "any."

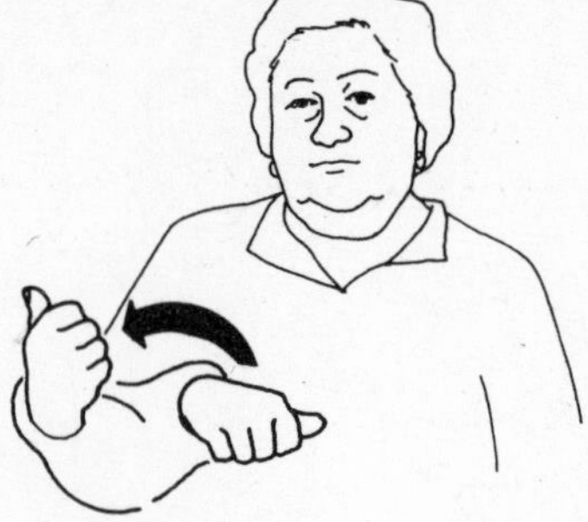

OTHER, ANOTHER, ELSE
Beginning with the right "10" hand in front of the chest, palm facing down, twist the wrist to the right, ending with palm facing left.
Hint: Pointing outward to another thing.

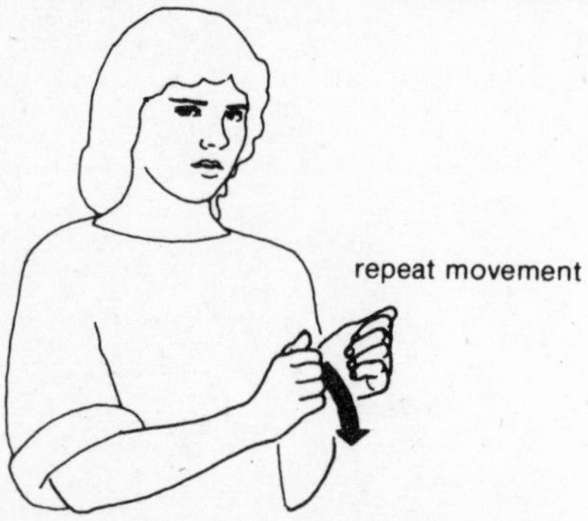

EVERY, EACH
Bring the knuckles of the right "10" hand, palm facing left, with a double movement down the thumb of the left "a" hand, palm facing right.

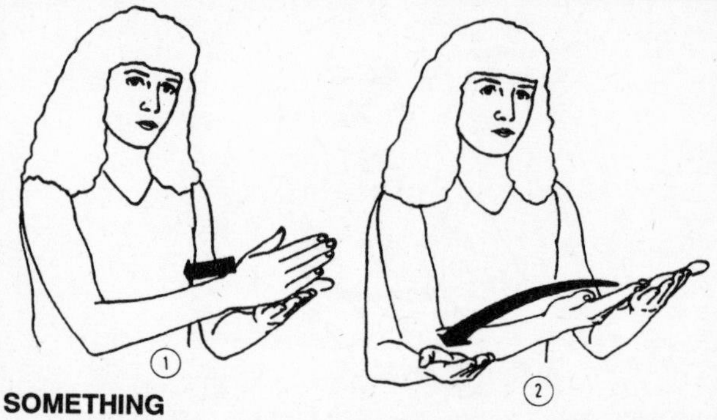

SOMETHING
Pull the little-finger side of the right hand, palm facing left, in toward the body across the open left palm. Then beginning with the back of the open right hand on the open left palm, both palms facing up, move the right hand to the right with a smooth movement.
Hint: "Some" plus "thing."

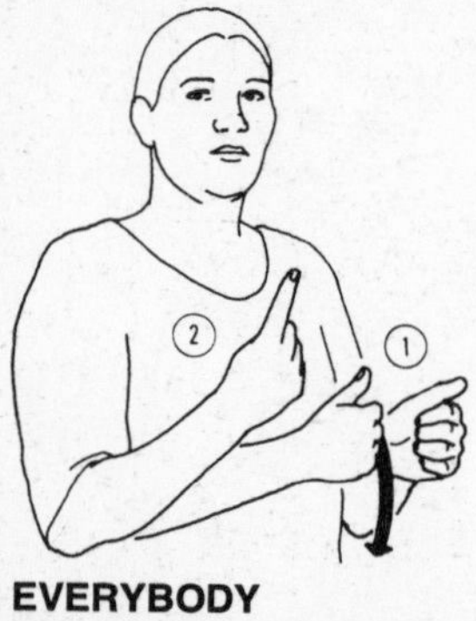

EVERYONE, EVERYBODY
Bring the knuckles of the right "10" hand, palm facing left, down the thumb of the left "a" hand, palm facing right. Then point the extended right index finger up in front of the chest, palm facing in.
Hint: "Every" plus "one."

HORDE, CROWD, AUDIENCE
Move both "claw" hand, palms facing down, from in front of the chest forward a short distance.
Hint: Rows of people.

four

FOODS AND EATING

Meals
Drinks
Desserts and Flavors
Fruits and Vegetables
Containers and Utensils

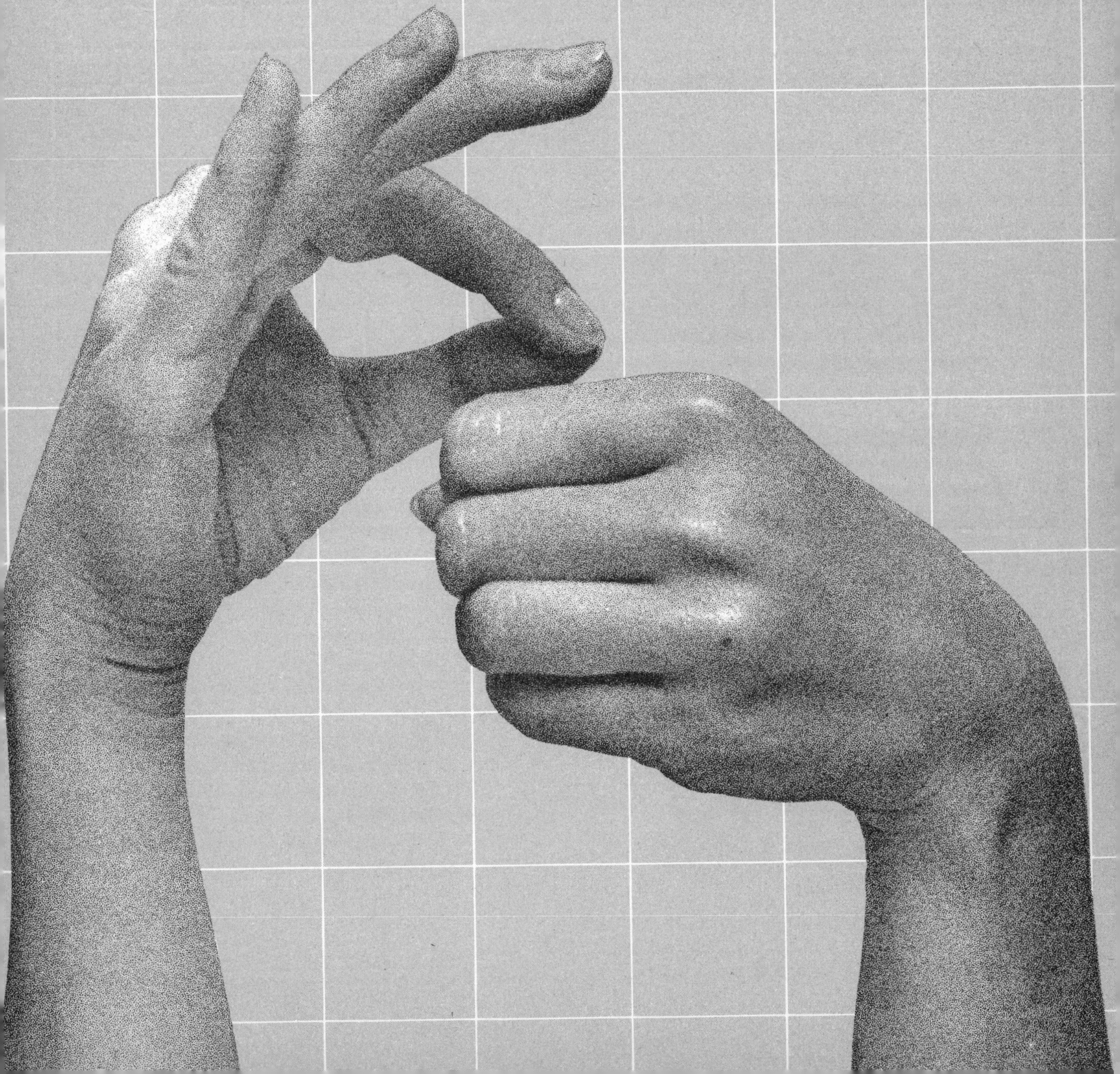

THE SIGNING SPACE

Signs are formed most frequently within an imaginary area that extends from the top of the head to the waist, extending on each side to the width of the shoulders. Signs which in the past were formed outside this area have been brought inward over time, probably because of ease in signing and greater visual clarity to the observer. Seventy-five percent of all signs are formed near the hear, face, or neck where the observer can see them most clearly.

SYMMETRY

Many signs use both hands moving independently of each other. Some examples of these signs are "let," "horse," and "place." Such signs almost always have the same handshape, location, and type of movement. Sometimes the movement is an alternating movement, with the hands moving in a similar fashion but in opposite directions.

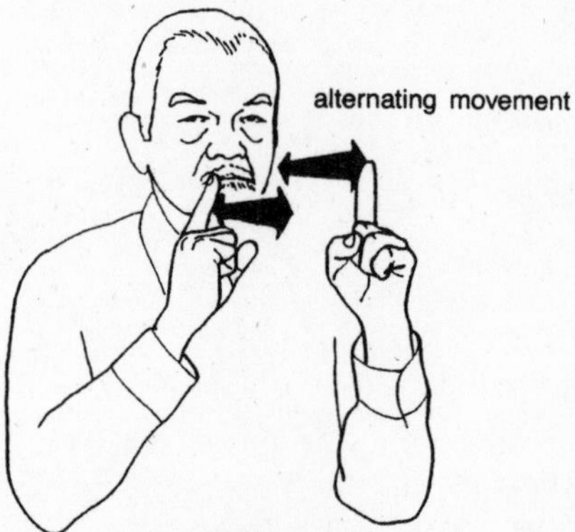

talk

THE DOMINANT HAND

Sometimes signs are formed with a different handshape for each hand. In those signs, the dominant hand moves while the other hand is held still. For a right-handed person, the dominant hand is the right hand; for a left-handed person, it is the left. Examples of such signs are "tea,""dollar," and "day."

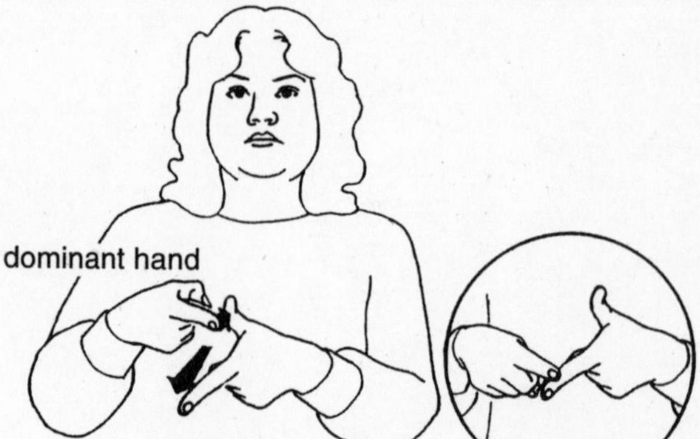

then

Meals

BREAKFAST
With the thumb and fingertips of the right hand together, palm facing down, move the fingers toward the lips. Then with the fingers of the open left hand in the crook of the bent right arm, move the open right palm upward toward the face.
Hint: "Eat" plus "morning."

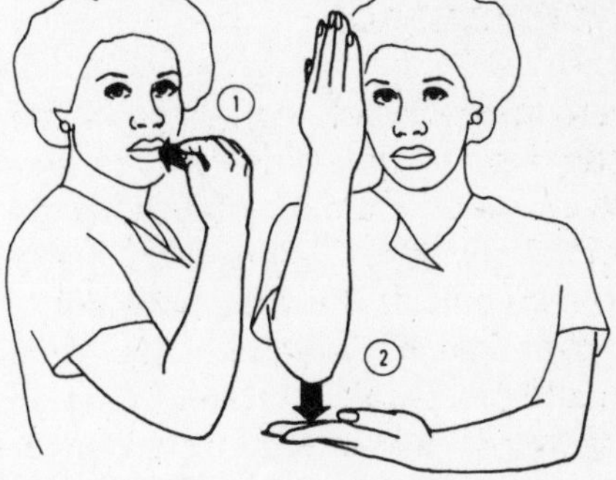

LUNCH
With the thumb and fingertips of the right hand together, palm facing down, move the fingers toward the lips. Then place the elbow of the bent right arm, hand extended straight up, on the palm of the open left hand held across the body.
Hint: "Eat" plus "noon."

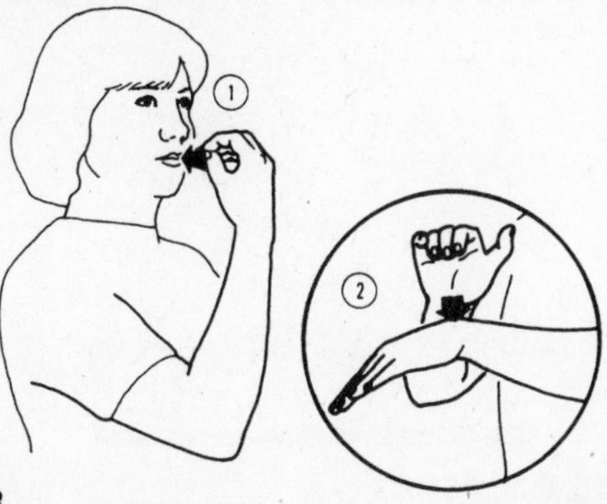

DINNER
With the thumb and fingertips of the right hand together, palm facing down, move the fingers toward the lips. Then place the wrist of the bent right hand on the back of the wrist of the open left hand held across the chest, both palms facing down.
Hint: "Eat" plus "night."

BREAD
Roll the fingers of the bent right hand, palm facing in, downward with a double movement over the back of the open left hand, ending with the palm facing up each time.
Hint: Slicing a loaf of bread.

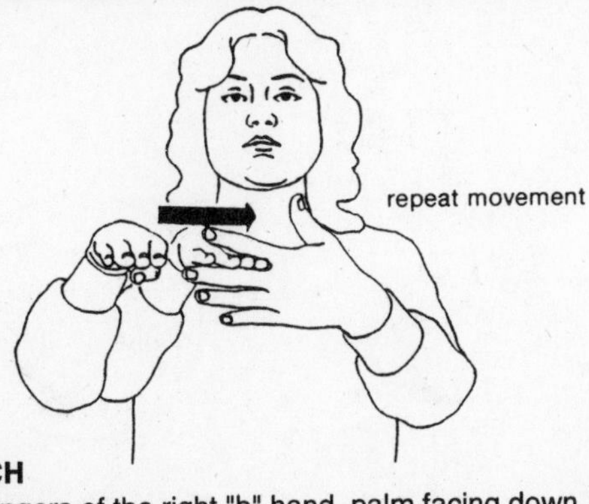

SANDWICH
Slide the fingers of the right "b" hand, palm facing down, between the index and middle fingers of the left "5" hand held in front of the chest, palm facing in and fingers pointing right.
Hint: Putting filling between slides of bread.

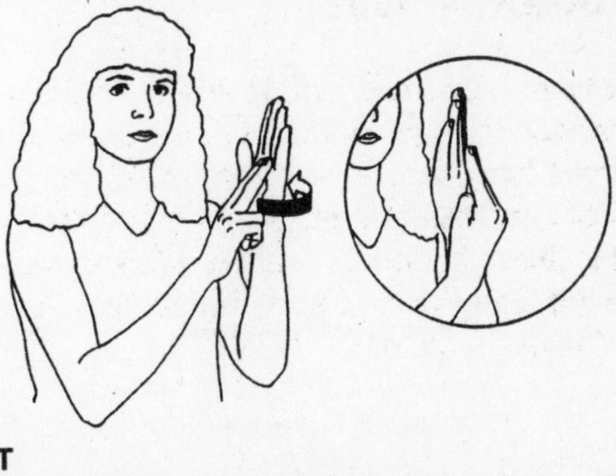

TOAST
Touch the fingertips of the right "v" hand first to the palm and then to the back of the open left hand held in front of the chest, palm facing right and fingers pointing up.
Hint: Holding bread with a fork to toast both sides.

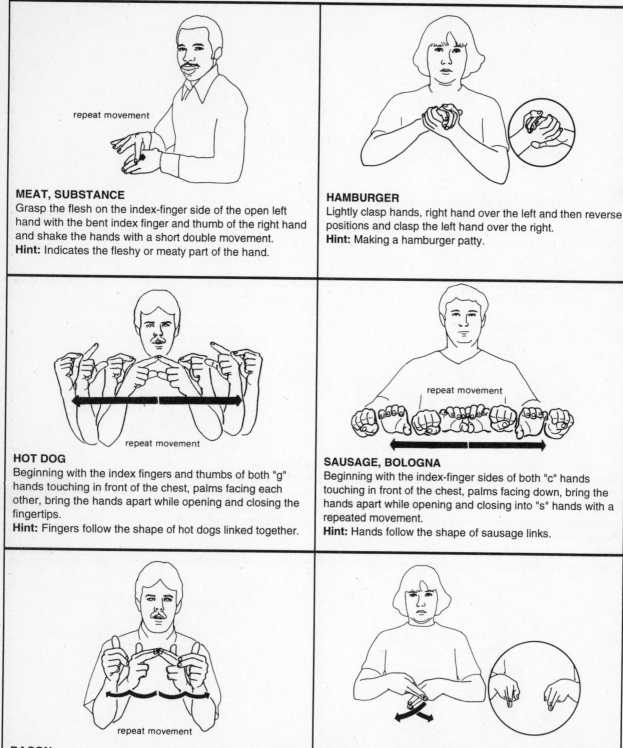

MEAT, SUBSTANCE
Grasp the flesh on the index-finger side of the open left hand with the bent index finger and thumb of the right hand and shake the hands with a short double movement.
Hint: Indicates the fleshy or meaty part of the hand.

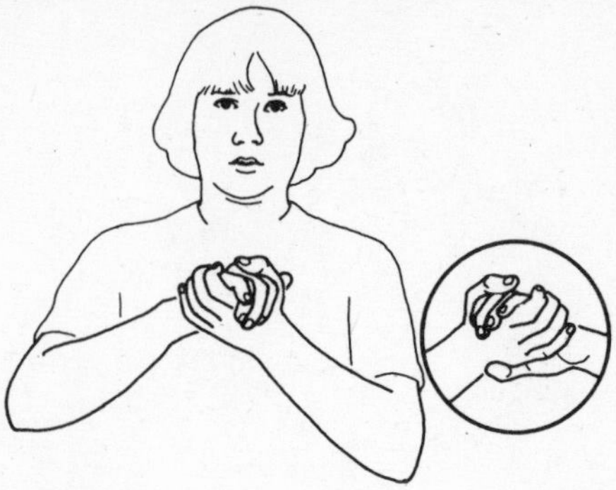

HAMBURGER
Lightly clasp hands, right hand over the left and then reverse positions and clasp the left hand over the right.
Hint: Making a hamburger patty.

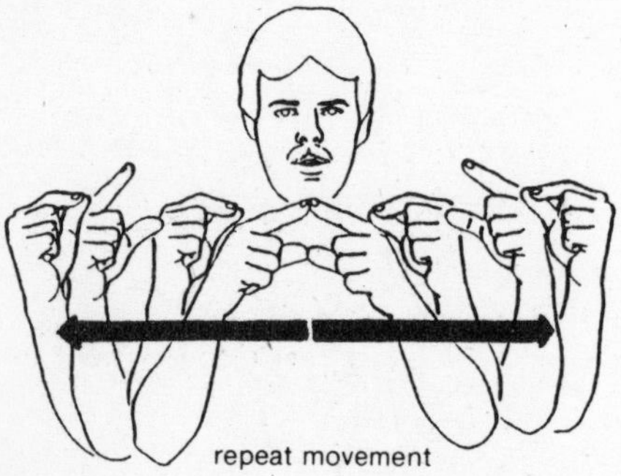

HOT DOG
Beginning with the index fingers and thumbs of both "g" hands touching in front of the chest, palms facing each other, bring the hands apart while opening and closing the fingertips.
Hint: Fingers follow the shape of hot dogs linked together.

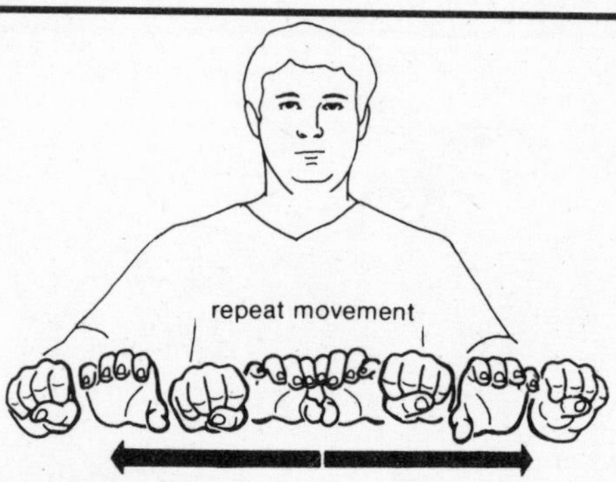

SAUSAGE, BOLOGNA
Beginning with the index-finger sides of both "c" hands touching in front of the chest, palms facing down, bring the hands apart while opening and closing into "s" hands with a repeated movement.
Hint: Hands follow the shape of sausage links.

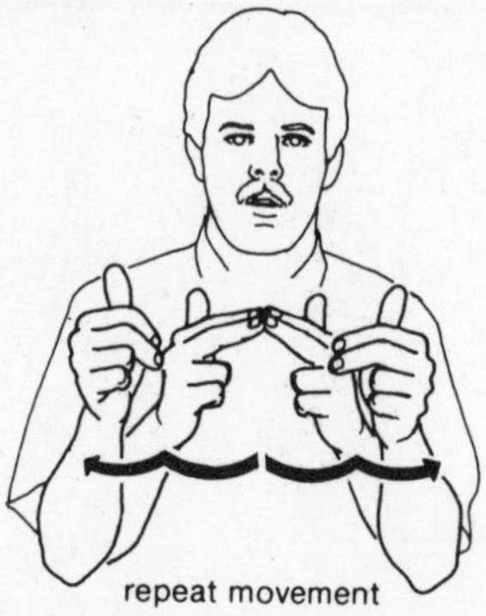

BACON
Beginning with the fingertips of both "h" hands touching in front of the chest, pull the hands apart while bending the fingers of each hand up and down with a double movement.
Hint: Shows the shape of bacon frying.

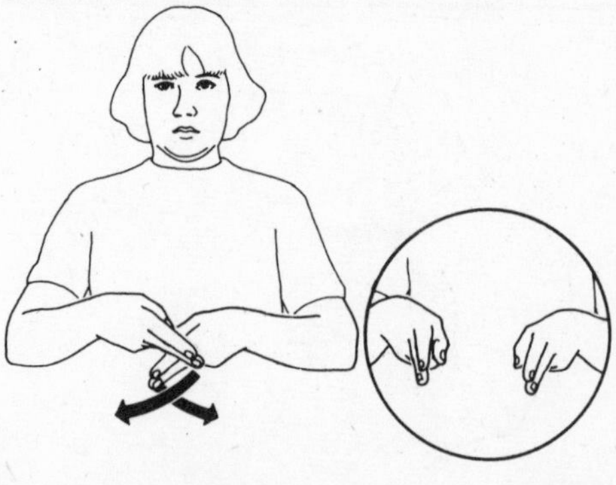

EGG
Beginning with the middle-finger side of the right hand across the index-finger side of the left "h" hand, drop the fingers down and apart from each other.
Hint: Breaking an egg into a bowl.

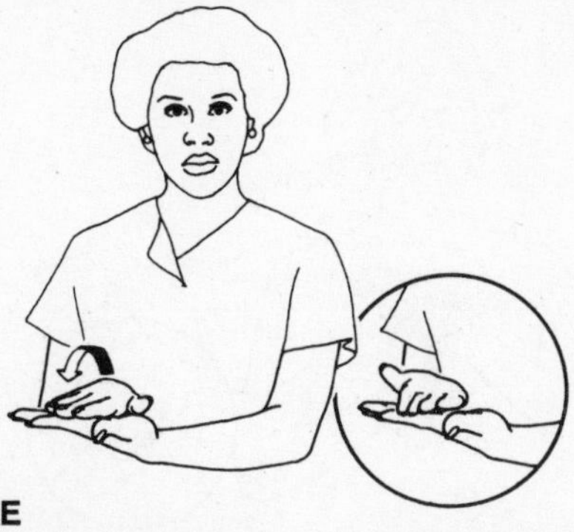

PANCAKE
Beginning with the palm of the open right hand, palm facing down, on the palm of the open left hand held in front of the chest, flip the right hand over, ending with the back of the right hand on the left palm.
Hint: Flipping pancakes while cooking.

SYRUP
Pull the extended right index finger from left to right under the nose, palm facing down.
Hint: Wiping syrup from the lips.

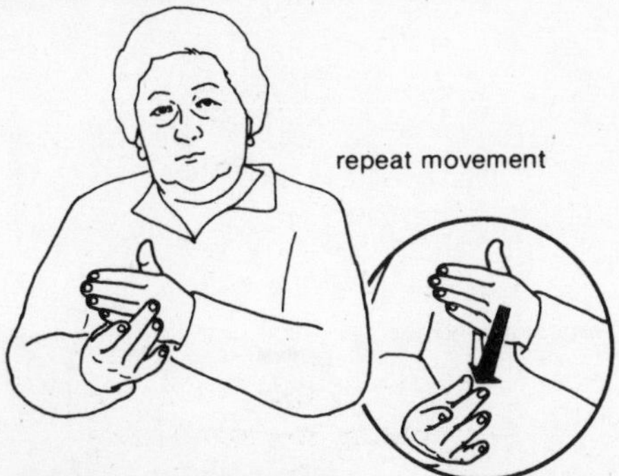

GRAVY, GREASE, GREASY, OIL
Grasp the little-finger side of the open left hand, palm angled right, with the thumb and middle finger of the right hand. Pull the right hand down with a double movement, pinching the middle finger and thumb together each time.
Hint: Grease dripping from meat.

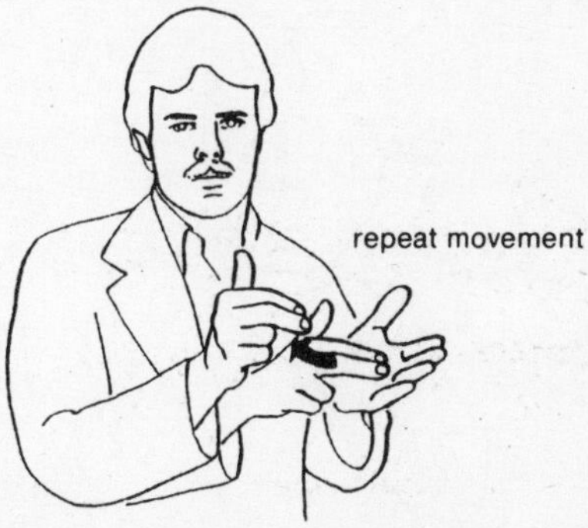

BUTTER
Pull the fingertips of the right "u" hand upward on the heel of the open left hand with a double movement bending the right fingers each time.
Hint: Spreading butter on bread.

FRENCH FRIES
Move the right "f" hand downward with a short movement in front of the right side of the body. Repeat slightly to the right.
Hint: Abbreviation "f-f."

SOUP
Bring the right "h" finger, palm facing up, across the palm of the open left hand, palm facing up in front of the chest, upward in a repeated circular movement toward the mouth.
Hint: Eating soup from a held bowl.

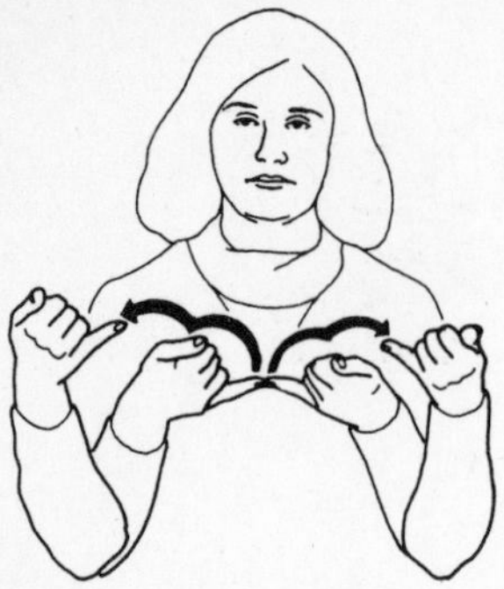

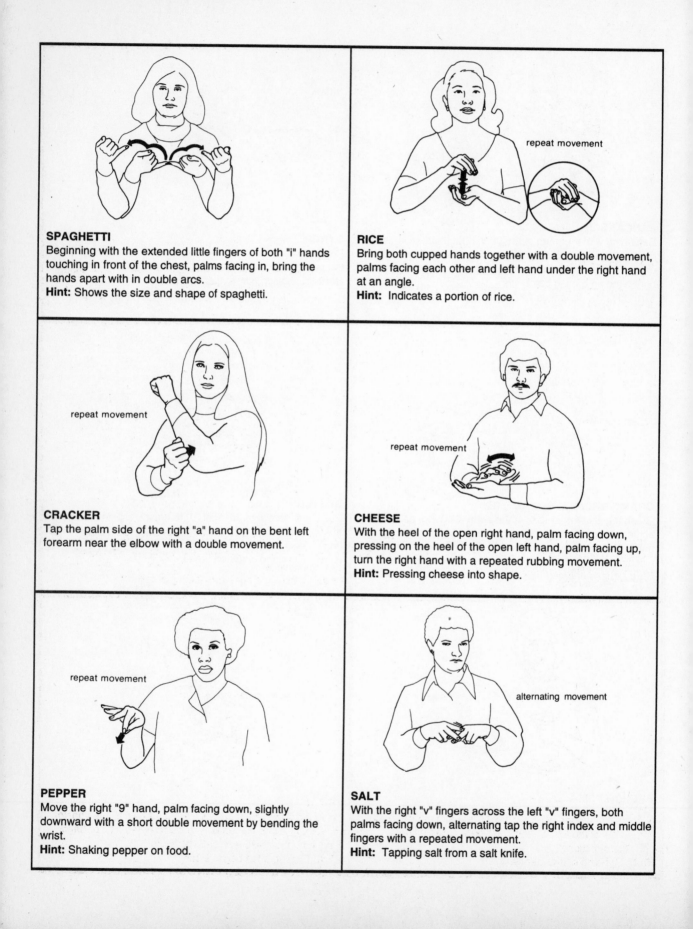

SPAGHETTI
Beginning with the extended little fingers of both "i" hands touching in front of the chest, palms facing in, bring the hands apart with in double arcs.
Hint: Shows the size and shape of spaghetti.

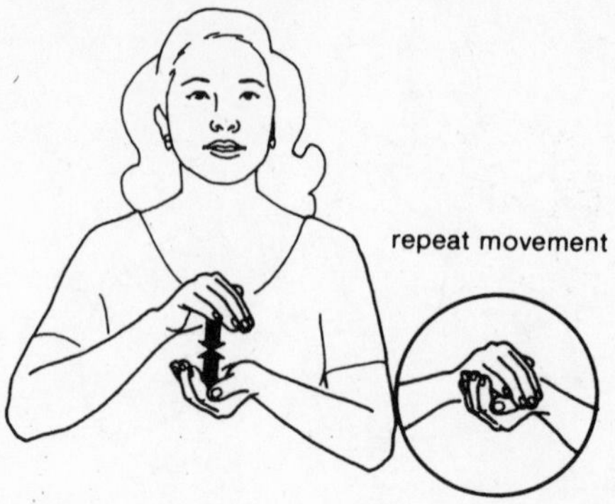

RICE
Bring both cupped hands together with a double movement, palms facing each other and left hand under the right hand at an angle.
Hint: Indicates a portion of rice.

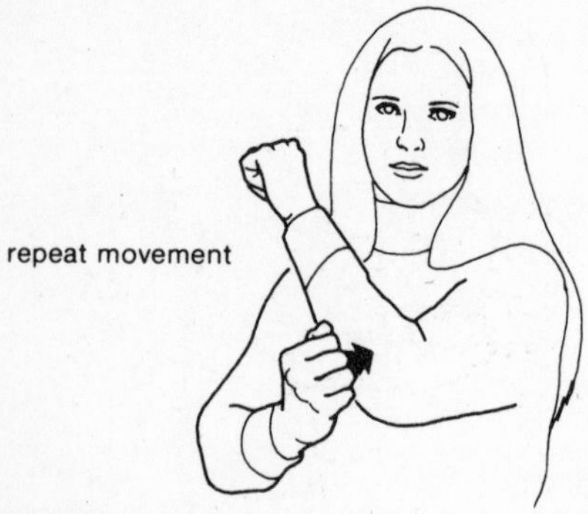

CRACKER
Tap the palm side of the right "a" hand on the bent left forearm near the elbow with a double movement.

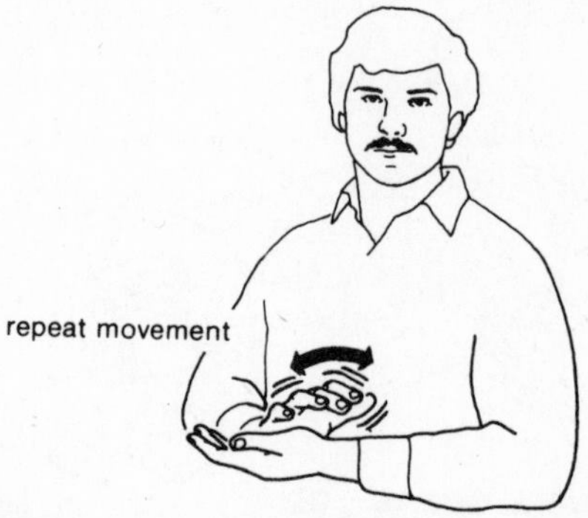

CHEESE
With the heel of the open right hand, palm facing down, pressing on the heel of the open left hand, palm facing up, turn the right hand with a repeated rubbing movement.
Hint: Pressing cheese into shape.

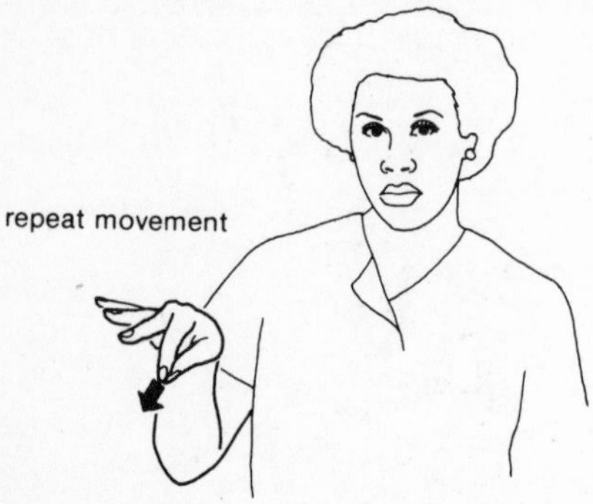

PEPPER
Move the right "9" hand, palm facing down, slightly downward with a short double movement by bending the wrist.
Hint: Shaking pepper on food.

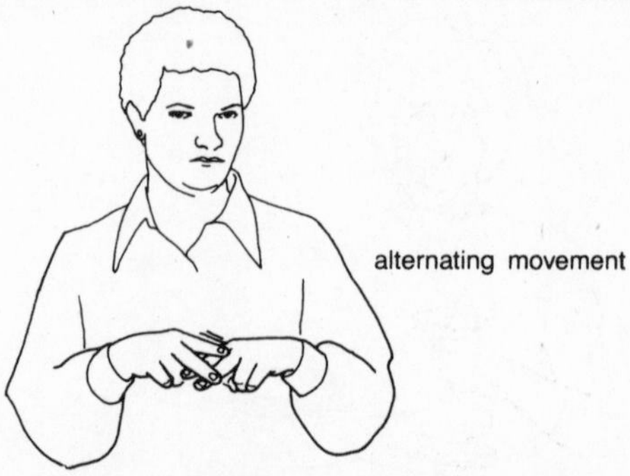

SALT
With the right "v" fingers across the left "v" fingers, both palms facing down, alternating tap the right index and middle fingers with a repeated movement.
Hint: Tapping salt from a salt knife.

Drinks

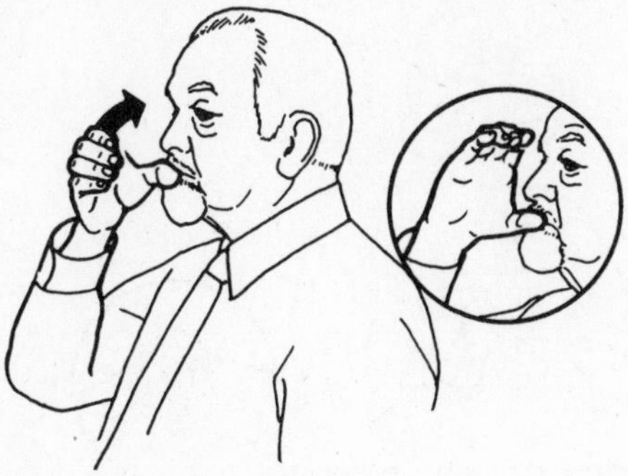

DRINK, BEVERAGE
With the thumb of the right "c" hand at the mouth, palm facing left, tip the right fingers upward toward the nose.
Hint: Mime taking a drink.

WATER
Tap the index-finger side of the right "w" hand, palm facing left, on the chin with a double movement.
Hint: Initialized sign from near where one drinks water.

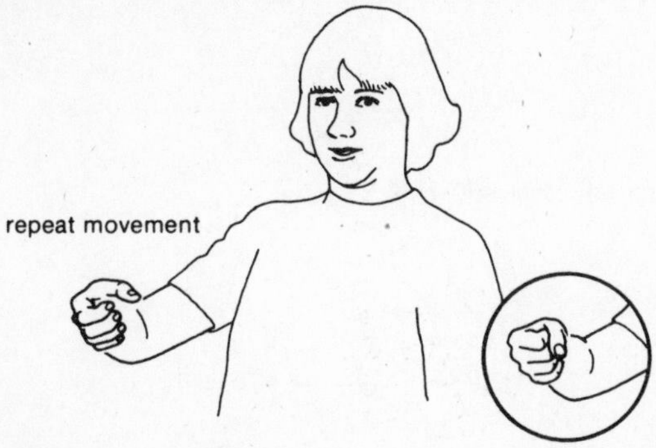

MILK
Beginning with the right "c" hand in front of the right side of the body, palm facing left, open and close the hand into an "s" with a repeated movement.
Hint: Milking a cow.

CREAM
Bring the little-finger side of the right "c" hand from the fingers to the heel of the open left hand, palm facing up in front of the chest.
Hint: Skimming cream from the top of milk.

COFFEE
Rub the little-finger side of the right "s" hand on the index-finger side of the left "s" hand, in small circles going opposite directions.
Hint: Grinding coffee beans.

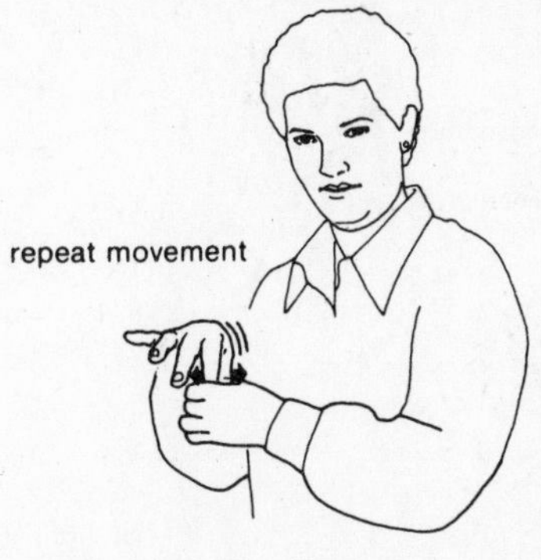

TEA
Move the fingertips of the right "9" hand with a little shaking movement inside the index-finger side of the left "o" hand held in front of the chest, palm facing in.
Hint: Dipping a tea bag in a cup.

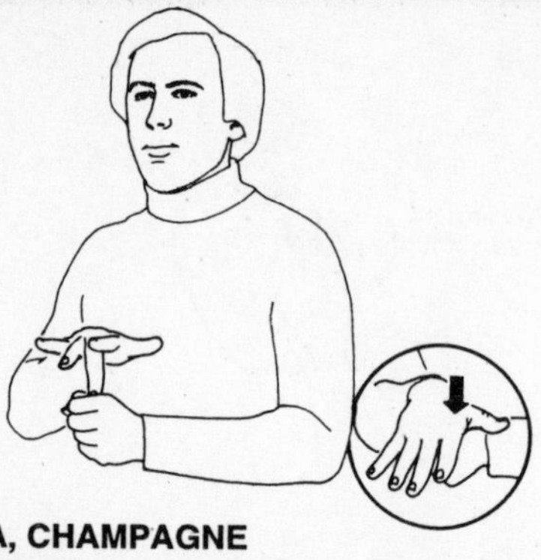

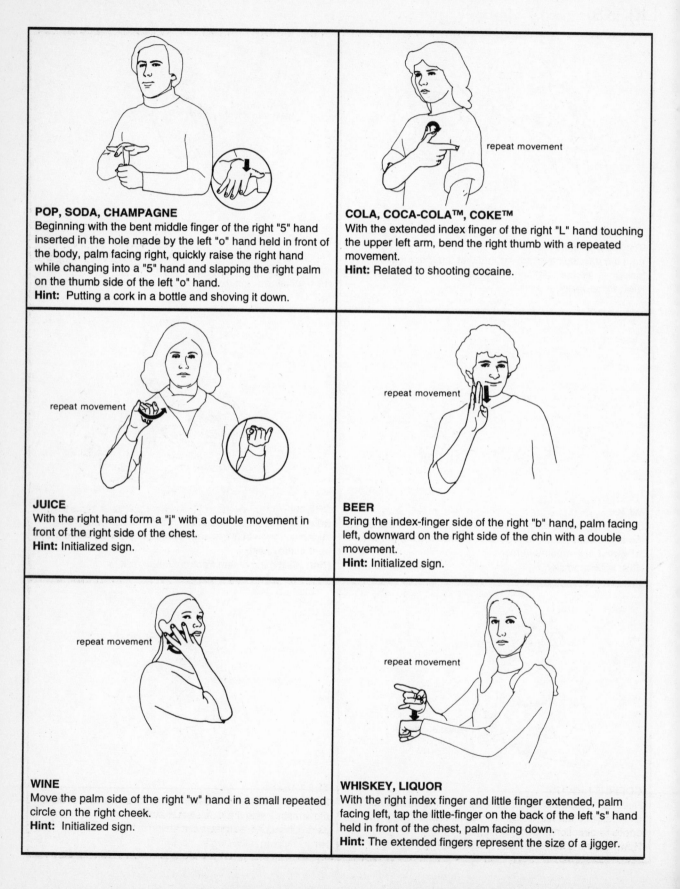

POP, SODA, CHAMPAGNE
Beginning with the bent middle finger of the right "5" hand inserted in the hole made by the left "o" hand held in front of the body, palm facing right, quickly raise the right hand while changing into a "5" hand and slapping the right palm on the thumb side of the left "o" hand.
Hint: Putting a cork in a bottle and shoving it down.

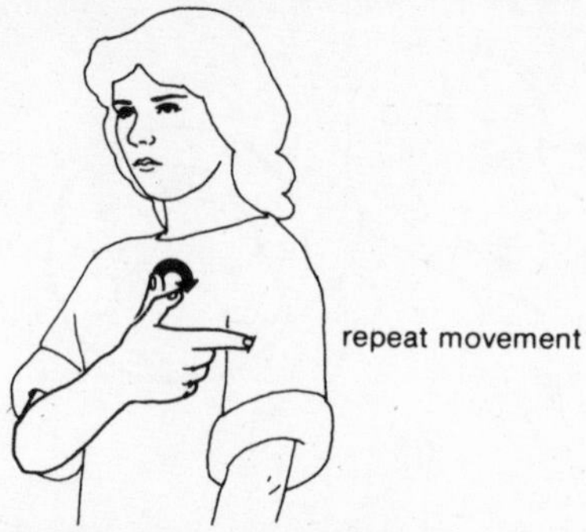

COLA, COCA-COLA™, COKE™
With the extended index finger of the right "L" hand touching the upper left arm, bend the right thumb with a repeated movement.
Hint: Related to shooting cocaine.

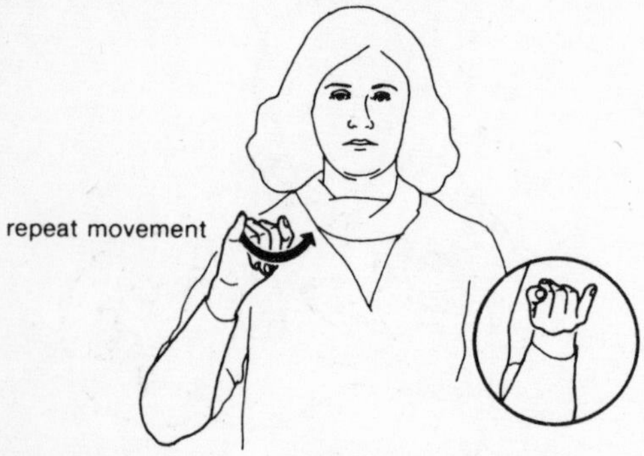

JUICE
With the right hand form a "j" with a double movement in front of the right side of the chest.
Hint: Initialized sign.

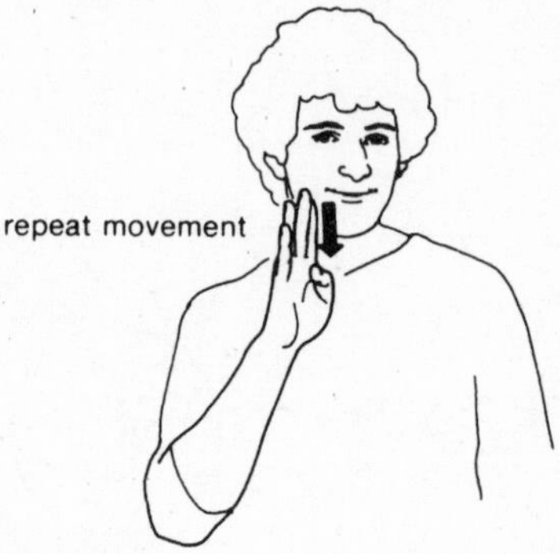

BEER
Bring the index-finger side of the right "b" hand, palm facing left, downward on the right side of the chin with a double movement.
Hint: Initialized sign.

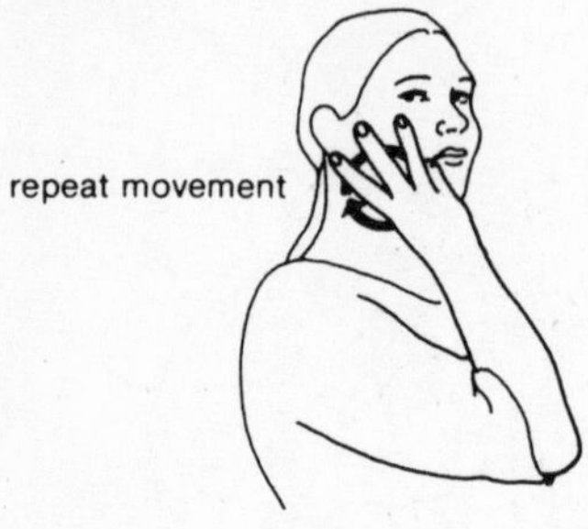

WINE
Move the palm side of the right "w" hand in a small repeated circle on the right cheek.
Hint: Initialized sign.

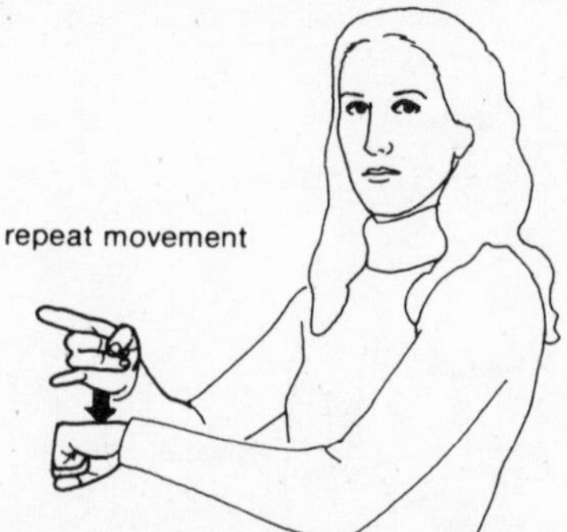

WHISKEY, LIQUOR
With the right index finger and little finger extended, palm facing left, tap the little-finger on the back of the left "s" hand held in front of the chest, palm facing down.
Hint: The extended fingers represent the size of a jigger.

Desserts and Flavors

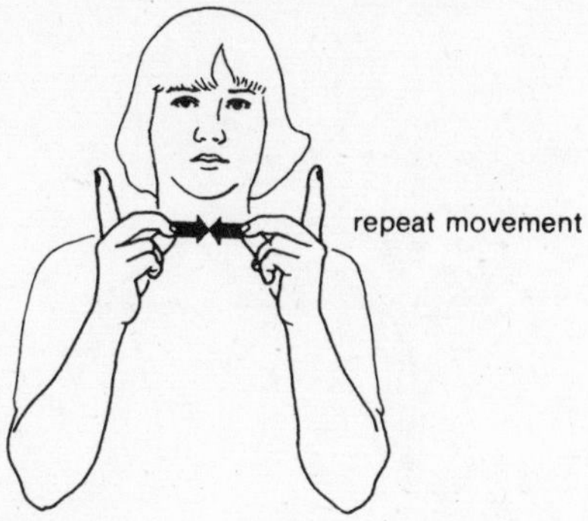

DESSERT
Tap the middle fingers of both "d" hands together with a double movement in front of the chest, palms facing each other.
Hint: Initialized sign.

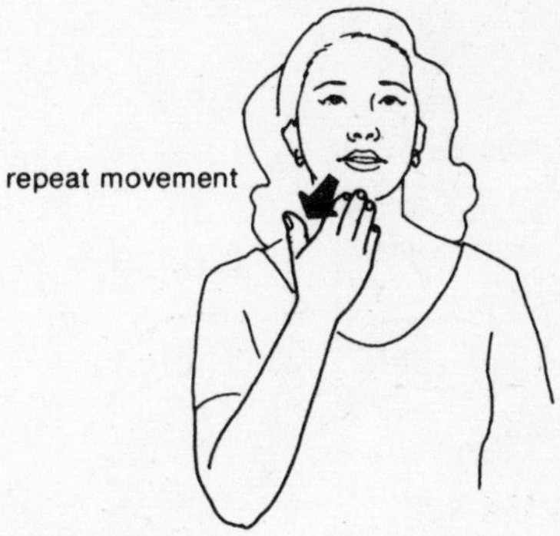

SUGAR, SWEET
Brush the fingertips of the open right hand, palm facing in, downward on the chin with a double movement, bending the fingers back toward the palm each time.

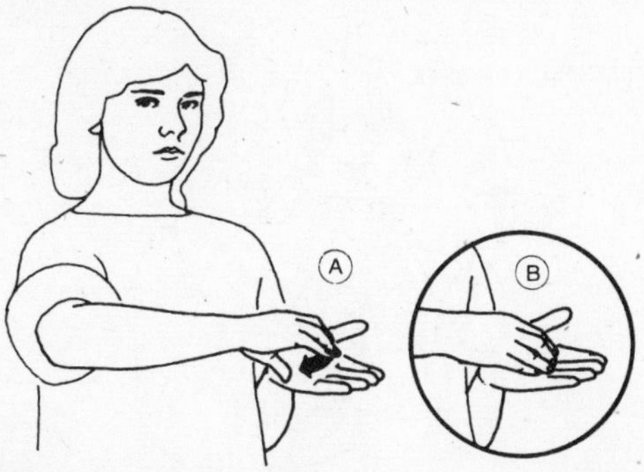

CAKE
Bring the fingertips of the right "c"hand across the palm of the open left hand held in front of the chest, palm facing up. Twist the right wrist and repeat at a different angle on the left palm.
Hint: Initialized sign representing cutting a piece of cake.

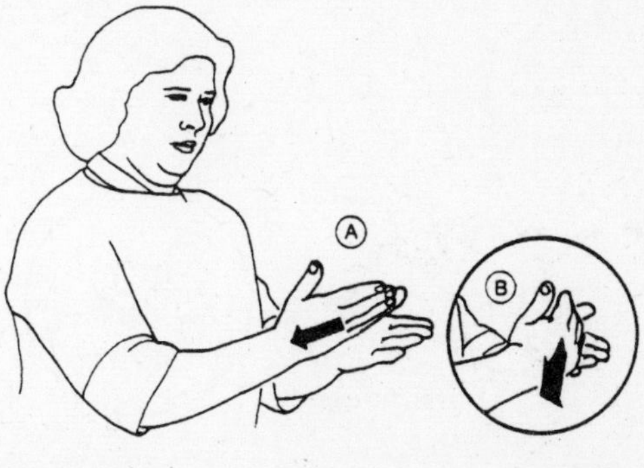

PIE
Slide the little-finger side of the open right hand across the palm of the open left hand held in front of the chest, palm facing up. Twist the right wrist and repeat at a different angle on the left palm.
Hint: Slicing a pie.

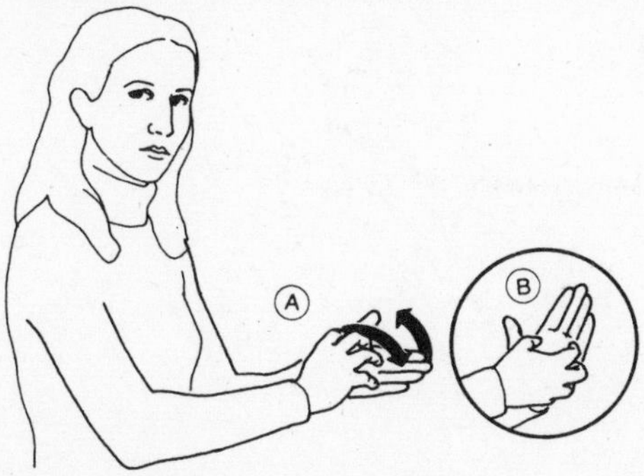

COOKIE, BISCUIT
Touch the fingertips of the right "claw" hand on the palm of the open left hand, palm facing up. Twist both hands in opposite directions and touch again.
Hint: Cutting cookies with a cookie cutter.

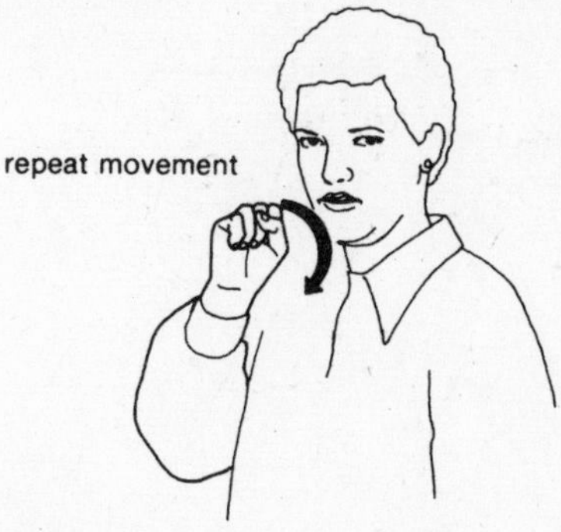

ICE CREAM
Bring the right "s" hand, palm facing left, downward in front of the mouth with a repeated movement.
Hint: Licking an ice cream cone.

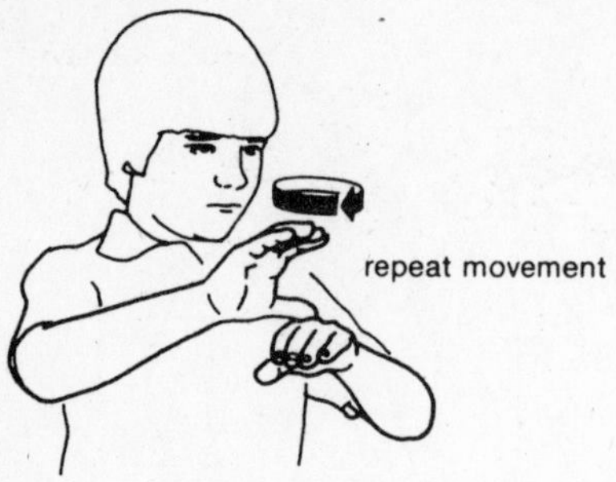

CHOCOLATE
Move the thumb side of the right "c" hand, palm facing forward, in a repeated circle on the back of the open left hand held in front of the chest, palm facing down.
Hint: Initialized sign.

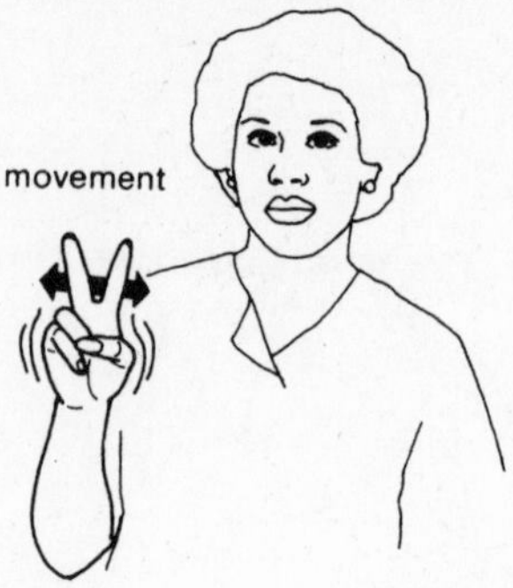

VANILLA, VITAMIN
Wiggle the right "v" hand, palm facing forward, from side to side with a slight movement in front of the right shoulder.
Hint: Initialized sign.

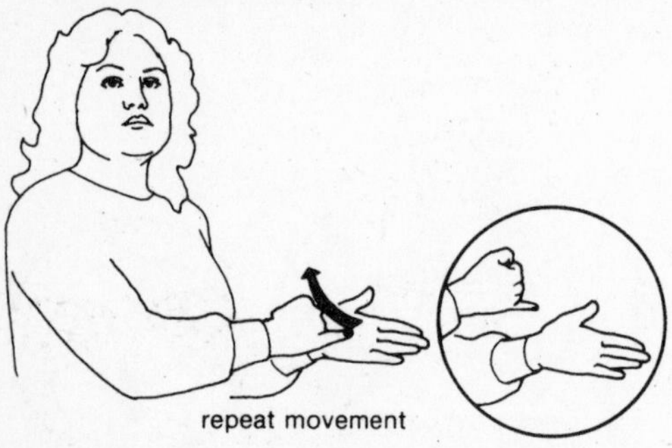

JELLY, JAM
With a twist of the wrist, move the extended right little finger upward with a quick movement on the heel of the open left hand.
Hint: Initialized sign; spreading jelly on bread.

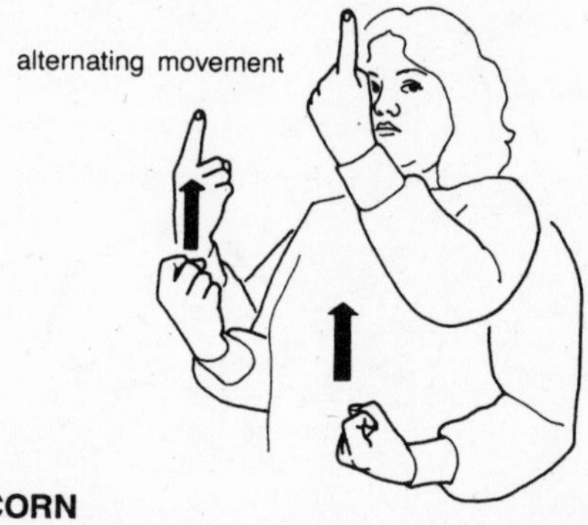

POPCORN
Beginning with both "s" hands in front of each side of the chest, alternately raise each hand with a repeated movement, flicking up the index finger as the each hand moves.
Hint: Represents kernels of popcorn popping.

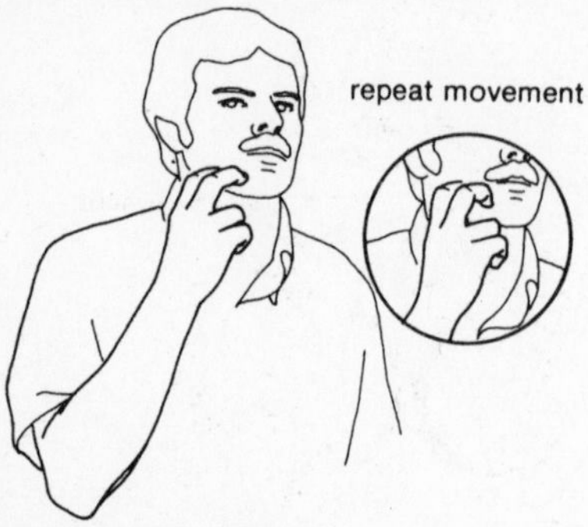

CHEWING GUM, GUM
With the right "v" fingertips on the right cheek, move the hand in toward the cheek with a repeated movement by bending the fingers.
Hint: Indicates the jaw movement when chewing gum.

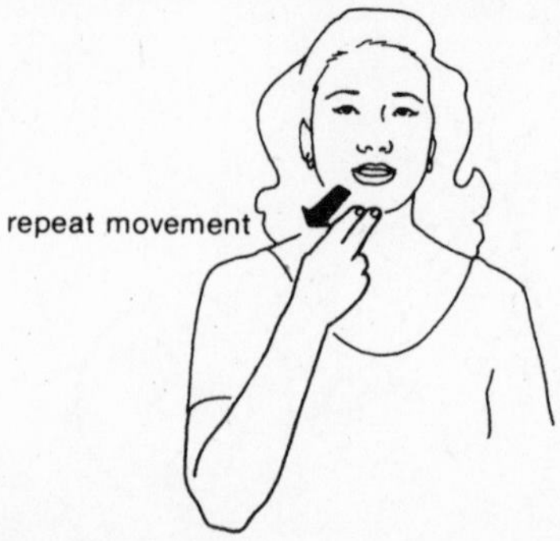

CANDY
Brush the fingertips of the right "u" hand, palm facing in, downward on the chin with a double movement, bending the fingers back toward the palm each time.
Hint: Licking a lollipop.

Fruits and Vegetables

VEGETABLE
Beginning with the index finger of the right "v" hand, palm facing left, touching the right side of the chin, twist the wrist to touch the right middle finger to the left side of the chin, ending with the palm facing right.
Hint: Initialized sign.

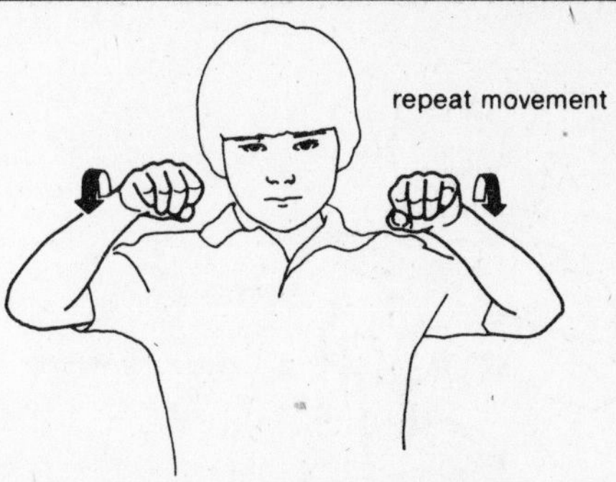

CORN, CORN-ON-THE-COB, EAT CORN
With both "s" hands near each side of the face, both palms facing down and elbows extended, twist the wrists forward with a double movement, turning the palms back each time.
Hint: Eating corn-on-the-cob.

PEAS
Move the index fingertip of the right "x" hand along the length of the extended left index finger with a repeated movement.
Hint: Pointing to the individual peas in a pod.

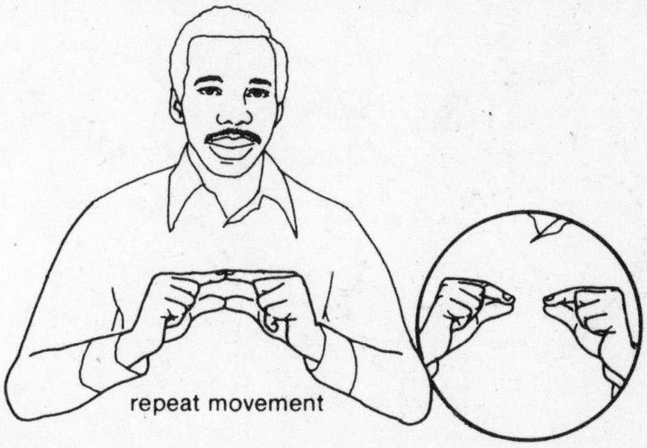

BEANS
Beginning with the extended fingers of both "g" hands touching in front of the chest, palms facing each other, bring the hands apart with a double movement, closing the fingers to the thumbs each time.
Hint: Fingers follow the shape of a bean.

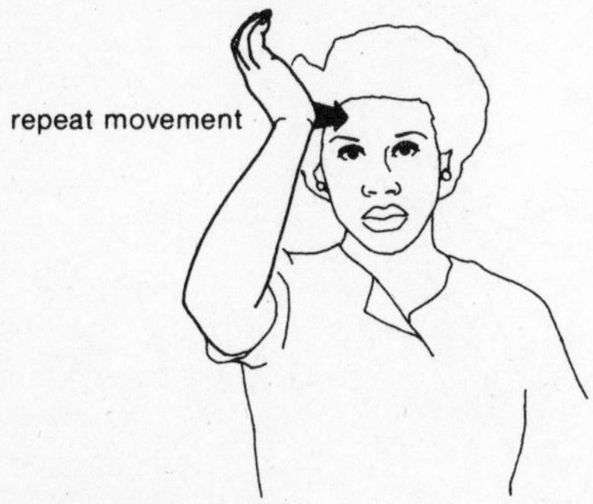

CABBAGE, LETTUCE
Tap the heel of the curved right hand, palm angled up, against the right side of the forehead with a double movement.
Hint: Indicates a head of cabbage or lettuce.

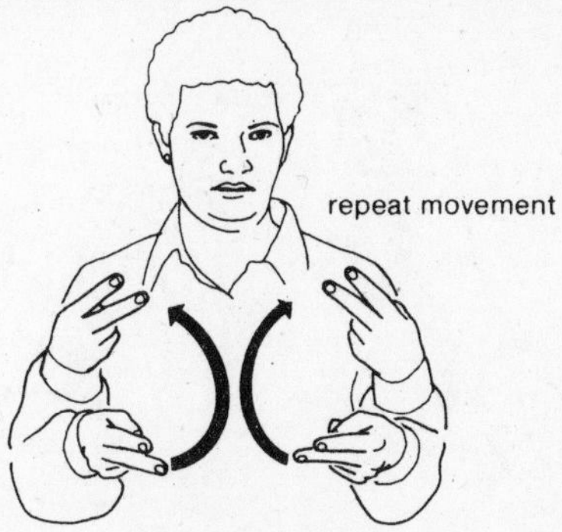

SALAD
Beginning with both "v" hands in front of the body, palms facing up and fingers pointing toward each other, move the hands toward each other and upward with a repeated movement. Note: Hands may be "claw" hands instead.
Hint: Initialized sign for "vegetable"' mime tossing a salad.

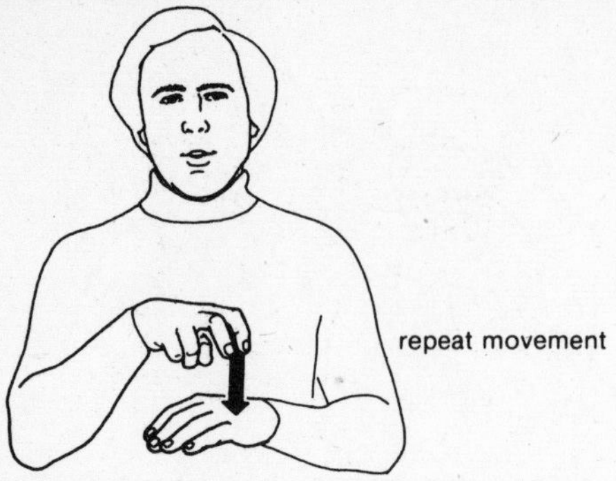

POTATO
Tap the fingertips of the right crooked "v" hand on the back of the open left hand with a double movement, both palms facing down.
Hint: Testing a potato with a fork to see if it is cooked.

CARROT
Move the right "s" hand, palm facing left, slowly to the right side of the mouth. Note: Sign is usually made with a quick clicking of the teeth as if biting or chewing on the carrot.
Hint: Mime eating a carrot.

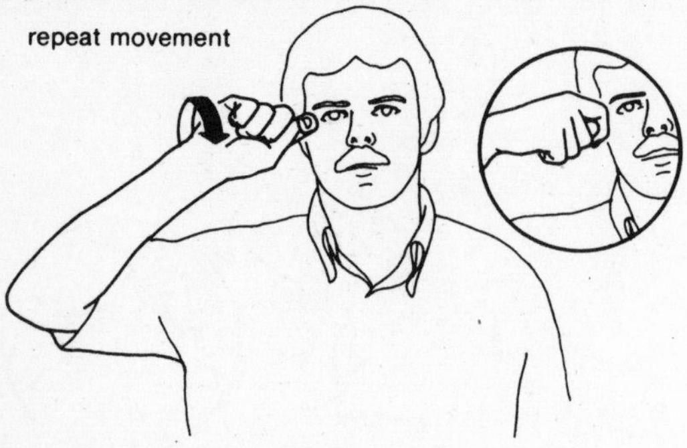

ONION
Twist the knuckle of the right "x" index finger downward with a double movement near the corner of the right eye.
Hint: Wiping a tear fro the eye caused by peeling onions.

TOMATO
Bring the extended right index finger, palm facing left, from the mouth downward across the index-finger side of the left "s" hand held in front of the body, palm facing right.
Hint: Slicing a tomato.

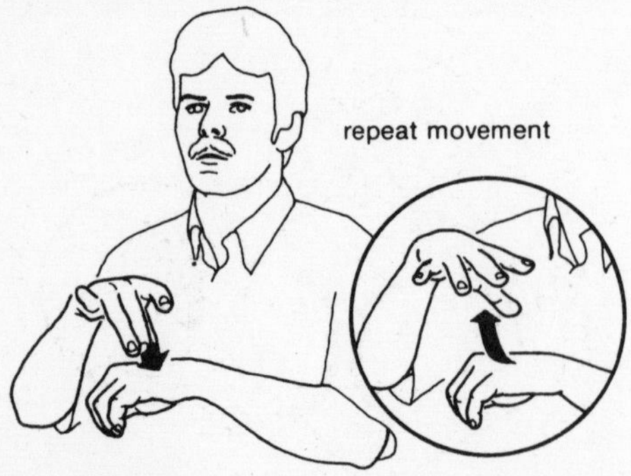

PUMPKIN, MELON
Flick the middle finger of the right "8" hand off the back of the back of the left hand with a double movement, both palms facing down, raising and opening the right hand each time.

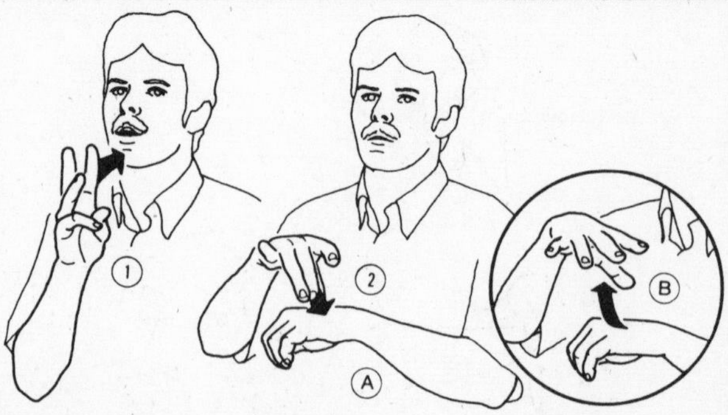

WATERMELON
Tap the index-finger side of the right "w" hand to the chin with a double movement, palm facing left. Then flick the middle finger of the right "8" hand off the back of the back of the left hand with a double movement, both palms facing down, raising and opening the right hand each time.

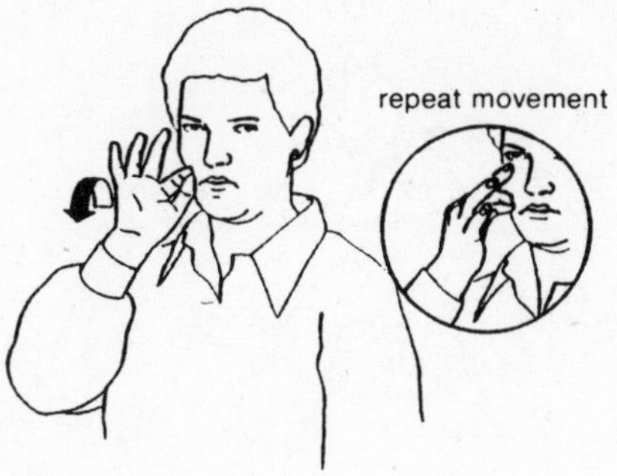

FRUIT
Twist the fingertips of the right "f" hand downward with a double movement on the right cheek.
Hint: Initialized sign.

APPLE
Twist the palm side of the right "a" hand downward with a double movement on the right side of the chin.
Hint: Initialized sign showing chewing an apple in the cheek.

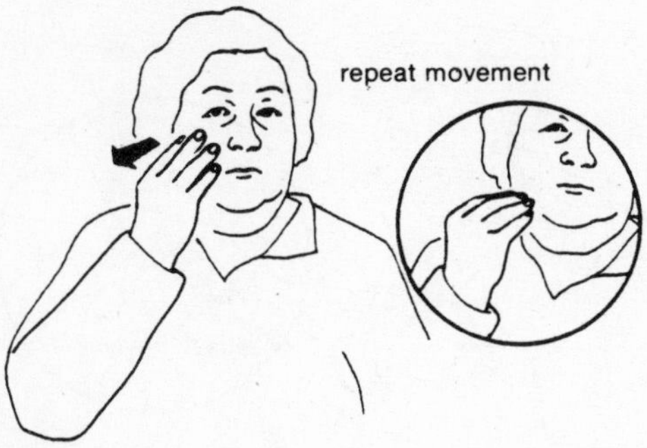

PEACH
Wipe the fingertips of the right "5" hand, palm facing in, downward on the right cheek with a double movement, closing the fingers to the thumb each time.
Hint: Feeling peach fuzz.

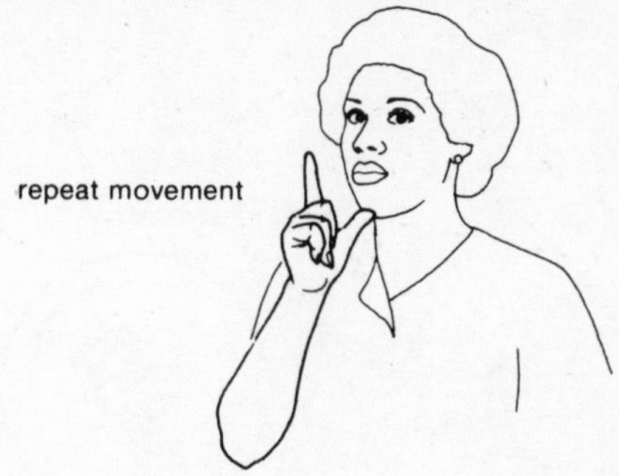

LEMON
Tap the thumb of the right "l" hand to the chin with a double movement, palm facing left.
Hint: Initialized sign.

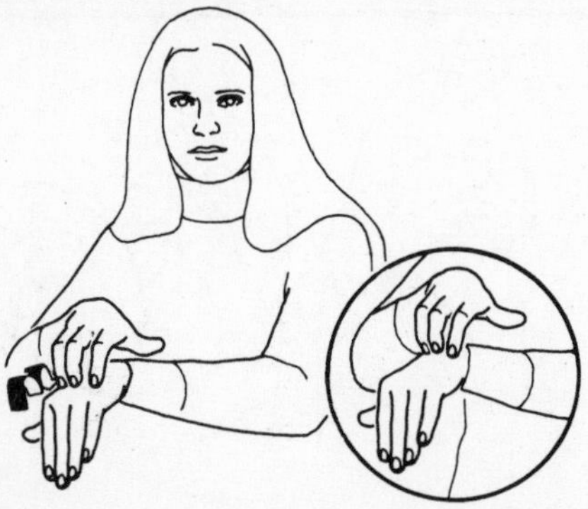

GRAPES
Touch the fingertips of the right "claw" hand on the back of the bent left hand in a couple of places as the right hand moves back toward the chest from the left knuckles to the wrist, both palms facing down.
Hint: Shows a bunch of grapes.

BANANA
Move the fingers of the right bent hand, palm facing forward, down the thumb side of the extended left index finger pointing up in front of the chest, palm facing right. Then turn the right hand, palm facing left, and repeat.
Hint. Mime peeling a banana.

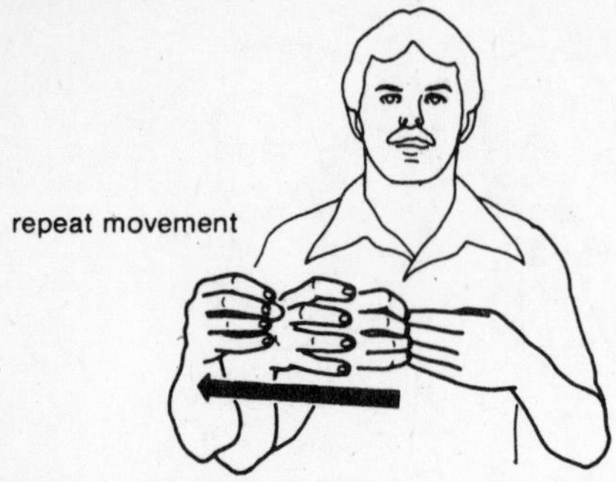

PEAR
Beginning with the right fingers around the left fingers and thumb, both palms facing in and fingers pointing toward each other in front of the chest, pull the right hand outward to the right while opening and then closing the right fingers.
Hint: Shows the shape of a pear.

COCONUT
While holding both "c" hands near the right side of the head, palms facing each other, shake the hands with a small repeated movement.
Hint: Mime shaking a coconut to hear the milk inside.

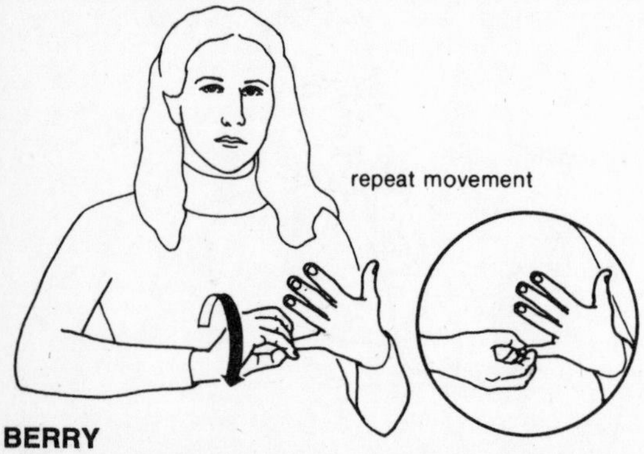

BERRY
While holding the little finger of the left "5" hand, palm facing in, with the right fingers, twist the right hand with a double movement. Note: Add "blue" to form blueberry.
Hint: Twisting a berry from the vine.

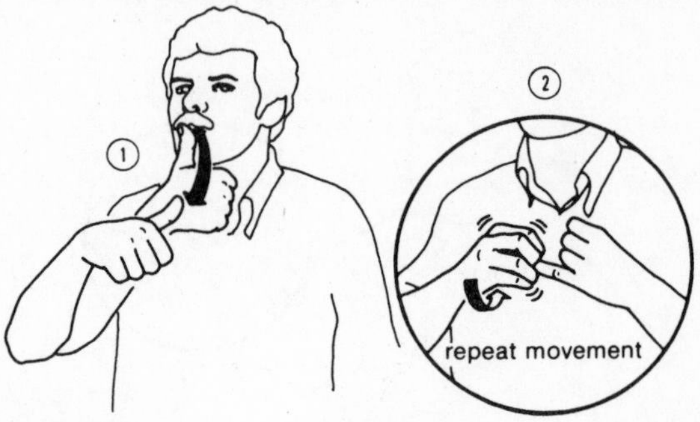

STRAWBERRY
Bring the extended thumb of the right "10" hand, palm facing in, from the mouth downward while turning the palm down. Then while holding the extended little finger of the left hand with the right fingers, twist the right hand with a double movement.
Hint: A modified sign for "red" plus "berry."

PEANUT, NUT
Flick the thumb of the right "a" hand off the edge of the front teeth.
Hint: Cracking nuts with the teeth.

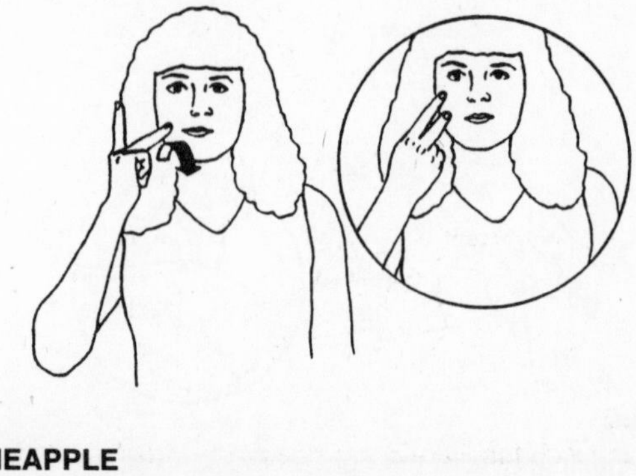

PINEAPPLE
With the middle finger of the right "p" hand on the cheek near the mouth, palm facing left, twist the hand to turn the palm back.
Hint: Initialized sign similar to sign for "apple."

Containers and Utensils

BOWL
Beginning with the little-finger sides of both cupped hands together in front of the chest, move the hand apart and upward while changing into "c" hands, ending with the palms facing each other.
Hint: Hands form the shape of a bowl.

PLATE
Hold the curved "L" hands several inches apart in front of the body, palms facing each other.
Hint: Fingers form the side borders of a plate.

CUP, CAN
Move the right "c" hand, palm facing left, down a short distance to land on the palm of the open left hand held in front of the chest, palm facing up.
Hint: Hands show the shape of a cup on a saucer.

GLASS
Beginning with little-finger side of the right "c" hand, palm facing left, on the palm of the open left hand, move the right hand upward a few inches.
Hint: Hand follows the height and shape of a glass.

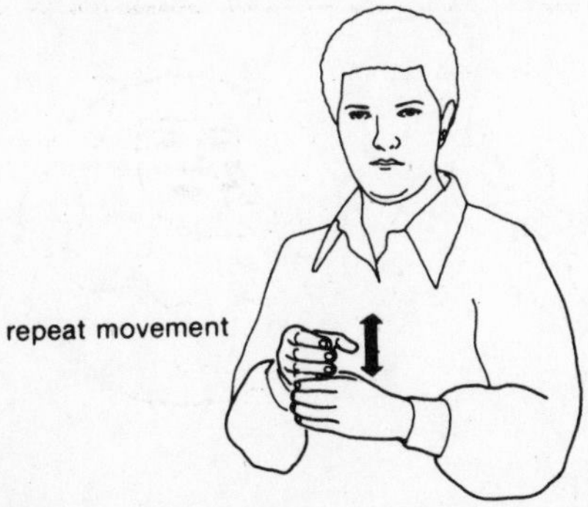

BOTTLE
Beginning with the little-finger side of the right "c" hand, palm facing left, on the index-finger side of the left "c" hand, palm facing right, move the right hand upward with a double movement.

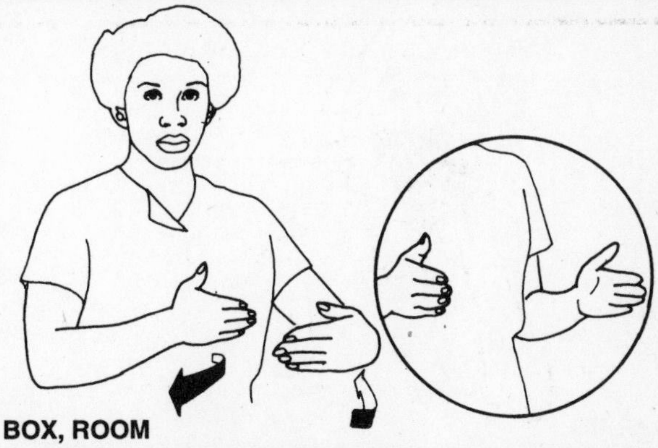

BOX, ROOM
Beginning with both open hands in front of chest, right hand closer to the body than the left hand, both palms facing in, move the hands to the sides, ending with the palms facing each other.
Hint: Hands form the shape of a box.

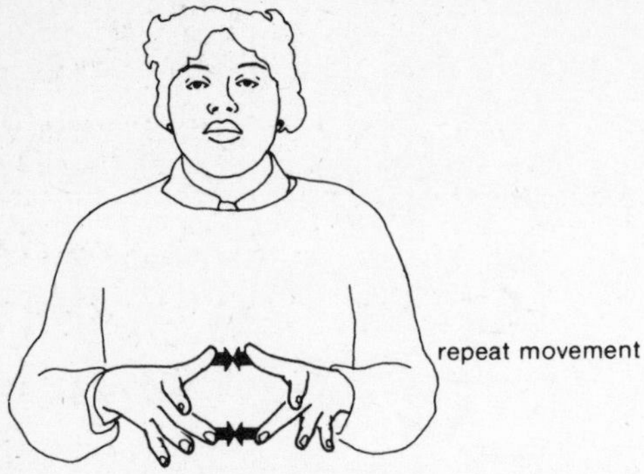

DISH
Tap the bent middle fingers and thumbs of both "5" hands together with a double movement in front of the chest.
Hint: shows the shape of a dish.

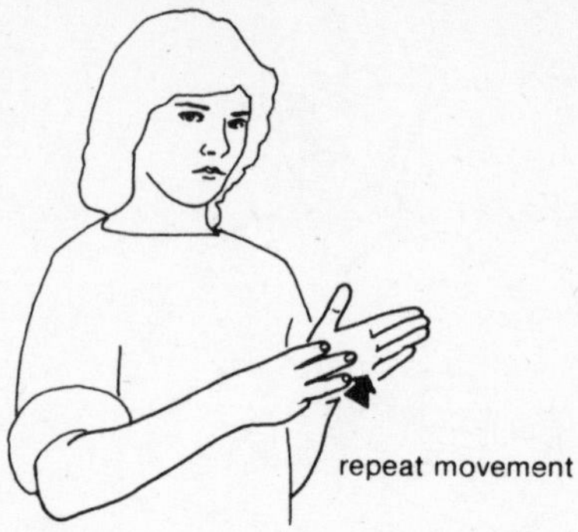

FORK
Tap the fingertips of the right "w" hand, palm facing in, with a repeated movement against the palm of the open left hand, palm facing right.
Hint: Represents the tines of a fork.

SPOON
Bring the back of the right "h" fingers, palm facing up, upward across the palm of the open left hand with a small repeated circular movement.

KNIFE
Slide the extended right index finger, palm facing down and finger pointing left, with a repeated movement along the length of the extended left index finger, palm facing right.
Hint: Sharpening a knife on a honing blade.

NAPKIN
Move the fingertips of the open right hand, palm facing in, back and forth with a double movement in front of the mouth.
Hint: Wiping the mouth with a napkin.

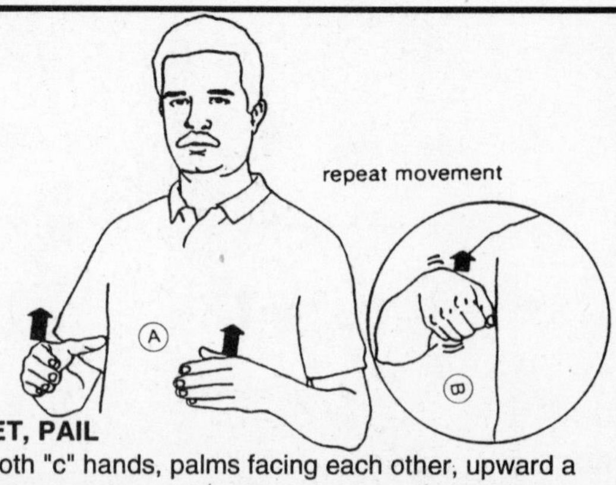

BUCKET, PAIL
Move both "c" hands, palms facing each other, upward a short distance in front of each side of the chest. Then move the right "s" hand upward with a short double movement near the right side of the body with the elbow extended.
Hint: The shape of a bucket and holding a bucket.

five

DESCRIPTIONS

Opposites
Other Descriptions
Colors

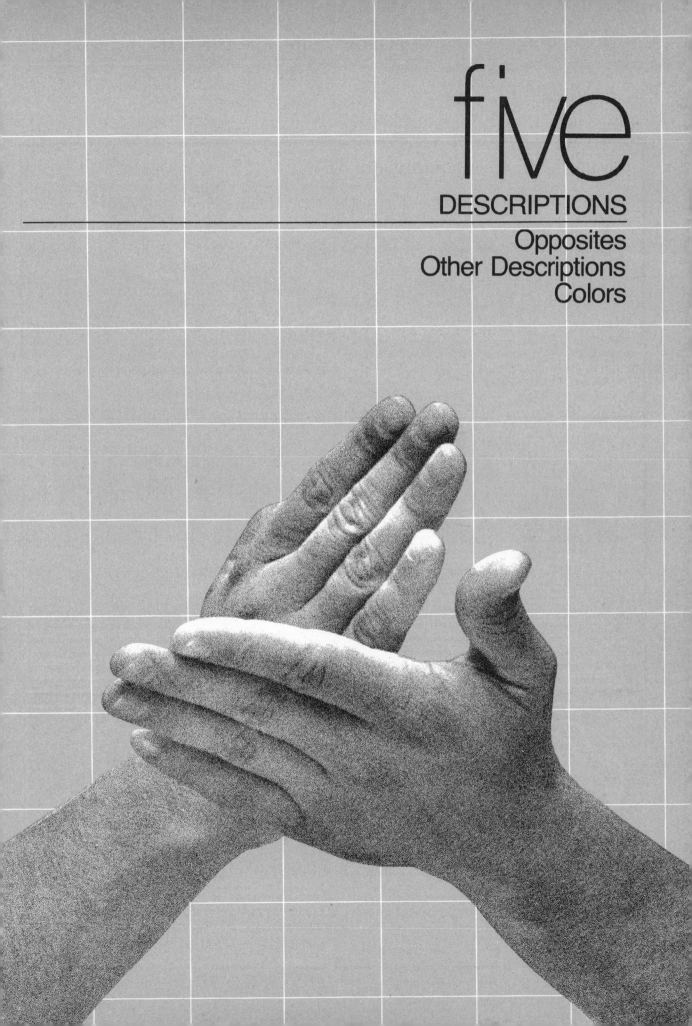

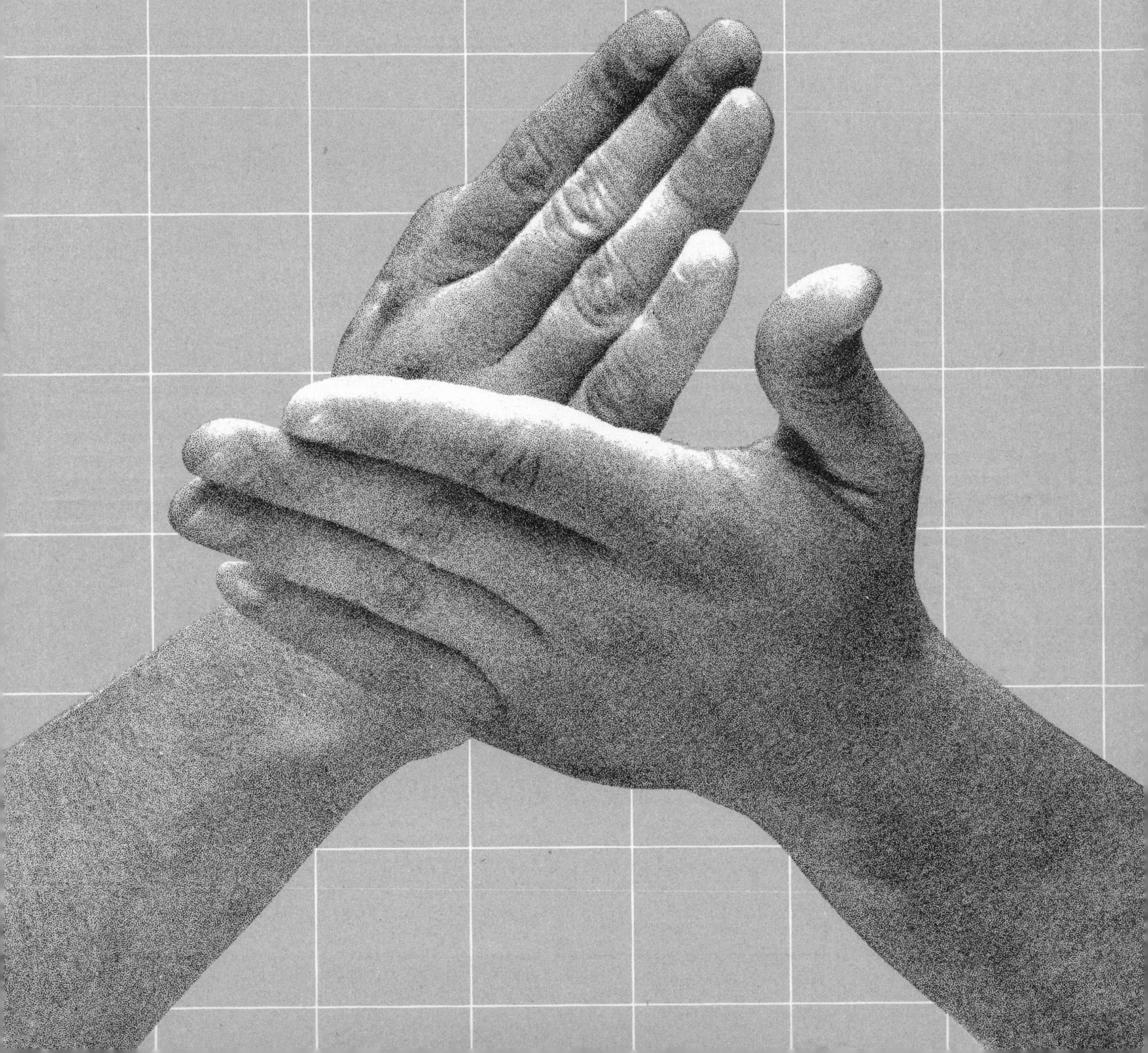

THE ORDER OF NOUNS AND ADJECTIVES

Whether the adjective or noun comes first is not a fixed rule in sign language. If the adjective is necessary to distinguish the noun from other similar nouns, the adjective usually comes last for emphasis. If a noun is used as an adjective, it always precedes the noun it modifies. For example, "baseball bat," "baby doll," and "bird cage."

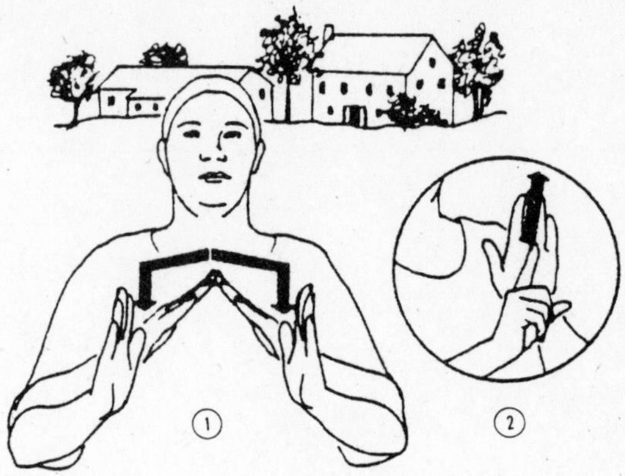

house tall

ADJECTIVES AND ADVERBS

Signs indicating size, shape, and other descriptive qualities can be incorporated into noun signs and into adjectives signs. For example, if "famous" is signed with large sweeping movements, it becomes "very famous." If "green" is signed with a very small light turning motion, it becomes "light green." "Fish," signed far from the body with a distasteful facial expression, communicates much more than can be described by an English adjective.

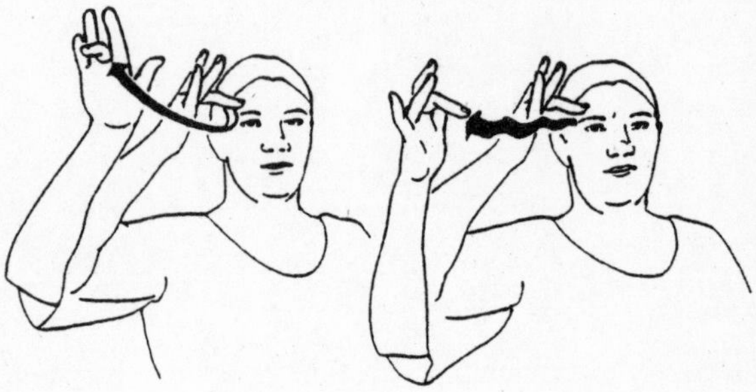

smart   brilliant or genius

KINSHIP SIGNS

There are some pairs of signs that use exactly the same handshape, but with reversed movements. Some of these signs are used as prepositions and some as verbs. The pairs of signs are usually opposites of each other. Some examples are "on" and "off"; "in" and "out"; "open" and "close"; and "come" and "go."

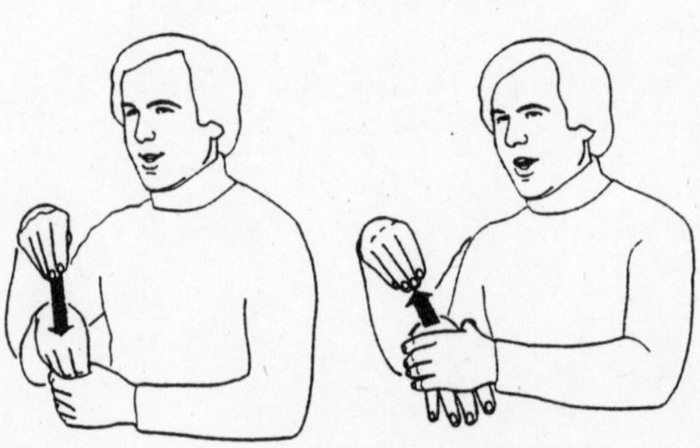

in   out

Opposites

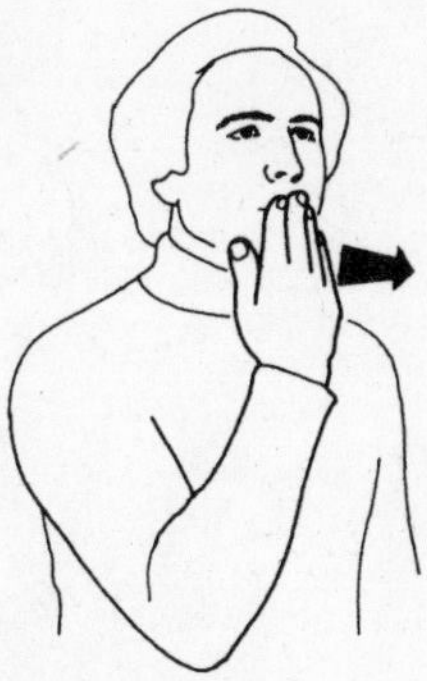

GOOD, WELL
Move the fingers of the open right hand from the mouth forward. Note: For emphasis, bring the back of the open right hand from the mouth downward to land in the open left palm held in front of the chest.
Hint: Something is tasted and presented as tasking good.

BAD
Beginning with the fingertips of the open right hand on the lips, fingers pointing up, turn the wrist and move the hand forward and down, ending with the palm facing down.
Hint: Something distasteful is thrown away from the mouth.

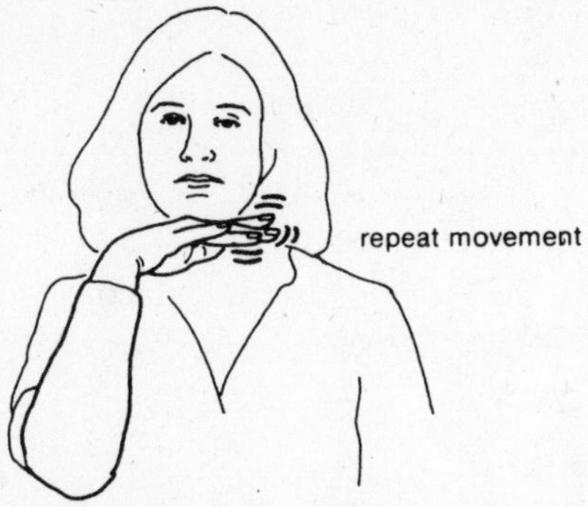

DIRTY, FILTHY, SOILED
With the back of right "5" hand under the chin, palm facing down and fingers pointing left, wiggle the fingers.

CLEAN, NICE, NEAT
Slide the palm of the open right hand from the heel to the fingers of the open left hand held in front of the chest, palm facing up.
Hint: Wiping something clean.

SLOW, SLOWLY
Slowly pull the fingers of the open right hand upward on the back of the open left hand from the fingers to the back of the wrist, both palms facing down.
Hint: Demonstrates a slow moving motion.

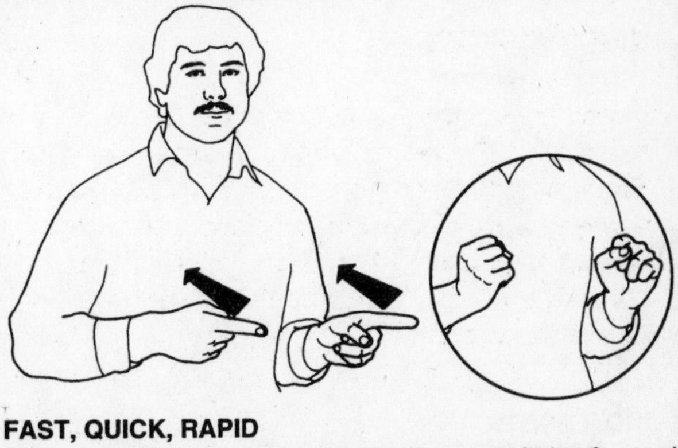

FAST, QUICK, RAPID
Beginning with both extended index fingers pointing forward, palms facing each other, pull the hands back quickly toward the chest while changing to "s" hands.
Hint: Shows a fast movement.

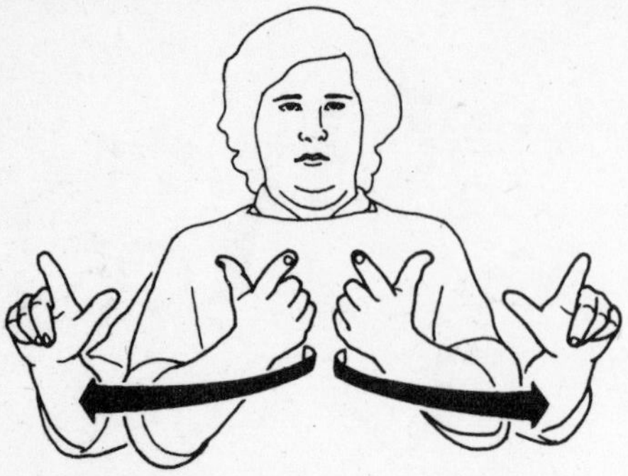

LARGE, BIG, HUGE
Beginning with both "I" hands near each other in front of the chest, palms facing in, twist the wrists and move the hands outward to in front of each side of the chest, palms facing forward.
Hint: Initialized sign showing a large area of space.

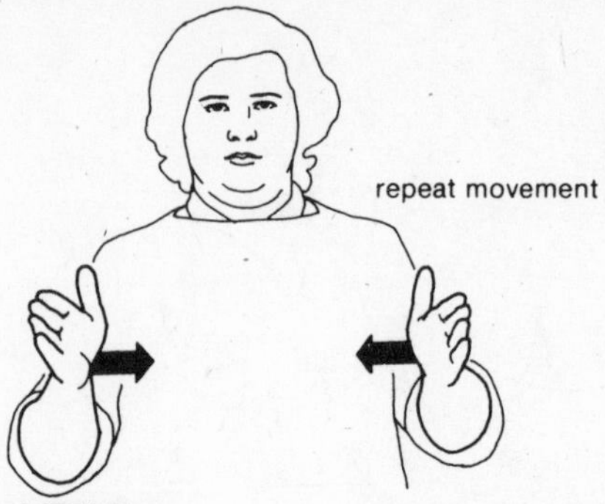

SMALL, LITTLE
Move both open hands held in front of each side of the body, palms facing each other and fingers pointing forward, toward each other with a short double movement.
Hint: Demonstrates a small size.

TALL
Move the thumb side of the extended right index finger, palm facing left, upward from the heel to the fingers of the open left hand held in front of the chest, palm facing forward.
Hint: Points the direction of height.

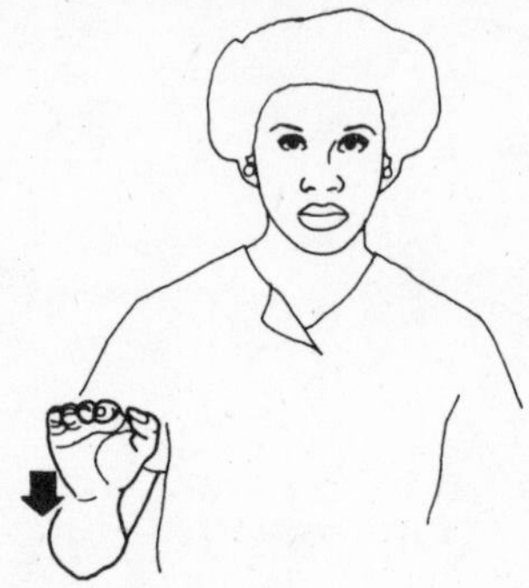

SHORT, LITTLE, SMALL
Move the bent right hand, palm facing down, downward with a short movement in front of the right side of the chest.
Hint: Demonstrates a short height.

LONG, LENGTH
Move the extended right index finger upward from the wrist to the upper arm of the extended left arm.
Hint: Demonstrates the length of one's arm.

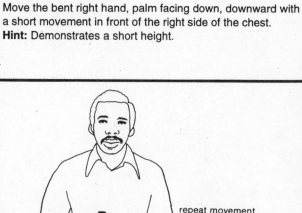

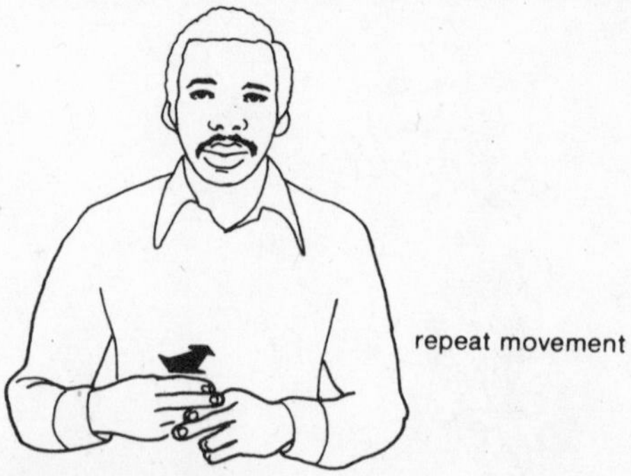

SHORT, SOON, BRIEF
Rub the middle-finger side of the right "h" fingers with a short repeated movement on the index-finger side of the left "h" fingers, palms facing each other at an angle.
Hint: Demonstrates a short distance on the fingers.

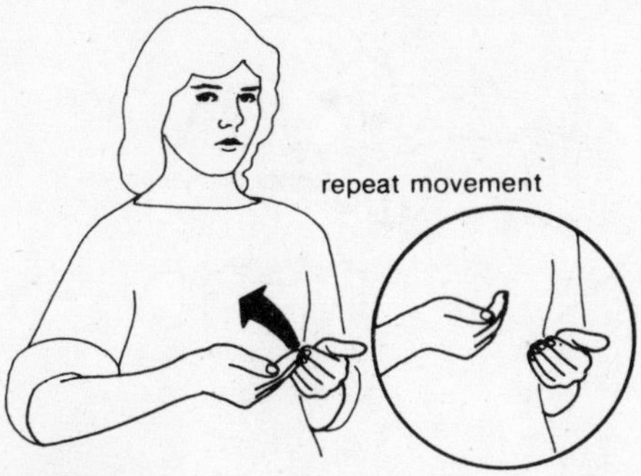

EASY, SIMPLE
Brush the fingertips of the bent right hand upward with a repeated movement on the back of the fingertips of the bent left hand, both palms facing up.
Hint: The smooth movement shows ease.

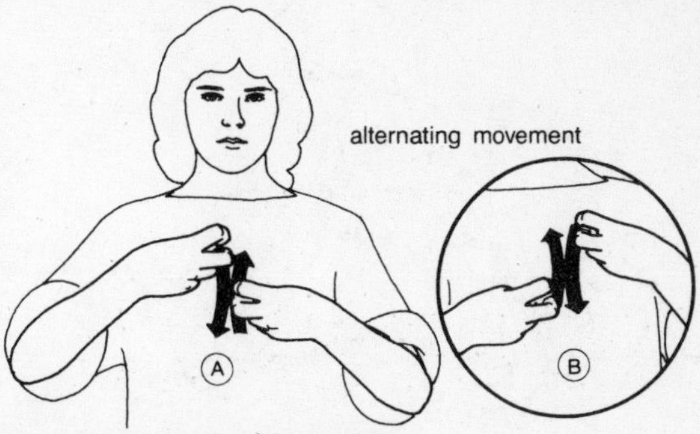

DIFFICULT, HARD, PROBLEM
Strike the knuckles of both bent "v" hands, palms facing in, against each other as the hand move up and down with a repeated movement.
Hint: Shows two hard things hitting each other.

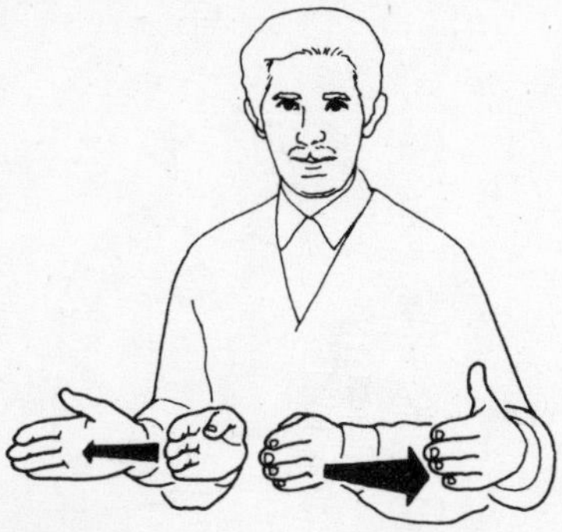

WIDE, BROAD
Beginning with both open hands near each other in front of the body, palms facing each other and fingers pointing forward, move the hands apart toward the sides of the body.
Hint: Demonstrates the size of something that is wide.

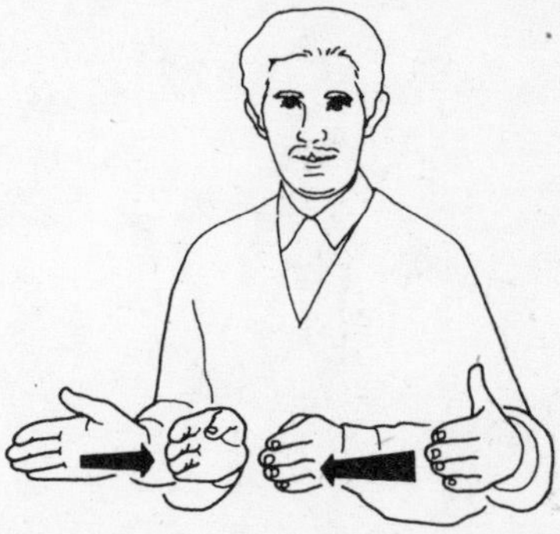

NARROW
Beginning with both open hands in front of the sides of the body, palms facing and fingers pointing forward, move the hands toward each other.
Hint: Demonstrates the size of something that is narrow.

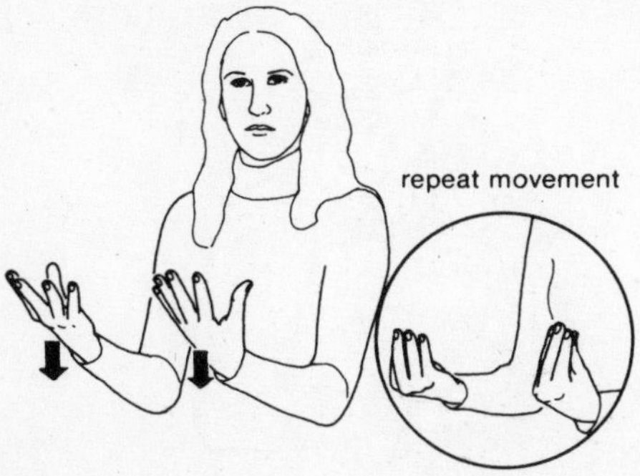

SOFT
Beginning with both curved "5" hands in front of the body, palms and fingers pointing up, bring the hands downward with a double movement closing the fingers to the thumbs each time.
Hint: Feeling something soft with the fingers.

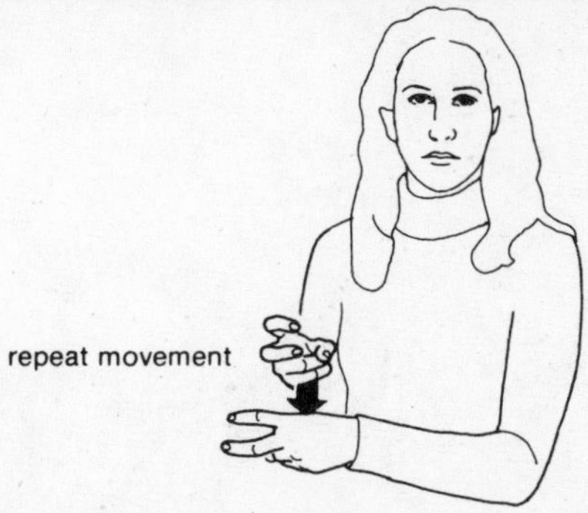

HARD
Hit the little-finger side of the right bent "v" hand, palm facing left, with a double movement on the thumb side of the left bent "v" hand.
Hint: Hitting something hard.

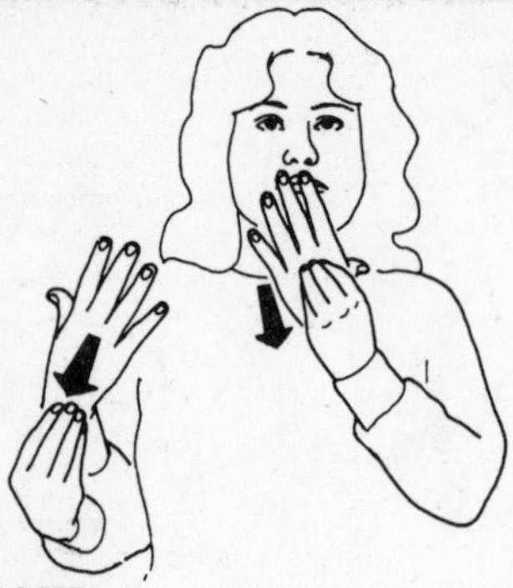

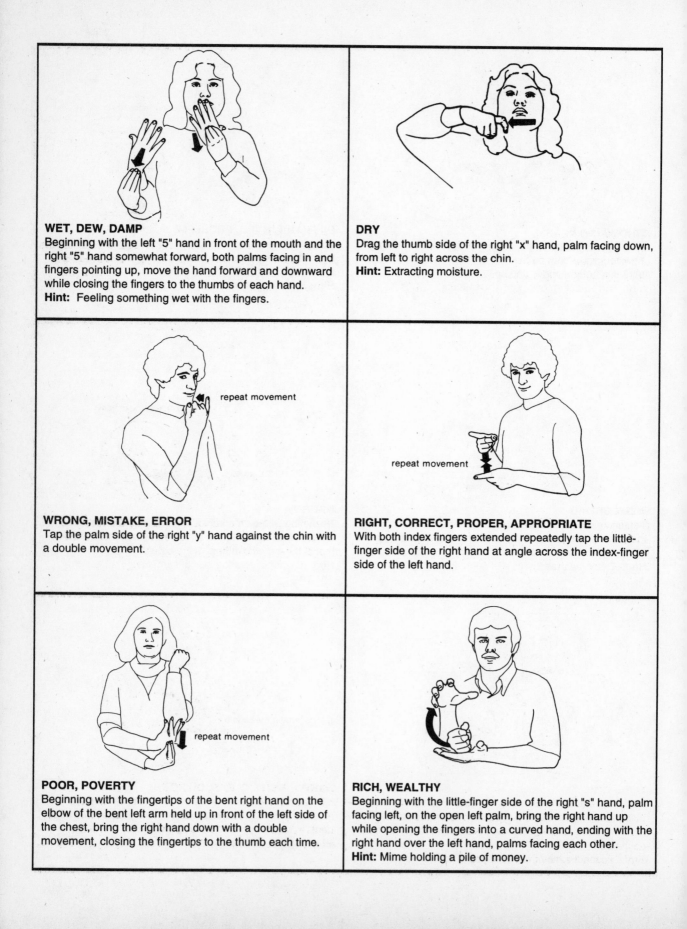

WET, DEW, DAMP
Beginning with the left "5" hand in front of the mouth and the right "5" hand somewhat forward, both palms facing in and fingers pointing up, move the hand forward and downward while closing the fingers to the thumbs of each hand.
Hint: Feeling something wet with the fingers.

DRY
Drag the thumb side of the right "x" hand, palm facing down, from left to right across the chin.
Hint: Extracting moisture.

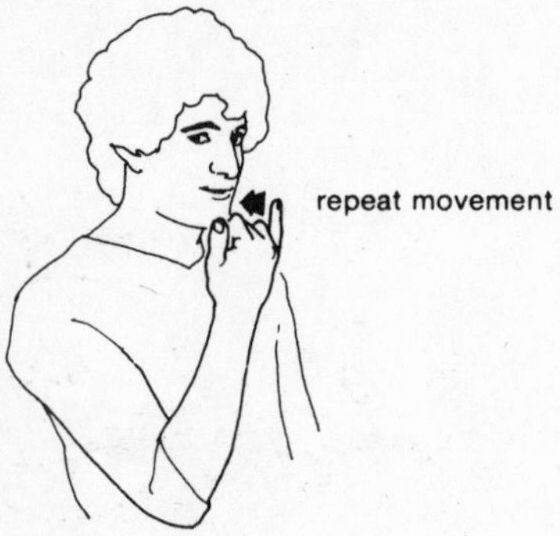

WRONG, MISTAKE, ERROR
Tap the palm side of the right "y" hand against the chin with a double movement.

RIGHT, CORRECT, PROPER, APPROPRIATE
With both index fingers extended repeatedly tap the little-finger side of the right hand at angle across the index-finger side of the left hand.

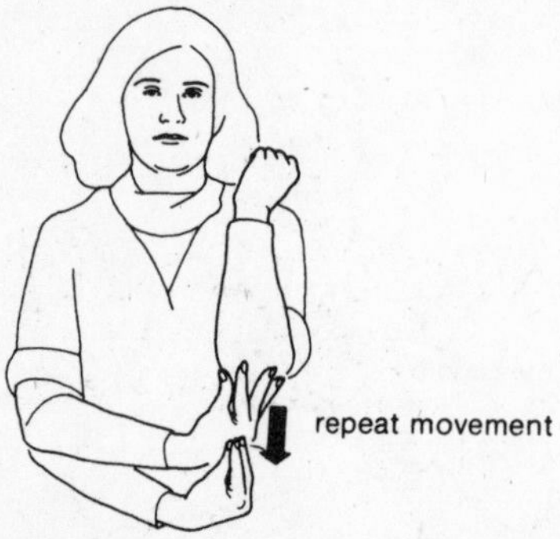

POOR, POVERTY
Beginning with the fingertips of the bent right hand on the elbow of the bent left arm held up in front of the left side of the chest, bring the right hand down with a double movement, closing the fingertips to the thumb each time.

RICH, WEALTHY
Beginning with the little-finger side of the right "s" hand, palm facing left, on the open left palm, bring the right hand up while opening the fingers into a curved hand, ending with the right hand over the left hand, palms facing each other.
Hint: Mime holding a pile of money.

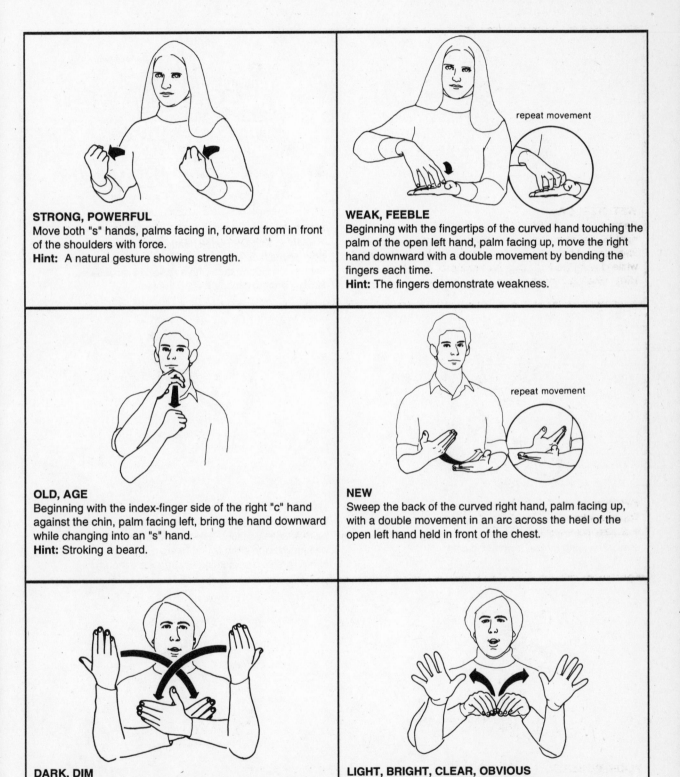

STRONG, POWERFUL
Move both "s" hands, palms facing in, forward from in front of the shoulders with force.
Hint: A natural gesture showing strength.

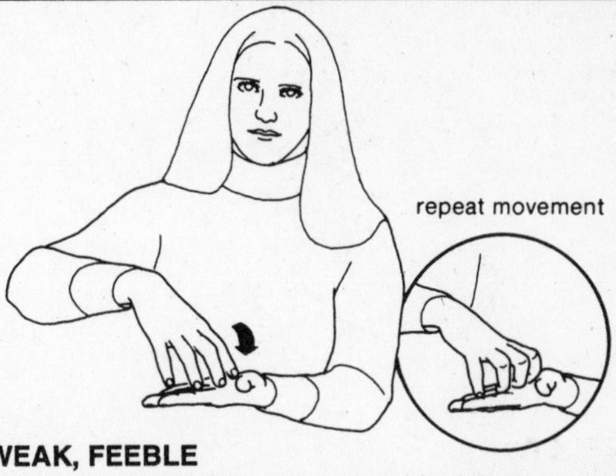

WEAK, FEEBLE
Beginning with the fingertips of the curved hand touching the palm of the open left hand, palm facing up, move the right hand downward with a double movement by bending the fingers each time.
Hint: The fingers demonstrate weakness.

OLD, AGE
Beginning with the index-finger side of the right "c" hand against the chin, palm facing left, bring the hand downward while changing into an "s" hand.
Hint: Stroking a beard.

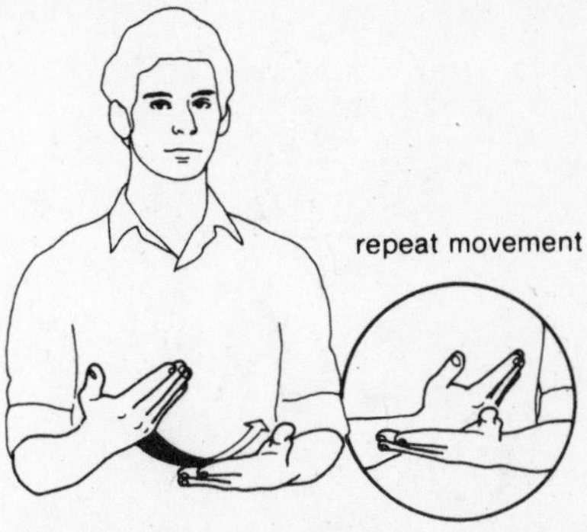

NEW
Sweep the back of the curved right hand, palm facing up, with a double movement in an arc across the heel of the open left hand held in front of the chest.

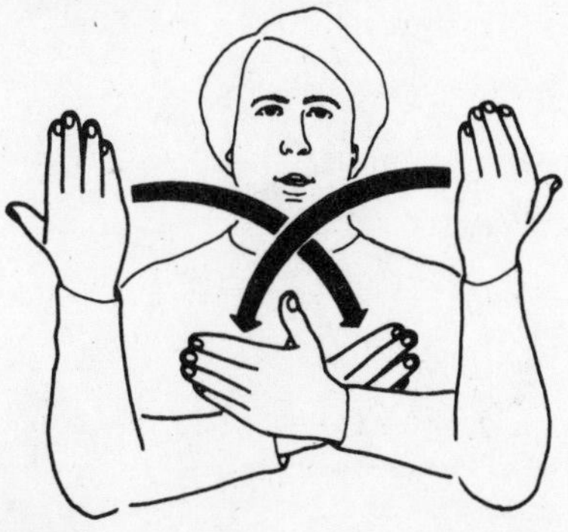

DARK, DIM
Beginning with both open hands near each side of the head, palms facing back, bring the hand toward each other and downward, ending with the hands crossed in front of the chest.
Hint: Closing the light from the eyes.

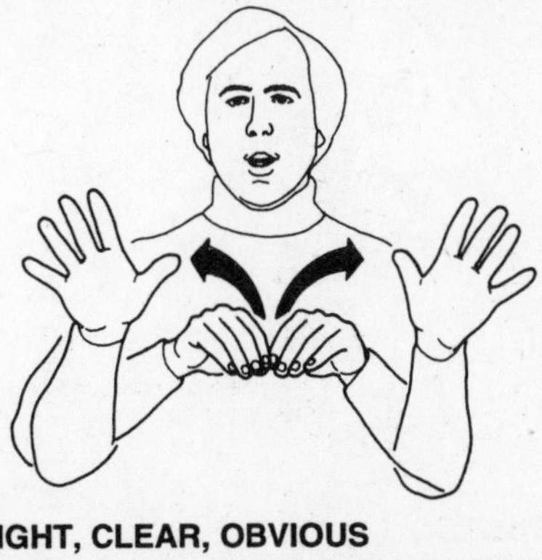

LIGHT, BRIGHT, CLEAR, OBVIOUS
With the index-finger side of both flattened "o" hands touching in front of the chest, palms facing down, move the hands apart and upward while opening into "5" hands, ending with the palms facing forward and fingers pointing up.

WARM
Beginning with the fingers of the loosely curled right hand in front of the mouth, palm facing in, move the hand upward and forward while opening the fingers.
Hint: Warming the fingers with heat from the mouth.

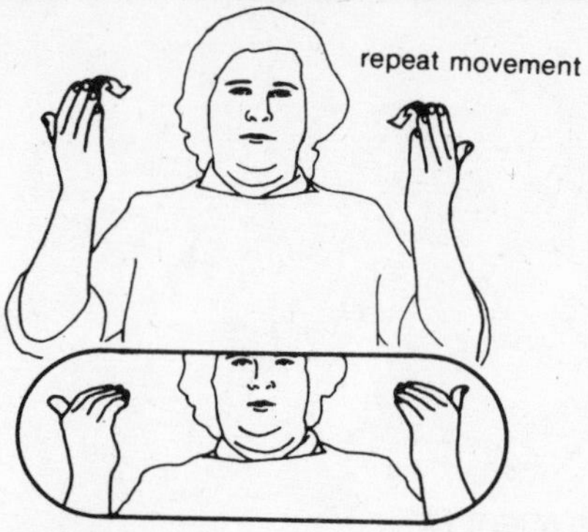

COOL, PLEASANT
Beginning with both open hands near each side of the head, both palms facing back and fingers pointing up, bend the fingers toward the face with a repeated movement.
Hint: Fanning cool air toward the face.

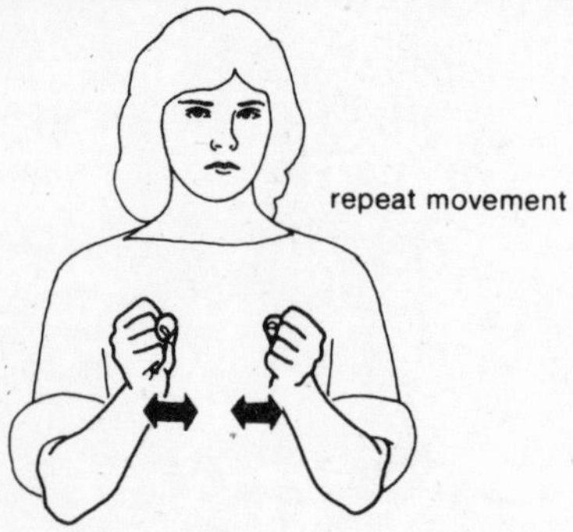

COLD, CHILLY
Shake both "s" hands toward each other with a repeated movement in front of the chest, palms facing each other.
Hint: Shivering motion from being cold.

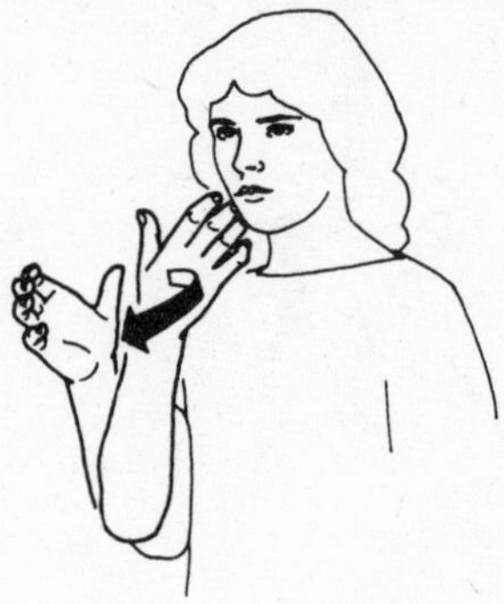

HOT, HEAT
Move the right curved "5" hand from in front of the mouth, palm facing in, quickly forward with a twist of the wrist, ending with the palm facing forward.
Hint: Throwing something hot out of the mouth.

TRUE, READ, REALLY, SURE
Move the extended right index finger, palm facing left, upward in front of the lips and forward in an arc.
Hint: Speaking straight from the mouth.

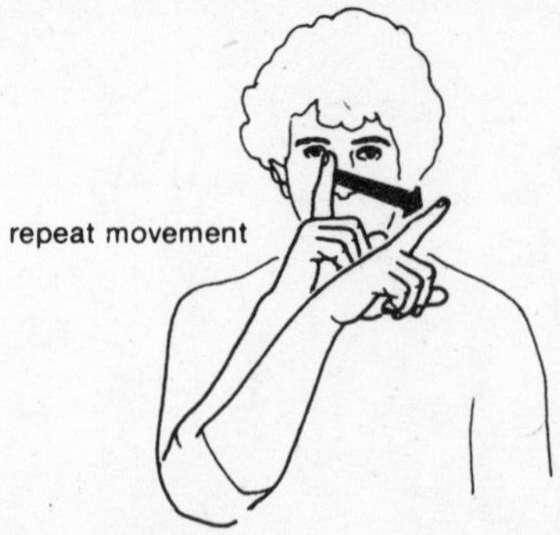

FALSE
Move the extended right index finger from pointing up near the right side of the nose, palm facing left, to the left with a double movement by bending the wrist.
Hint: Pushing the true aside.

FAT, CHUBBY
Move both "c" hands from near each cheek, palms facing each other, outward to each side with a short movement.
Hint: Shows the cheeks of a fat person.

THIN, SKINNY, SLENDER, LEAN
Beginning with the extended little fingers of both "i" hands touching in front of the chest, palms facing in and right hand above the left hand, pull the hands apart from each other.
Hint: Fingers indicate thinness.

UGLY
Pull the extended right index finger, palm facing down and finger pointing left, from left to right under the nose while changing into an "x" hand.
Hint: Pulling the face into an ugly distortion.

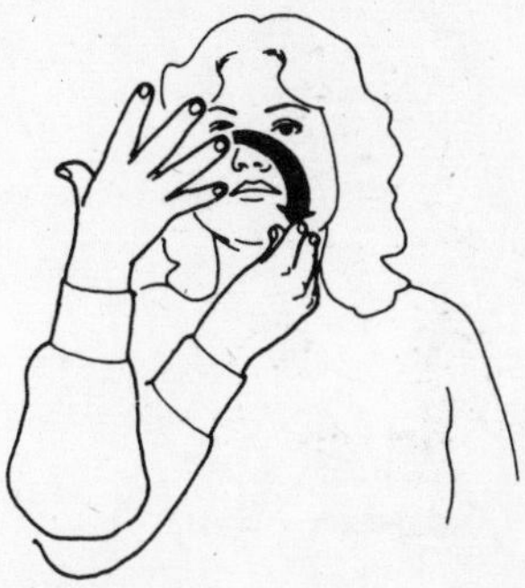

PRETTY, BEAUTIFUL, LOVELY
Beginning with the right "5" hand in front of the face, palm facing up, bring the hand in an arc to the left while closing into a flattened "o" hand.
Hint: Showing a pretty face.

LIGHT
Beginning with the bent middle fingers of the both "5" hands in front of each side of the body, palms facing down, twist the wrists to flick the hand quickly upward, ending with the palms facing up.
Hint: Hands move delicately and lightly.

HEAVY
With both open hands in front of each side of the body, palms facing up, drop the hands slightly.
Hint: Mime holding something heavy.

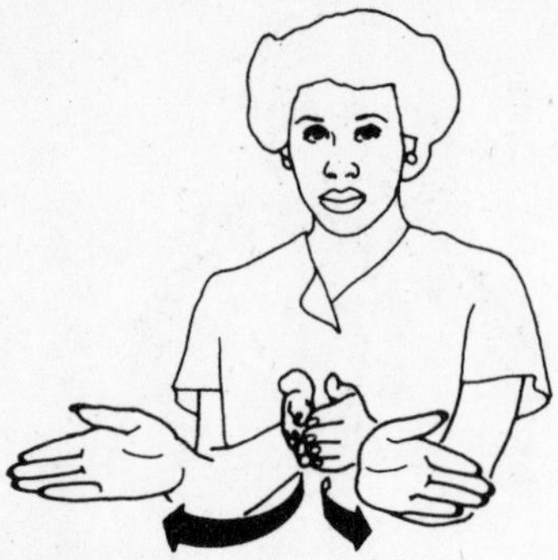

GENERAL, BROAD
Beginning with the palms of both open hands together in front of the body, move the hands forward and apart turning the palms forward.
Hint: Demonstrates a broad direction.

SPECIFIC, POINT
Move the extended right index finger, palm facing left, forward from the shoulder toward the extended left index finger held in front of the body, palm facing right.
Hint: Pinpointing a specific point.

SAME, ALIKE, SIMILAR, LIKE
Beginning with both extended index fingers pointing forward, both palms facing down, bring the fingers together in front of the chest.
Hint: Bringing together things that are the same.

DIFFERENT, DIFFER
Beginning with the extended index fingers of both hands crossed in front of the chest, palms facing down, swing the hands apart.
Hint: Separating things that are not the same.

PARALLEL
Move both extended index fingers, palms facing down, forward simultaneously.
Hint: Demonstrates things parallel to each other.

OPPOSITE, OPPOSE, CONTRARY
Beginning with both extended index fingers touching each other, palms facing the chest, pull the hands apart.
Hint: Pulling things apart that are not alike.

QUIET, CALM, PEACEFUL
Beginning with both "b" hands crossed in front of the face, palms facing in opposite directions and fingers pointing up, move the hands smoothly apart and downward, ending with both palms facing down in front of each side of the body.

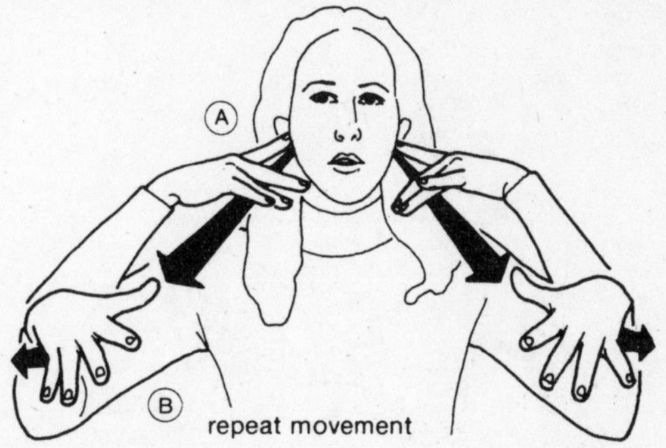

NOISY, SOUND, LOUD
Beginning with the index fingers of both "5" hands near each ear, palms facing down, move the hands downward and outward to shake the hands loosely in front of each side of the chest, palms facing down.
Hint: Blocking out loud noise.

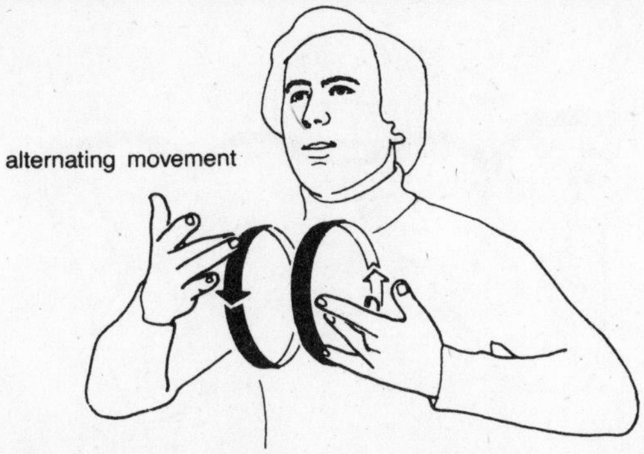

EXCITE, EXCITING, THRILL, THRILLING
Move the bent middle finger of both "5" hands, palms facing in, upward in alternating circles on each side of the chest.
Hint: Stimulation flowing through the body.

BORING, BORED, DULL
With the extended right index finger touching the right side of the nose, palm facing forward, twist the hand down turning the palm back.
Hint: Keeping one's nose to the grindstone.

ROUGH, SCRATCH, DRAFT
Move the fingertips of the right "claw" hand, palm facing down, with a double movement from the heel to the fingers of the left palm held up in front of the body.
Hint: Showing a rough surface.

SMOOTH, FLAT
Slide the palm of the open right hand across the back of the open left hand from the wrist to the fingers, both palms facing down.
Hint: Showing a smooth surface.

Other Descriptions

PERFECT
Move the right "p" hand in a circle above the left "p" hand, palms facing each other, ending with both middle fingers touching.
Hint: Initialized sign similar to sign for "exact."

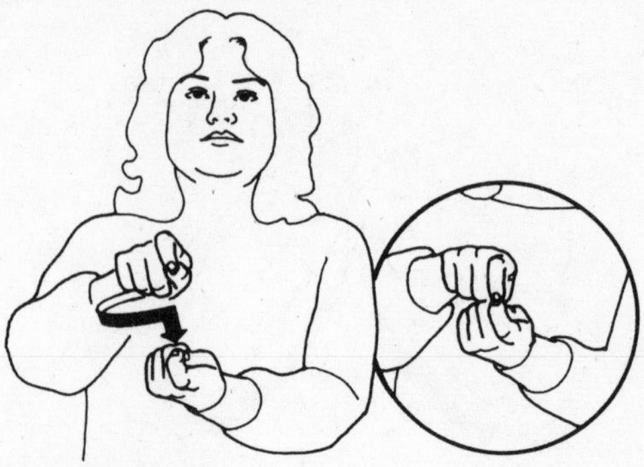

EXACT, PRECISE, FIT
With the thumbs and index fingers of both hands pinched together, move the right hand in a circle above the left hand, palms facing each other, ending with the hands touching.
Hint: Hitting a nail on the head.

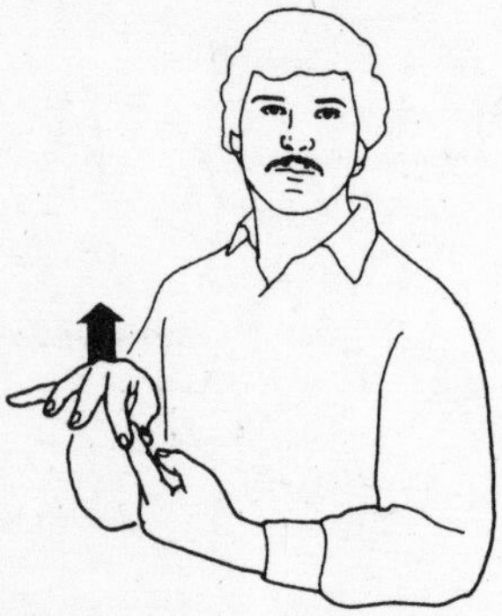

SPECIAL, EXCEPTIONAL, EXCEPT
With the right thumb and index finger, grasp and pull up the extended left index finger pointing up in front of the chest.
Hint: Pulling one thing into view for special attention.

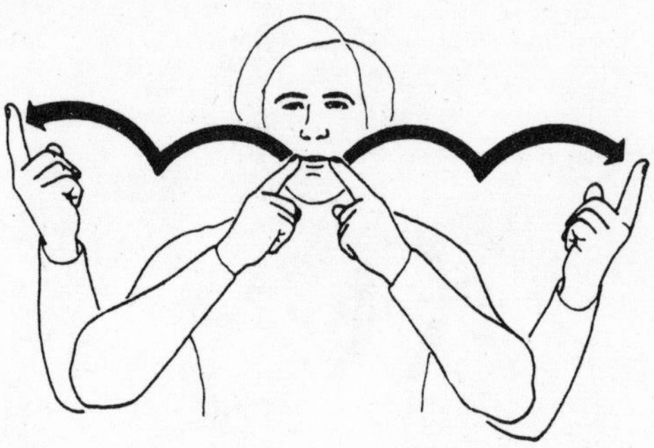

FAMOUS
Beginning with both extended index fingers pointing up to each side of the mouth, palms facing in, move the hands outward in large arcs, ending with the palms facing each other above each shoulder.

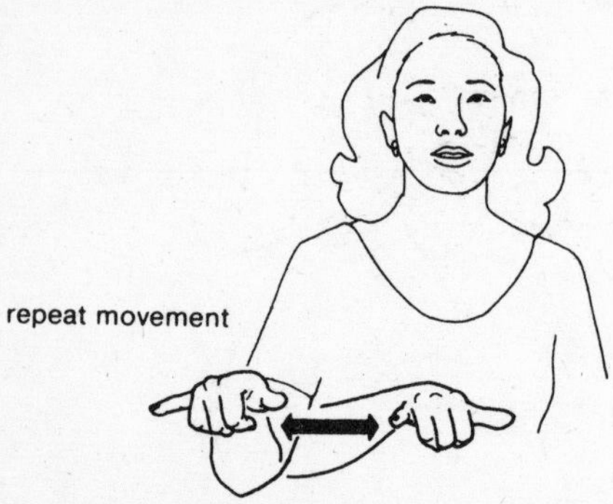

SAME, THE SAME AS, SIMILAR
Move the right "y" hand, palm facing down, from side to side with a repeated movement in front of the chest.
Hint: The hand compares the similarity between two things.

STANDARD, UNIFORM, COMMON
Move the right "y" hand, palm facing down, in a large circle in front of the body.
Hint: The sign for "same" moving around to show that everything is similar.

LUCKY, LUCK
Beginning with the bent middle finger of the right "5" hand touching the chin, move the hand forward by quickly twisting the wrist, ending with the palm facing forward.

FAVORITE, FAVOR
Tap the bent middle finger of the right "5" hand to the chin with a short double movement.
Hint: Pointing to the taste buds.

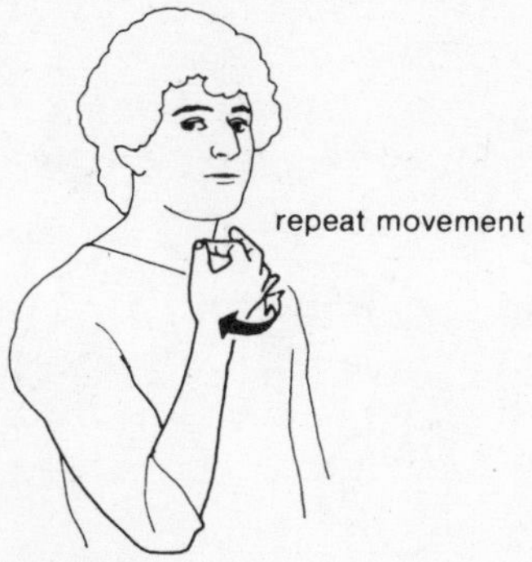

CURIOUS, CURIOSITY
While pinching a little skin of the neck with the right thumb and index finger, wiggle the hand back and forth with a little movement.
Hint: Straining the neck from curiosity.

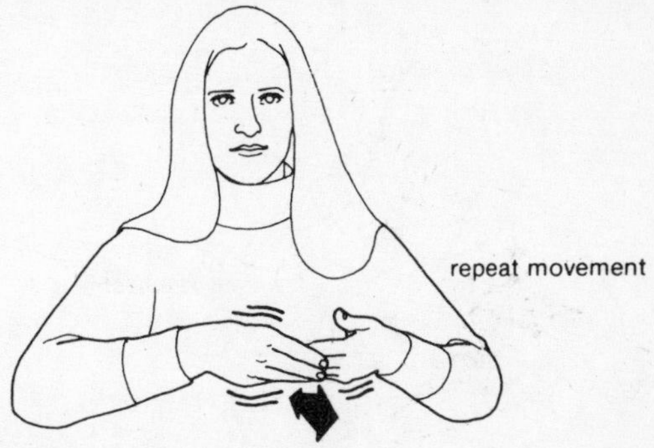

FLEXIBLE, FLOPPY
While holding the fingers of the open left hand with the right fingers, both palms facing the chest, loosely wiggle the hands forward and back with a repeated movement.
Hint: Demonstrates flexible fingers.

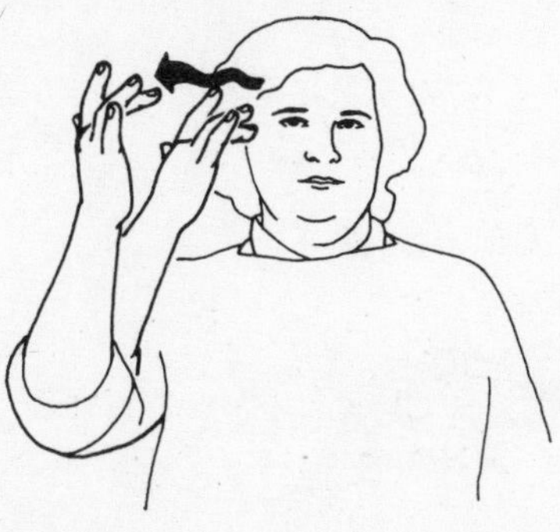

SILVER
Beginning with the bent middle finger of the right "5" hand touching the right side of the forehead, move the hand away with a wiggly movement.
Hint: Pointing to a silver earring.

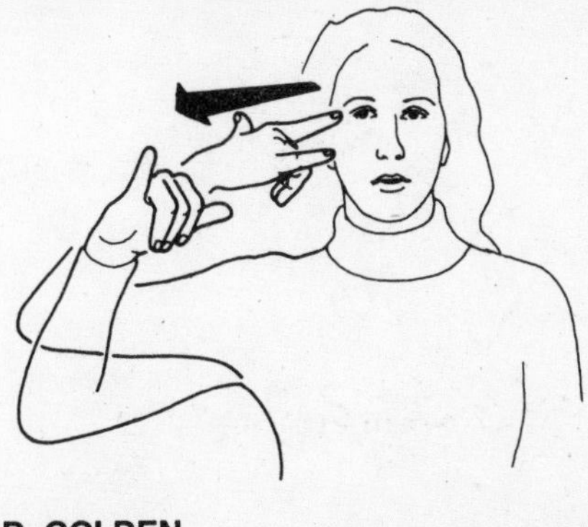

GOLD, GOLDEN
With the right thumb, index finger and little fingers extended, touch the index finger near the right each, palm facing down. Then move the hand outward with a twist of the wrist while changing into a "y" hand.
Hint: Pointing to a gold earring.

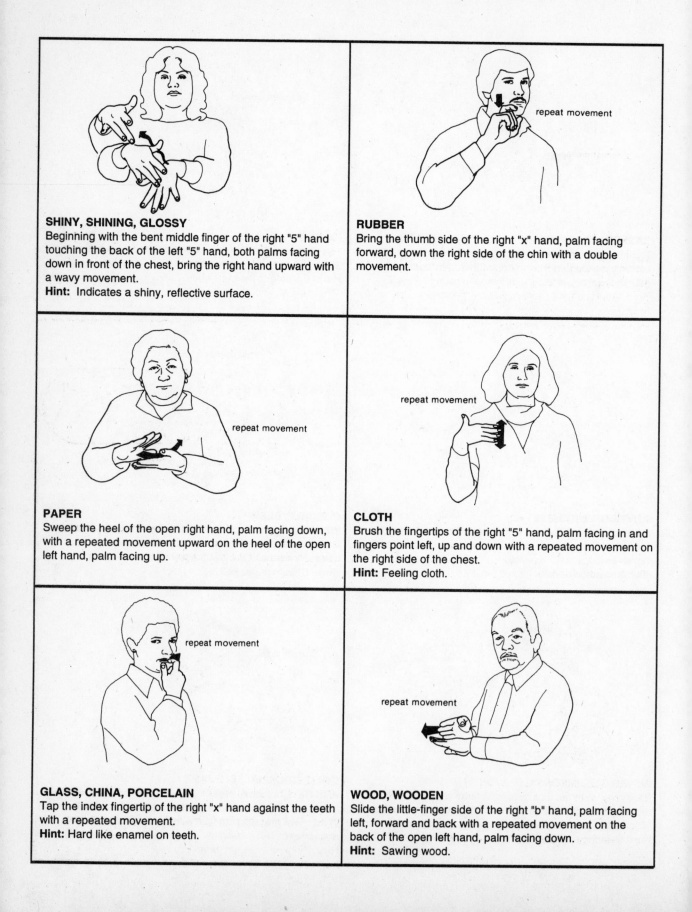

SHINY, SHINING, GLOSSY
Beginning with the bent middle finger of the right "5" hand touching the back of the left "5" hand, both palms facing down in front of the chest, bring the right hand upward with a wavy movement.
Hint: Indicates a shiny, reflective surface.

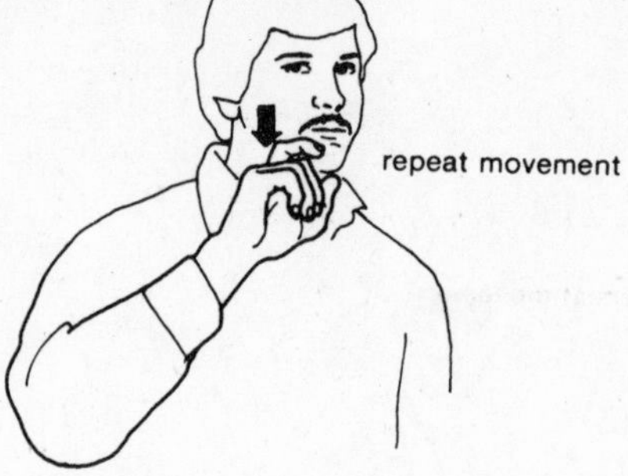

RUBBER
Bring the thumb side of the right "x" hand, palm facing forward, down the right side of the chin with a double movement.

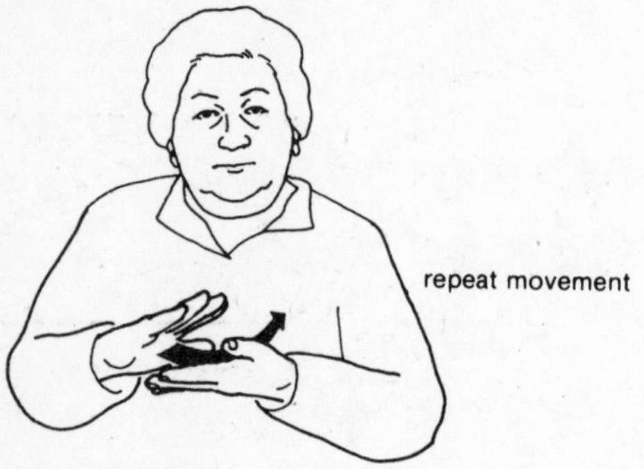

PAPER
Sweep the heel of the open right hand, palm facing down, with a repeated movement upward on the heel of the open left hand, palm facing up.

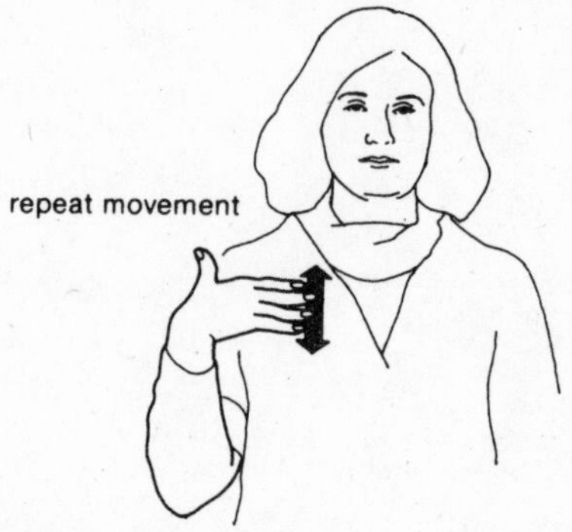

CLOTH
Brush the fingertips of the right "5" hand, palm facing in and fingers point left, up and down with a repeated movement on the right side of the chest.
Hint: Feeling cloth.

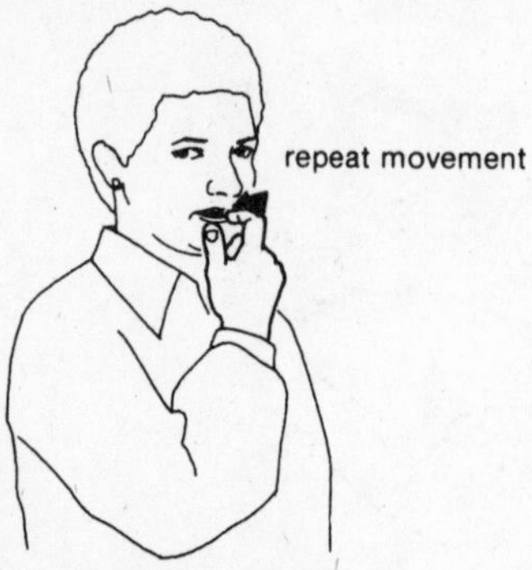

GLASS, CHINA, PORCELAIN
Tap the index fingertip of the right "x" hand against the teeth with a repeated movement.
Hint: Hard like enamel on teeth.

WOOD, WOODEN
Slide the little-finger side of the right "b" hand, palm facing left, forward and back with a repeated movement on the back of the open left hand, palm facing down.
Hint: Sawing wood.

CAREFUL, CAUTIOUS
Tap the little-finger side of the right "v" hand, palm facing left, with a repeated movement on the thumb side of the left "v" hand, palm facing right.
Hint: Represents a combination of the signs "watch" and "warn."

CUTE
Brush the fingertips of the right "u" hand downward on the chin, changing into an "a" hand as the hand moves.

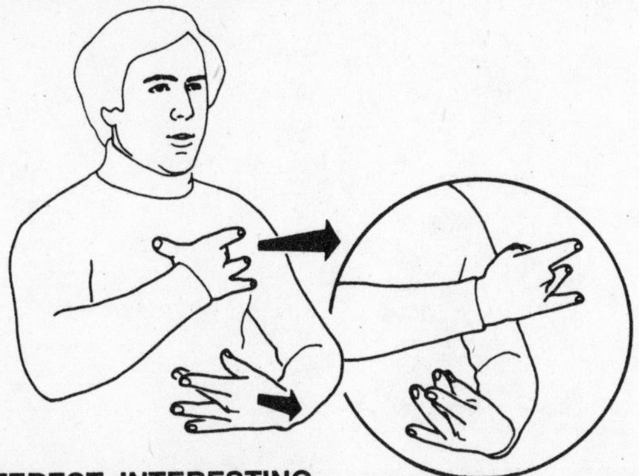

INTEREST, INTERESTING
Beginning with the bent middle fingers of both "5" hands on the chest, right hand higher than the left hand, bring the hands forward while pinching the middle fingers to the thumb of each hand.

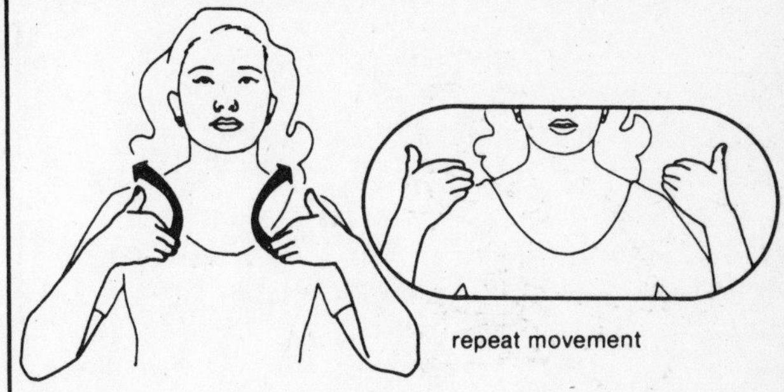

YOUNG, YOUTH
Brush the fingertips of both bent hands upward with a repeated movement near each shoulder.
Hint: Indicates vitality in the body.

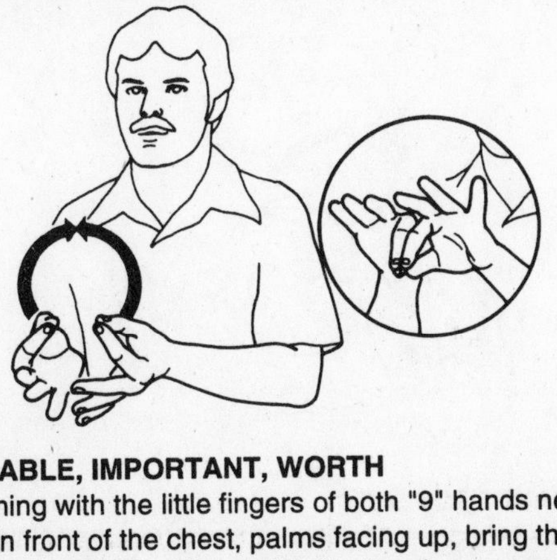

VALUABLE, IMPORTANT, WORTH
Beginning with the little fingers of both "9" hands near each other in front of the chest, palms facing up, bring the hands apart and upward while turning the hands over, ending with the index-finger sides of both hands touching, palms facing down.

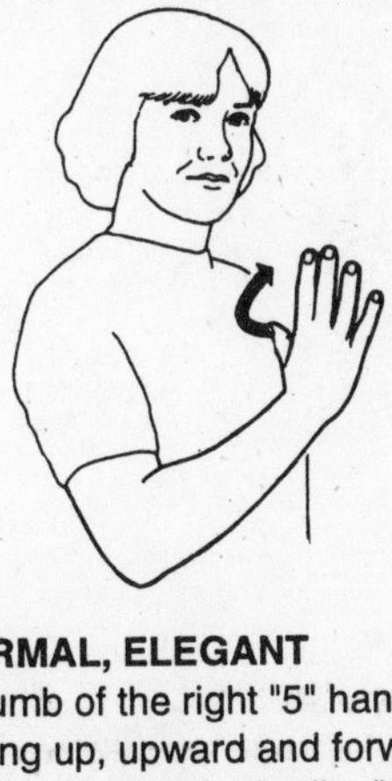

FANCY, FORMAL, ELEGANT
Brush the thumb of the right "5" hand, palm facing left and fingers pointing up, upward and forward on the chest.
Hint: Similar to the sign for "polite," but with an upward movement.

SHARP
Move the bent middle finger of the right "5" hand, palm facing down, forward across the back of the left "s" hand held in front of the chest, palm facing down.
Hint: Feeling a sharp knife blade.

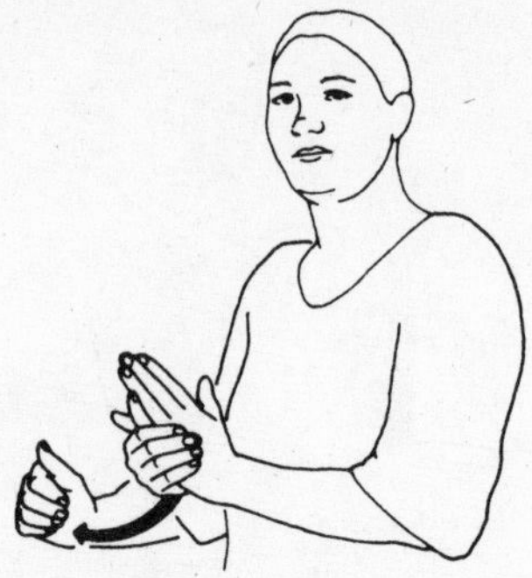

EXPERT, SKILL, COMPETENT, ABILITY
Beginning with the right hand grasping the little-finger side of the open left hand, palm facing right, pull the right hand downward and forward in an arc.

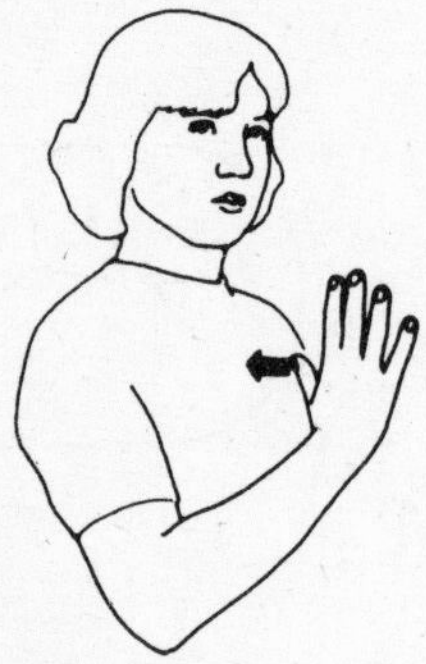

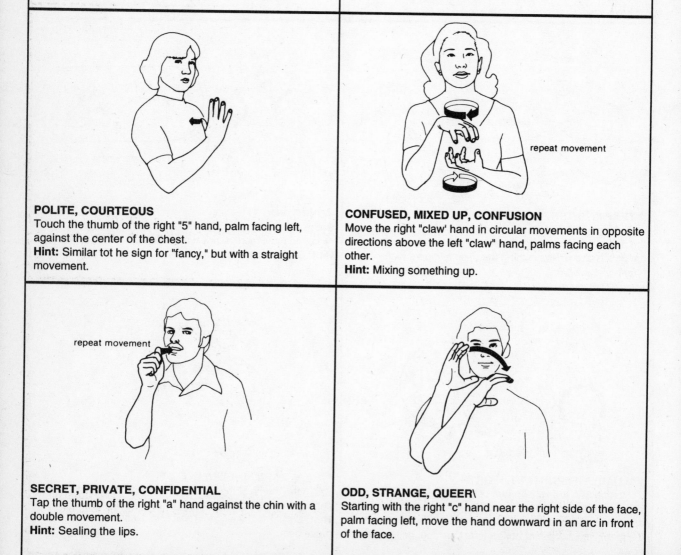

POLITE, COURTEOUS
Touch the thumb of the right "5" hand, palm facing left, against the center of the chest.
Hint: Similar tot he sign for "fancy," but with a straight movement.

CONFUSED, MIXED UP, CONFUSION
Move the right "claw' hand in circular movements in opposite directions above the left "claw" hand, palms facing each other.
Hint: Mixing something up.

SECRET, PRIVATE, CONFIDENTIAL
Tap the thumb of the right "a" hand against the chin with a double movement.
Hint: Sealing the lips.

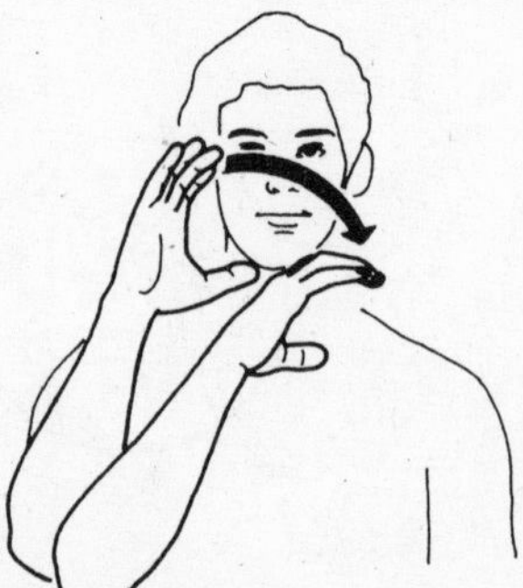

ODD, STRANGE, QUEER
Starting with the right "c" hand near the right side of the face, palm facing left, move the hand downward in an arc in front of the face.

Colors

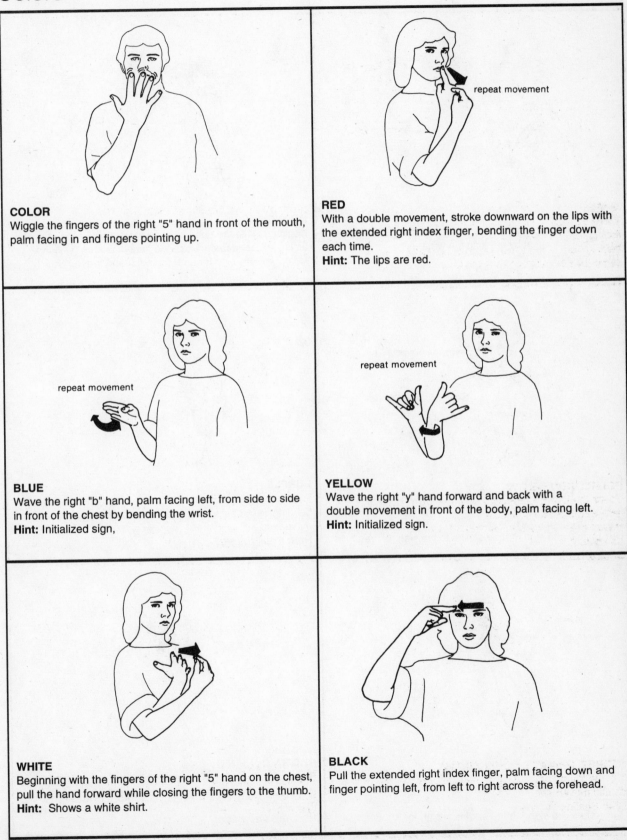

COLOR
Wiggle the fingers of the right "5" hand in front of the mouth, palm facing in and fingers pointing up.

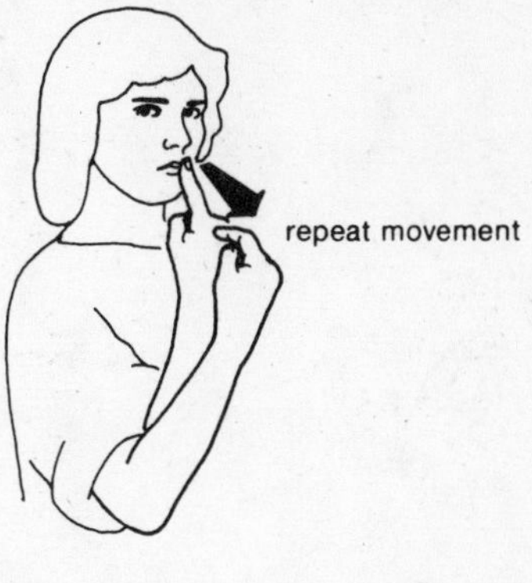

RED
With a double movement, stroke downward on the lips with the extended right index finger, bending the finger down each time.
Hint: The lips are red.

BLUE
Wave the right "b" hand, palm facing left, from side to side in front of the chest by bending the wrist.
Hint: Initialized sign,

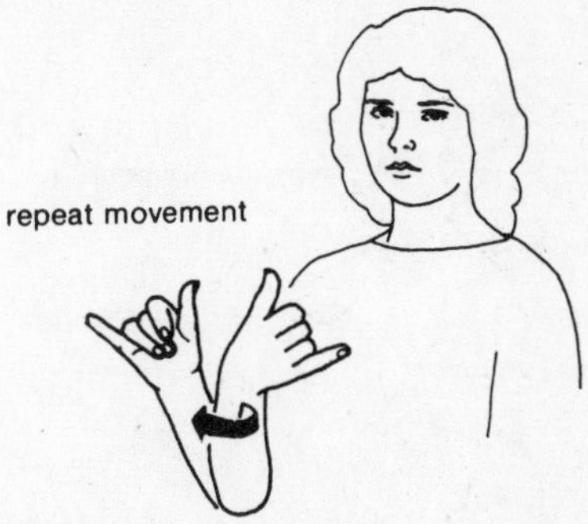

YELLOW
Wave the right "y" hand forward and back with a double movement in front of the body, palm facing left.
Hint: Initialized sign.

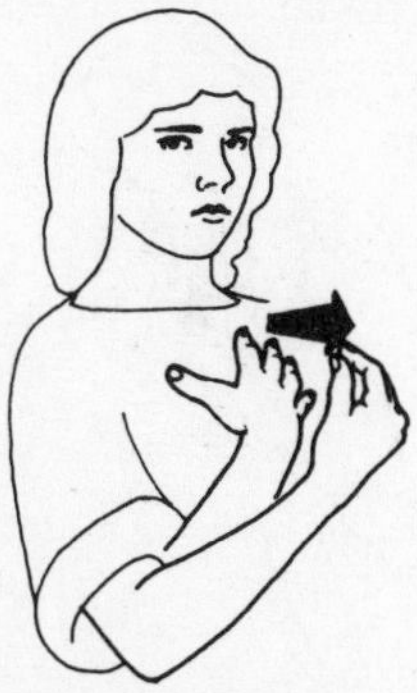

WHITE
Beginning with the fingers of the right "5" hand on the chest, pull the hand forward while closing the fingers to the thumb.
Hint: Shows a white shirt.

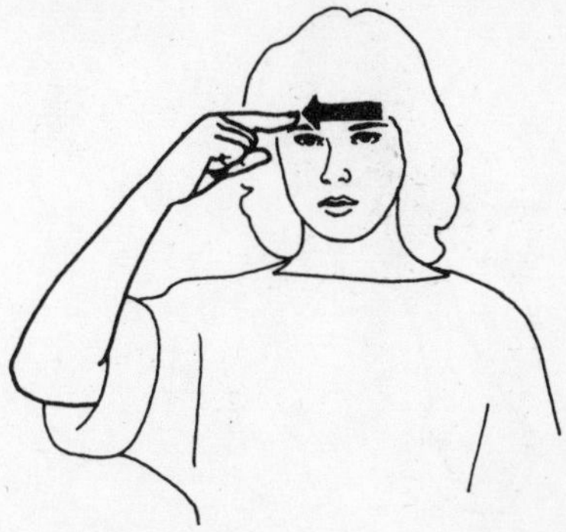

BLACK
Pull the extended right index finger, palm facing down and finger pointing left, from left to right across the forehead.

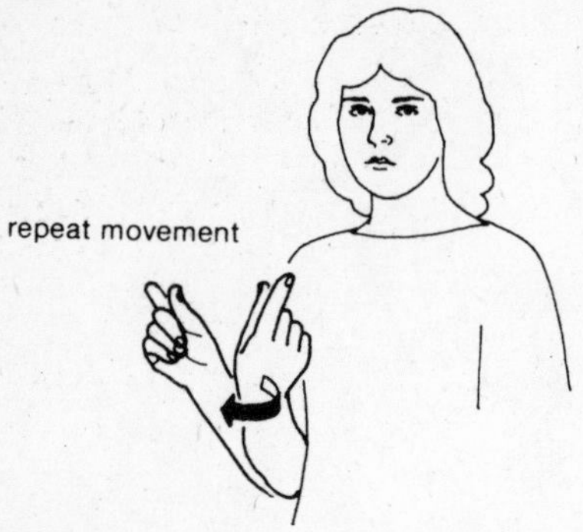

GREEN
Wave the right "g" hand, palm facing left, from side to side in front of the chest by bending the wrist.
Hint: Initialized sign.

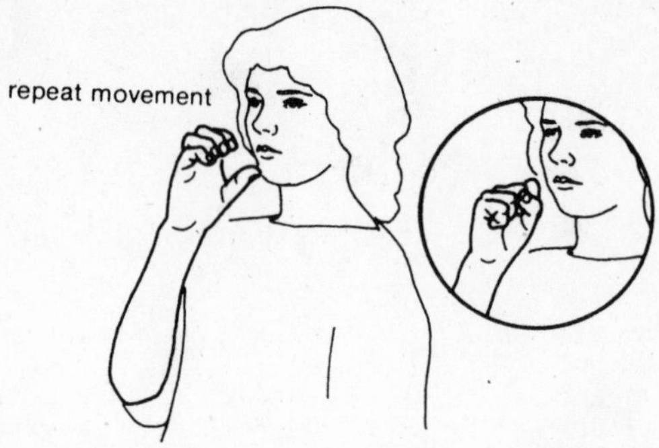

ORANGE
Beginning with the right "c" hand in front of the mouth, palm facing left, repeatedly close the fingers into an "s" hand.
Note: Use this sign for both the color and the fruit.

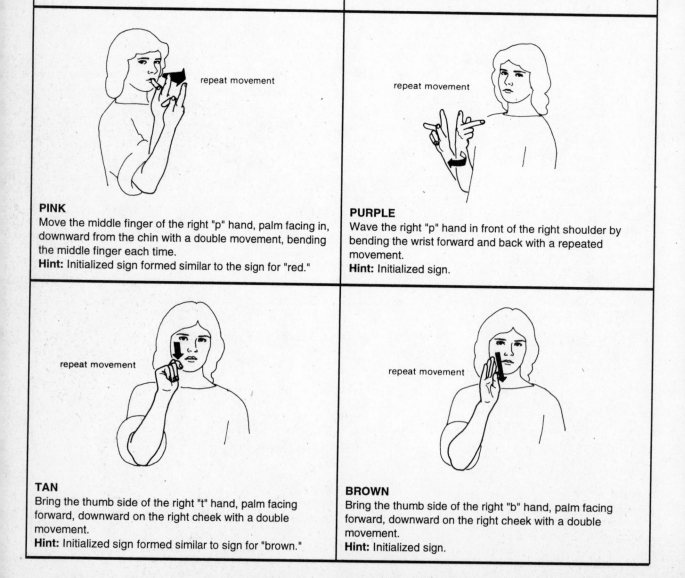

PINK
Move the middle finger of the right "p" hand, palm facing in, downward from the chin with a double movement, bending the middle finger each time.
Hint: Initialized sign formed similar to the sign for "red."

PURPLE
Wave the right "p" hand in front of the right shoulder by bending the wrist forward and back with a repeated movement.
Hint: Initialized sign.

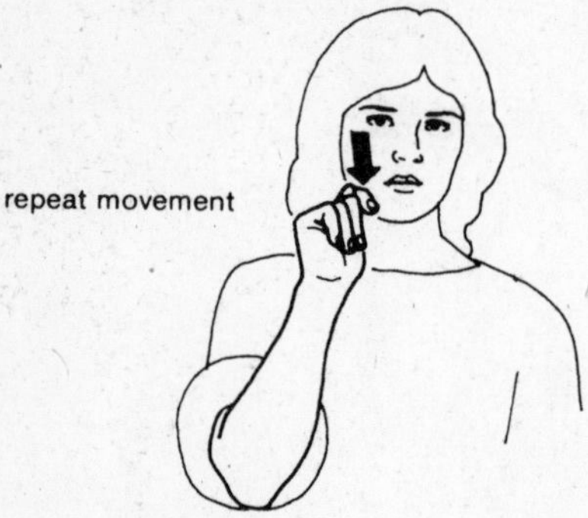

TAN
Bring the thumb side of the right "t" hand, palm facing forward, downward on the right cheek with a double movement.
Hint: Initialized sign formed similar to sign for "brown."

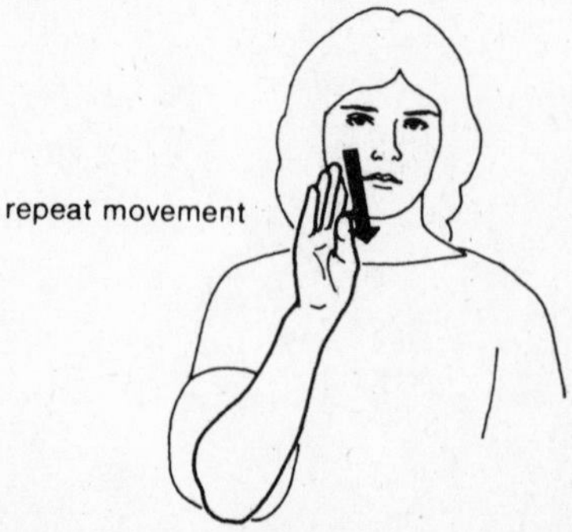

BROWN
Bring the thumb side of the right "b" hand, palm facing forward, downward on the right cheek with a double movement.
Hint: Initialized sign.

SIX

NUMBERS, MONEY, AND MATH

Numbers
Quantity
Money and Math

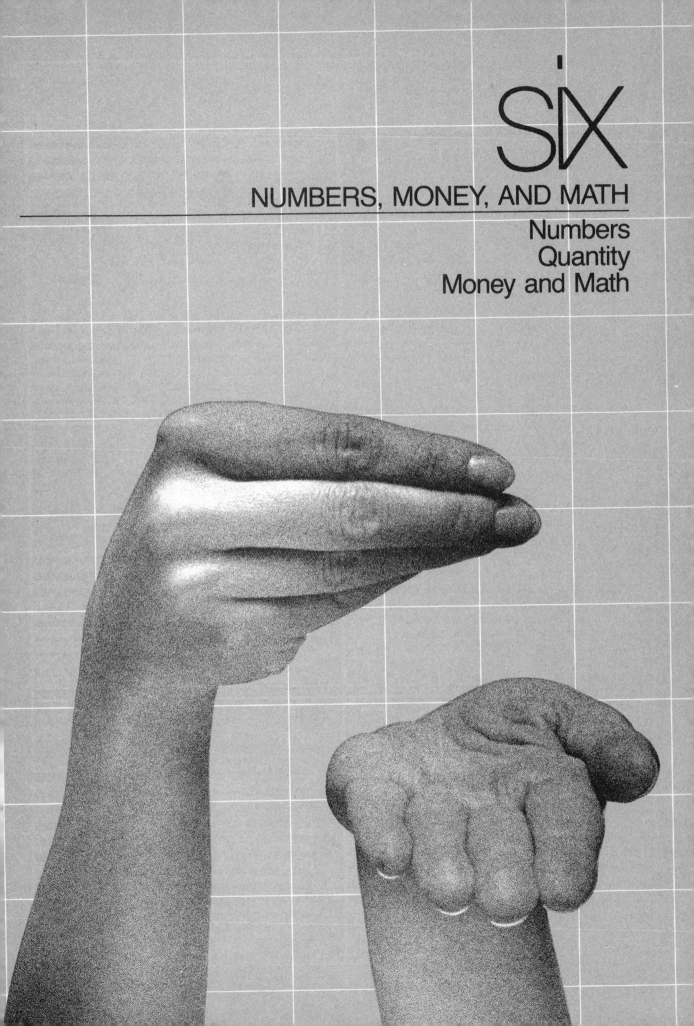

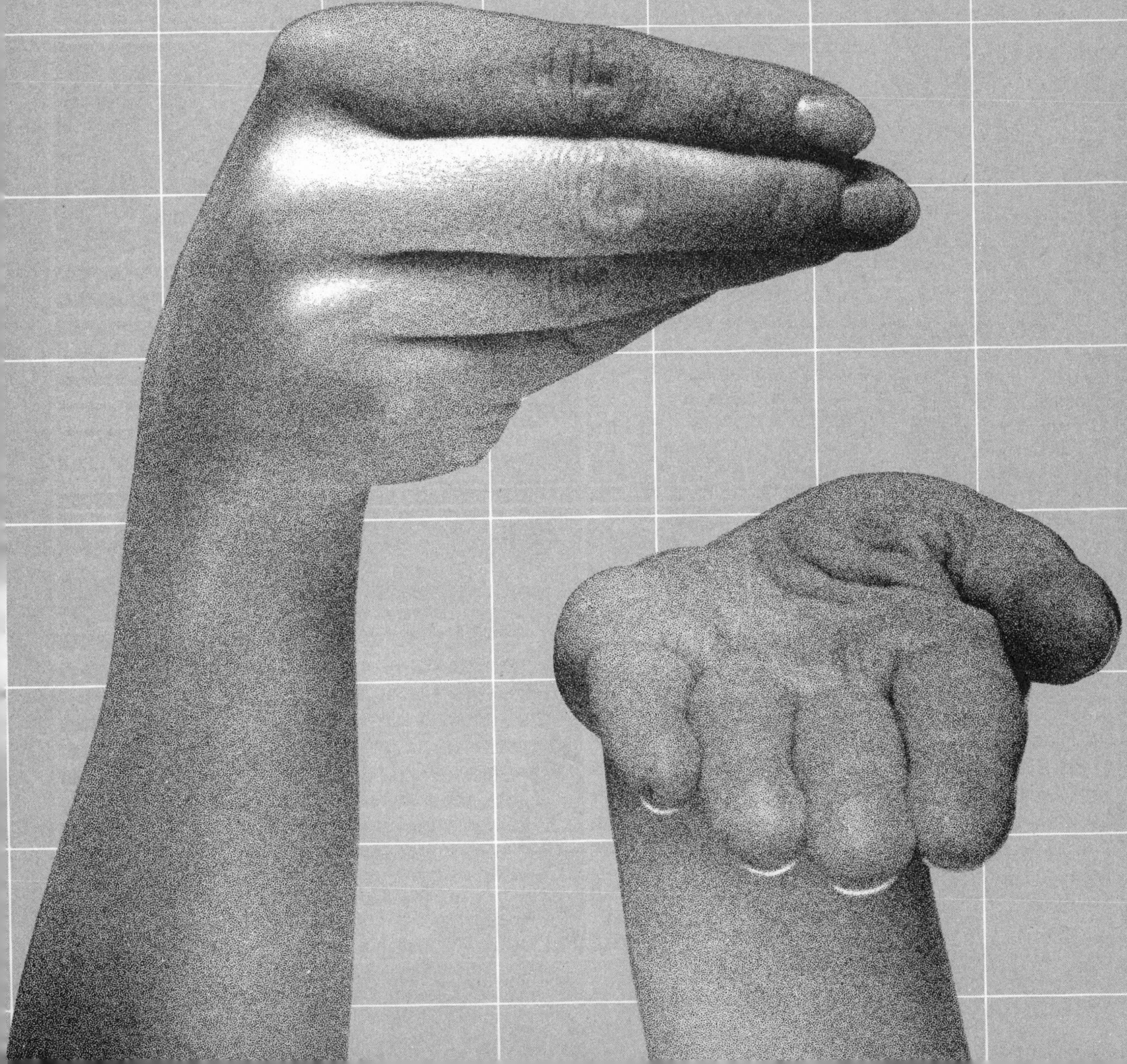

YEARS, HOUSE NUMBERS, AND MONEY

Years, house numbers, and money amounts are usually signed like they are spoken in English. For example, "1995" is signed "19" and then "95." Even money amounts less than $11.00 can be expressed by signing the numeral and twisting the palm sharply inward. Monetary amounts greater than $11.00 must be followed by the sign for "dollar." Uneven amounts of money of any size are signed as they are spoken. For example, $67.52 is signed "67" "dollar" "52" "cents."

five dollars

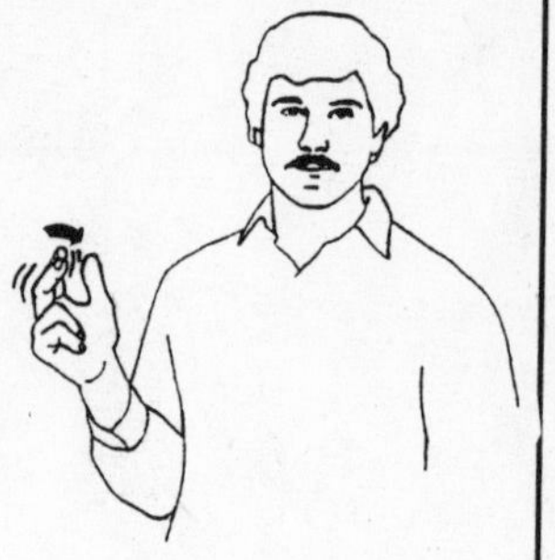

thirteen dollars

THE TEENS

The signs for the numerals sixteen, seventeen, and eighteen may be made as demonstrated in this chapter, or they may be formed by rubbing the thumb along the inside edge of the little finger for sixteen, the inside edge of the fourth finger for seventeen, and the inside edge of the middle finger for eighteen, while holding the other fingers extended in each case. The rubbing movement is the only thing that distinguishes six from sixteen, seven from seventeen, and eight from eighteen.

six

sixteen

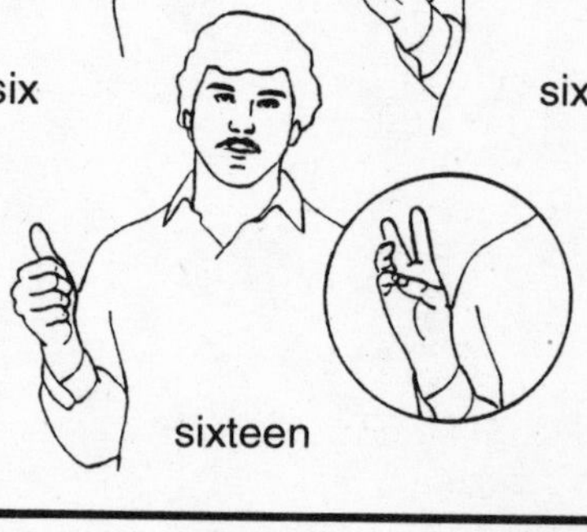

sixteen

FIRST, SECOND, THIRD . . .

Ordinals may be signed in any of three ways. The signs illustrated in this chapter use the fingers of the left hand as the primary source of information as they are struck by the index finger of the right hand. Another way of expressing ordinal numerals is to sign a numeral and twisting the palm sharply toward the right shoulder. In that way "one" becomes "first,' "two" become "second," and so forth. Ordinals formed by twisting the wrist are usually used as nouns, while the two-handed ordinals are used as adjectives. The third way to sign ordinals is to move a horizontally held numeral sign across the chest from left to right.

third

third

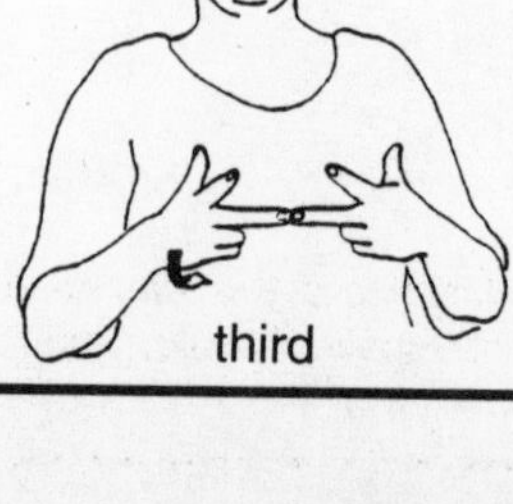

third

Numbers

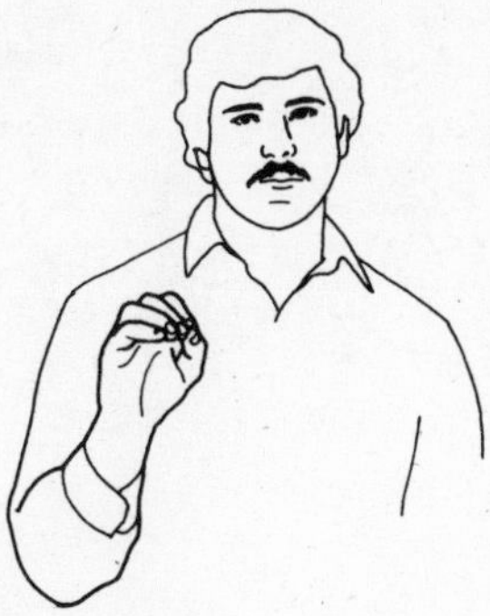

ZERO
Form an "o" right hand, palm facing forward, in front of the right side of the chest.

ONE
Hold the extended right index finger up in front of the body. Note: The palm may face either forward or in.

TWO
Hold the extended index finger and middle finger of the right hand up in front of the body. Note: The palm may face either forward or in.

THREE
Hold the extended index and middle fingers and thumb up in front of the body. Note: The palm may face either forward or in.

FOUR
Hold the four extended fingers of the right hand up in front of the body, thumb bent across the palm. Note: The palm may face either forward or in.

FIVE
Hold all four extended fingers and thumb of the right hand up in front of the body. Note: The palm may face either forward or in.

SIX
With the thumb touching the little finger of the right hand, hold the other three fingers up in front of the body, palm facing forward.

SEVEN
With the thumb touching the ring finger of the right hand, hold the other three fingers up in front of the body, palm facing forward.

EIGHT
With the thumb touching the middle finger of the right hand, hold the other three fingers up in front of the body, palm facing forward.

NINE
With the thumb touching the index finger of the right hand, hold the other three fingers up in front of the body, palm facing forward.

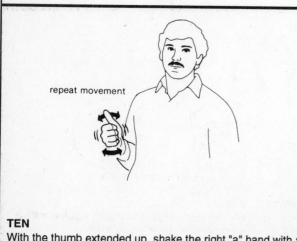

TEN
With the thumb extended up, shake the right "a" hand with a short repeated movement in front of the body, palm facing left.

ELEVEN
With a double movement, flick the index finger off the thumb of the right hand, palm facing in, extending the index finger up each time.

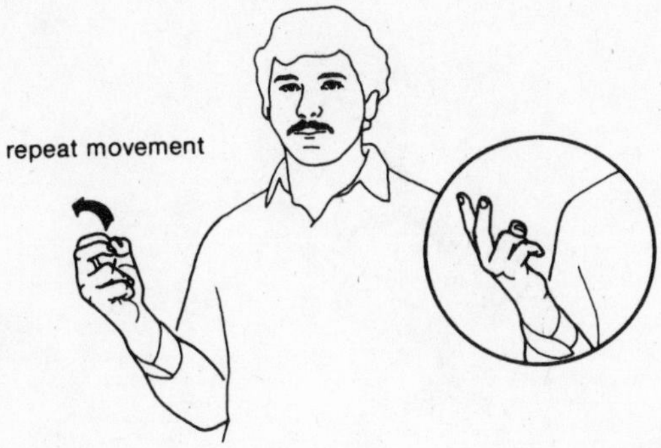

TWELVE
With a double movement, flick the index and middle fingers off the thumb of the right hand, palm facing in, extending the index and middle fingers up each time.

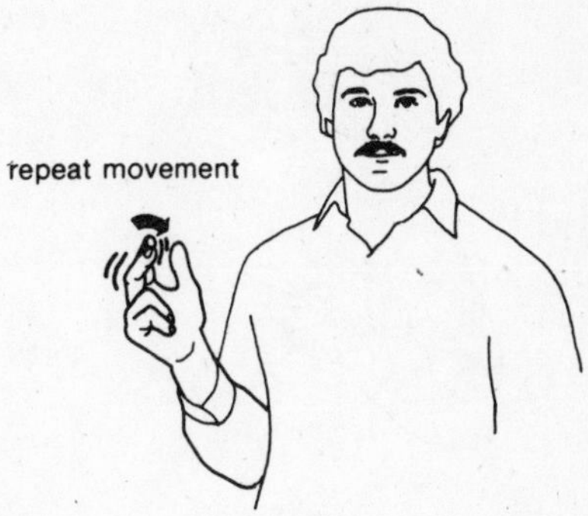

THIRTEEN
With the thumb, middle and index fingers of the right hand extended, palm facing in, wiggle the fingers with a repeated movement.

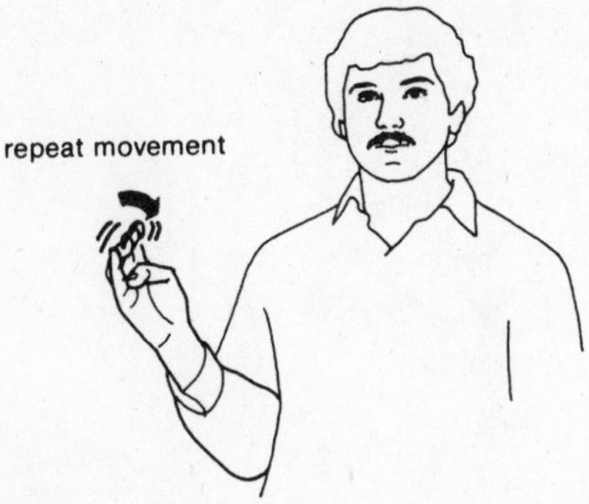

FOURTEEN
With all four fingers together and thumb across the palm, bend the fingers with a short repeated movement.

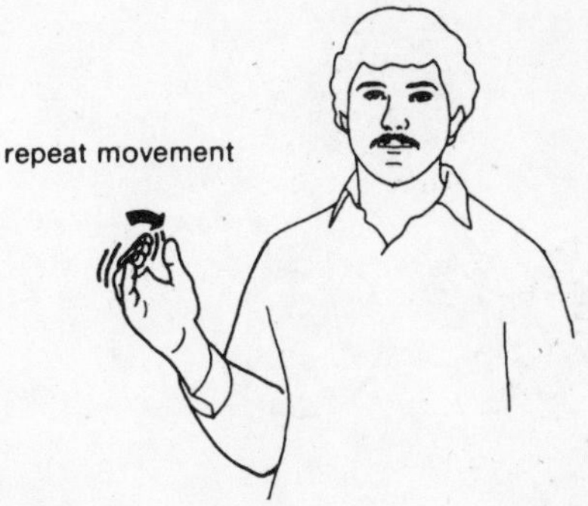

FIFTEEN
With all four fingers together and the thumb extended, palm facing in, bend the fingers with a short repeated movement.

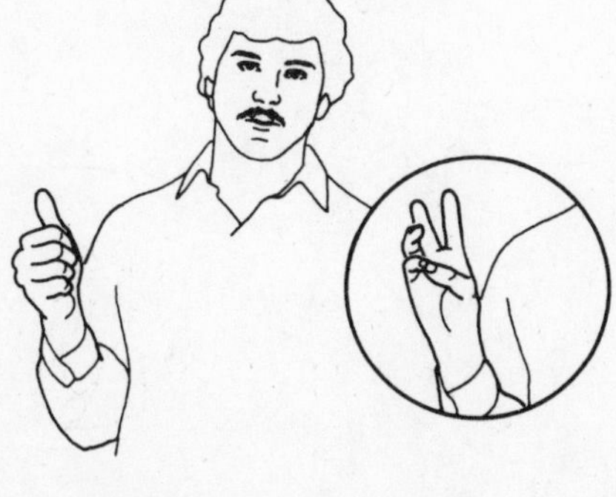

SIXTEEN
With the thumb of the right "a" hand extended up in front of the right shoulder, palm facing in, twist the hand quickly and touch the thumb to the little finger, palm facing forward.
Hint: "Ten" plus "six."

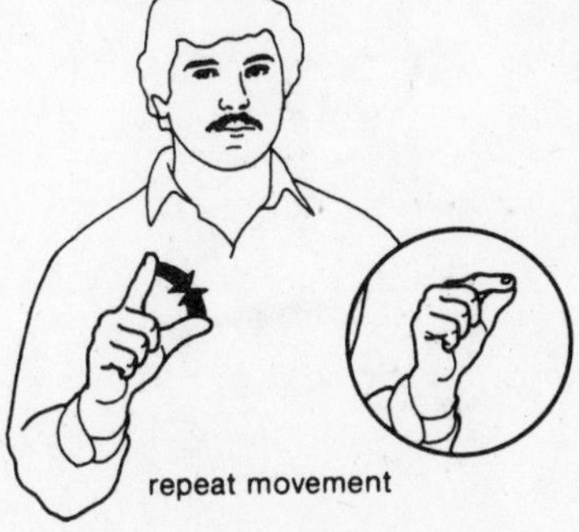

TWENTY
Close the extended index finger and thumb together with a short repeated movement, palm facing forward.

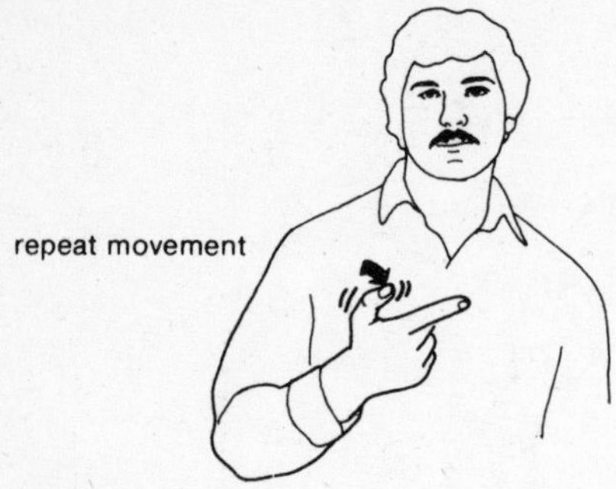

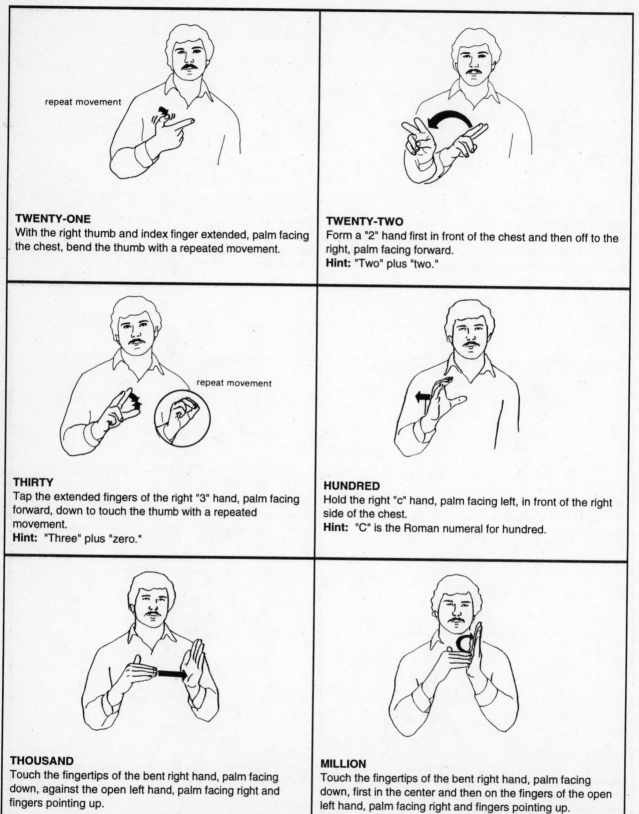

TWENTY-ONE
With the right thumb and index finger extended, palm facing the chest, bend the thumb with a repeated movement.

TWENTY-TWO
Form a "2" hand first in front of the chest and then off to the right, palm facing forward.
Hint: "Two" plus "two."

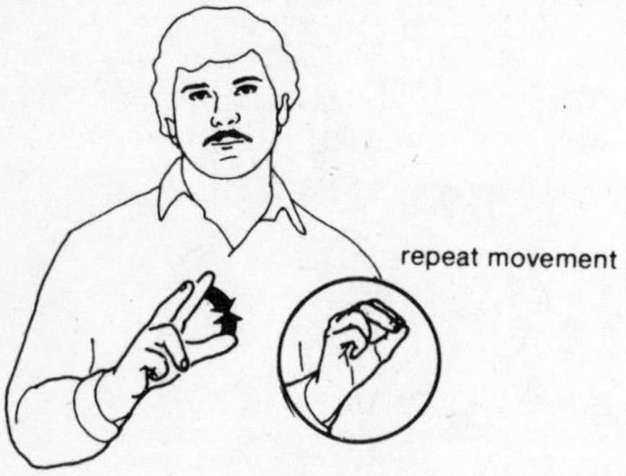

THIRTY
Tap the extended fingers of the right "3" hand, palm facing forward, down to touch the thumb with a repeated movement.
Hint: "Three" plus "zero."

HUNDRED
Hold the right "c" hand, palm facing left, in front of the right side of the chest.
Hint: "C" is the Roman numeral for hundred.

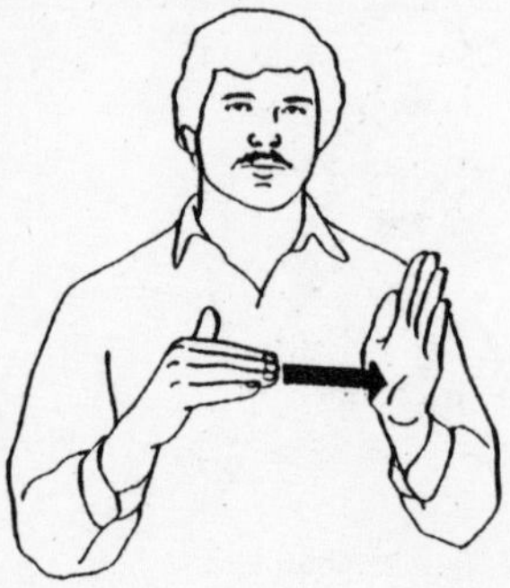

THOUSAND
Touch the fingertips of the bent right hand, palm facing down, against the open left hand, palm facing right and fingers pointing up.

MILLION
Touch the fingertips of the bent right hand, palm facing down, first in the center and then on the fingers of the open left hand, palm facing right and fingers pointing up.

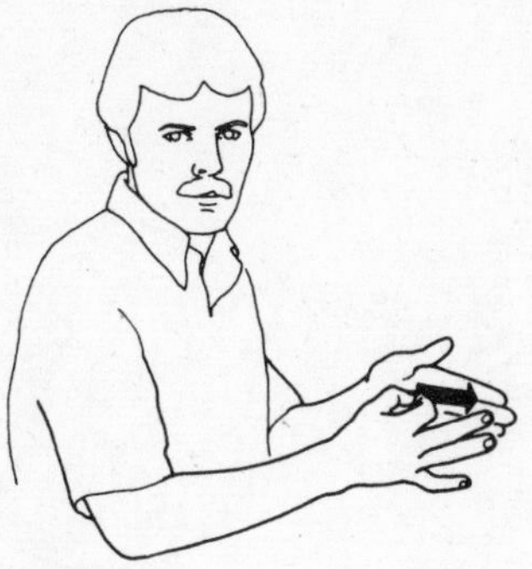

COUNT
Move the fingertips of the right "9" hand from the heel to the fingertips of the palm of the open left hand, palm facing up.
Hint: Moving across a column of numbers.

FIRST
Bring the extended right index finger, palm facing in, back to touch the extended thumb of the left "10" hand, palm facing right.
Hint: Pointing to the first finger.

SECOND
Touch the middle finger of the right "2" hand to the extended index finger of the left "L" hand, both palms facing in.
Hint: Pointing to the second finger.

THIRD
Touch the middle finger of the right "3" hand to the middle finger of the left "3" hand, both palms facing in.
Hint: Pointing to the third finger.

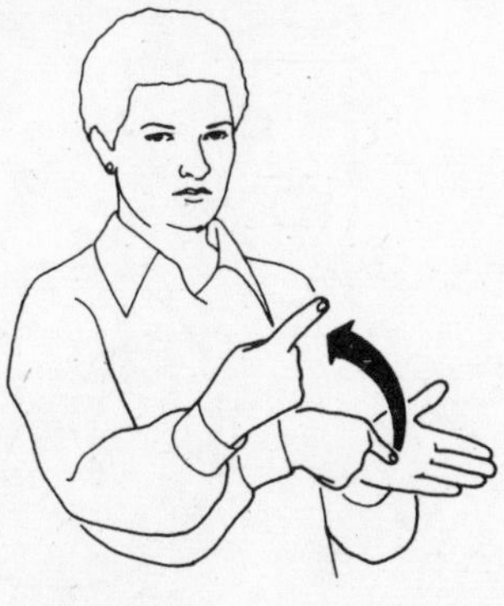

ONCE
Beginning with the extended right index finger touching the palm of the open left hand, bring the right hand upward with a quick movement.

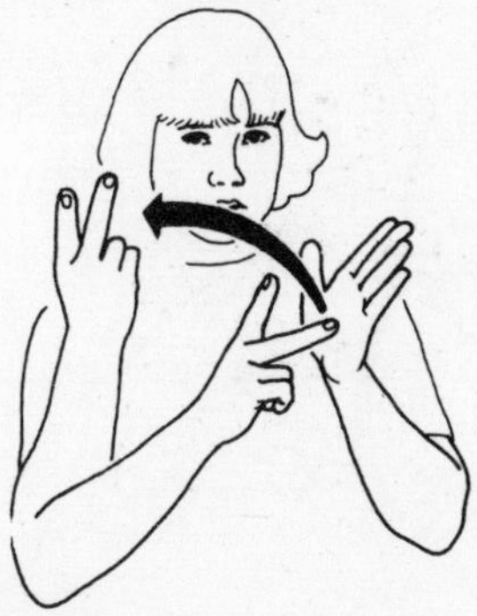

TWICE, DOUBLE
Brush the middle finger of the right "2" hand, palm facing left upward across the palm of the open left hand, palm facing right.

Quantity

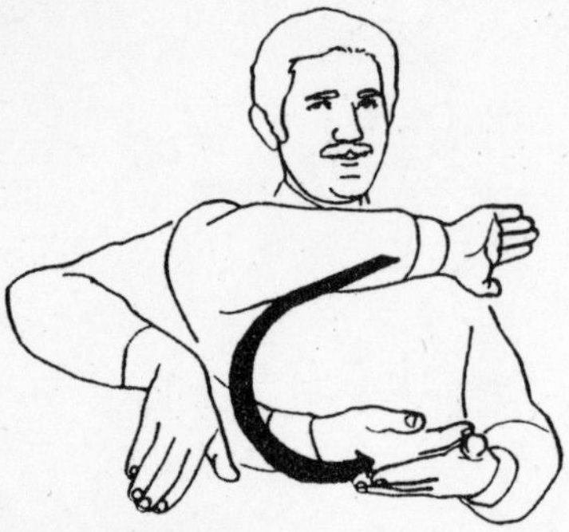

ALL, WHOLE, ENTIRE
Move the open right from in front of the left side of the body, palm facing forward, in a large circular movement to the right, ending with the back of the right hand in the palm of the open left hand, both palms facing up.
Hint: The right hand seems to encompass everything as it moves.

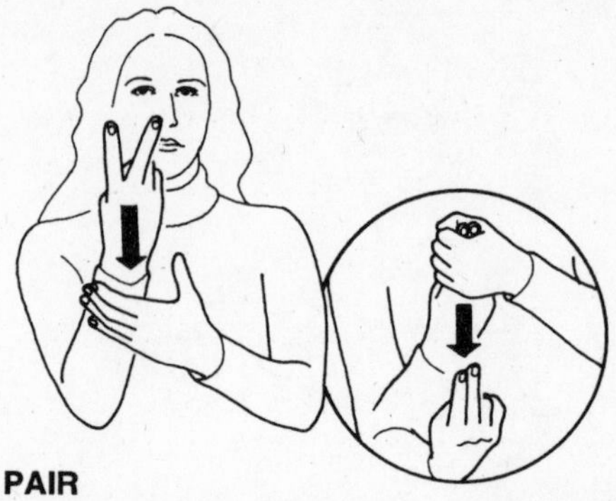

BOTH, PAIR
Bring the right "2" hand, palm facing in, downward through the curved left hand, palm facing in. As the right hand moves downward, the left fingers close to squeeze the extended right fingers together into a "u" shape.
Hint: Two things join together to become a pair.

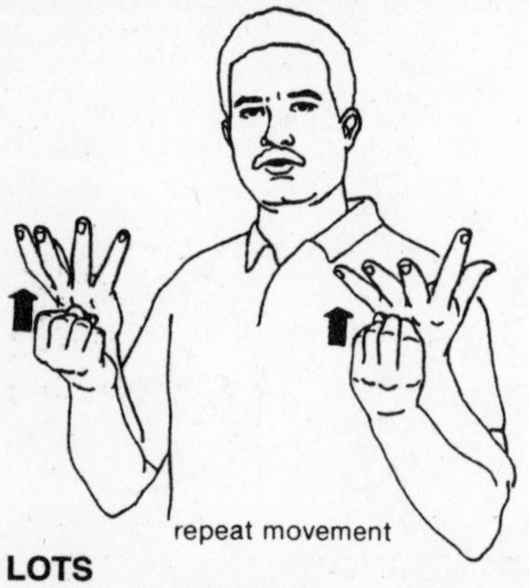

MANY, LOTS
With both "s" hands in front of each side of the chest, palms facing in, flick the fingers upward with a double movement.
Hint: The flicking of the fingers indicates an indeterminable number.

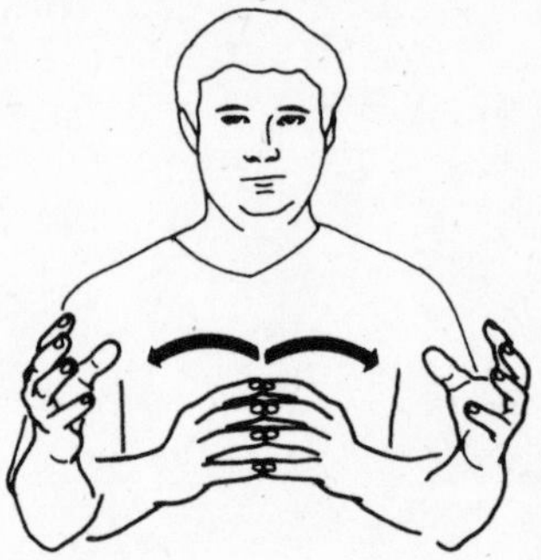

MUCH, A LOT
Beginning with the fingertips of both curved "5" hands touching in front of the chest, palms facing each other, move the hands outward to about shoulder width.
Hint: Hands show a large amount of something.

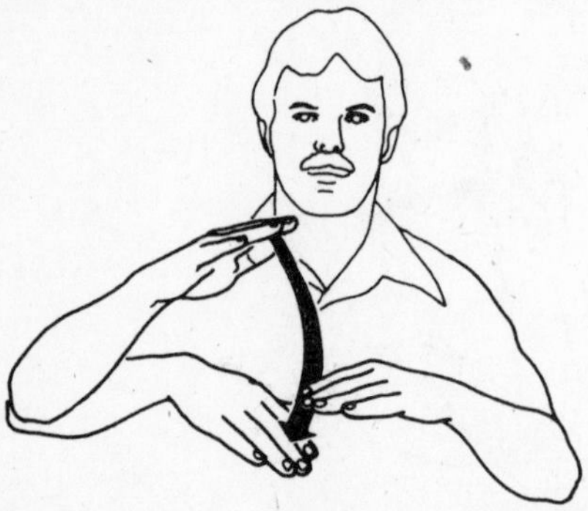

THAN
Move the open right hand downward hitting the fingers of the open left as the right hand moves down, both palms facing down and fingers pointing toward each other.

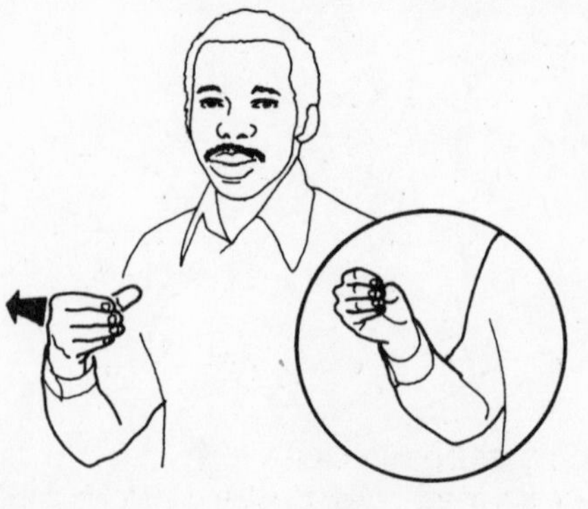

AND
Bring the right "c" hand, palm facing left, from in front of the chest outward to the right while closing the fingers to the thumb.

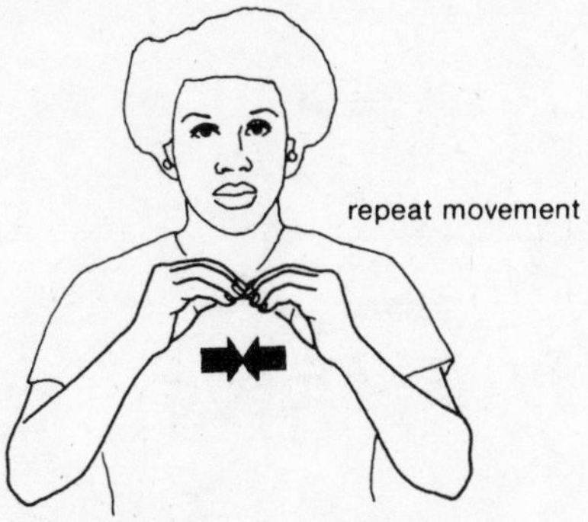

MORE
Tap the fingertips of both flattened "o" hands together in front of the chest with a repeated movement.
Hint: Similar in handshape and concept to the sign for "add."

MOST
Beginning with the knuckles of both "a" hands touching in front of the chest, both palms facing in, bring the right hand upward in an arc to the right.
Hint: This is the movement used for "-est" endings or "the greatest" when comparing things.

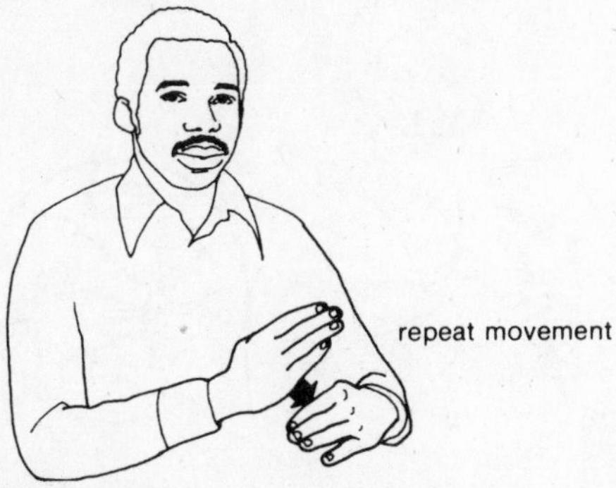

MEDIUM, MODERATE
Tap the little-finger side of the right "b" hand, palm facing left, with a double movement across the index-finger side of the left "b" hand, palm facing right.
Hint: Shows the middle of the finger or a medium location.

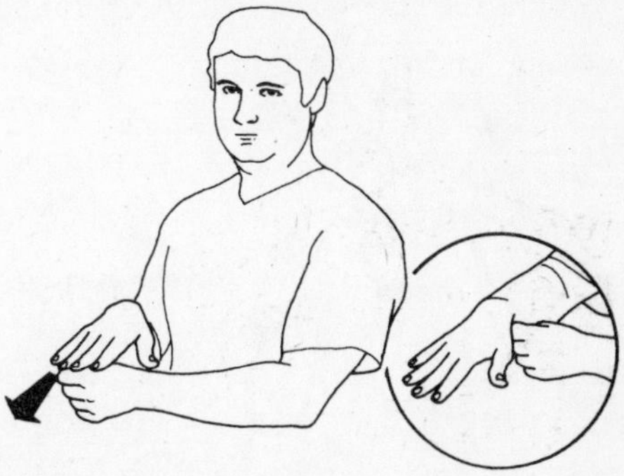

ENOUGH, PLENTY, SUFFICIENT
Push the palm of the open right hand, palm facing down, forward across the index-finger side of the left "s" hand, palm facing right.
Hint: Pushing away the excess.

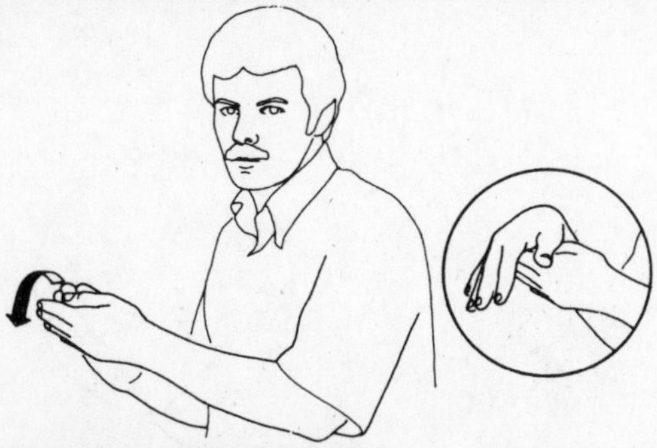

OVERFLOW, RUNNING OVER
Move the palm of the open right hand, palm facing down, forward over the index-finger side of the open left hand, palm facing in, spreading the right fingers as they move down the back of the left fingers.
Hint: Shows something overflowing.

FULL
Slide the palm of the open right hand, palm facing down, from right to left across the index-finger side of the left "s" hand held in front of the chest, palm facing right.
Hint: Shows something full to the top.

SOME, PART, PORTION
Slide the little-finger side of the open right hand, palm facing left, to the right across the open left hand, palm facing up.
Hint: Dividing something into part.

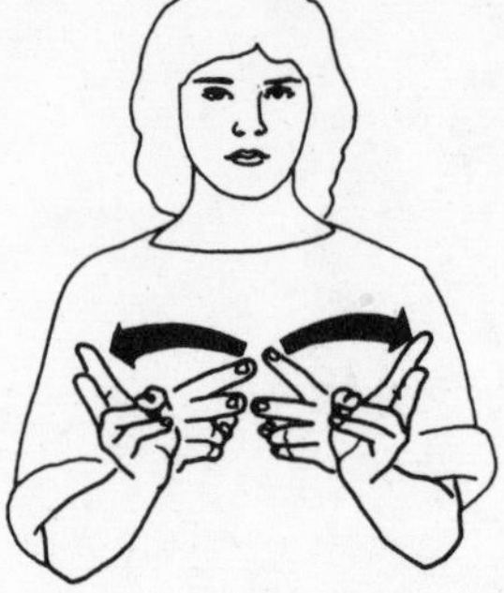

VERY
Beginning with extended fingers of both "v" hands touching in front of the chest, palms facing each other, move the fingers apart by bending the wrists back.
Hint: Initialized sign formed similar to the sign for "much."

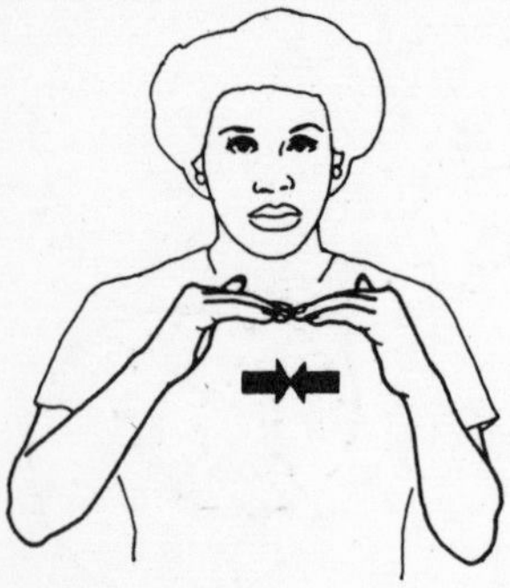

EQUAL, FAIR, EVEN
Tap the fingertips of both bent hands together in front of the chest with a double movement.
Hint: Shows two things at an equal level with each other.

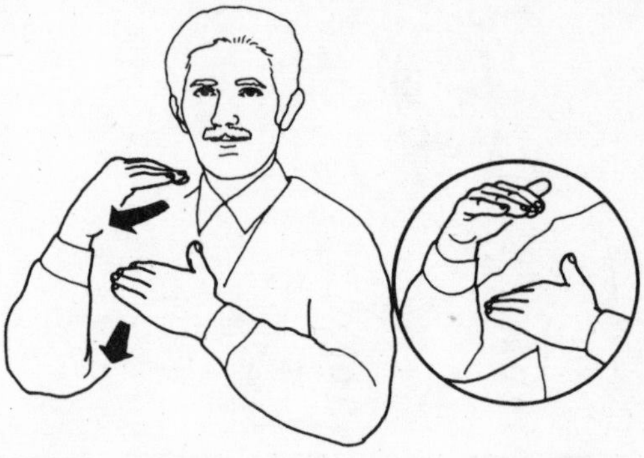

LIMIT, RESTRICT
With the right bent hand several inches above the left bent hand, both palms facing down, swing the fingertips of both hand outward a short distance.
Hint: The hands demonstrate the outside limits permitted.

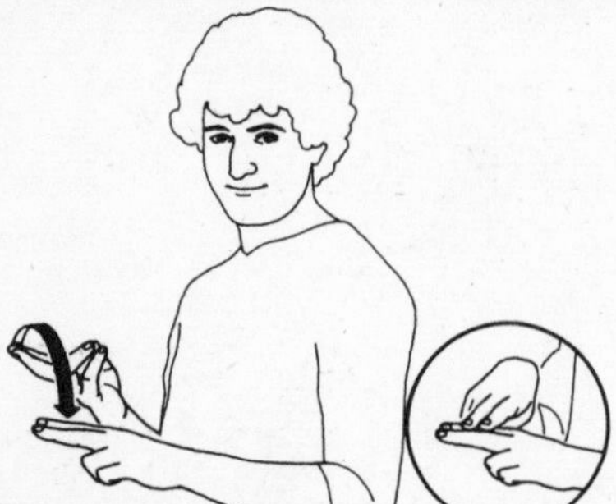

INCREASE, GAIN WEIGHT
Beginning with right "h" hand, palm facing up, next to the left "h" hand, palm facing down, turn the right hand over, ending with the extended right fingers across the extended left fingers.
Hint: Formed similar to the sign for "weigh"; shows an increase of pounds.

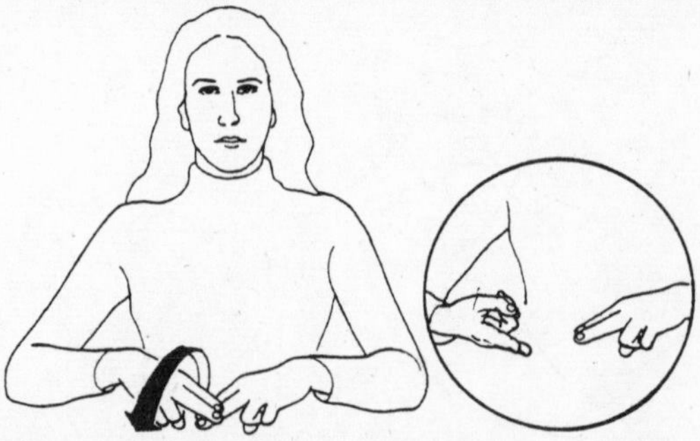

DECREASE, REDUCE
Beginning with the extended fingers of the right "h" hand across the extended fingers of the left "h" hand, both palms facing down, move the right fingers forward by twisting the right wrist over, ending with the right palm facing up.
Hint: Formed similar to the sign for "weight"; shows a decrease of pounds.

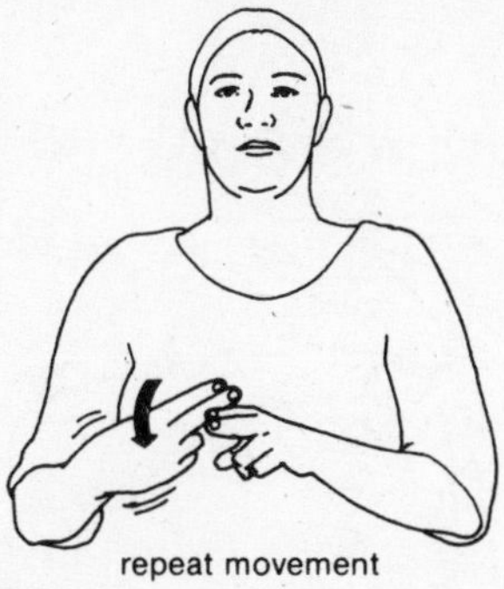

WEIGH, WEIGHT
With the middle-finger side of the right "h" fingers, palm angled left, across the index-finger side of the left "h" fingers, palm angled right, rock the right hand up and down with a short repeated movement.
Hint: Balancing things on a scale.

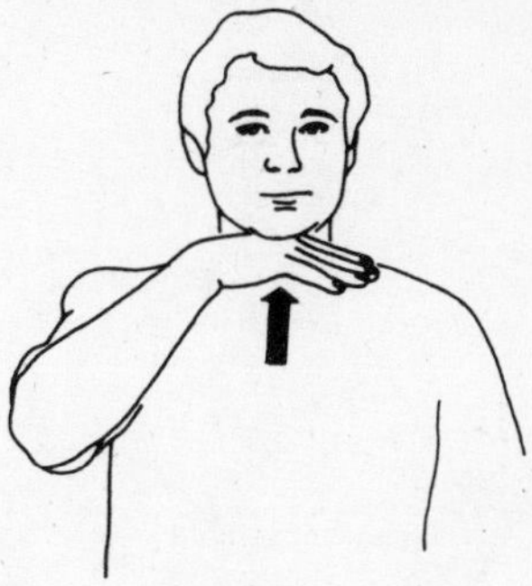

FULL, FED UP
Bring the back of the open right hand up to under the chin, palm facing down and fingers pointing left.
Hint: Shows that you are full to the chin.

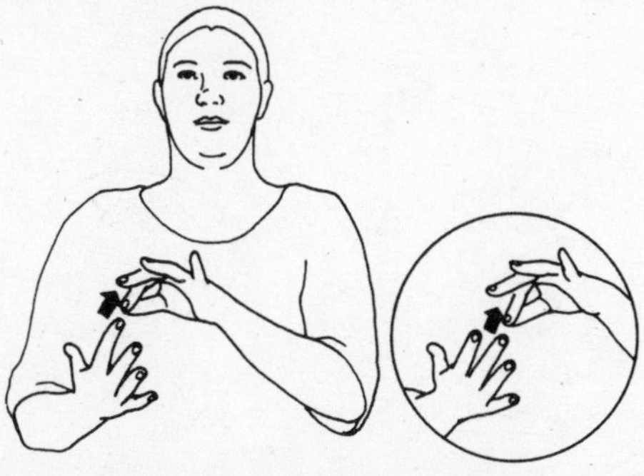

EITHER, CHOOSE, PICK, OPTION, SELECT
Pull the bent index finger and thumb of the left "5" hand, palm facing down, upward first off the index fingertip and then the middle fingertip of right "5" hand held in front the chest, palm facing in and fingers pointing up.
Hint: Trying to decide between one or another.

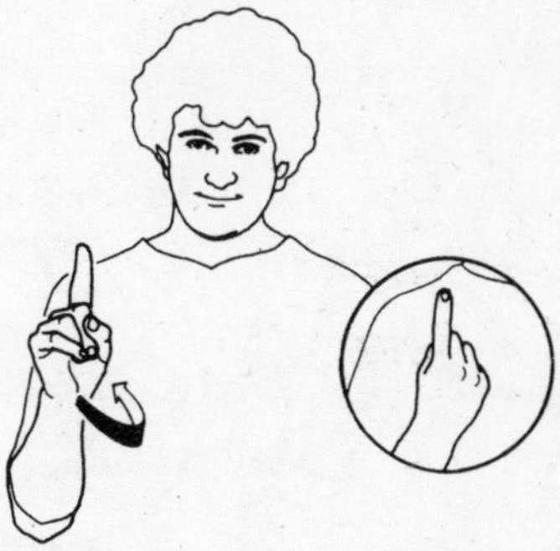

ONLY
Beginning with the right "one" hand in front of the right shoulder, palm facing forward, twist the wrist, ending with the palm facing in.
Hint: Shows only one thing.

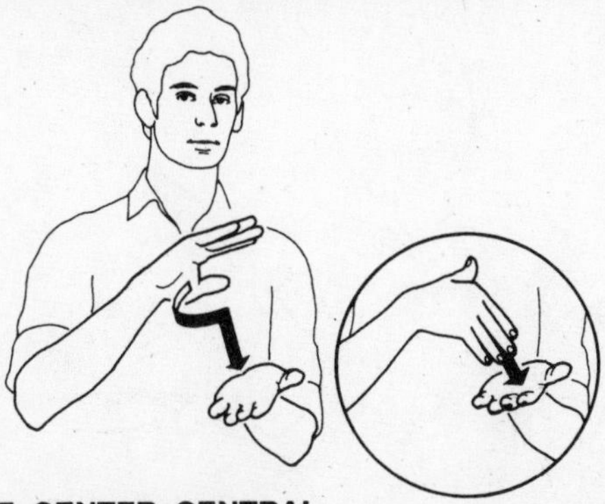

MIDDLE, CENTER, CENTRAL
Beginning with the open right hand several inches above the open left hand, palms facing each other, move the right hand in a circular movement while bending the fingers and bringing them sharply downward into the left palm.
Hint: Indicates the center of the palm.

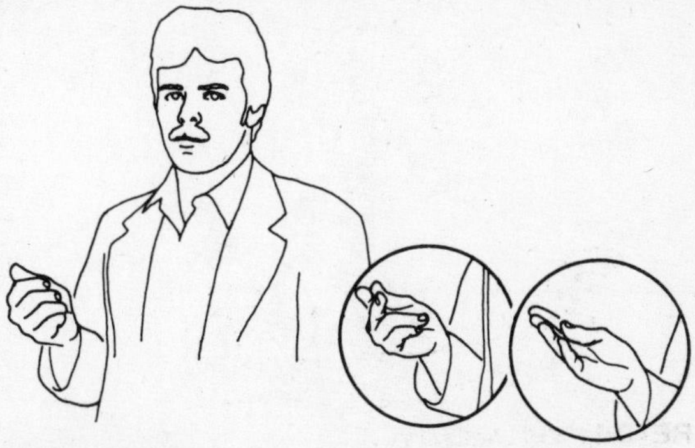

FEW, SEVERAL
Beginning with the right "a" hand in front of the right side of the body, palm facing up, smoothly uncurl each finger, starting with the index finger while moving the thumb in toward the palm.
Hint: The fingers seem to count out a few things.

Flick thumb + pinky

TINY BIT, IOTA, MINUTE
Rub the thumb on the little fingertip of the right hand, palm facing up.
Hint: Feeling a tiny amount of something.

EMPTY, BARE, NAKED, BLANK, VACANT
Move the bent middle finger of the right "5" hand, palm facing down, from the wrist across the back of the left "s" hand held across the chest, palm facing down.
Hint: The finger feels a bare spot on the back of the hand.

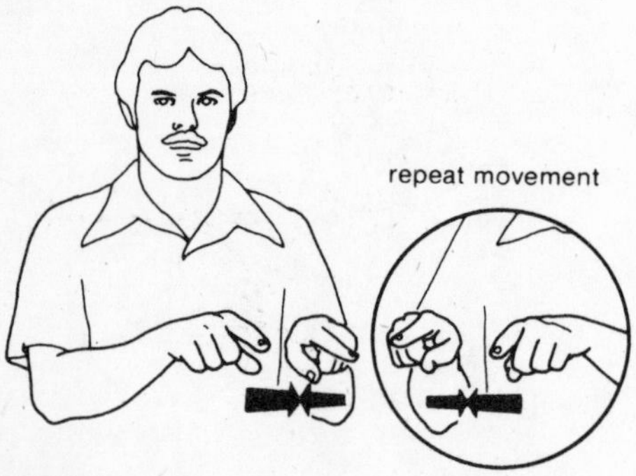

TOO, ALSO
With the index fingers of both hands extended, palms facing down, tap the thumb side of both hands together first in front of the left side of the body and then the right side.
Hint: "Same" signed twice, showing that something is the same as something else.

LESS, DECREASE, DISCOUNT
Beginning with the open right hand, palm facing down, several inches above the open left hand, palm facing up, bring the right hand downward a short distance.
Hint: Demonstrates a decrease in distance.

ALMOST, NEARLY
Brush the fingers of the right curved hand upward from under the left curved hand, both palms facing up, brushing the left fingers as the right hand moves.

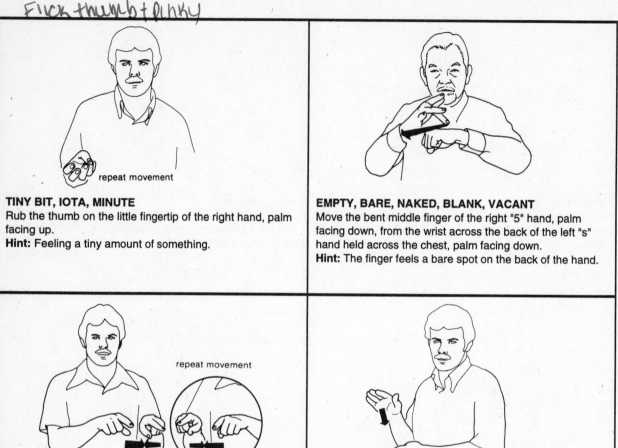

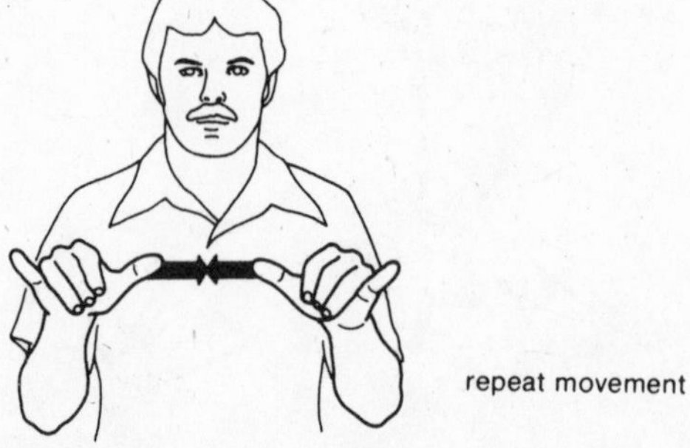

MEASURE, SIZE
Tap the thumbs of both "y" hands together in front of the chest with a repeated movement, both palms facing down.
Hint: The little fingers indicate a unit of measure.

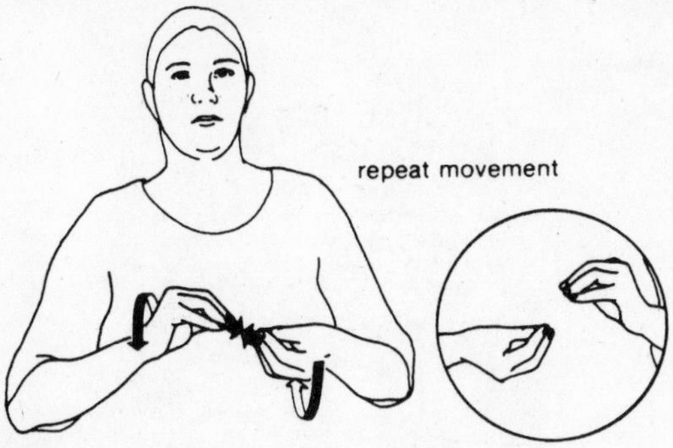

NUMBER
Beginning with the fingertips of both flattened "o" hands touching in front of the chest, right palm facing down and left palm facing up, twist the wrists in opposite directions with a double movement keeping the fingertips together.

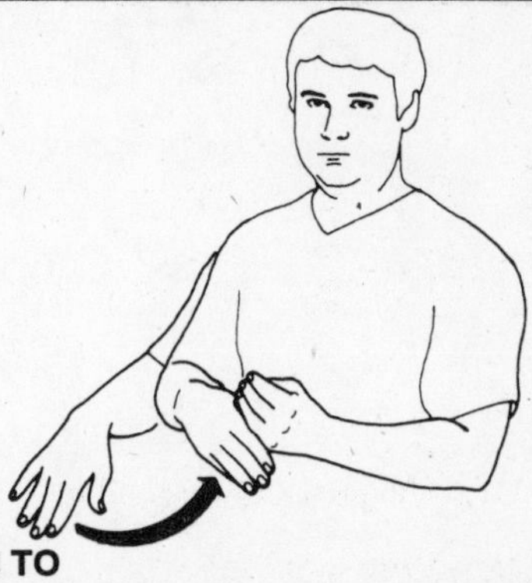

ADD, ADD ON TO
Beginning with the right "5" hand hanging down in front of the right side of the body, palm facing back, swing the hand upward to the left while closing into a flattened "o" hand, ending with the index-finger side of the right hand under the little-finger side of the left flattened "o" hand.

PERCENT
Dip the right "o" hand outward to in front of the right shoulder, palm facing left, and then downward.
Hint: Trace the shape of a percentage sign in the air.

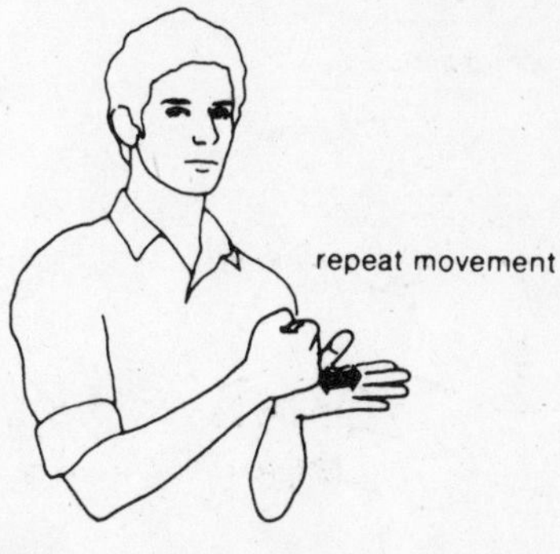

CREDIT CARD
Move the little-finger side of the right "s" hand, palm facing left, back and forth with a double movement across the length of the open left palm.
Hint: Shows the action of a credit card machine taking an impression.

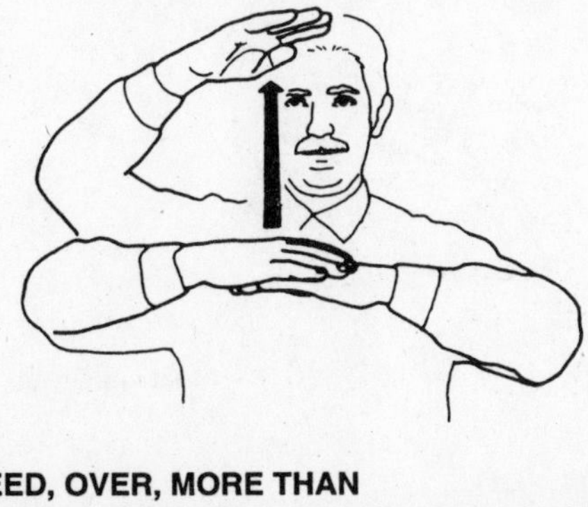

EXCEED, OVER, MORE THAN
Beginning with the right "b" hand on the back of the left "b" hand, both palms facing down and fingers pointing in opposite directions, move the right hand upward.
Hint: The right hand moves above a limit set by the left hand.

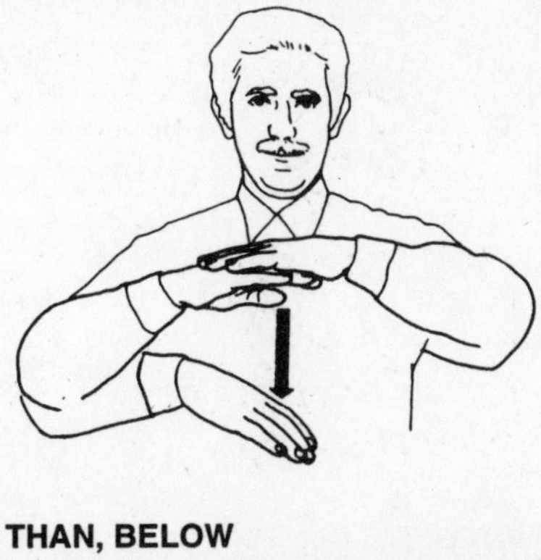

LESS THAN, BELOW
Move the right "b" hand from under the left "b" hand, both palms facing down and fingers pointing in opposite directions, move the right hand downward.
Hint: The right hand moves to a position less than the limit set by the left hand.

Money and Math

or rub finger tips

MONEY
Tap the back of the right flattened "o" hand on the open left hand, both palms facing up, with a repeated movement.
Hint: Holding money and laying it in the other hand.

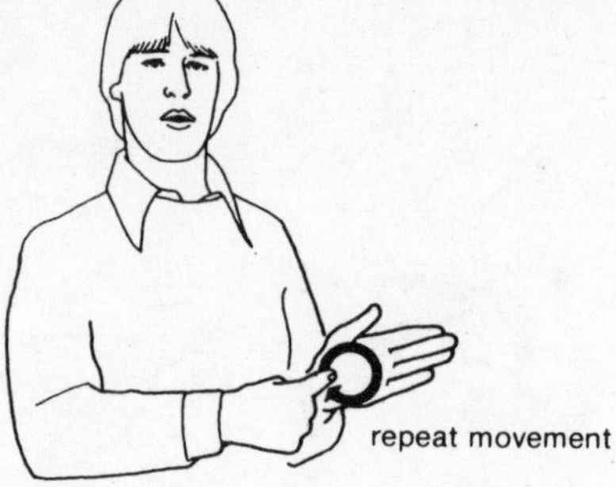

COIN
With the extended right index finger, draw a small circle on the palm of the open left hand.
Hint: Shows the shape of a coin held in the hand.

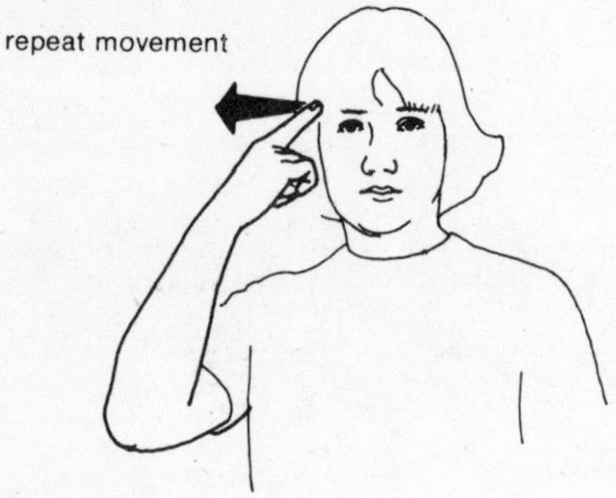

PENNY, ONE CENT, CENTS
Bring the extended right index finger from touching the right side of the forehead forward a short distance.

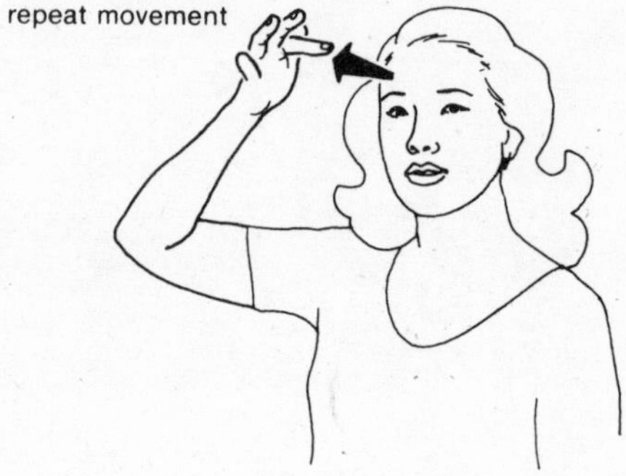

NICKEL, FIVE CENTS
Bring the bent middle finger of the right "5" hand from touching the right side of the forehead forward a short distance.

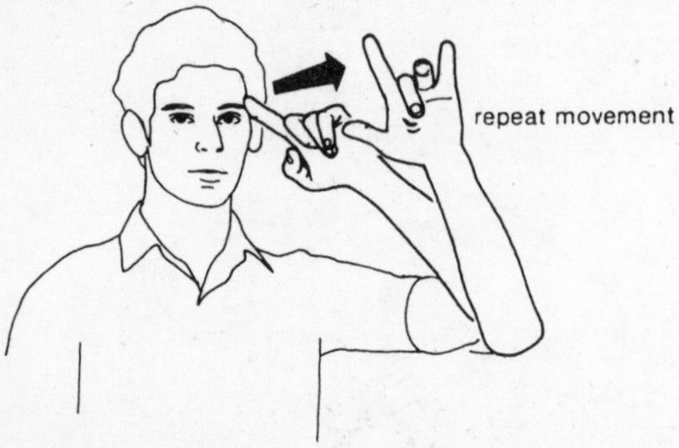

QUARTER, TWENTY-FIVE CENTS
Beginning with the extended right index finger touching the right side of the forehead, palm facing forward, move the hand forward, ending with the right thumb, index and middle fingers extended and wiggling the middle and ring fingers, palm facing forward.

DIME, TEN CENTS
Beginning with the extended right index finger touching the right side of the forehead, palm facing back, move the hand forward while changing into a "10" and wiggling it, palm facing back.

DOLLAR
Beginning with the right fingers grasping the index-finger side of the open left hand, palm facing in, slide the right hand the length of the left index finger from near the thumb outward to off the fingertip.
Hint: Feeling the shape of a dollar bill.

ONE DOLLAR
Beginning with the right "1" hand in front of the right shoulder, palm facing left, twist the wrist, ending with the palm facing back.
Hint: "One" plus a twist that is used to represent "dollar" for amounts under eleven dollars.

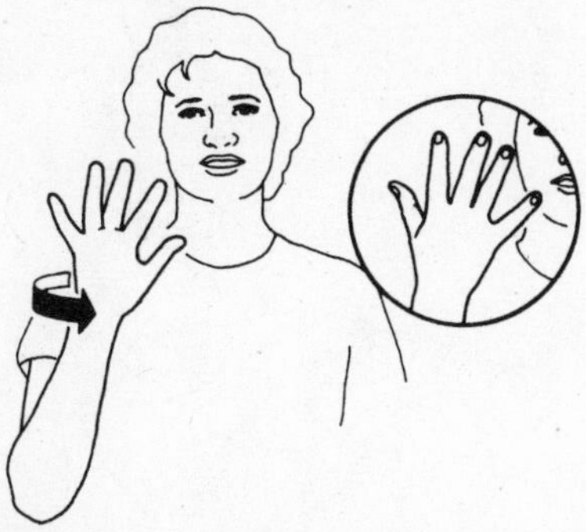

FIVE DOLLARS
Beginning with the right "5" hand in front of the right shoulder, palm facing left, twist the wrist, ending with the palm facing back.
Hint: "Five" plus a twist that is used to represent "dollar" for amounts under eleven dollars.

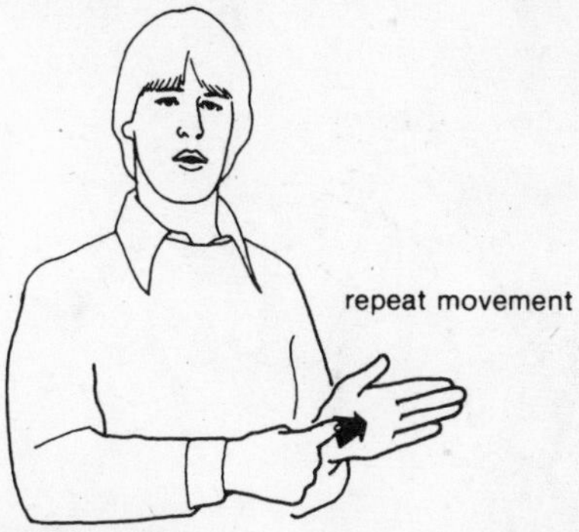

OWE, DEBT, OWE
Tap the extended right index with a repeated movement into the palm of the open left hand held in front of the chest, palm facing right.
hint: Similar to the movement for the sign "against."

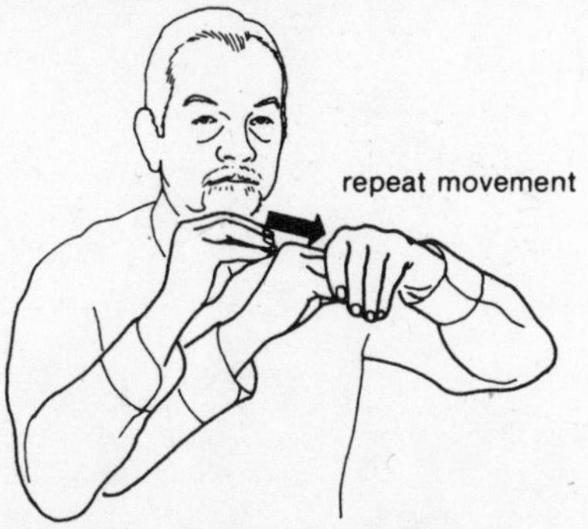

SAVE, SAVINGS, BANK, STORE, INVEST
Insert the right flattened "o" hand, palm facing down, with a double movement into the thumb-side opening of the left "c" hand held in front of the chest, palm facing down.
Hint: Putting money away to save it.

DEPOSIT
With the thumb of the right "a" hand on the thumbnail of the left "a" hand, palms facing in, move the hands downward and apart by twisting the wrists.

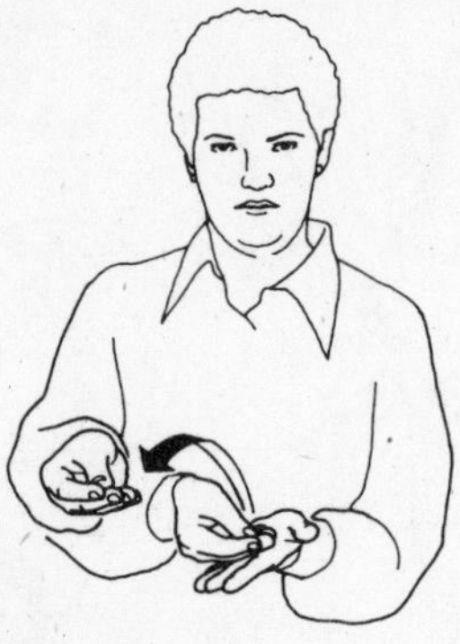

BUY, PURCHASE
Beginning with back of the right flattened "o" hand on the open left hand, both palms facing up, move the right hand forward in an arc.
Hint: "Money" plus giving it to another.

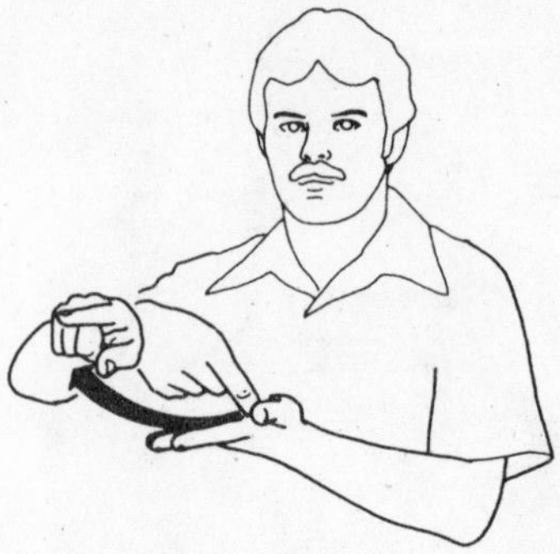

PAY
Sweep the extended right index finger across the palm of the open left hand held in front of the chest, palm facing up, from the heel to off the fingertips.
Hint: Directing a pay off of what is owed.

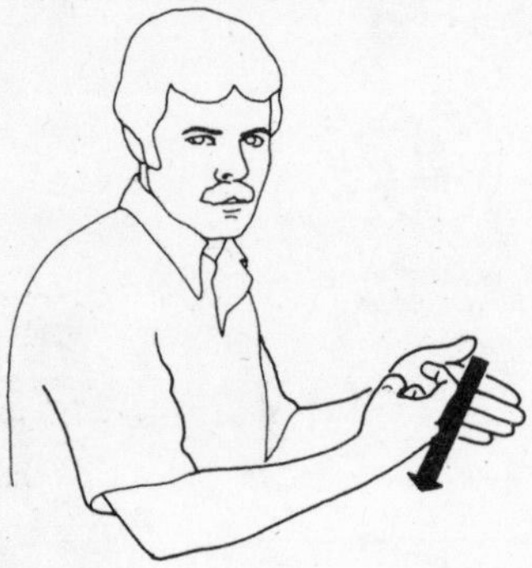

CHARGE, COST, FINE, TAX
Bring the index finger of the right "x" hand, palm facing in, downward on the palm of the open left hand held in front of the chest, palm facing right.

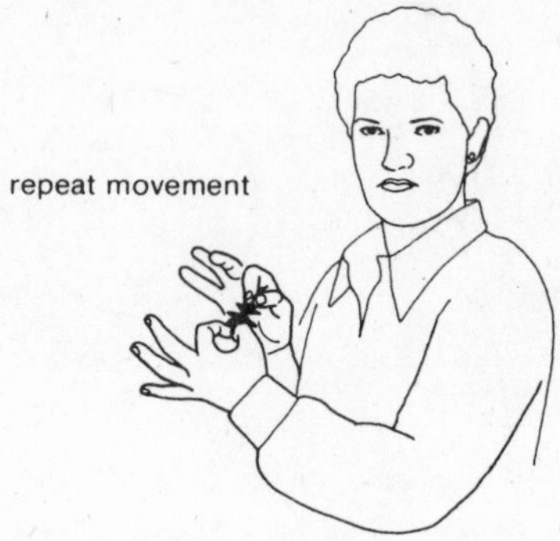

PRICE, COST
Tap the fingertips of both "9" hands together with a repeated movement, palms facing each other.

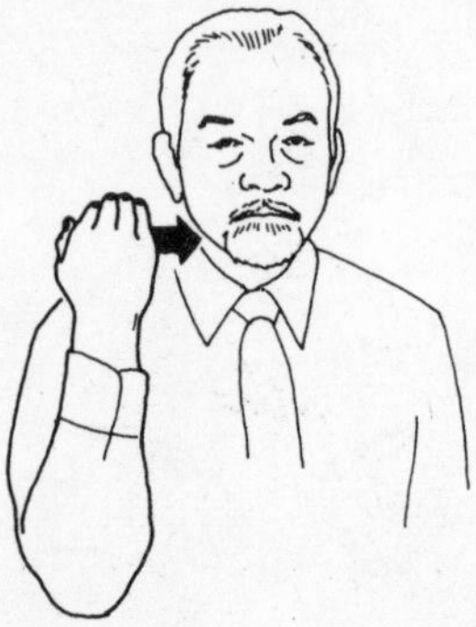

BROKE
Tap the little-finger side of the open right hand, palm facing down and finger pointing back, against the right side of the neck.
Hint: Breaking the neck.

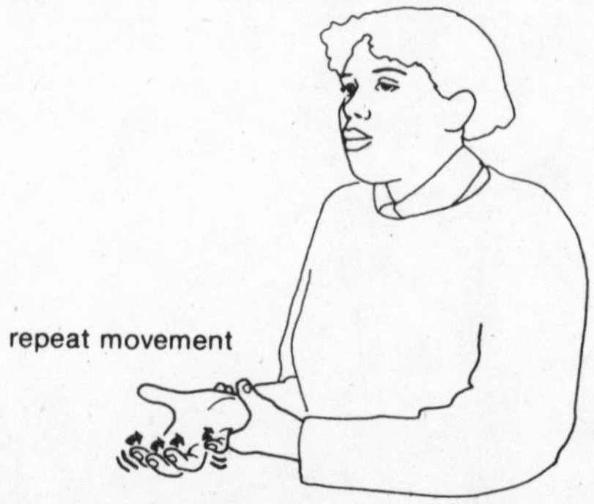

BEG
While holding the wrist of the right "claw" hand with the left hand, both palms facing up, bend the right fingers with a small repeated movement.
Hint: Mime a traditional beggar's movement when asking for a handout.

EARN, SALARY, INCOME
Beginning with the little-finger side of the right "c" hand, palm facing left, on the fingers of the open left hand, palm facing up, bring the right hand toward the left heel while closing to an "s" hand.
Hint: Gathering money together.

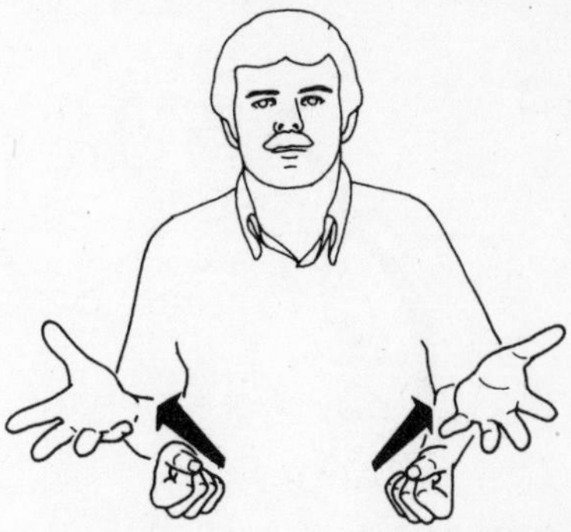

SPEND
Beginning with both "s" hands in front of each side of the body, both palms facing up, move the hands upward to each side while opening into "5" hands.
Hint: Taking money and spreading it around.

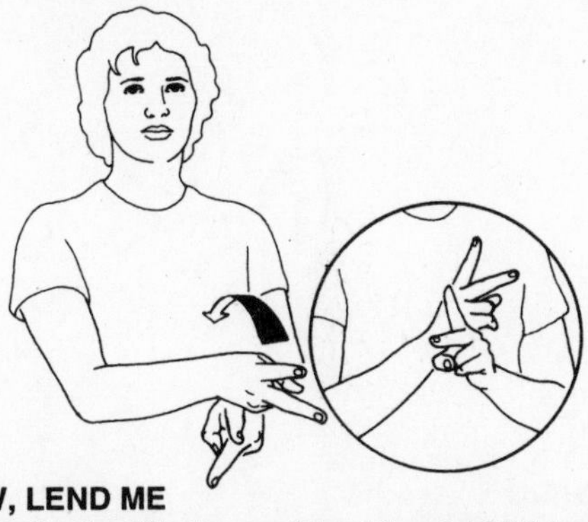

BORROW, LEND ME
Beginning with the little-finger side of the right "k" hand on the index-finger side of the left "k" hand, palms facing in opposite directions, move the hands back toward the body.
Note: This means "I borrow from you" and "You lend to me."
Hint: Bringing something borrowed to the body.

LEND
Beginning with the little-finger side of the right "k" hand on the index-finger side of the left "k" hand, palms facing in opposite directions, move the hands from the body forward.
Note: This means "I lend to you" and "You borrow from me."
Hint: Giving something lent to another person.

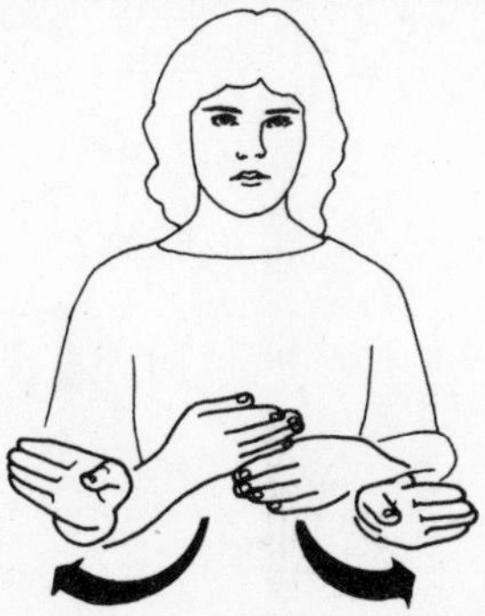

DIVIDE, SPLIT
Beginning with the little-finger side of the right "b" hand across the index-finger side of the left "b" hand, palms angled in, move the hands downward and apart, ending with the palms angled forward.
Hint: Moving things apart when dividing them.

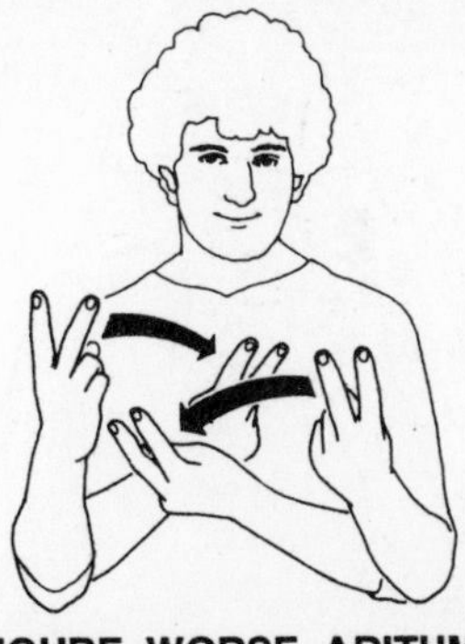

MULTIPLY, FIGURE, WORSE, ARITHMETIC
Beginning with both "k" hands in front of each side of the chest, move the hands in opposite directions past each other touching each other as they pass.

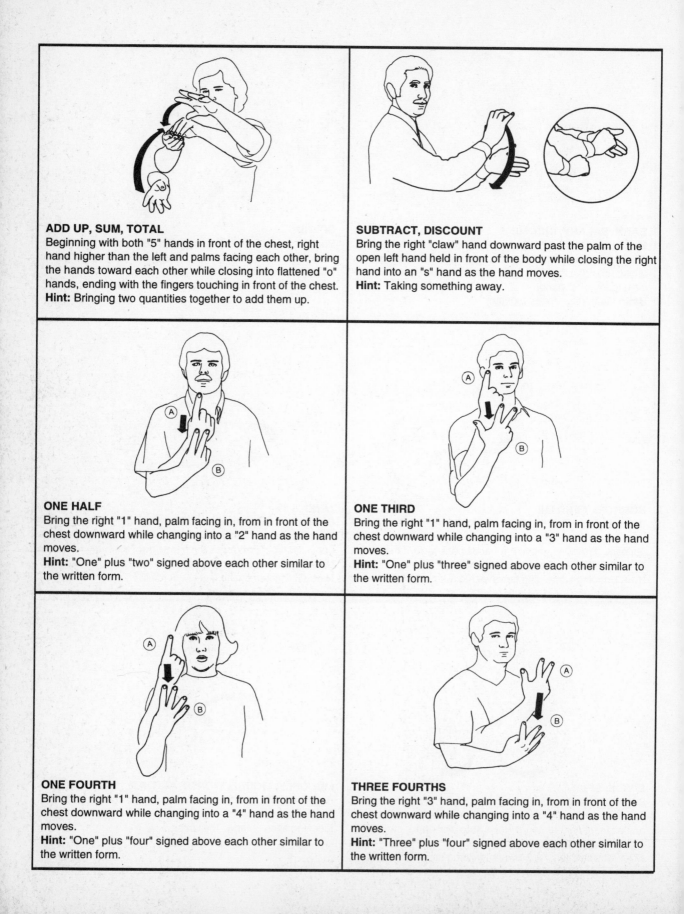

ADD UP, SUM, TOTAL
Beginning with both "5" hands in front of the chest, right hand higher than the left and palms facing each other, bring the hands toward each other while closing into flattened "o" hands, ending with the fingers touching in front of the chest.
Hint: Bringing two quantities together to add them up.

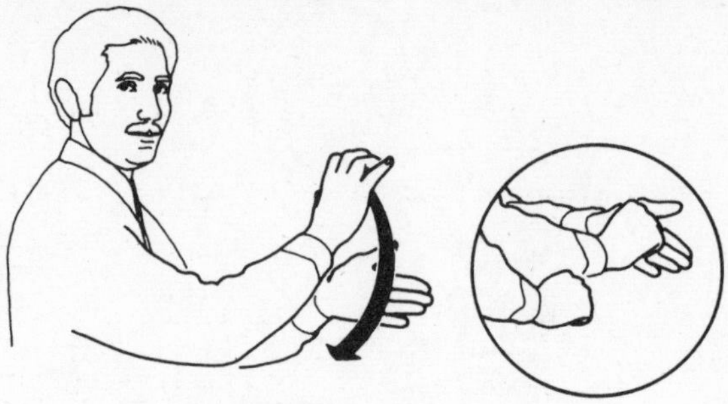

SUBTRACT, DISCOUNT
Bring the right "claw" hand downward past the palm of the open left hand held in front of the body while closing the right hand into an "s" hand as the hand moves.
Hint: Taking something away.

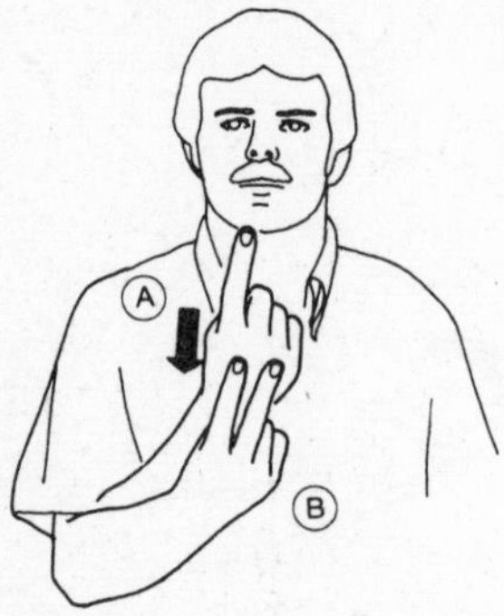

ONE HALF
Bring the right "1" hand, palm facing in, from in front of the chest downward while changing into a "2" hand as the hand moves.
Hint: "One" plus "two" signed above each other similar to the written form.

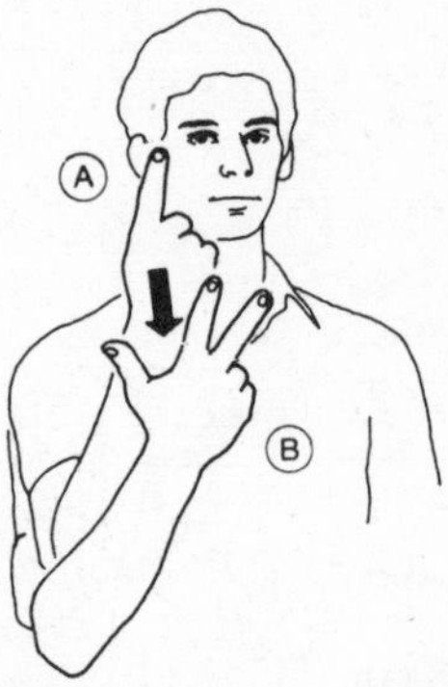

ONE THIRD
Bring the right "1" hand, palm facing in, from in front of the chest downward while changing into a "3" hand as the hand moves.
Hint: "One" plus "three" signed above each other similar to the written form.

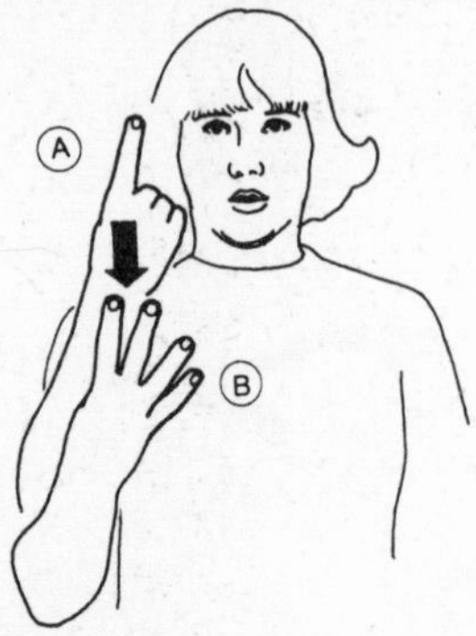

ONE FOURTH
Bring the right "1" hand, palm facing in, from in front of the chest downward while changing into a "4" hand as the hand moves.
Hint: "One" plus "four" signed above each other similar to the written form.

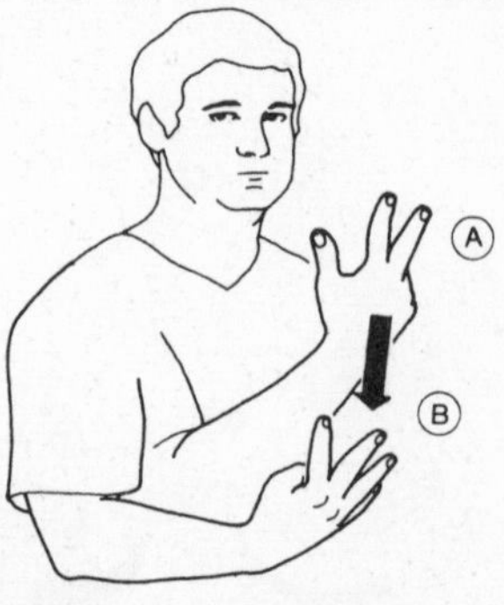

THREE FOURTHS
Bring the right "3" hand, palm facing in, from in front of the chest downward while changing into a "4" hand as the hand moves.
Hint: "Three" plus "four" signed above each other similar to the written form.

seven

TIME, DAYS, AND SEASONS

Time
Days and Holidays
Seasons and Weather

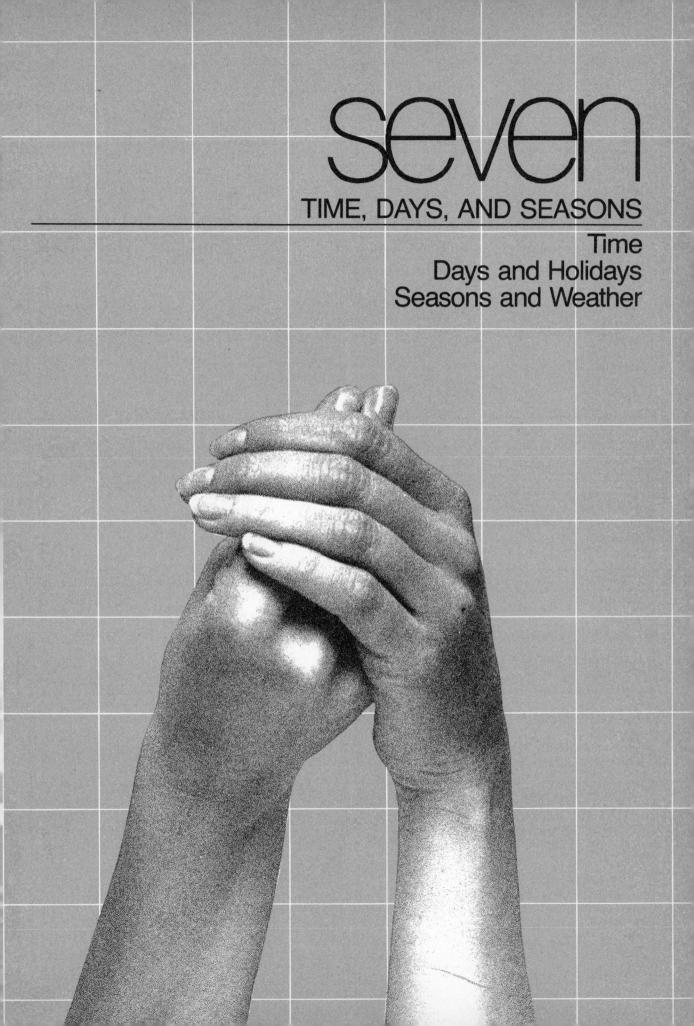

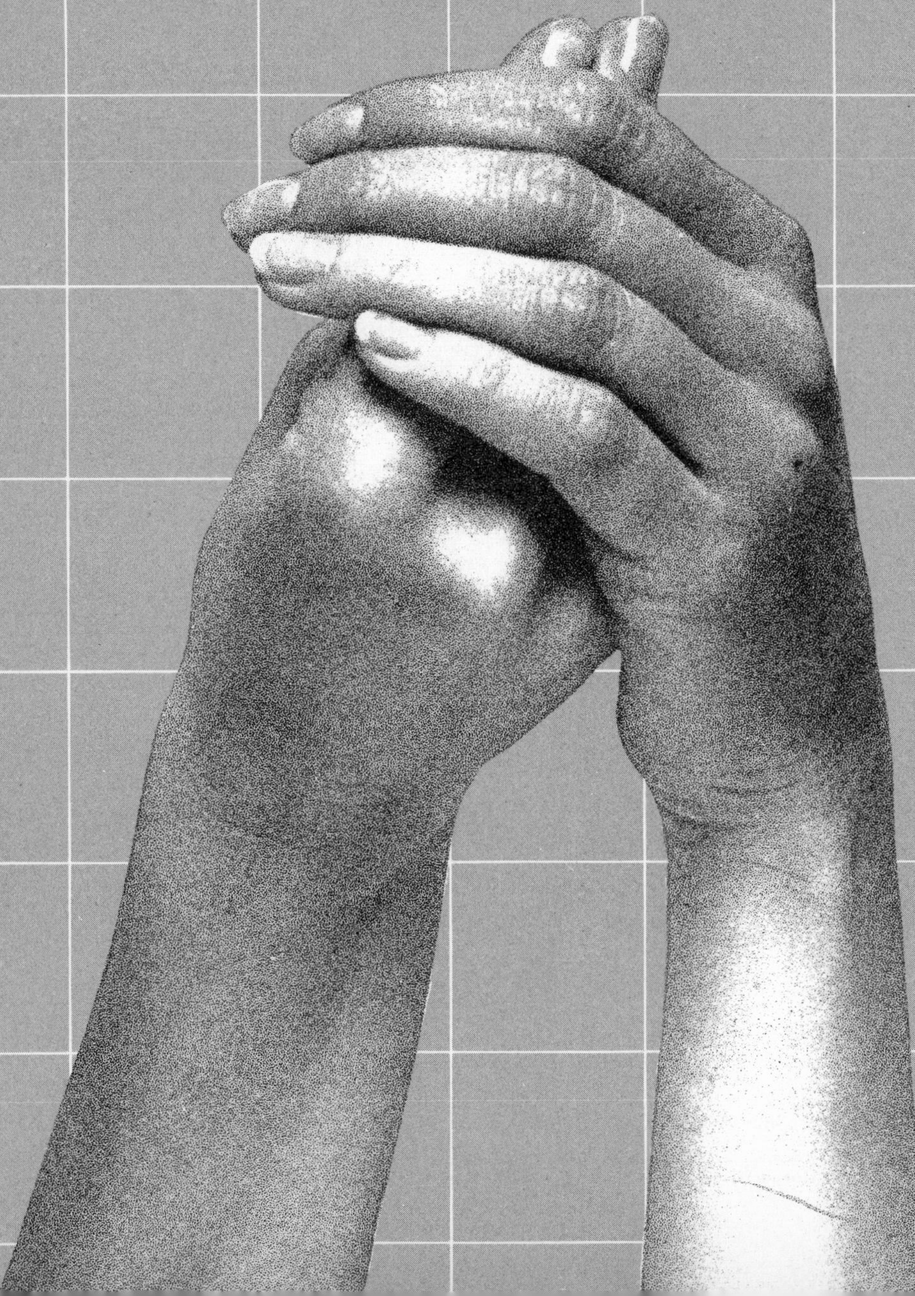

PAST, PRESENT, AND FUTURE TIME

Using the body as a present time referent, many of the time expressions fit logically into a pattern. Expressions that have a future connotation, such as "tomorrow," "later," and "still," have a forward movement from the body. Expressions indicating the past, such as "yesterday," "recently," and "previous," have a backward movement. Present time expressions, such as "today," "now," and "always," are formed directly in front of the body.

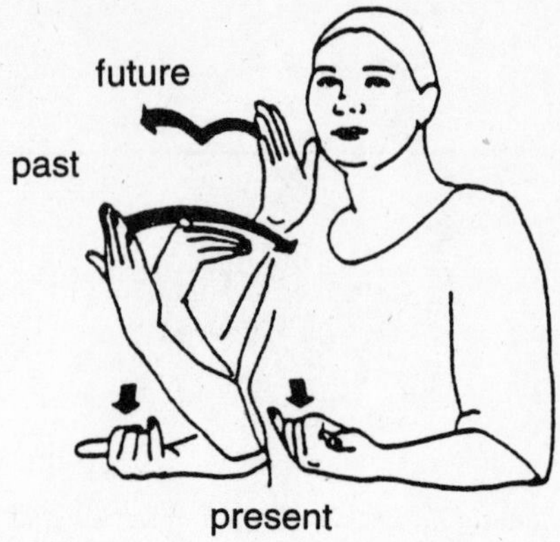

TIME OF DAY

With the left arm as an imaginary horizon, it is easy to visualize signs that indicate the time of day. The right hand becomes the position of the sun over the horizon. Thus, "morning" brings the sun up over the horizon toward the body, and "afternoon" takes the sun down over the horizon away from the body. At "noon" the sun, hence the right hand, is up overhead, and at "midnight," it is directly below the horizon on the other side of the earth.

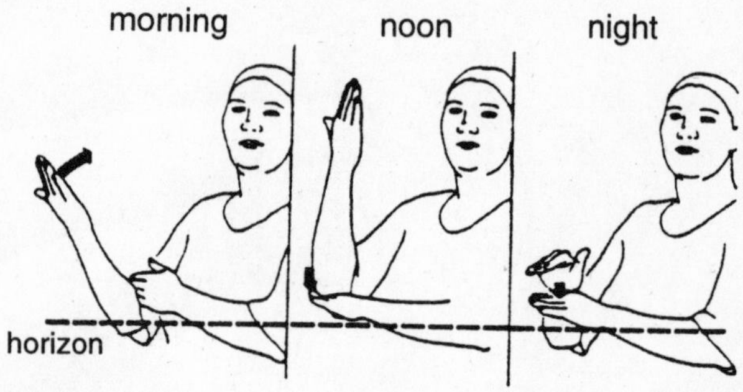

ADDING NUMBERS TO TIME

The numerals one through nine can be incorporated into the time signs "minute," "hour," "day," "week," and "month," forming signs like "six months" or five days." In the same way, "next week," "last week," "last year," and "next year" can incorporate numbers into form concepts like "four years from now" and "three weeks ago."

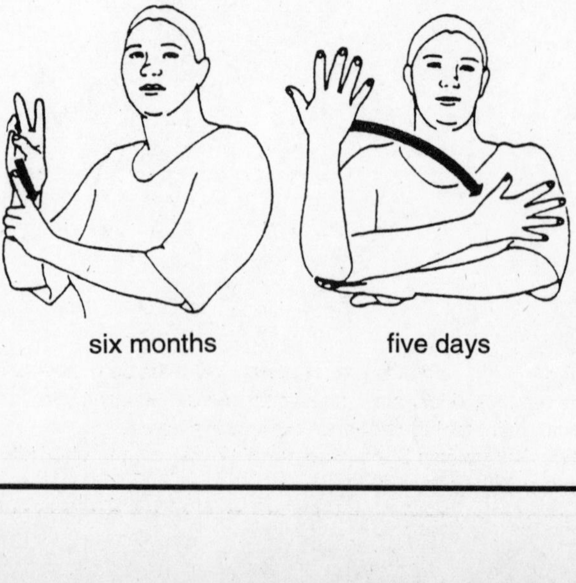

Time

TIME
Tap the bent right index finger on the back of the left wrist held in front of the body. Then hold both "c" hands, palms angled forward near each side of the face.
Hint: "Time" plus the shape of a large clock face.

WATCH
Place the palm side of the right "9" hand on the back of the left wrist held in front of the body.
Hint: The fingers encircle an imaginary wristwatch.

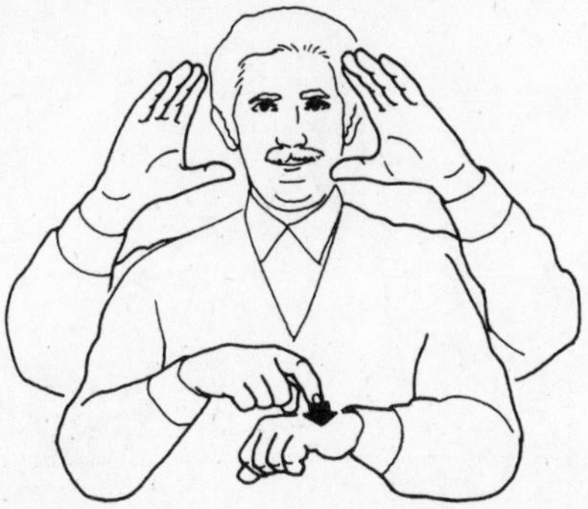

CLOCK
Tap the bent right index finger to the back of the left wrist. Then place both "c" hands, palms facing forward near each side of the face.
Hint: "Time plus showing the size of a large clock face.

HOUR
With the right index finger extended, move the palm side of the right hand in a circle on the open left palm held in front of the chest, palm facing right and fingers pointing up.
Hint: Represents the minute hand making a complete hour movement around the clock.

MINUTE
With the right index finger extended, pivot the palm side of the right hand forward a short distance on the open left hand, palm facing right and fingers pointing up.
Hint: Represents the minute hand moving a short distance on a clock.

SECOND
With the right index finger extended, pivot the palm side of the right hand slightly forward on the open left hand, palm facing right and fingers pointing up.
Hint: Represents the movement of the second hand on a clock.

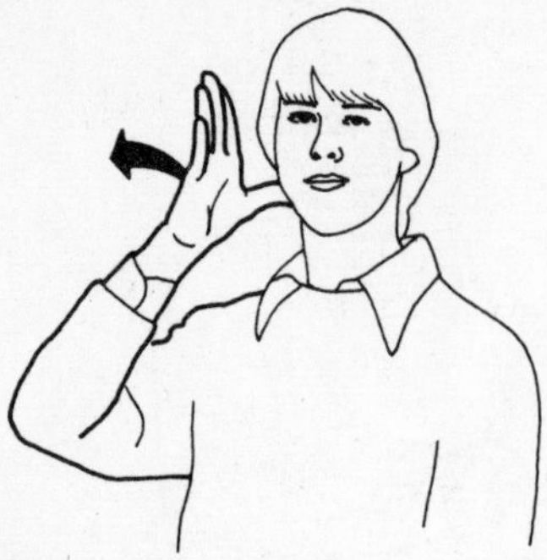

WILL, SHALL
Bring the open right hand, palm facing left and fingers pointing up, forward from the right side of the face.
Hint: The hand moves forward into the future.

FUTURE
Bring the open right hand, palm facing left and fingers pointing up, forward in a double arc from the right side of the face.
Hint: The hand moves forward into the future.

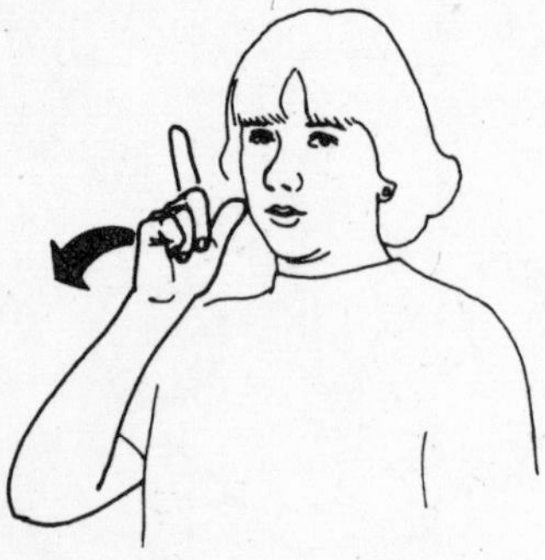

LATER, AFTER A WHILE
Move the right "I" hand, palm facing left, forward from the right side of the face.
Hint: Initialized sign moving forward into the future.

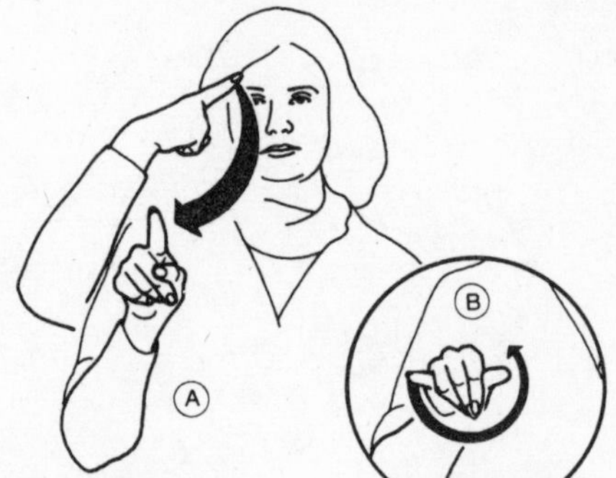

FOREVER
Move the extended right index finger from touching the right side of the forehead downward while changing into a "y" hand. Then move the right "y" hand, palm facing down, it in a small arc to the left.
Hint: "For" plus a modified form of "still."

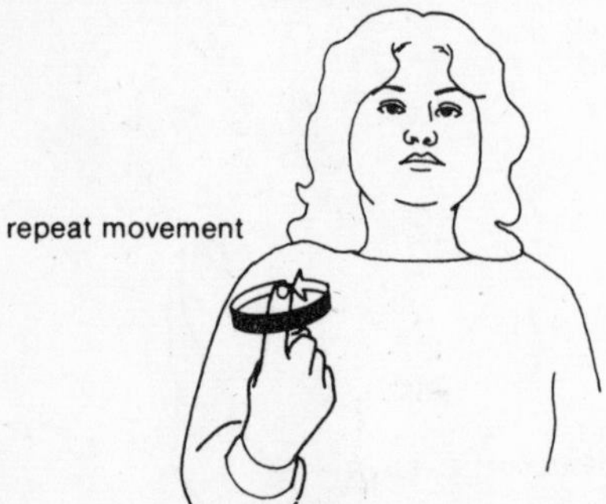

ALWAYS
Move the extended right index finger in a small circle in front of the right shoulder by moving the whole arm, palm facing in and finger pointing up.
Hint: The circular movement shows something never ending.

LAST, FINAL, FINALLY
Bring the extended right little finger downward in front of the chest, striking the extended left little finger as the right hand moves, both palms facing in.
Hint: Shows the last finger of the hand.

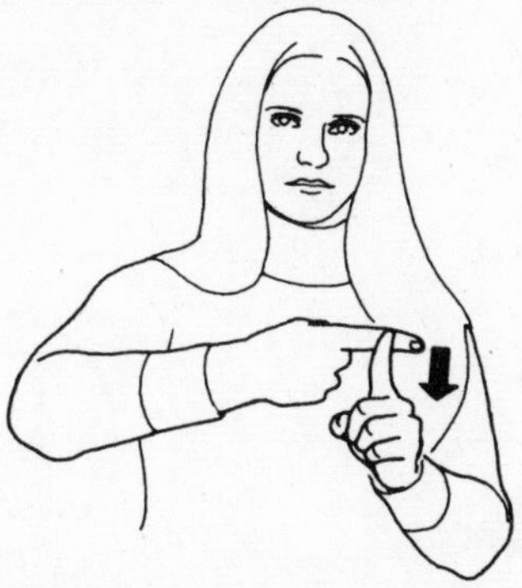

MONTH
Bring the back of the extended right index finger, palm facing in, downward on the thumb side of the extended left index finger held up in front of the body, palm facing right.
Hint: The left hand represents the weeks of a month and the right hand shows the passage of time over them.

WEEK
With the right index finger extended, move the palm side of the right hand across the palm of the open left hand from the heel to the fingers.
Hint: With the left hand representing a calendar, the right hand shows one row or week of dates.

NEXT WEEK, ONE WEEK FROM NOW
Beginning with the right hand with the right index finger extended on the palm of the open left hand, move the right hand forward in an arc.

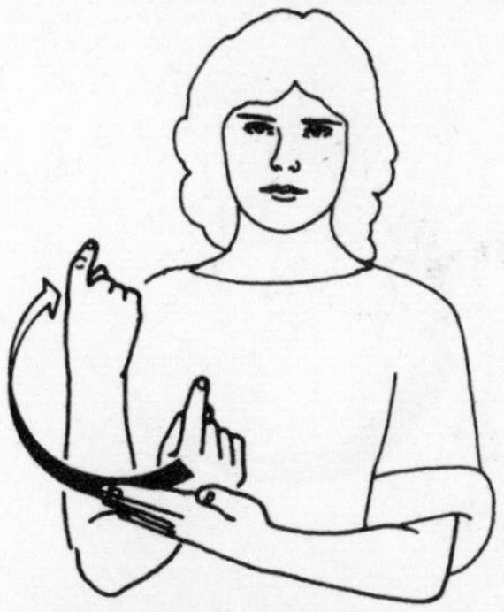

LAST WEEK, ONE WEEK AGO
With the right index finger extended, move the back of the of the right hand across the left palm and back over the right shoulder, both palms facing up.
Hint: "Week" plus a movement back into the past.

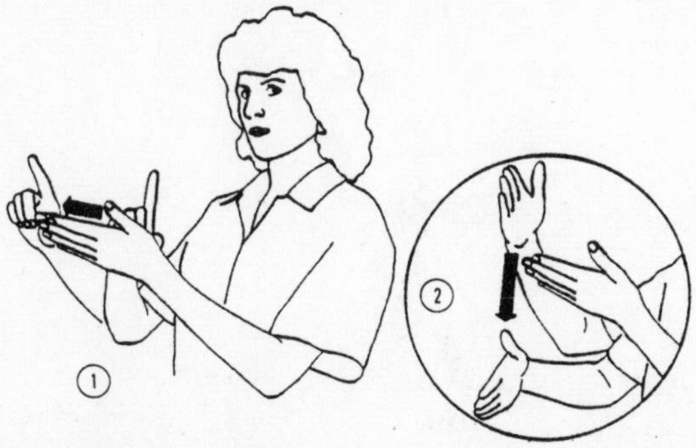

WEEKEND
Move the palm side of the right "1" hand from the heel to the fingers of the open left hand, palm facing in and fingers pointing right. Then move the open right hand, palm facing left, downward near the fingertips of the open left hand.
Hint: "Week" plus "end."

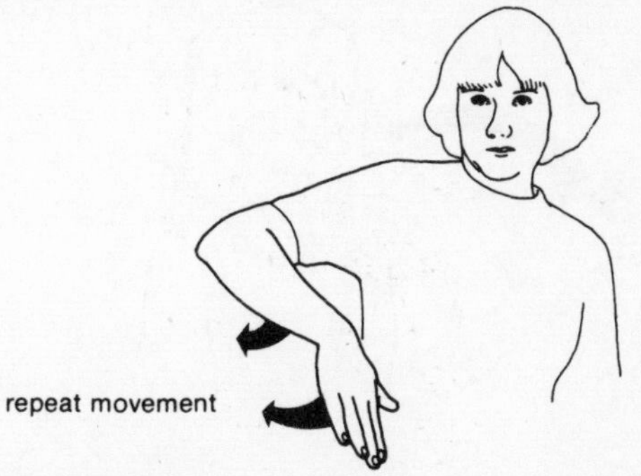

LATE, NOT YET
With the fingers of the right open hand pointing down near the right side of the body, palm facing back and elbow extended, move the right arm back past the waist with a double movement.
Hint: The hand moves back into the past.

PAST, AGO
Move the open right hand, palm facing back, from near the right side of the face back over the right shoulder.
Hint: The hand moves back into the past.

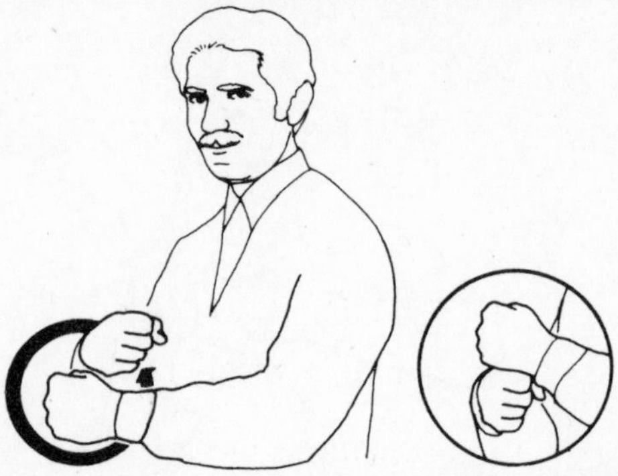

YEAR
Beginning with the right "s" hand over the left "s" hand, both palms facing in, move the right hand in a full circle forward over the left hand, ending with the little-finger side of the right hand on the thumb side of the left hand.
Hint: The earth's movement around the sun.

LAST YEAR
Beginning with the little-finger side of the right "s" hand on the thumb side of the left "s" hand, palms facing in opposite directions, move the right hand back over the right shoulder, extending the right index finger as the hand moves.
Hint: "year plus "one" in the past position.

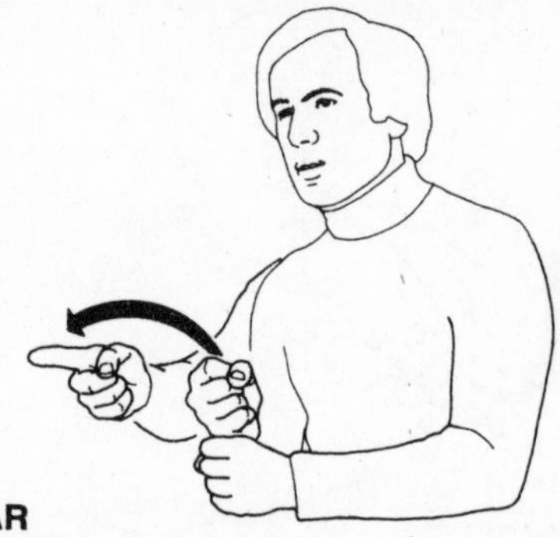

NEXT YEAR
Beginning with the little-finger side of the right "s" hand on the thumb side of the left "s" hand, palms facing in opposite directions, move the right hand forward in an arc while extending the right index finger.
Hint: "Year" plus "one" in the future position.

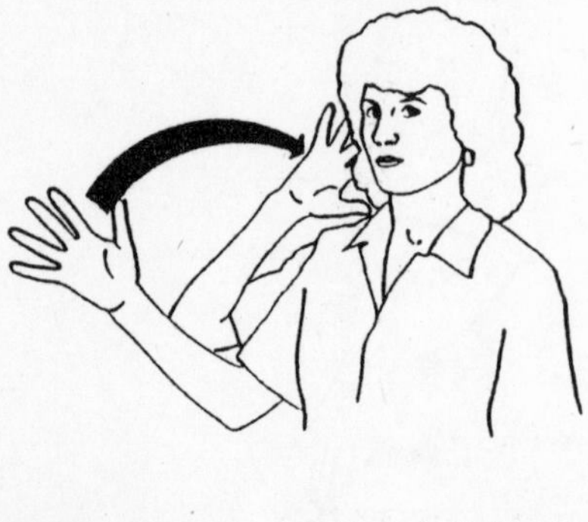

LONG TIME AGO
Move the right "5" hand in a large arc back over the right shoulder, palm facing left.
Hint: The hand moves far back into the past.

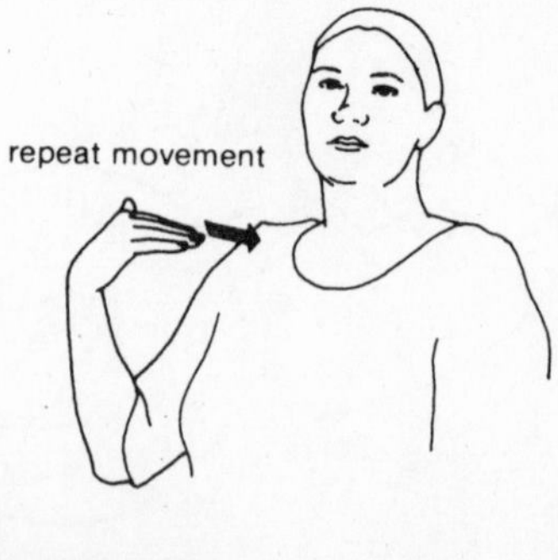

PREVIOUS, USED TO
Tap the fingertips of the bent right hand, palm facing down, against the right shoulder with a double movement.
Hint: The hand moves toward the past.

REGULARLY, REGULAR, APPROPRIATE
With the index fingers of both hands extended, palms facing in opposite directions, tap the little-finger side of the right hand on the thumb side of the left hand with a repeated movement.
Hint: Indicates repeated action.

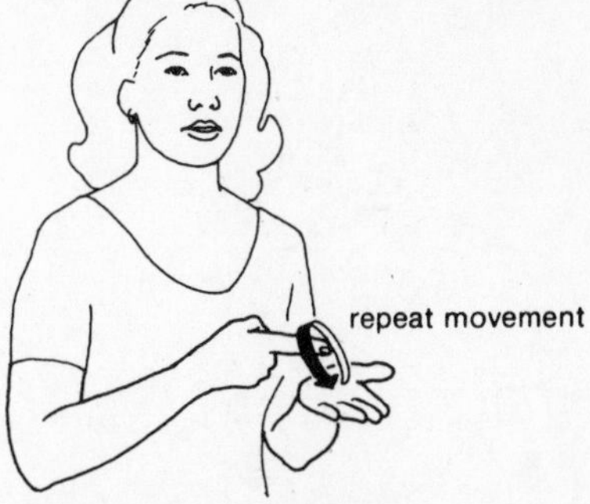

SOMETIMES, OCCASIONALLY
Brush the extended right index finger, palm facing left, upward with a repeated movement on the palm of the open left hand held in front of the chest, palm facing up.
Hint: Represents a periodic repetition.

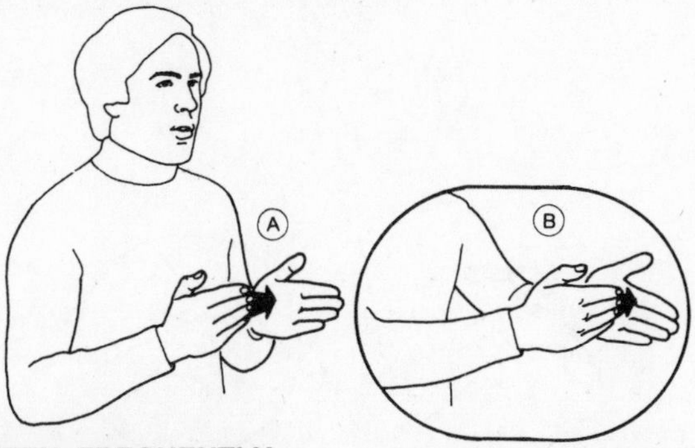

OFTEN, FREQUENTLY
Move the fingertips of the bent right hand against the open left palm held in front of the body, palm facing right and fingers pointing forward. Move the left hand forward a short distance and repeat.
Hint: "Again" repeated to show a repeated activity.

AGAIN, REPEAT
Beginning with the bent right hand next to the open left hand in front of the body, both palms facing up, flip the right hand over and touch the right fingertips into the left palm.

RECENTLY, LATELY, JUST
With the palm facing back, rub the inside of the right "x" index finger with a repeated small movement back on the right cheek.
Hint: Shows a very short time back toward the past.

DAILY, EVERYDAY, EVERY DAY
With the palm side of the right "a" hand on the cheek, twist the hand forward with a repeated movement.
Hint: "Tomorrow" repeated several times.

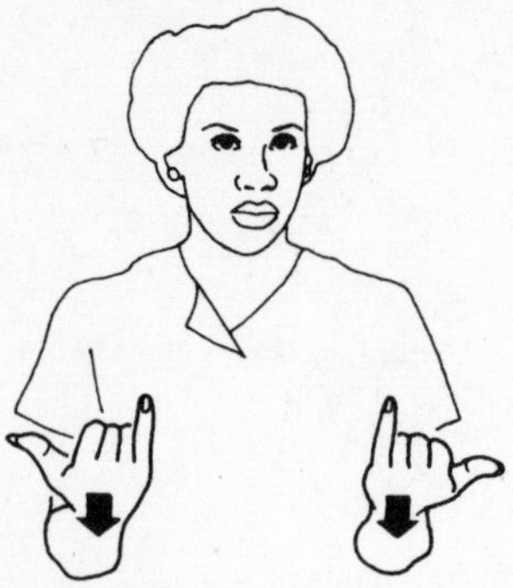

CURRENT, TODAY, PRESENT
Bring both "y" hands, palms facing up, downward with a deliberate movement in front of each side of the body.
Hint: In the present position.

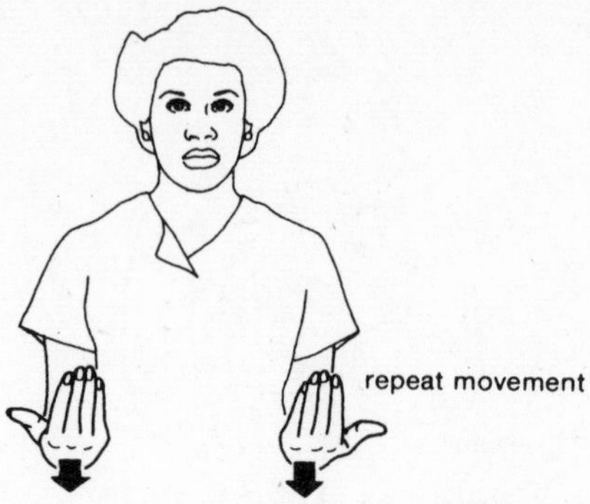

NOW
Bring both bent hands, palms facing up, downward with a deliberate movement in front of each side of the body.
Hint: In the present position.

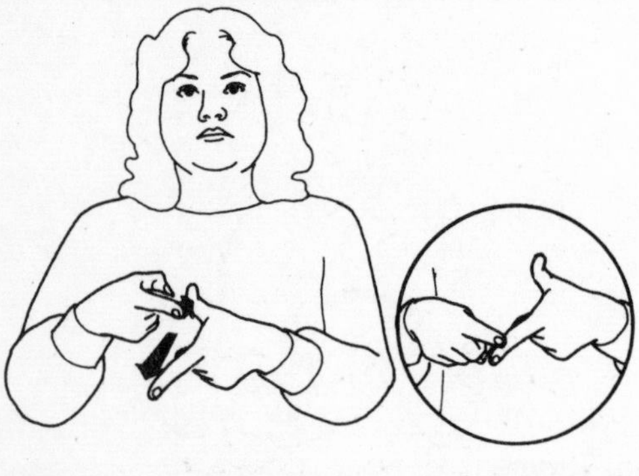

THEN, OR
Touch the extended right index finger first to the thumb and then to the index finger of the left "I" hand held in front of the chest, palm facing right.
Hint: First one and then the other.

EARLY
Push the bent middle finger of the right "5" hand forward across the back of the open left hand held across the chest, both palms facing down.
Hint: The sun going over the horizon.

DURING, WHILE
With both index fingers extended and pointing forward in front of each side of the body, palms facing down, move the hands forward in parallel arcs.
Hint: Shows simultaneous movement into the future.

STILL, YET
Beginning with both "y" hands in front of each side of the chest, palms facing in, move the hands downward toward each other and forward, ending with the palms facing down.
Hint: Shows continuous future action.

UNTIL
Move the extended right index finger, palm facing down, in a forward arc to touch the extended left index finger held up in front of the chest, palm facing right.
Hint: Shows movement of time.

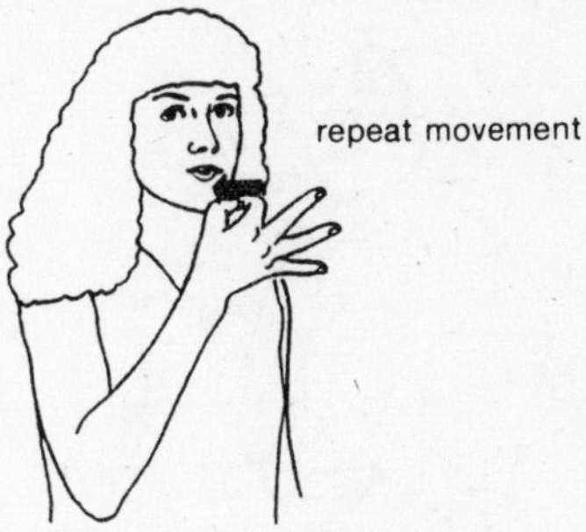

SOON
Tap the fingertips of the right "f" hand, palm facing in, against the chin with a short double movement.

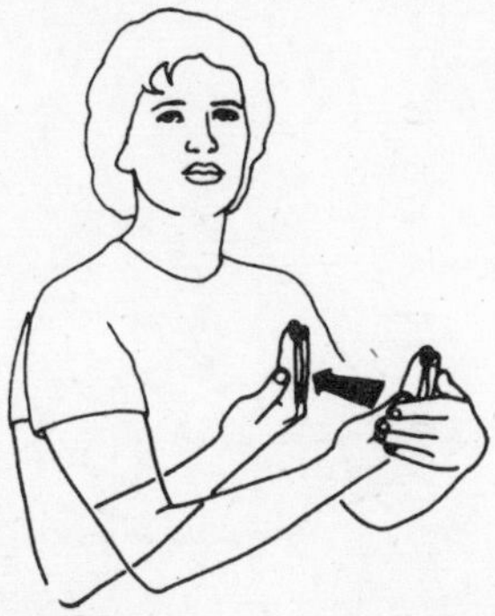

BEFORE
Beginning with the back of the curved right hand in the palm of the open left hand, both palms facing in, bring the right hand in toward the chest.
Hint: Something happening in the past prior to another thing.

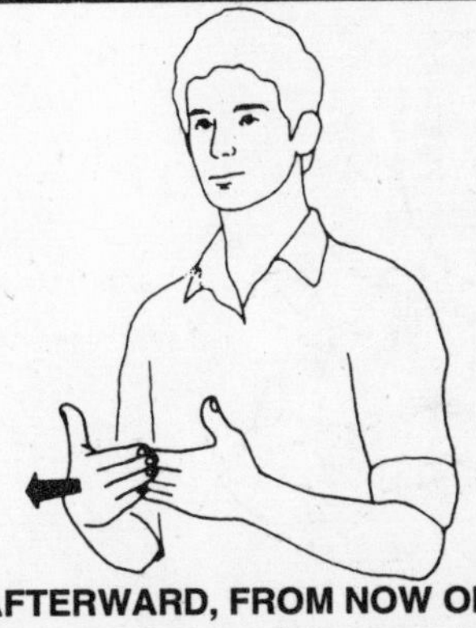

AFTER, AFTERWARD, FROM NOW ON
Beginning with the fingers of the open right hand on the back of the fingers of the open left hand, both palms facing in and the fingers pointing in opposite directions, move the right hand smoothly forward.
Hint: Something happening after another thing in the future.

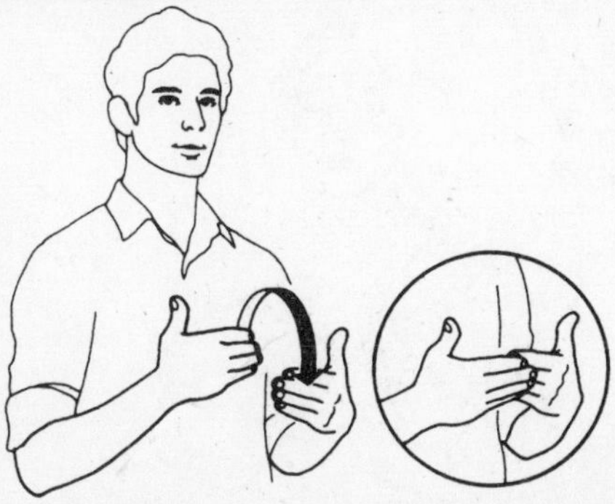

NEXT
Beginning with both open hands in front of the chest, right hand closer to the chest than the left hand and both palms facing in, move the right hand in an arc over the left hand, ending directly behind it.
Hint: Shows something nearby.

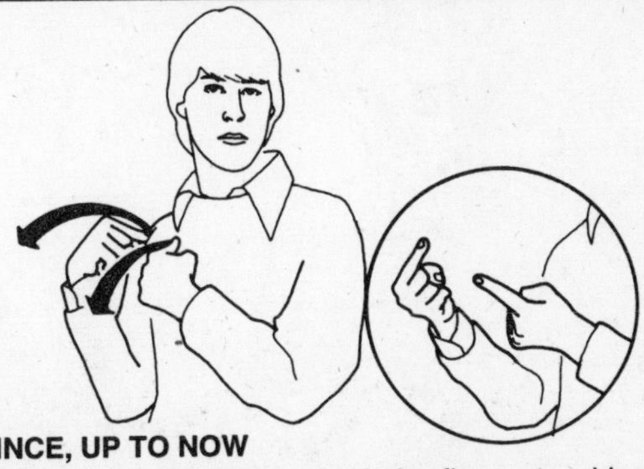

SINCE, UP TO NOW
Beginning with both extended index fingers touching near the right shoulder, move the hands forward by turning the hands over, ending with the fingers pointing forward, palms facing up.
Hint: Indicates a passage of time from the past forward to another point in time.

Days and Holidays

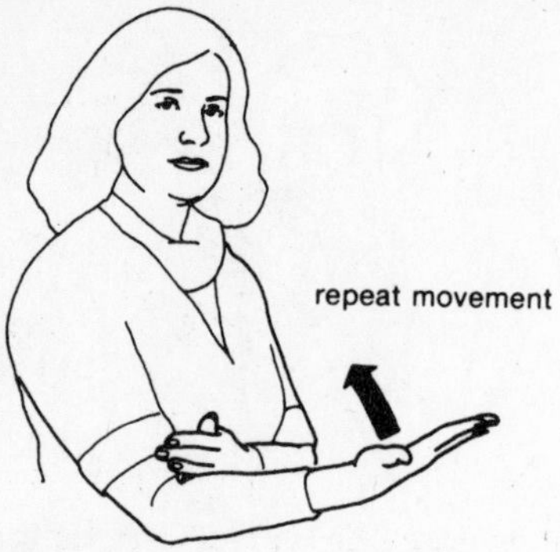

MORNING
With the fingers of the open left hand in the crook of the extended right arm, bring the right open palm upward toward the face.
Hint: Shows the movement of the sun coming up over the horizon in the morning.

NOON, MIDDAY
Place the bent right arm, right open hand extended straight up, on the palm of the open left hand held across the chest, palm facing up.
Hint: Shows the sun straight up above the horizon.

AFTERNOON
With the forearm of the somewhat bent extended right arm on the back of the open left hand, palm facing down, lower the open right hand slightly with a double movement, palm facing down.
Hint: Shows the movement of the sun going down toward the horizon in the afternoon.

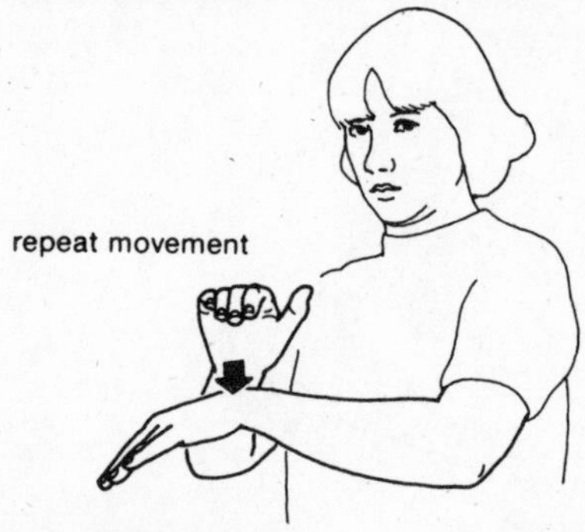

NIGHT, EVENING
Tap the wrist of the bent right hand, palm facing forward, with a double movement on top of the wrist of the open left hand held across the chest, palm facing down.
Hint: Shows the sun setting below the horizon.

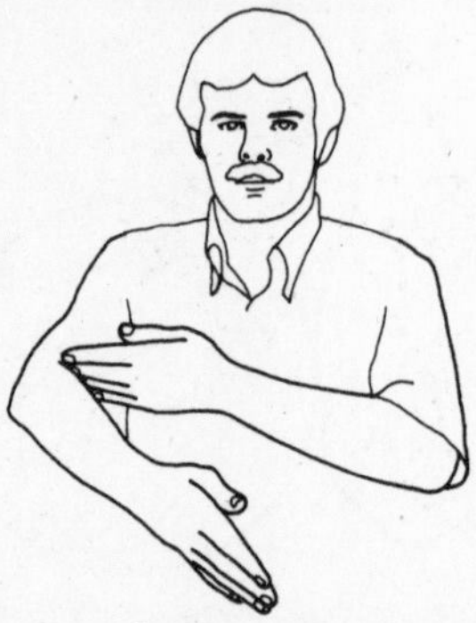

MIDNIGHT
Place the fingertips of the open left hand in the crook of the bent right arm extended downward, palm facing right.
Hint: Shows the sun halfway through its nighttime cycle.

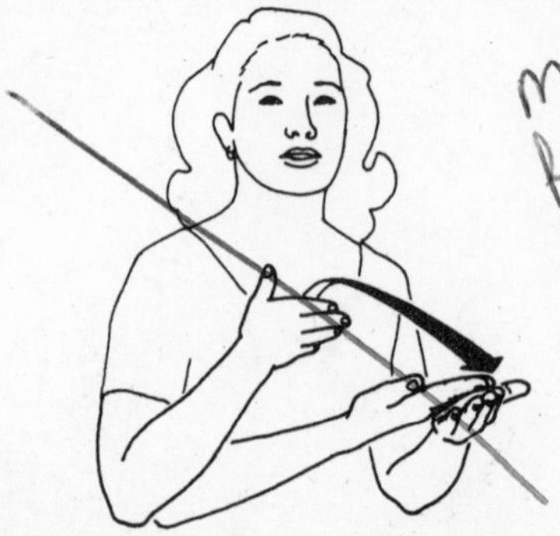

middle finger chin, chest

BIRTHDAY
Move the open right hand from near the chest, palm facing in, downward to land in the palm of the open left hand held in front of the chest, palm facing up.
Hint: "Happy" plus "born."

DAY, ALL DAY
With the extended right index pointing up, place the elbow of the bent right arm on the back of open left hand, palm facing down. Then move the right hand downward toward the left elbow while keeping the right elbow in place. Note: "All day" is generally signed slower than "day."
Hint: The sun moving across the horizon.

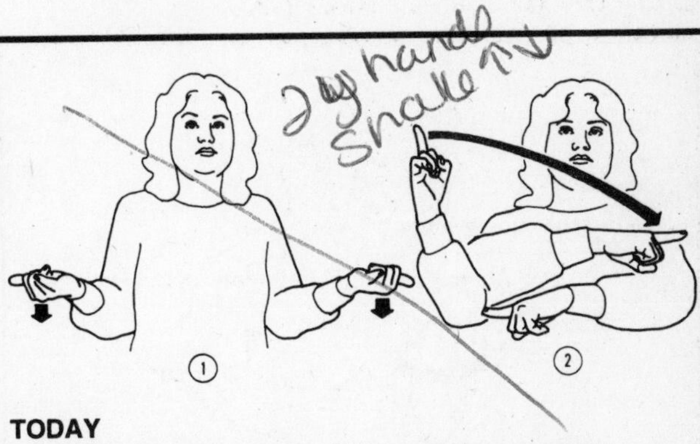

TODAY
Bring both "y" hands, palms facing up, downward with a deliberate movement in front of each side of the body. Then with the extended right index pointing up, place the elbow of the bent right arm on the back of open left hand, palm facing down. Then move the right hand downward toward the left elbow while keeping the right elbow in place.
Hint: "Current" plus "day."

TOMORROW
Move the thumb of the right "10" hand, palm facing left, from the right side of the chin forward in an arc.
Hint: Moving forward into the future.

YESTERDAY
Touch the thumb of the right "10" hand, palm facing left, first to the right side of the chin and then to the right cheek.
Hint: Moving back into the past.

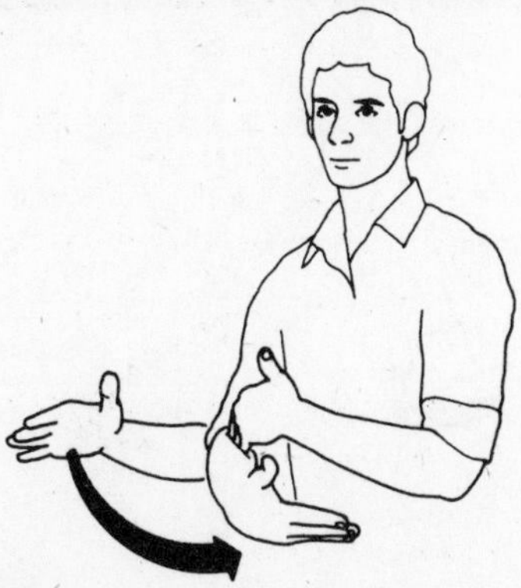

ALL NIGHT
With the fingers of the open left hand in the crook of the bent right arm, move the open right hand, palm facing in, back toward the body under the left arm.
Hint: The movement of the sun through the nighttime cycle.

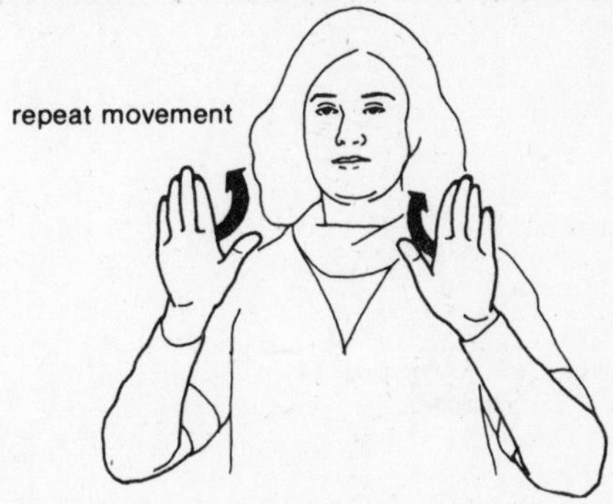

SUNDAY
Move both open hands, palms facing forward, in small circular repeated movements toward each other in front of each shoulder.

MONDAY
Move the right "m" hand, palm facing in, in a small repeated circle in front of the right shoulder.
Hint: Initialized sign.

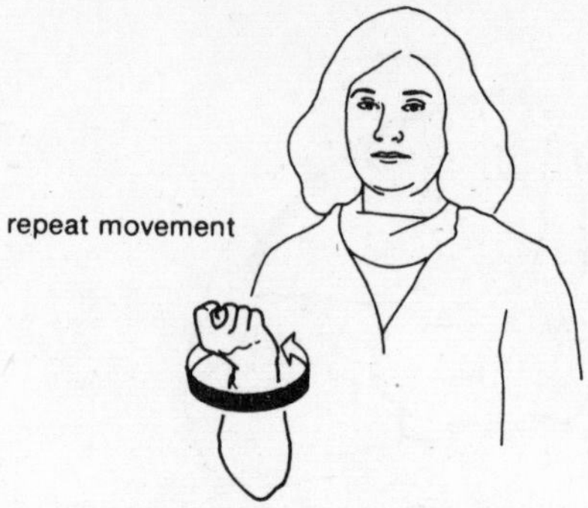

TUESDAY
Move the right "t" hand, palm facing in, in a small repeated circle in front of the right shoulder.
Hint: Initialized sign.

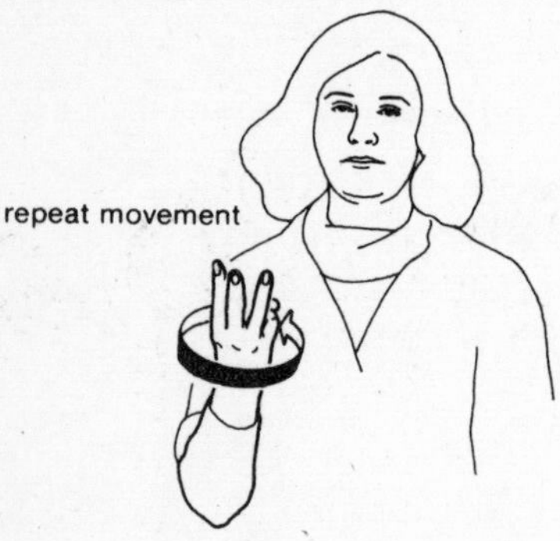

WEDNESDAY
Move the right "w" hand, palm facing in, in a small repeated circle in front of the right shoulder.
Hint: Initialized sign.

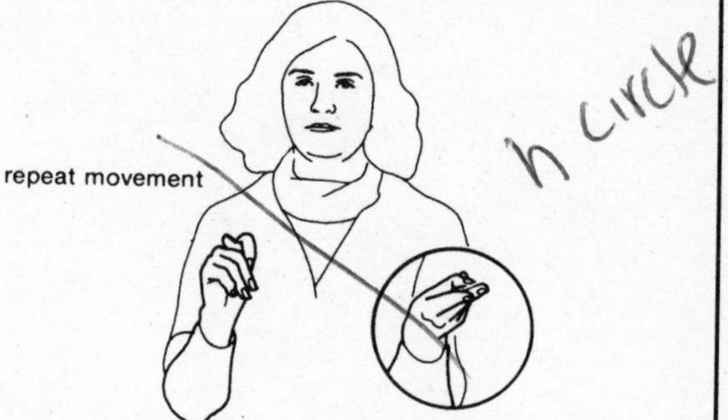

THURSDAY
Beginning with the right "t" hand, palm facing left, in front of the right shoulder, flick the fingers forward forming an "h" hand.
Hint: Abbreviation "t-h."

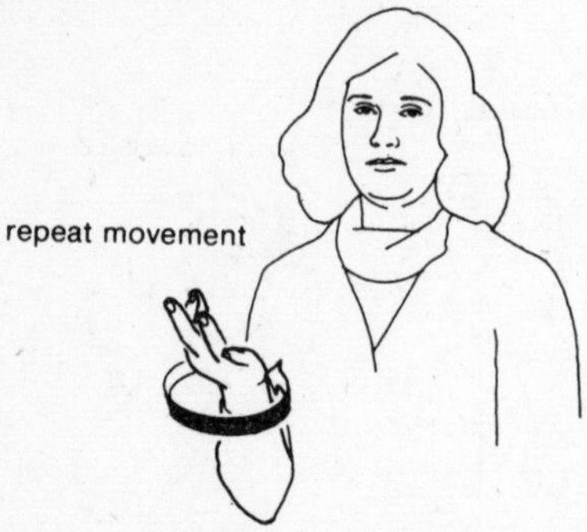

FRIDAY
Move the right "f" hand, palm facing in, in a small repeated circle in front of the right shoulder.
Hint: Initialized sign.

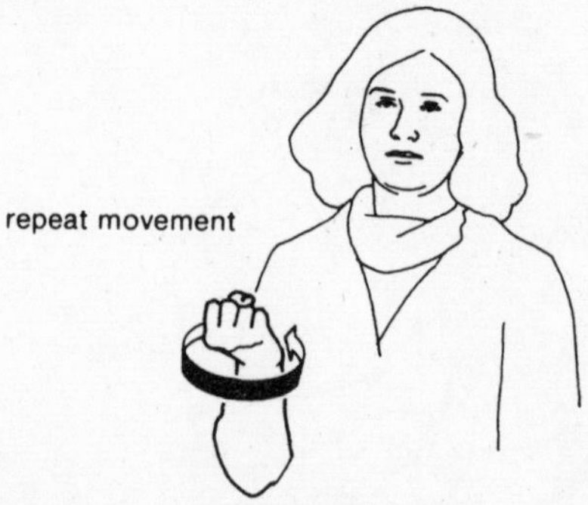

SATURDAY
Move the right "s" hand, palm facing in, in a small repeated circle in front of the right shoulder.
Hint: Initialized sign.

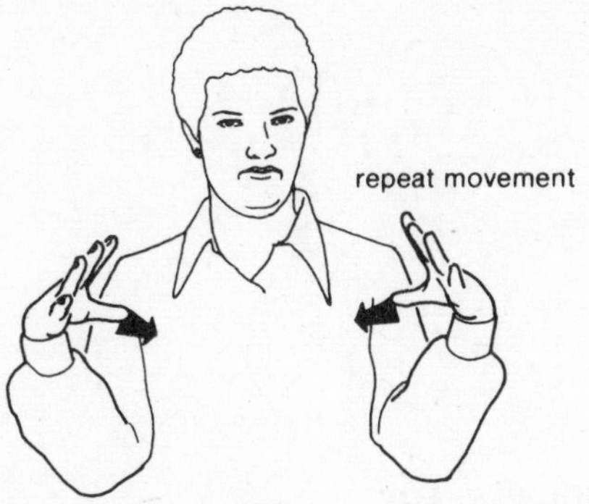

HOLIDAY, VACATION, IDLE
Tap the thumbs of both "5" hands, palms angled in, to near the armpits with a short repeated movement.
Hint: Mime tucking one's thumbs under one's suspenders when having nothing to do.

VALENTINE
Trace the shape of a heart on the chest with the fingertips of both "v" hands.
Hint: Initialized sign showing the location and shape of one's heart.

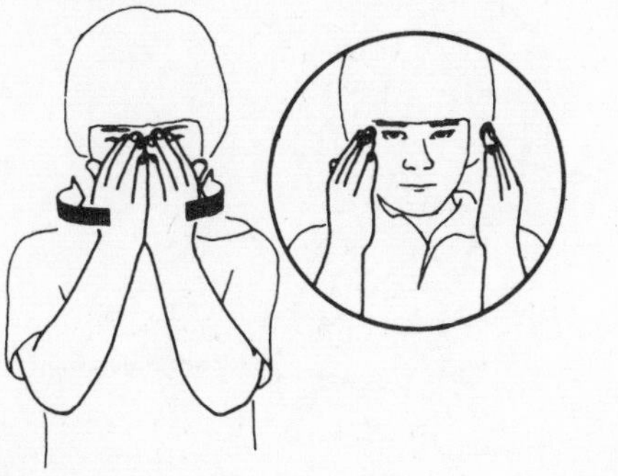

HALLOWEEN
Beginning with the little-finger sides of both curved hands touching in front of the face, fingers pointing up, move the hands outward to each side of the face.
Hint: Removing a mask.

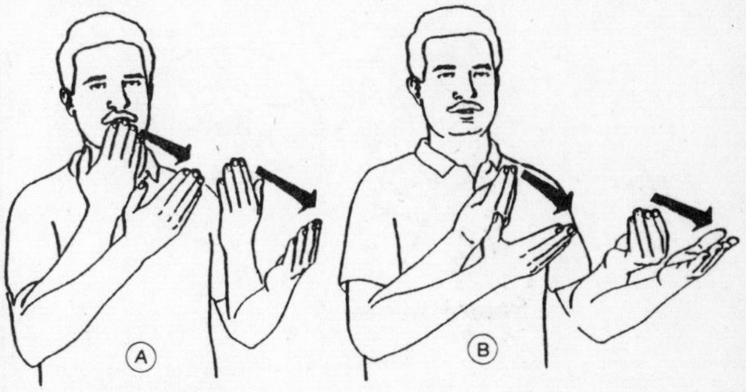

THANKSGIVING
Beginning with the open right hand in front of the mouth and the open left hand somewhat forward, both palms facing in and fingers pointing up, move both hands forward while closing the fingers to each thumb. Then move both hands forward again while changing to open hands again.
Hint: "Thank you" plus "give" directed toward God.

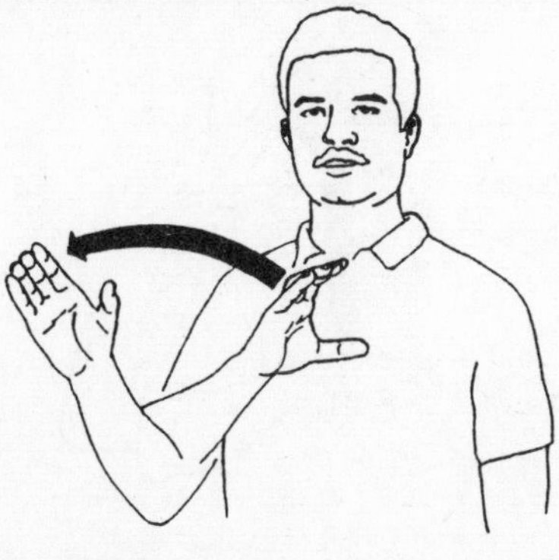

CHRISTMAS
Move the right "c" hand, palm facing left, from in front of the chest in an arc to the right.
Hint: Initialized sign with a gesture as if opening a present.

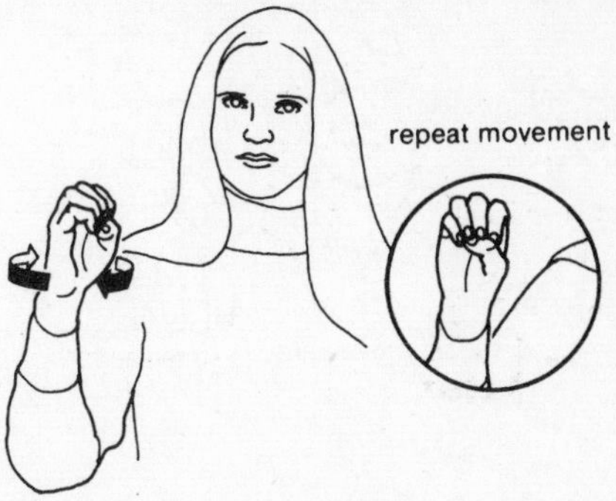

EASTER
Twist the right "e" hand forward and back in front of the right shoulder.
Hint: Initialized sign.

Seasons and Weather

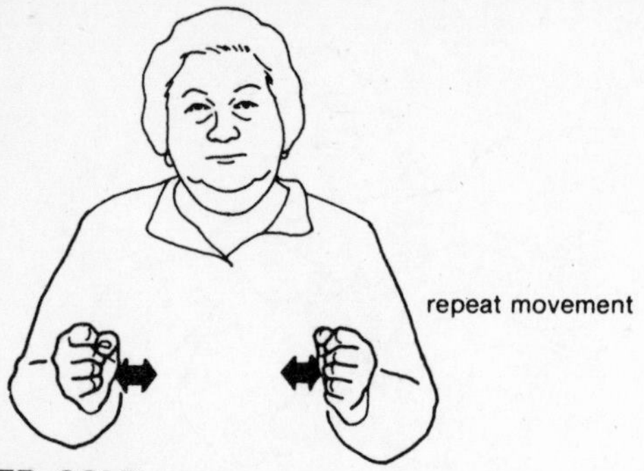

WINTER, COLD
Shake both "s" hand, palms facing each other, back and forth with a short repeated movement in front of each side of the chest.
Hint: Shivering in winter.

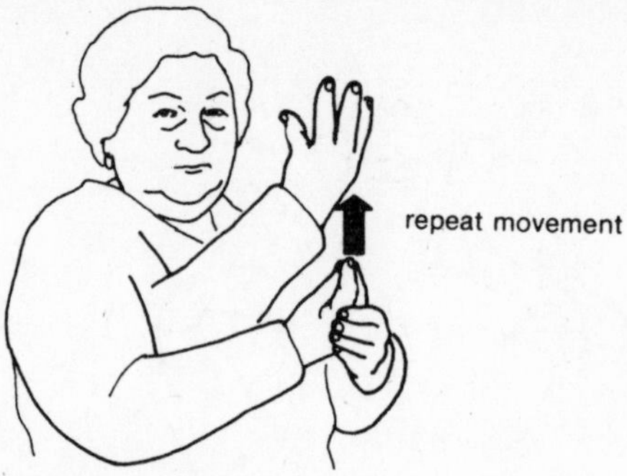

SPRING, GROW, PLANT
Beginning with the left hand cupped around the right flattened "o" hand, palm facing up, move the right hand upward with a repeated movement opening into a "5" hand each time.
Hint: A plant sprouting through the soil.

SUMMER
Bring the extended right index finger, palm facing down and finger pointing left, across the forehead with a double movement changing into an "x" hand each time as the hand moves.
Hint: Wiping sweat off the brow.

FALL, AUTUMN
Bring the index-finger side of the right "b" hand, palm facing down, downward with a double movement on the bent left arm near the elbow.
Hint: Leaves falling from a tree.

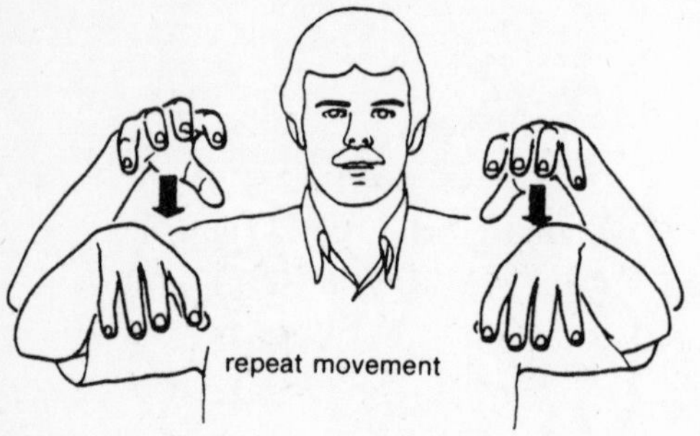

RAIN
Beginning with both loose "claw" hands in front of each shoulder, palms facing down, bring the hands downward with a double movement.
Hint: Raindrops falling.

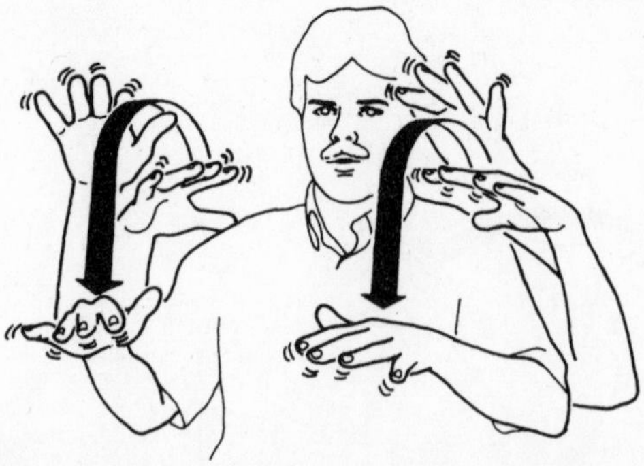

SNOW
Beginning with both "5" hands in front of each shoulder, palms facing down, move the hands forward and downward in large arcs while wiggling the fingers.
Hint: Snowflakes falling.

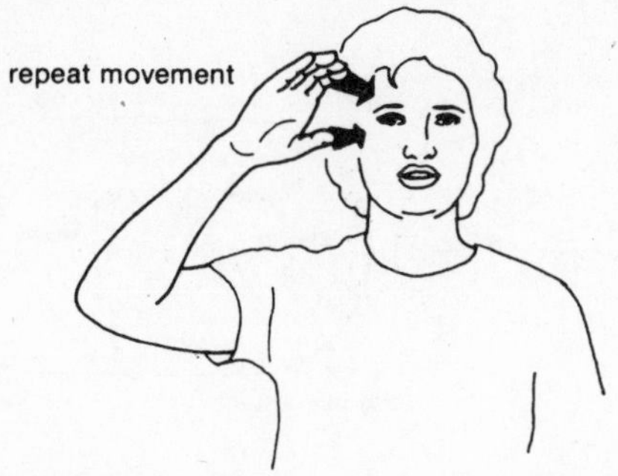

SUN
Bring the index-finger side of the right "c" hand, palm facing forward, against the right side of the forehead with a double movement.
Hint: Shading the eyes from the sun.

MOON
Place the curved right index finger and thumb at the right temple encircling the right eye.
Hint: Fingers represent the crescent shape of the moon.

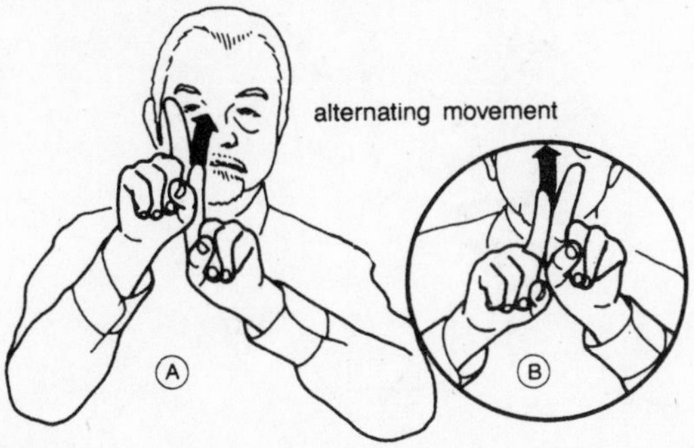

STARS
Brush the sides of both extended index fingers together with an alternating movement as the hands move upward, palms facing forward.
Hint: Indicate the twinkling rays radiating from stars.

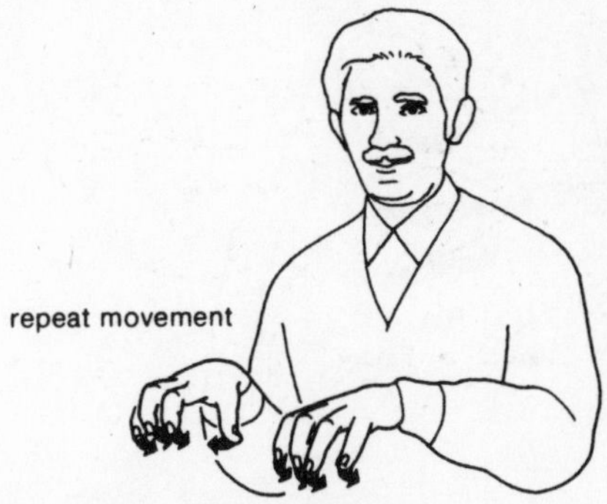

FROST, FREEZE, FROZEN, ICE
With both "claw" hands in front of the body, palms facing down, constrict the fingers with a repeated movement.
Hint: A stiffening frozen position.

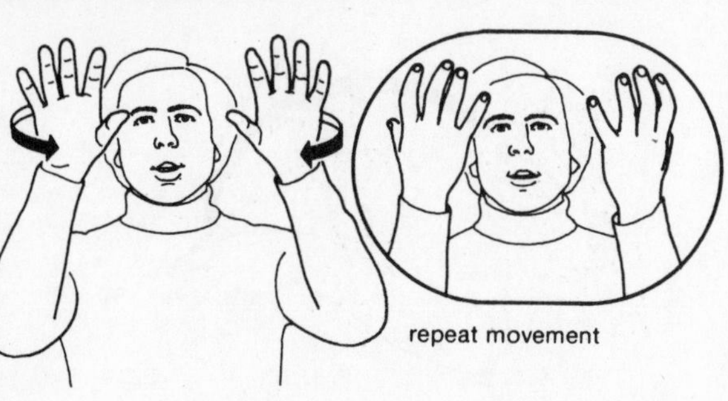

CLOUD
Beginning with both "5" hands in front of each side of the head, palms facing forward, move the hands forward in a outward arcs, ending with the palms facing in. Repeat.
Hint: Follows the shape of fluffy, billowy clouds.

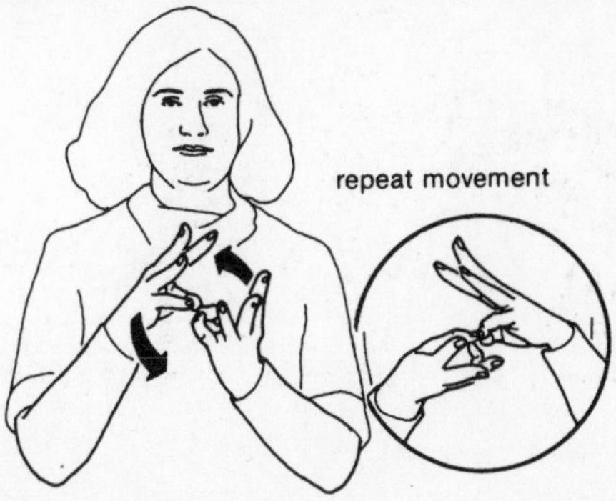

WEATHER
With the bent fingertips of both "w" hands touching in front of the chest, palms facing each other, twist the wrists with a repeated movement.
Hint: Initialized sign formed with a movement like the sign for "change" indicating that the weather changes so much.

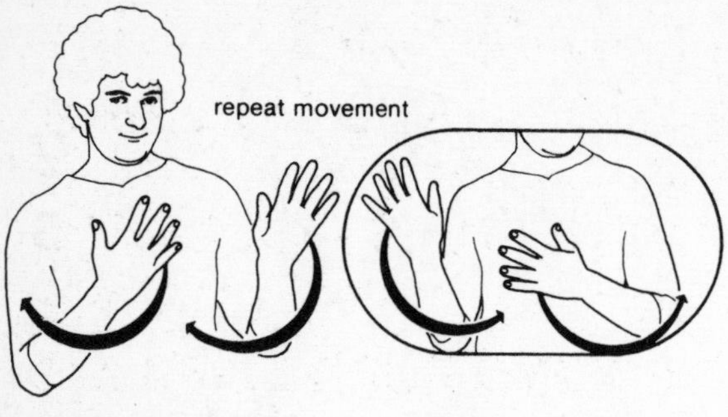

WIND, BREEZE
Beginning with both "5" hands in front of the left side of the body, palms facing each other and fingers pointing up, swing the hands in arcs across the chest with a repeated movement.
Hint: Shows the movement of air.

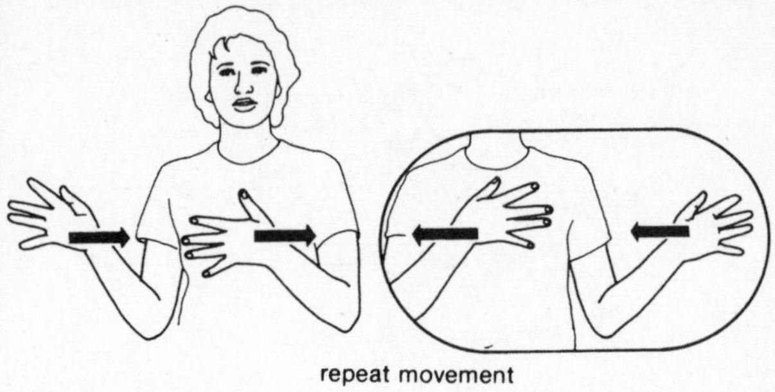

STORM
Beginning with the left "5" hand in front of the chest, palm facing in, and the right "5" hand to the right side of the body, palm facing forward, move the hands with a smooth repeated movement from side to side in front of the body, reversing hand positions on opposite sides of the body.
Hint: Wind whipping the air around.

TORNADO
Beginning with the right extended index finger pointing down in front of the right shoulder and the left extended index finger pointing up in front of the body, move the right finger upward in a spiraling movement.
Hint: Follows the shape of a tornado funnel.

HURRICANE
Beginning with the right "claw" hand above the left "claw" hand in front of the chest, palms facing each other, move the right hand upward in a spiraling movement.
Hint: Shows the whipping winds of a hurricane.

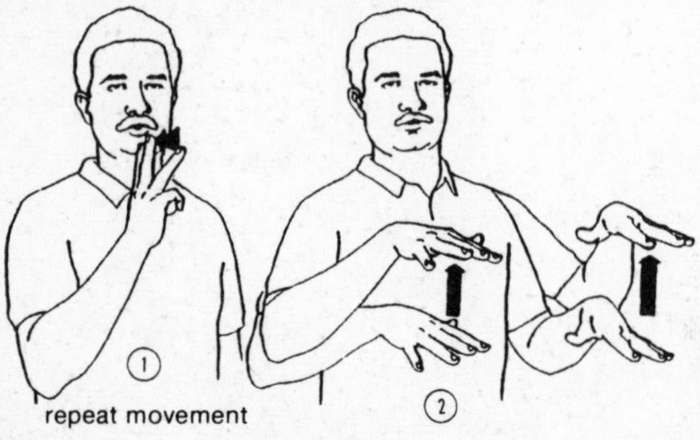

FLOOD
Tap the index-finger side of the right "w" hand, palm facing left, against the chin with a double movement. Then beginning with both "5" hands in front of the chest, fingers pointing forward and both palms facing down, raise both hands simultaneously.
Hint: "Water" plus showing the water rising.

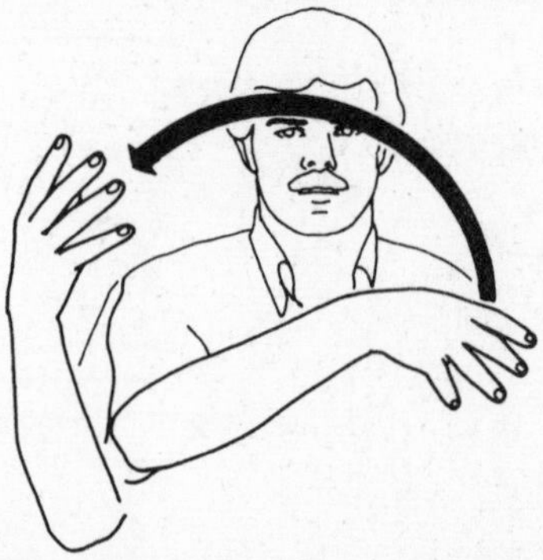

RAINBOW
Move the right "4" hand from in front of the left shoulder in an arc in front of the face, palm facing in and fingers pointing left.
Hint: The fingers follow the colors and shape of a rainbow.

eight

PLACES

Cities and States
Countries
Location and Direction
Buildings

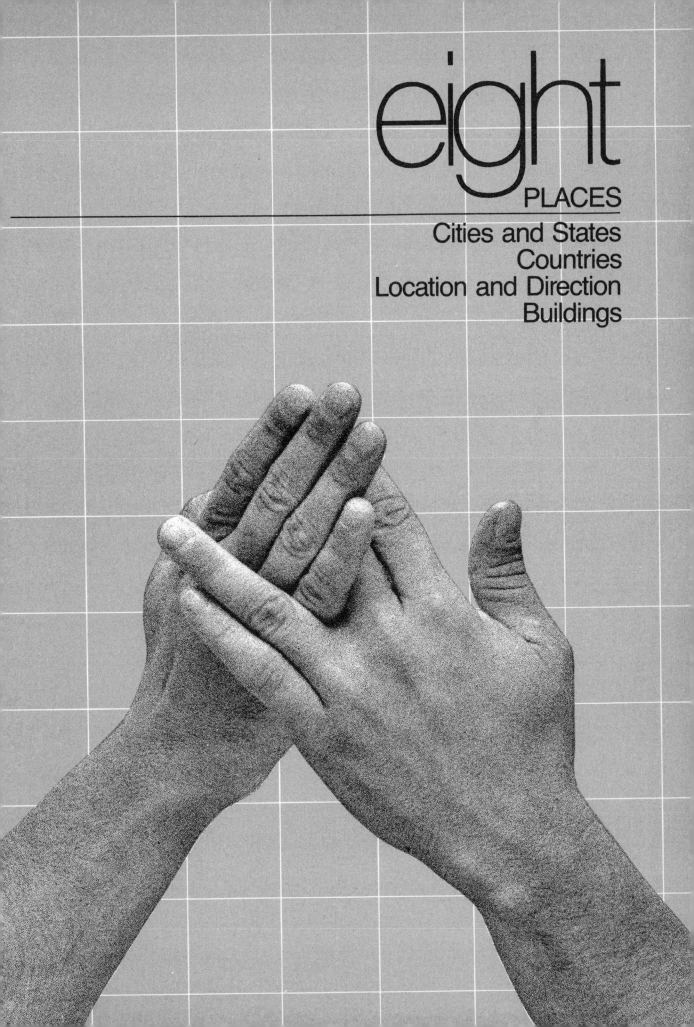

SIGNS FOR COUNTRIES

For many years, the signs in American Sign Language for the names of countries were signs developed in the United States generally based on some identifiable feature of people or activities from the various countries. These signs were not necessarily the signs that people from those countries used in referring to themselves. As deaf people traveled and attended international meetings, they became more sensitive to using the signs preferred by natives of other countries and began to use them as a part of American Sign Language.

Africa
(old American sign based on facial feature)

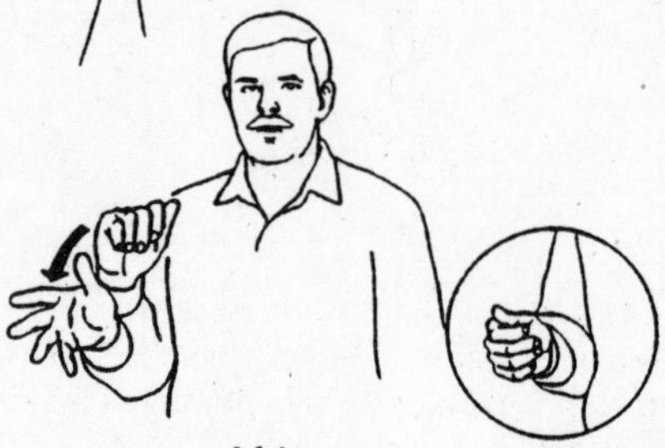

Africa
(new preferred sign based on shape of country)

DIRECTION WITH "LOOK"

Using the extended index and middle fingers of either or both hands to represent the eyes, point them in the direction of the object you are referring to. The hands should be held in front of the face at about nose level, and your eyes should peer down the fingers in the direction they are pointing. In the way you can form "look at," "look around," "look down," "look back," and so forth.

look at (the bat)

USING CLASSIFIERS TO SHOW MOVEMENT

Special handshapes, called classifiers, can be used to represent various objects, vehicles, people, etc. It is possible to represent an object on each hand at the same time. For example, the classifier for vehicles uses a "3" handshape. By using the Classifier 3 on each hand you can demonstrate two vehicles and how their movement and location is related. The vehicles can follow , pass, or race each other and thus clearly describe what is happening just by moving the two hands.

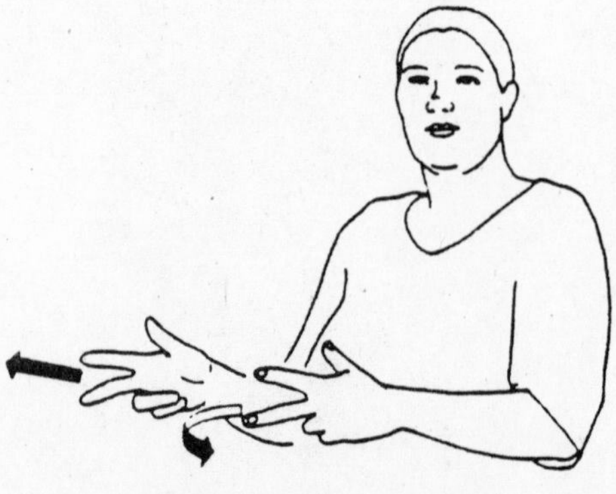

The car behind me turned left.

Cities and States

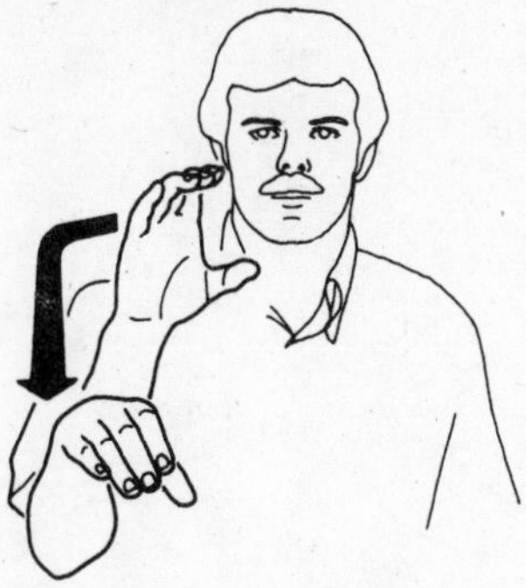

CHICAGO
Move the right "c" hand, palm facing forward, from in front of the right shoulder first to the right and then downward.
Hint: Initialized sign.

NEW YORK
Move the palm side of the right "y" hand with a repeated movement across the palm of the open left hand held in front of the chest, palm facing up.
Hint: Initialized sign.

ATLANTA
Touch the thumb side of the right "a" hand, palm facing left, first to the left side of the chest and then to the right.
Hint: Initialized sign.

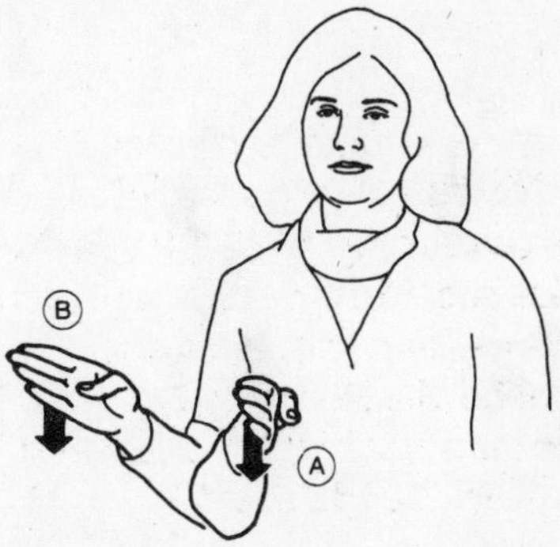

BALTIMORE
Move the right "b" hand, palm facing left and fingers pointing forward, downward first in front of the right side of the body and then to the right.
Hint: Initialized sign.

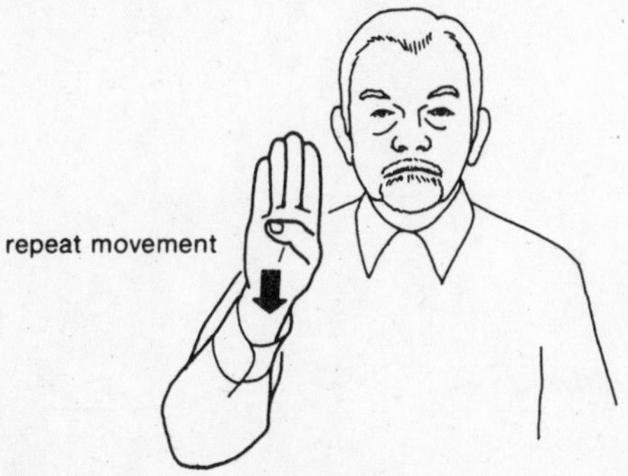

BOSTON
Bring the right "b" hand, palm facing forward, downward with a short double movement in front of the right shoulder.
Hint: Initialized sign.

DETROIT
Move the right "d" hand, palm facing forward, from in front of the chest to the right and then downward.
Hint: Initialized sign.

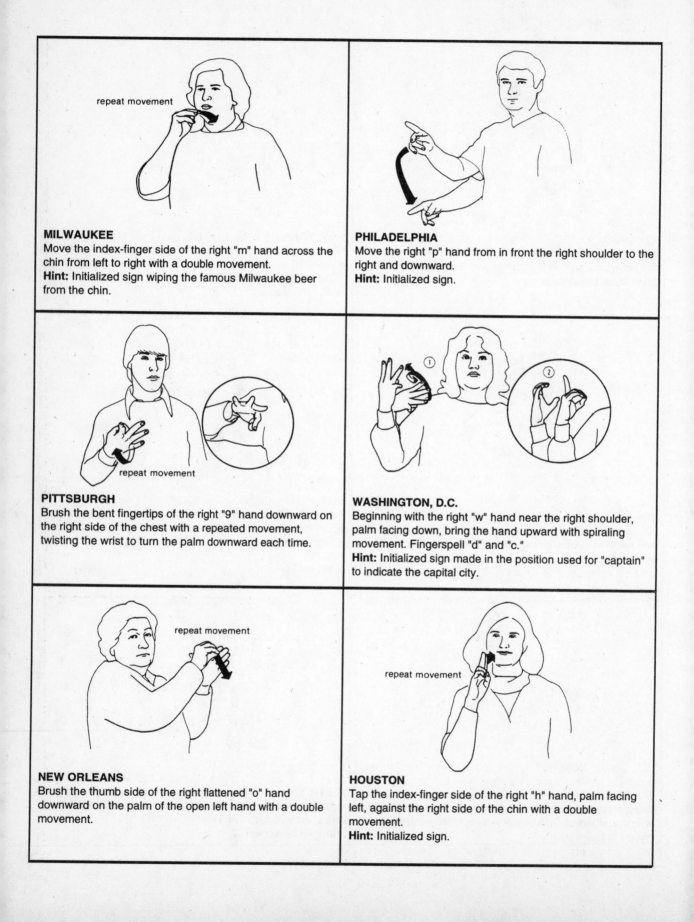

MILWAUKEE
Move the index-finger side of the right "m" hand across the chin from left to right with a double movement.
Hint: Initialized sign wiping the famous Milwaukee beer from the chin.

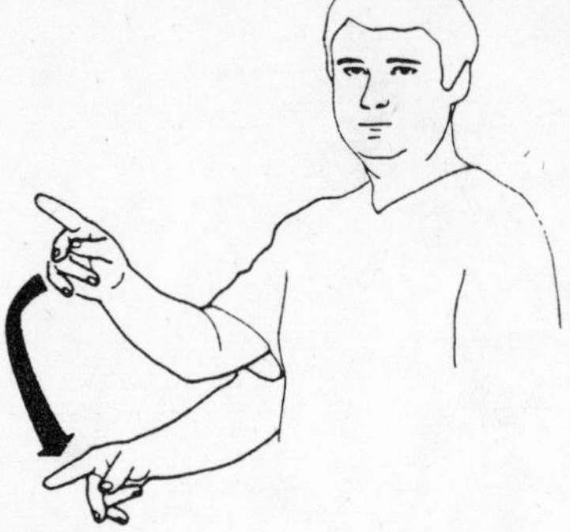

PHILADELPHIA
Move the right "p" hand from in front the right shoulder to the right and downward.
Hint: Initialized sign.

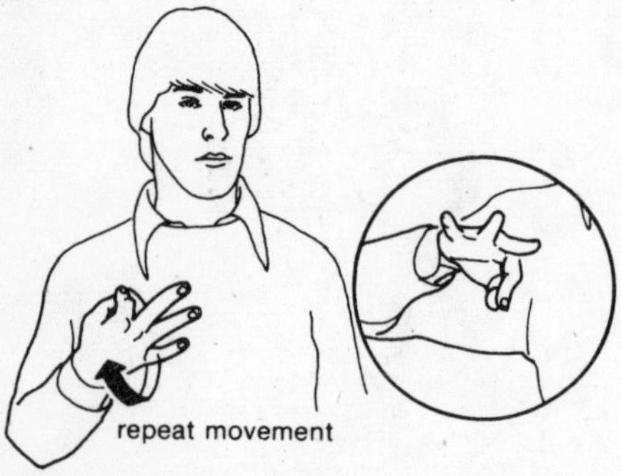

PITTSBURGH
Brush the bent fingertips of the right "9" hand downward on the right side of the chest with a repeated movement, twisting the wrist to turn the palm downward each time.

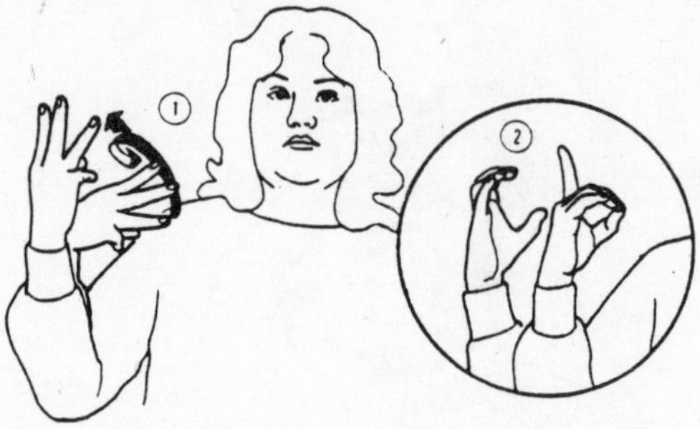

WASHINGTON, D.C.
Beginning with the right "w" hand near the right shoulder, palm facing down, bring the hand upward with spiraling movement. Fingerspell "d" and "c."
Hint: Initialized sign made in the position used for "captain" to indicate the capital city.

NEW ORLEANS
Brush the thumb side of the right flattened "o" hand downward on the palm of the open left hand with a double movement.

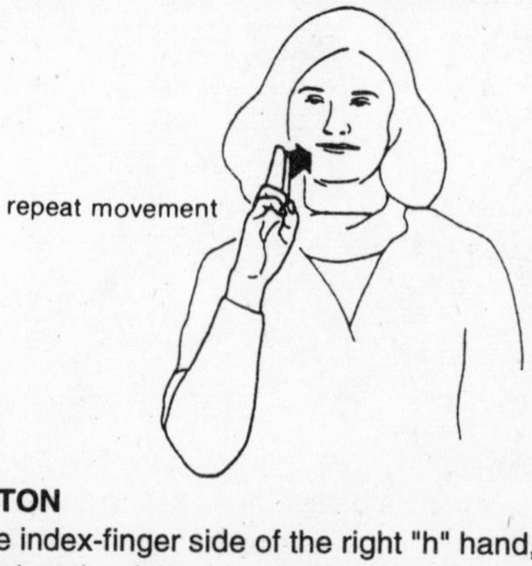

HOUSTON
Tap the index-finger side of the right "h" hand, palm facing left, against the right side of the chin with a double movement.
Hint: Initialized sign.

ARIZONA
Touch the thumb of the right "a" hand, palm facing left, first to the right side and then the left side of the chin.
Hint: Initialized sign formed similar to the sign for "dry" symbolizing the weather in Arizona.

TEXAS
Move the right "x" hand, palm facing forward, to the right and then downward in front of the body.

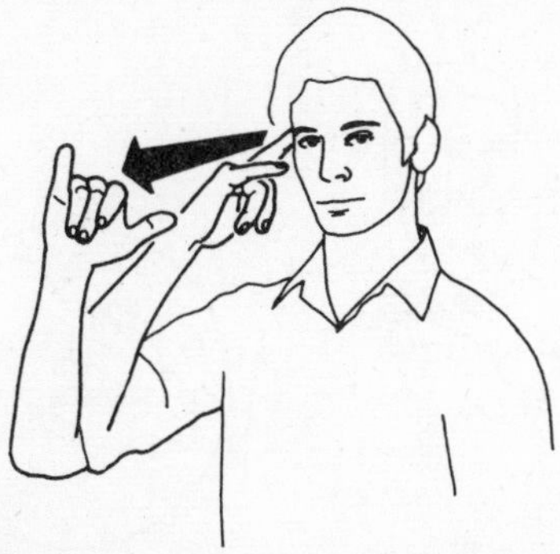

CALIFORNIA
With the right thumb, index finger, and little fingers extended, touch the index finger near the right ear. Then twist the wrist quickly forward while changing into a "y" hand, ending with the palm facing forward.
Hint: Similar to the sign for "gold," symbolizing California's gold rush.

HAWAII, HAWAIIAN
With the fingers of the right "h" hand, palm facing in, draw a circle around the face.
Hint: Initialized sign.

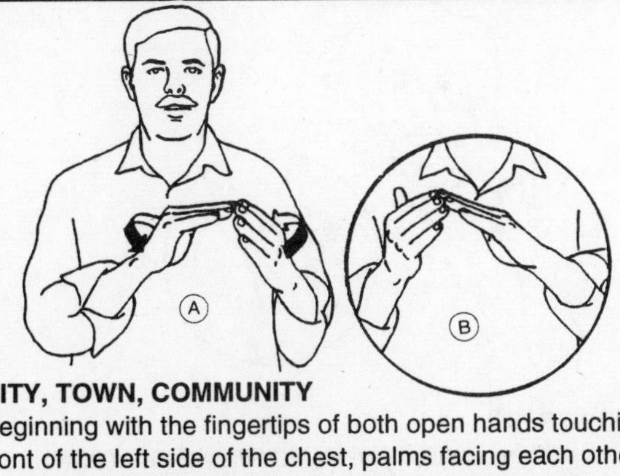

CITY, TOWN, COMMUNITY
Beginning with the fingertips of both open hands touching in front of the left side of the chest, palms facing each other at an angle, separate the hands slightly, twist the wrists and touch the fingertips again while moving the hands to the right.
Hint: Represents the roofs of buildings.

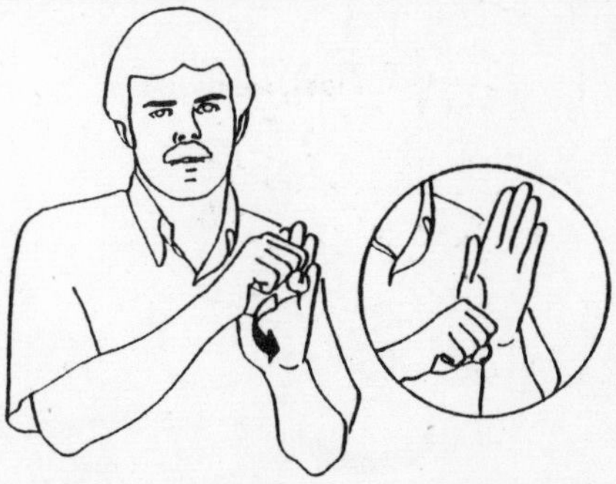

STATE
Touch the thumb side of the right "s" hand, palm facing forward, first on the fingers and then on the heel of the palm of the left open hand held in front of the chest, palm facing right and fingers pointing up.
Hint: Initialized sign.

Countries

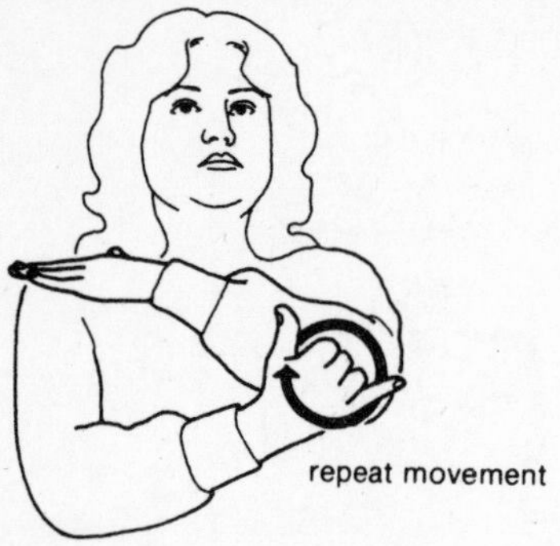

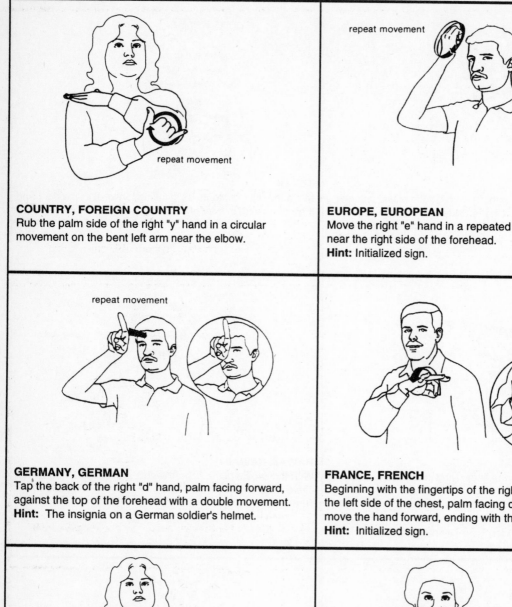

COUNTRY, FOREIGN COUNTRY
Rub the palm side of the right "y" hand in a circular movement on the bent left arm near the elbow.

EUROPE, EUROPEAN
Move the right "e" hand in a repeated circular movement near the right side of the forehead.
Hint: Initialized sign.

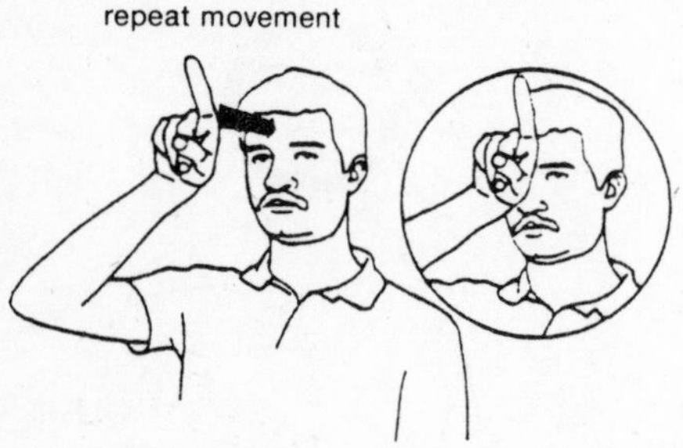

GERMANY, GERMAN
Tap the back of the right "d" hand, palm facing forward, against the top of the forehead with a double movement.
Hint: The insignia on a German soldier's helmet.

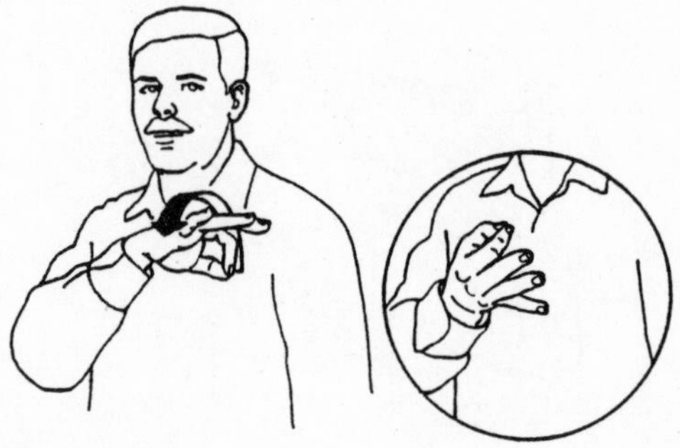

FRANCE, FRENCH
Beginning with the fingertips of the right "f" hand touching the left side of the chest, palm facing down, twist the wrist to move the hand forward, ending with the palm facing up.
Hint: Initialized sign.

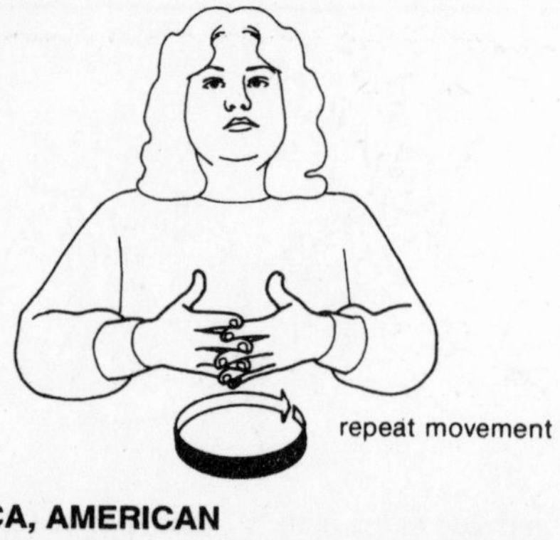

AMERICA, AMERICAN
With the fingers of both "5" hands meshed together, palms angled toward each other, move the hands in a repeated flat circle in front of the body.
Hint: The split-rail fences of early America.

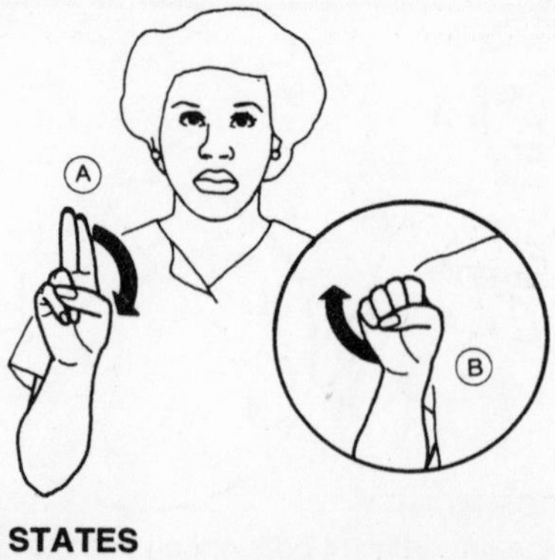

UNITED STATES
Move the right "u" hand, palm facing forward, downward slightly in front of the right shoulder. Then move the right "s" hand, palm facing forward, upward slightly in front of the right shoulder.
Hint: Abbreviation "u-s."

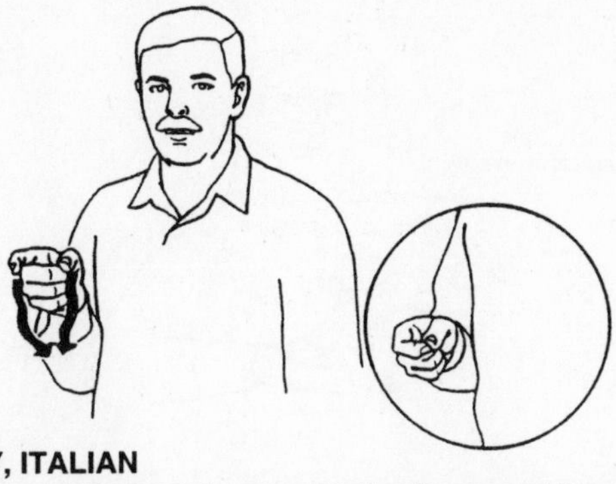

ITALY, ITALIAN
Beginning with the right curved index finger and thumb held in front of the right shoulder, palm facing forward, move the hand downward while pinching the index finger and thumb together.
Hint: Shape of Italy.

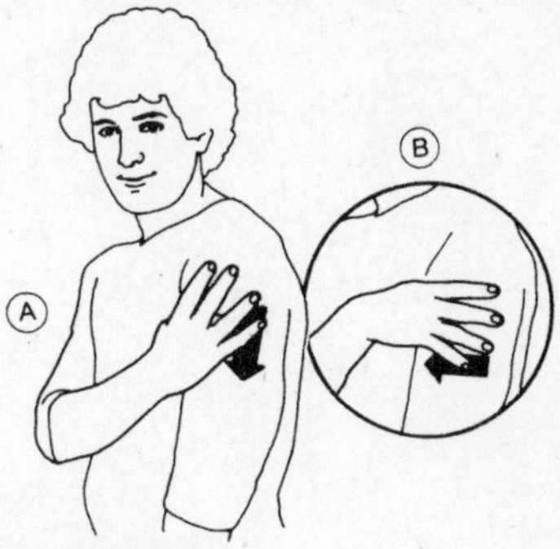

SCOTLAND, SCOTTISH
Bring the fingers of the right "4" hand, fingers pointing up, downward on the upper left arm and then from back to front in the same location.
Hint: Fingers show the plaid pattern of Scottish fabric.

reach shoulder then touch

SPAIN, SPANISH
Beginning with the curved right fingers touching the right side of the body, palm facing in, move the hand up while opening the fingers into a "b" hand, ending with the thumb side of the right "b" hand touching the left side of the chest, palm facing down.
Hint: The Spanish flag.

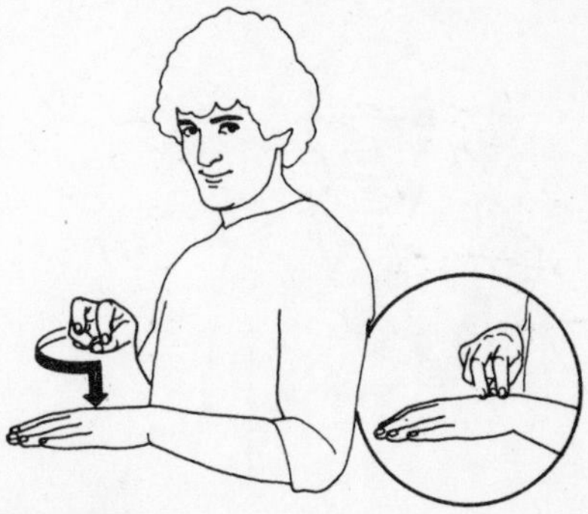

IRELAND, IRISH
Bring the fingertips of the bent "v" hand, palm facing down, in a circular movement down to touch the back of the open left hand, palm facing down.
Hint: Similar to the sign for "potato" symbolizing the Irish potato.

HOLLAND, DUTCH, NETHERLANDS
Beginning with the thumb of the right "y" hand on the forehead, palm facing left, move the hand downward and forward in a sweeping arc.
Hint: The shape of the traditional Dutch hat.

GREAT BRITAIN, UNITED KINGDOM, ENGLAND
Place the curved index finger and thumb on the chin, palm facing in.

RUSSIA, RUSSIAN, SOVIET
With the right index finger extended, palm facing down and finger pointing left, pull the index finger from left to right in front of the chin.

SWEDEN, SWEDISH
Beginning with the fingertips of the bent right "5" hand on the back of the open left hand, both palms facing down, bring the right hand upward with a double movement closing the fingers into a flattened "o" hand each time.

NORWAY, NORWEGIAN
Beginning with the right "n" hand in front of the chest, palm facing down, move the hand to the right with a large up and down movement, ending in front of the right shoulder.
Hint: Initialized sign.

DENMARK, DANE, DANISH
Move the right "3" hand, palm facing in and fingers pointing left, from left to right across the chest with a wavy movement.
Hint: A boat in the Danish fleet.

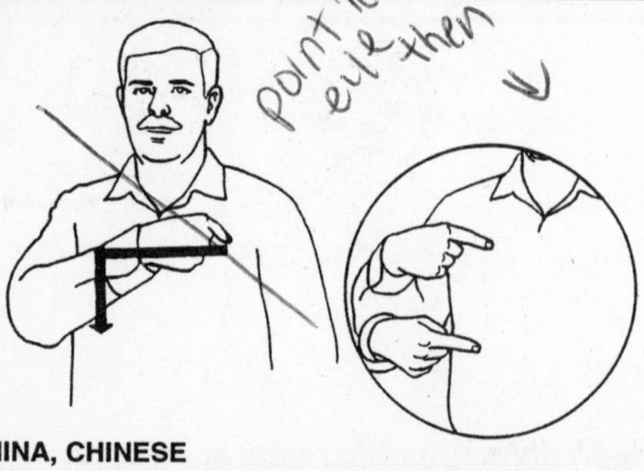

CHINA, CHINESE
Move the extended right index finger from touching the left side of the chest, palm facing in, to the right side of the chest and then straight down.
Hint: The shape of a Chinese soldier's uniform.

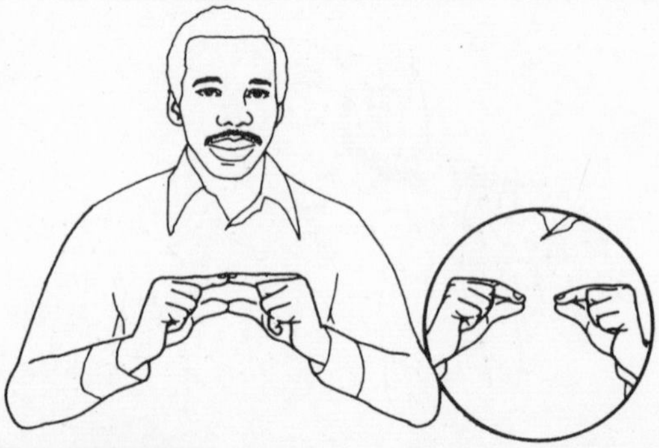

JAPAN, JAPANESE
Beginning with the fingertips of both "g" hands touching in front of the chest, palms facing each other, bring the hands apart while pinching the index finger and thumb of each hand together.
Hint: The shape of the country.

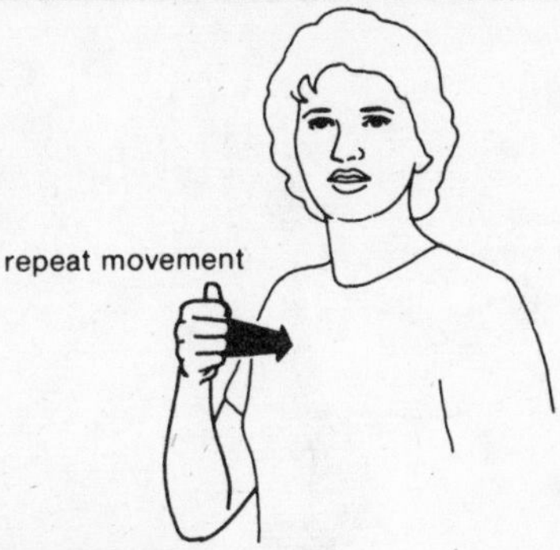

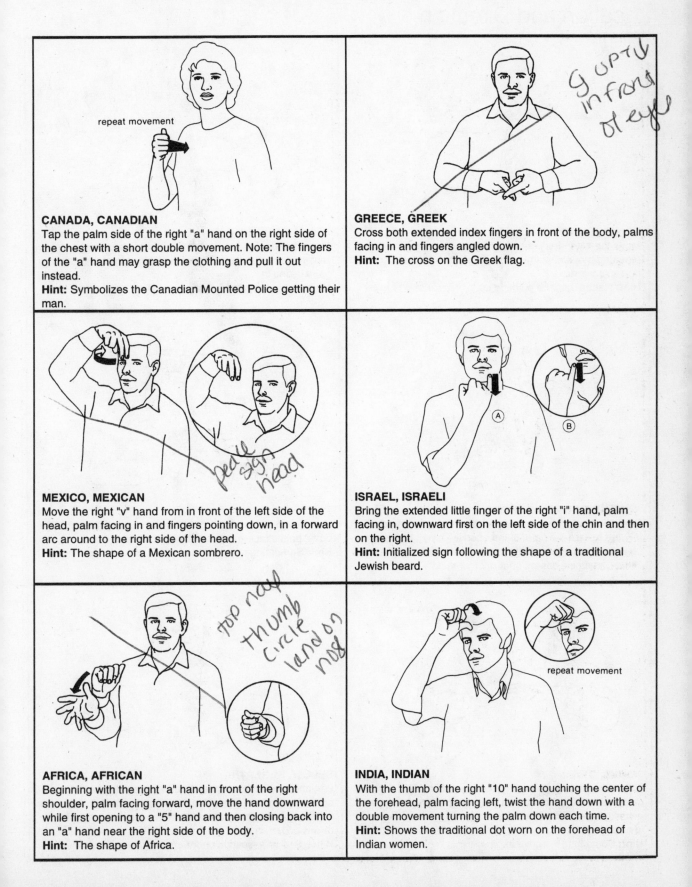

CANADA, CANADIAN
Tap the palm side of the right "a" hand on the right side of the chest with a short double movement. Note: The fingers of the "a" hand may grasp the clothing and pull it out instead.
Hint: Symbolizes the Canadian Mounted Police getting their man.

GREECE, GREEK
Cross both extended index fingers in front of the body, palms facing in and fingers angled down.
Hint: The cross on the Greek flag.

MEXICO, MEXICAN
Move the right "v" hand from in front of the left side of the head, palm facing in and fingers pointing down, in a forward arc around to the right side of the head.
Hint: The shape of a Mexican sombrero.

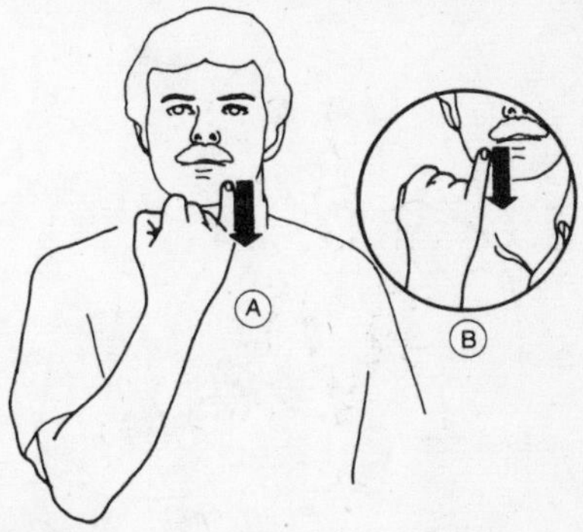

ISRAEL, ISRAELI
Bring the extended little finger of the right "i" hand, palm facing in, downward first on the left side of the chin and then on the right.
Hint: Initialized sign following the shape of a traditional Jewish beard.

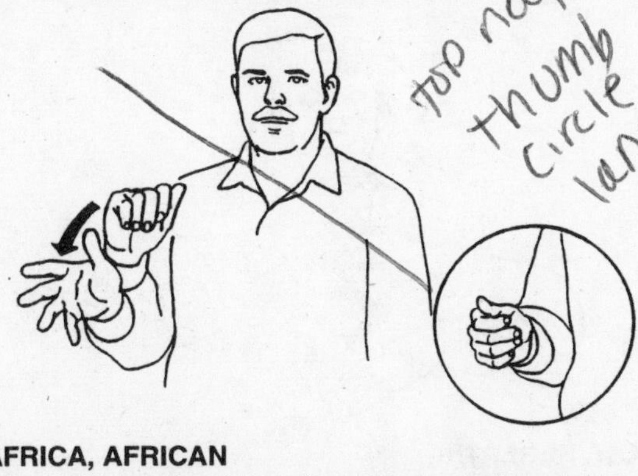

AFRICA, AFRICAN
Beginning with the right "a" hand in front of the right shoulder, palm facing forward, move the hand downward while first opening to a "5" hand and then closing back into an "a" hand near the right side of the body.
Hint: The shape of Africa.

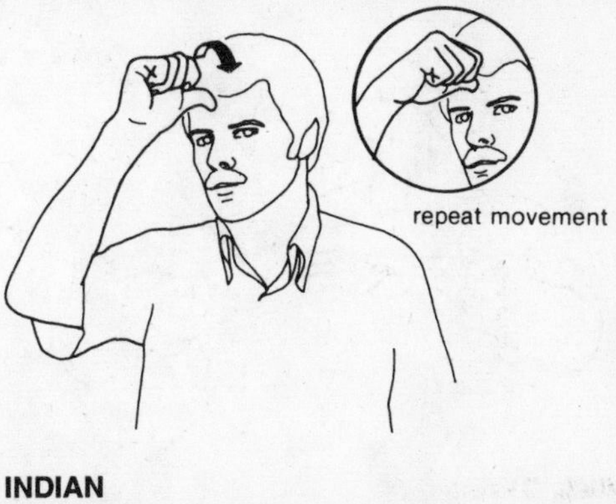

INDIA, INDIAN
With the thumb of the right "10" hand touching the center of the forehead, palm facing left, twist the hand down with a double movement turning the palm down each time.
Hint: Shows the traditional dot worn on the forehead of Indian women.

Location and Direction

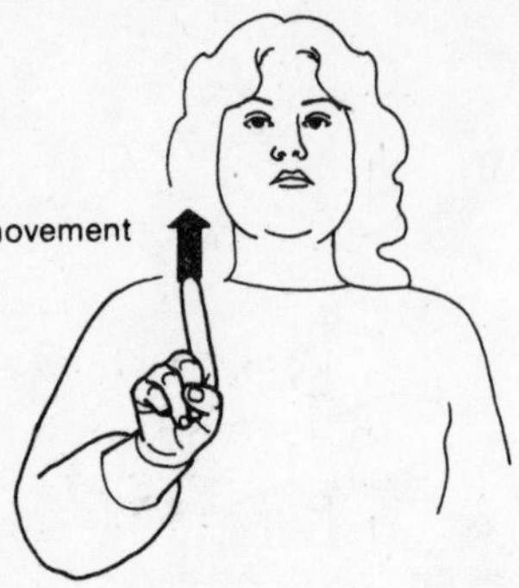

UP, UPSTAIRS
Move the extended right index finger upward with a short repeated movement in front of the right shoulder, palm facing forward.
Hint: Natural gesture pointing up.

DOWN, DOWNSTAIRS
Move the extended right index finger downward with a short repeated movement in front of the right side of the body, palm facing in.
Hint: Natural gesture pointing down.

NEAR, CLOSE TO, APPROACH
Bring the back of the open right hand from near the chest forward toward the palm of the open left hand, both palms facing in and fingers pointing in opposite directions.
Hint: Something comes near another thing.

FAR
With the knuckles of both "10" hands touching in front of the body, palms facing in, move the right hand forward.
Hint: Something is a distance away from another thing.

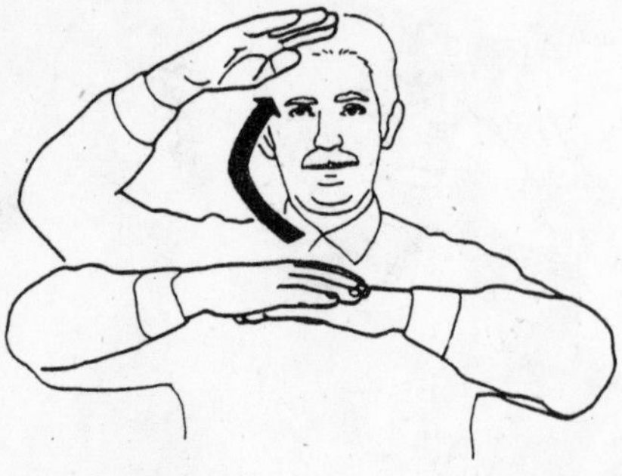

ABOVE, OVER
Beginning with the palm of the open right hand on the back of the open left hand, both palms facing down and fingers pointing in opposite directions, bring the right hand upward in an arc.
Hint: Something is above another thing.

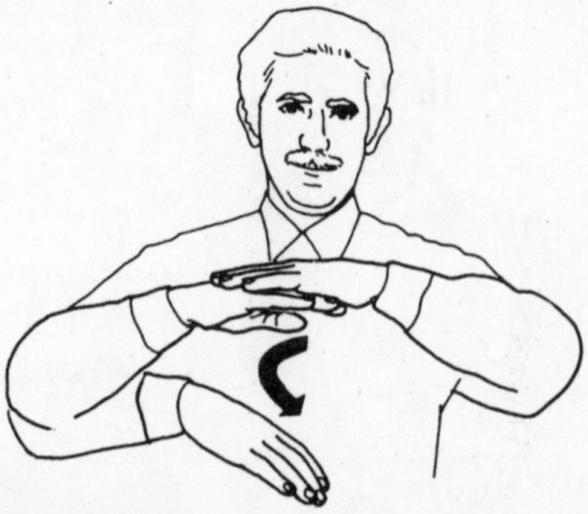

BELOW, BENEATH
Beginning with the open right hand under the palm of the left open hand in front of the chest, both palms facing down and fingers pointing in opposite directions, move the right hand downward in an arc.
Hint: Shows a location under another thing.

TOGETHER
With the palm sides of both "a" hands together, move the hands in a flat circle in front of the body.
Hint: Two things moving together.

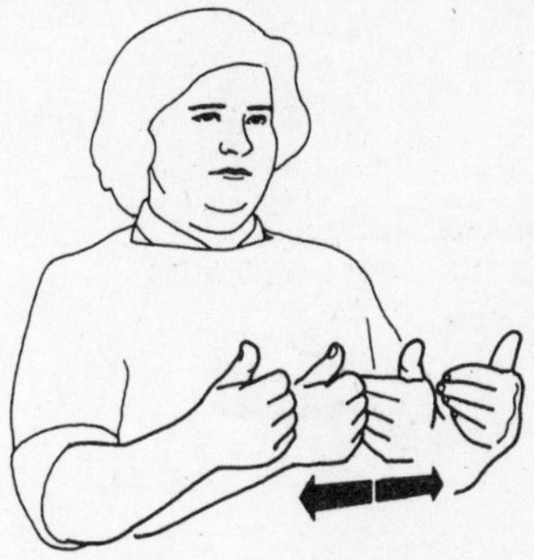

SEPARATE, APART
Beginning with the knuckles of both bent hands together, palms facing the chest, bring the hands apart.
Hint: Two things moving apart.

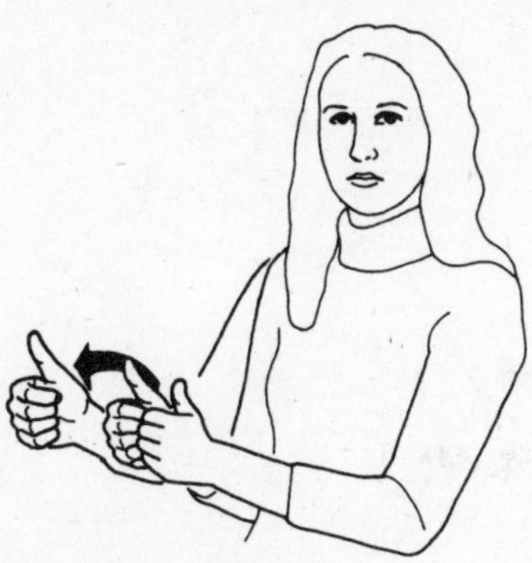

AHEAD, BEFORE
Beginning with the palm sides of both "10" hands together, move the right hand in a short arc forward.
Hint: Something moves ahead of another thing.

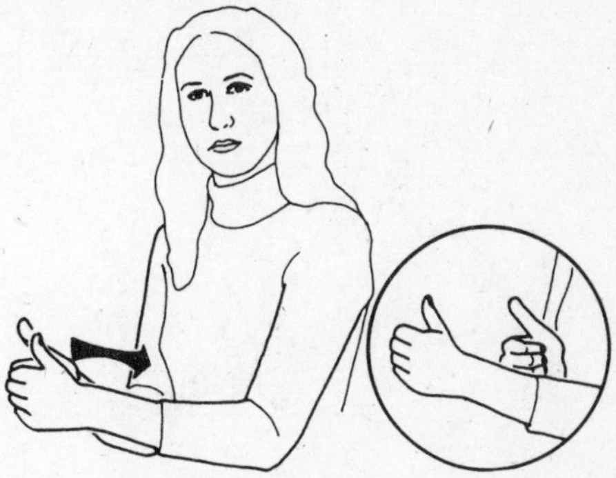

BEHIND
Beginning with the palm sides of both "10" hands together, move the right hand back toward the chest.
Hint: Something moves behind another thing.

OUT
Beginning with the left "c" hand, palm facing right, around the right "5" hand hanging down in front of the body, palm facing right, pull the right hand upward while closing the fingers of both hands into flattened "o" hands.
Hint: Taking something out of another thing.

OUTSIDE
Beginning with the left "c" hand around the right "5" hand hanging down in front of the body, both palms facing right, pull the right hand upward with a double movement, closing the fingers of both hands into flattened "o" hands each time.
Hint: Taking something out of another thing.

AROUND, SURROUND
With the extended right index finger pointing down over the extended left index finger, pointing up in front of the chest, move the right finger around the left finger.
Hint: Something moving around another thing.

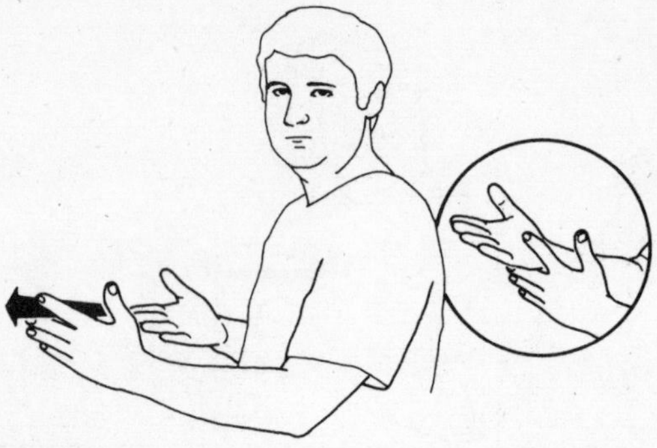

THROUGH
Move the fingers of the open right hand, palm facing up, between the index and middle fingers of the open left hand, palm facing right.
Hint: Something goes through another thing.

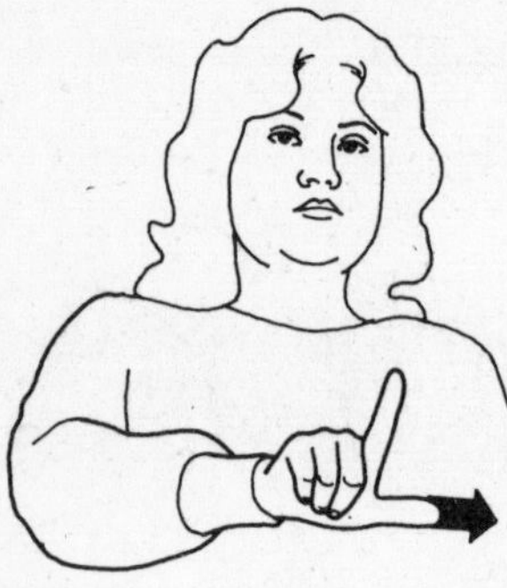

LEFT
Move the right "l" hand, palm facing forward, from right to left in front of the chest. Note: The sign may be formed with the left hand instead.
Hint: Initialized sign showing a left direction.

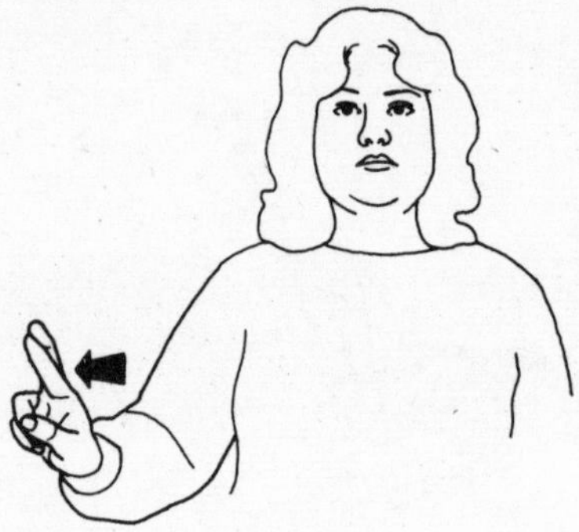

RIGHT
Move the right "r" hand, palm facing forward, to the right with a deliberate movement.
Hint: Initialized sign pointing right.

IN
Beginning with the right flattened "o" hand, fingers pointing down, above the left "c" hand, palm facing right, move the right hand down to insert the right fingers in the left "c" fingers.
Hint: Put something in another thing.

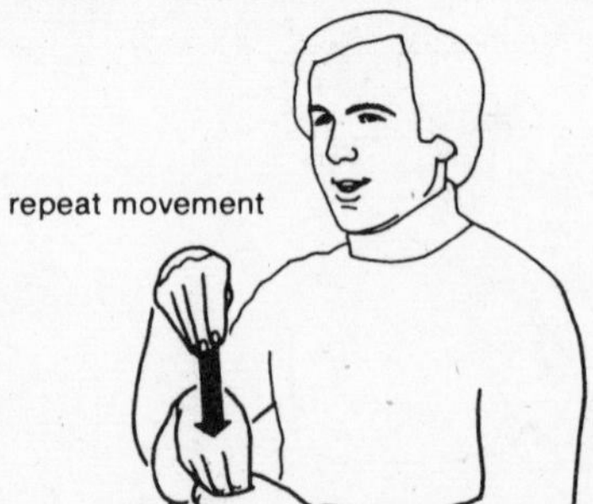

INSIDE
Beginning with the right flattened "o" hand, fingers pointing down, above the left "c" hand, palm facing right, move the right hand down with a double movement to insert the right fingers in the left "c" fingers each time.
Hint: Put something inside another thing.

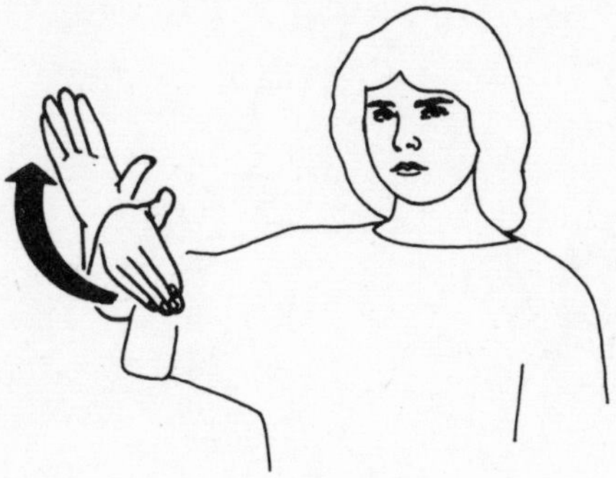

AWAY
With the open right hand held down somewhat forward of the chest, twist the wrist to move the open right hand forward and upward.
Hint: Brushing something away.

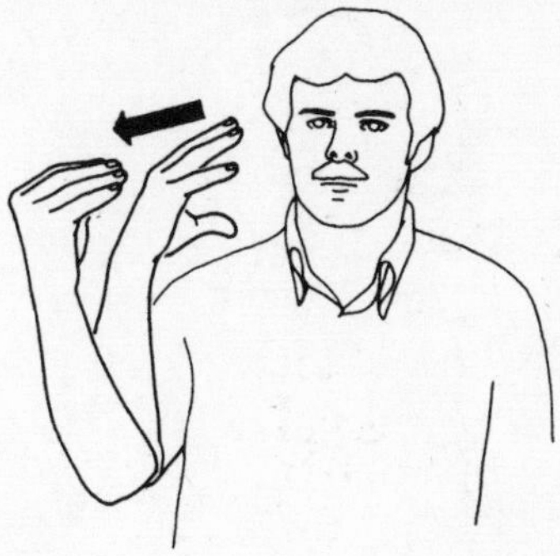

GONE, LEFT
Beginning with the curved right hand in front of the right shoulder, palm facing left, move the hand quickly to the right while closing the fingers into a flattened "o" hand.
Hint: Something disappearing into the distance.

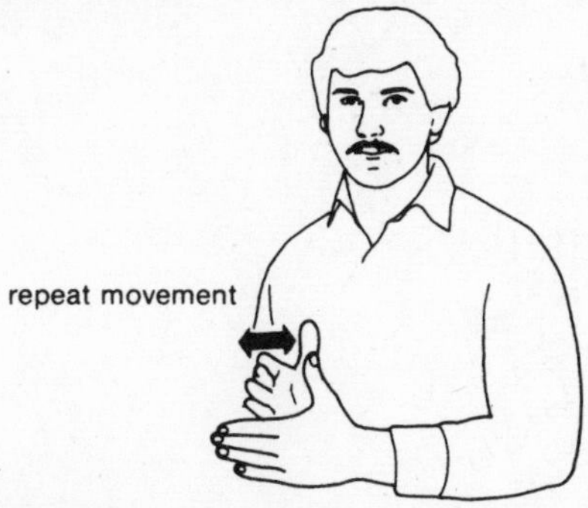

BETWEEN
Move the little-finger side of the open right hand, palm facing left and fingers pointing forward, with a repeated back and forth movement on the index-finger side of the open left hand held in front of the body, palm facing in.
Hint: Shows a location between the thumb and the end of the finger.

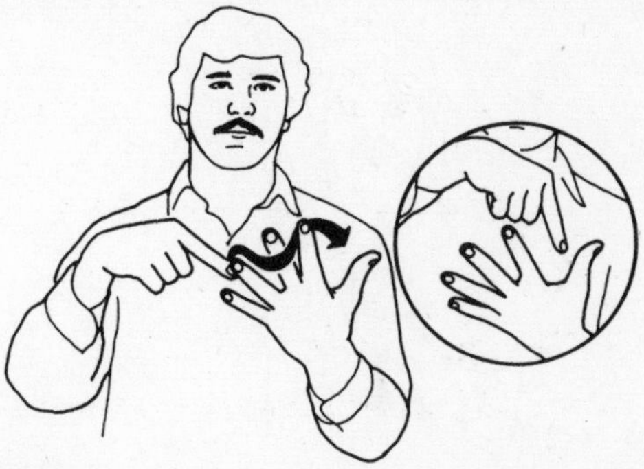

AMONG
Move the extended right index finger in and out between the fingers of the left "5" hand held in front of the chest, palm facing in and fingers pointing up.
Hint: Something moving among other things.

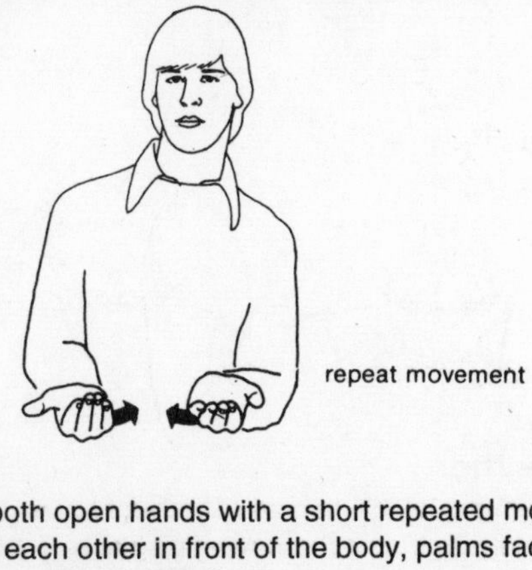

HERE
Move both open hands with a short repeated movement toward each other in front of the body, palms facing up and fingers pointing forward.
Hint: Indicates a location in the present location.

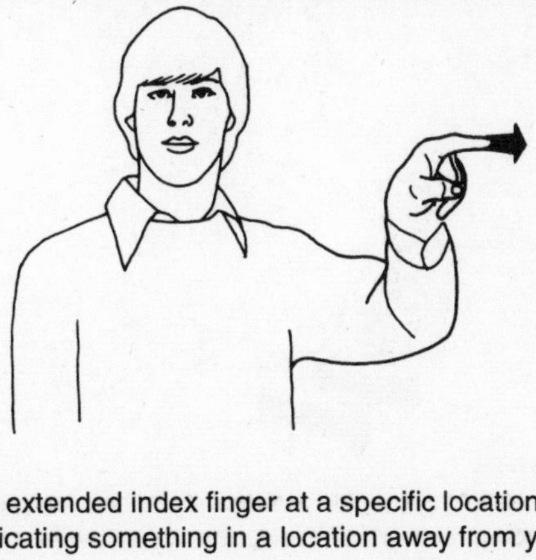

THERE
Point the extended index finger at a specific location.
Hint: Indicating something in a location away from you.

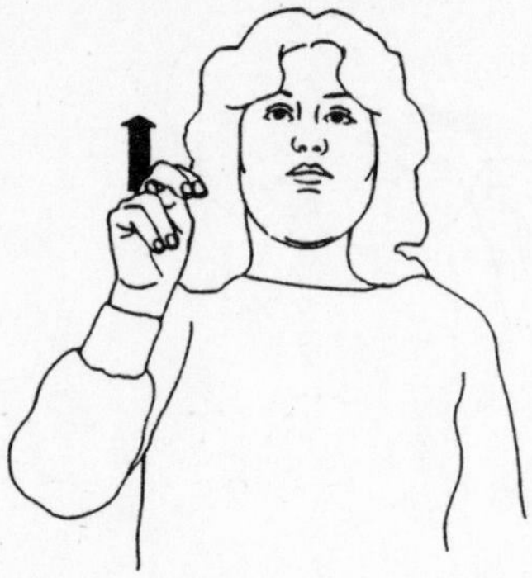

NORTH
Move the right "n" hand, palm facing forward, upward in front of the right shoulder.
Hint: Initialized sign moving north on a map.

EAST
Move the right "e" hand, palm facing forward, to the right in front of the right shoulder.
Hint: Initialized sign moving east on a map.

SOUTH
Move the right "s" hand, palm facing forward, downward in front of the body.
Hint: Initialized sign moving south on a map.

WEST
Move the right "w" hand, palm facing forward, to the left in front of the chest.
Hint: Initialized sign moving west on a map.

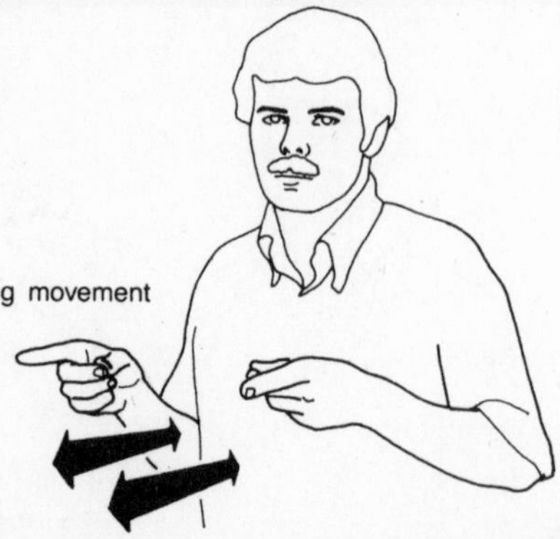

DIRECTION
Move both "d" hands, index fingers pointing forward and palms facing each other, forward and back with an alternating movement.
Hint: Initialized sign indicating movement in a non-specific direction.

PLACE, POSITION
Beginning with the middle fingers of both "p" hands touching in front of the body, both palms facing up, move the hands outward in a circular movement back to touch middle fingers again near the body.
Hint: Initialized sign outlining an area or place.

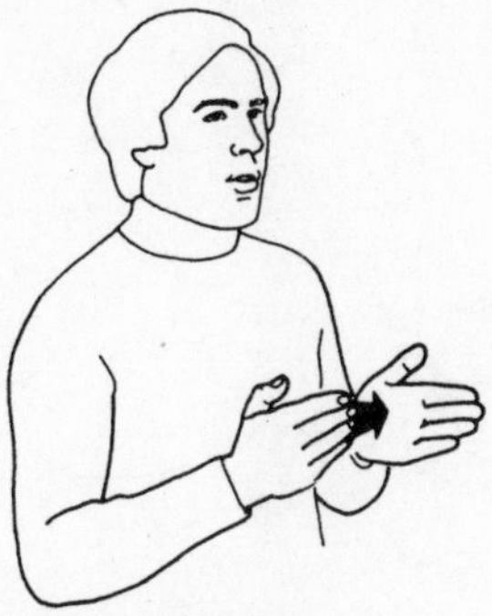

AGAINST, SUE, DISCRIMINATION
Bring the fingertips of the bent right hand, palm facing in, against the palm of the open left hand held in front of the chest, palm facing right.
Hint: Something coming up against another thing.

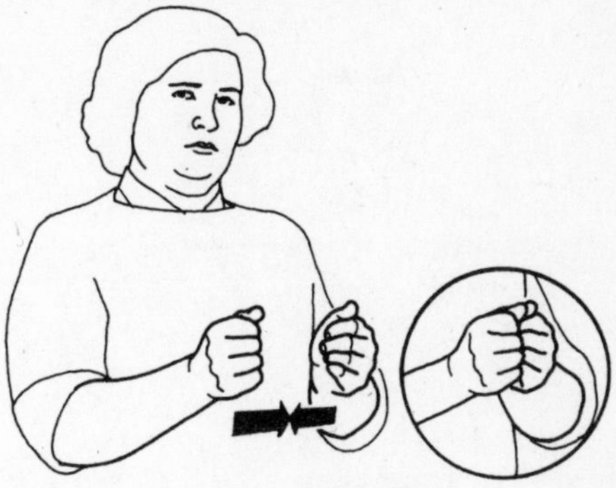

WITH
Bring the palm sides of both "a" hand together in front of the chest.
Hint: Something moves with another thing.

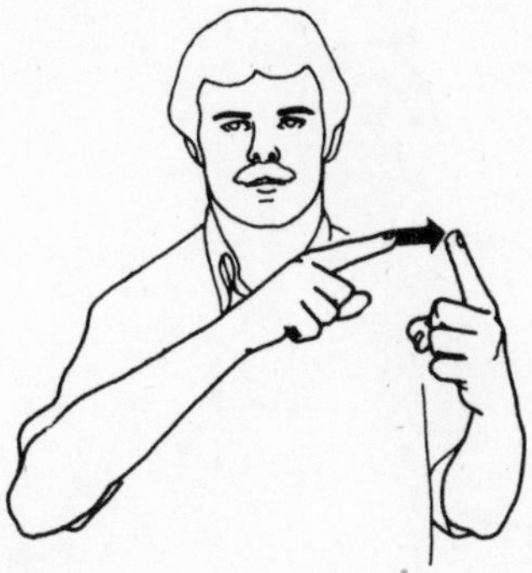

TO
Bring the extended right index finger, palm facing down, a short distance to the left to touch the extended left index finger held up in front of the chest, palm facing right.
Hint: Bringing something to another thing.

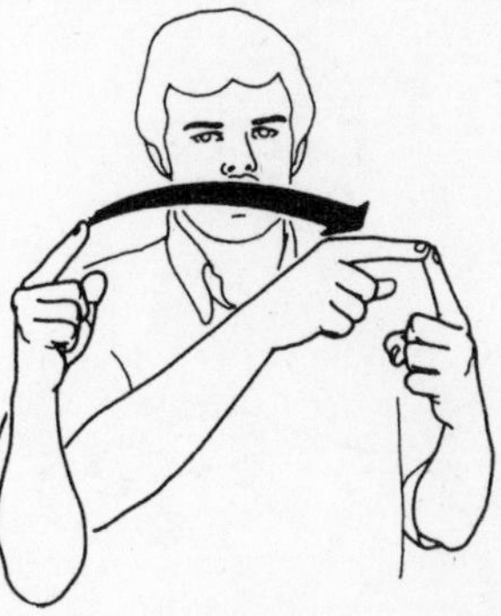

TOWARD
Bring the extended right index finger, palm facing down, in an arc to the left to touch the extended left index finger held up in front of the chest, palm facing right.
Hint: Bringing something toward another thing.

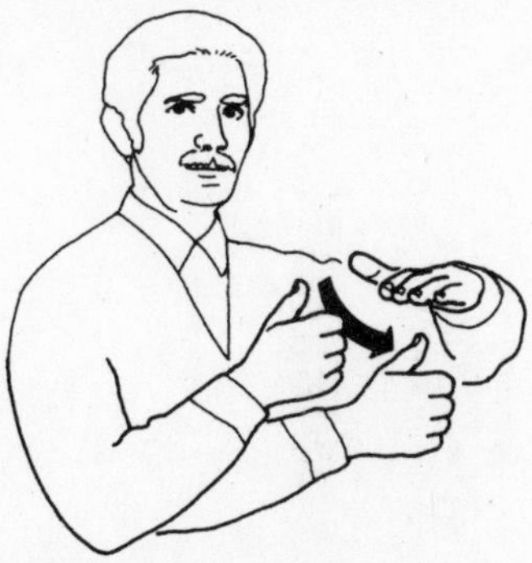

UNDER
Move the right "a" hand, palm facing left, forward in an arc under the open left hand held across the chest, palm facing down and fingers pointing right.
Hint: Something moves under another thing.

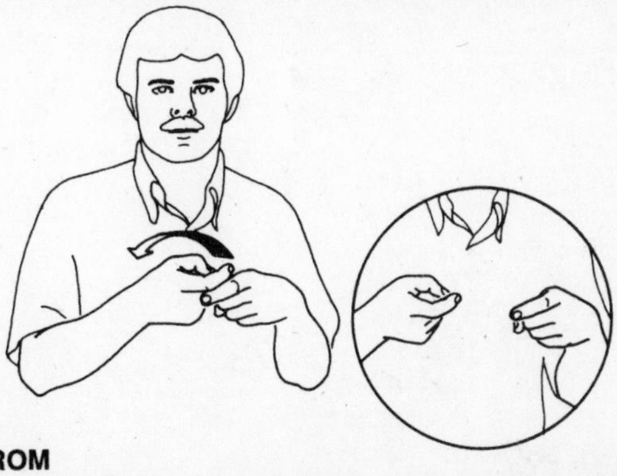

FROM
Beginning with the index fingers of both "x" hands touching in front of the chest, palms facing in opposite directions, move the right hand back toward the body.
Hint: Taking something from another thing.

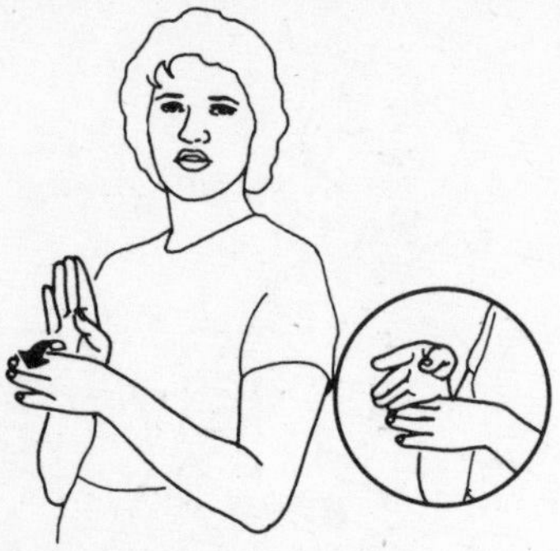

OVER, AFTER, ACROSS
Beginning with little-finger side of the right "b" hand, palm facing left and fingers pointing up, against the palm side of the left "b" hand held in front of the body, palm facing in and fingers pointing right, move the right hand in a tight arc over the index-finger side of the left hand.
Hint: Something moves over another thing.

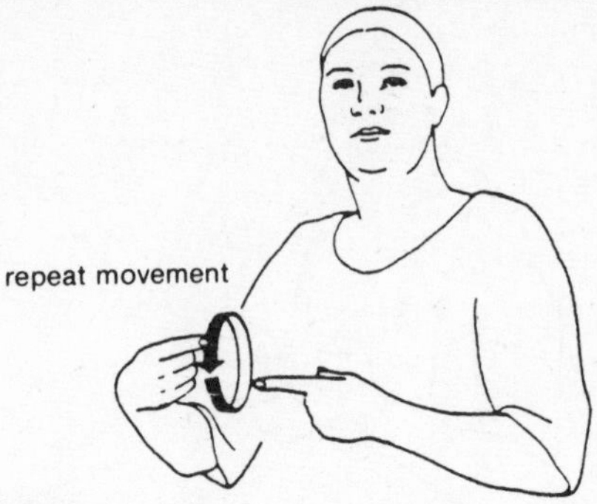

ABOUT
Move the extended right index finger in a repeated circle around the extended left index finger held in front of the chest, both palms facing in and fingers pointing toward each other.
Hint: Something moving about another thing.

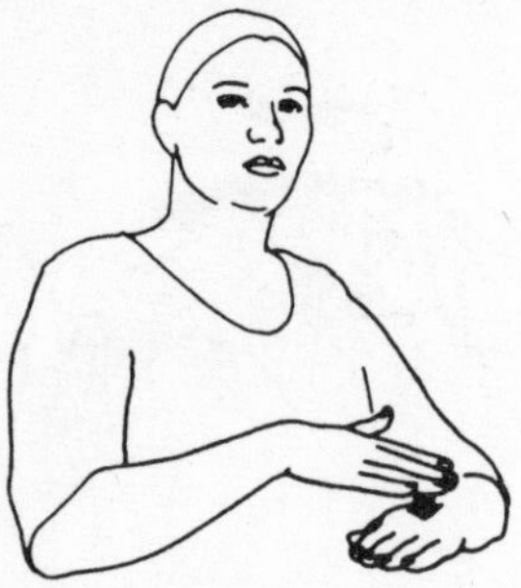

ON
Place the fingers of the open right hand on the back of the open left hand held in front of the body, both palms facing down.
Hint: Shows the location of something on another thing.

OFF
Beginning with the fingers of the open right hand on the back of the open left hand held in front of the body, both palms facing down, move the right hand up a short distance.
Hint: Shows something moving off another thing.

APPEAR, SHOW UP
Bring the extended right index finger, palm facing forward and finger pointing up, upward between the index and middle fingers of the open left hand held across the chest, palm facing down.
Hint: Pop up out of nowhere.

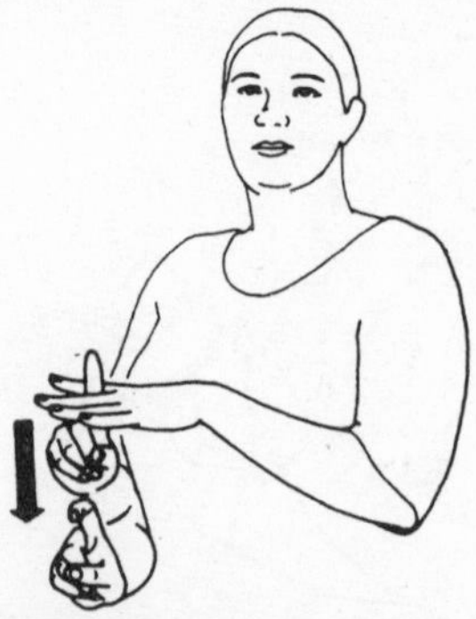

DISAPPEAR, DROP OUT
Pull the extended right index finger, palm facing forward and finger pointing up, downward from between the index and middle fingers of the open left hand held across the chest, palm facing down.

Buildings

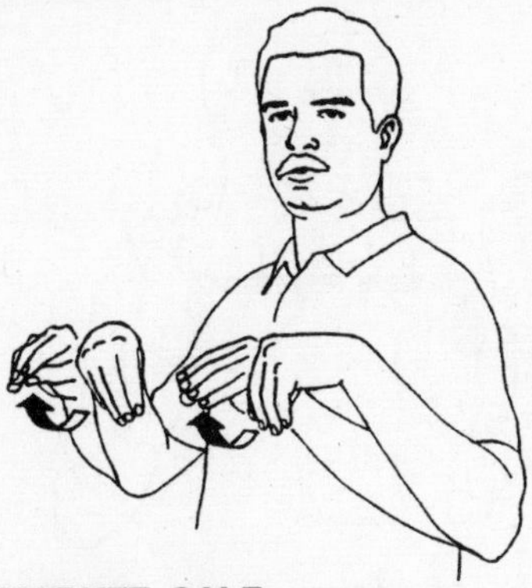

STORE, MARKET, SALE
Swing the fingertips of both flattened "o" hands forward from in front of each side of the chest, both palms facing down.
Hint: Similar to the sign "sell" only made with a single movement.

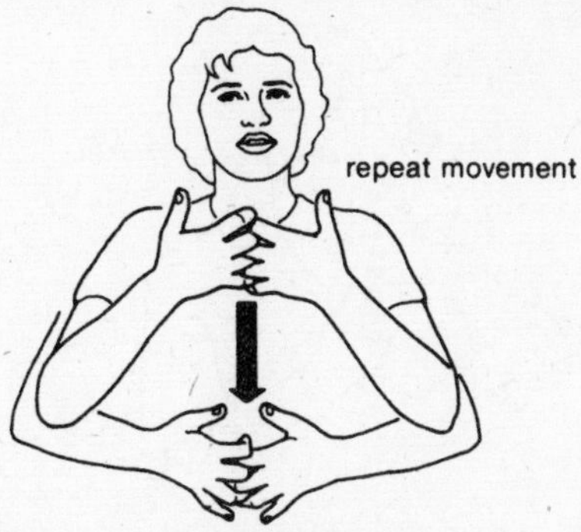

FACTORY, MACHINE, INDUSTRY
With the fingers of both curved hands loosely curved together, palms facing in, shake the up and down with a repeated movement in front of the chest.
Hint: Shows the moving gears in machinery.

LIBRARY
Move the right "l" hand, palm facing forward, in an outward circle in front of the right shoulder.
Hint: Initialized sign.

RESTAURANT
Touch the fingers of the right "r" hand, palm facing left, first to the right side of the chin and then to the left side.
Hint: Initialized sign formed near where one eats.

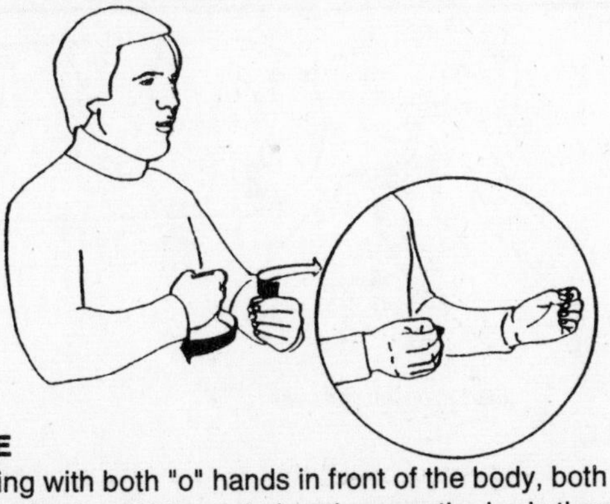

OFFICE
Beginning with both "o" hands in front of the body, both palms facing in and the right hand nearer the body than the left, move the hands to each side, ending with the palms facing each other.
Hint: Initialized sign formed similar to the sign for "box."

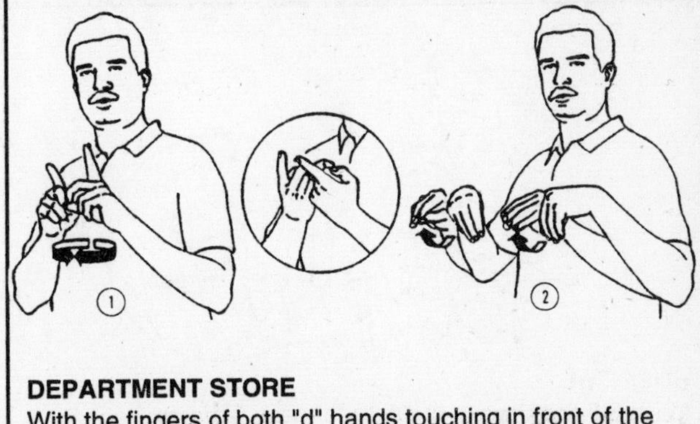

DEPARTMENT STORE
With the fingers of both "d" hands touching in front of the chest, move the hands apart and forward in a circular movement, ending with the little fingers touching. Then swing the fingertips of both flattened "o" hands forward from in front of each side of the chest, both palms facing down.
Hint: "Department" is an initialized sign plus "store."

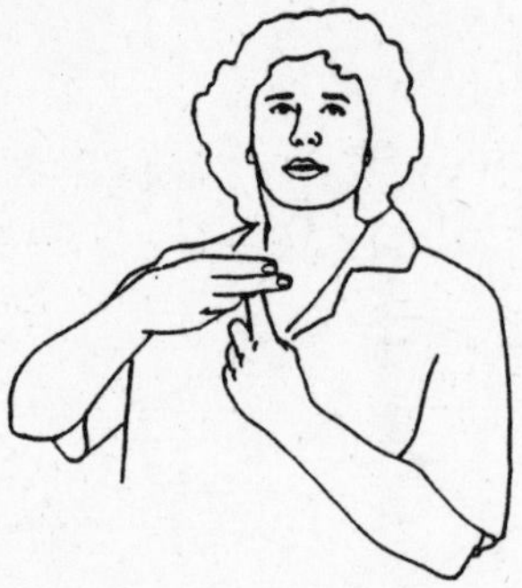

HOTEL

Bring the right "h" fingers toward the chest to hit the extended left index finger held up in front of the chest.
Hint: Initialized sign.

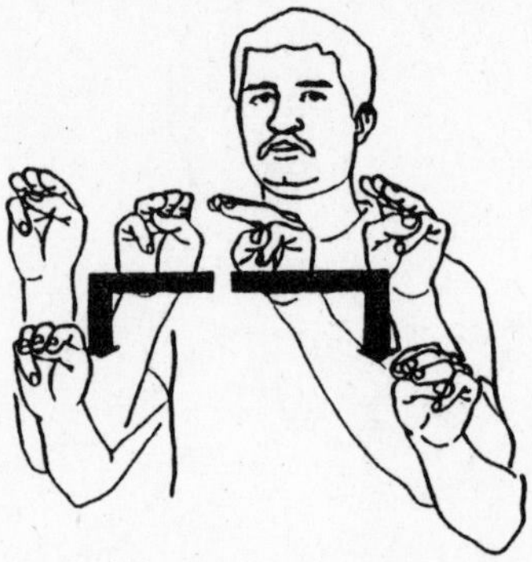

MUSEUM

Beginning with the index-finger side of both "m" hands touching in front of the chest, palms facing forward, move the hands apart to in front of the sides of chest and then straight down.
Hint: Initialized sign showing the shape of a museum.

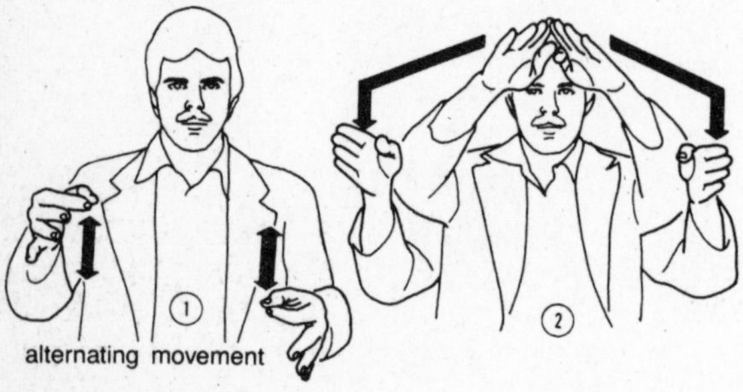

COURTHOUSE

Move both "f" hands, palms facing each other, up and down with an alternating movement. Then beginning with the index-finger sides of both "b" hands touching in front of the forehead, bring the hands down at an angle to about shoulder width and then straight down, ending with the palms facing each other.
Hint: "Judge" plus "house."

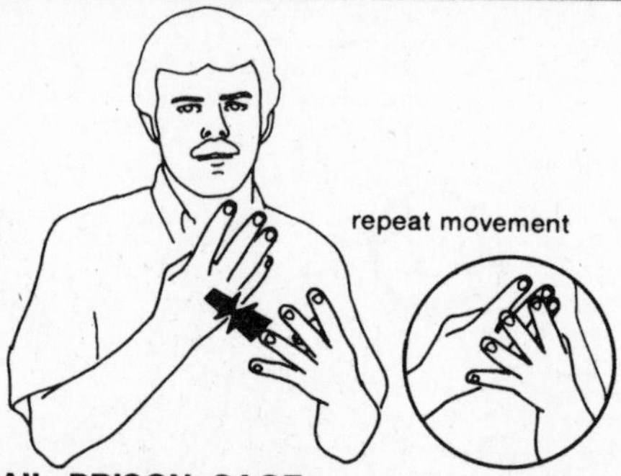

JAIL, PRISON, CAGE

Bring the back of the right "4" hand and the palm side of the left "4" hand toward each other to meet each other with a double movement.
Hint: Fingers represent cell bars.

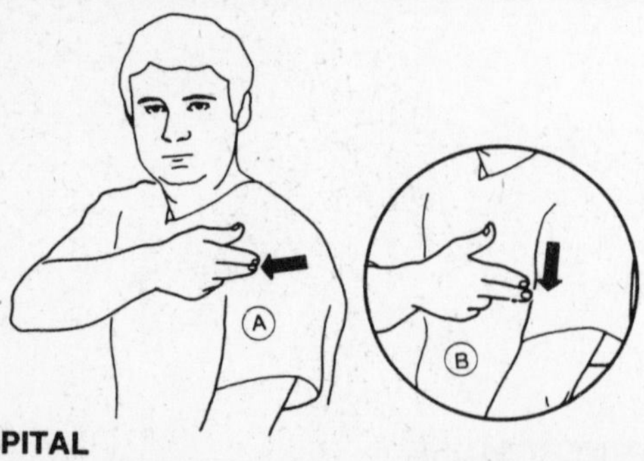

HOSPITAL

Move the fingertips of the right "h" hand first from back to front and then up to down on the upper left arm.
Hint: Initialized sign tracing the symbolic cross of some medical personnel's uniforms.

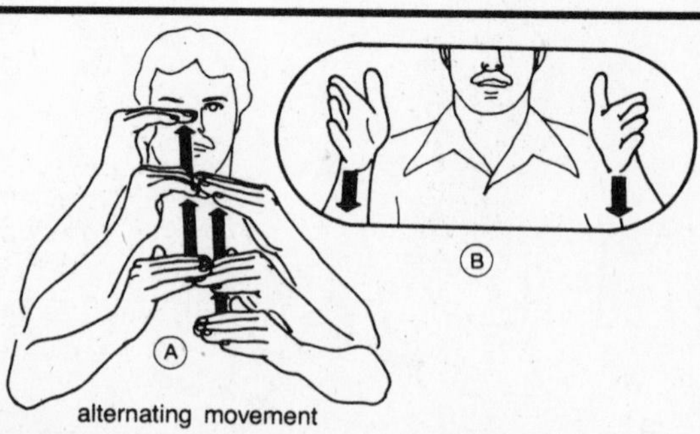

BUILDING

With the fingertips of both bent hands overlapping slightly, alternatingly move the hands over each other as the hands move upward in front of the chest. Then move both open hands downward along the sides of the body, palms facing each other.
Hint: "Build" plus the shape of the walls of a building.

nine

HEALTH AND SURVIVAL

Health and Medical
Parts of the Body
Survival

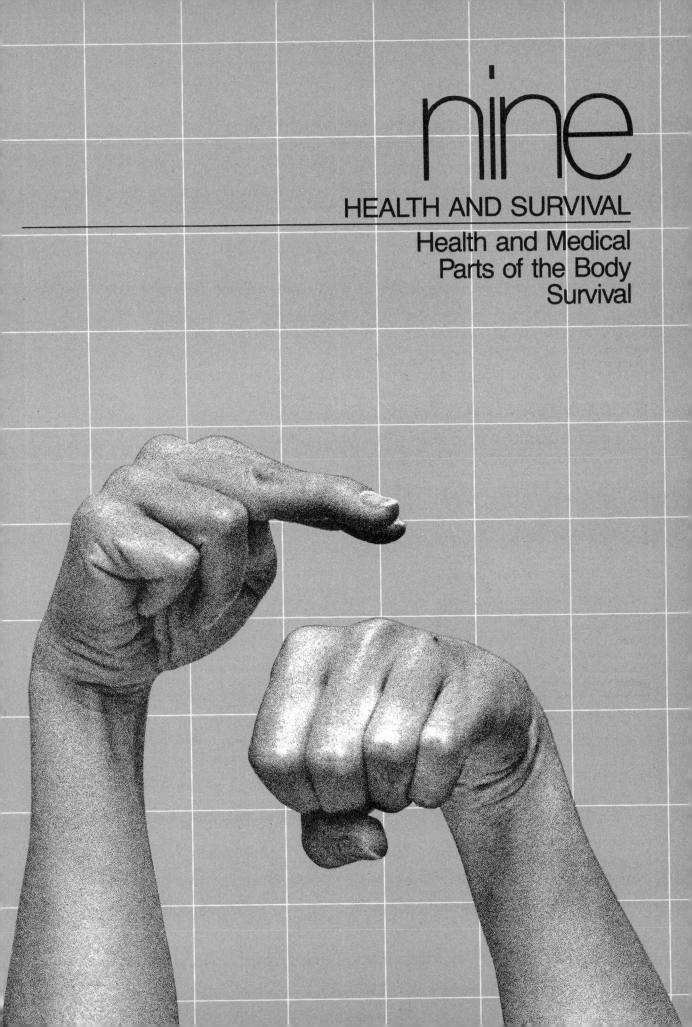

SIGNS THAT EXPRESS DIFFICULTY

Many signs that express difficulty are formed with a bent "v" handshape. Some examples are "hard," "strict," "difficult," and "problem."

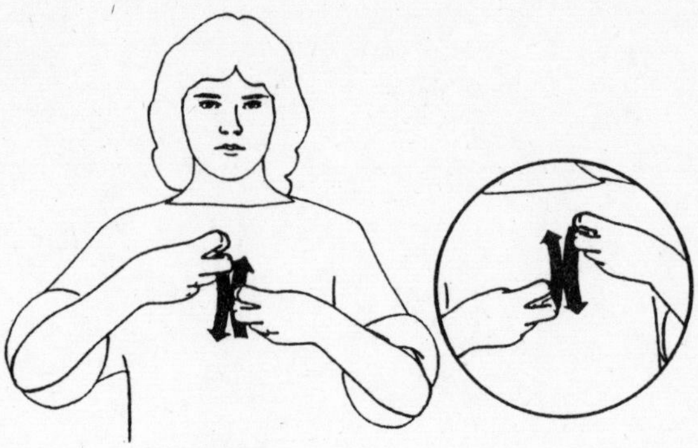

difficult

SIGN PLACEMENT

Some verbs can carry additional information by their placement on the body. For example, "hurt," "sore," "cut," and "operation" will be understood more easily if you sign them near the location on the body where the pain or surgery has occurred.

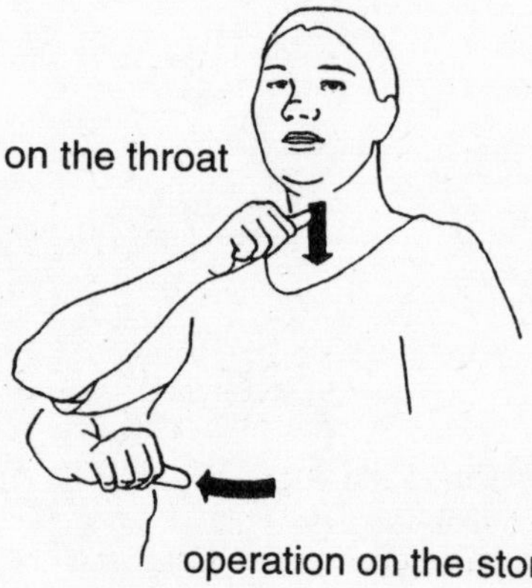

operation on the throat

operation on the stomach

COMPOUNDS

Compounds are formed in spoken language by joining two words together to form a new word with a different meaning from that of either contributing word. For example, "notebook" has a completely different meaning than either "note" or "book." Similarly, in sign language, two signs may be combined to form a new sign with a different meaning. An example of a sign compound is "pale," which is made up of the two signs "white" plus "face." Often knowing the two signs that make up a compound helps you remember it.

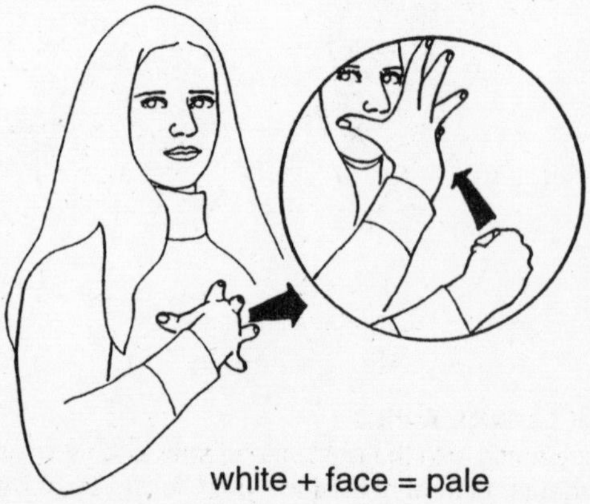

white + face = pale

Health and Medical

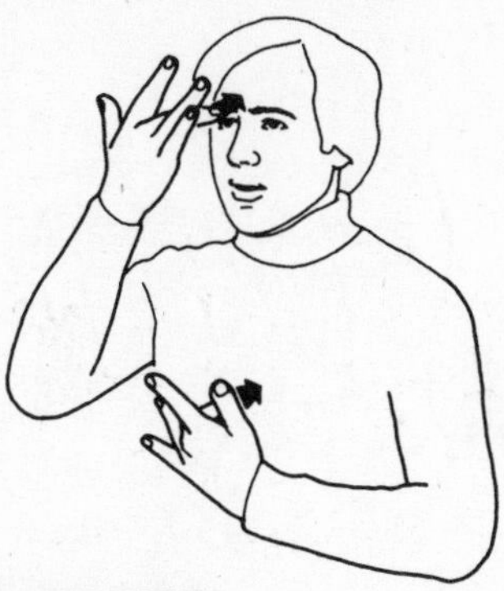

SICK, ILL, DISEASE
Touch the bent middle finger of the right "5" hand to the forehead while touching the bent middle finger of the left "5" hand to the lower chest.
Hint: Shows that one feels bad in the head and stomach.

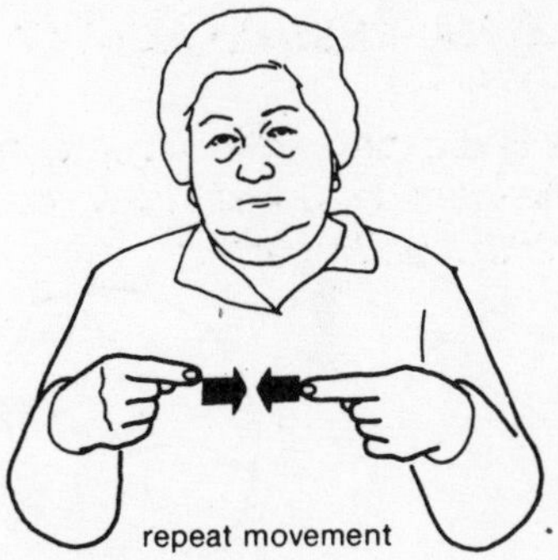

HURT, PAIN, ACHE, SORE
Move the extended index fingers of both hands toward each other in front of the chest with a short repeated movement, palms facing in.
Hint: Shows piercing pains when one hurts.

OPERATION, SURGERY
Pull the thumbnail of the right "a" hand, palm facing down, toward the body from the fingers to the heel of the open left hand, palm facing up. Note: The sign can be made on the body wherever surgery occurs.
Hint: Shows where the incision occurred.

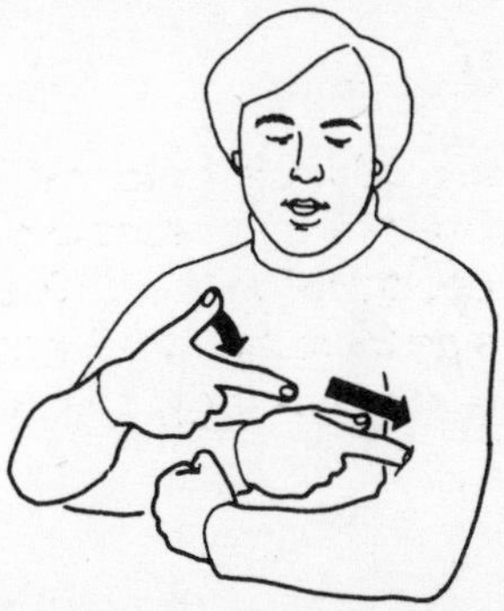

INJECTION, SHOT, VACCINATION
Bring the index finger of the right "l" hand, palm facing in, to touch the upper part of the bent left arm while lowering the right thumb.
Hint: Mime giving oneself an injection.

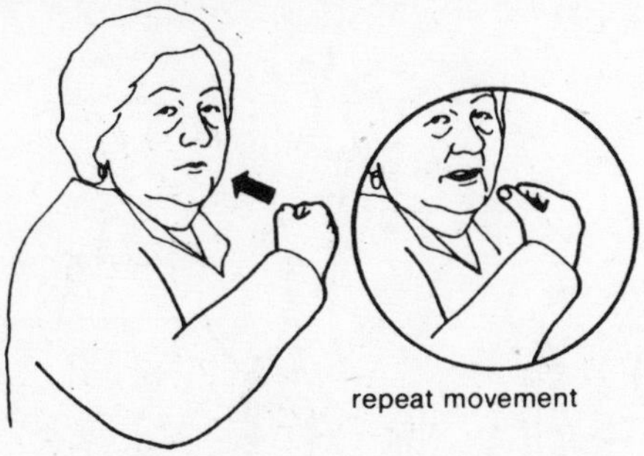

PILL, TAKE A PILL
Beginning with the right index finger and thumb pinched together in front of the face, palm facing in, move the hand together the mouth with a double movement, opening the thumb and index finger each time.
Hint: Dispensing a pill into the mouth.

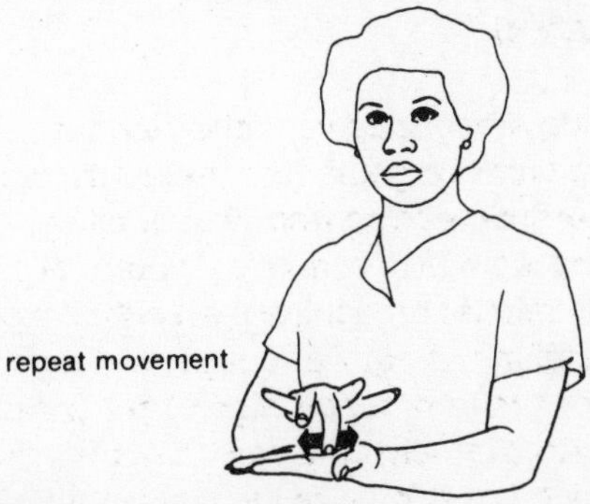

MEDICINE
Rub the fingertip of the bent middle finger of the right "5" hand with a short repeated movement on the palm of the open left hand held in front of the body.
Hint: Indicates the grinding action of making medicine with a pestle and mortar.

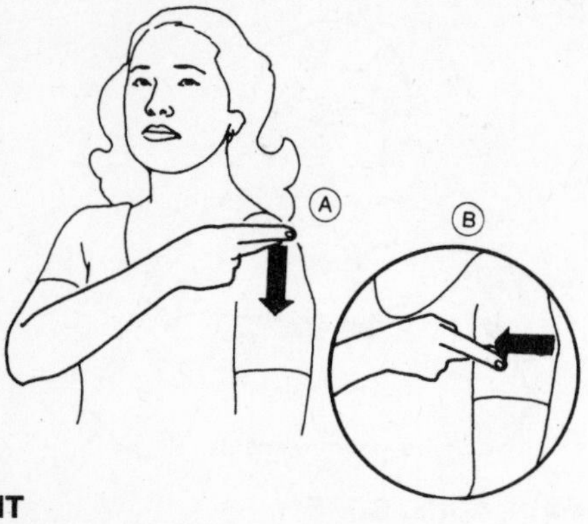

PATIENT
Move the middle finger of the right "p" hand downward and then from back to front on the upper left arm.
Hint: Initialized sign formed similar to sign for "hospital."

AMBULANCE
Move the right flattened "o" hand in a circular movement near the right side of the head by repeated twisting the wrist and opening the fingers into a "5" hand each time.
Hint: Represents the flashing lights on an ambulance.

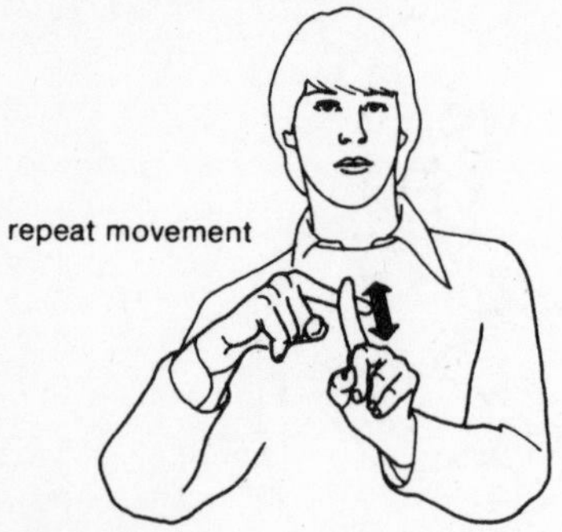

TEMPERATURE
Move the extended right index finger, palm facing down, up and down with a repeated movement on the extended left index finger held up in front of the chest, palm facing forward.
Hint: Shows the mercury moving in a thermometer.

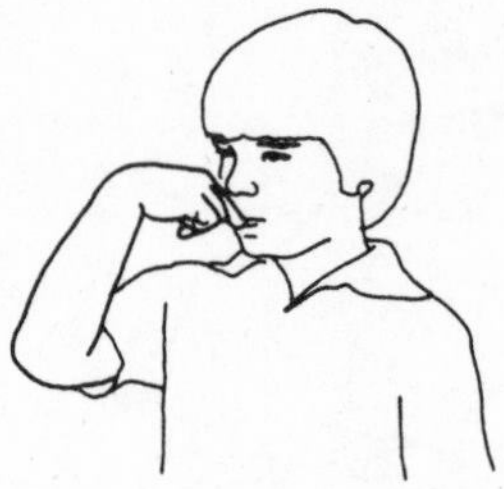

THERMOMETER
Insert the extended right index finger between the lips, palm facing down.
Hint: Mime taking a person's temperature.

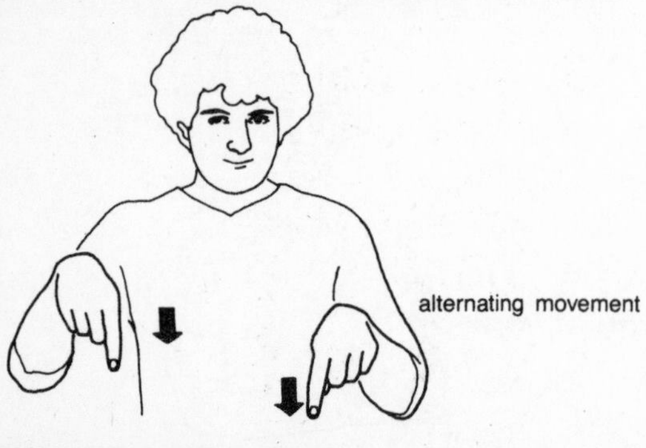

CRIPPLED, LAME, LIMP
With both extended index fingers pointing down in front of each side of the chest, palm facing in, move the hands up and down with a repeated alternating movement.
Hint: The fingers represent two legs limping.

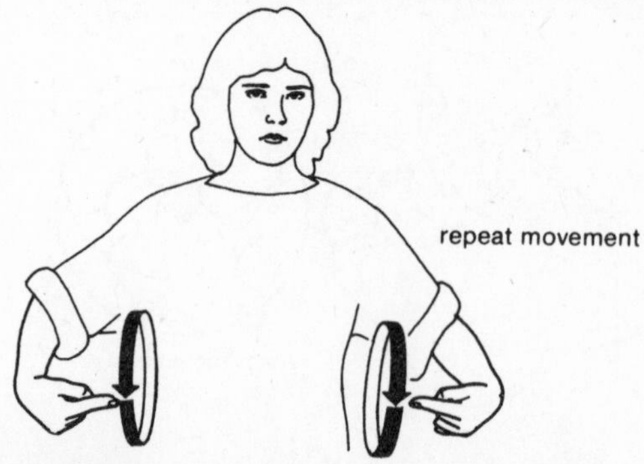

WHEELCHAIR
With both extended index fingers pointing toward each other near each side of the body, palms facing up, move the hands forward in large circles.
Hint: The fingers follow the movement of a wheelchair's wheels.

BLIND
Move the right bent "v" fingers close in toward the eyes.
Hint: The eyes are put out by the fingers.

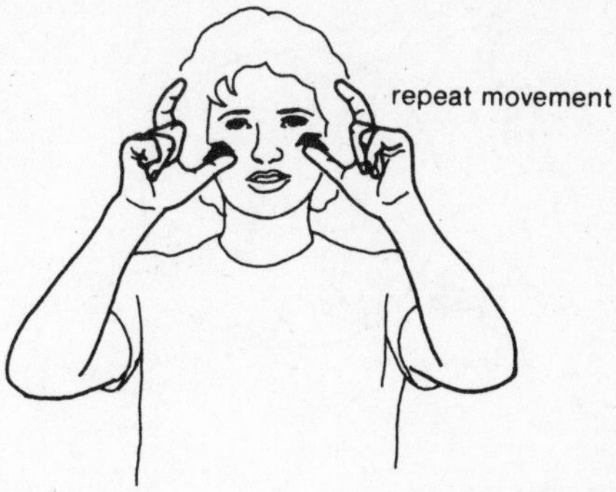

GLASSES
With the curved index fingers and thumbs of both hands encircling the outside of both eyes, tap the thumbs against each cheek with a double movement.
Hint: The fingers show the shape of glasses frames.

DEAF
Bring the extended right index finger from touching near the ear downward while changing into a "b" hand, ending with the index-finger sides of both "b" hands together in front of the body, palms facing down.
Hint: Shows that the ear is closed.

DEAF
Touch the extended right index finger first near the mouth and then near the right ear.
Hint: The mouth and ear are closed.

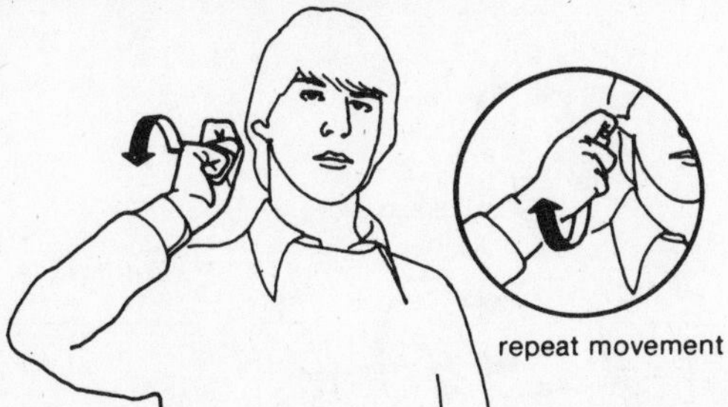

HEARING AID
With the right index finger and thumb pinched together, twist the right palm back with a double movement near the right ear.
Hint: Screwing a hearing aid mold firmly in the ear canal.

HEALTH
Touch the fingertips of both "h" hands, palms facing in, first on each side of the chest and then to each side of the waist.
Hint: Initialized sign formed similar to sign for "body."

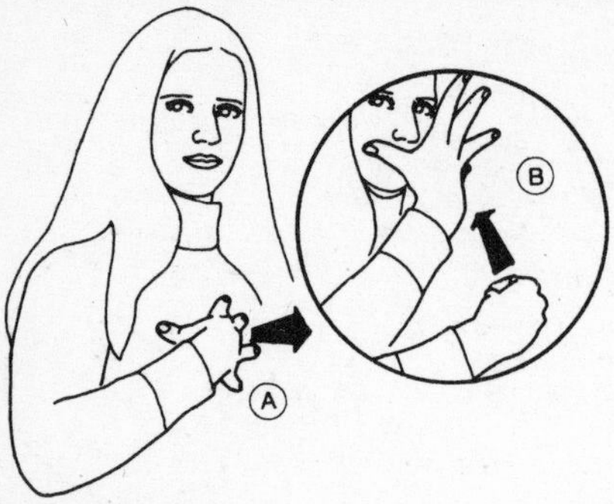

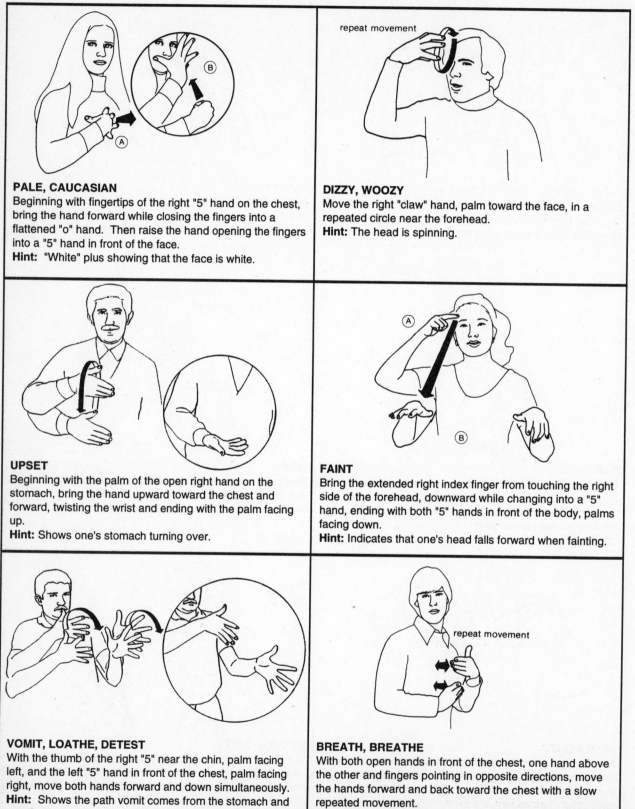

PALE, CAUCASIAN
Beginning with fingertips of the right "5" hand on the chest, bring the hand forward while closing the fingers into a flattened "o" hand. Then raise the hand opening the fingers into a "5" hand in front of the face.
Hint: "White" plus showing that the face is white.

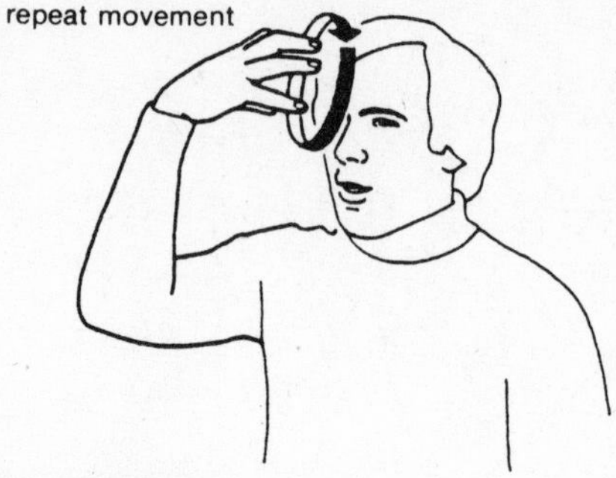

DIZZY, WOOZY
Move the right "claw" hand, palm toward the face, in a repeated circle near the forehead.
Hint: The head is spinning.

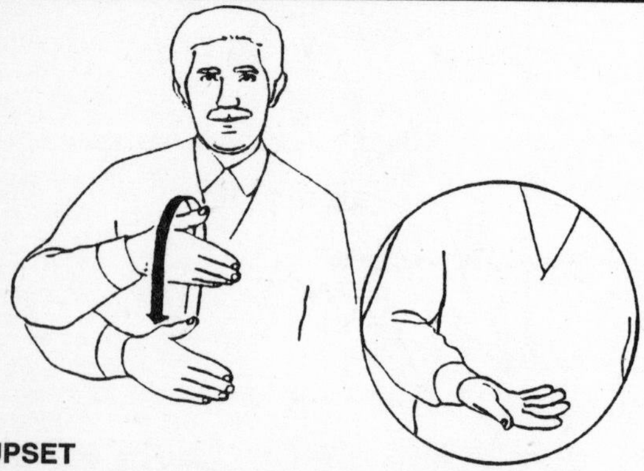

UPSET
Beginning with the palm of the open right hand on the stomach, bring the hand upward toward the chest and forward, twisting the wrist and ending with the palm facing up.
Hint: Shows one's stomach turning over.

FAINT
Bring the extended right index finger from touching the right side of the forehead, downward while changing into a "5" hand, ending with both "5" hands in front of the body, palms facing down.
Hint: Indicates that one's head falls forward when fainting.

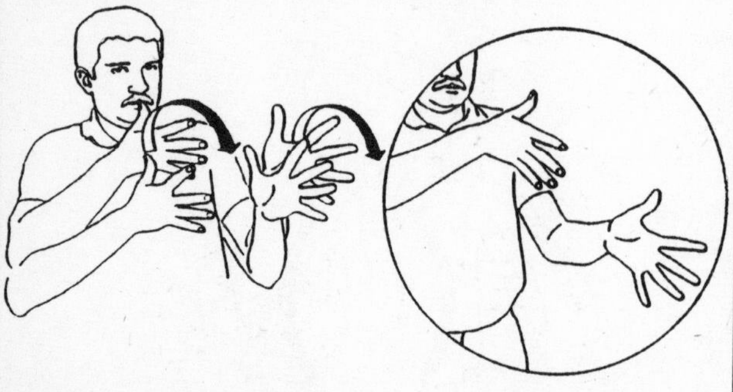

VOMIT, LOATHE, DETEST
With the thumb of the right "5" near the chin, palm facing left, and the left "5" hand in front of the chest, palm facing right, move both hands forward and down simultaneously.
Hint: Shows the path vomit comes from the stomach and mouth.

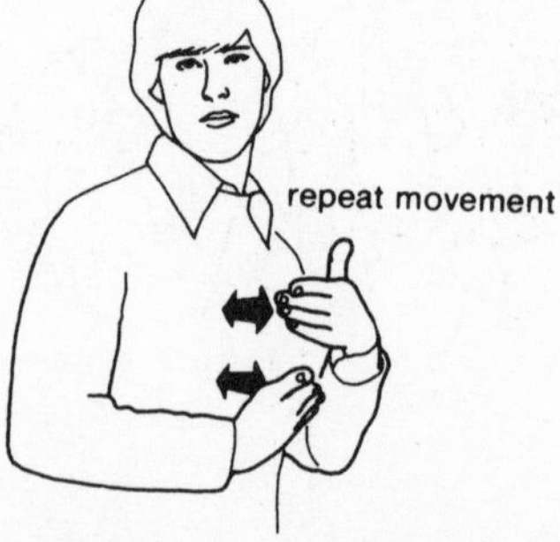

BREATH, BREATHE
With both open hands in front of the chest, one hand above the other and fingers pointing in opposite directions, move the hands forward and back toward the chest with a slow repeated movement.
Hint: Shows the movement of one's lungs when breathing.

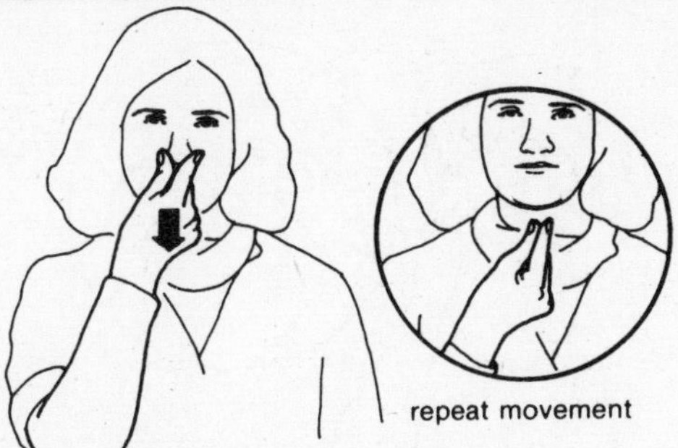

COLD, HANDKERCHIEF, TISSUE
Grasp the bottom of the nose with the right thumb and index finger and pull downward with a double movement, closing the index finger and thumb each time.
Hint: Mime wiping the nose with a handkerchief.

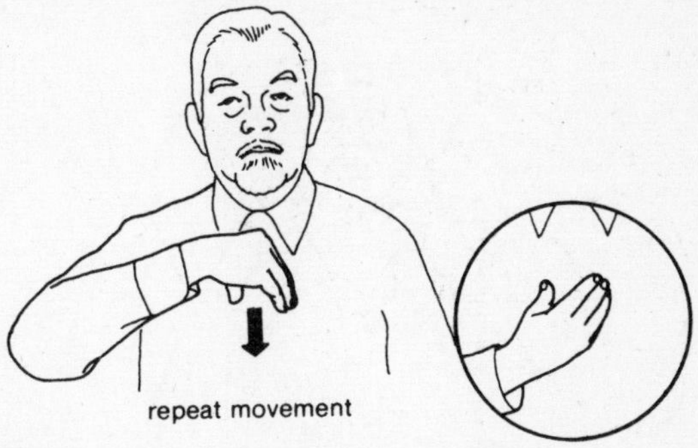

COUGH
While keeping the fingertips of the right "c" on the chest, move the hand up and down with a repeated movement.
Hint: Shows the action of a cough deep in the chest.

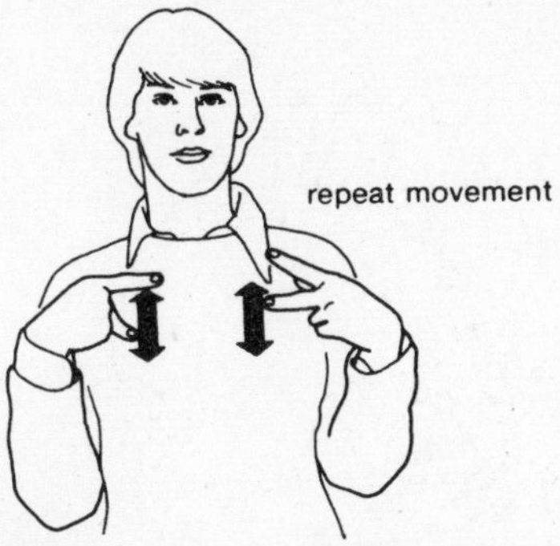

PNEUMONIA
With the middle fingers of both "p" hands on each side of the chest, palms facing in, move the hands up and down with a repeated movement.
Hint: Initialized sign indicating the location of pneumonia in the lungs.

HEART
Tap the bent middle finger of the right "5" hand to the left side of the chest with a small repeated movement.
Hint: Shows the location of the heart.

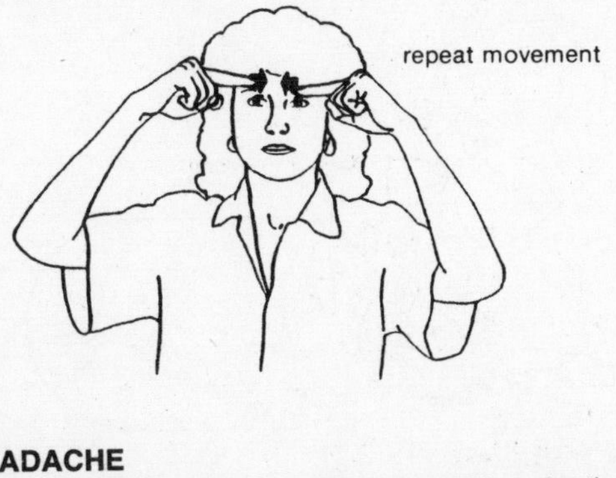

HEADACHE
Move both extended index fingers toward each other with a short double movement in front of the forehead, palms facing down.
Hint: "Hurt" formed near the head.

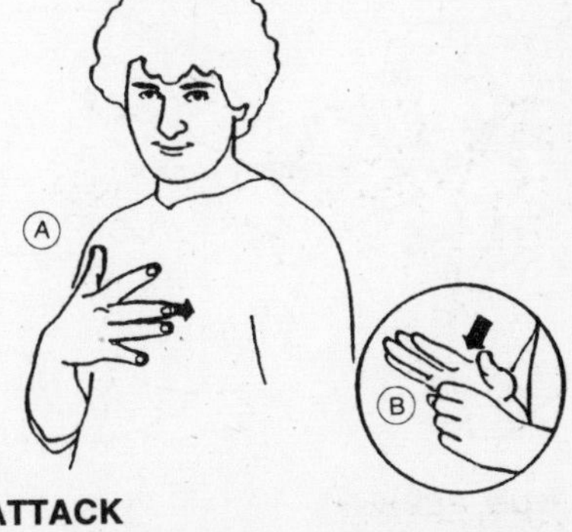

HEART ATTACK
Touch the bent middle finger of the right "5" hand to the left side of the chest. Then push the palm of the open right hand downward on the index-finger side of the left "s" hand forcing it downward.
Hint: "Heart" plus the pressure felt during a heart attack.

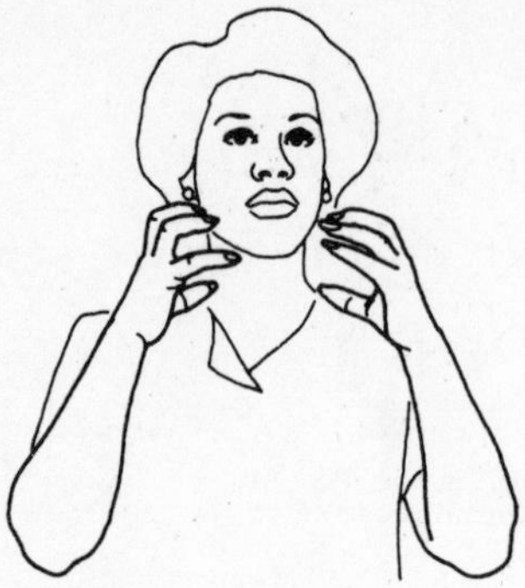

MUMPS
Hold both "claw" hands near each jaw, palms facing each other.
Hint: Shows the shape and location of mumps.

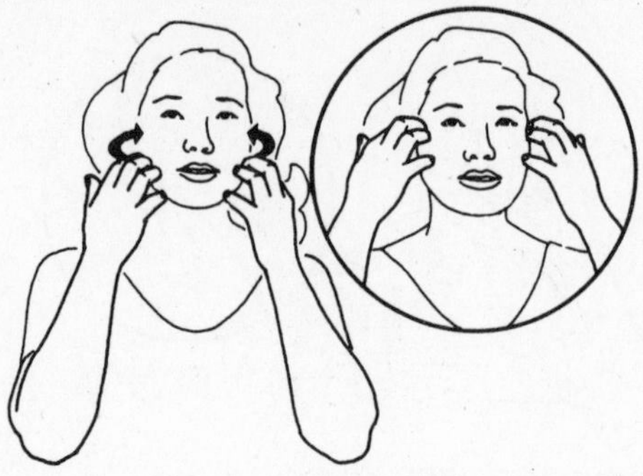

MEASLES
Lightly touch the fingertips of both loose "claw" hands on the cheeks in several places.
Hint: Shows the spots on the face from measles.

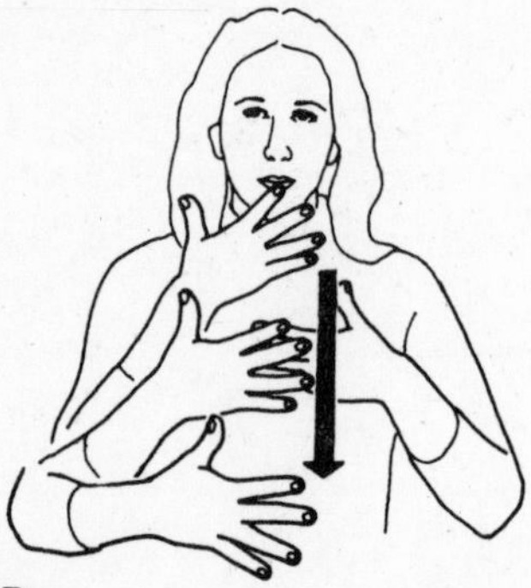

BLOOD, BLEED
With the left "5" hand in front of the chest, palm facing in and fingers pointing right, move the right "5" hand, palm facing in and fingers pointing left, from the lips downward past the back of the left hand, wiggling the fingers as the hand moves.
Hint: Blood streaming down.

PREGNANT
Bring the right curved hand forward from the stomach, palm facing in and fingers pointing down.
Hint: Shows the size and shape of a pregnant woman's belly.

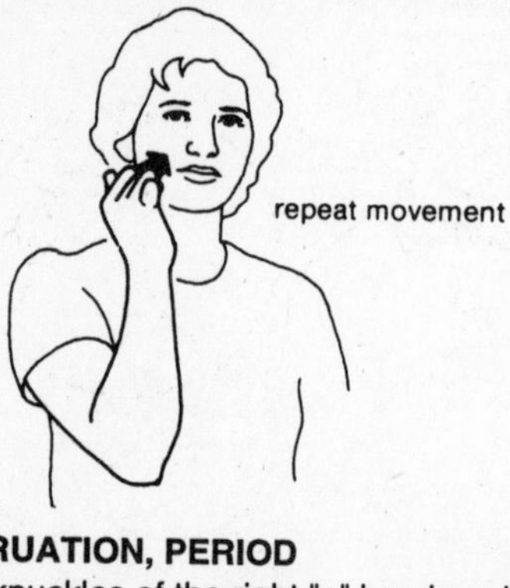

MENSTRUATION, PERIOD
Tap the knuckles of the right "a" hand against the right cheek with a double movement.

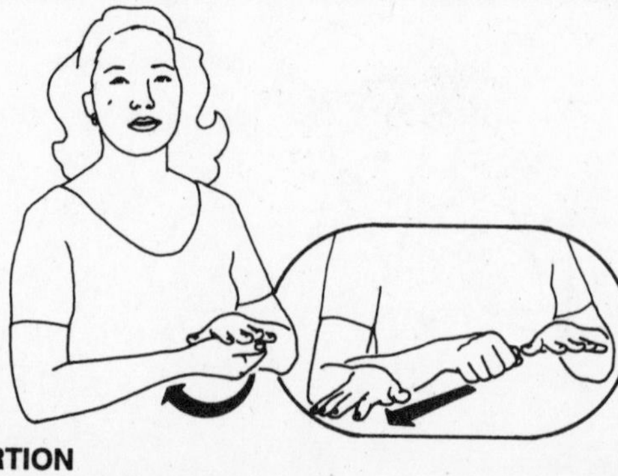

ABORTION
Beginning with the right "a" hand, palm facing up, under the open left hand held in front of the chest, palm facing down, move the right hand outward to the right while turning the palm down and opening into a "5" hand.
Hint: Shows removing a fetus and throwing it away.

Parts of the Body

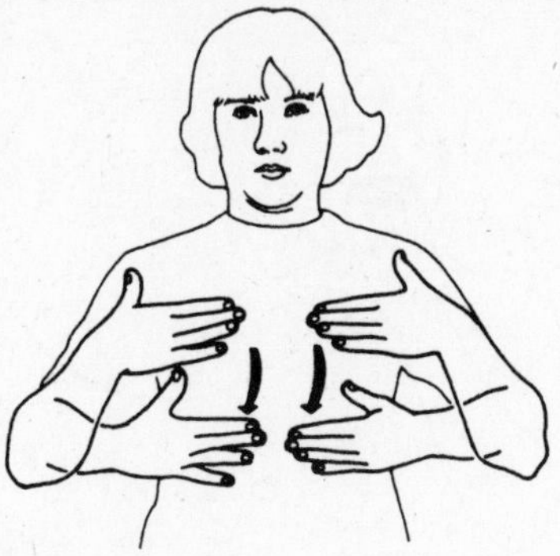

BODY
Touch the upper chest and then the lower chest with the fingers of both open hands, palms facing in and fingers pointing toward each other.
Hint: Shows the location of the body.

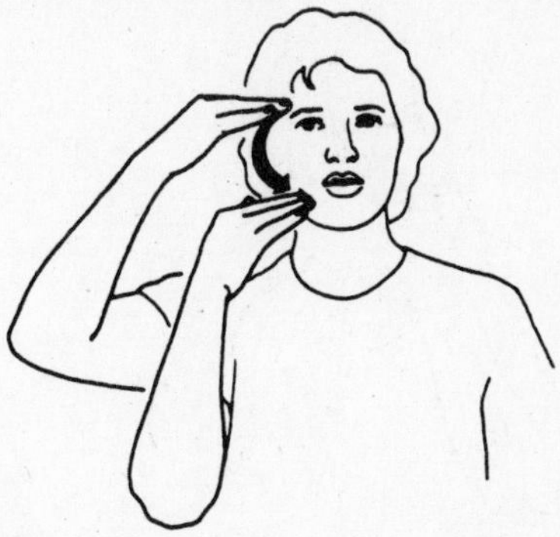

HEAD
Touch the fingers of the bent right hand, palm facing down, first to the right temple and then to the right lower cheek.
Hint: Shows location of the head.

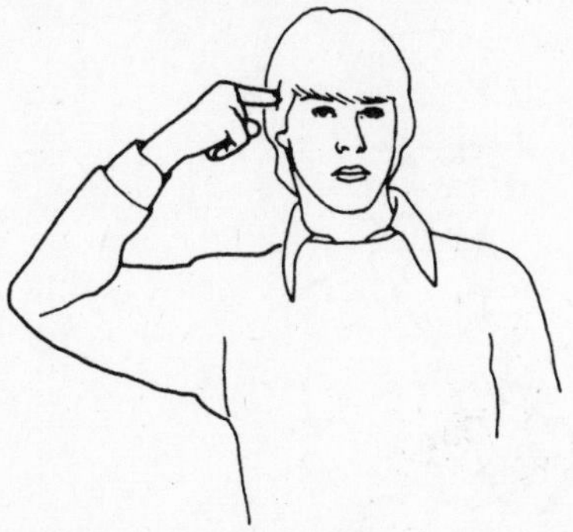

BRAIN, MIND
Touch the extended right index finger to the right side of the head.
Hint: Shows the location of the brain.

FACE, LOOKS, APPEARANCE
With the extended right index finger make a circle around the face.
Hint: The finger outlines the shape of the face.

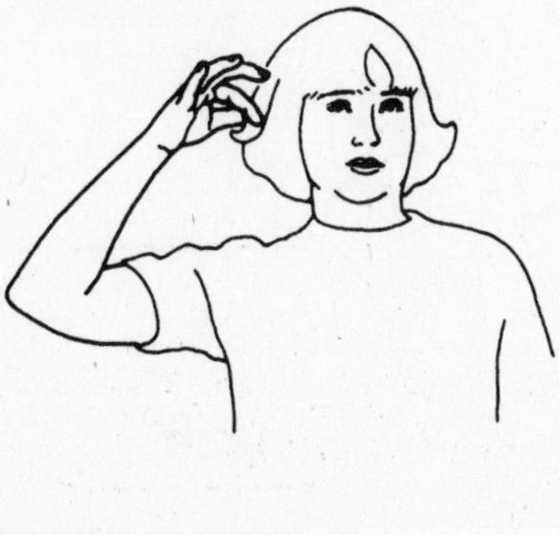

HAIR
Hold a few strands of hair between the index finger and thumb of the right "f" hand.
Hint: Shows the location of hair.

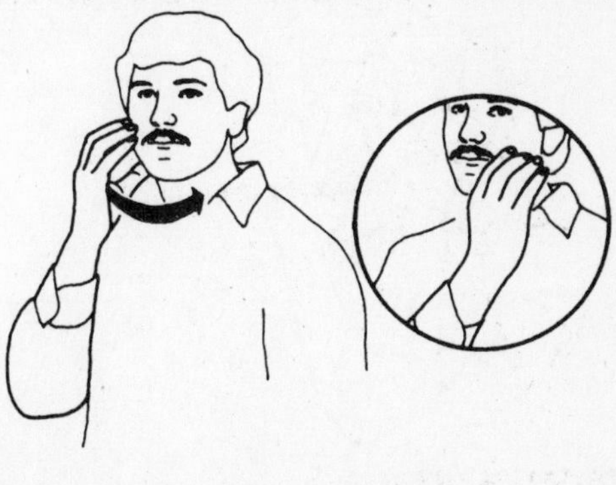

BEARD
Move the thumb and fingertips of the right "c" hand, palm facing in, from the right cheek along the jawline, ending with the index finger side of the "c" hand against the left cheek.
Hint: Shows the location and shape of a beard.

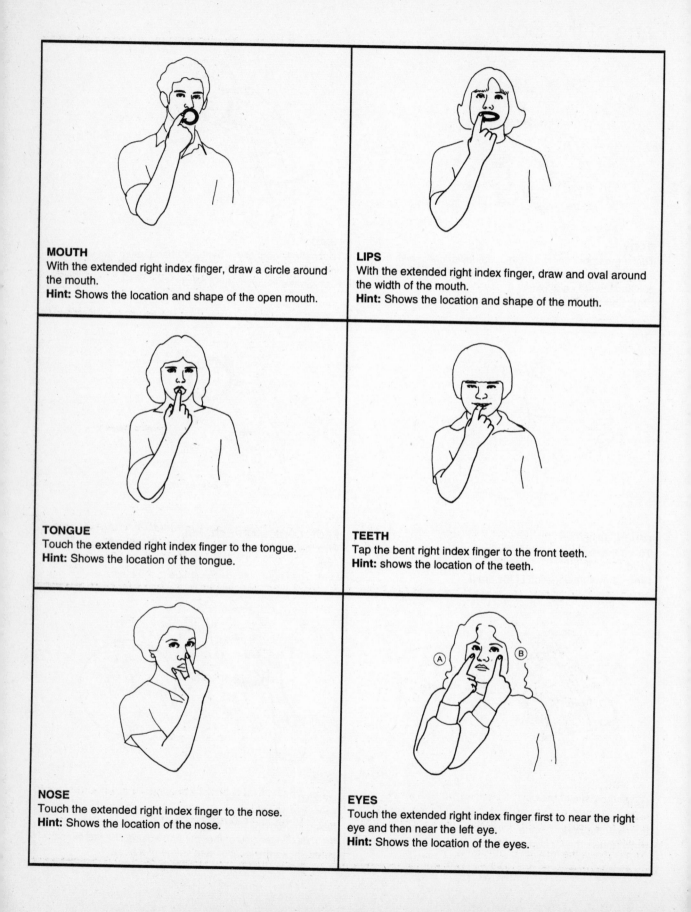

MOUTH
With the extended right index finger, draw a circle around the mouth.
Hint: Shows the location and shape of the open mouth.

LIPS
With the extended right index finger, draw and oval around the width of the mouth.
Hint: Shows the location and shape of the mouth.

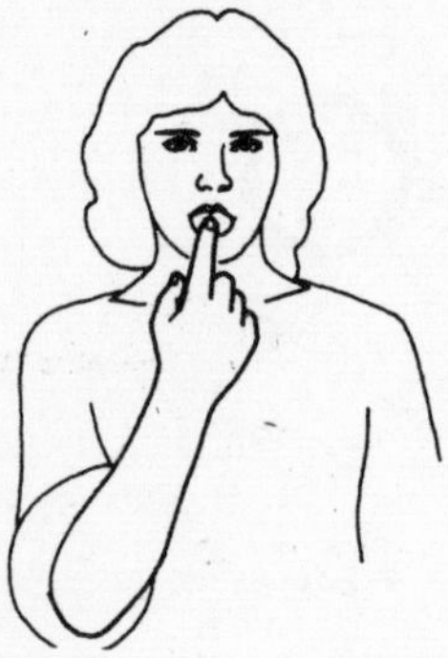

TONGUE
Touch the extended right index finger to the tongue.
Hint: Shows the location of the tongue.

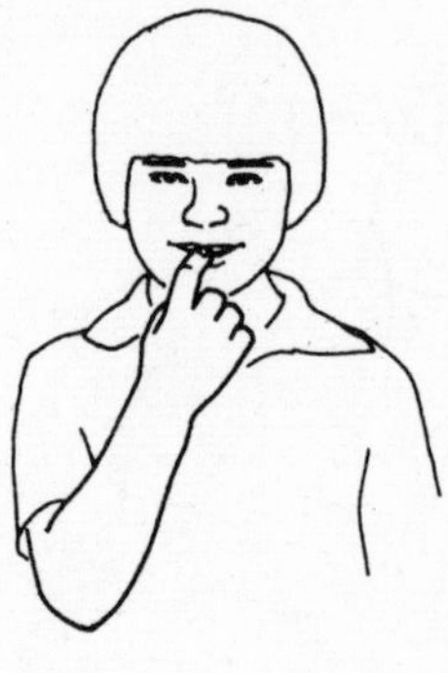

TEETH
Tap the bent right index finger to the front teeth.
Hint: shows the location of the teeth.

NOSE
Touch the extended right index finger to the nose.
Hint: Shows the location of the nose.

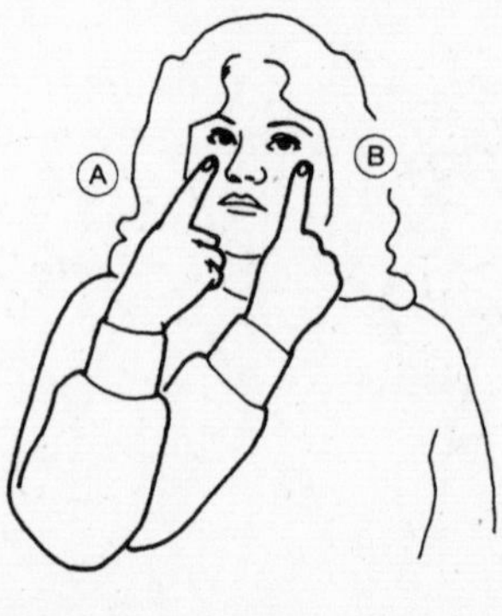

EYES
Touch the extended right index finger first to near the right eye and then near the left eye.
Hint: Shows the location of the eyes.

EAR
Grasp the right earlobe with the thumb and index finger of the closed right hand.
Hint: Shows the location of one's ear.

NECK
Tap the fingertips of the bent right hand, palm facing down, against the right side of the neck with a double movement.
Hint: Shows the location of the neck.

BACK
Tap the fingers of the open right hand, palm facing down, on the back of the right shoulder.
Hint: Shows the location of the back.

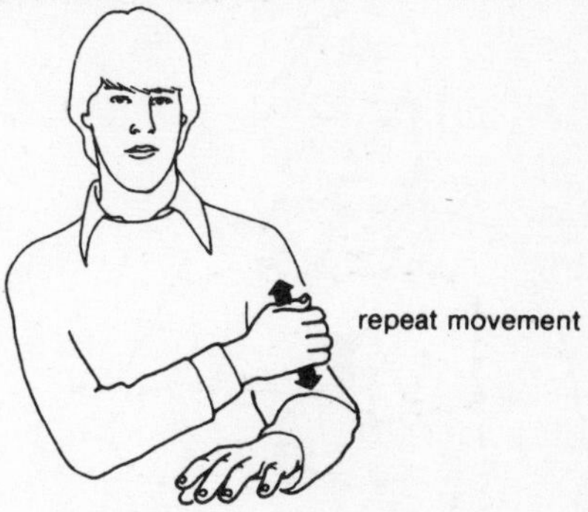

ARM
Move the palm side of the right curved hand up and down with a repeated movement on the upper left arm.
Hint: Shows the location and shape of the arm.

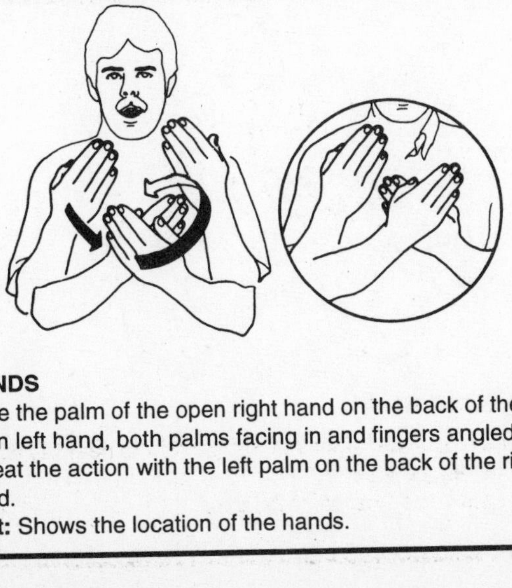

HANDS
Wipe the palm of the open right hand on the back of the open left hand, both palms facing in and fingers angled up; repeat the action with the left palm on the back of the right hand.
Hint: Shows the location of the hands.

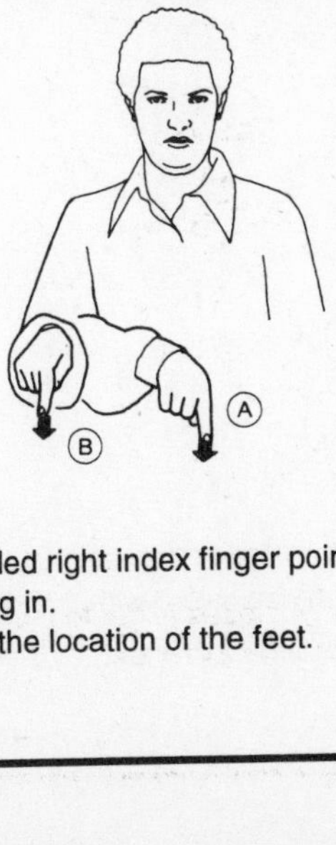

FEET
With the extended right index finger point downward at each foot, palm facing in.
Hint: Points to the location of the feet.

Survival

SURVIVE
Move the palm sides of both "10" hands upward on the body to the chest.
Hint: Formed similar to the sign for "live."

LIVE, LIFE
Move the palm sides of both "l" hands, index fingers pointing toward each other, upward on the body to the chest.
Hint: Initialized sign showing life moving through the body.

HELP, AID, ASSIST
With the little-finger side of the left "a" hand, palm facing in, on the palm of the open right hand, raise both hands in front of the chest.
Hint: The right hand gives help to the left hand.

DEFEND, PROTECT, GUARD
With both "s" hands crossed at the wrists in front of the chest, palms facing in opposite directions, move the hands forward with a short double movement.
Hint: The hands are help up to protect the body.

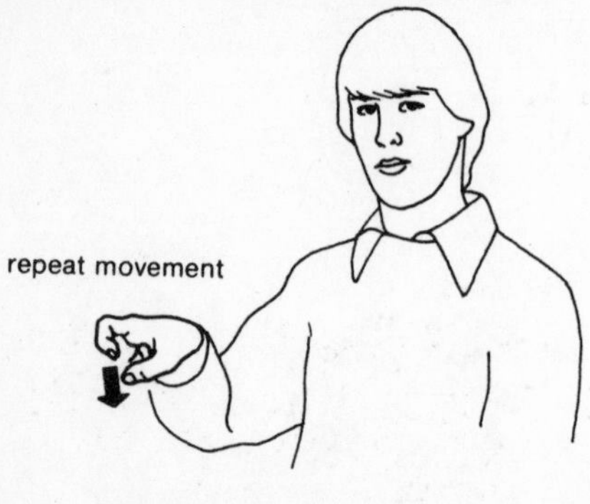

NEED, NECESSARY, OUGHT TO, SHOULD
Bring the right "x" hand downward with a short double movement in front of the right side of the body, palm facing down.

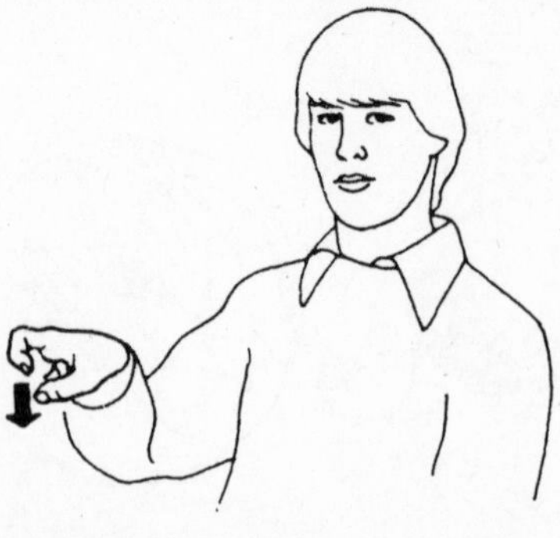

MUST, HAVE TO
Bring the right "x" hand downward in front of the right side of the body, palm facing down.

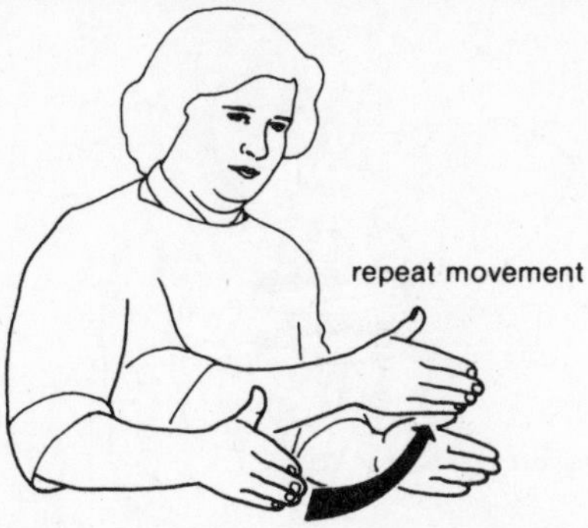

SPANK
Swing the open right hand, palm facing left and fingers pointing forward, with a double movement to the left against the palm of the open left hand held in front of the body, palm facing right and fingers pointing forward.
Hint: Mime spanking the hand on someone's bottom.

PUNISH, PENALTY
With the extended right index finger, palm facing down, strike downward on the elbow of the bent left arm.

HIT, STRIKE, PUNCH
With the knuckles of the right "s" hand, palm facing in, with a deliberate movement hit the extended left index finger held up in front of the chest, palm facing right.
Hint: Demonstrates striking something.

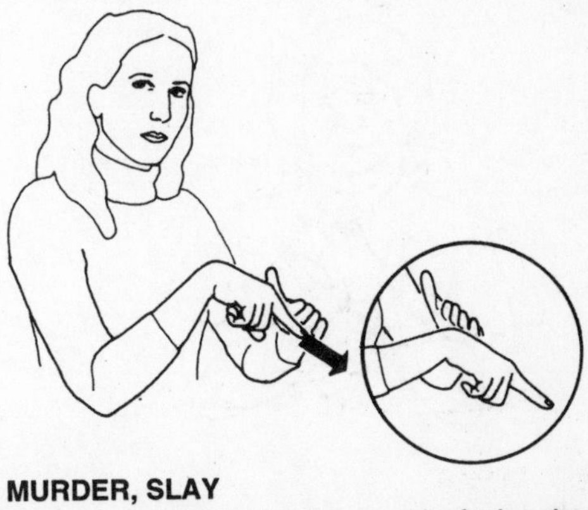

KILL, MURDER, SLAY
Push the extended right index finger, palm facing down, under the palm of the open left hand, palm angled right.
Hint: Stabbing someone.

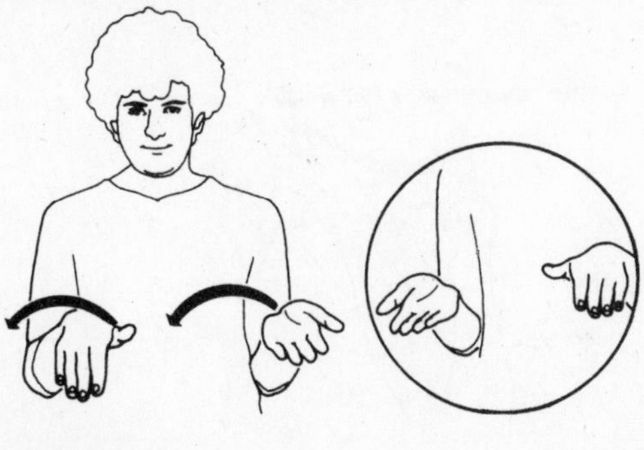

DIE, DEATH, DEAD
Beginning with both open hands held side by side in front of the chest, right palm facing down and left palm facing up, flip the hands over to the right so that the right palm faces up and the left palm faces down.
Hint: Represents a bug turning over to die.

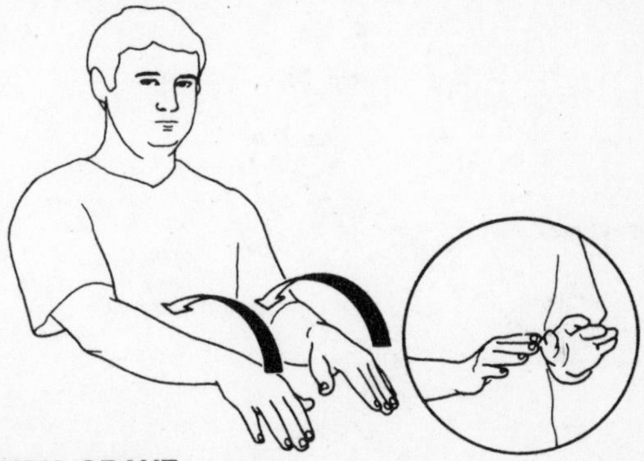

BURY, GRAVE
Beginning with both curved hands in front of the body, palms facing down and fingers pointing forward, bring the hands in arcs back toward the body.
Hint: Hands follow the shape of a mound of dirt on a grave.

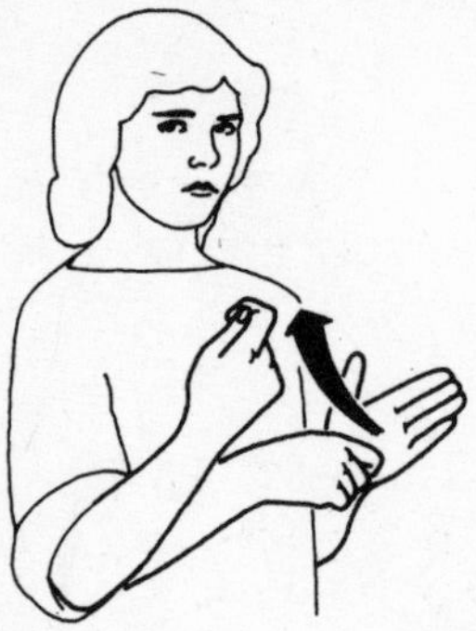

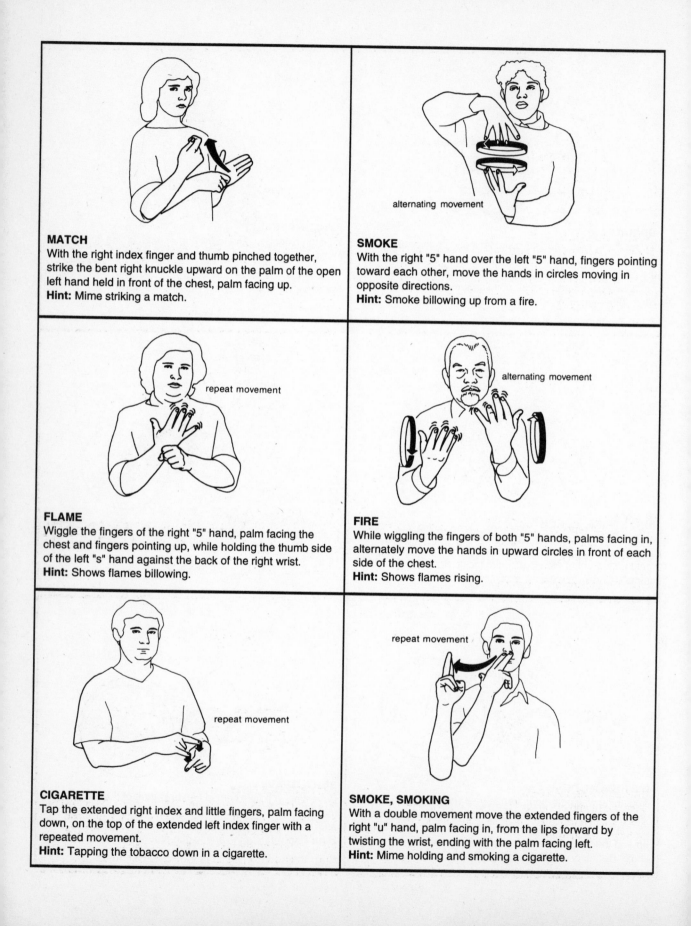

MATCH
With the right index finger and thumb pinched together, strike the bent right knuckle upward on the palm of the open left hand held in front of the chest, palm facing up.
Hint: Mime striking a match.

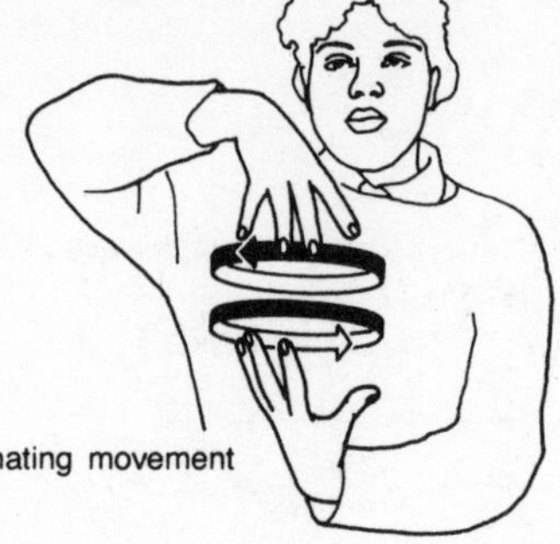

SMOKE
With the right "5" hand over the left "5" hand, fingers pointing toward each other, move the hands in circles moving in opposite directions.
Hint: Smoke billowing up from a fire.

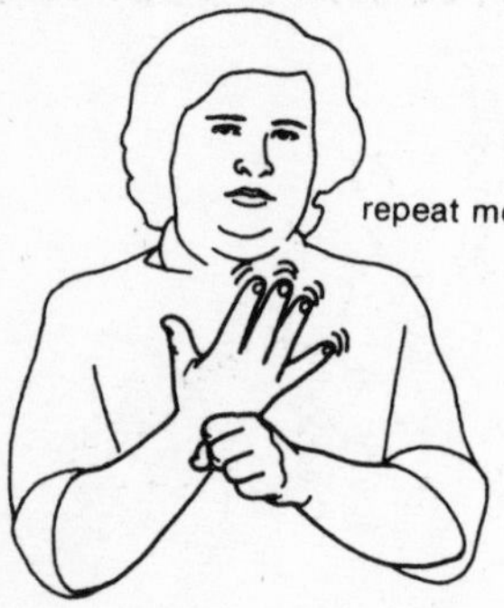

FLAME
Wiggle the fingers of the right "5" hand, palm facing the chest and fingers pointing up, while holding the thumb side of the left "s" hand against the back of the right wrist.
Hint: Shows flames billowing.

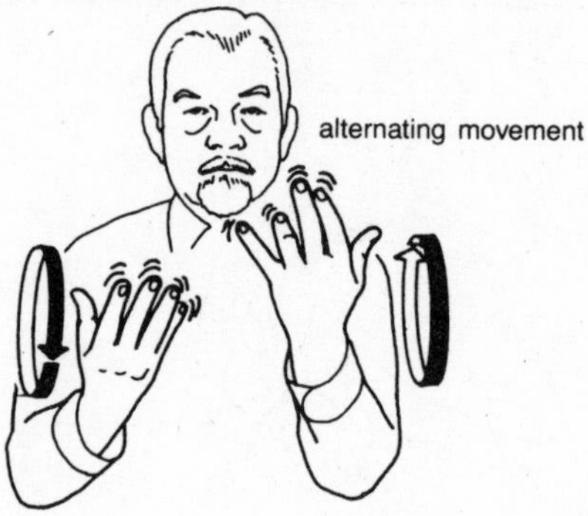

FIRE
While wiggling the fingers of both "5" hands, palms facing in, alternately move the hands in upward circles in front of each side of the chest.
Hint: Shows flames rising.

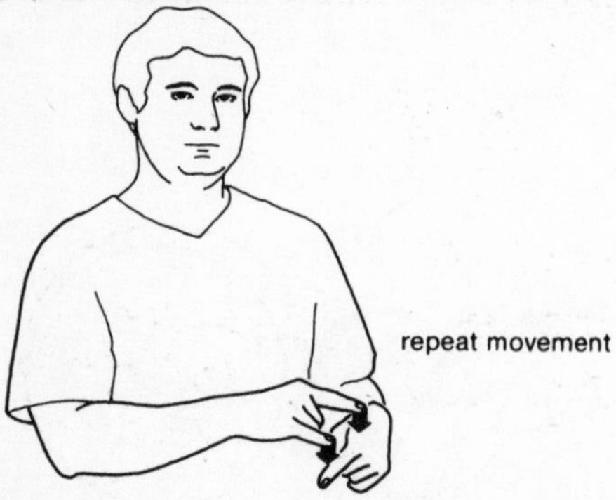

CIGARETTE
Tap the extended right index and little fingers, palm facing down, on the top of the extended left index finger with a repeated movement.
Hint: Tapping the tobacco down in a cigarette.

SMOKE, SMOKING
With a double movement move the extended fingers of the right "u" hand, palm facing in, from the lips forward by twisting the wrist, ending with the palm facing left.
Hint: Mime holding and smoking a cigarette.

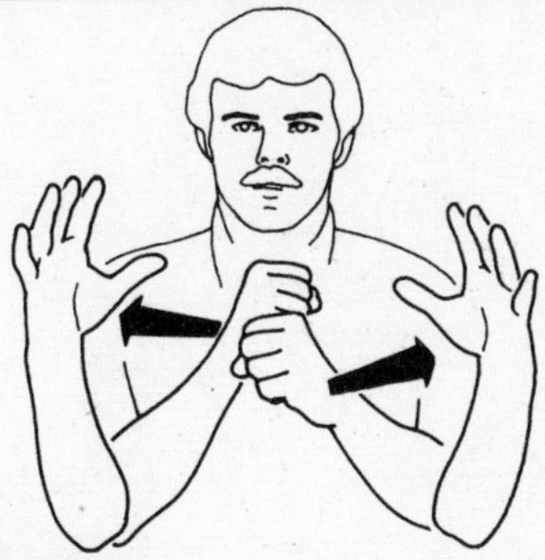

BOMB, EXPLODE
Beginning with the little-finger side of the right "s" hand on the index-finger side of the left "s" hand, palms facing in opposite directions, bring the hands apart with a sudden movement to in front of each side of the chest while opening to curved "5" hands.
Hint: A bomb exploding outward.

HURRY
Move both "h" hands, palms facing each other and fingers pointing forward, in an up and down bouncing movement while the hands move forward.
Hint: Initialized sign moving forward in a hurry.

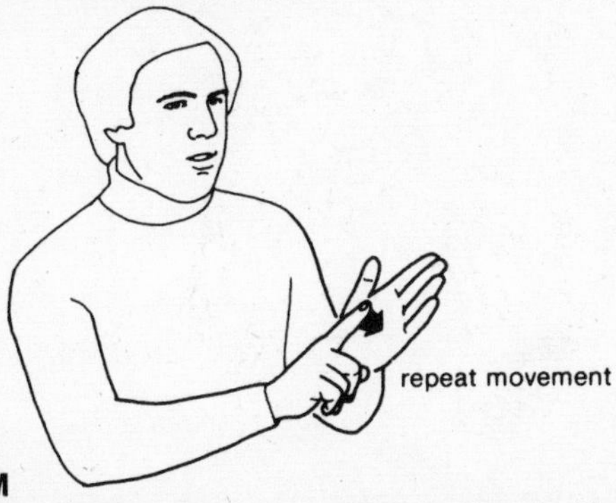

ALARM
With a quick repeated movement tap the thumb side of the extended right index finger, palm facing down, against the palm of the open left hand held in front of the chest, palm facing right.
Hint: The striking of the bell on an alarm.

WARNING, SIGNAL
With the fingers of the open right hand strike the back of the left "s" hand, both palms facing down, bringing the right hand back up after hitting.
Hint: Slapping someone to warn them.

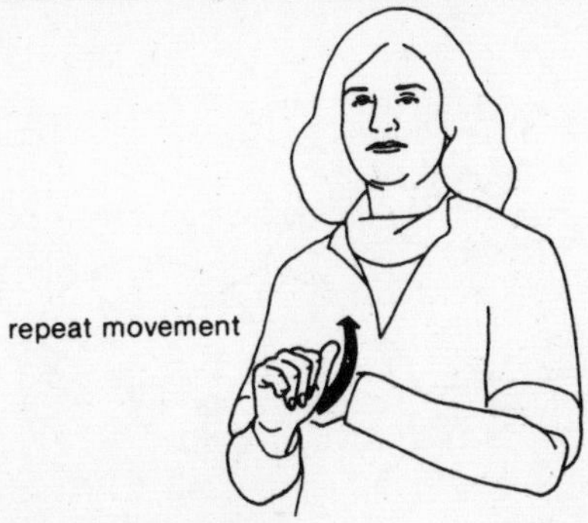

DANGEROUS, DANGER
Bring the thumb of the right "a" hand, palm facing left, upward with a repeated movement on the back of the left "s" hand held in front of the chest.

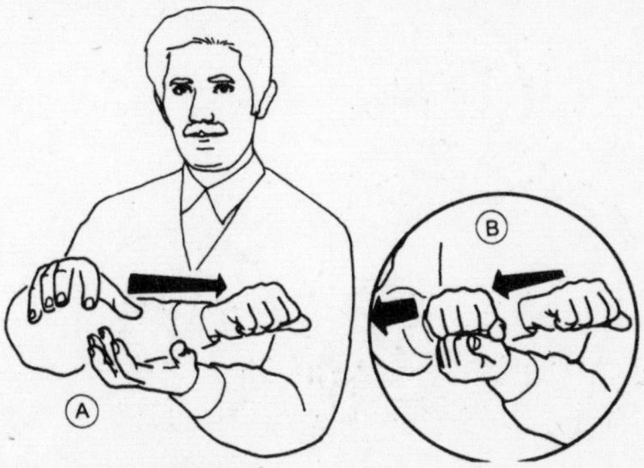

DAMAGE, DESTROY
Move the right "claw" hand, palm facing down, back toward the chest over the left "claw" hand palm facing up, while closing the hands into "a" hands. Then bring the right "a" hand forward brushing over the left "a" hand.
Hint: Taking something and tearing it into shreds.

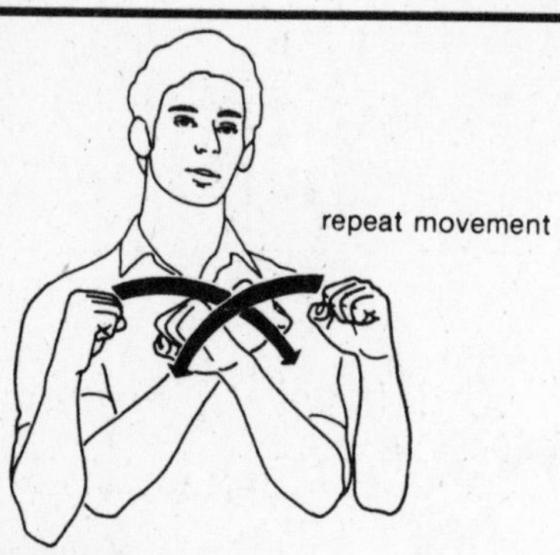

FIGHTING, FIGHT
Beginning with both "s" hands in front of each side of the chest, palms facing each other, bring the hands past each other with a double movement, brushing the right little finger across the left index finger each time.
Hint: Mime fighting.

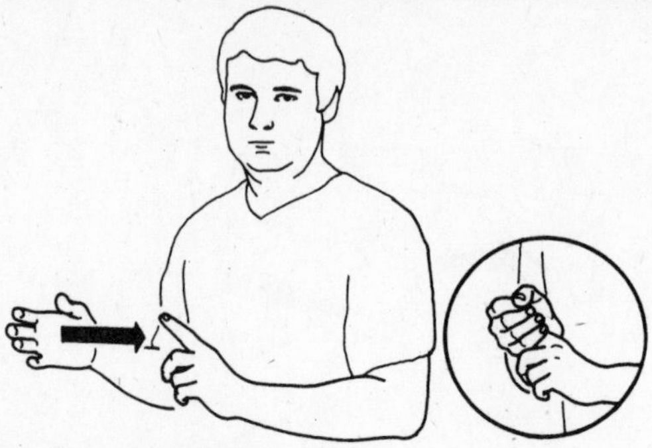

CAPTURE, ARREST, CATCH
Bring the curved right hand to the left to grasp the extended left index finger held up in front of the chest.
Hint: Surrounding and capturing someone.

STEAL
Beginning with the index-finger side of the right "v" hand, palm facing down, near the elbow of the bent left arm, pull the right hand back toward the left wrist while bending the extended right fingers.
Hint: Stealthily taking something.

GUN
Move the right "l" hand, palm facing left, forward in an arc in front of the right side of the body.
Hint: Mime holding a gun.

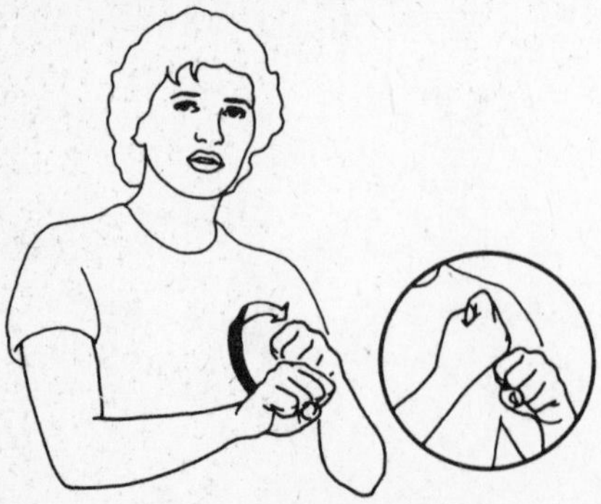

LOCK
Beginning with the right "s" hand under the left "s" hand, both palms facing down, twist the wrist to move the right hand up to land on the back of the left hand, ending with right palm facing up.
Hint: Turning the lock for protection.

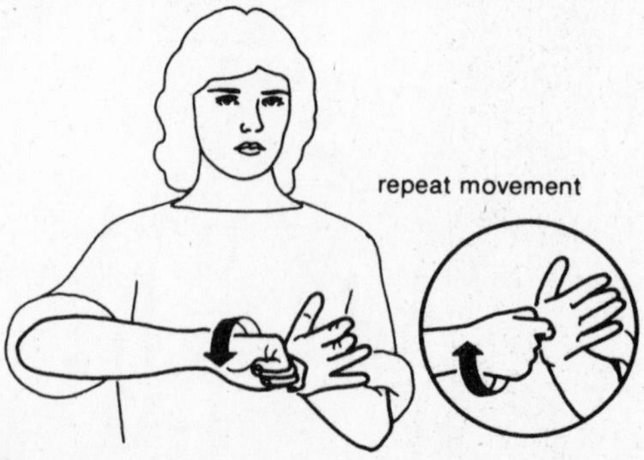

KEY
Twist the knuckle of the right "x" hand, palm facing down, with a double movement back on the palm of the open left hand, turning the right palm in each time.
Hint: Turning the key in a lock.

ten
RECREATION

Sports
Leisure and Hobbies
Travel and Transportation
Geography

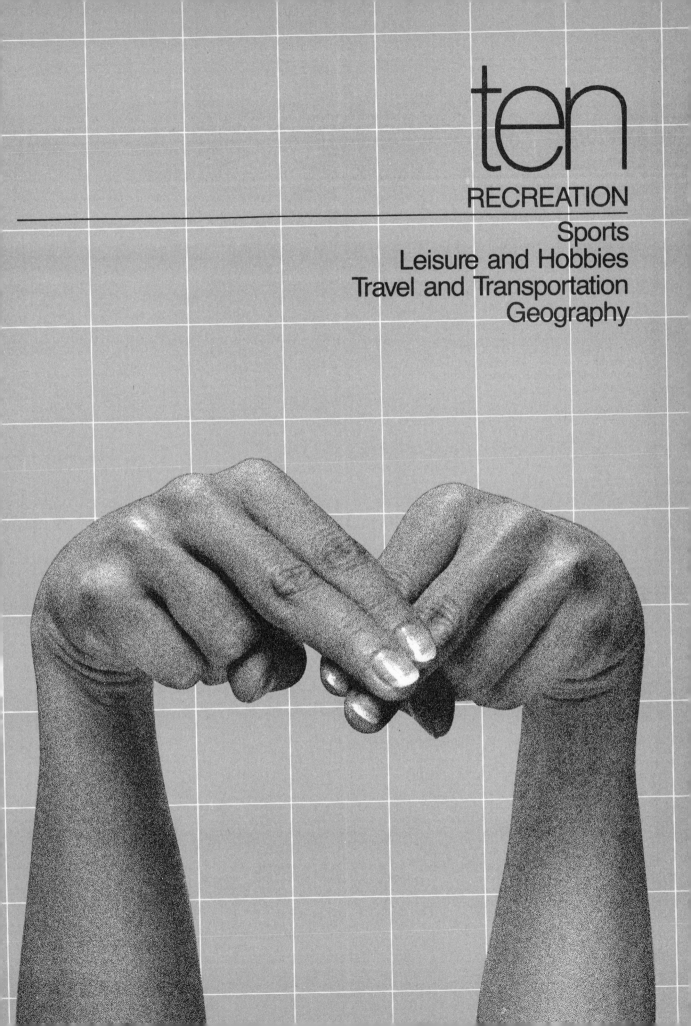

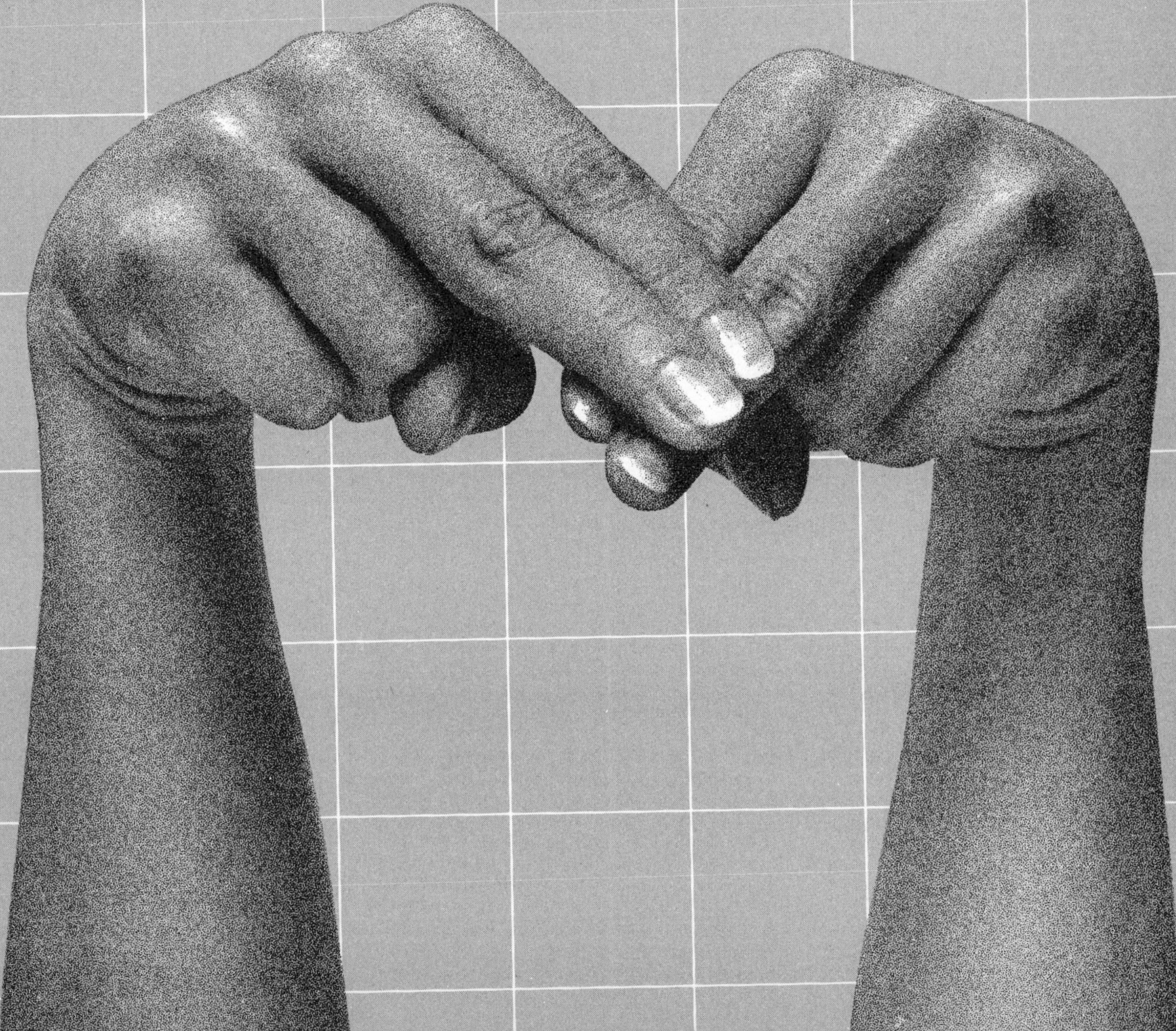

INITIALIZED SIGNS

The sign for "class" is formed with both "c" hands, palms facing each other, moving out and around until the little fingers touch and the palms are facing the body. The sign for "group" is formed in exactly the same way, except the hands have "g" handshapes. "Family" is formed the same way, except with "f" handshapes, "association" is the same except having "a" handshapes, and so forth. These signs are formed with the handshape from the manual alphabet that matches the first letter of the English gloss. The initialized formation helps distinguish the literal meaning of many signs.

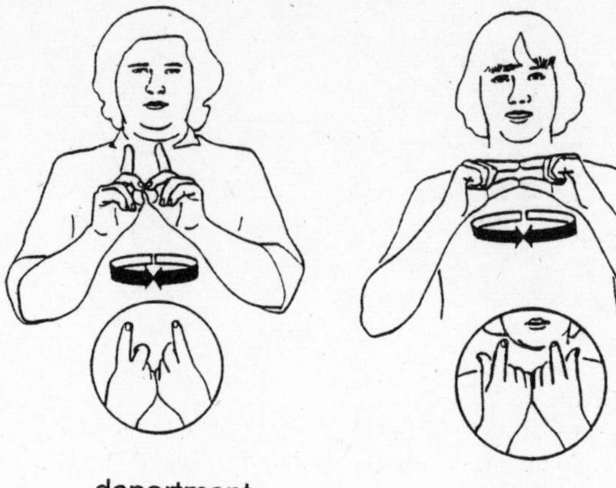

department   group

REPEATING SIGNS

Many signs, when they are repeated three or more times, indicate that the action or feeling lasted a long time, or that is happens habitually. A verb sign executed with a repeated slow circular orbit toward the body means "a continuous action." A verb sign quickly repeated means "a repeated action." For example, "wait, wait, wait" signed with a slow circular movement toward the body means "I waited for a long time." If you sign "worry, worry, worry" quickly, it means "I keep worrying."

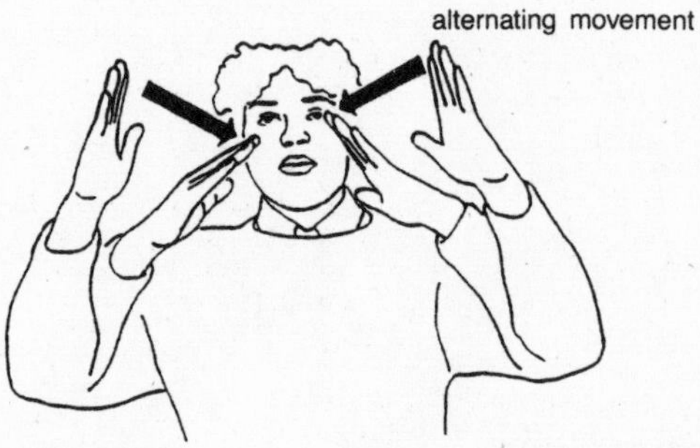

worry—worry—worry = I keep worrying.

THE ICONICITY OF SIGNS

Many signs resemble some aspect of the objects they represent. These signs are said to be "iconic' or "transparent." Often people unfamiliar with sign language will recognize and guess the meaning of these signs. Most signs for sports are iconic. For example, "baseball" looks like you are ready to swing your bat, and for "basketball," your hands seem to encircle and throw an imaginary basketball. Many other signs are less iconic, but once the relationship between the sign and its meaning is explained, they are easier to remember than those signs that seem to be more arbitrarily formed.

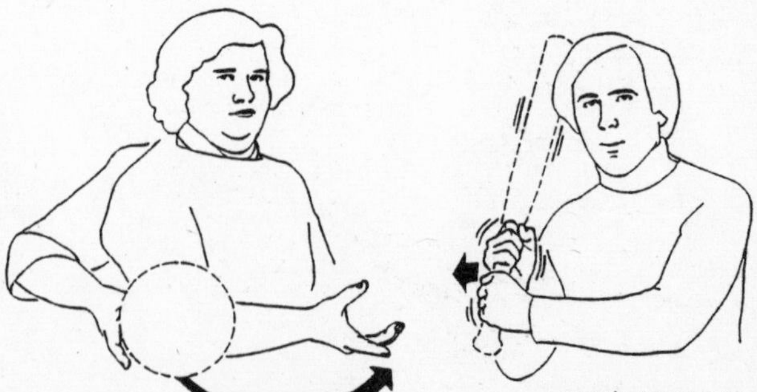

bowling   baseball

Sports

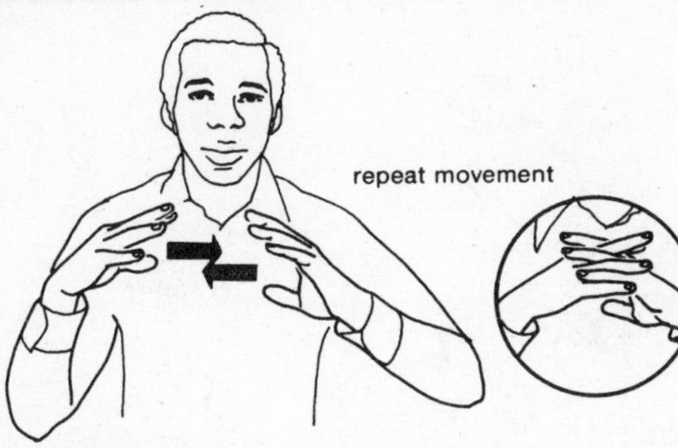

FOOTBALL
Beginning with both "5" hands in front of each side of the chest, bring he hands together with a double movement, meshing the fingers together each time.
Hint: The fingers represent the lines of scrimmage on the football field.

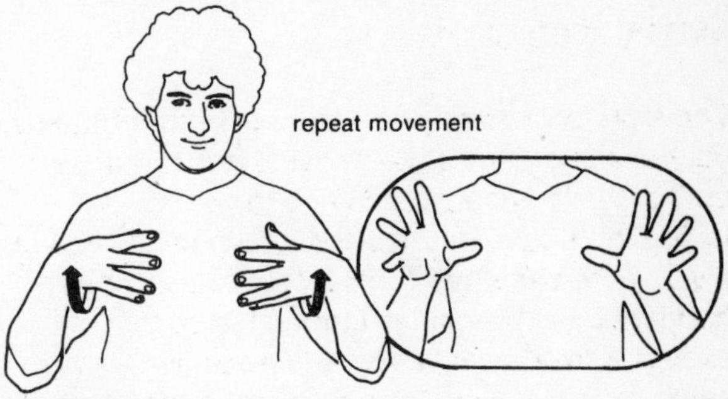

BASKETBALL
Beginning with both "5" hands in front of each side of the chest, palms facing in, twist the wrists with a double movement, turning the palms forward each time.
Hint: Mime throwing a basketball.

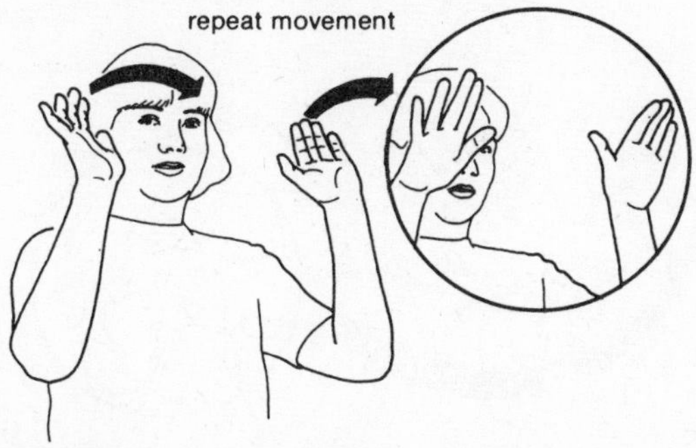

VOLLEYBALL
With the open hands above each shoulder, palms facing up, move the hands forward with a double movement, turning the wrists down each time.
Hint: Mime hitting a volleyball.

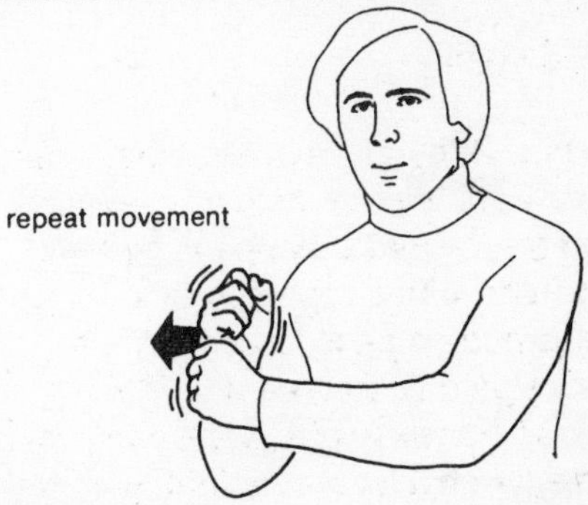

BASEBALL
With the little-finger side of the right "s" hand on the index-finger side of the left "s" hand, palms facing in opposite directions, in front of the right shoulder shake the hands forward with a short repeated movement.
Hint: Mime holding a baseball bat.

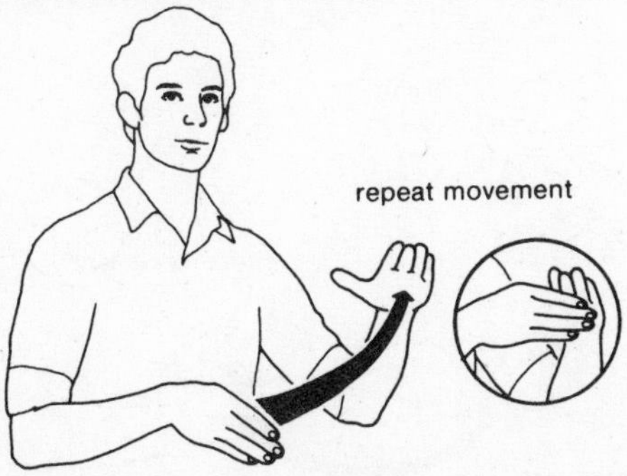

SOCCER
Bring the index-finger side of the right "b" hand, palm facing in, from in front of the right side of the body upward with a swinging movement to hit the palm of the open left hand held across the chest, palm facing down.
Hint: Kicking a soccer ball.

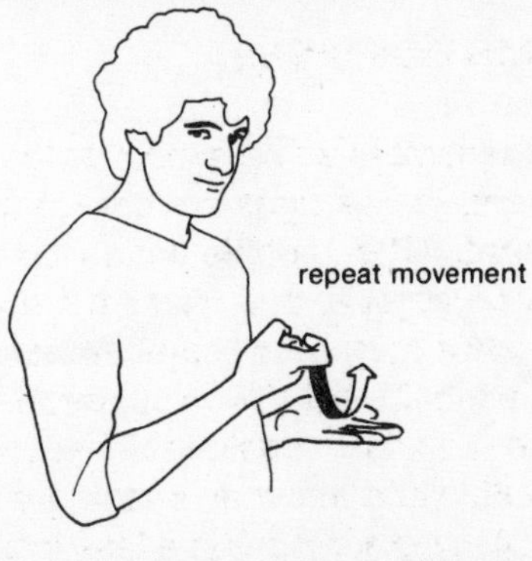

HOCKEY
Bring the knuckle of the right "x" hand, palm facing up, upward with a double movement across the palm of the open left hand, palm facing up.
Hint: The hockey stick striking the puck.

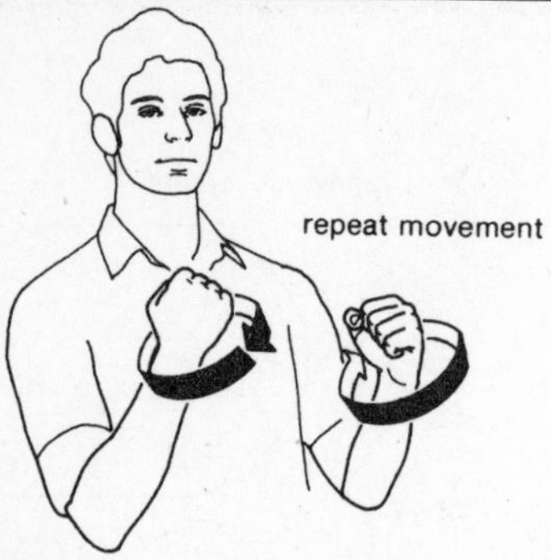

BOX, BOXING
With both "s" hands in front of each side of the chest, palms angled in, move the hands forward in alternating circles.
Hint: Mime defending oneself during boxing.

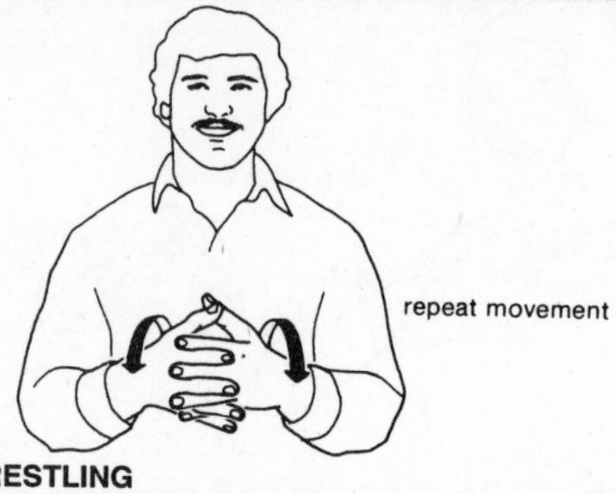

WRESTLING
With the fingers of both "5" hands meshed together in front of the body, palms facing in, move the hands forward and downward by twisting the wrists, turning the palms up each time.
Hint: Shows the limbs of two people intertwined.

ARCHERY, ARROW
Beginning with the right "a" hand above the right shoulder, palm facing up, and the left "s" hand forward of the left shoulder, move the right hand forward past the right cheek and then back again while moving the left hand forward,
Hint: Mime shooting an arrow with a bow.

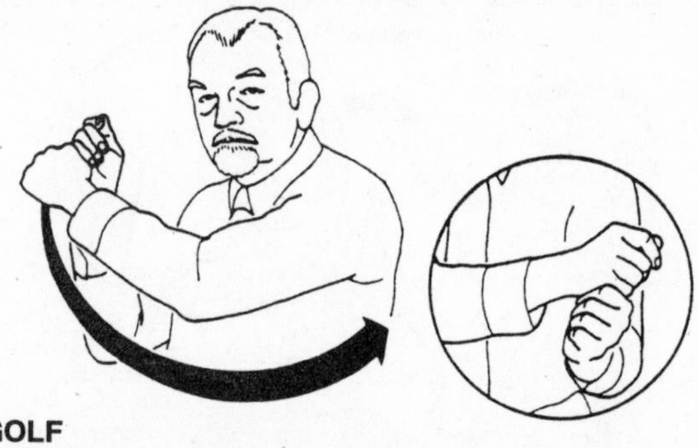

GOLF
With the little-finger side of the right "a" hand on the index-finger side of the left "s" hand, palms facing in opposite directions, swing the hands from near the right shoulder downward across the body to the left.
Hint: Mime swinging a golf club.

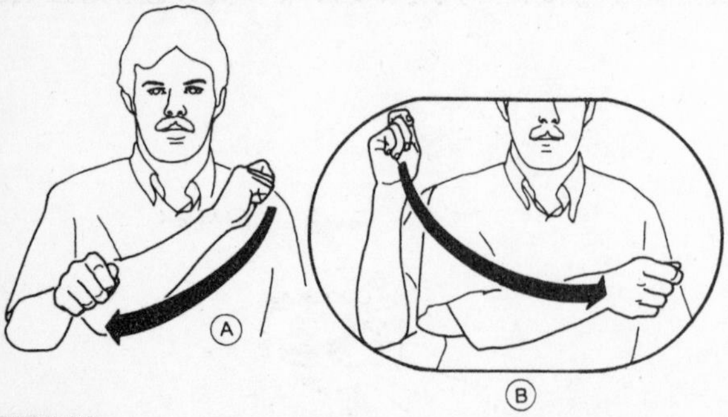

TENNIS
Bring the right "a" hand, palm facing left, from near the left shoulder downward across the body to the right and then from near the right shoulder downward across the body to the left.
Hint: Mime swinging a tennis racquet.

BOWL, BOWLING
With the right thumb, index finger, and middle finger extended, swing the right hand forward from near the right side of the body, palm facing up.
Hint: Mime throwing a bowling ball.

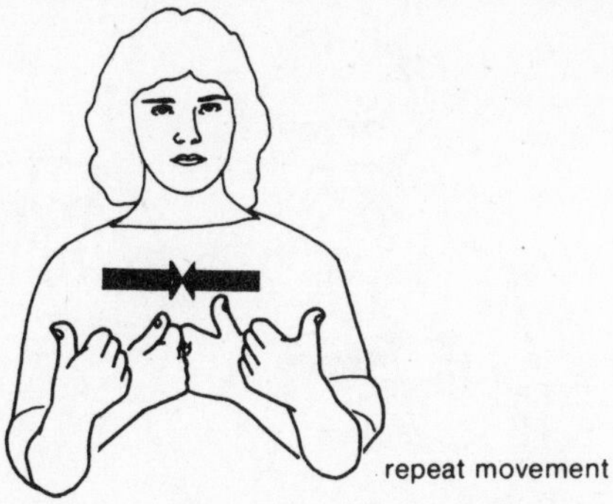

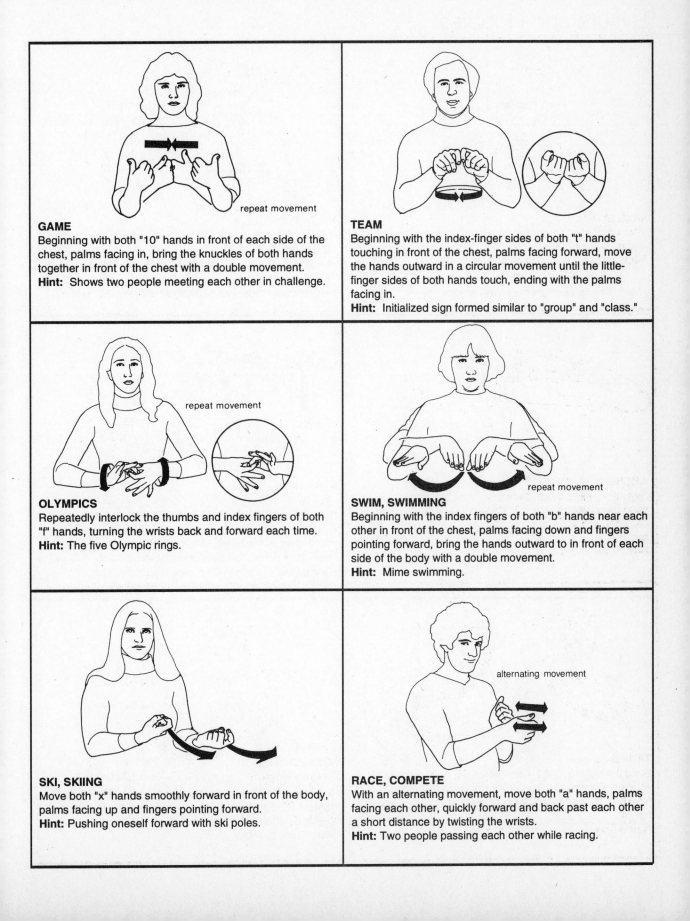

GAME
Beginning with both "10" hands in front of each side of the chest, palms facing in, bring the knuckles of both hands together in front of the chest with a double movement.
Hint: Shows two people meeting each other in challenge.

TEAM
Beginning with the index-finger sides of both "t" hands touching in front of the chest, palms facing forward, move the hands outward in a circular movement until the little-finger sides of both hands touch, ending with the palms facing in.
Hint: Initialized sign formed similar to "group" and "class."

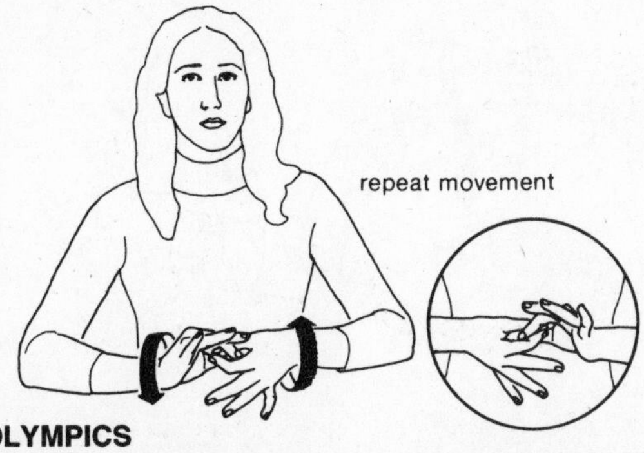

OLYMPICS
Repeatedly interlock the thumbs and index fingers of both "f" hands, turning the wrists back and forward each time.
Hint: The five Olympic rings.

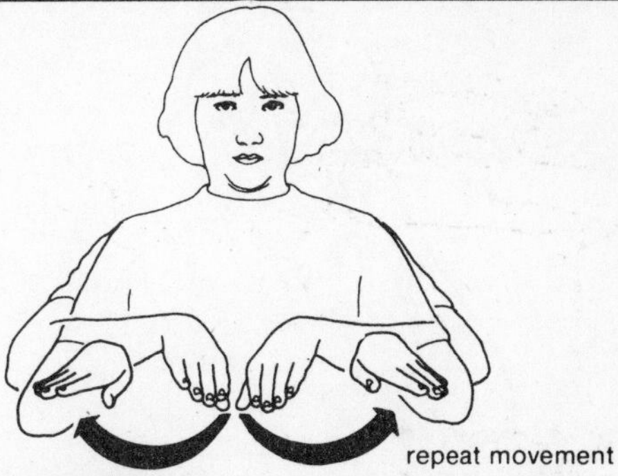

SWIM, SWIMMING
Beginning with the index fingers of both "b" hands near each other in front of the chest, palms facing down and fingers pointing forward, bring the hands outward to in front of each side of the body with a double movement.
Hint: Mime swimming.

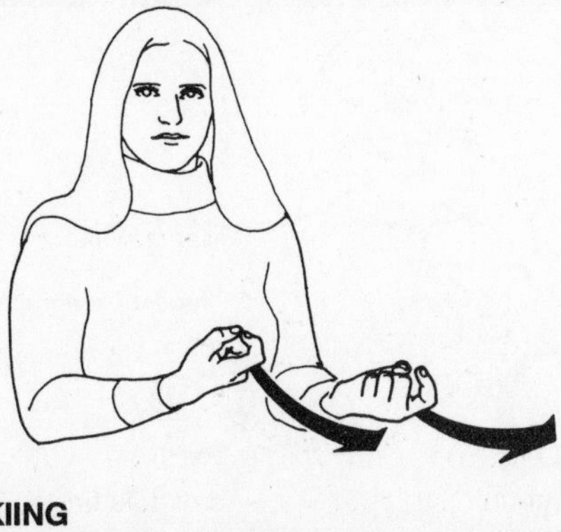

SKI, SKIING
Move both "x" hands smoothly forward in front of the body, palms facing up and fingers pointing forward.
Hint: Pushing oneself forward with ski poles.

RACE, COMPETE
With an alternating movement, move both "a" hands, palms facing each other, quickly forward and back past each other a short distance by twisting the wrists.
Hint: Two people passing each other while racing.

Leisure and Hobbies

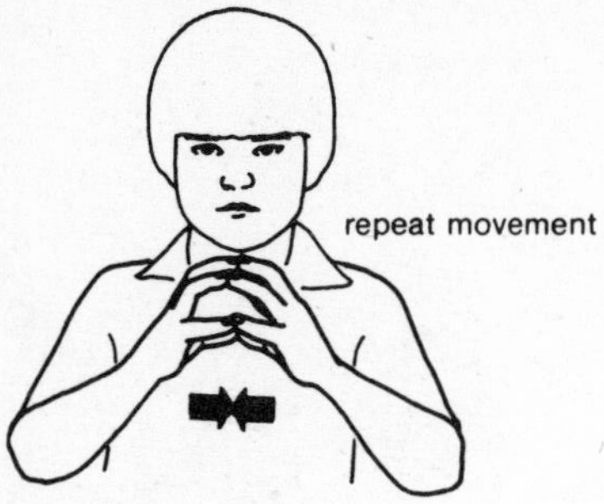

BALL
Tap the fingertips of both "claw" hands together with a double movement in front of the chest.
Hint: The fingers form the shape of a ball.

BALLOON
Move both curved hands, palms facing each other, from in front of the mouth forward in a circular movement, ending with the little fingers together and the palms facing in.

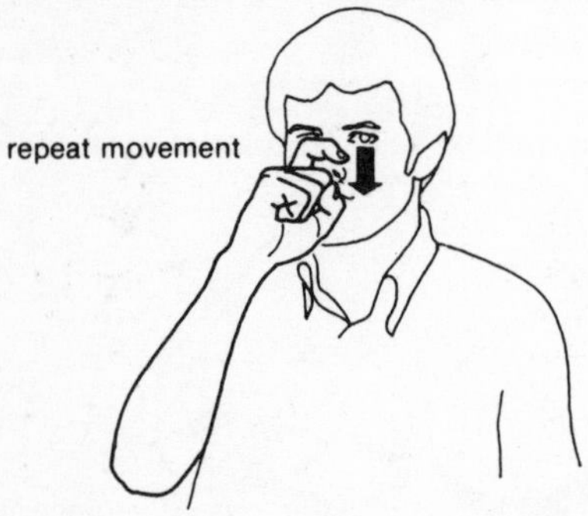

DOLL
Bring the thumb side of the right "x" hand, palm facing left, downward on the nose with a double movement.

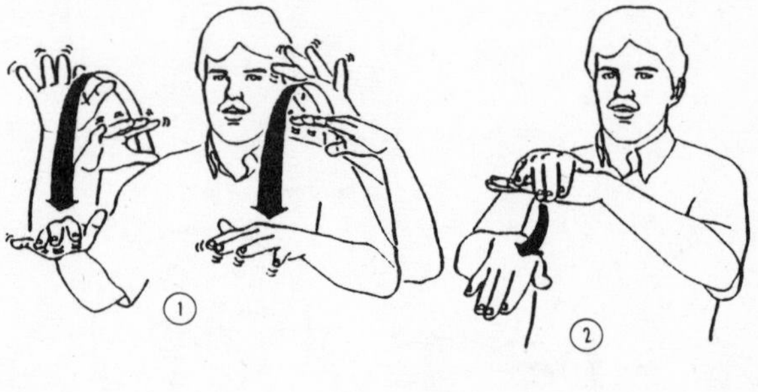

SLED
Bring both "5" hands from near each side of the head, palms facing down, forward and downward in a large arc, wiggling the fingers as the hands move. Then move the open right hand from across the back of the open left hand, both palms facing down, forward with a swooping movement.
Hint: "Snow" plus showing the movement of a sled.

FUN
Bring the index-finger side of the right "h" hand, palm facing down, forward and then downward from the nose tapping the fingers of the left "h" hand held in front of the chest as the right hand passes.

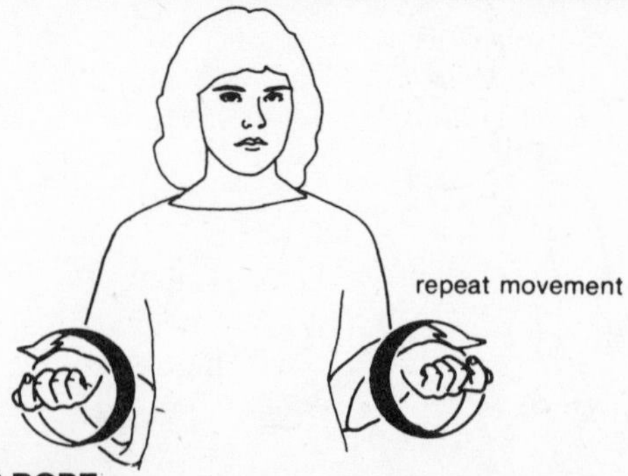

JUMP ROPE
With the index fingers and thumbs of both hands pinched together, move both "a" hands, palms facing up, in repeated outward circles in front of each side of the body.
Hint: Mime turning a jump rope.

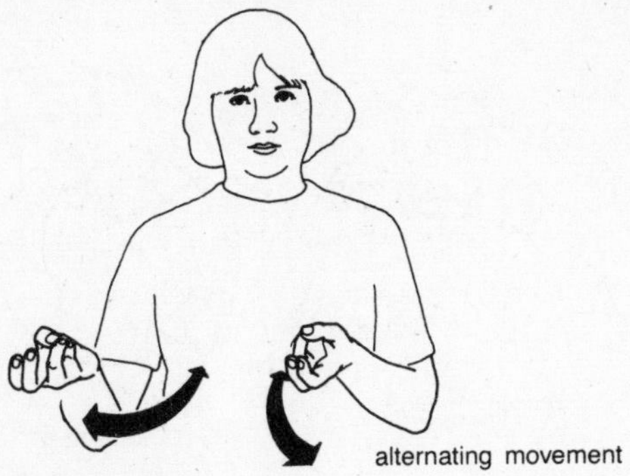

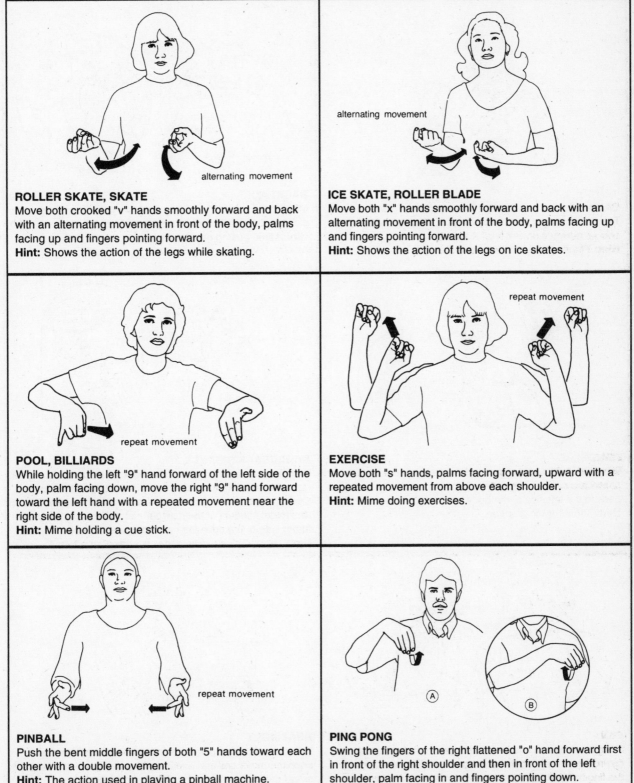

ROLLER SKATE, SKATE
Move both crooked "v" hands smoothly forward and back with an alternating movement in front of the body, palms facing up and fingers pointing forward.
Hint: Shows the action of the legs while skating.

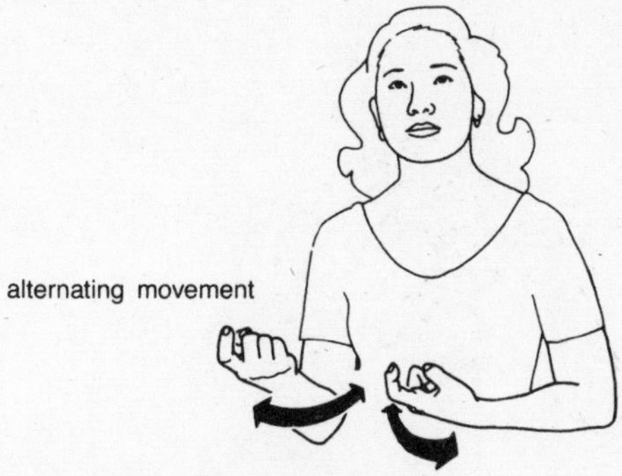

ICE SKATE, ROLLER BLADE
Move both "x" hands smoothly forward and back with an alternating movement in front of the body, palms facing up and fingers pointing forward.
Hint: Shows the action of the legs on ice skates.

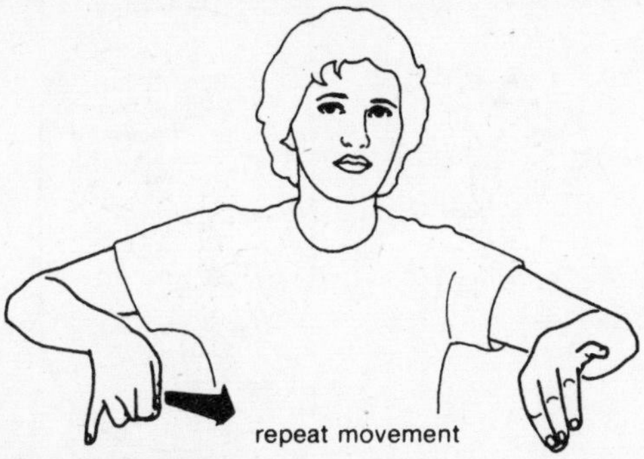

POOL, BILLIARDS
While holding the left "9" hand forward of the left side of the body, palm facing down, move the right "9" hand forward toward the left hand with a repeated movement near the right side of the body.
Hint: Mime holding a cue stick.

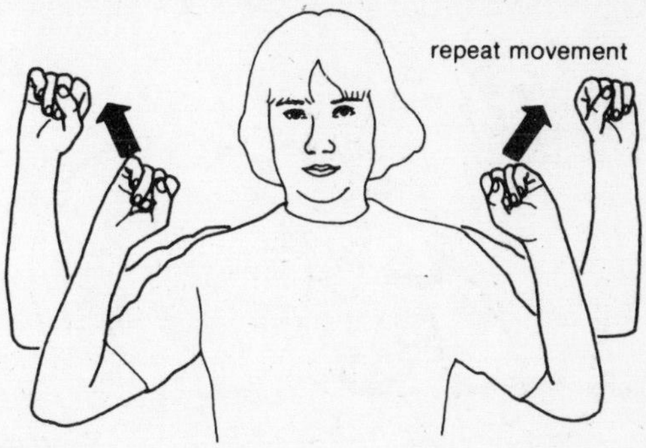

EXERCISE
Move both "s" hands, palms facing forward, upward with a repeated movement from above each shoulder.
Hint: Mime doing exercises.

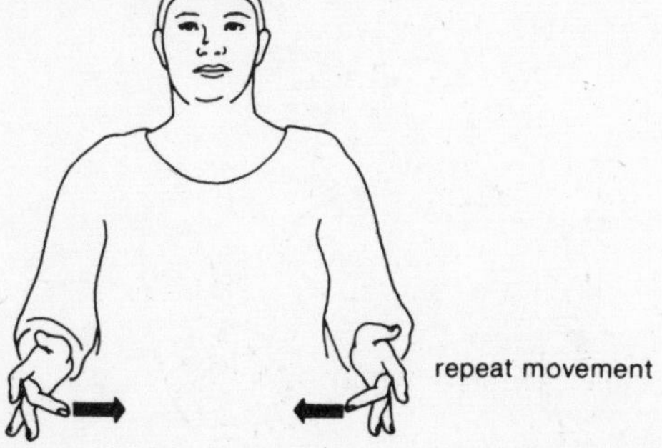

PINBALL
Push the bent middle fingers of both "5" hands toward each other with a double movement.
Hint: The action used in playing a pinball machine.

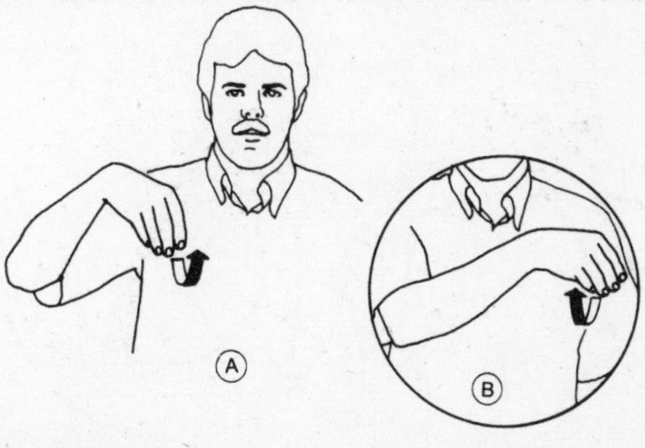

PING PONG
Swing the fingers of the right flattened "o" hand forward first in front of the right shoulder and then in front of the left shoulder, palm facing in and fingers pointing down.
Hint: Mime the action used in playing ping pong.

TENT
Beginning with the extended index and little fingers of both hands touching in front of the face, palms facing each other, bring the hands downward and apart.
Hint: Fingers follow the shape of a tent.

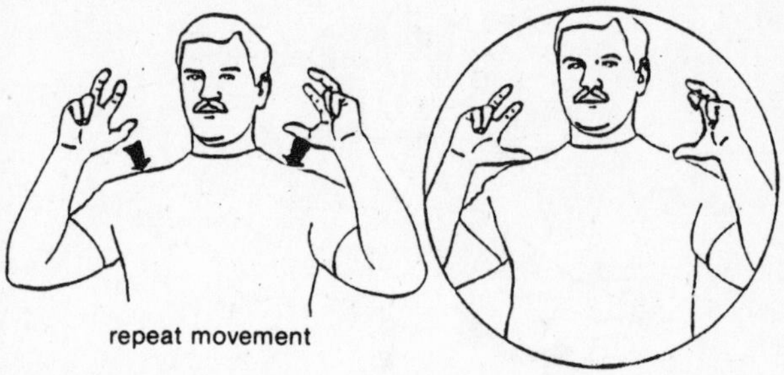

BACKPACK
Move the curved "3" hands, palms facing forward, back over each shoulder with a short double movement.
Hint: Mime putting on a backpack.

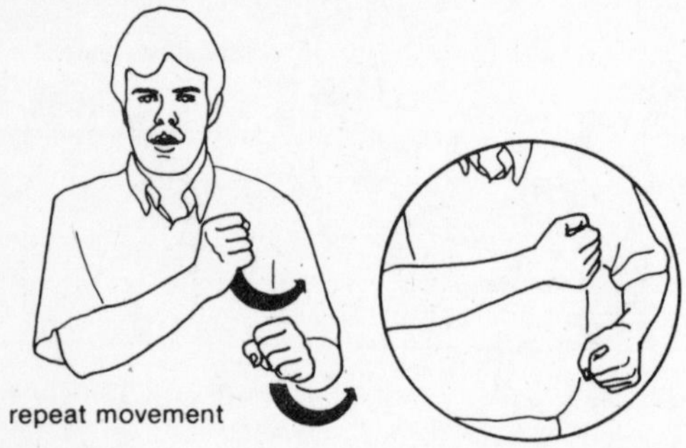

CANOEING
With both "s" hands in front of the left side of the body, palms facing in and right hand over the left, move the hands back to the left side of the body with a double movement.
Hint: Mime rowing a canoe.

HORSEBACK RIDING
With the extended thumbs of the right "u" hands touching the right side of the head, palm facing forward, bend the fingers up and down with a double movement. Then with the index and middle fingers of the right "3" hand straddling the index-finger side of the open left hand, move both hands forward.
Hint: "Horse" plus represents legs straddling a horse.

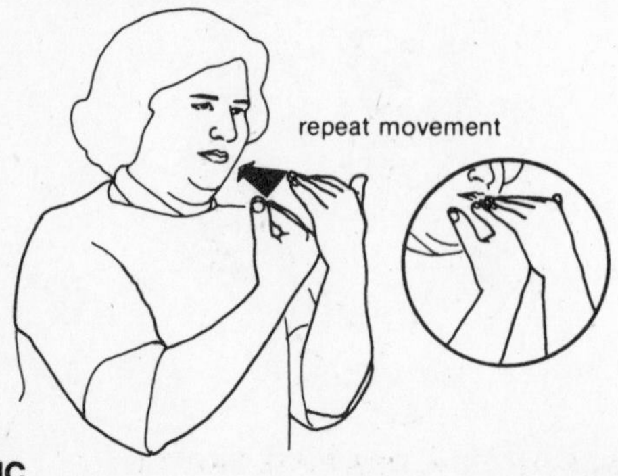

PICNIC
With the bent left fingers over the bent right fingers, palms facing down and fingers pointing toward the mouth, move the hands back toward the mouth with a double movement.
Hint: Shoving food in one's mouth at a picnic.

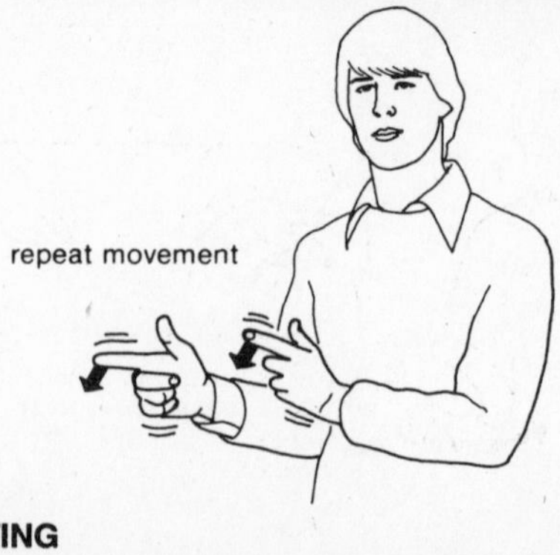

HUNTING
With both "l" hands in front of the body, palms facing in opposite directions and one hand closer to the body than the other, shake the hands downward with a short double movement.
Hint: Mime shooting at something.

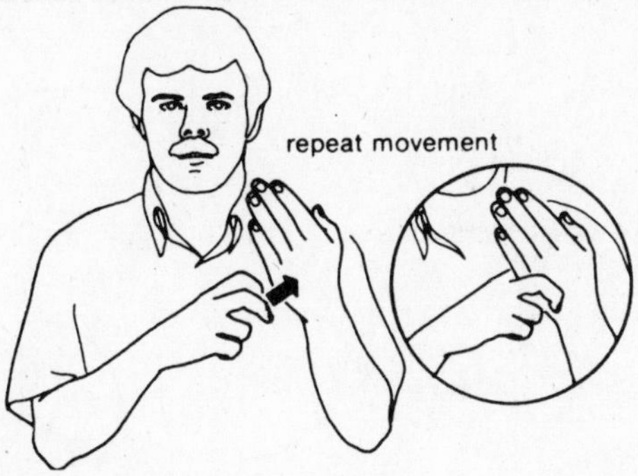

TICKET
Move the fingers of the right crooked "v" hand, palm facing down, with a double movement against each side of the little-finger side of the open left hand held up in front of the chest, palm facing in.
Hint: Punching a used ticket.

FIREWORKS
Beginning with both "s" hands in front of each side of the body, palms facing forward, move the hands together in front of the chest and then upward while opening into "5" hands in front of each side of the body, palms facing forward and fingers pointing up.
Hint: Represents fireworks exploding.

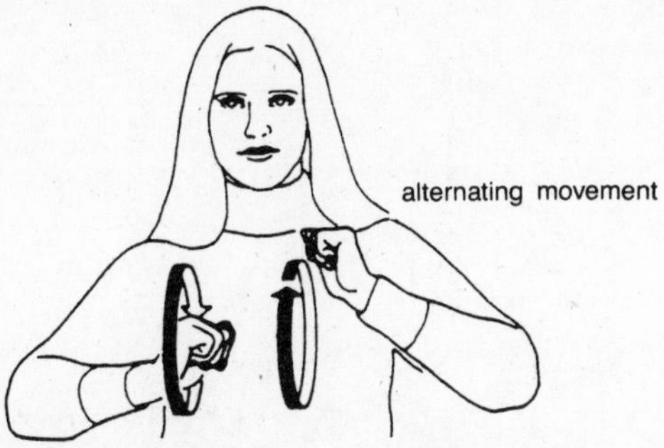

THEATER, DRAMA, PLAY, ACT
Move the thumbs of both "a" hands, palms facing each other, in alternating circles forward in front of each side of the chest.

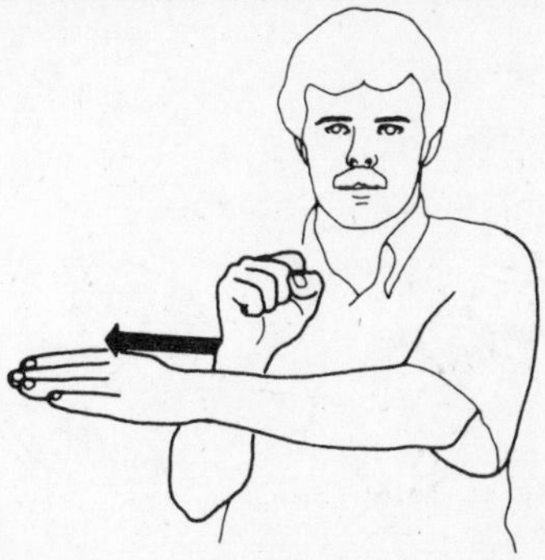

STAGE
With the left arm extended in front of the body, move the right "s" hand, palm facing forward, from the wrist across the back of the open left hand, palm facing down and fingers pointing right.
Hint: Initialized sign showing the shape of a stage floor.

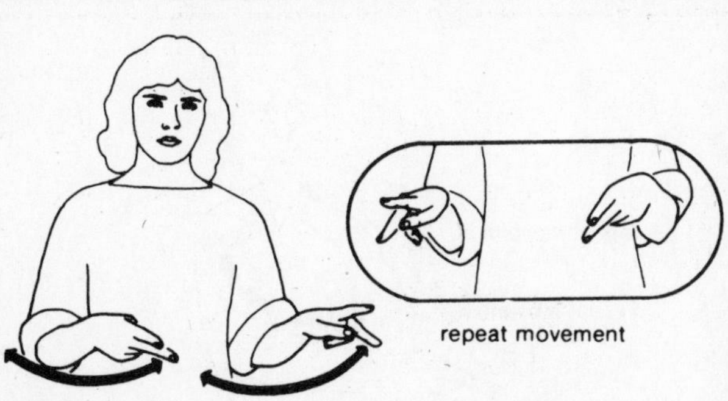

PARTY
Swing both "p" hands, palms facing down, from side to side with a repeated movement in front of the body.
Hint: Initialized sign.

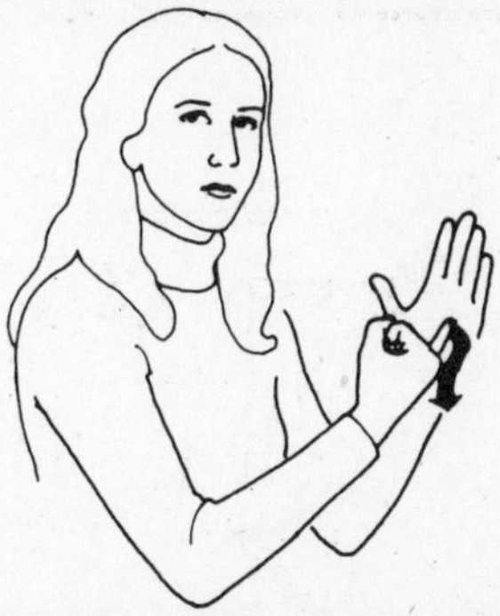

ART, ILLUSTRATION, DRAWING, SKETCH
Move the extended little finger of the right "i" hand, palm facing in, downward in a wiggly movement on the palm of the open left hand held in front of the chest, palm facing right.
Hint: Drawing a line on paper.

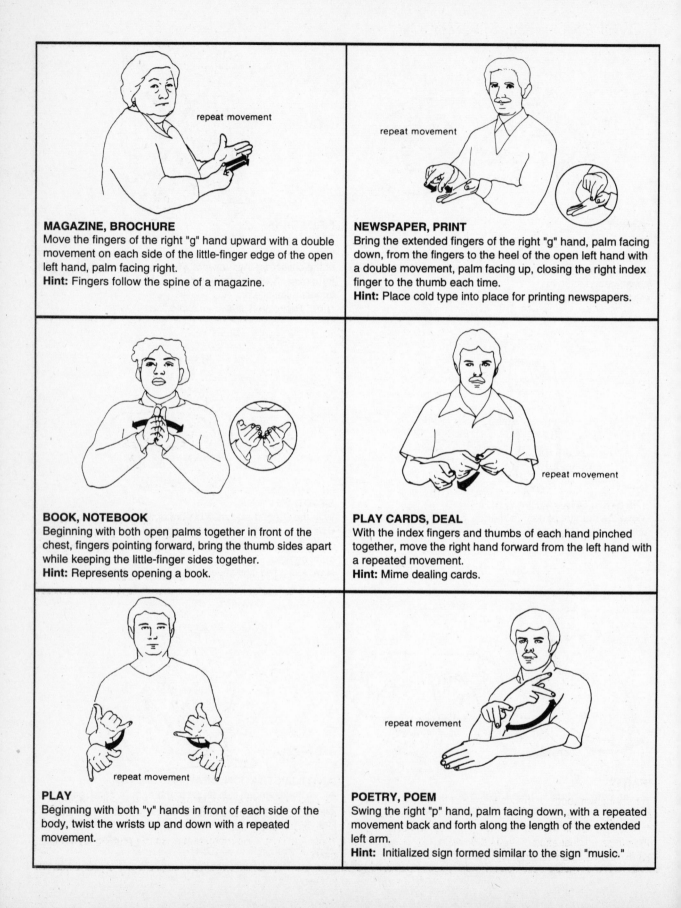

MAGAZINE, BROCHURE
Move the fingers of the right "g" hand upward with a double movement on each side of the little-finger edge of the open left hand, palm facing right.
Hint: Fingers follow the spine of a magazine.

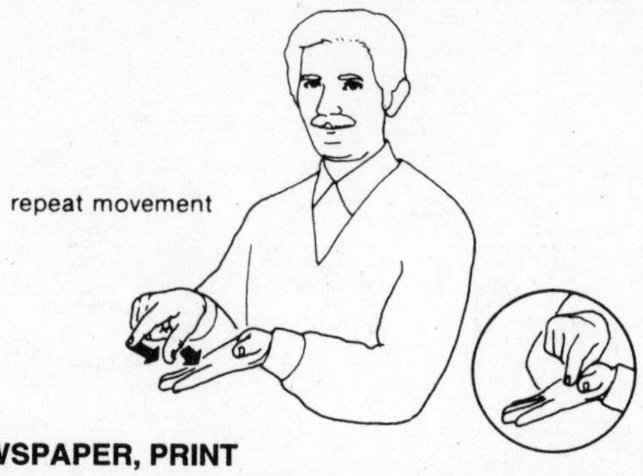

NEWSPAPER, PRINT
Bring the extended fingers of the right "g" hand, palm facing down, from the fingers to the heel of the open left hand with a double movement, palm facing up, closing the right index finger to the thumb each time.
Hint: Place cold type into place for printing newspapers.

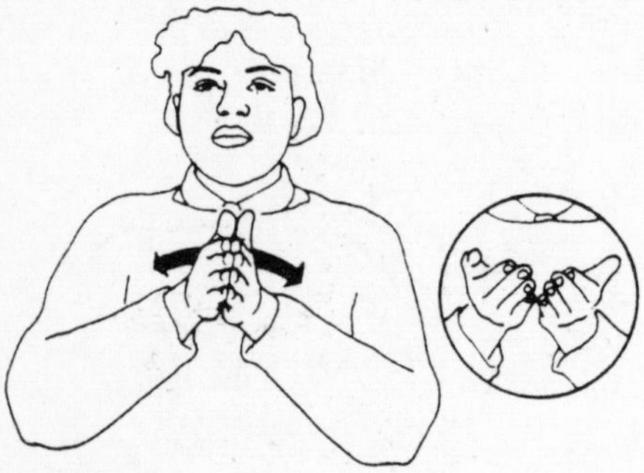

BOOK, NOTEBOOK
Beginning with both open palms together in front of the chest, fingers pointing forward, bring the thumb sides apart while keeping the little-finger sides together.
Hint: Represents opening a book.

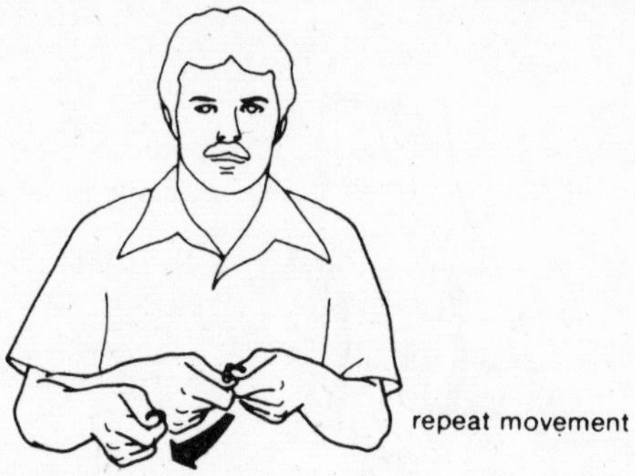

PLAY CARDS, DEAL
With the index fingers and thumbs of each hand pinched together, move the right hand forward from the left hand with a repeated movement.
Hint: Mime dealing cards.

PLAY
Beginning with both "y" hands in front of each side of the body, twist the wrists up and down with a repeated movement.

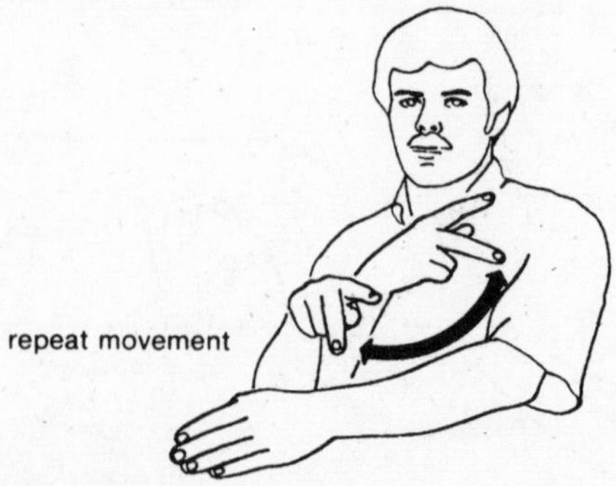

POETRY, POEM
Swing the right "p" hand, palm facing down, with a repeated movement back and forth along the length of the extended left arm.
Hint: Initialized sign formed similar to the sign "music."

Travel and Transportation

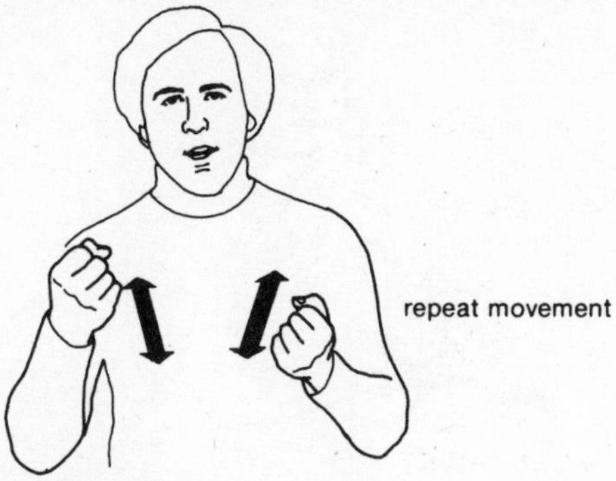

CAR, AUTOMOBILE
Move both "s" hands, palms facing in, up and down at an angle with an alternating movement in front of each side of the chest.
Hint: Mime driving a car.

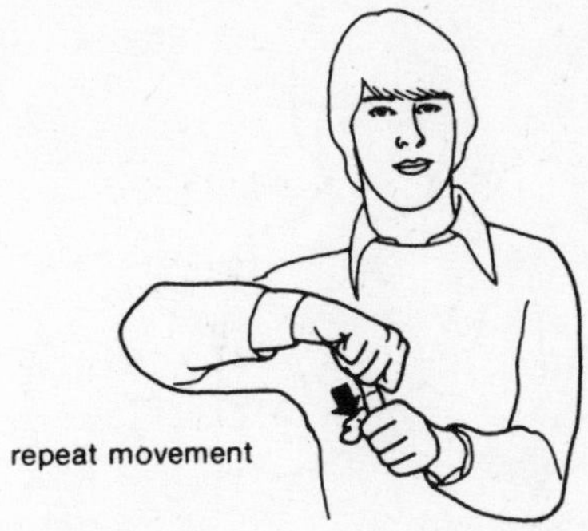

GASOLINE, FILL UP
Dip the thumb of the right "10" hand, palm facing right, downward with a double movement into the top opening of the left "s" hand, palm facing right.
Hint: Pouring gas into the gas tank.

STREET, HIGHWAY, ROAD
Move both open hands, palms facing each other and fingers pointing forward, from near the body straight forward.
Hint: Shows the shape of a street.

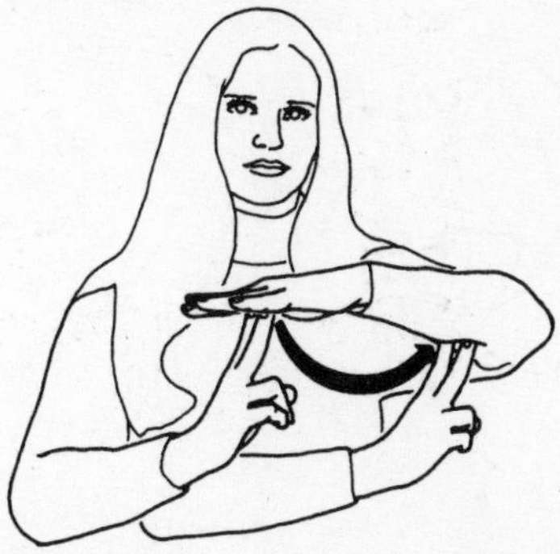

BRIDGE
With the open left hand extended across the chest, palm facing down, touch the fingertips of the right "v" hand, palm facing left and fingers pointing up, first to left palm and then to near the bent left elbow.
Hint: Shows the span of a suspension bridge.

TRAFFIC
Beginning with both "5" hands in front of the chest, palms facing each other and fingers pointing up, move the hands forward and back with an alternating movement, brushing the palms against each other as they pass.
Hint: Shows cars whizzing past each other.

PARK
Tap the little-finger side of the right "3" hand, palm facing left, with a double movement on the palm of the open left hand, palm facing up.
Hint: The right hand represents a vehicle parking on the left hand.

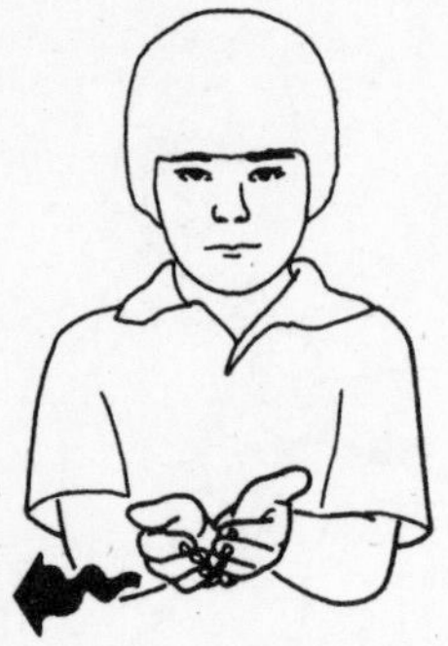

BOAT
With the little-finger sides of both curved hands together in front of the chest, palms angled toward each other and fingers pointing forward, move the hands forward from the body in a wavy movement.
Hint: The hands form the hull of a boat moving on water.

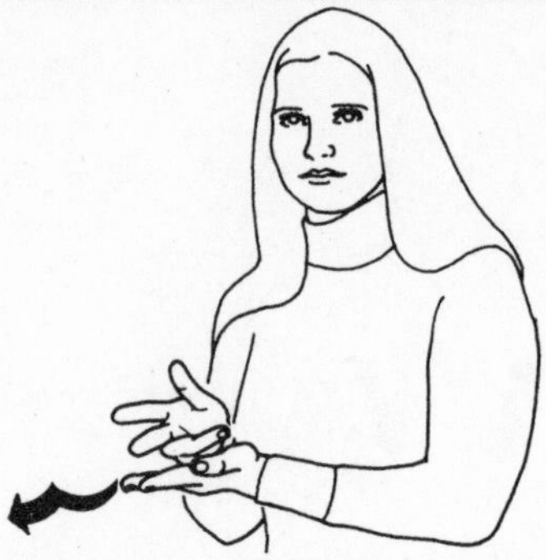

SHIP
With the little-finger side of the right "3" hand, palm facing left, on the palm of the open left hand, move the hands forward in a series of small arcs.
Hint: The right hand represents a ship moving forward on the waves.

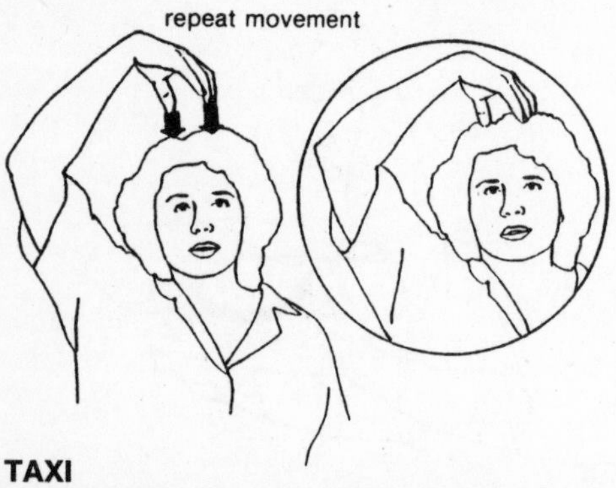

CAB, TAXI
Place the fingertips of the right "c" hand, palm facing down, on the top of the head with a double movement.
Hint: Initialized sign showing the dome on a taxi.

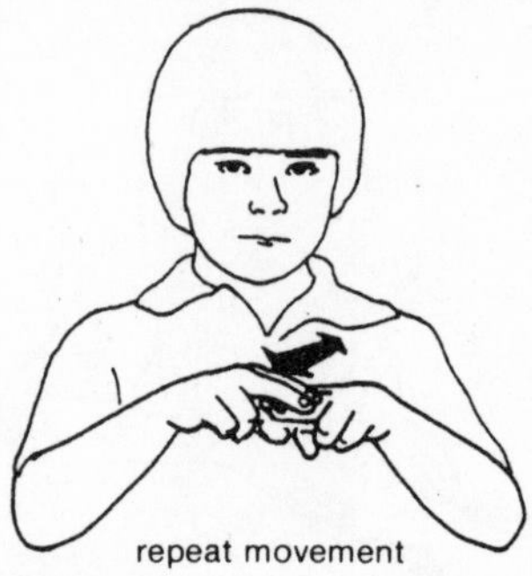

TRAIN, RAILROAD
Move the extended fingers of the right "h" hand with a repeated movement back and forth on the back of the back of the extended fingers of the left "h" hand, both palms facing down.
Hint: Shows the cross-ties on a railroad.

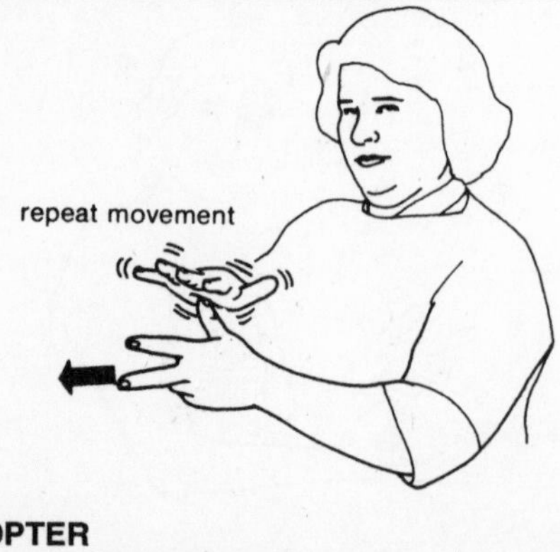

HELICOPTER
With the right "5" hand, palm facing down, on the thumb of the left "3" hand, palm facing right, move both hands forward while wiggling the right fingers.
Hint: The right hand represents the propeller turning on a helicopter.

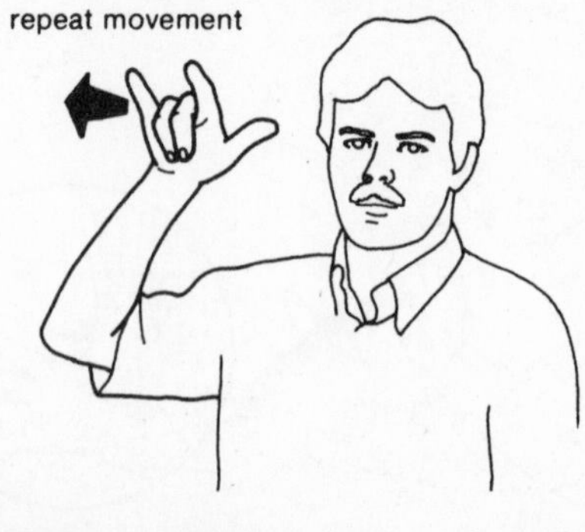

AIRPLANE, JET, PLANE
With the right little finger, index finger, and thumb extended, palm facing down, move the hand forward with a short double movement in front of the right shoulder.
Hint: The hand represents an airplane moving.

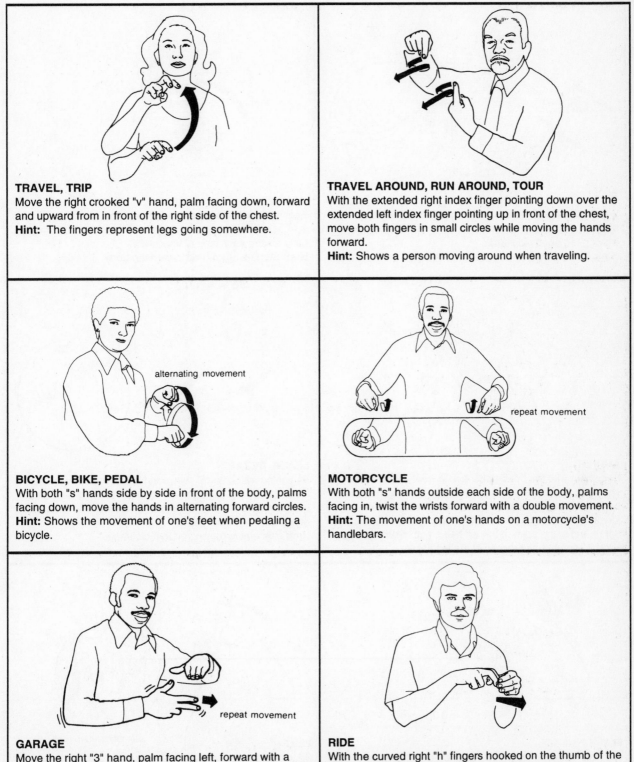

TRAVEL, TRIP
Move the right crooked "v" hand, palm facing down, forward and upward from in front of the right side of the chest.
Hint: The fingers represent legs going somewhere.

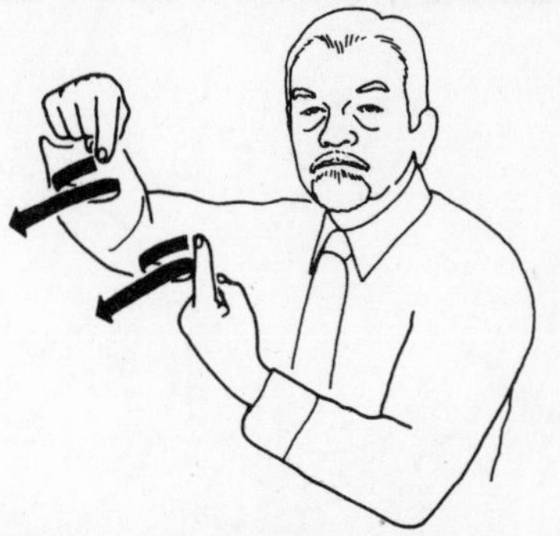

TRAVEL AROUND, RUN AROUND, TOUR
With the extended right index finger pointing down over the extended left index finger pointing up in front of the chest, move both fingers in small circles while moving the hands forward.
Hint: Shows a person moving around when traveling.

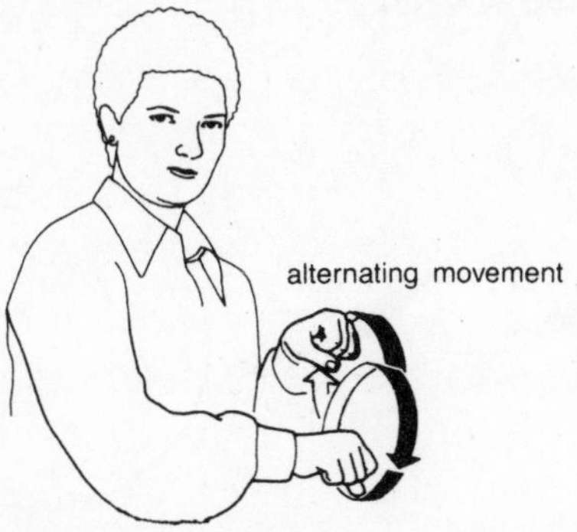

BICYCLE, BIKE, PEDAL
With both "s" hands side by side in front of the body, palms facing down, move the hands in alternating forward circles.
Hint: Shows the movement of one's feet when pedaling a bicycle.

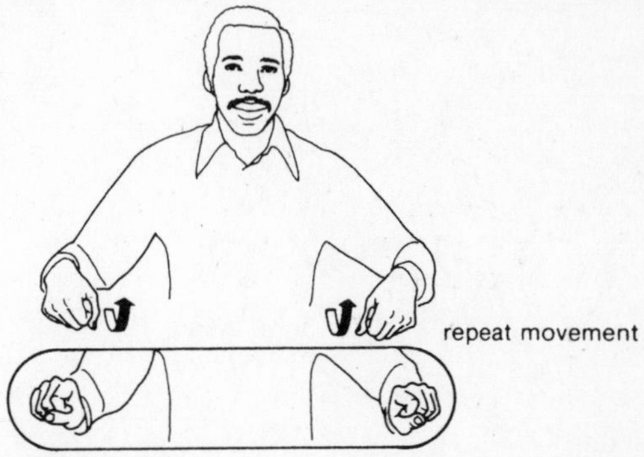

MOTORCYCLE
With both "s" hands outside each side of the body, palms facing in, twist the wrists forward with a double movement.
Hint: The movement of one's hands on a motorcycle's handlebars.

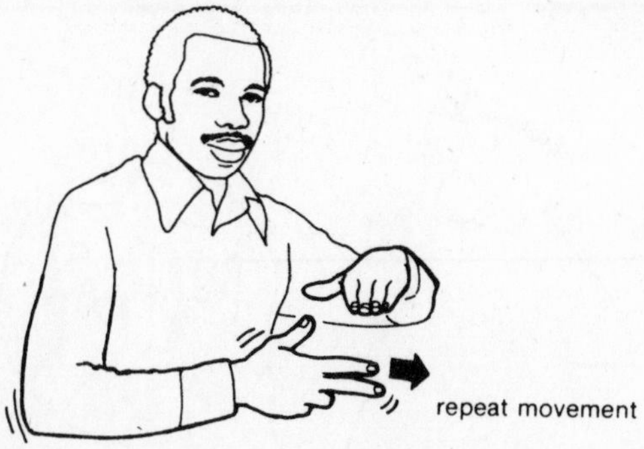

GARAGE
Move the right "3" hand, palm facing left, forward with a double movement under the palm of the open left hand held across the chest, palm facing down and fingers pointing right.
Hint: Represents a vehicle moving into the garage.

RIDE
With the curved right "h" fingers hooked on the thumb of the left "c" hand, palm facing right, move both hands forward.
Hint: The curved fingers represent one's legs sitting in a moving vehicle.

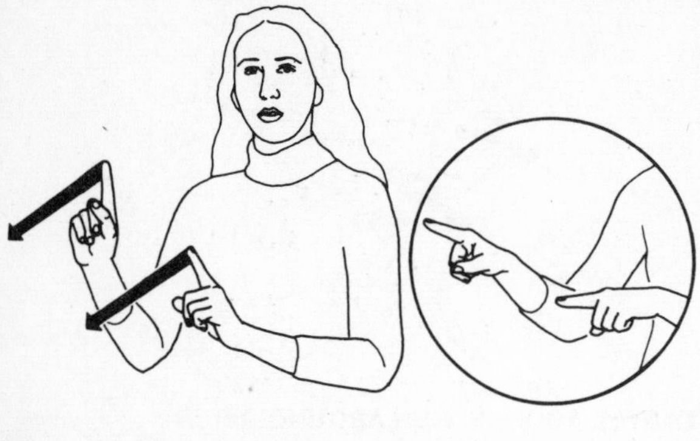

GO
With both extended index fingers pointing up in front of the body, palms facing forward, turn the wrists down while moving the hands forward.
Hint: Something going away from the body.

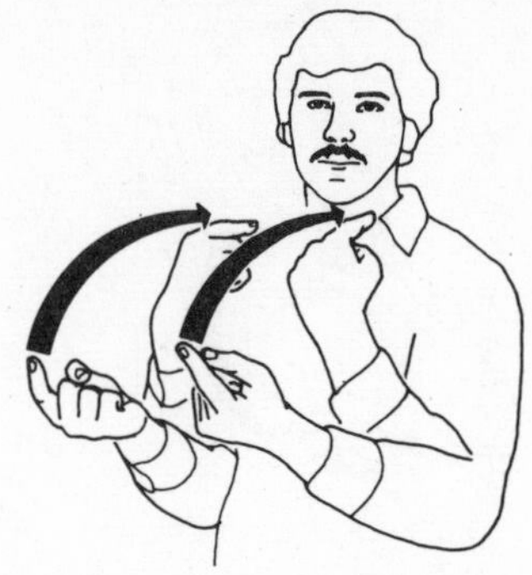

COME
Beginning with both extended index fingers pointing forward in front of the body, palms facing up, bring the index fingers back toward each side of the chest.
Hint: Something coming toward the body.

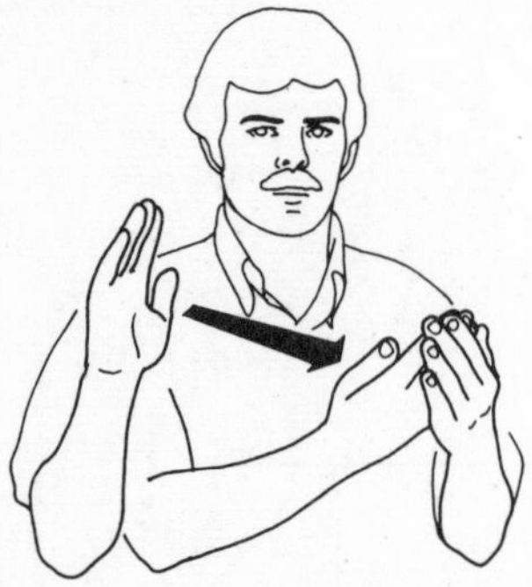

ARRIVE
Beginning with the open right hand in front of the right shoulder, palm facing forward, and the left open hand in front of the body, palm facing in, move the right hand forward while twisting the wrist, ending with the back of the right hand in the palm of the left hand, both palms facing in.
Hint: The right hand arrives at the left hand.

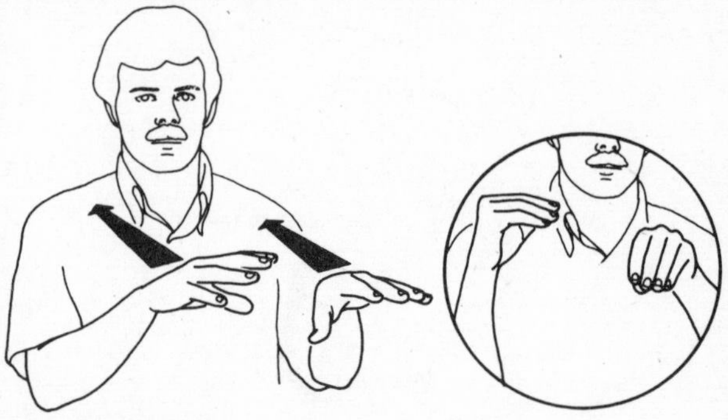

LEAVE, DEPART
Beginning with both "5" hands in front of the body, palms facing down and fingers pointing forward, bring the hands back toward the right shoulder while closing into flattened "o" hands as the hands move.
Hint: Something moving off in a distance.

FLY
With the right little finger, index finger, and thumb extended, palm facing down, move the hand forward in front of the right shoulder.
Hint: The hand represents an airplane moving.

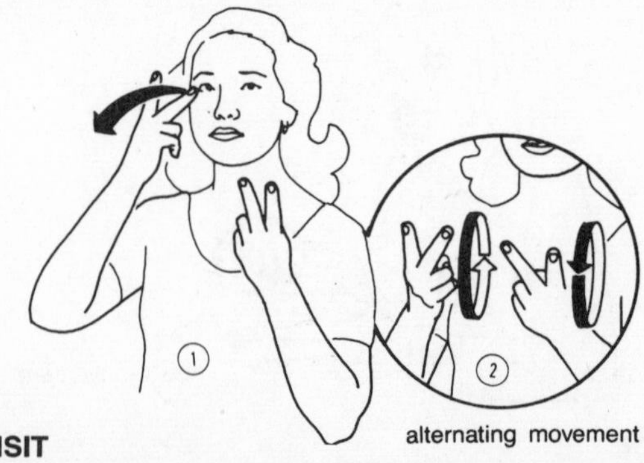

VISIT
Bring the right "v" hand forward from near the right eye, palm facing in. Then move both "v" hands in alternating circles forward in front of the chest, palms facing in.
Hint: Initialized sign representing people seeing each other.

BUS
Beginning with the little-finger side of the right "b" hand touching the index-finger side of the left "b" hand, palms facing in opposite directions and fingers pointing up, bring the right hand back toward the chest.
Hint: Initialized sign showing the long shape of a bus.

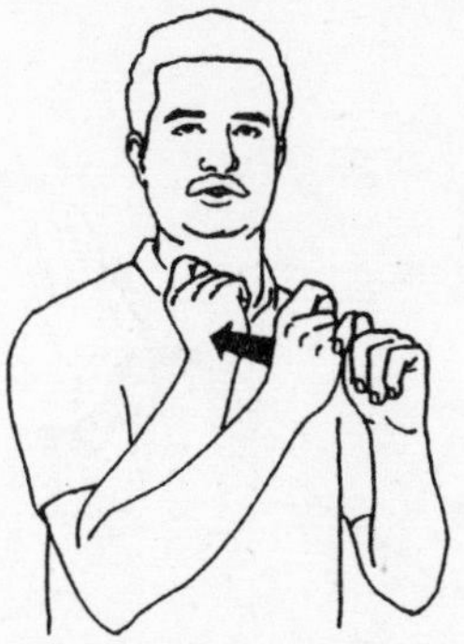

TRUCK
Beginning with the little-finger side of the right "t" hand touching the index-finger side of the left "t" hand, palms facing in opposite directions and fingers pointing up, bring the right hand back toward the chest.
Hint: Initialized sign showing the long shape of a truck.

SUBWAY
Move the right "s" hand, palm facing left, forward with a double movement under the open left hand held across the chest, palm facing down.
Hint: Initialized sign moving beneath the ground.

AIRPORT
With the little finger, index finger, and thumb of the right hand extended, palm facing down, move the right hand forward with a small repeated movement in front of the right shoudler.
Hint: Similar to sign for airplane except smaller movement.

ACCIDENT, COLLISION, CRASH
Beginning with both "claw" hands in front of each side of the chest, palms facing in, bring the hands together while changing into "s" hands.
Hint: Two things running into each other.

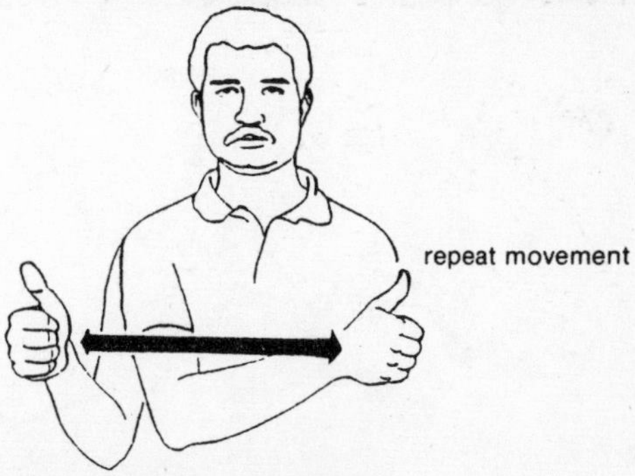

COMMUTE, BACK AND FORTH
Move the right "10" hand, palm facing left, with a repeated movement from side to side in front of the body.
Hint: Represents one going back and forth repeatedly.

Geography

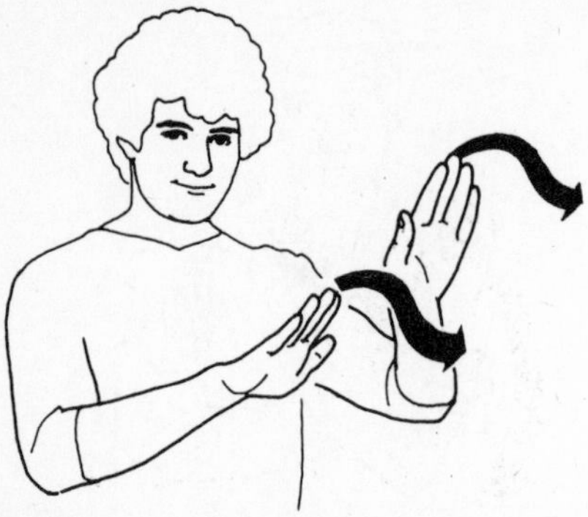

HILL
Move both open hands upward with a wavy movement, palms angled forward and one hand higher than the other.
Hint: The hands follow the shape of a hill.

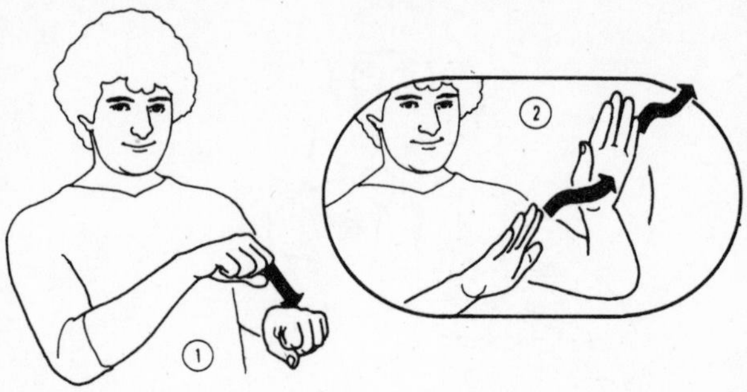

MOUNTAIN
Tap the palm side of the right "s" hand on the back of the left "s" hand held in front of the chest, both palms facing down. Then move both open hands, palms angled forward, upward in a wavy movement, left hand higher than the right.
Hint: "Rock" plus the shape of a rocky mountainside.

VALLEY
Beginning with both "b" hands in front of each shoulder, palms facing down and fingers pointing forward, move the hands downward toward each other in front of the body.
Hint: The hands outline the shape of a valley.

ISLAND
With the extended right little finger, palm facing in, draw a circle on the back of the open left hand held in front of the chest, palm facing down.
Hint: Initialized sign showing the shape of a small area surrounded by water.

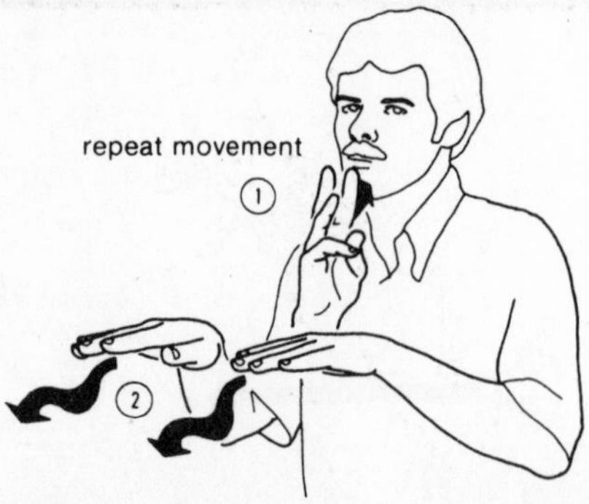

RIVER
Tap the index-finger side of the right "w" hand to the chin with a double movement, palm facing left. Then move both open hands, palms facing down, forward from in front of each side of the chest with a wavy movement, one hand somewhat forward of the other hand.
Hint: "Water" plus the shape of a rolling river.

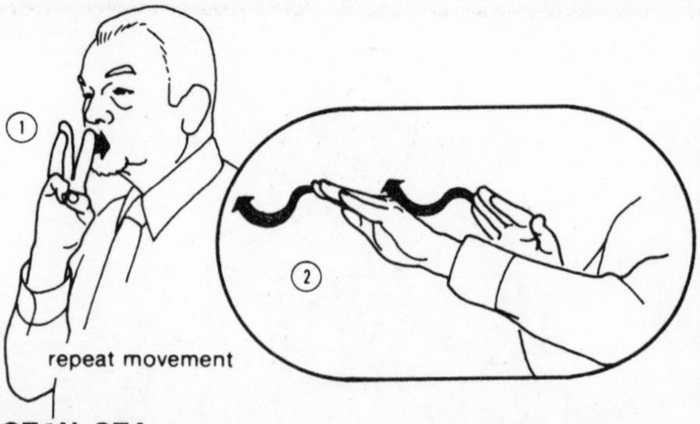

OCEAN, SEA
Tap the index-finger side of the right "w" hand to the chin with a double movement, palm facing left. Then move both open hands, palms facing down, forward from in front of each side of the chest with a large wavy movement, one hand somewhat forward of the other hand.
Hint: "Water" plus the action of ocean waves.

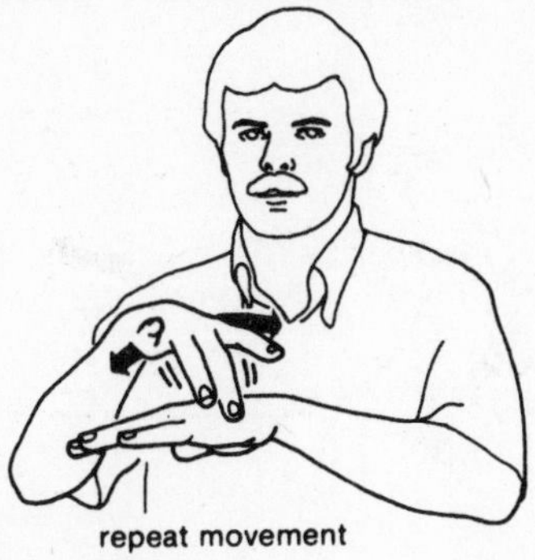

EARTH
While holding the sides of the open left hand held in front of the chest with the bent thumb and middle finger of the right "5" hand, both palms facing down, rock the right hand forward and back with a short repeated movement.
Hint: The earth moving on it axis.

WORLD
Bring the right "w" hand, palm facing left, in a circle around the left "w" hand, palm facing right, ending with the little-finger side of the right hand on the index-finger side of the left hand.
Hint: Initialized sign following the shape of a globe.

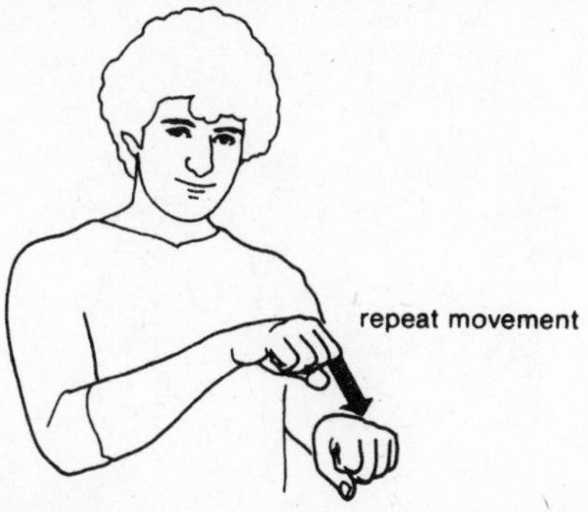

ROCK, STONE
Tap the palm side of the right "s" hand on the back of the left "s" hand held in front of the chest, both palms facing down.
Hint: Knocking on a rock to show its hardness.

NATURAL, NATURE, NATION
Move the right "n" hand in a circle over and down on the back of the open left hand held in front of the chest, both palms facing down.
Hint: Initialized sign.

GRASS, HAY
Bring the heel of the curved right hand, palm facing up, upward with a double movement under the chin.

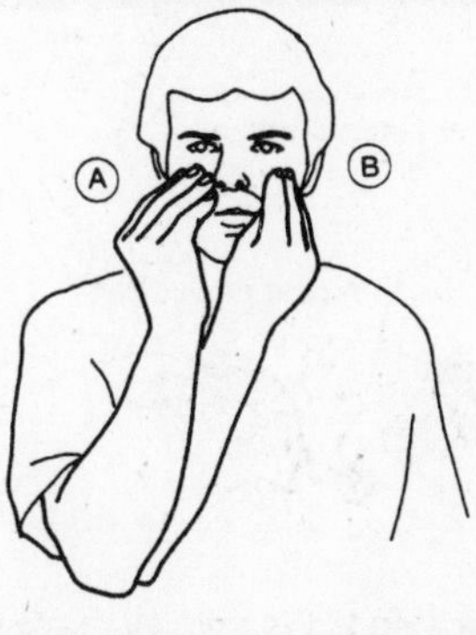

FLOWER
Touch the fingers of the right flattened "o" hand, palm facing in, first to the right side of the nose and then to the left side of the nose.
Hint: Swelling a flower.

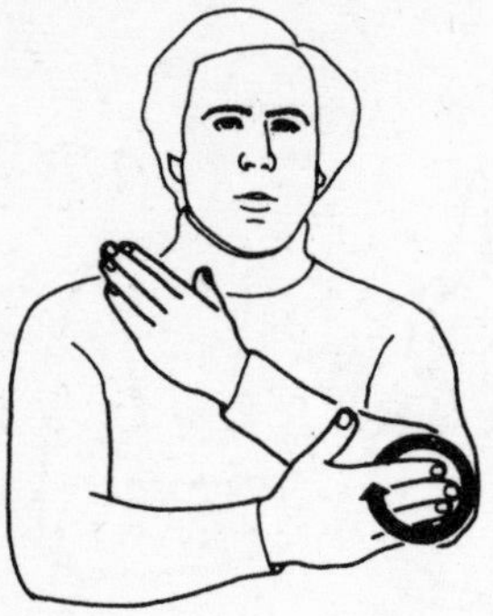

COUNTRY, RURAL
Rub the fingers of the open right hand in a circular movement near the elbow of the bent left arm held across the chest.

FARM
Drag the thumb of the right "5" hand, palm facing left, from left to right across the chin.

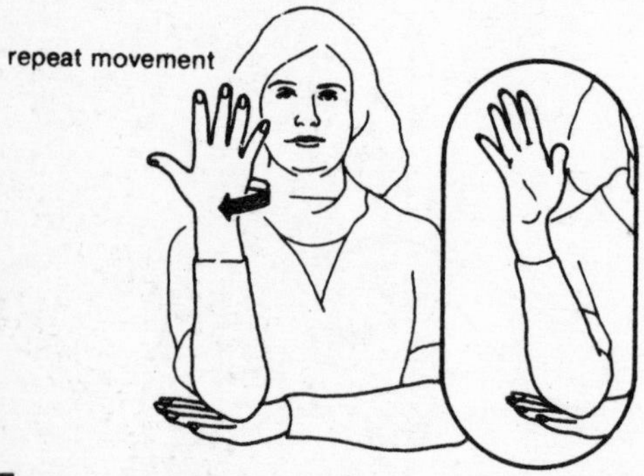

TREE
With the elbow of the right raised arm, palm facing back, on the back of the open left hand held across the body, palm facing down, twist the right palm forward and back with a repeated movement.
Hint: The arm represents the tree trunk and the hand represents its branches.

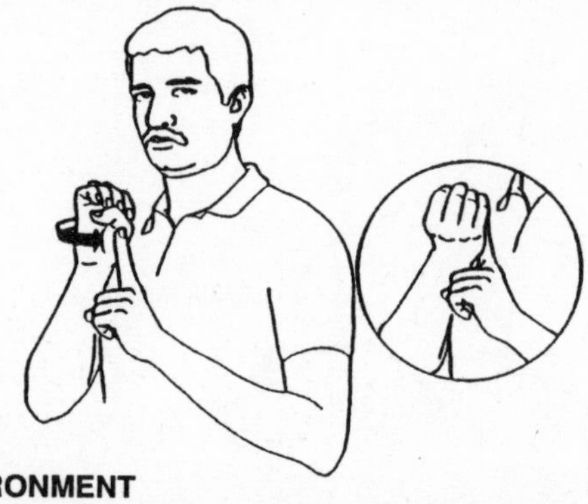

ENVIRONMENT
Beginning with the right "e" hand, palm facing left, near the extended left index finger held up in front of the chest, palm facing right, move the right hand around the left finger, ending with the right palm facing in.
Hint: Initialized sign representing the space around something.

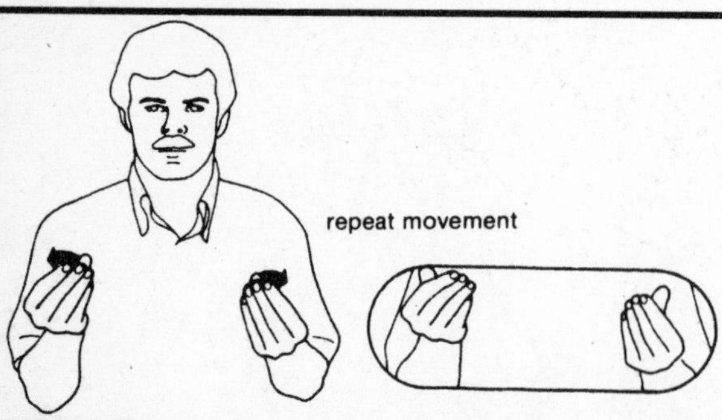

DIRT, SOIL
With a double movement rub the thumbs of both flattened "o" handsacross the fingertips from the little fingers to the index fingers, palms facing up.
Hint: Feeling soil between the fingers.

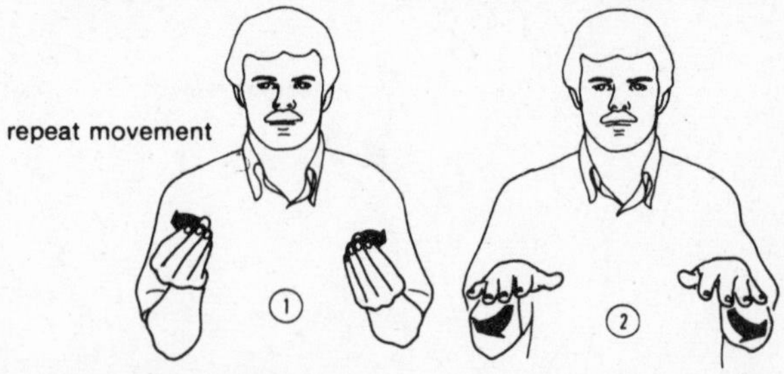

LAND, FIELD, PROPERTY
With a double movement rub the thumbs of both flattened "o" hands across the fingertips from the little fingers to the index fingers, palms facing up. Then move both open hands, palms facing down, forward in front of each side of the chest.
Hint: "Dirt" plust showing the flat land before you.

eleven

ACTIONS

Actions of the Body
Actions at School and Work
Other Actions

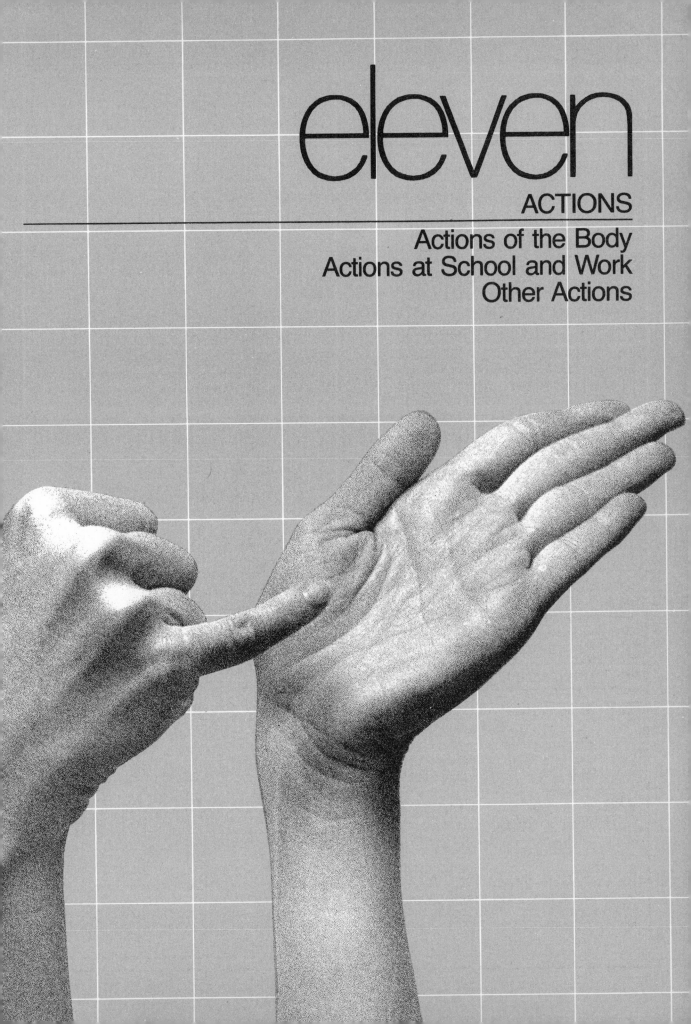

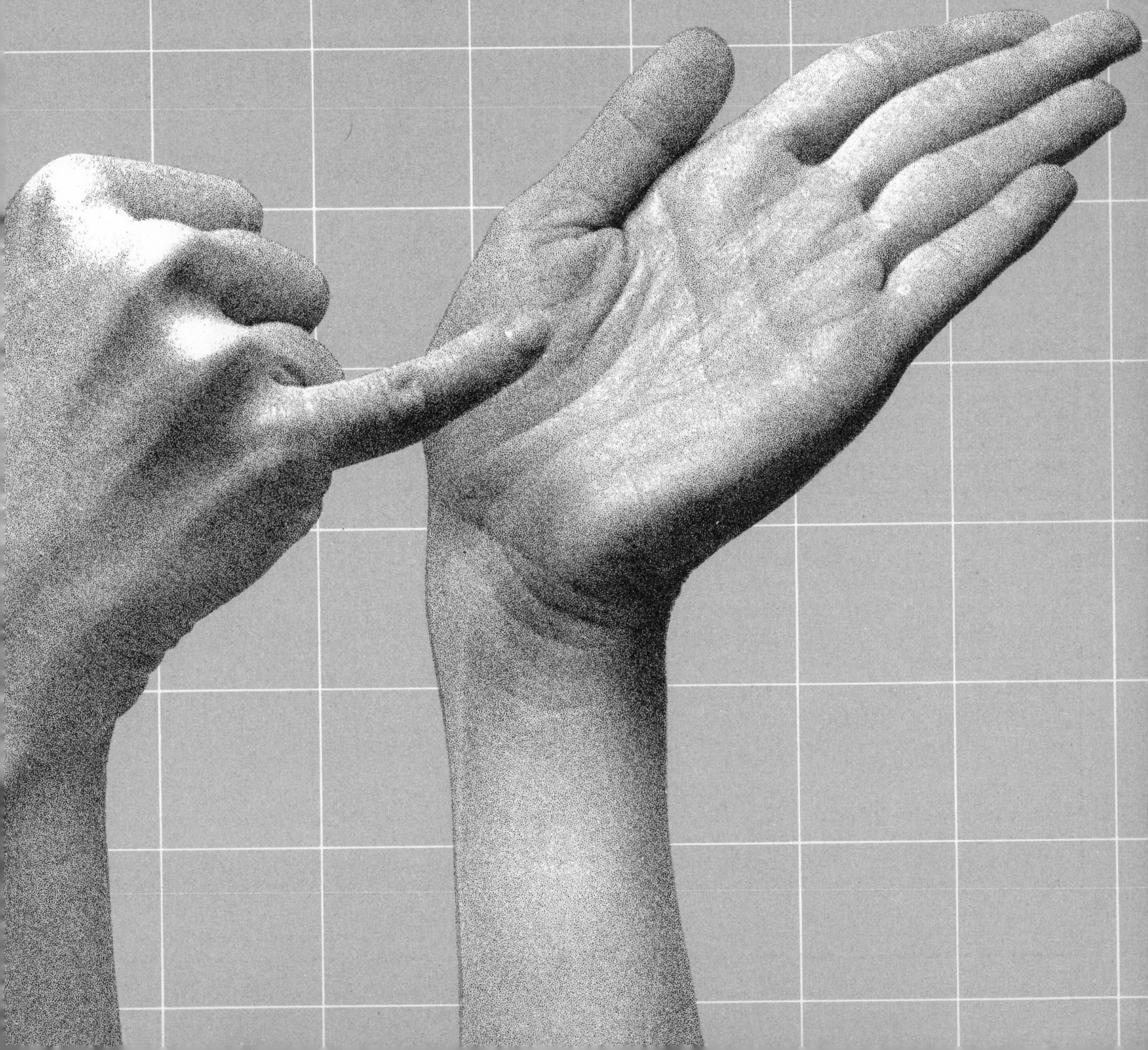

THE DIRECTION OF THE SIGN

Some verbs can carry information about the subject and object of the sentence by the direction in which the sign moves. For example, if the sign "show" is pulled back toward the body, it means that "you showed something to me." If "show" moves forward from the body, it means that "I showed something to you." Other verbs in this category are "inform," "ask," "help," "tell," "give," "send," and "look at."

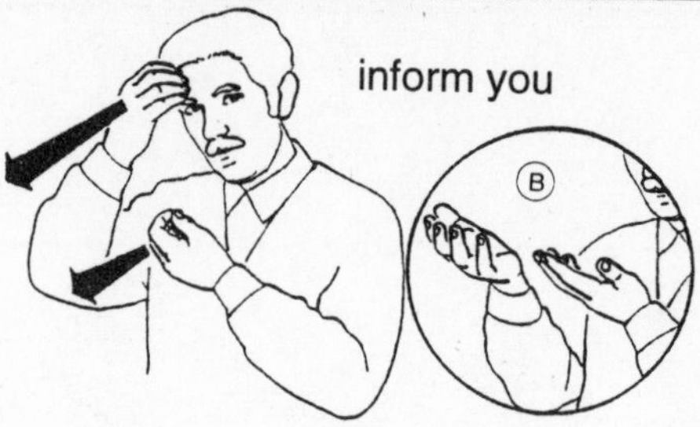

inform you

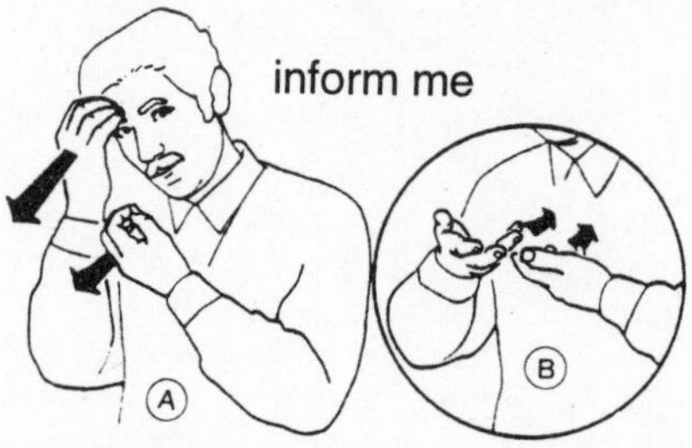

inform me

PAST, PRESENT, AND FUTURE VERBS

In English, verb tense is expressed by changing the verb form to indicate past, present, or future. In sign language, verb tense is indicated by establishing a time reference. All discussion remains in the established time frame until a new one is introduced. The time reference may be set by signing "past," "now," "future," or any other indication of time, such as "two weeks ago."

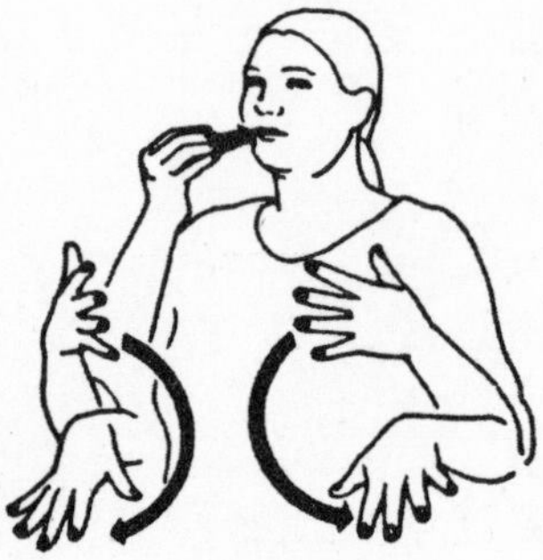

eat + finished = ate

eat + now = is eating

THE "TO BE" VERB

Native sign language users do not always sign a form of the verb "to be" because verb tenses are designated by establishing a time frame. When "to be" is used, the same sign is used for all tenses. That sign is similar in formation to the sign for "true" and is often used to add emphasis to the sentence.

Many new signers prefer using initialized forms of "to be" for "am," "is," "are," "was," or "were," especially when they are signing in an English word order.

am; be; is; are; was; were

Actions of the Body

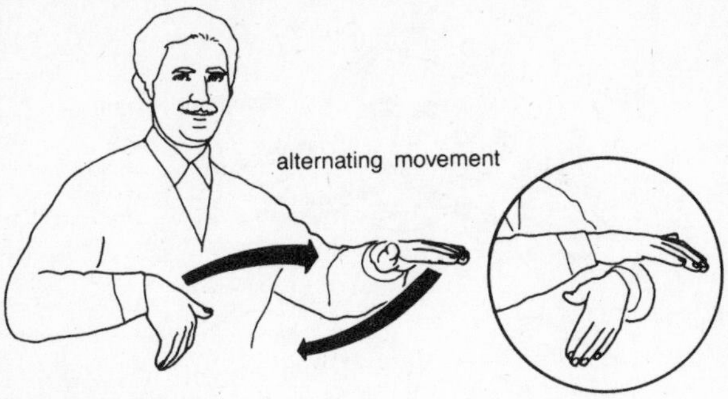

WALK, STROLL
Alternately swing both open hands forward and back in front of each side of the body, bending the wrist each time the hand goes back.
Hint: The arms represent the movement of the legs while walking.

STAND
Place the fingertips of the right "v" hand, palm facing in and fingers pointing down, on the palm of the open left hand in front of the chest.
Hint: The fingers represent legs standing up.

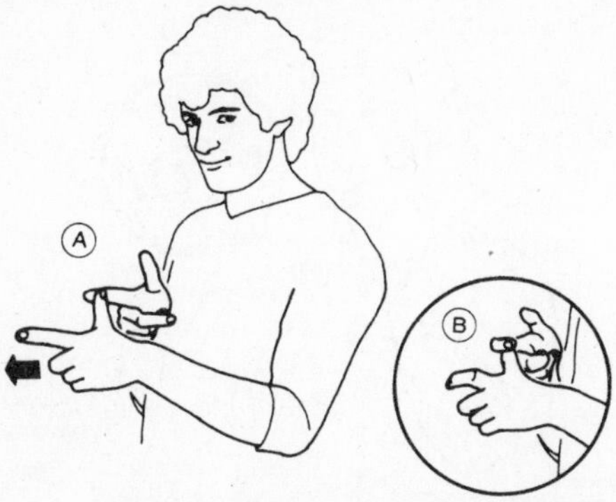

RUN
With the index finger of the right "l" hand touching the thumb of the left "l" hand, palms facing each other and index fingers pointing forward, crook both the index fingers and the right thumb while moving the hands forward.

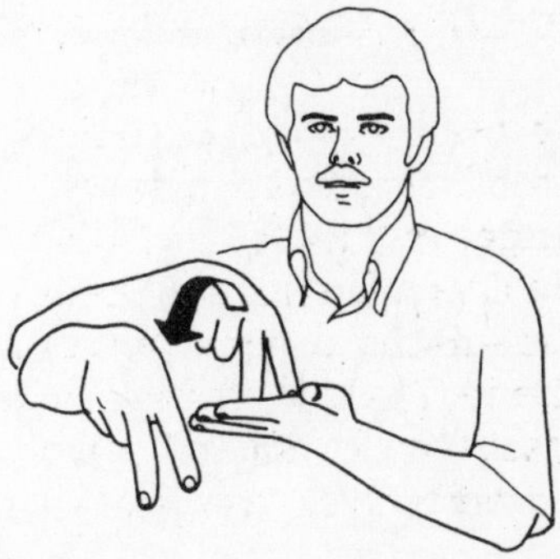

JUMP
Beginning with the fingers of the right "v" hand, palm facing in and fingers pointing down, on the palm of the open left hand, palm facing up, move the right fingers forward off the palm in an arc.
Hint: The fingers represent legs jumping off something.

THROW, THROW AWAY
Beginning with the right "s" hand in front of the right side of the body, palm facing in, move the hand forward and downward while thrusting the index and middle fingers forward forming an "h" hand, palm facing left.

CATCH
Beginning with the loosely curved right "5" hand, palm facing down, in front of the right shoulder, bring the hand downward while closing into an "s" hand, ending with the palm side of the right "s" hand on the back of the left "s" hand.
Hint: Mime catching something.

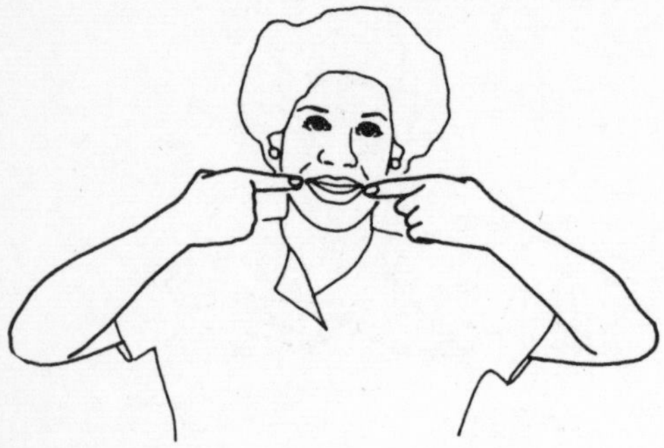

SMILE
Point the both extended index fingers to the corners of the mouth while smiling.
Hint: Pointing to the expanse of a smile.

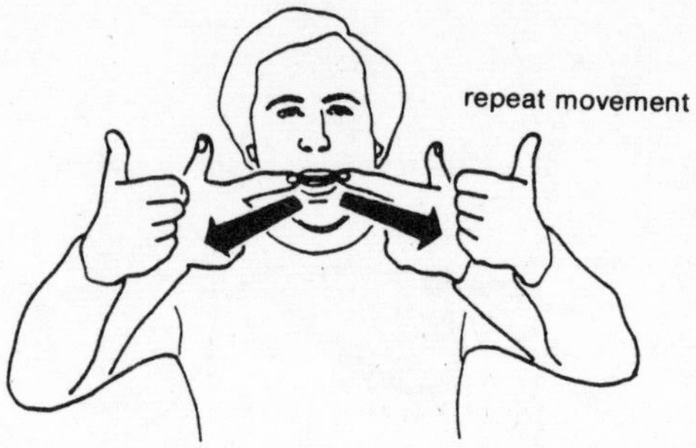

LAUGH
Beginning with the index fingers of both "I" hands touching each side of the mouth, palms facing back, flick the index fingers back toward each palm with a repeated movement.
Hint: Initialized sign; shows a smile broadening into a laugh.

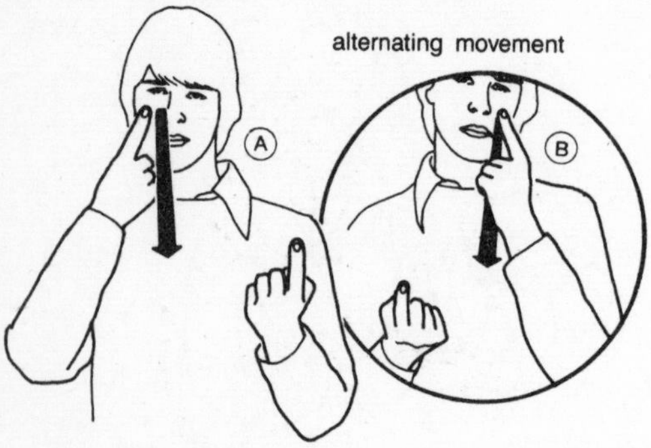

CRY, TEARS, WEEP
Using first the right extended index finger and then the left extended index finger, palms facing in, alternately stroke downward on each cheek.
Hint: Tears streaming down the face.

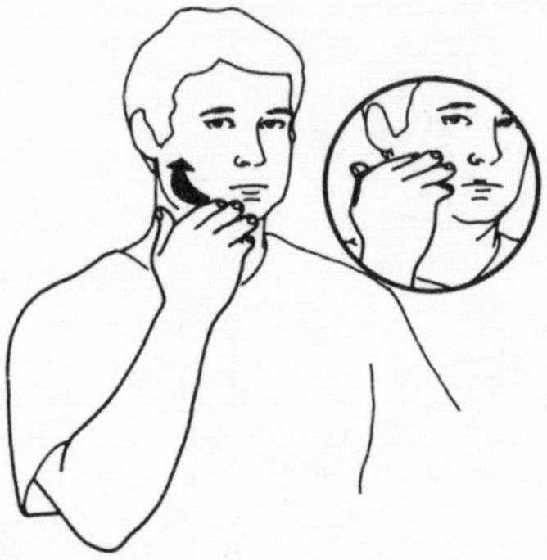

KISS
Touch the fingertips of the bent right hand, palm facing down, first to the right side of the chin and then to the right cheek.
Hint: Planting a kiss on the cheek.

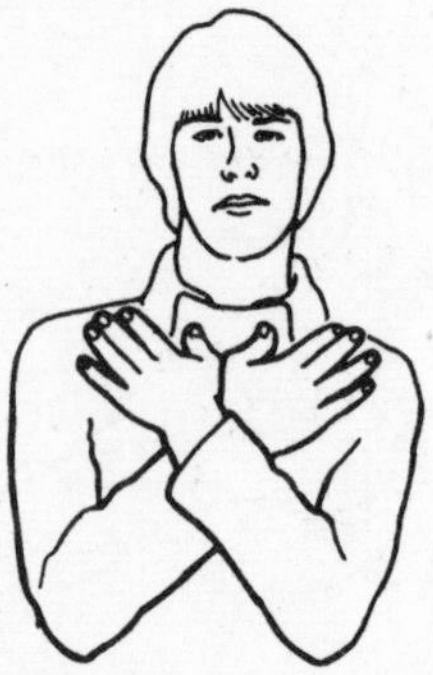

REST, RETIRE
Lay the palms of both open hands near the opposite shoulder, with the arms crossed at the wrists.
Hint: Laying back to rest.

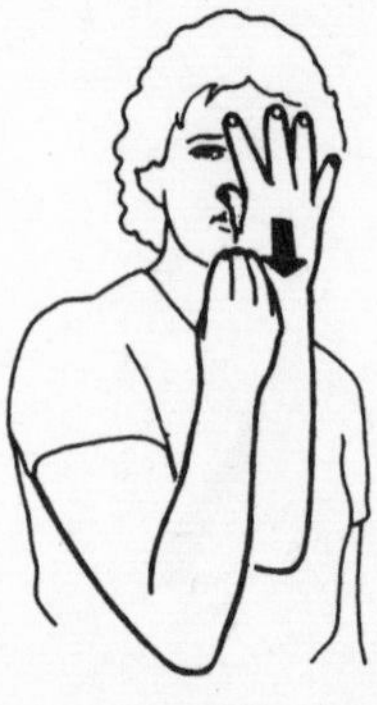

SLEEP, NAP
Beginning with the right "5" hand in front of the face, palm facing in and fingers pointing up, bring the hand downward while closing the fingers into a flattened "o" hand.
Hint: Drawing the eyes closed for sleep.

WASH
With the right "a" hand over the left "a" hand, rub the knuckles together back and forth with a repeated movement.
Hint: Rubbing something to wash it.

DUST
Move the right "a" hand, palm facing down, from left to right in front of the chest with a large wavy movement.
Hint: Mime cleaning with a dust rag.

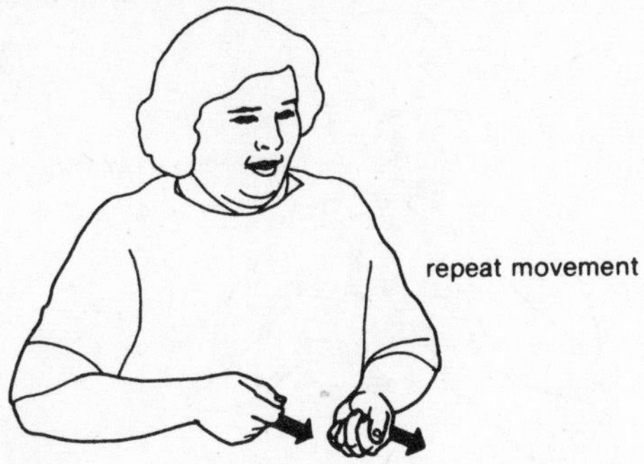

MOP
With both "a" hands in front of the body, right hand closer to the body than the left, push both hands forward with a short double movement.
Hint: Mime pushing a mop.

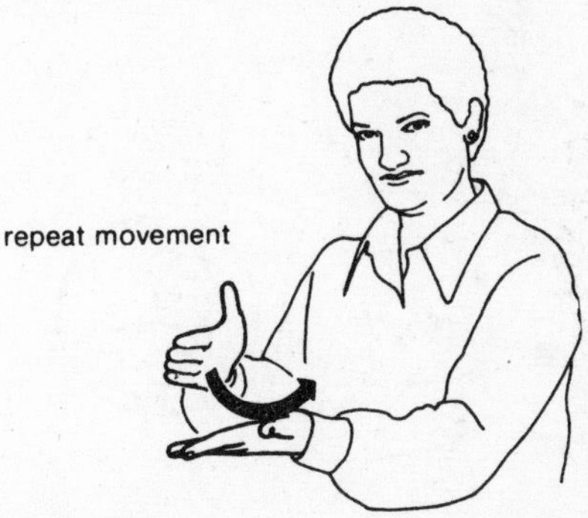

SWEEP, BROOM
Brush the little-finger side of the open right hand, palm facing left, across the left palm to the heel with a repeated movement by twisting the right wrist.
Hint: The right hand is sweeping away dirt.

BAKE, OVEN
Beginning with the right open hand above the left open hand in front of the body, palms facing each other, move the right hand forward under the left hand.
Hint: Putting something in the oven.

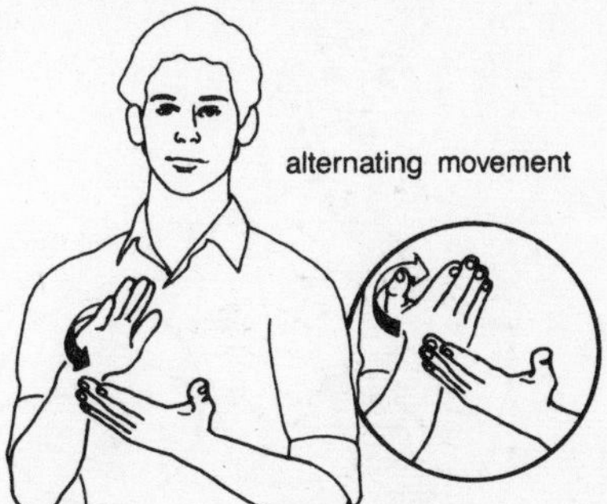

COOK
Beginning with the open right hand above the open left hand in front of the chest, palms facing each other, flip the right hand over and back with a double movement.
Hint: Flipping food over to cook both sides.

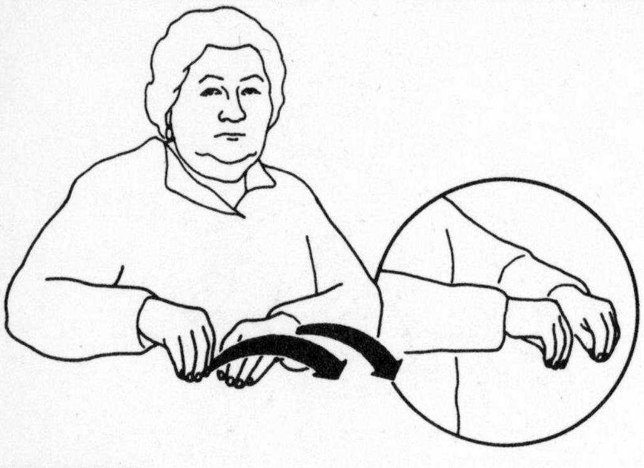

PUT, MOVE
Move both flattened "o" hands, palms facing down, forward and to the left in arcs from in front of the body.
Hint: Mime moving something from one place to another.

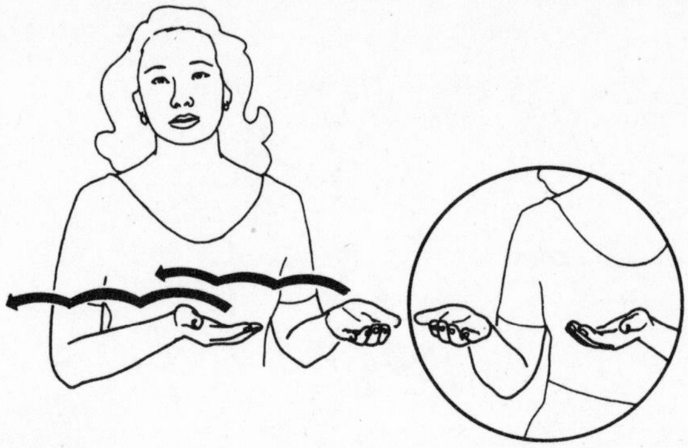

CARRY
Beginning with both curved hands in front of the body, palms facing up, from left to right in front of the body in a series of small arcs.
Hint: Mime carrying something.

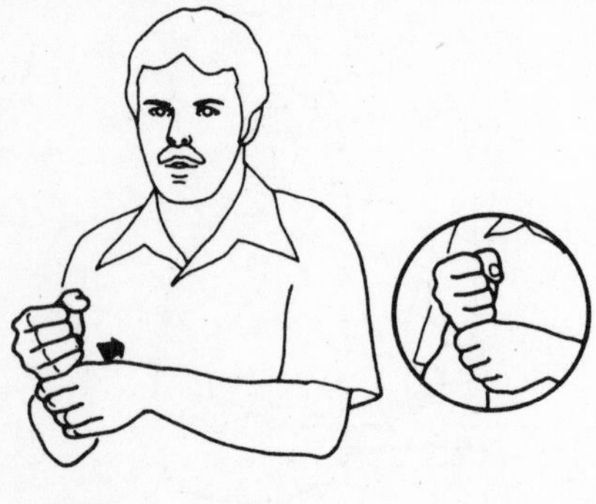

HOLD
With the little-finger side of the right "s" hand on the index-finger side of the left "s" hand, palms facing in opposite directions, move the hands toward the chest.
Hint: Mime holding on to something.

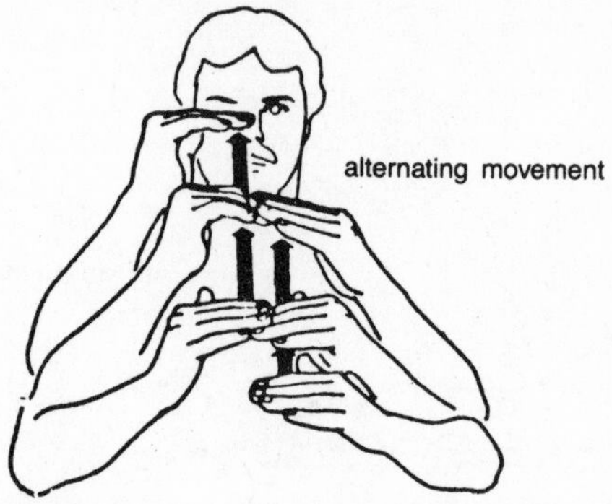

BUILD
With the fingertips of both bent hands overlapping slightly, alternatingly move the hands over each other as the hands move upward in front of the chest.
Hint: The hands move as if constructing something.

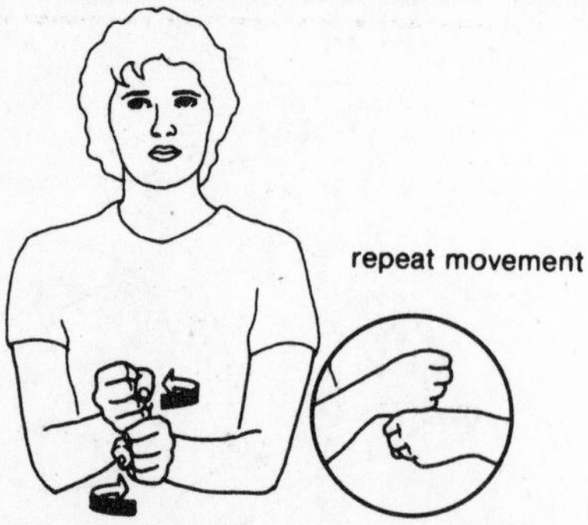

MAKE, CREATE, PRODUCE, FORM
With the little-finger side of the right "s" hand on the index-finger side of the left "s" hand, palms facing opposite directions, keep the hands together while twisting them in opposite directions with a repeated small movement.
Hint: Molding something.

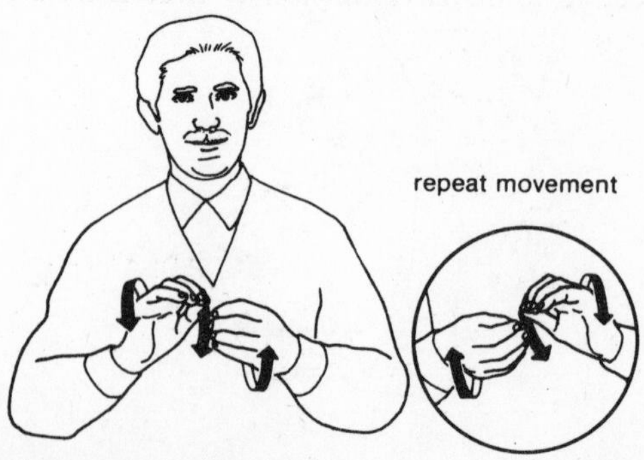

FIX, REPAIR, MAINTENANCE
Repeatedly touch the fingertips of both "o" hands as the wrists are twisted with a repeated movement in opposite directions.
Hint: Putting the parts of something together.

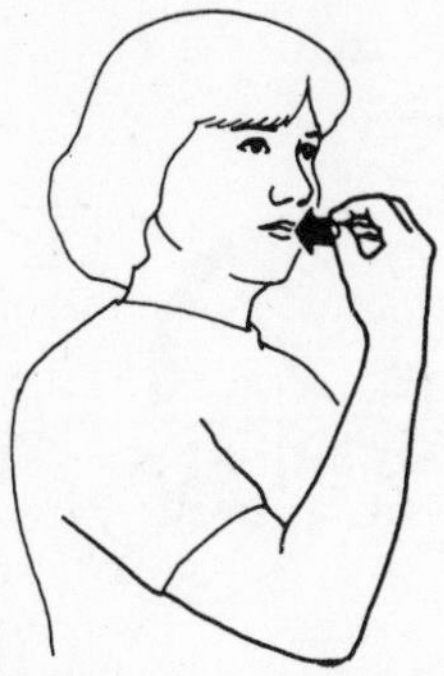

EAT, FOOD
Bring the fingers of the right flattened "o" hand toward the mouth. Note: "Food" is made with a short repeated movement.
Hint: Putting food in the mouth.

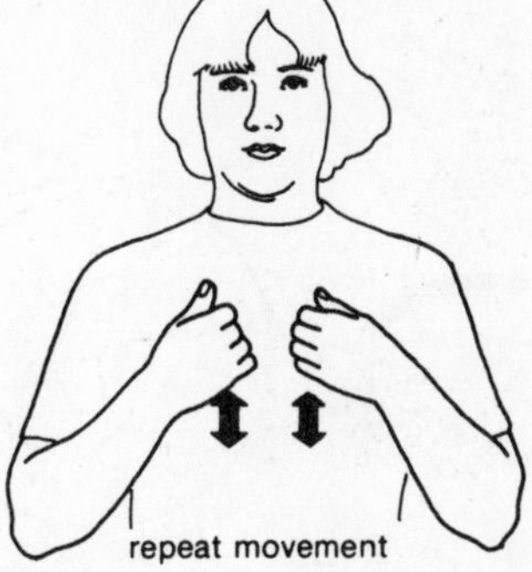

BATHE, BATH
Rub the knuckles of both "a" hands up and down with a repeated movement on each side of the chest, palms facing in.
Hint: Mime washing the chest during a bath.

CUT, CUT OFF
Move the right "3" hand, fingers pointing forward and palm facing left, forward near the fingertips of the open left hand held in front of the chest, palm facing down and fingers pointing right, while deliberately closing the index and middle fingers of right hand.
Hint: Mime cutting with scissors.

SIT
Place the extended fingers of the right "h" hand across the extended finger of the left "h" hand, both palms facing down.
Hint: The right fingers represent legs resting on something.

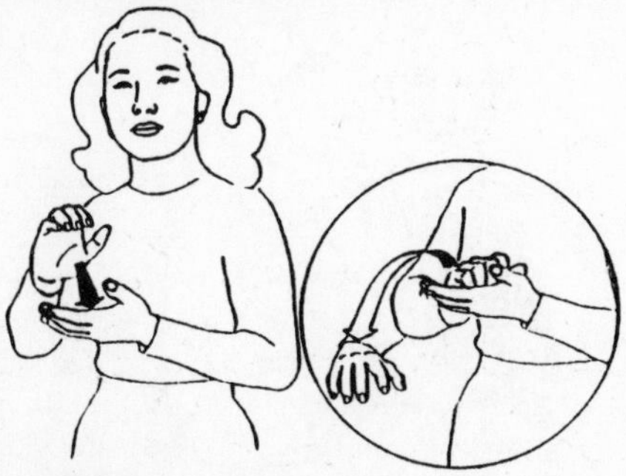

REMOVE, REMOVAL
Bring the palm of the curved right hand down on the open left palm while changing to an "a" right hand. Then move the right hand downward off the left palm while opening into a "5" hand, palm facing down.
Hint: Taking something and discarding it.

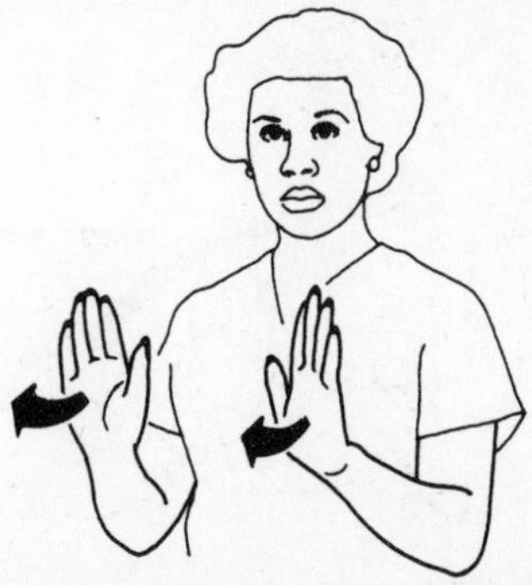

PUSH
Move both open hands, palms facing forward and fingers pointing up, forward in front of the chest with a short deliberate movement.
Hint: Mime pushing something.

Actions at School and Work

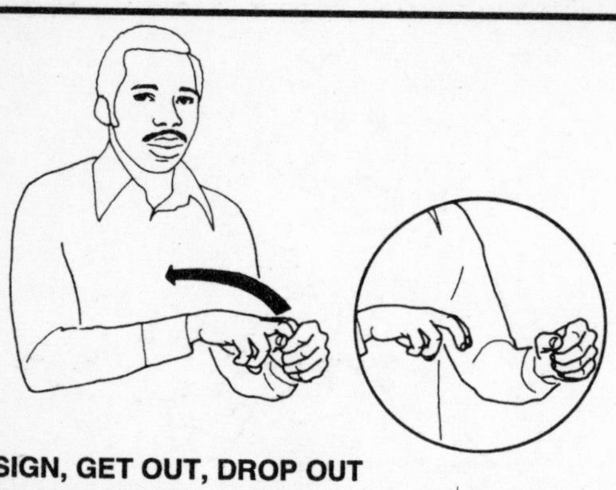

RESIGN, GET OUT, DROP OUT
Beginning with the bent fingers of the right "h" hand, palm facing down, inserted in the thumb side opening of the left "s" hand held in front the chest, palm facing right, pull the right fingers out back toward the chest.
Hint: The fingers represent legs which you are withdrawing from a situation.

QUIT
Beginning with the extended fingers of the right "h" hand, palm facing left, inside the top opening of the left "s" hand, palm facing right, bring the right hand upward in an arc toward the chest.
Hint: The fingers represent legs pulling away from a situation.

STOP
Bring the little-finger side of the open right hand, palm facing left, downward on the palm of the open left hand, palm facing up.
Hint: A natural gesture for stopping something.

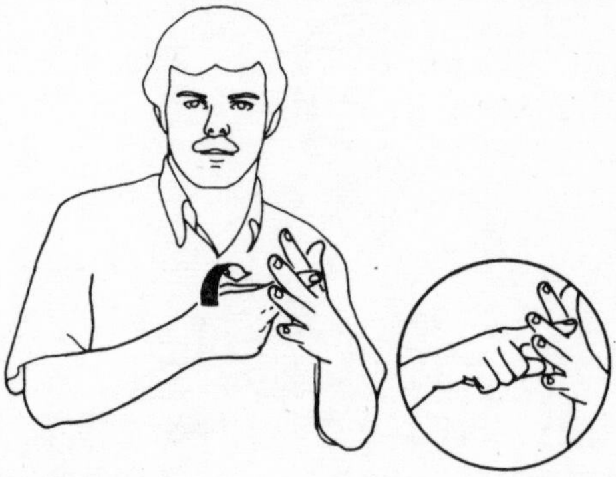

START, BEGIN, INITIATE
With the extended right index finger, palm facing the chest, inserted between the index and middle fingers of the left "5" hand, palm facing right, twist the right hand downward, ending with the palm facing down.

PARTICIPATE, JOIN
Beginning with the right "h" hand in front of the chest, palm facing left and fingers pointing up, move the hand downward to land on the thumb of the left "c" hand, palm facing right.
Hint: The fingers represent legs moving into a situation.

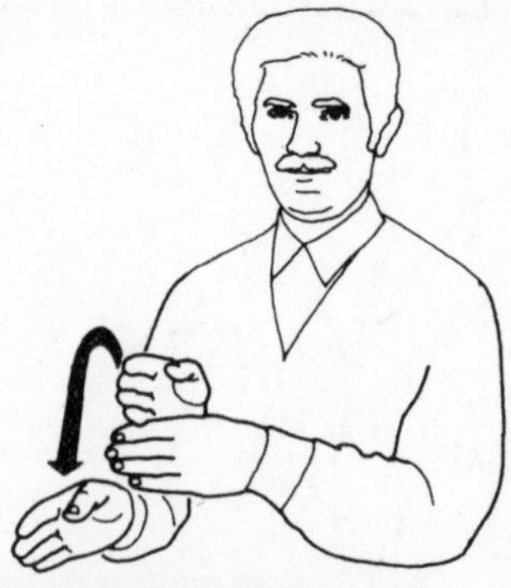

COMPLETE, END, FINISH, DONE
Beginning with the little-finger side of the right "b" hand, palm facing left, across the index-finger side of the left "b" hand, palm facing in, move the right hand slightly upward and then sharply downward near the left fingertips.
Hint: Showing the end of something.

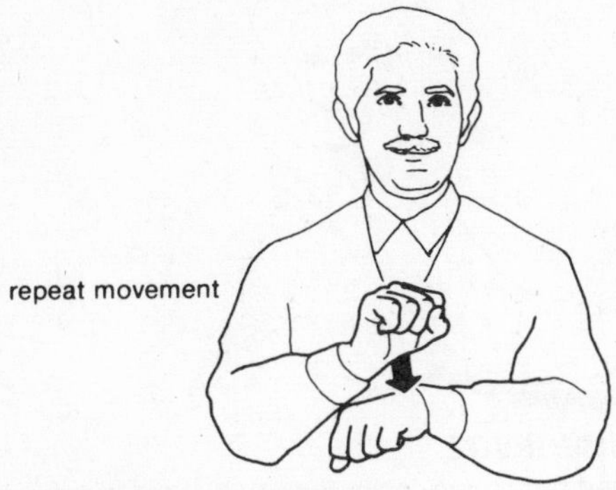

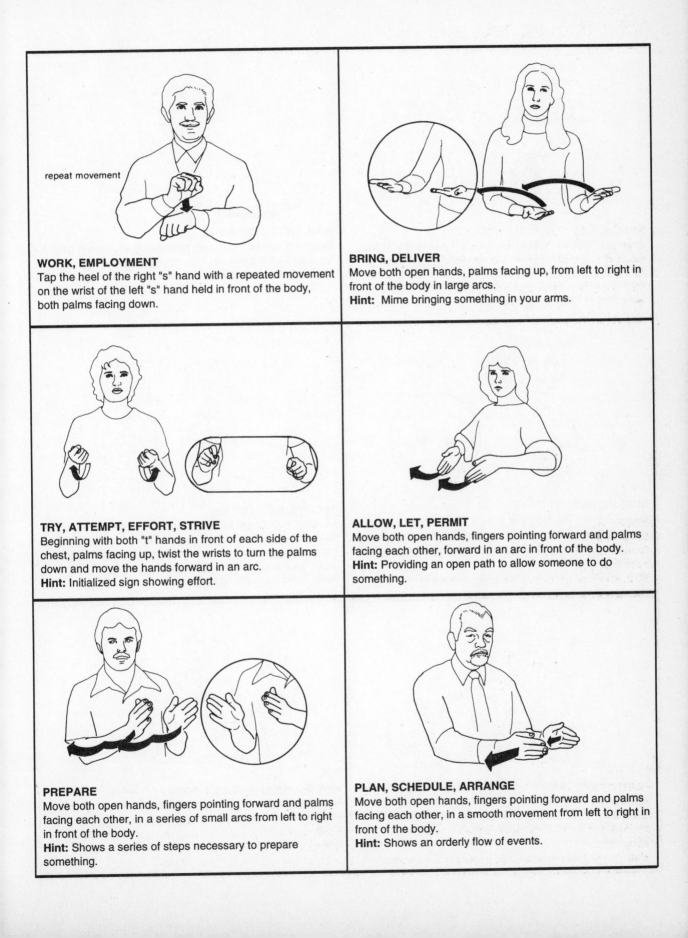

WORK, EMPLOYMENT
Tap the heel of the right "s" hand with a repeated movement on the wrist of the left "s" hand held in front of the body, both palms facing down.

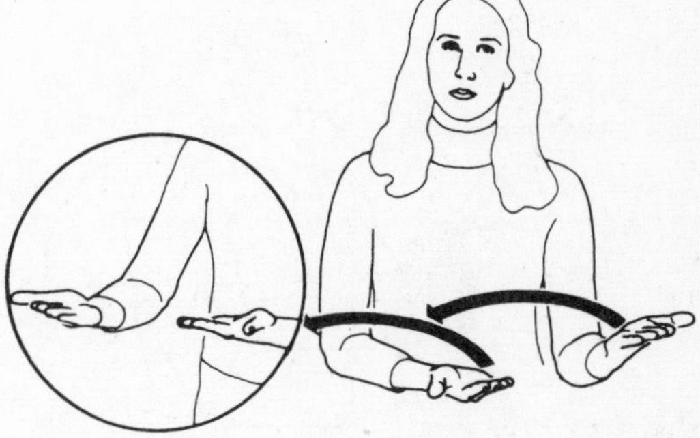

BRING, DELIVER
Move both open hands, palms facing up, from left to right in front of the body in large arcs.
Hint: Mime bringing something in your arms.

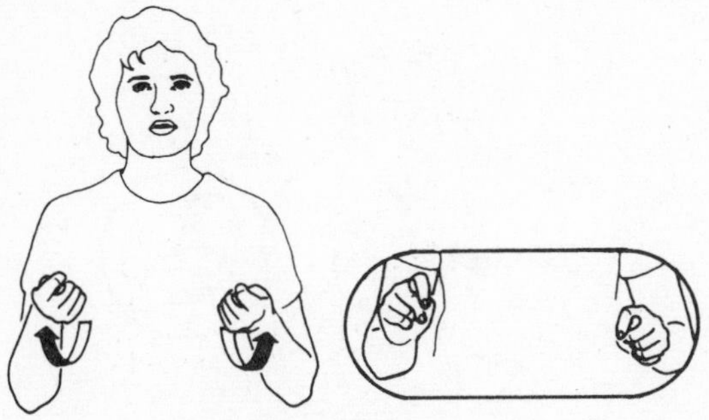

TRY, ATTEMPT, EFFORT, STRIVE
Beginning with both "t" hands in front of each side of the chest, palms facing up, twist the wrists to turn the palms down and move the hands forward in an arc.
Hint: Initialized sign showing effort.

ALLOW, LET, PERMIT
Move both open hands, fingers pointing forward and palms facing each other, forward in an arc in front of the body.
Hint: Providing an open path to allow someone to do something.

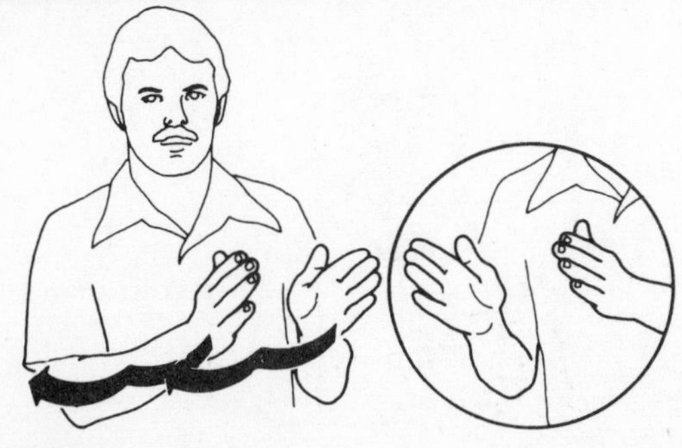

PREPARE
Move both open hands, fingers pointing forward and palms facing each other, in a series of small arcs from left to right in front of the body.
Hint: Shows a series of steps necessary to prepare something.

PLAN, SCHEDULE, ARRANGE
Move both open hands, fingers pointing forward and palms facing each other, in a smooth movement from left to right in front of the body.
Hint: Shows an orderly flow of events.

KEEP
Tap the little-finger side of the right "k" hand, palm facing left, with a double movement on the index-finger side of the left "k" hand, palm facing right.
Hint: Initialized sign showing eyes looking in different directions to keep something safe.

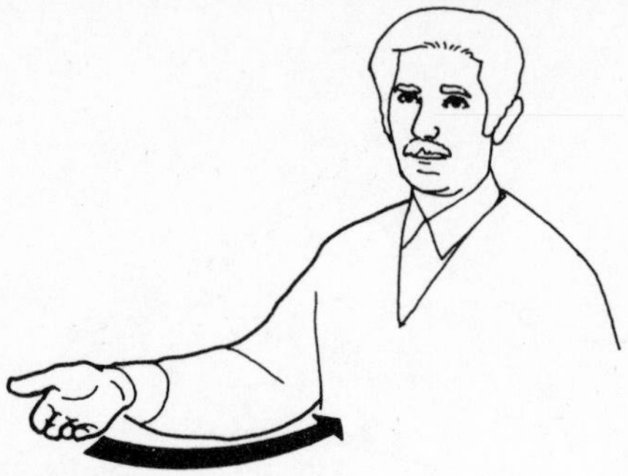

HIRE, WELCOME, INVITE
Swing the curved right hand, palm facing up, from in front of the right side of the body, in to near the waist.
Hint: Bringing something in close relationship.

ACCEPT, RECEIVE
Beginning with the fingers of both "5" hands loosely hanging down in front of each side of the chest, palms facing down, bring the fingers back toward the chest while changing into flattened "o" hands.
Hint: Bringing something to oneself in acceptance.

RECEIVE, GET, OBTAIN
Move both "5" hands from in front of the chest, palms facing each other, back toward the chest while changing into "s" hands, ending with the little-finger side of the right "s" hand on the thumb side of the left "s" hand.
Hint: Taking something for yourself.

REJECT
Beginning with the fingertips of the bent right hand, palm facing in, touching the heel of the open left hand, palm facing up, flick the right fingers forward over the left palm, ending with the palms facing each other.
Hint: Pushing away something that you reject.

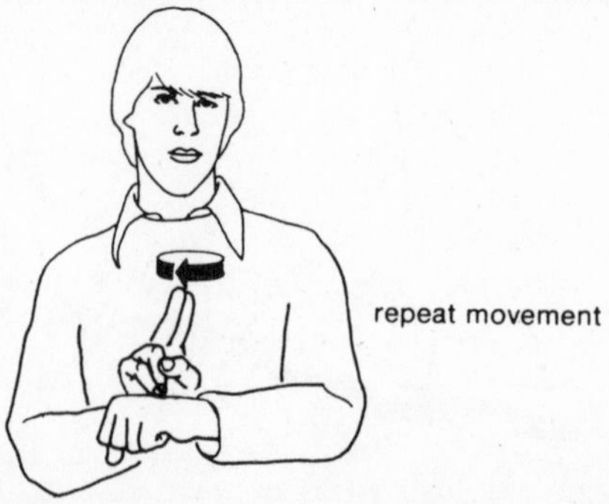

USE
Move the heel of the right "u" hand, palm facing forward and fingers pointing up, in a repeated circular movement on the back of the left "s" hand held across the chest, palm facing down.
Hint: Initialized sign.

INVESTIGATE, INSPECT, EXAMINE, CHECK
Bring the extended right index finger from near the right eye down and across the length of the open left hand held palm facing up in front of the body.
Hint: Moving one's vision from the eye down to examine something.

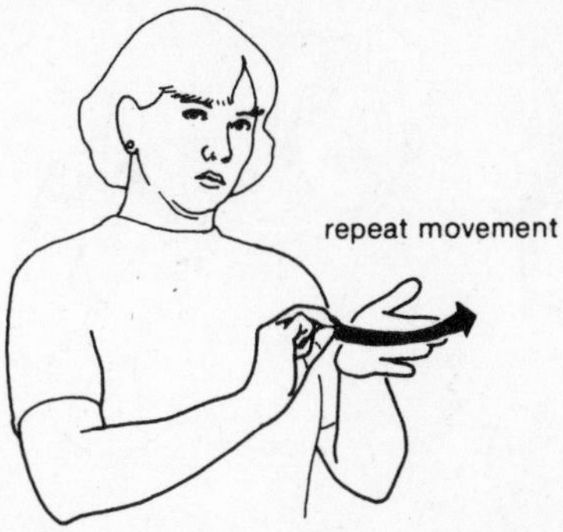

WRITE
Move the fingertips of the right thumb and index finger pinched together, with a repeated movement from the heel to the fingers of the open left palm held palm facing up in front of the body.
Hint: Mime holding a pencil and writing on paper.

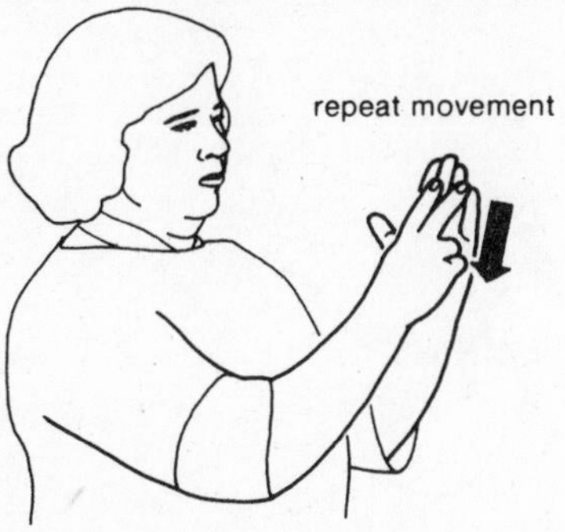

READ
Move the fingers of the right "v" hand with a repeated movement from the fingers to the heel of the open left hand held up in front of the body.
Hint: The fingers represent the eyes moving across a page.

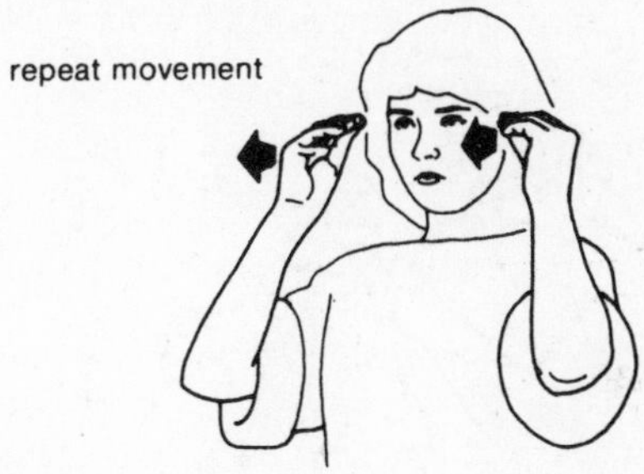

TEACH
Move both flattened "o" hands, palms facing each other, forward with a short double movement from near each side of the head.
Hint: Taking information from one's head and giving it to others.

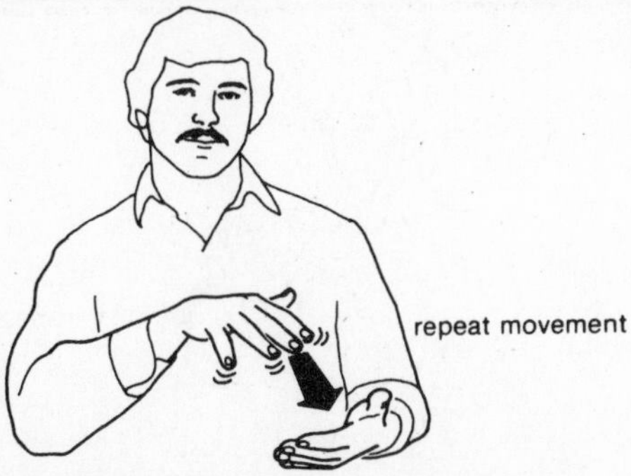

STUDY
While wiggling the fingers, move the right "5" hand downward with a repeated movement toward the open left hand held palm facing up in front of the body.
Hint: Reading and rereading while studying.

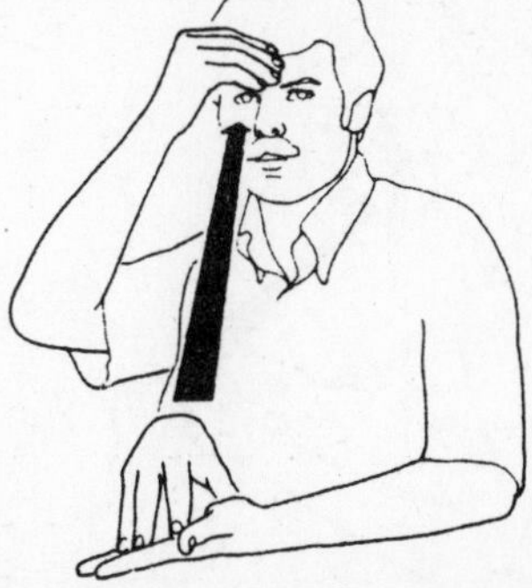

LEARN
Beginning with the fingers of the right "5" hand touching the palm of the open left hand held in front of the body, bring the right hand up to the forward while closing into a flattened "o" hand as the hand moves.
Hint: Taking information from the page and putting it in the head.

SUCCEED, FINALLY, AT LAST
Beginning with both extended index fingers pointing toward each other in front of each shoulder, palms facing in, twist the palms forward, ending with index fingers pointing up.
Hint: A natural gesture for success.

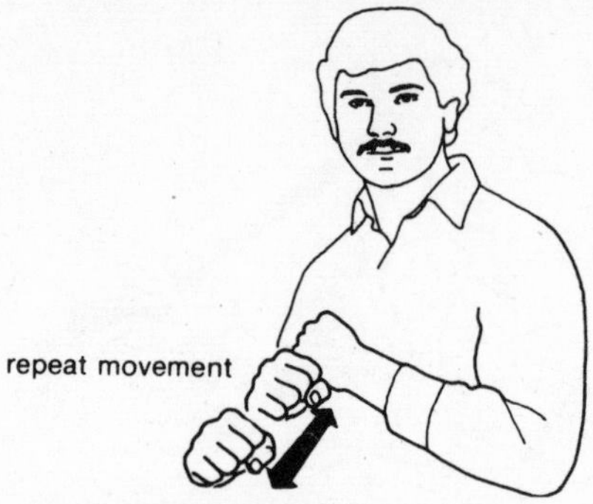

ADVERTISE, PUBLICIZE, COMMERCIAL
Beginning with the index-finger side of the right "s" hand, palm facing left, under the little-finger side of the left "s" hand, palm facing right,

CHOOSE, PICK, SELECT
Beginning with the fingertips of the right "g" hand touching the index finger of the left "5" hand, palms facing each other, bring the right hand back toward the right shoulder while pinching the thumb and index finger together.
Hint: Making a selection of the fingers on the left hand.

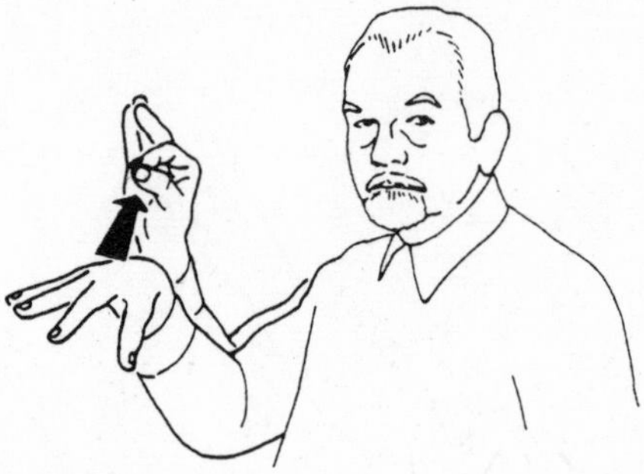

FIND, DISCOVER
Beginning with the right "5" hand hanging down in front of the right shoulder, palm facing down, bring the hand upward while pinching the thumb and index finger together.
Hint: Picking up something you found.

PROVE
Bring the open right hand, palm facing back, from near the right cheek forward and down, landing the back of the right hand on the open left palm held up in front of the body.
Hint: Taking something and laying it out for examination.

DEMONSTRATE, SHOW, EXAMPLE
With the extended right index finger, palm facing in, touching the palm of the open left hand, palm facing right, move the hands forward.
Hint: Pointing out something as an example.

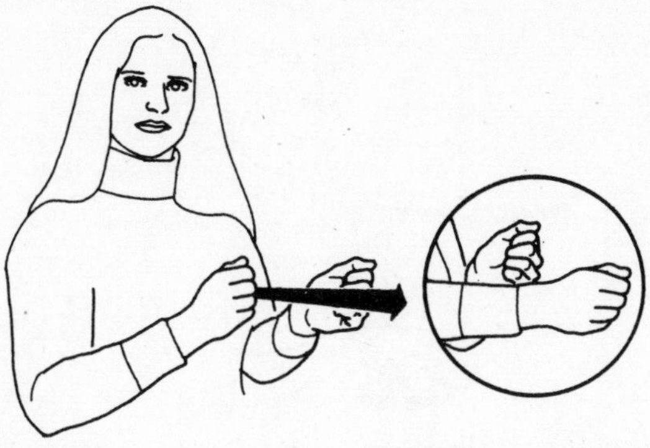

PASS, BY
Move the right "a" hand, palm facing left, from near the body forward past the left "a" hand, palm facing right.
Hint: Something passing another thing.

FAIL
Move the back of the right "k" hand, palm facing up, from the heel to the fingers of the open left palm held up in front of the body.

CANCEL, CORRECT, CRITICIZE
Using the extended right index finger, palm facing left, draw a large X across the open left palm held up in front of the body.
Hint: Cross out something that is incorrect.

ESTABLISH, APPOINT, APPOINTMENT
Beginning the right "a" hand, palm facing down, over the open left hand held across the chest, palm facing down, twist the wrist of the right hand to turn the palm in, ending with the little-finger side of the right hand on the back of the left hand.
Hint: Take something and set it down firmly to establish it.

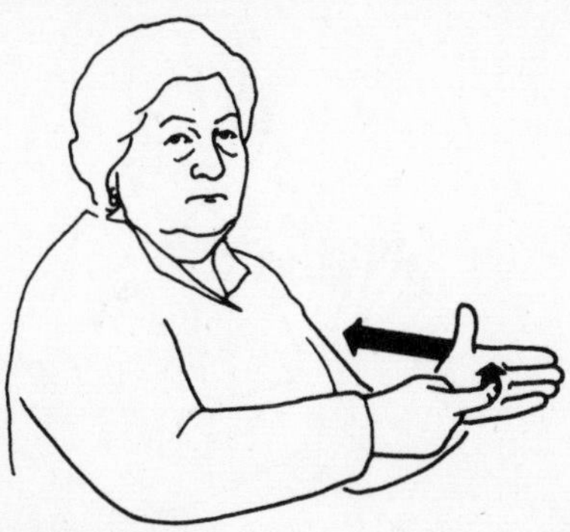

REQUIRE, DEMAND
Tap the index fingertip of the right "x" hand against the open left palm held in front of the body, palm facing right, and then pull both hands toward the body.
Hint: Demanding that something be placed in your palm as required.

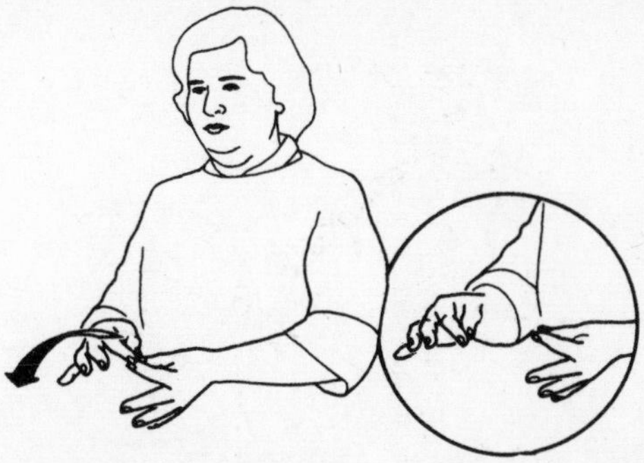

POSTPONE, DELAY
Beginning the fingertips of both "f" hands touching in front of the body, palms facing each other, move the right hand forward a short distance in an arc.
Hint: Put something off from the present into the future.

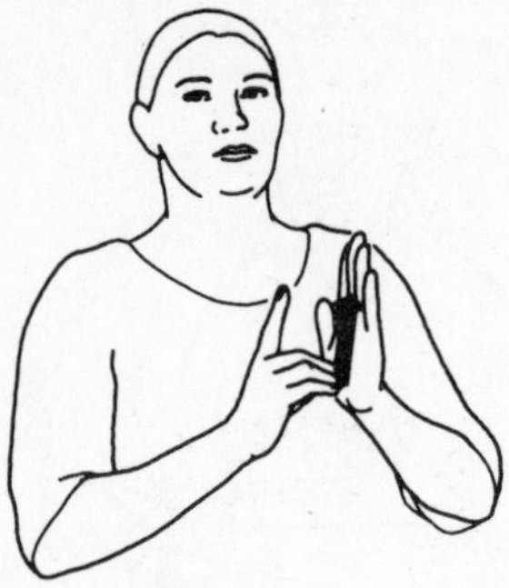

DEVELOP
Move the fingertips of the right "d" hand, from the heel to the fingers of the open left hand held in front of the chest, palms facing each other and fingers pointing up.
Hint: Initialized sign showing an idea growing upward.

SUPERVISE, TAKE CARE OF
With the little-finger side of the right "k" hand on the index-finger side of the left "k," palms facing in opposite directions, move the hands in a repeated flat circle in front of the body.
Hint: The fingers represent eyes looking in every direction.

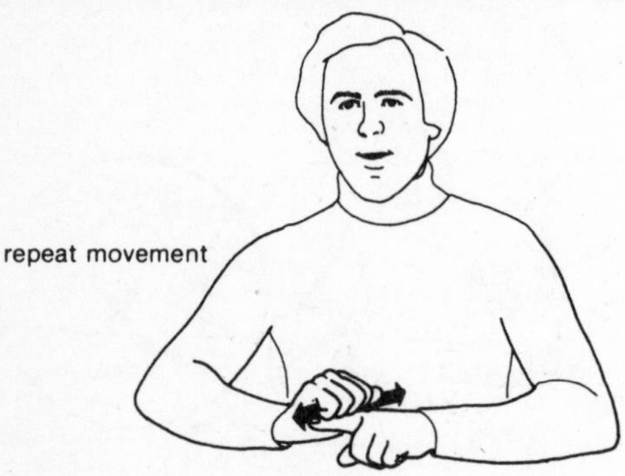

PRACTICE, TRAIN, TRAINING
Rub the knuckles of the right "a" hand with a repeated movement across the length of the extended index finger of the left hand held across the chest, both palms facing down.
Hint: Repetitive action as when practicing.

MANAGE, DIRECT, CONTROL, RULE, REIGN
Move both "x" hand, palms facing each other, forward and back with a repeated alternating movement in front of each side of the body.
Hint: Holding the reins to control a horse.

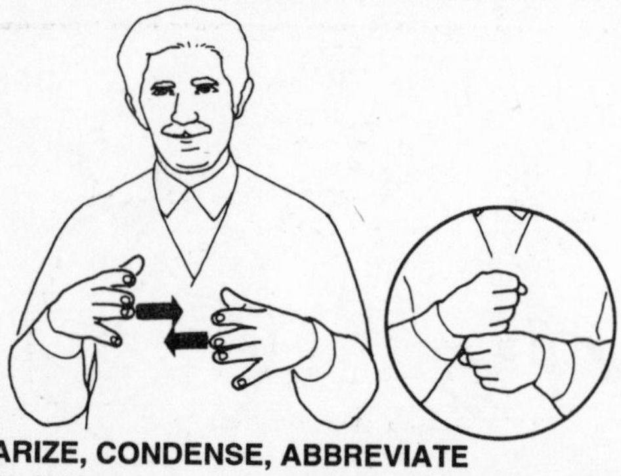

SUMMARIZE, CONDENSE, ABBREVIATE
With both "5" hands in front of the body, palms facing each other, bring the hands together while closing into "s" hands, ending with the little-finger side of the right "s" hand on the index-finger side of the left "s" hand.
Hint: Bring information together in a summary.

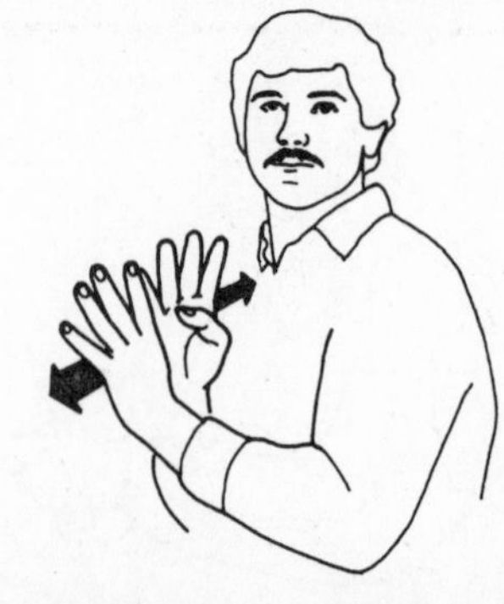

LINE UP
Beginning with the little-finger side of the right "4" hand touching the index-finger side of the left "4" hand, palms facing outward in opposite directions and right hand closer to the chest than the left hand, plus the hands apart, right hand in toward the chest and the left hand forward.
Hint: People standing in a line.

CHALLENGE, DARE
Beginning with both "10" hands in front of each shoulder, palms facing forward, bring the hands toward each other in front of the chest while turning the palms in.
Hint: Two things coming together in order to compete.

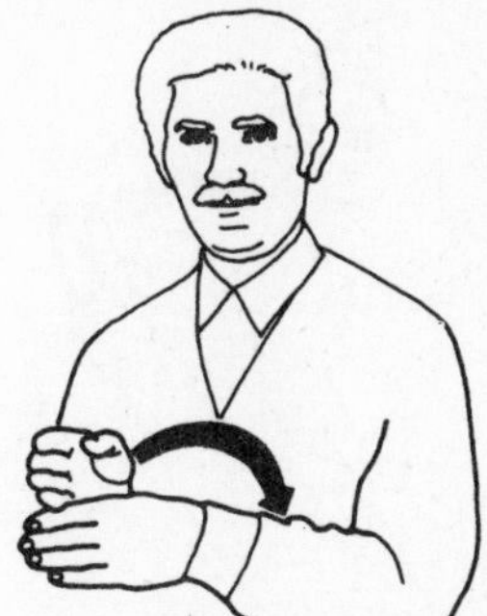

IMPROVE
Beginning with the little-finger side of the right "b" hand at an angle across the index-finger side of the left "b" hand, move the right hand in an arc up to touch again on the left forearm.
Hint: Showing improvement by moving up on the chart

LOSE, LOST
Beginning with the knuckles of both "c" hands touching in front of the chest, palms facing in, bring the hands downward and apart while opening the fingers into open hands.
Hint: Dropping or losing what you have.

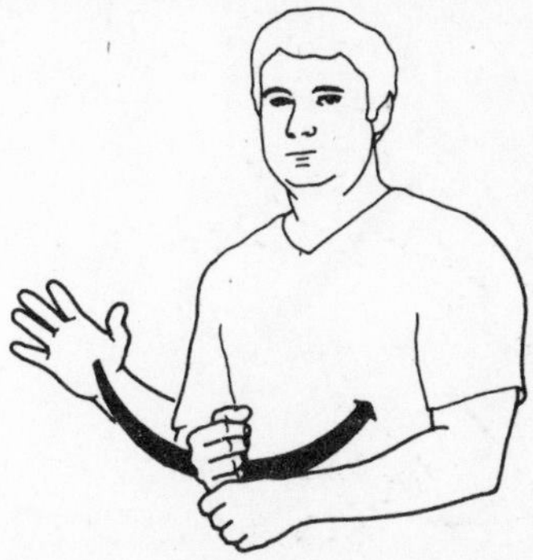

WIN
Move the right "5" hand from in front of the right side of the body, palm facing left, with a swinging movement to the left while closing into an "s" hand, ending with the little-finger side of the right "s" hand on the index-finger side of the left "s" hand, palms facing in opposite directions.
Hint: Grabbing to take the trophy.

SUPPORT, FAVOR, ADVOCATE
Push the knuckles of the right "s" hand up under the little-finger side of the left "s" hand held in front of the chest, both palms facing in, forcing the left hand to move upward to the left.
Hint: The right hand is giving support to the left hand.

CELEBRATE, VICTORY, FESTIVAL
With the index fingers and thumbs of both hands pinched together near each side of the head, palms facing each other, move the hands in small repeated circles.
Hint: Waving a flag to celebrate.

Other Actions

SEE
Move the fingers of the right "v" hand forward from pointing toward the eyes, palm facing in.
Hint: The fingers vision from the eyes looking at something.

WATCH
Move the right "v" hand forward from in front of the face, palm facing down and fingers pointing forward.
Hint: The fingers represent the eyes looking at something.

NOTICE, OBSERVE
Move the extended right index finger from near the right eye, palm facing in, downward to touch the open left palm held up in front of the chest.
Hint: Direct one's eyes to inspect something in the hand.

WATCH
Place the heel of the right "v" hand on the back of the left "s" hand held across the chest, both palms facing down and the right fingers pointing forward.

PREDICT, FORESEE, PREDICTION, PROPHECY
Move the right "v" hand from in front of the face, palm facing in and fingers pointing up, forward under the open left hand held in front of the chest, palm facing down.
Hint: Looking into the future.

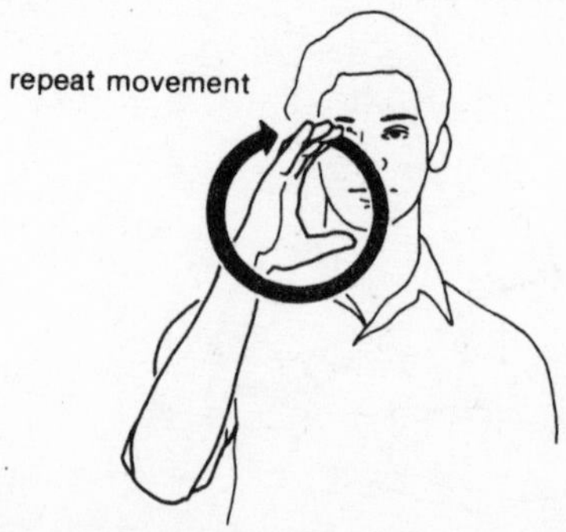

SEARCH, EXAMINE, LOOK FOR
With the right "c" hand, palm facing left, make a large repeated circle in front of the face.
Hint: Moving things aside to search everywhere.

OPEN
Beginning with the index-finger sides of both "b" hands touching in front of the body, palms facing down, turn the hands over and bring the hands upward and apart to in front of each side of the chest, palms facing each other.
Hint: Pulling the lid back on each side of a container.

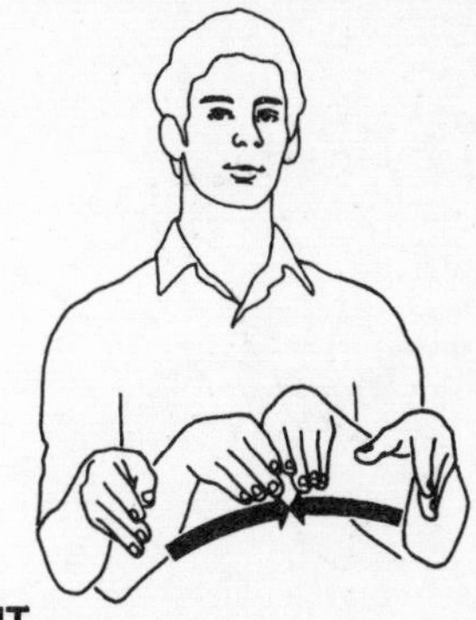

CLOSE, SHUT
Beginning with both "b" hands in front of each side of the body, palms facing each other, bring the index-finger side of both hands together, ending with palms facing down.
Hint: Closing the lid on a container.

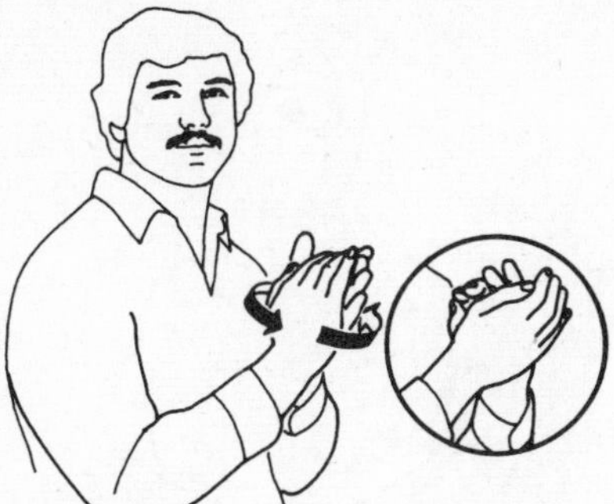

BECOME, TURN INTO
With the palms of both open hands together in front of the chest, right hand over the left, twist the wrists, ending with the left hand over the right hand.
Hint: Change one thing into something else.

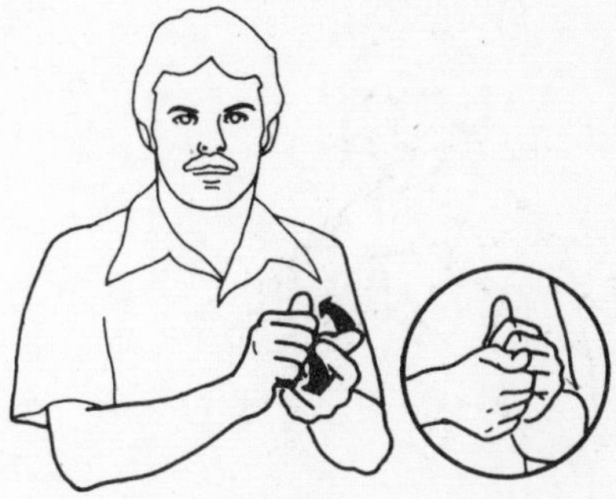

CHANGE, ADAPT, ALTER
With the palm side of both "a" hands together, right hand over the left, twist the wrists, ending with the left hand over the right hand.
Hint: Turn something into something else.

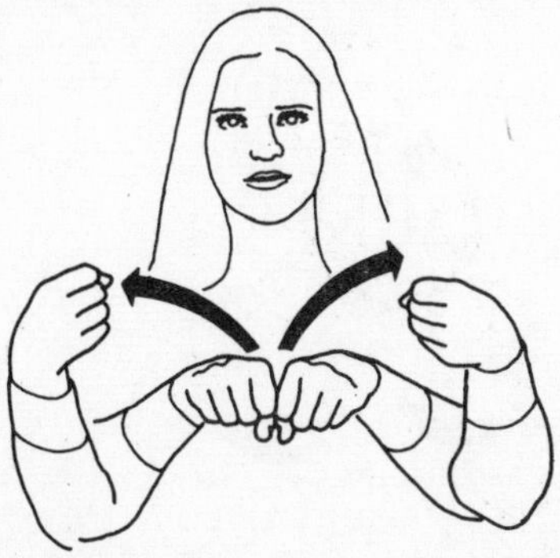

BREAK
Beginning with the index-finger sides of both "s" hands together in front of the chest, palms facing down, twist the wrists and bring the hands upward and apart to in front of each side of the chest, ending with the palms facing in.

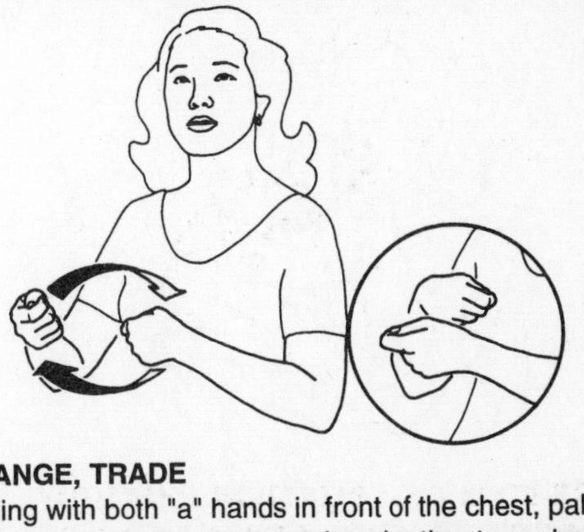

EXCHANGE, TRADE
Beginning with both "a" hands in front of the chest, palms facing in, move the hands around each other to exchange places.
Hint: Taking one thing and exchanging its location for another's.

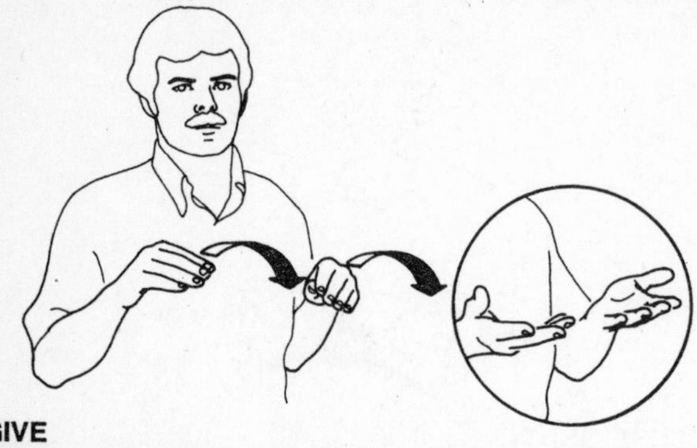

GIVE
Beginning with both flattened "o" hands in front of the chest, palms facing down, flip the hands over while opening into "5" hands, ending with palms facing up.
Hint: Taking something and presenting it to another person.

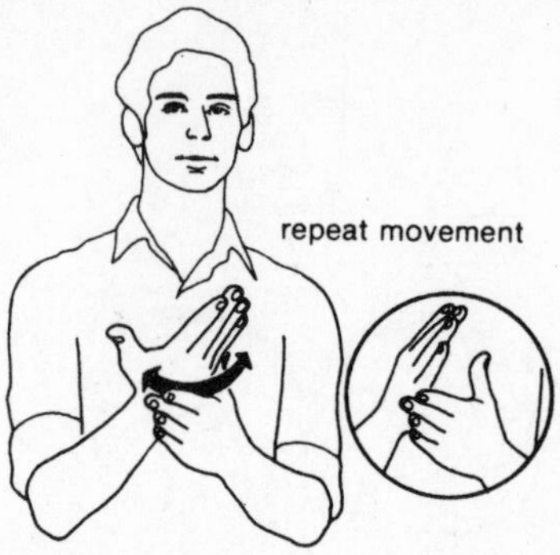

SHARE
Brush the little-finger side of the open right hand, palm facing left, back and forth with a repeated movement on the index-finger side of the open left hand, palm angled in, by twisting the right wrist.
Hint: Dividing something to give out shares.

HAVE, POSSESS
Bring the fingertips of both bent hands against the chest, palms facing outward in opposite directions.
Hint: Bringing something you own in toward yourself.

OFFER
Bring both open hands upward and slightly forward in front of the chest, palms facing up.
Hint: Taking something and offering it to another.

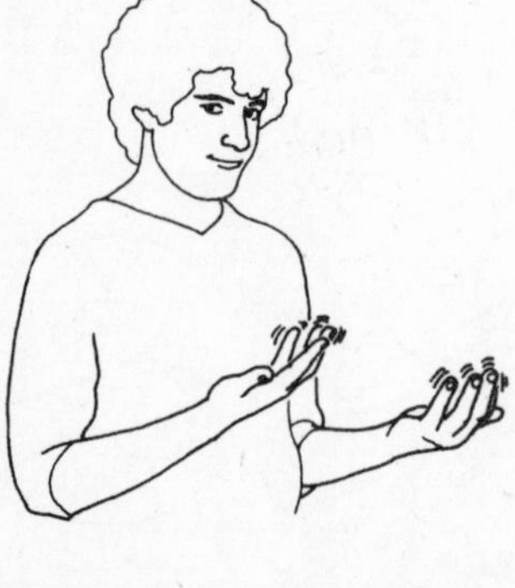

WAIT
With both "5" hands in front of the chest, palms facing up, wiggle the fingers repeatedly.
Hint: Drumming the fingers in boredom while waiting.

SAVE, SAFE, SAVIOR, SALVATION
Beginning with both "s" hands together in front of the chest, palms facing in, bring the hands apart to in front of each side of the chest, ending with palms facing forward.
Hint: Unloosing the chains binding a prisoner's wrists.

HIDE
Beginning with the thumb side of the right "a" hand touching the lips, palm facing left, move the hand downward and forward, ending with the right hand under the open left hand held in front of the chest, palm facing down.
Hint: "Secret" plus hiding something out of sight.

AVOID
Beginning with the right "a" hand, palm facing left, near the thumb of the left "a" hand, palm facing right, bring the right hand to the right back toward the chest with wavy movement.
Hint: Moving away from something to avoid it.

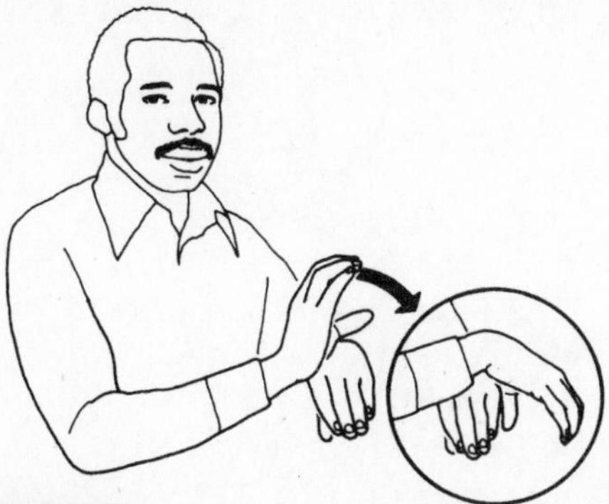

FORCE, DEFEAT
Beginning with the heel of the right "c" hand, palm facing forward, on the back of the open left hand, palm facing down, roll the right hand forward over the left hand while keeping the right heel in place.
Hint: The right hand forces something down.

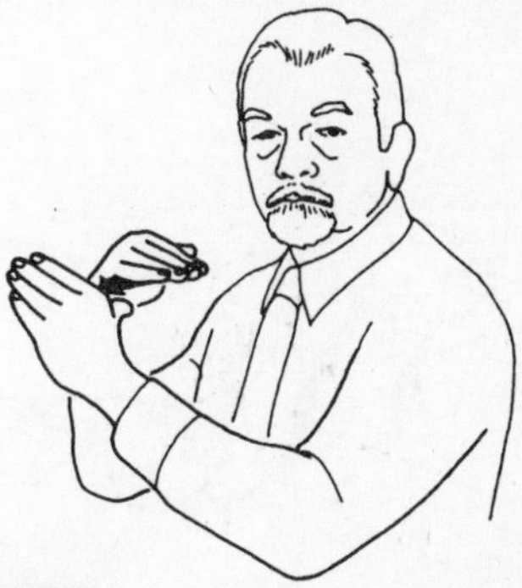

PREVENT, BLOCK
Hit the little-finger side of the open right hand at an angle against the index-finger side of the open left hand, both palms angled out in opposite directions.
Hint: Put up a barricade.

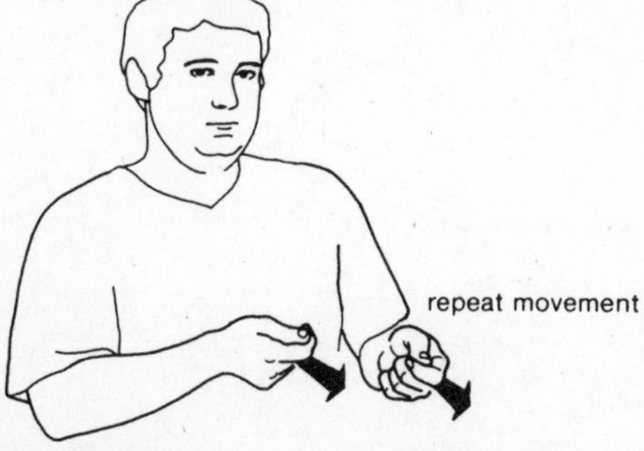

URGE, PERSUADE
With the index fingers and thumbs of both hands pinched together, palms facing each other and the right hand closer to the chest than the right, move the hands forward with a short repeated movement.
Hint: Using the reins to urge a horse forward.

MISS
Move the right "c" hand, palm facing left, across the face to the left while changing into an "s" hand.
Hint: Something gets away that you grab for.

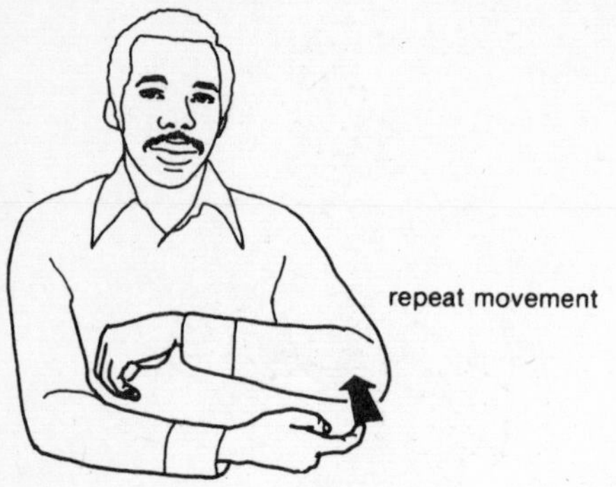

TEMPT
Tap the elbow of the bent left arm with the index fingertip of the right "x" hand.
Hint: Direct someone's attention away to tempt him or her.

BLAME, ACCUSE, AT FAULT
Slide the little-finger side of the right "a" hand, palm facing left, forward across the back of the left "s" hand held in front of the chest, palm facing down.
Hint: Pushing the blame away from oneself toward another.

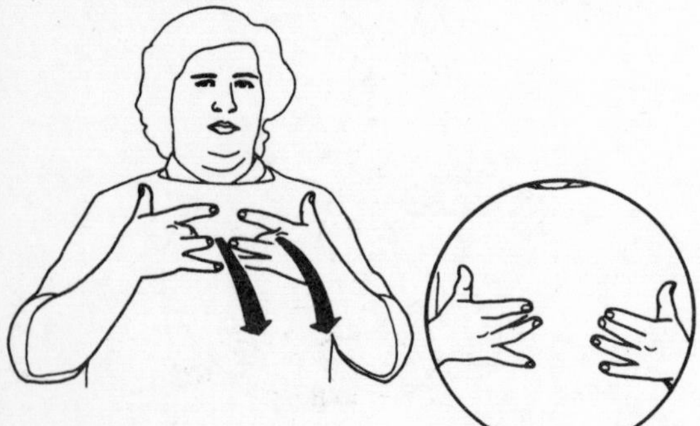

TEND, INCLINED TO
Beginning with the bent middle fingers of both "5" hands touching near each other on the chest, bring the hands forward.
Hint: Bring the heart forward toward something.

SEND, MAIL
Beginning with the fingertips of the bent right hand touching the back of the open left hand, both palms facing down, flick the right fingers forward while opening into an open hand.
Hint: Brush something away to send it.

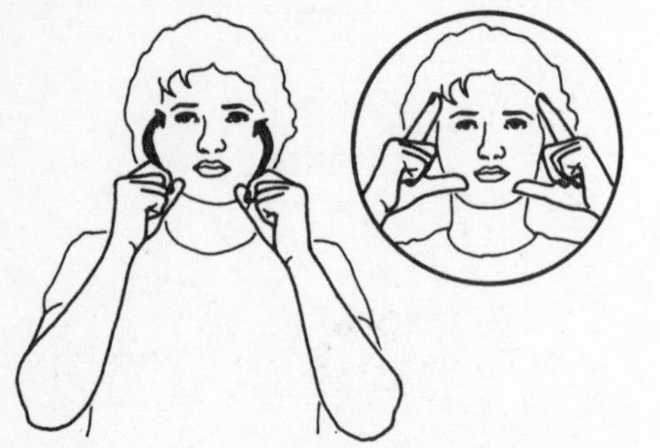

BLUSH
Beginning with the thumbs holding down the index fingers of both hands near each side of the face, palms facing each other, raise the index fingers forming "l" hands.
Hint: Fingers indicate a blush rising in the cheeks.

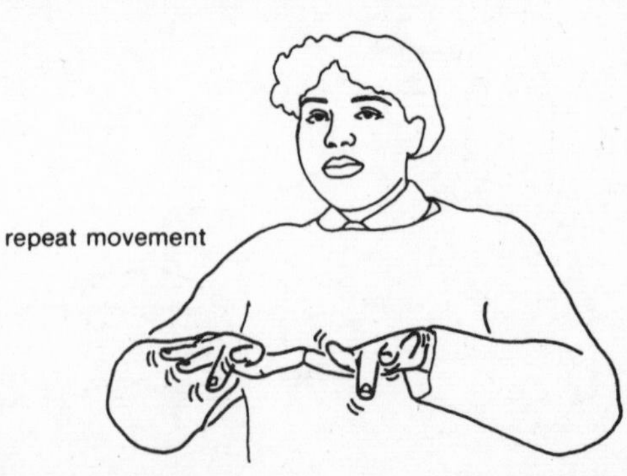

FLIRT
With the thumbs of both "5" hands touching, palms facing down and fingers pointing forward, wiggle the fingers with a repeated movement.
Hint: Mime fluttering your eyelashes when flirting.

CONTINUE, ENDURE, PERSEVERE
With the thumb of the right "a" hand on the thumb of the left "a" hand, move the hands forward in a double arc.
Hint: Moving action into the future.

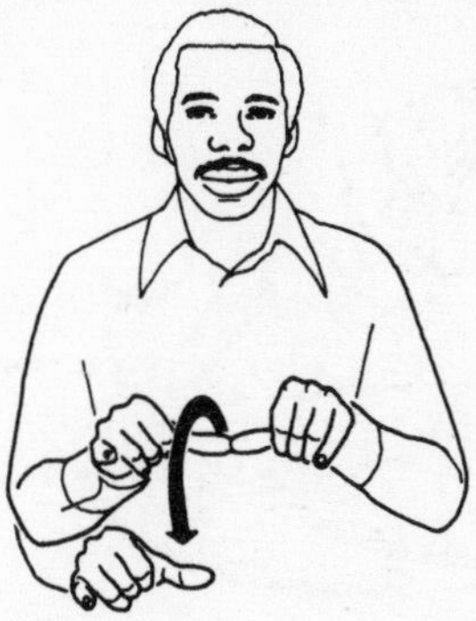

STAY
Beginning with the thumbs of both "y" hands touching in front of the chest, palms facing down, move the right hand forward and downward.
Hint: Moving something into a location to stay.

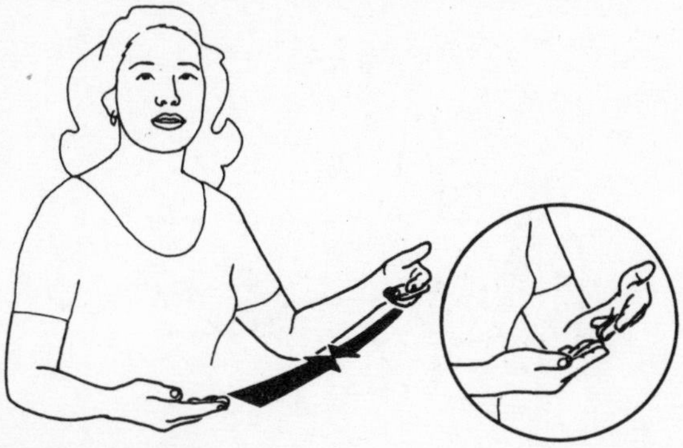

INTRODUCE
Bring both open hands from in front of each side of the body toward each other to meet in front of the body, palms facing up.
Hint: Bring two people together to meet each other.

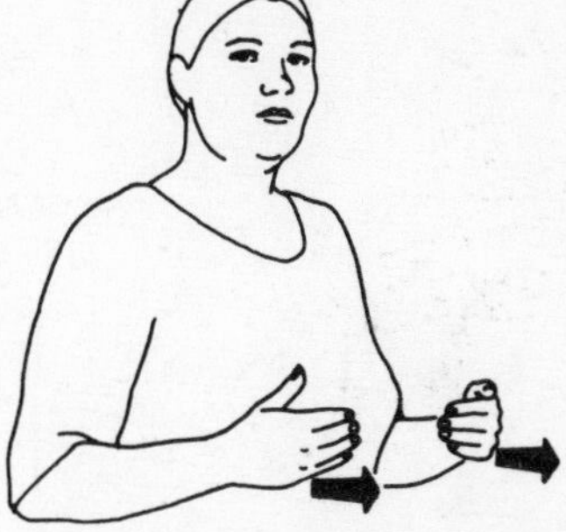

MOVE ON, FORWARD, CONTINUE, GO AHEAD
With both open hands in front of the body, palms facing in and fingers pointing toward each other, move the hands forward with a smooth action.
Hint: Moving on with things; a natural action.

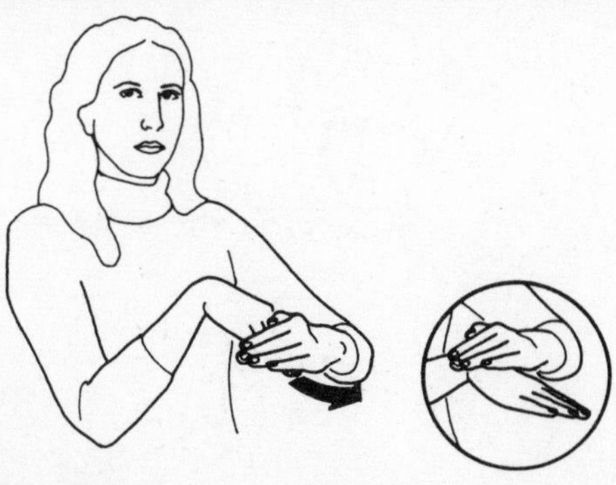

ENTER, INTO
Beginning with the fingers of the open right hand, palm facing down, in the opening of the left "c" hand, palm facing right, move the right hand forward from under the left hand.
Hint: Something moving into another thing.

INCLUDE, CONSIST OF
Move the right "5" hand, palm facing down, downward into the palm side of the left "c" hand held in front of the chest, palm facing right.
Hint: Taking something and including it with others.

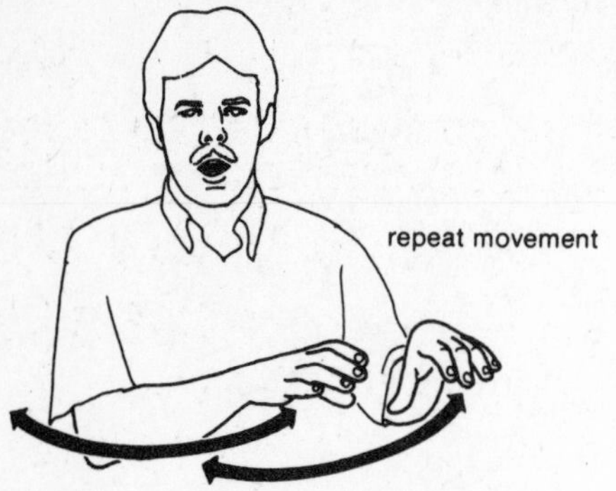

DO, ACT, ACTION, PERFORM, DEED, PERFORMANCE
Swing both curved hands, palms facing down, back and forth in front of the body with a repeated movement.
Hint: Shows the hands actively doing something.

MEET
With both extended index fingers pointing up, bring them toward each other until they meet in front of the chest, palms facing each other.
Hint: Two people walking up to each other.

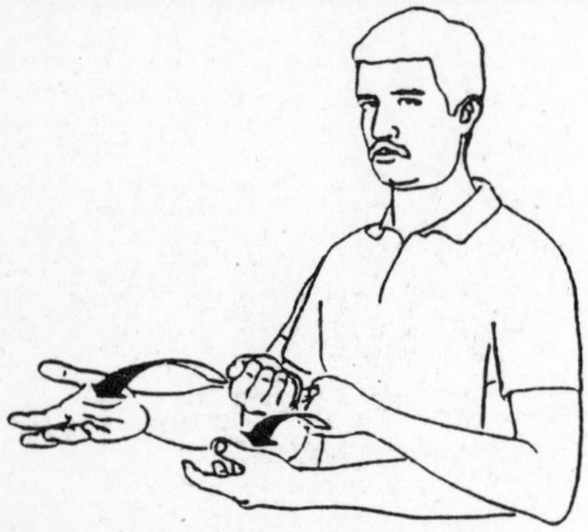

CAUSE
Beginning with both "s" hand near each other in front of the body, palms facing up, move the hands forward while opening into "5" hands.
Hint: Represents spreading an influence.

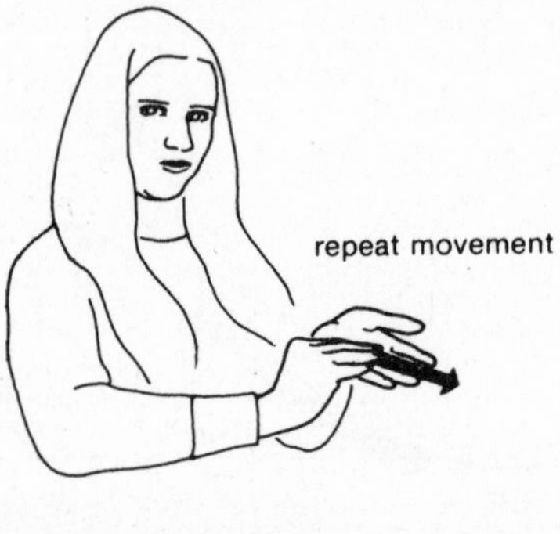

EXCUSE, FORGIVE, PARDON
Brush the fingertips of the bent right hand, palm facing down, with a repeated movement from the heel to the fingers of the open left palm held up in front of the body.
Hint: Brushing aside a mistake.

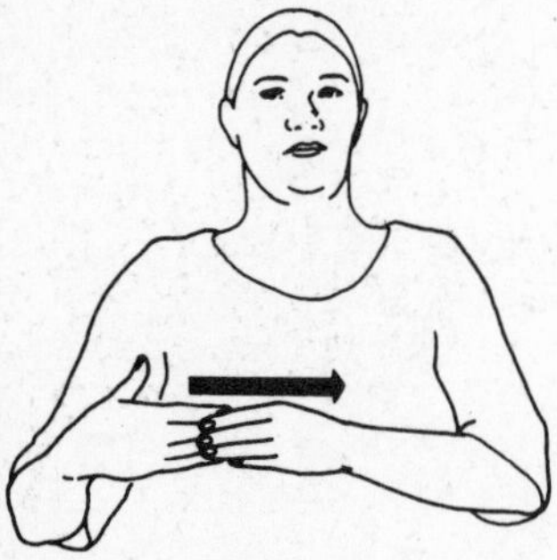

GUIDE, LEAD
While holding the fingertips of the right open hand with the fingers of the left open hand, palms facing the body, move the hands from right to left in front of the body.
Hint: The right hand guides the left hand.

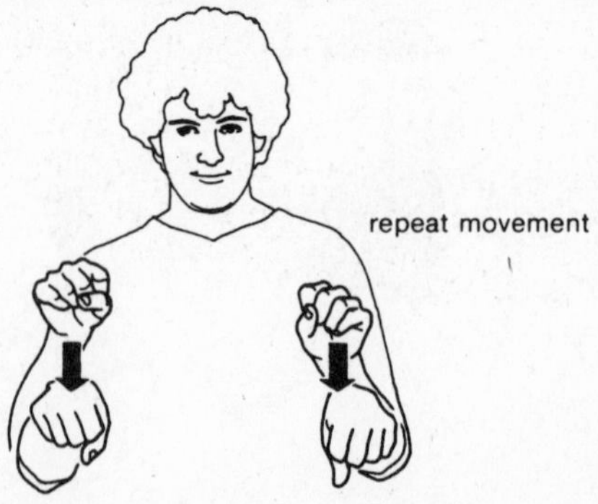

CAN
Move both "s" hands, palms facing forward, downward with a deliberate movement by bending the wrists.
Hint: The hands represent the head nodding in affirmative.

twelve

BEING AND FEELING

Actions of the Mind
Feelings

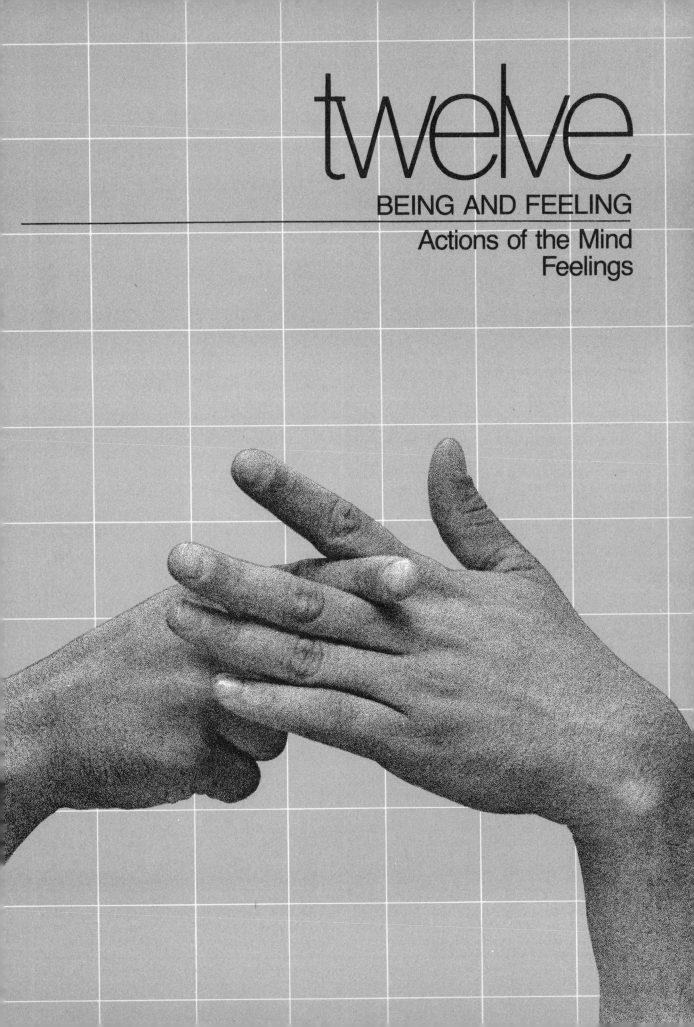

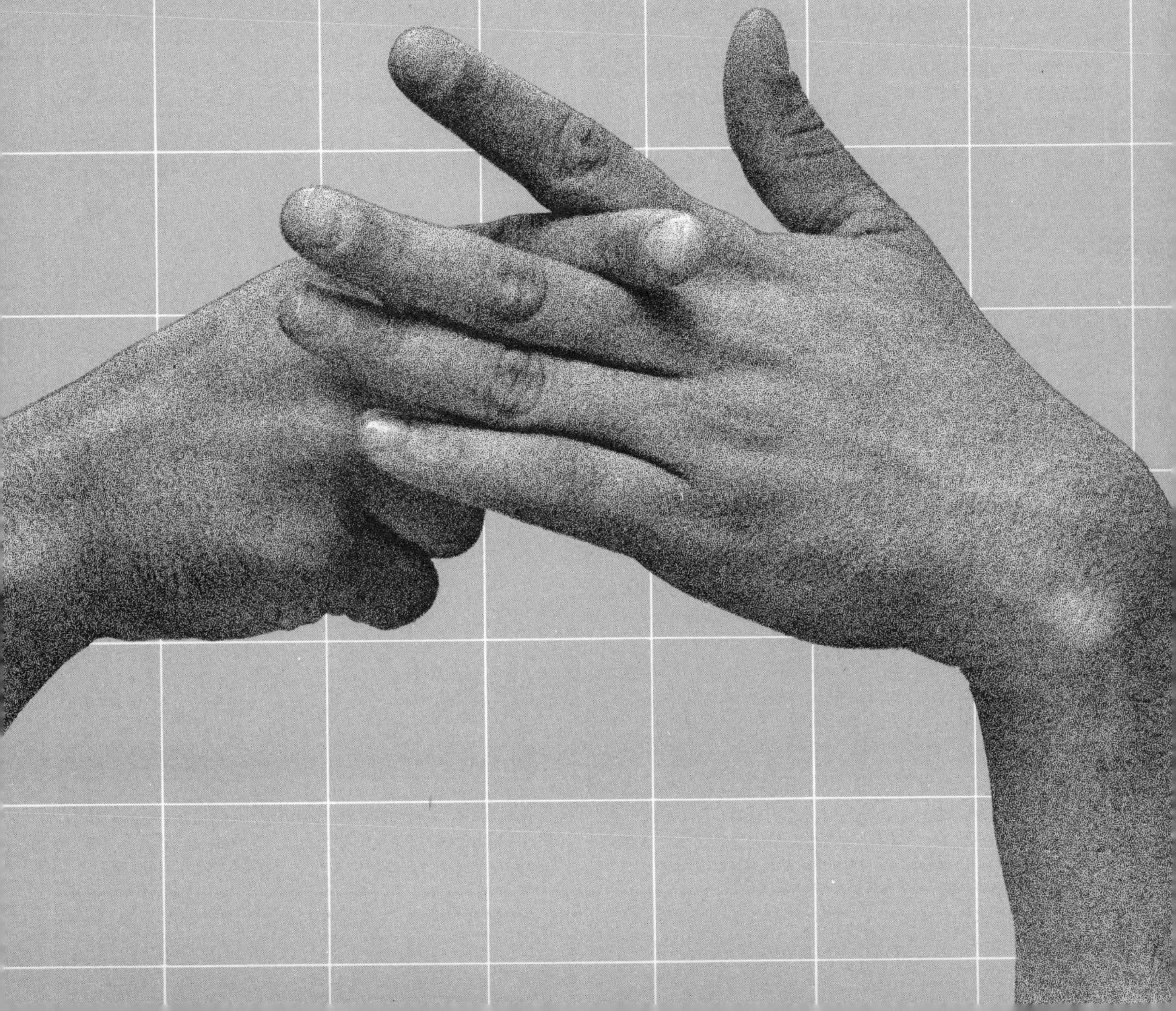

SIGNS FOR THINKING ACTIVITIES

The signs for many mental activities are formed against the forehead near the brain. Some example of mental signs are "think," "remember," "stupid," "memory," "dream," and "forget."

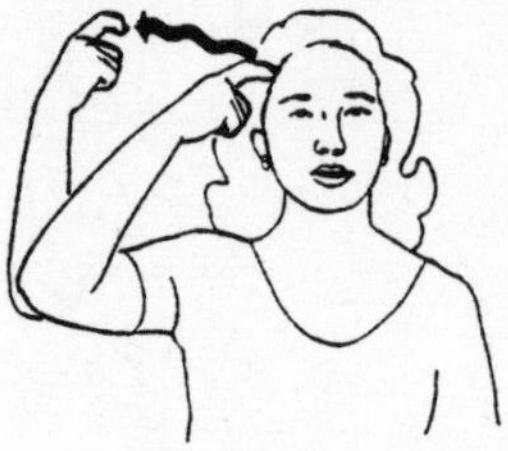

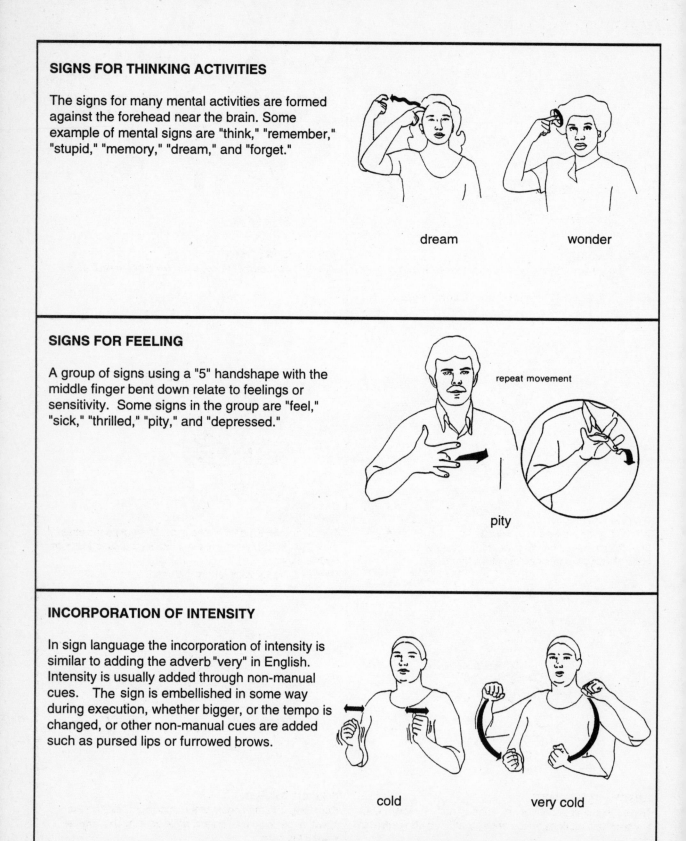

dream

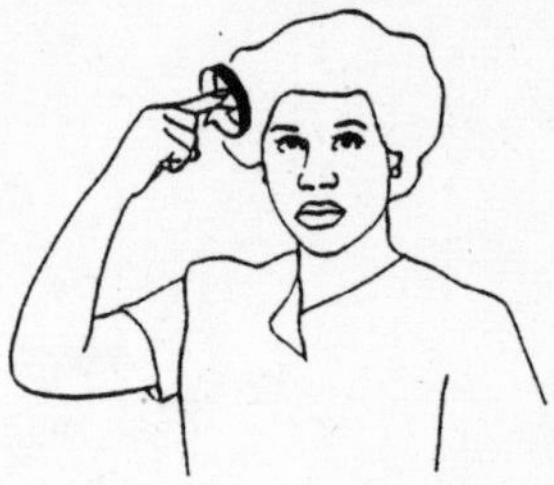

wonder

SIGNS FOR FEELING

A group of signs using a "5" handshape with the middle finger bent down relate to feelings or sensitivity. Some signs in the group are "feel," "sick," "thrilled," "pity," and "depressed."

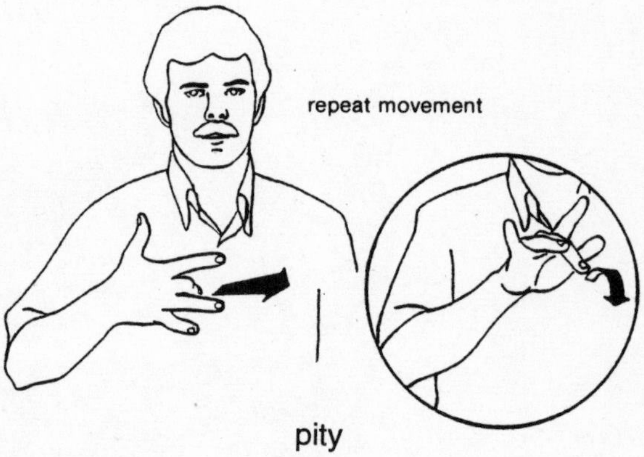

pity

INCORPORATION OF INTENSITY

In sign language the incorporation of intensity is similar to adding the adverb "very" in English. Intensity is usually added through non-manual cues. The sign is embellished in some way during execution, whether bigger, or the tempo is changed, or other non-manual cues are added such as pursed lips or furrowed brows.

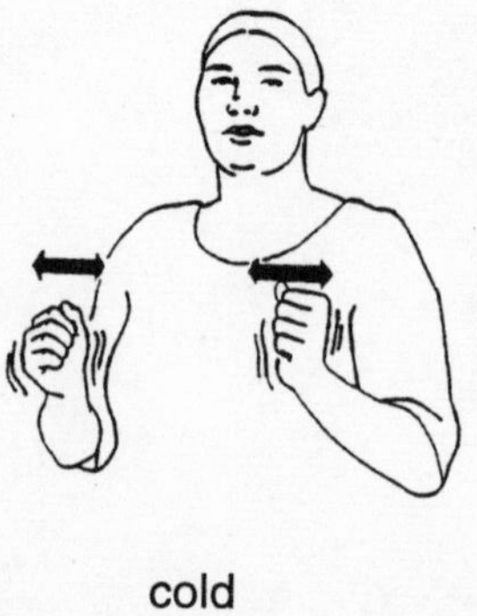

cold

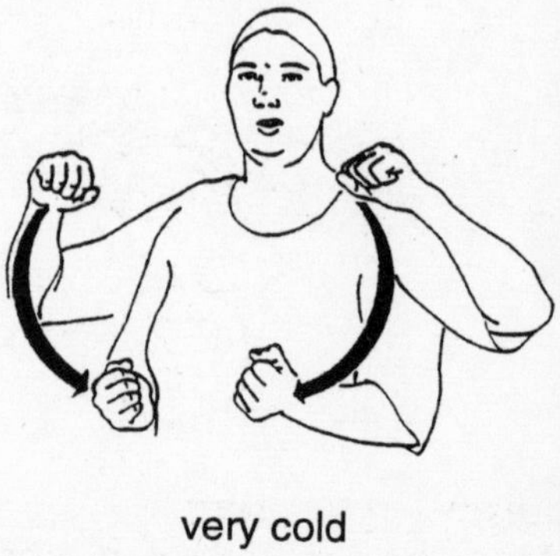

very cold

Actions of the Mind

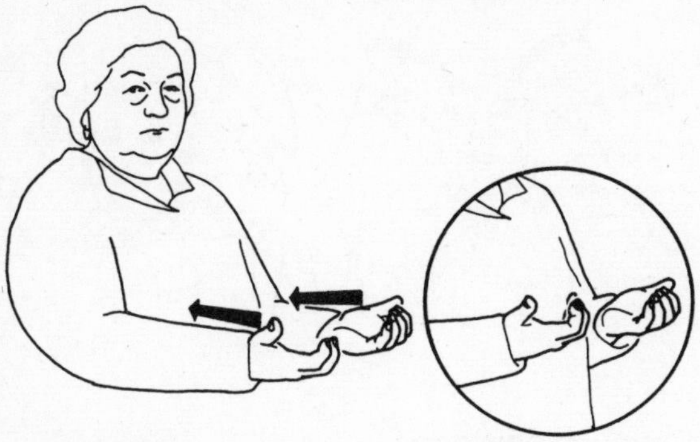

WANT, DESIRE
Bring both "claw" hands back toward the waist, palms facing up.
Hint: Bringing something to yourself that you want.

WISH, DESIRE, CRAVE
Move the fingertips of the right "c" hand downward on the chest.

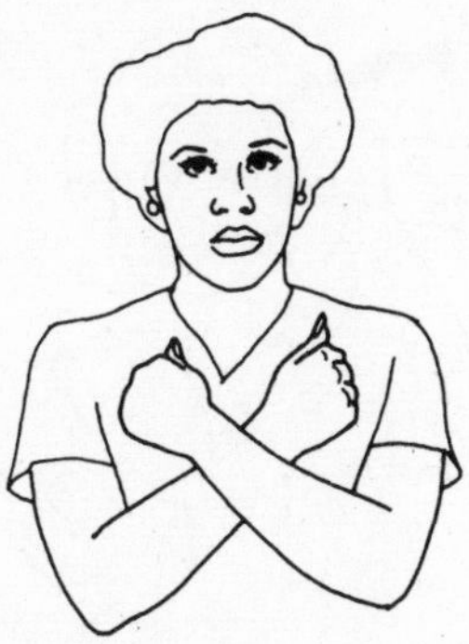

LOVE, HUG
With the arms crossed at the wrists, lay the palm sides of both "a" hands on the chest near the opposite shoulder.
Hint: Holding something dear close to oneself.

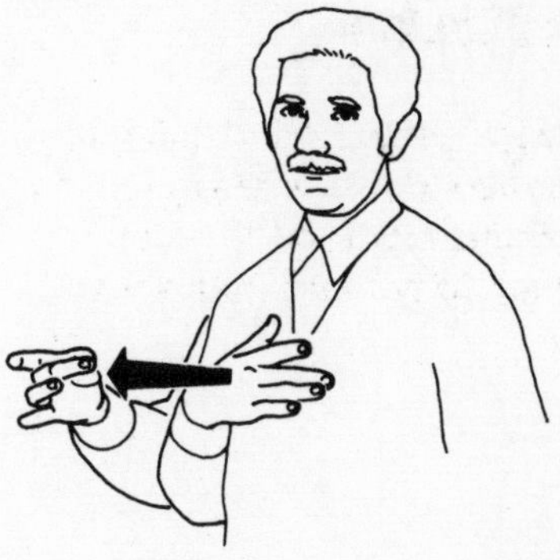

LIKE
Beginning with the palm of the right "5" hand on the chest, move the hand forward while closing the thumb to the bent middle finger.
Hint: Taking something from the heart.

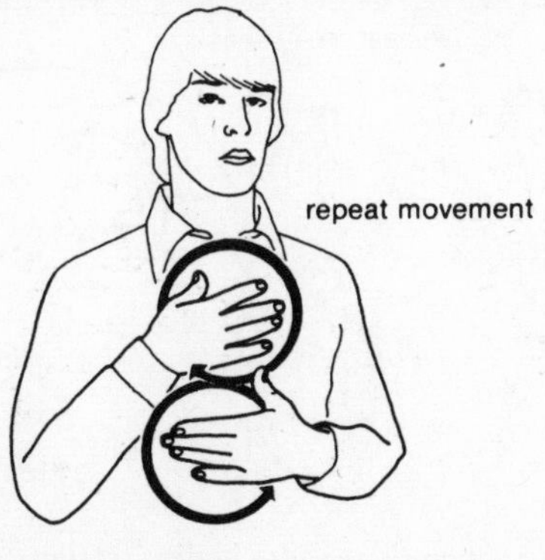

ENJOY, APPRECIATE
Move the palms of both open hands in circular movements in opposite directions on the body, right hand above the left hand.
Hint: Rubbing the chest in pleasure.

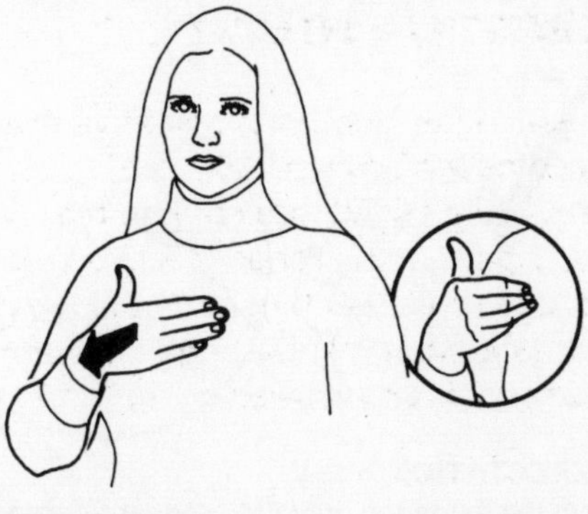

PREFER, RATHER
Beginning with the fingers of the open right hand on the chest, move the hand forward while bending the fingers toward the palm.

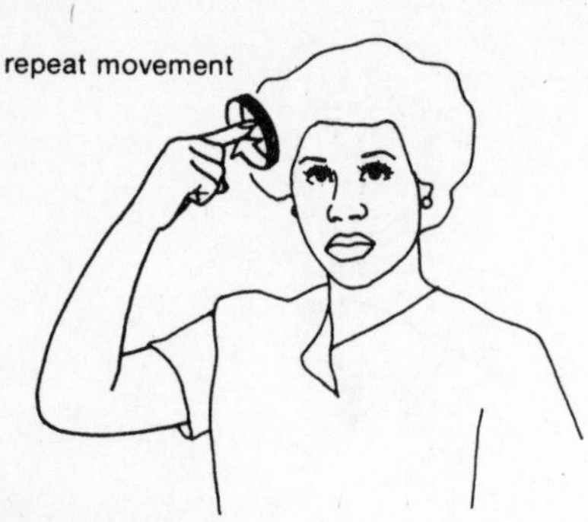

WONDER, CONSIDER
Move the extended right index finger in a small circle near the right side of the forehead.
Hint: Shows the brain pondering over something in a continuous manner.

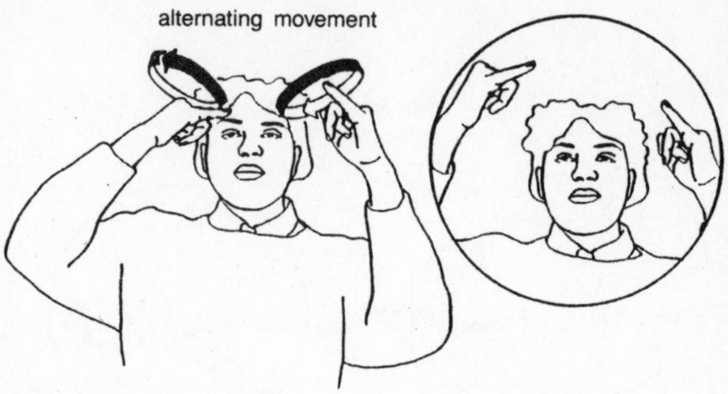

IMAGINE, IMAGINATION
Beginning with extended little fingers of both "i" hands near each side of the forward, palms facing each other, bring with hands upward with alternating movements.
Hint: Taking thoughts from the head.

INVENT, CREATE
Beginning with the index finger of the right "4" hand near the right side of the head, palm facing left, move the hand forward in an arc.

DREAM, DAYDREAM
Bring the extended right index finger from the right side of the forehead, palm facing in, forward while bending the index finger up and down repeatedly.
Hint: Taking a thought away as if in a dream.

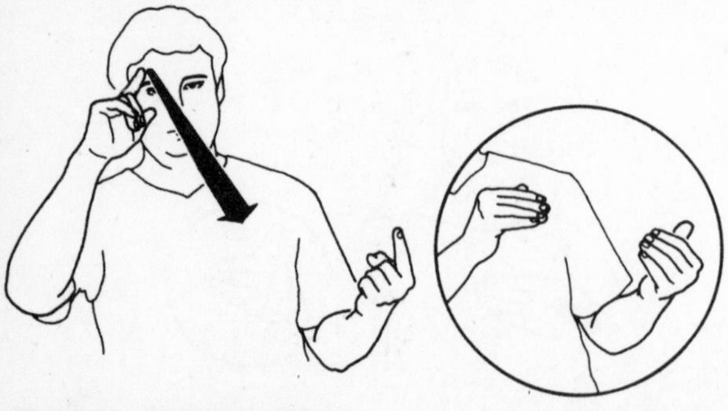

EXPECT, EXPECTATION
Beginning with the extended right index finger touching the right side of the forehead, palm facing forward, and the extended left index finger held in front of the right side of the body, palm facing in, bring the right hand downward while changing both hands into bent hands, palms facing each other in front of the left shoulder.

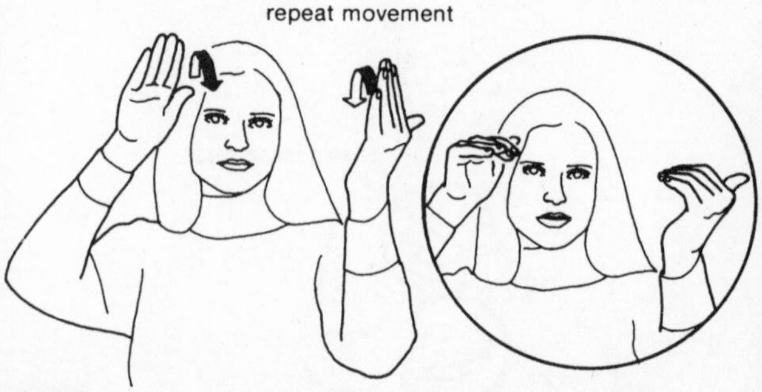

HOPE
With the open right hand near the right side of the head and the open left hand somewhat forward, palms facing each other, bend the fingers downward toward each other with a repeated movement.
Hint: Taking a thought and looking for it in the future.

KNOW, KNOWLEDGE
Tap the fingertips of the curved right hand to the right side of the forehead with a repeated movement, palm facing in.
Hint: The hand indicates that knowledge is in the brain.

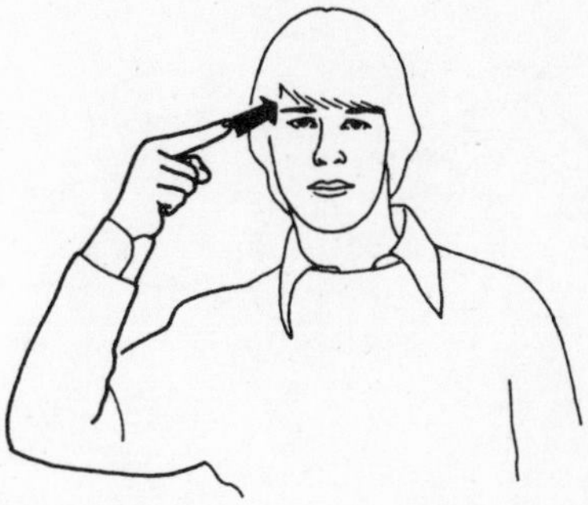

THINK, THOUGHTS
Touch the extended right index finger to the right side of the forehead.
Hint: Pointing to where thinking takes place.

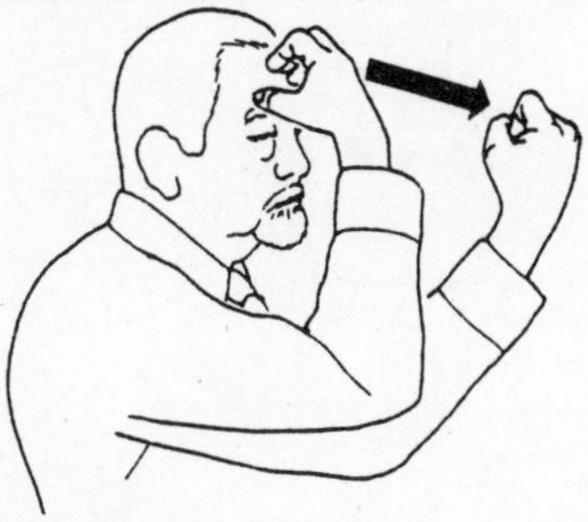

MEMORIZE, MEMORY
Beginning with the fingertips of the right "c" hand near the forehead, palm facing in, bring the hand forward while closing the fingers into an "s" hand.
Hint: Taking information from the brain and holding on to it.

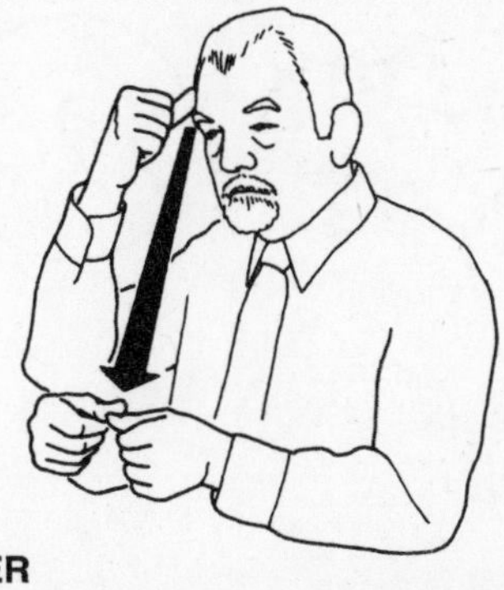

REMEMBER
Bring the thumb of the right "10" hand, palm facing left, downward from the right side of the forehead to touch the thumbnail of the left "10" hand held in front of the body, palm facing right.
Hint: Taking something from the head and looking at it.

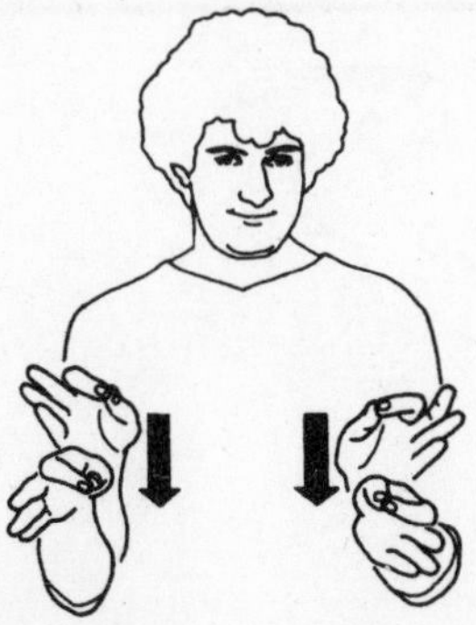

DECIDE, DECISION
Bring both "f" hands downward with a deliberate movement in front of each side of the body, palms facing each other.
Hint: Taking thoughts and setting them down firmly.

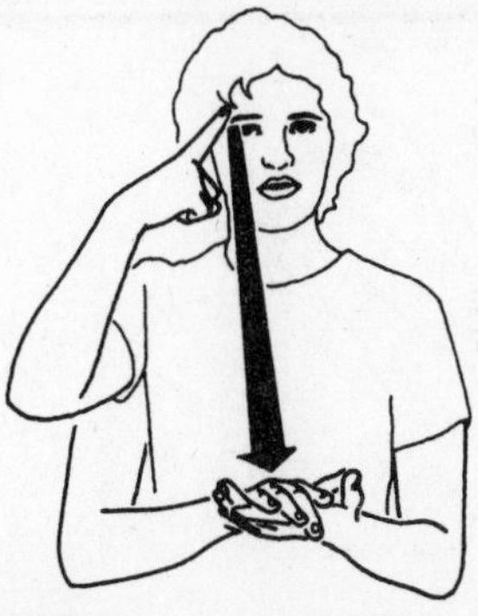

BELIEVE, BELIEF
Bring the extended right index finger from the right side of the forehead downward to clasp the left hand held palm up in front of the body.
Hint: Taking a thought from the head and holding on to it.

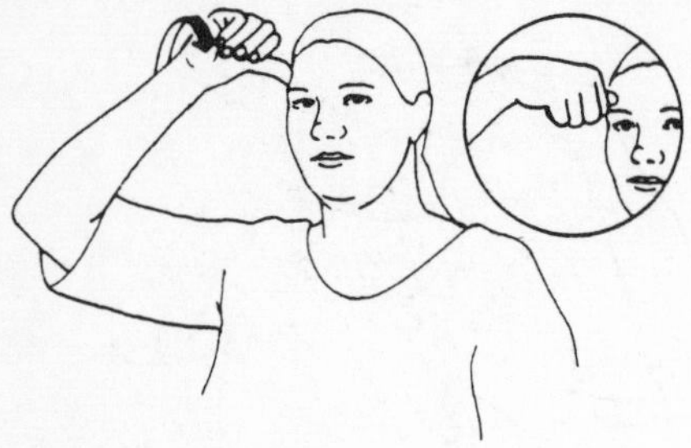

REMIND, REMEMBER
With the thumb of the right "10" hand against the right side of the forehead, palm facing left, twist the wrist down.
Hint: Embedding a thought in the mind.

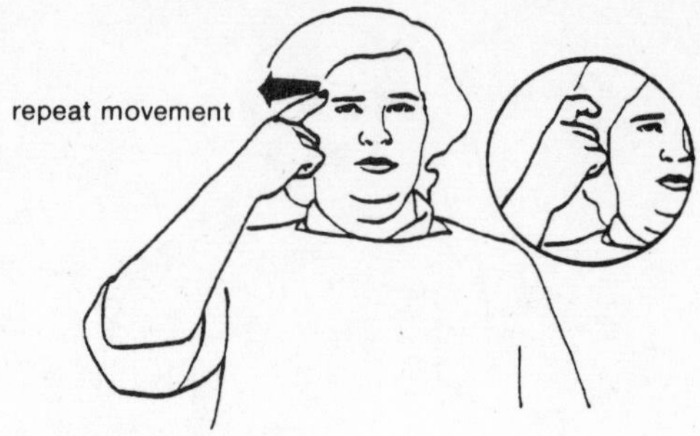

SUSPECT, SUSPICION
Move the extended right index finger from touching the right side of the forehead outward to the right with a double movement bending the finger as the hand moves each time.
Hint: Taking something from the mind and questioning it.

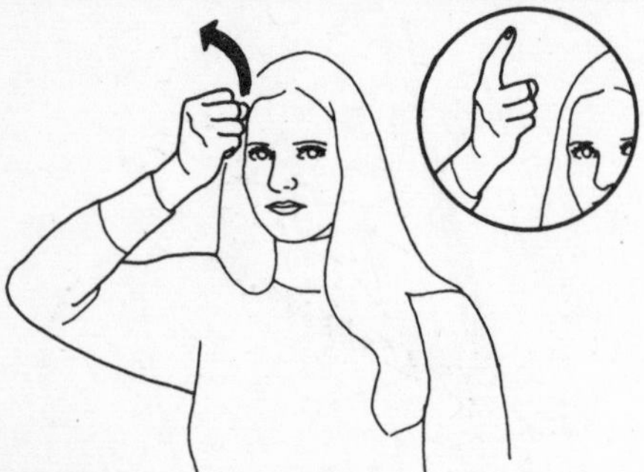

UNDERSTAND
Beginning with the right "s" hand near the right side of the forehead, palm facing in, flick the index finger upward.
Hint: A light goes on in the hear.

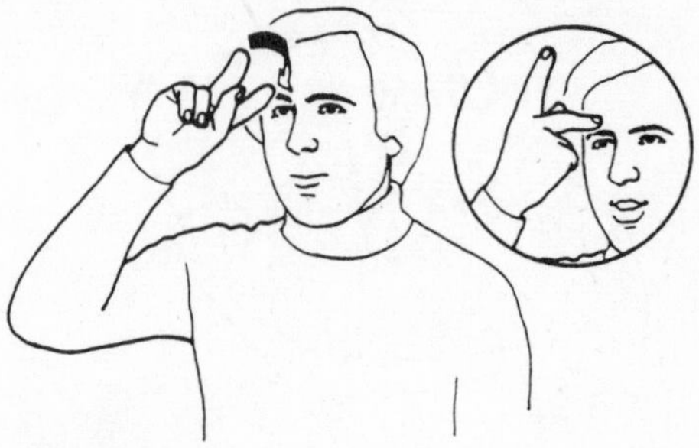

MISUNDERSTAND
Beginning with index finger of the right "k" hand touching the forehead, palm facing forward, twist the wrist to turn the palm back and touch the middle finger of the right "k" hand to the forehead.
Hint: Taking something and turning it around in the head.

GUESS, ASSUME, ESTIMATE
Move the right "c" hand, palm facing left, from in front of the right side of the face in an arc to the left while closing into an "a" hand.
Hint: Grabbing at a thought.

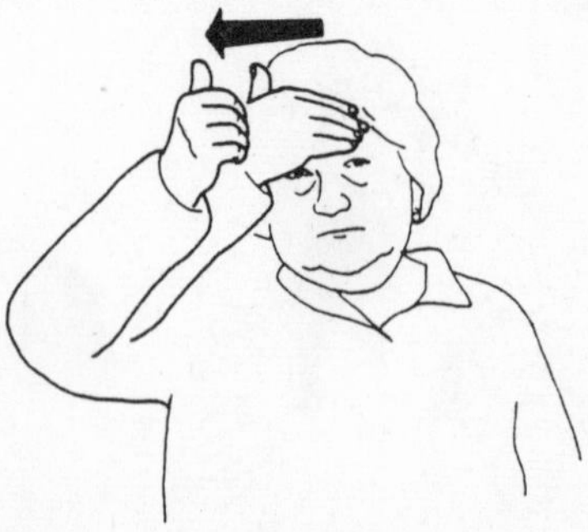

FORGET
Beginning with the fingers of the open right hand on the forehead, palm facing in, bring the hand across the forehead to the right, closing into an "10" hand as the hand moves.
Hint: Wiping a thought out the mind.

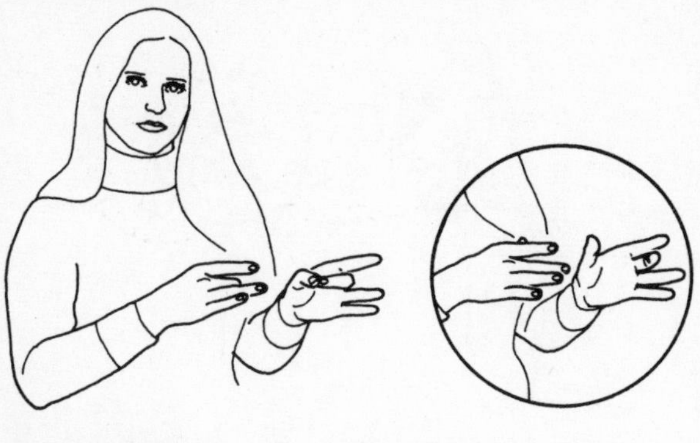

HATE, DESPISE
Beginning with both "8" hands in front of the body, palms facing each other, flick the middle fingers off the thumbs forward with a deliberate movement.
Hint: Flick something distasteful away from the body.

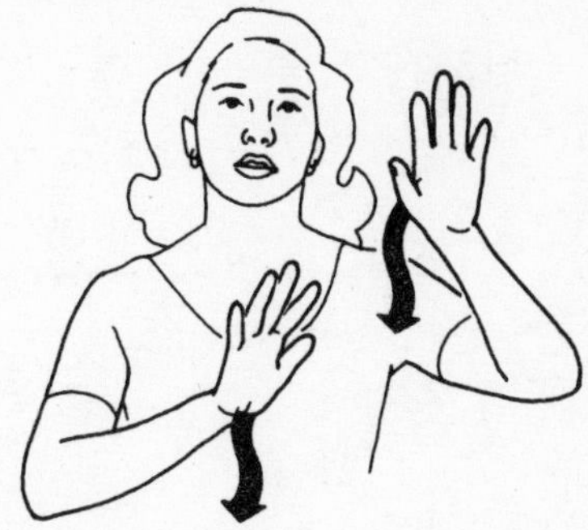

FEAR, DREAD
Beginning with both "5" hands held in front of the chest, one hand higher than the other and palms facing forward, move the hands downward simultaneously with wavy movements.
Hint: Hands are held up to protect the body against unknown fear.

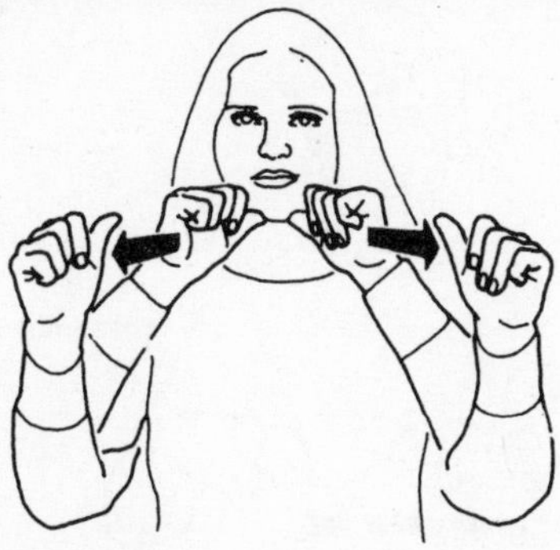

DENY
Bring the thumbs of both "10" hands, palms facing each other, forward and outward with a deliberate movement.
Hint: The sign for "not" formed with both hands for emphasis.

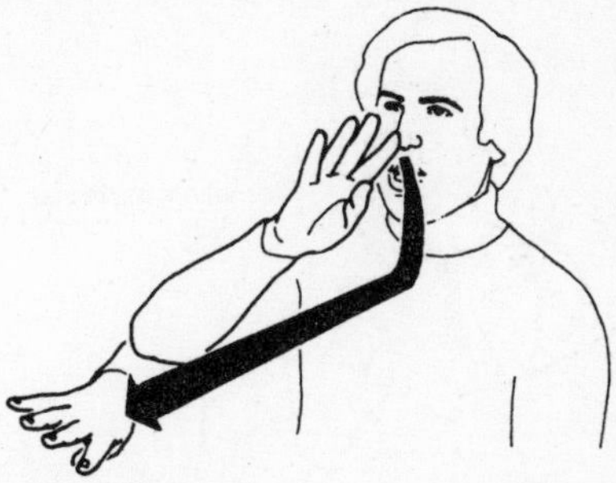

IGNORE, NEGLECT
Beginning with the index finger of the right "4" hand near the nose, palm facing left, bring the hand down to the left and then sharply to the right, ending with the palm facing down in front of the right side of the body.

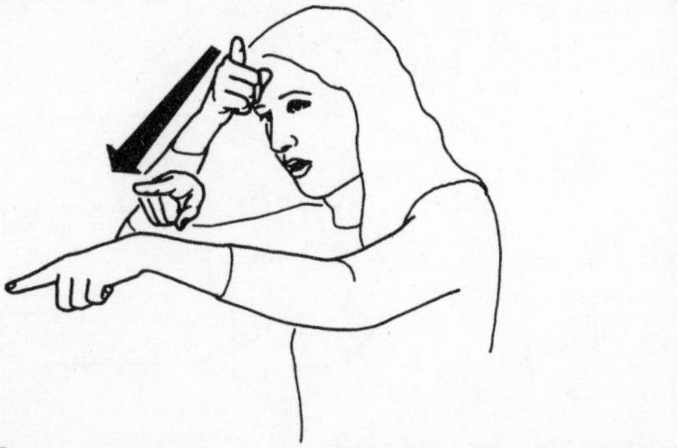

AGREE
Bring the extended right index finger from near the forehead downward to near the extended left index finger held some distance in front of the chest, ending with both palms facing down.
Hint: Bringing one's thoughts together to match another person's thoughts.

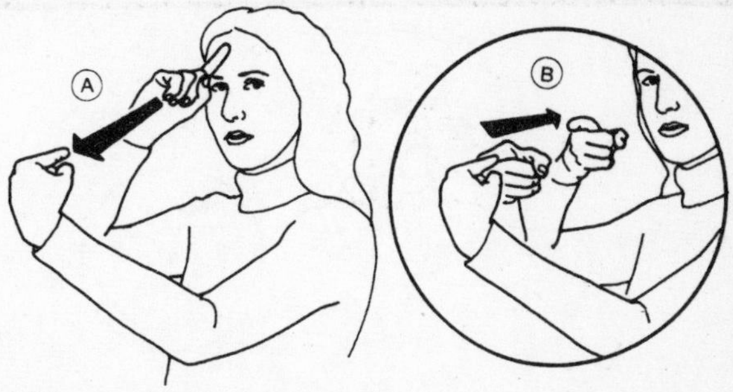

DISAGREE, CONTRARY
Bring the extended right index finger from near the forehead downward to touch the extended left index finger held some distance in front of the chest. Then pull the right extended index finger back toward the right shoulder.
Hint: Pulling your thoughts away from another's thoughts with whom you disagree.

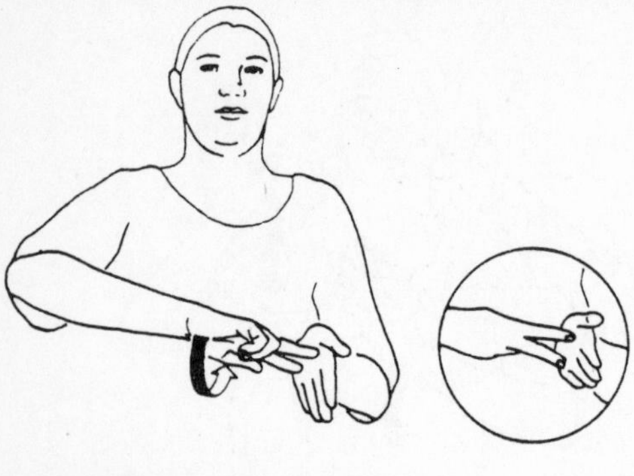

MEAN, INTEND
Beginning with the fingertips of the right "v" fingers, palm facing down and right elbow extended, touching the palm of the open left hand held in front of the chest, twist the right hand back, ending with the palm facing in.

SUFFER, BEAR, TOLERATE
Beginning with the thumbnail of the right "a" hand on the bottom lip, palm facing left, twist the wrist, ending with the palm facing in.
Hint: Silently bearing a burden.

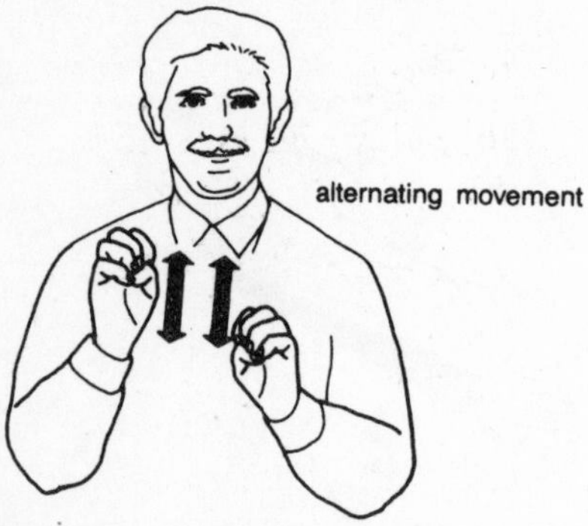

EVALUATE, EVALUATION
Beginning with both "e" hands near each other in front of the chest, palms facing forward, move the hands up and down repeatedly with an alternating movement.
Hint: Initialized sign showing indecision.

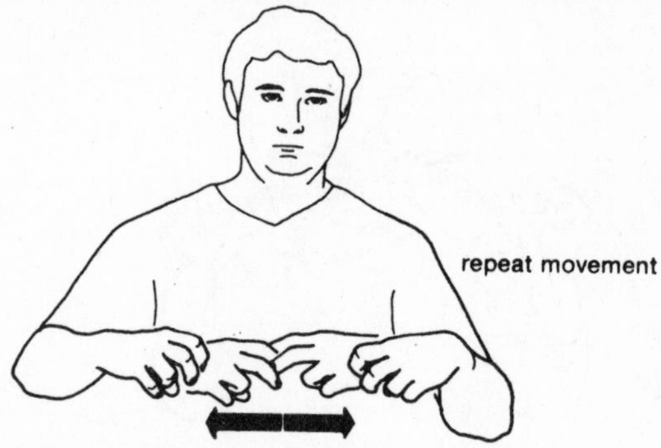

ANALYZE, ANALYSIS
Beginning with the knuckles of both bent "v" hands touching in front of the chest, palms facing down, pull the hands apart with a double movement.
Hint: Tearing something apart to inspect it.

SEEM, APPEAR
Twist the palm of the right curved hand back toward the face in front of the right shoulder.
Hint: Similar to the sign for "mirror."

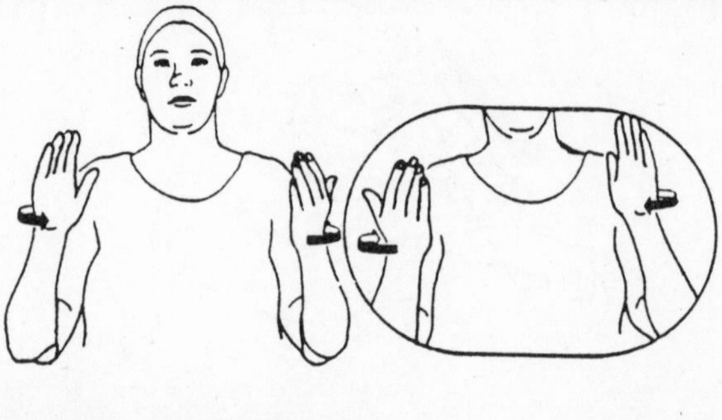

COMPARE, COMPARISON
Beginning with both curved hands in front of each shoulder, palms facing each other and fingers pointing up, twists the hands in opposite directions forward and back while keeping the palms facing each other.
Hint: Taking two things and looking first at one and then the other to compare them.

DUMB
Hit the palm side of the right "a" hand against the forehead.
Hint: Showing that something is thick-headed and dumb.

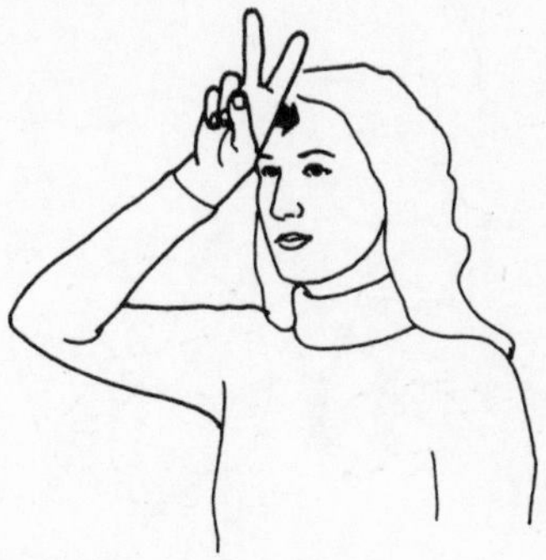

IGNORANT, STUPID
Hit the back of the right "v" hand against the forehead, palm facing forward.
Hint: Blocking the head from ideas.

CLEVER
Bring the bent middle finger of the right "5" hand from touching the forehead forward by twisting the wrist, ending with the palm facing forward.
Hint: Shows clever thoughts coming from the head.

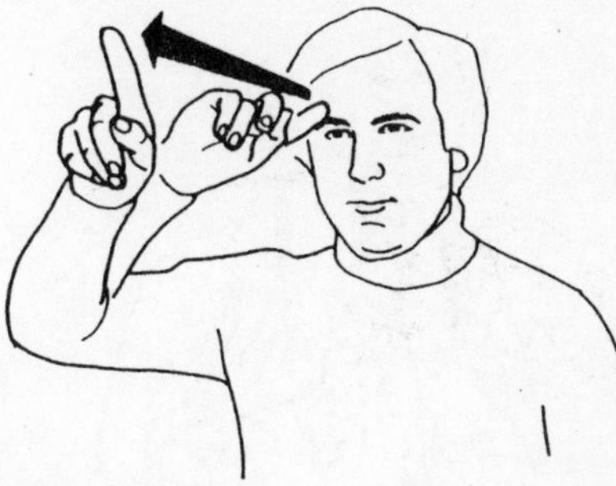

SMART, BRILLIANT
Beginning with the extended right index finger from touching the right side of the forehead, palm facing left, bring the hand forward by bending the wrist, ending with the index finger pointing forward.
Hint: Shows smart thoughts coming out of the brain.

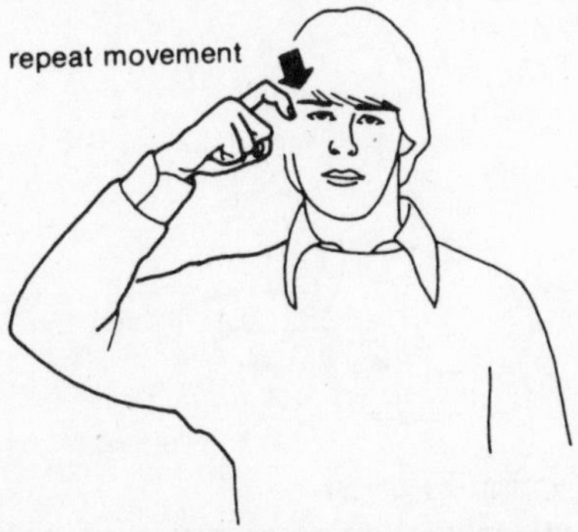

WISE
Bring the bent index finger of the right "x" hand downward with a double movement in front of the forehead, palm facing left.
Hint: Shows very deep thinking.

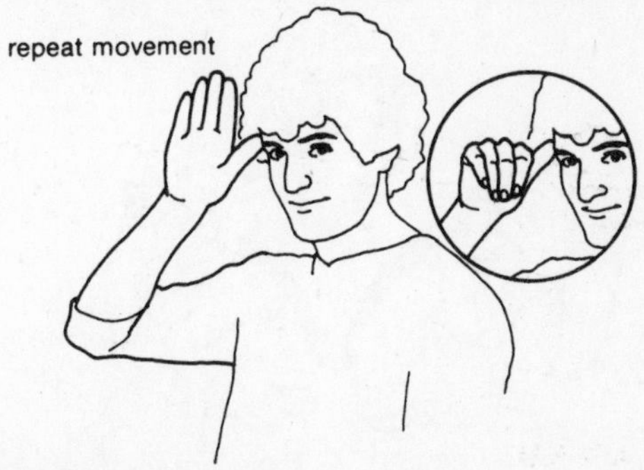

STUBBORN, OBSTINATE
With the thumb of the right "5" hand touching the right side of the forehead, palm facing forward, bend the fingers downward with a double movement.
Hint: This sign is formed similar to the sign for "donkey," indicating "stubborn like a mule."

Feelings

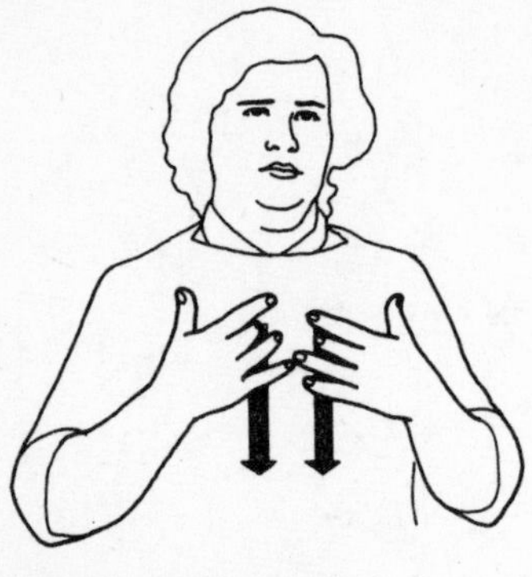

DISCOURAGED, DISAPPOINTED
Bring the bent middle fingers of both "5" hands downward from the upper chest to near the waist.
Hint: Feelings that are pulling the mood down.

DEPRESSED, DEPRESSION
Bring the thumbs of both "5" hands downward from the upper chest to near the waist.
Hint: Feelings that are suppressed and down.

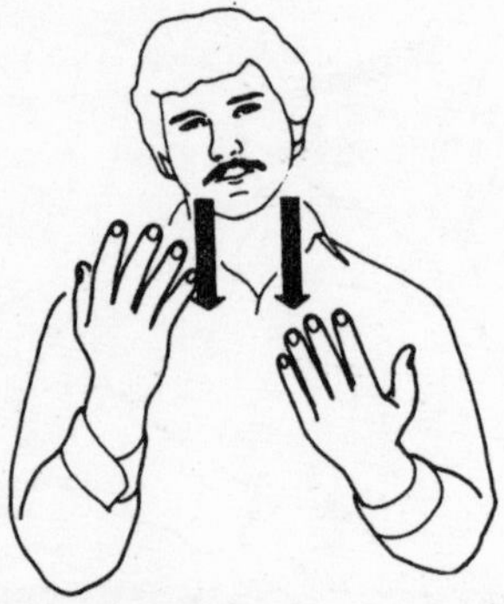

SAD, SORROWFUL, SORROW
Bring both loose "5" hands downward from the sides of the face, palms facing in and fingers pointing up.

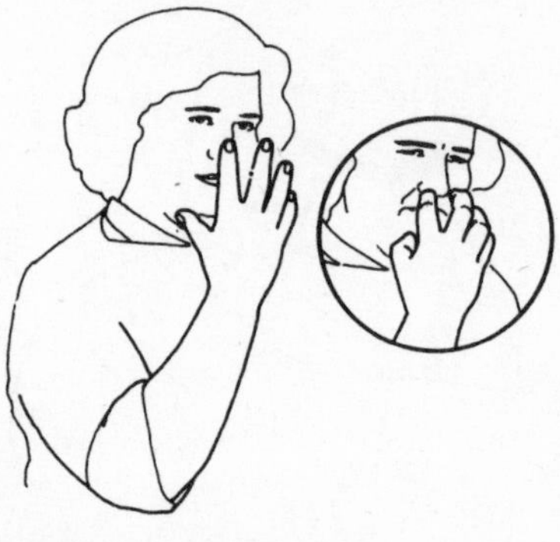

CROSS, GROUCHY, ANGRY, MAD
With the palm of the loose "5" hand in front of the face, bend the fingers down into a "claw" hand.
Hint: Shows bringing the facial features into an angry shape.

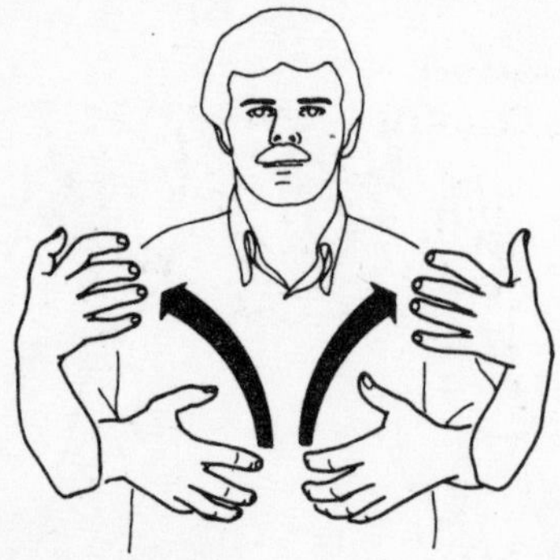

ANGER, ANGRY, MAD
Beginning with the fingers of both "claw" hands near each other on the lower chest, fingers pointing toward each other, bring the hands upward simultaneously, ending with hands in front of each shoulder.
Hint: Shows angry feelings rising up in the body.

BOILING MAD, BURNING MAD, FUME
Move the right "5" hand, palm facing up, in a circular movement while wiggling the fingers under the palm of open left hand held across the chest, palm facing down.
Hint: Deep penetrating feeling smoldering in the body.

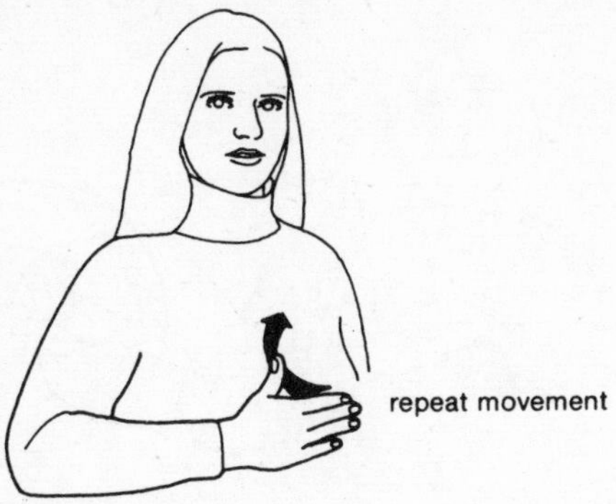

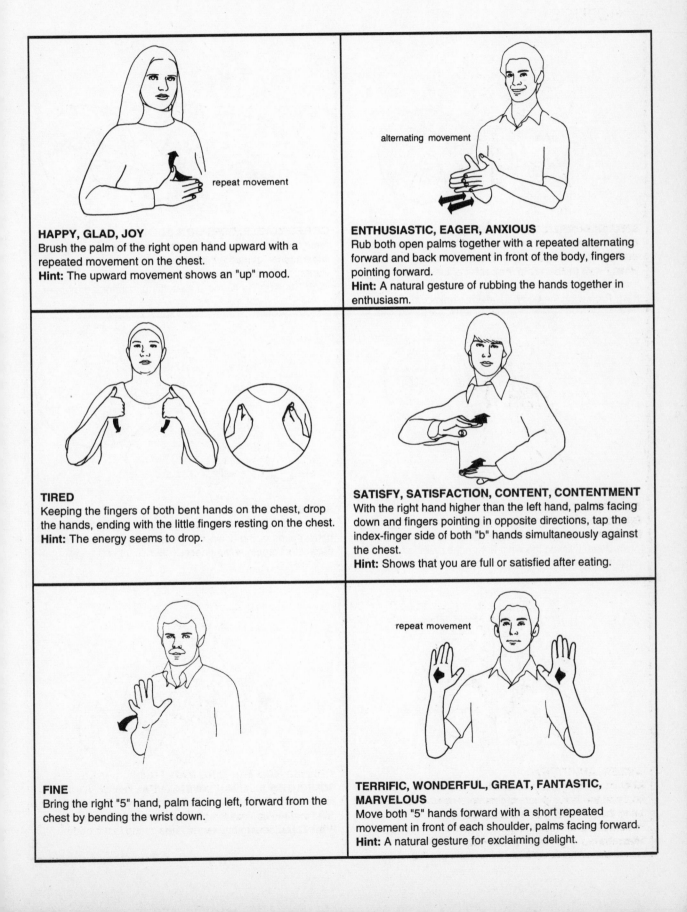

HAPPY, GLAD, JOY
Brush the palm of the right open hand upward with a repeated movement on the chest.
Hint: The upward movement shows an "up" mood.

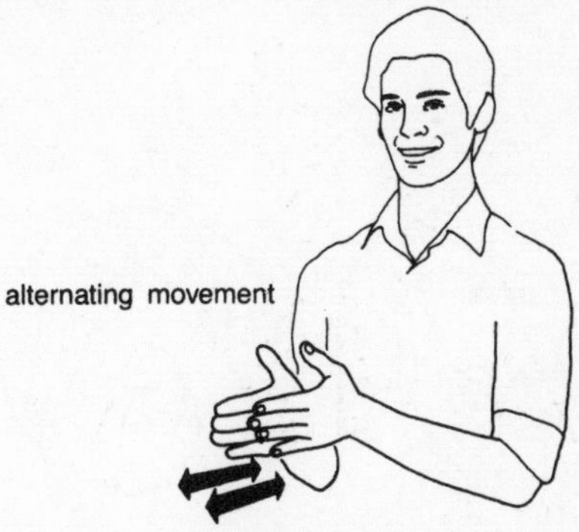

ENTHUSIASTIC, EAGER, ANXIOUS
Rub both open palms together with a repeated alternating forward and back movement in front of the body, fingers pointing forward.
Hint: A natural gesture of rubbing the hands together in enthusiasm.

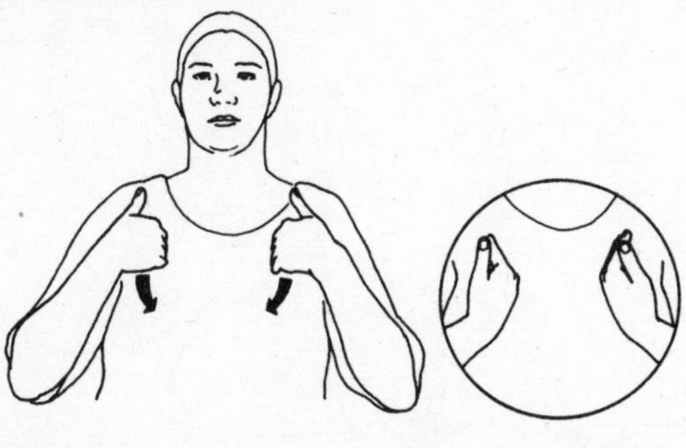

TIRED
Keeping the fingers of both bent hands on the chest, drop the hands, ending with the little fingers resting on the chest.
Hint: The energy seems to drop.

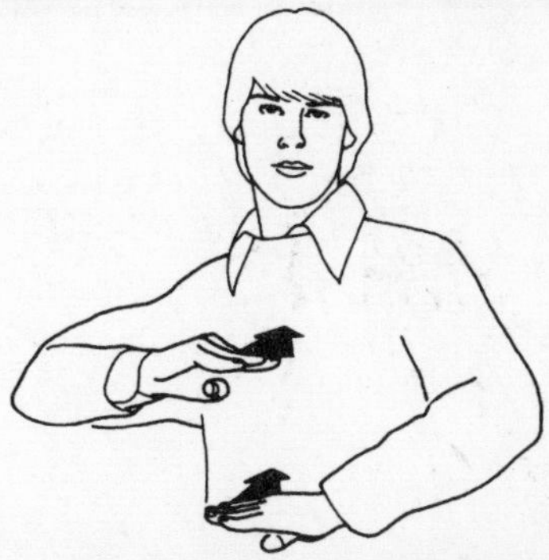

SATISFY, SATISFACTION, CONTENT, CONTENTMENT
With the right hand higher than the left hand, palms facing down and fingers pointing in opposite directions, tap the index-finger side of both "b" hands simultaneously against the chest.
Hint: Shows that you are full or satisfied after eating.

FINE
Bring the right "5" hand, palm facing left, forward from the chest by bending the wrist down.

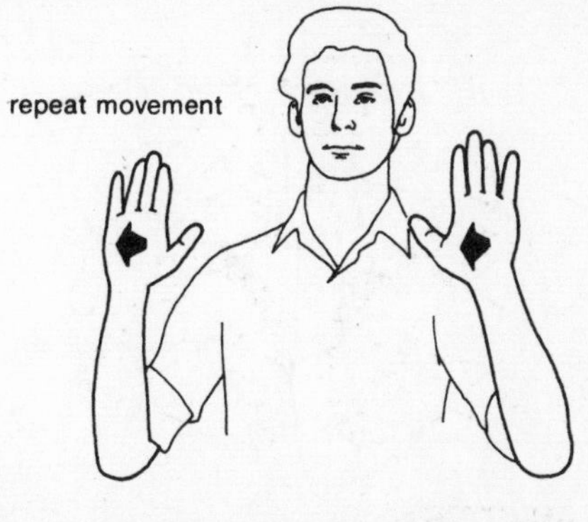

TERRIFIC, WONDERFUL, GREAT, FANTASTIC, MARVELOUS
Move both "5" hands forward with a short repeated movement in front of each shoulder, palms facing forward.
Hint: A natural gesture for exclaiming delight.

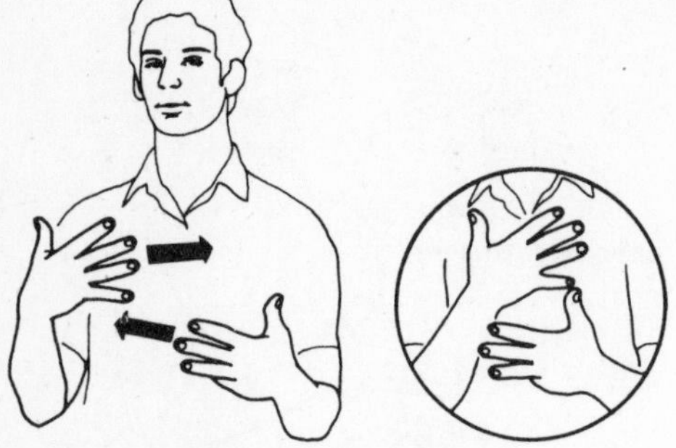

AFRAID, SCARED, FRIGHTENED
Beginning with both "5" hands in front of each side of the chest, palms facing in and fingers pointing toward each other, move the hands to the center of the chest with a deliberate movement.
Hint: Protecting the body against the unknown.

COMFORTABLE, COMFORT, SOOTHE
Wipe the palm of the curved right hand down over the fingers of the curved left hand, both palms facing down. Repeat with the left hand over the right.
Hint: Stroking the hands in a soothing, comforting manner.

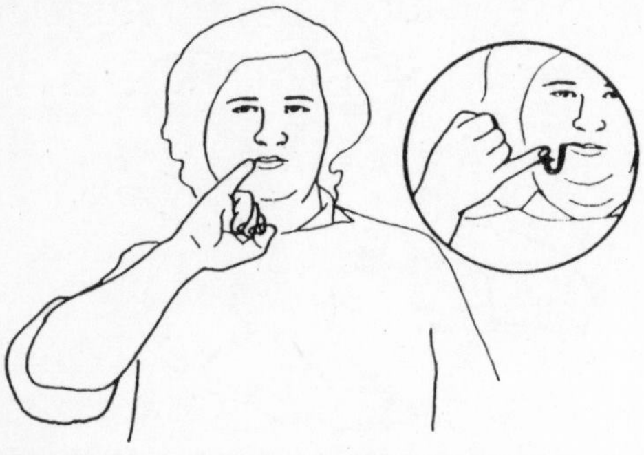

JEALOUS
With the extended right little finger, make a small "j" near the right side of the mouth, beginning with the palm facing forward and twisting the wrist to turn the palm in.
Hint: Initialized sign showing drooling when jealous.

SELFISH
Beginning with both '3" hands in front of each side of the body, palms facing down, bring the hands back toward the body while crooking the fingers.

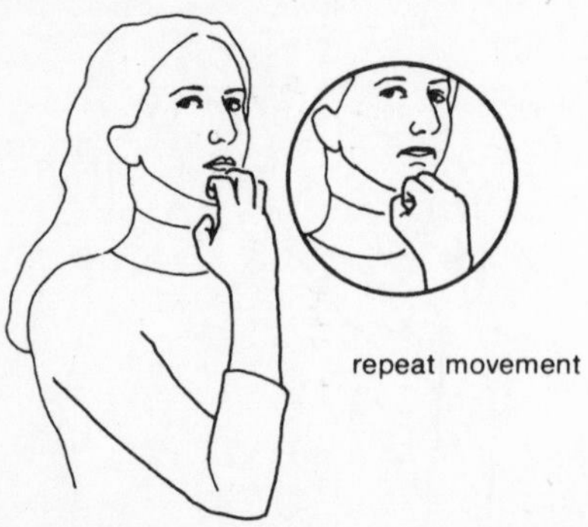

STINGY, MISERLY, PRECIOUS
Beginning with the fingers of the right "claw" hand in front of the chin, close the fingers into an "s" hand.
Hint: Holding something tight in one's hand so as to keep in for oneself.

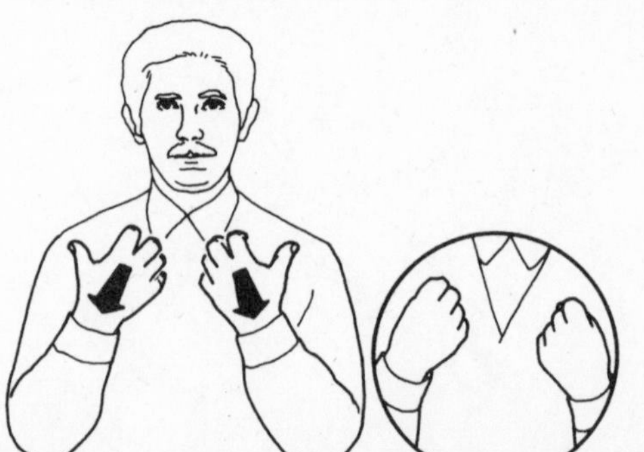

COURAGEOUS, BRAVE, WELL, HEALTHY
Beginning with the fingers of both "claw" hands on the chest, bring the hands forward while closing into "s" hands.
Hint: Taking strength from the body.

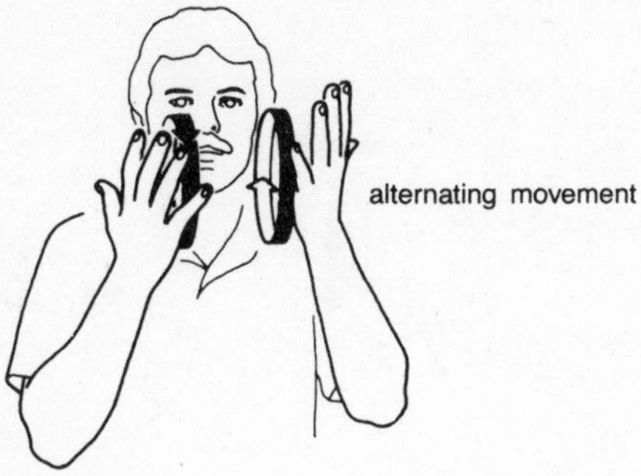

EMBARRASS
Bring the palms of both "5" hands upward in alternating circular movement in front of each side of the face, fingers pointing up.
Hint: Shows a blush from embarrassment rising in the face.

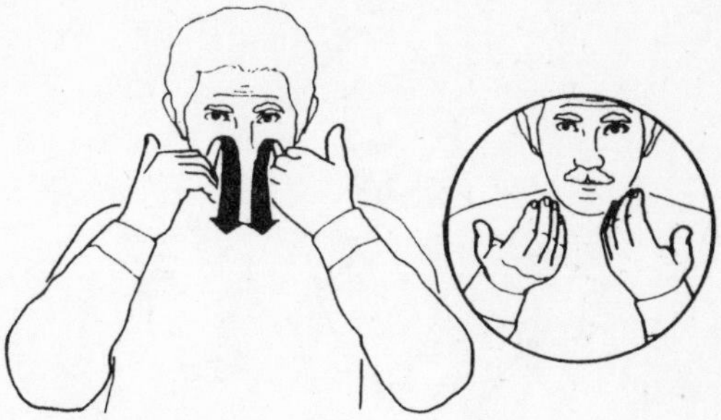

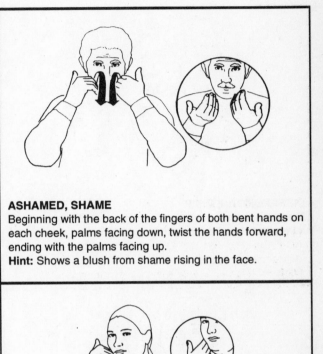

ASHAMED, SHAME
Beginning with the back of the fingers of both bent hands on each cheek, palms facing down, twist the hands forward, ending with the palms facing up.
Hint: Shows a blush from shame rising in the face.

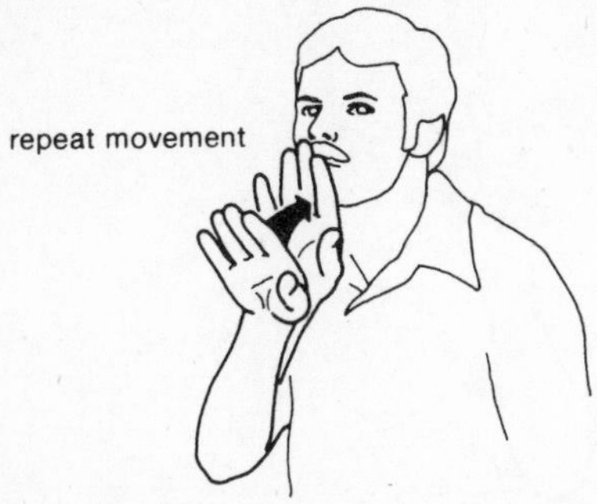

FRUSTRATED
Bring the back of the right open hand back to in front of the mouth, palm facing forward and fingers pointing up.
Hint: Coming up to an obstacle.

SHY
Beginning with the back of the bent right hand on the right cheek, palm facing down, twist the wrist to turn the wrist back while keeping the fingers in place.
Hint: A blush rising in the cheeks.

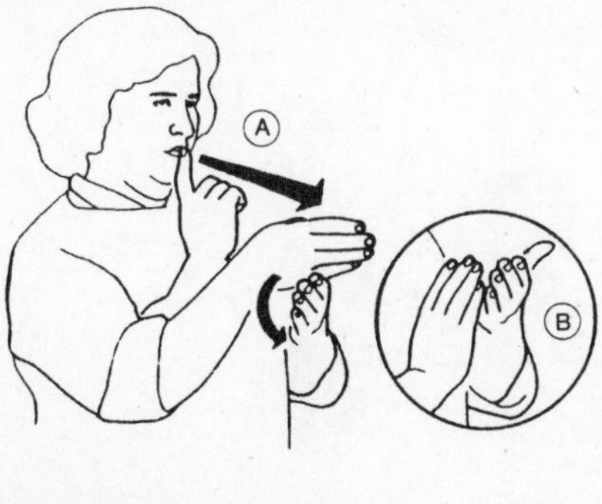

HUMBLE, MEEK
Move the extended right index finger from in front of the mouth forward while opening into a "b" hand, Then slide the little-finger side of the right "b" hand across the index-finger side of the open left hand downward across the left palm.
Hint: Placing yourself beneath others.

FEEL, FEELING, SENSATION
Bring the bent middle finger of the right "5" hand, palm facing in, upward on the chest.
Hint: Bringing feeling out from the heart.

DISAPPOINTED, MISS
Touch the extended right index finger to the chin with a deliberate movement, palm facing down.

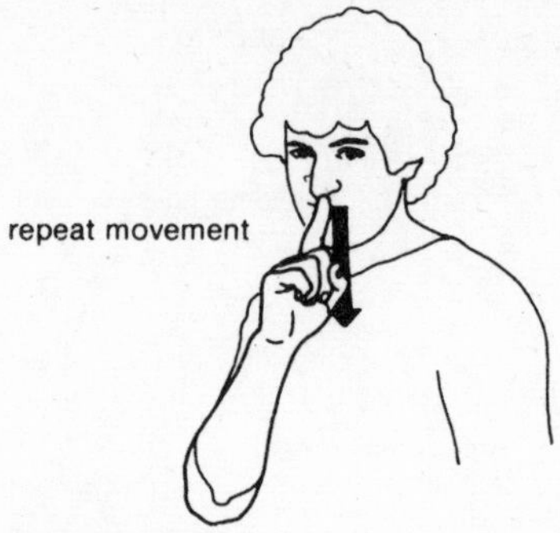

LONELY, LONESOME
Move the extended right index finger, palm facing left, from in front of the lips downward with a slow smooth movement.
Hint: A combination of using the handshape for the sign "alone" signed with a movement like "patience."

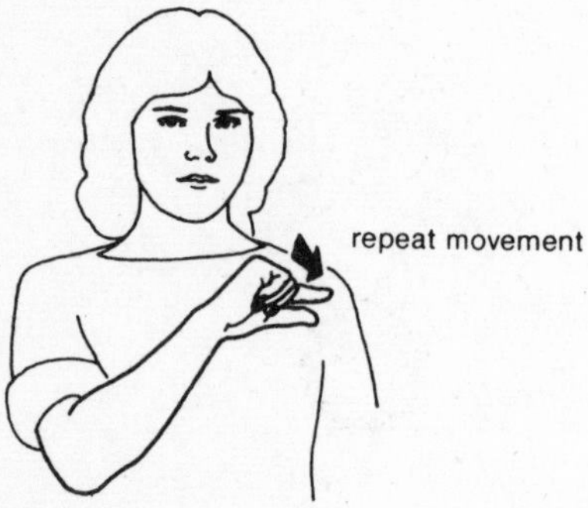

GUILT, GUILTY, CONSCIENCE
Tap the index-finger side of the right "g" hand, palm facing left, against the left side of the chest with a double movement.
Hint: Initialized sign made over the heart.

PATIENT, PATIENCE, ENDURE
Bring the thumbnail of the right "a" hand, palm facing left, from in front of the lips downward with a slow smooth movement.
Hint: Silently enduring a burden.

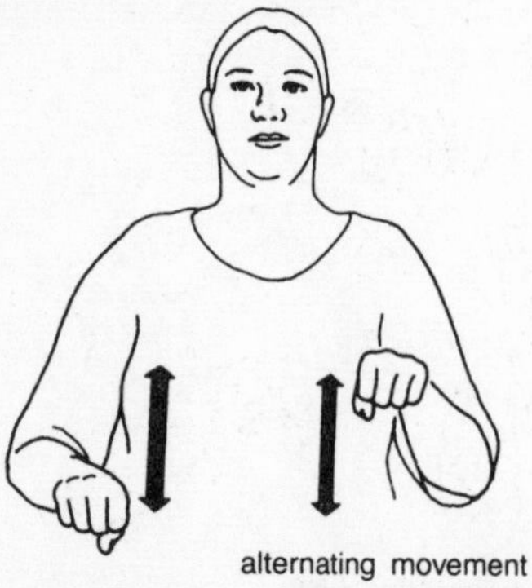

DOUBT, DOUBTFUL, DISBELIEF
Move both "s" hands, palms facing down, with an alternating up and down movement in front of each side of the body.
Hint: The alternating movement indicates indecision.

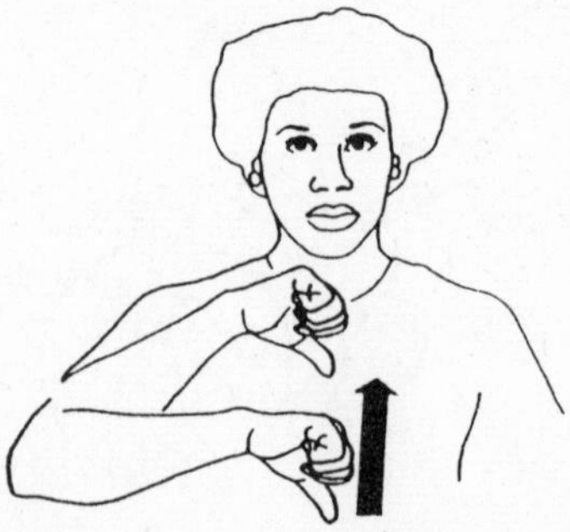

PROUD, PRIDE
Drag the thumb of the right "a" hand, thumb pointing down and palm facing right, upward in the center of the chest.
Hint: Feelings rising from within.

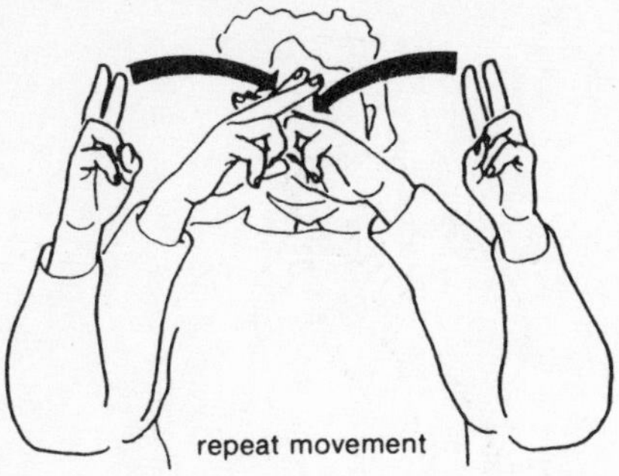

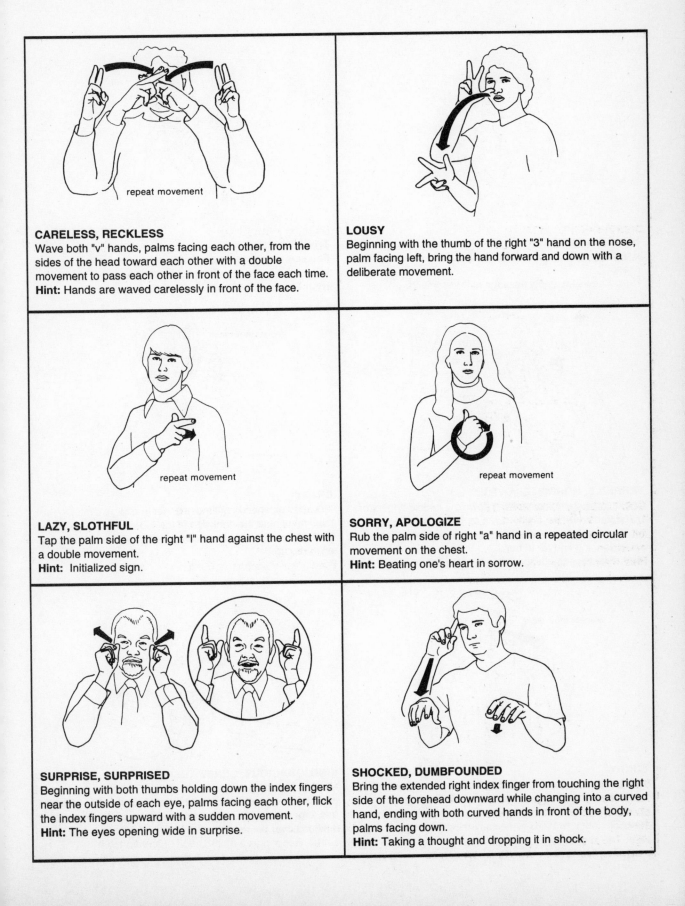

CARELESS, RECKLESS
Wave both "v" hands, palms facing each other, from the sides of the head toward each other with a double movement to pass each other in front of the face each time.
Hint: Hands are waved carelessly in front of the face.

LOUSY
Beginning with the thumb of the right "3" hand on the nose, palm facing left, bring the hand forward and down with a deliberate movement.

LAZY, SLOTHFUL
Tap the palm side of the right "l" hand against the chest with a double movement.
Hint: Initialized sign.

SORRY, APOLOGIZE
Rub the palm side of right "a" hand in a repeated circular movement on the chest.
Hint: Beating one's heart in sorrow.

SURPRISE, SURPRISED
Beginning with both thumbs holding down the index fingers near the outside of each eye, palms facing each other, flick the index fingers upward with a sudden movement.
Hint: The eyes opening wide in surprise.

SHOCKED, DUMBFOUNDED
Bring the extended right index finger from touching the right side of the forehead downward while changing into a curved hand, ending with both curved hands in front of the body, palms facing down.
Hint: Taking a thought and dropping it in shock.

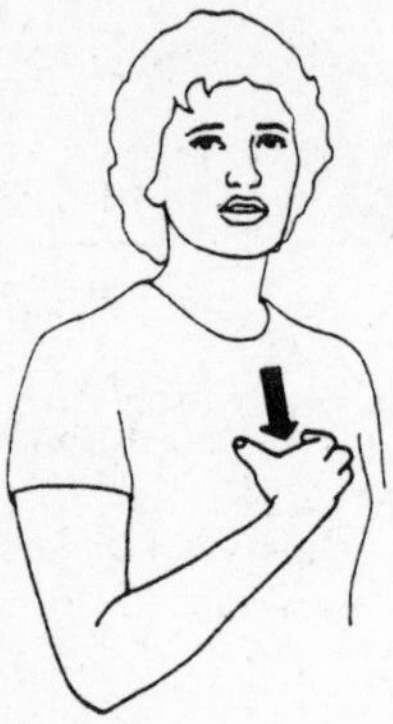

HUNGRY, STARVED
Bring the fingertips of the right "c" hand downward on the chest.
Hint: Shows an empty passage to the stomach.

THIRSTY
Bring the extended right index finger downward on the throat.
Hint: Shows a dry throat.

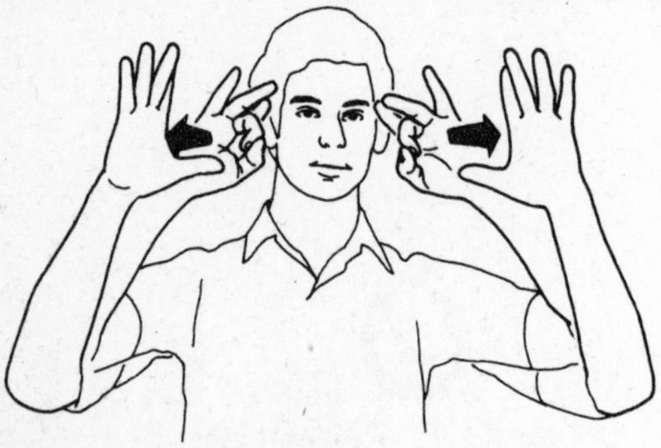

TERRIBLE, HORRIBLE, AWFUL
Beginning with thumbs holding down the middle fingers of both hands near each side of the face, palms facing forward, move the hands forward with a sudden movement while opening into "5" hands.
Hint: Flicking something terrible away from the mind.

CRAZY
Move the extended right index finger in a large circular movement near the right side of the face, palm facing down.
Hint: Natural gesture for showing that someone's brains are all mixed up.

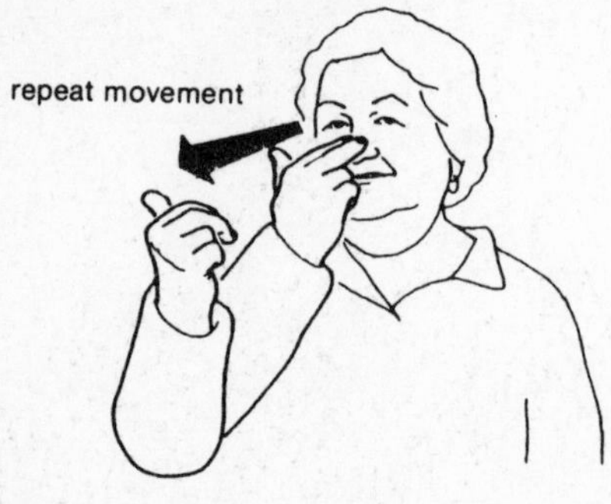

FUNNY
With a repeated movement bring the right extended index and middle fingers from the nose forward bending the fingers down each time.
Hint: The nose twitches when something is funny.

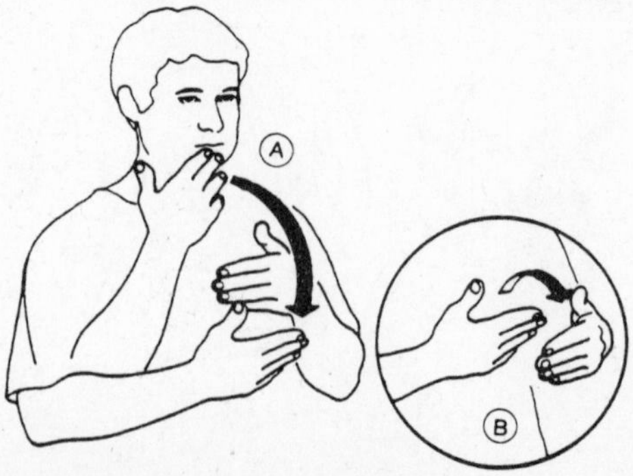

KIND, GRACIOUS, GENEROUS
Move the open right hand from the lips downward over the open left hand held in front of the chest, both palms facing in and fingers pointing in opposite directions, while moving the left hand over the right hand to exchange places.
Hint: "Good" plus a modification of "comfortable."

thirteen

RELIGION AND COMMUNICATION

Religion
Abstract Concepts
Communication

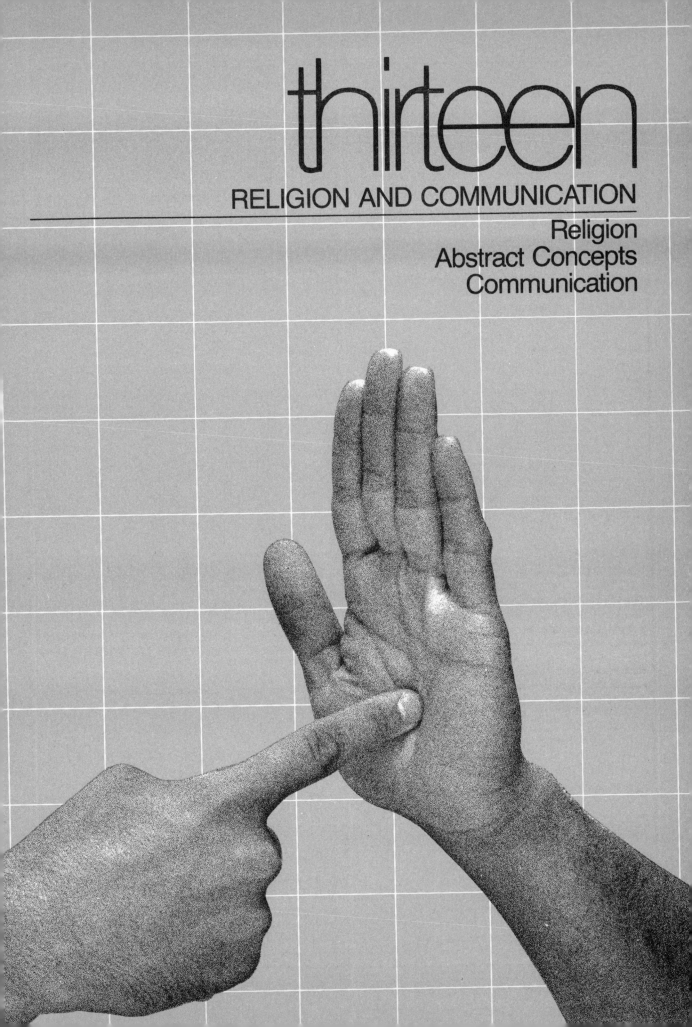

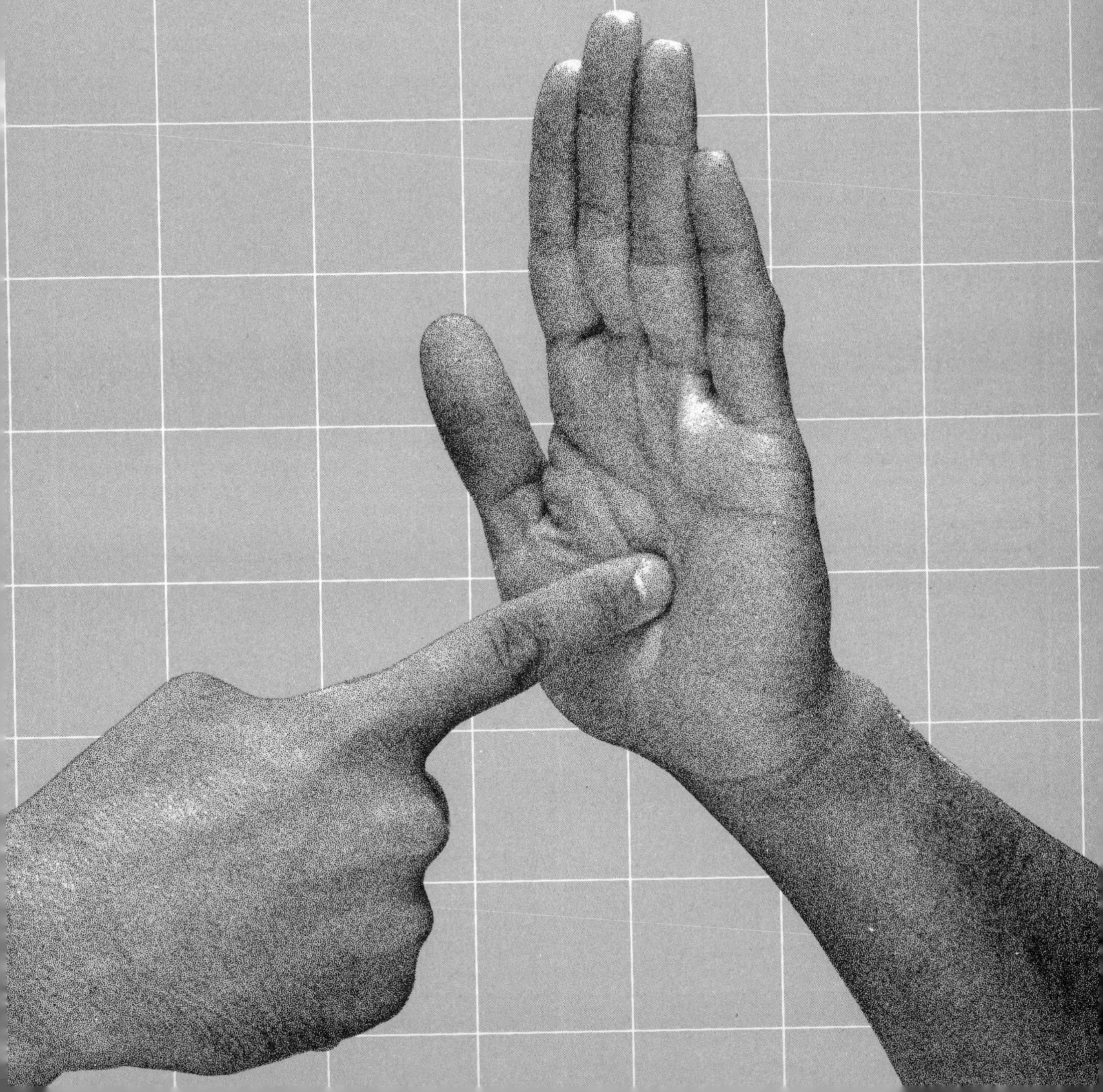

EMPHASIS

Emphasis can be added to any word in a signed sentence in one of four ways. One way is to add the sign for "true" or "really" before the sign. A second way is to added the sign for "whew" or "wow" after the sign that is to be emphasized. A third way is to execute the sign itself in an emphatic way. Or, fourth, you can fingerspell the word to add emphasis.

heroic + whew = very heroic

SIGNS SHOWING JUDGMENT

There is group of signs that are formed with two hands moving in an alternating movement to indicate indecisiveness. Some of the signs in this group are "maybe," "judge," "which," and "doubt."

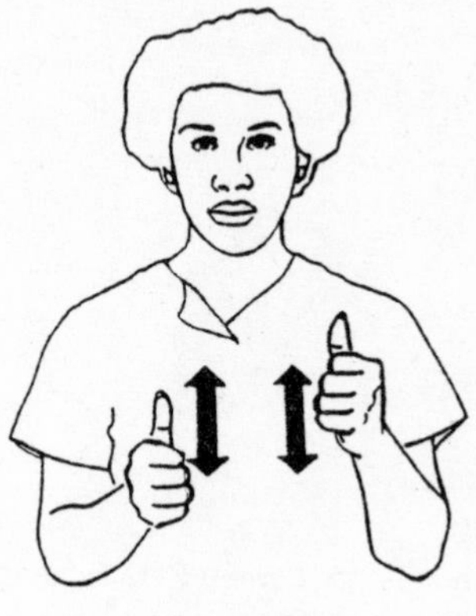

which

RELIGIOUS SIGNS

Many religious signs are governed by the specific beliefs of the religion for which they are used. In other words, the same English word may be signed in different ways depending on which religion is being discussed. A Protestant "Bible" is a compound of "Jesus" plus "book," whereas, a Jewish "Bible" is signed as the compound "God" plus "book." The sign for "baptism" depends on whether the religion requires immersion or not.

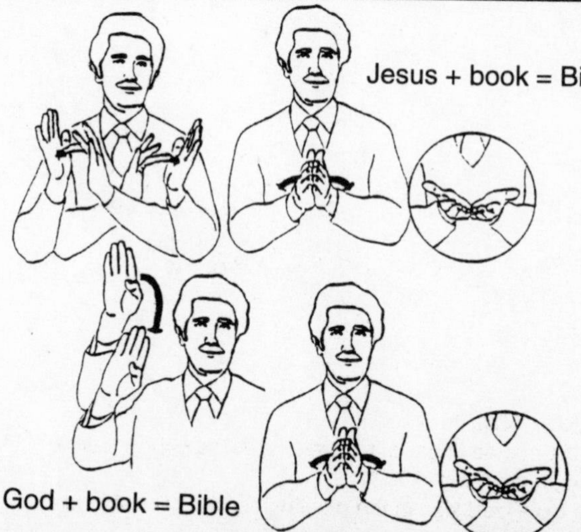

Jesus + book = Bible

God + book = Bible

Religion

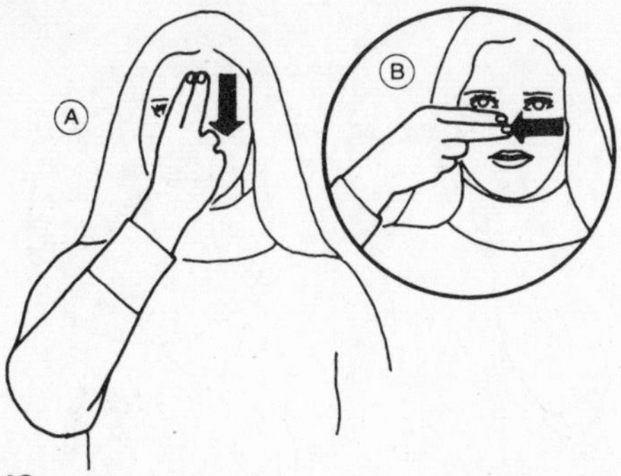

CATHOLIC
Move the fingers of the right "u"hand, palm facing in, first downward and then from left to right across the forehead.
Hint: Crossing oneself.

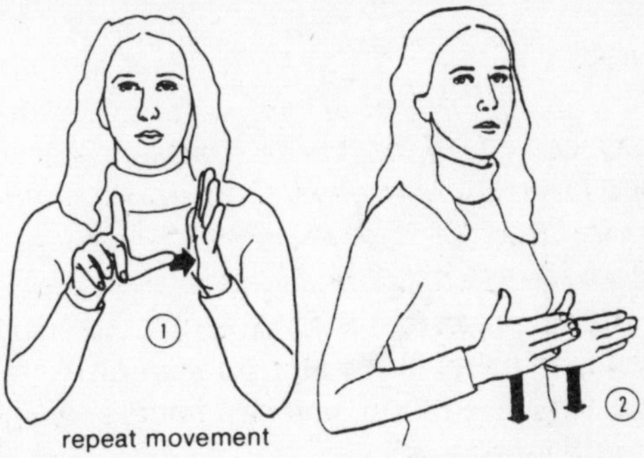

LUTHERAN
Tap the thumb of the right "l" hand, palm facing forward, with a double movement against the open left palm. Then move both open hands downward along the sides of the body, palms facing each other.
Hint: Initialized sign in the position used for the sign for "Jesus" plus "person marker."

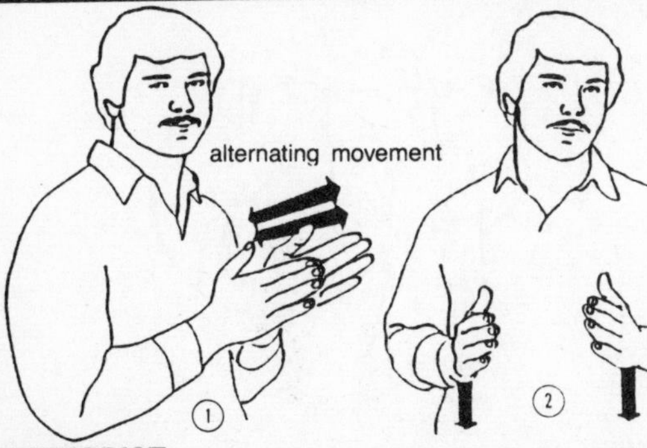

METHODIST
Rub the palms of both open hands together with an alternating forward and back movement, fingers pointing forward. Then move both open hands downward along the sides of the body, palms facing each other.

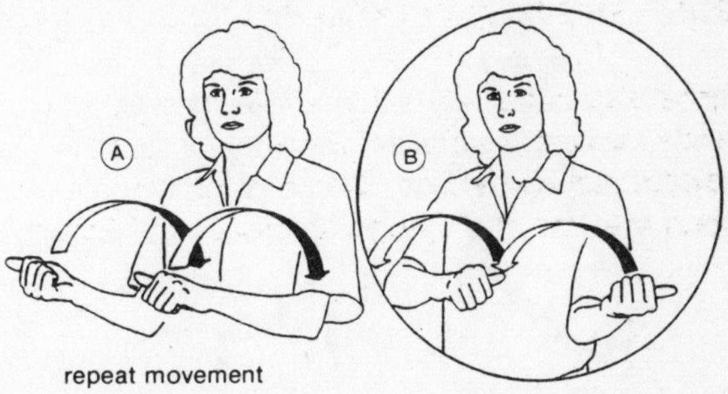

BAPTIST, BAPTIZE
Beginning with both "10" hands in front of each side of the chest, palms facing each other, dip the hands to the left with a double movement turning the right palm down and the left palm up each time.
Hint: Dipping the head under water for baptism.

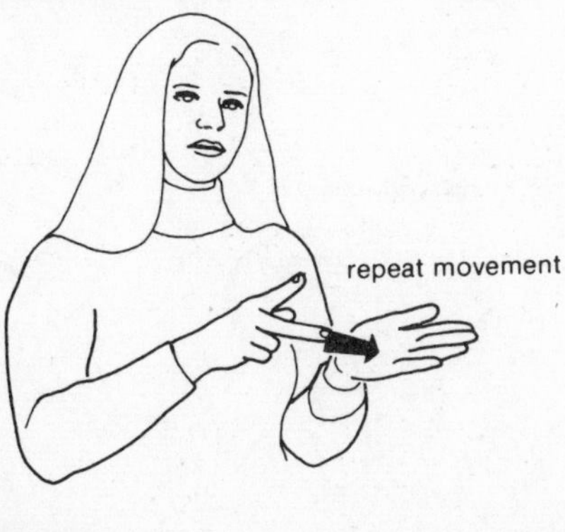

PRESBYTERIAN
Tap the middle finger of the right "p" hand on the palm of the open left hand.
Hint: Initialized sign in the position used for the sign for "Jesus."

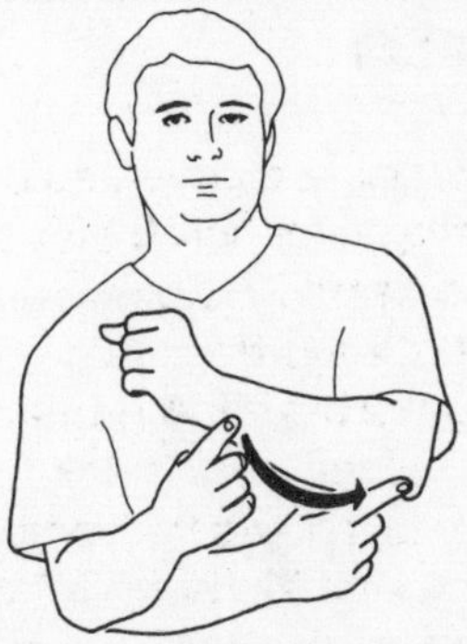

EPISCOPAL
Touch the extended right index finger, palm facing in, first to the wrist and then near the elbow of the bent left arm held across the body.
Hint: Follows the shape of the sleeve of a minister's robe.

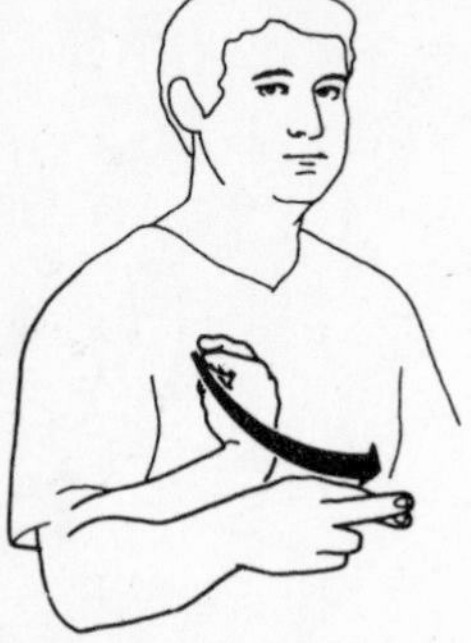

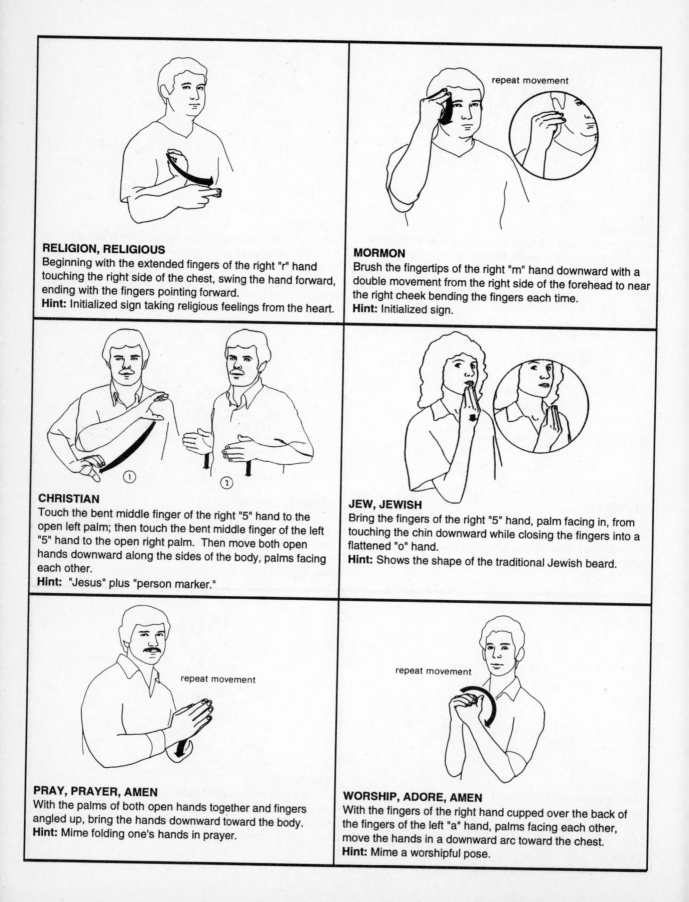

RELIGION, RELIGIOUS
Beginning with the extended fingers of the right "r" hand touching the right side of the chest, swing the hand forward, ending with the fingers pointing forward.
Hint: Initialized sign taking religious feelings from the heart.

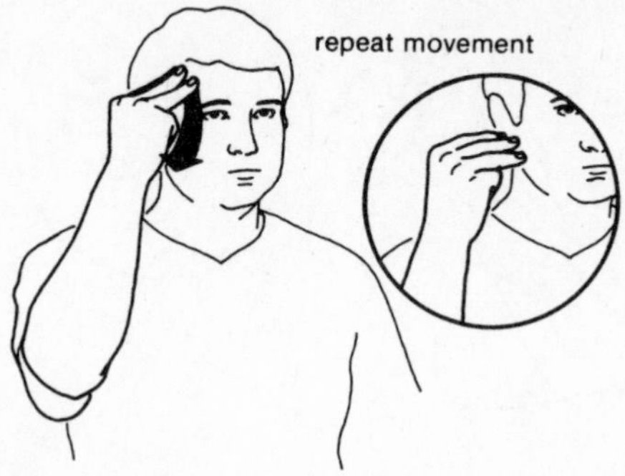

MORMON
Brush the fingertips of the right "m" hand downward with a double movement from the right side of the forehead to near the right cheek bending the fingers each time.
Hint: Initialized sign.

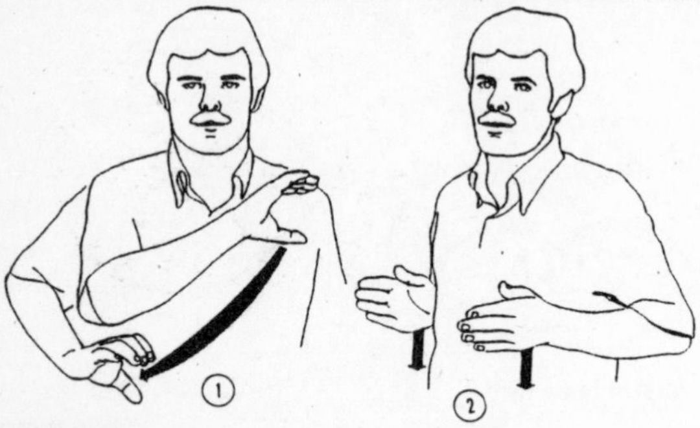

CHRISTIAN
Touch the bent middle finger of the right "5" hand to the open left palm; then touch the bent middle finger of the left "5" hand to the open right palm. Then move both open hands downward along the sides of the body, palms facing each other.
Hint: "Jesus" plus "person marker."

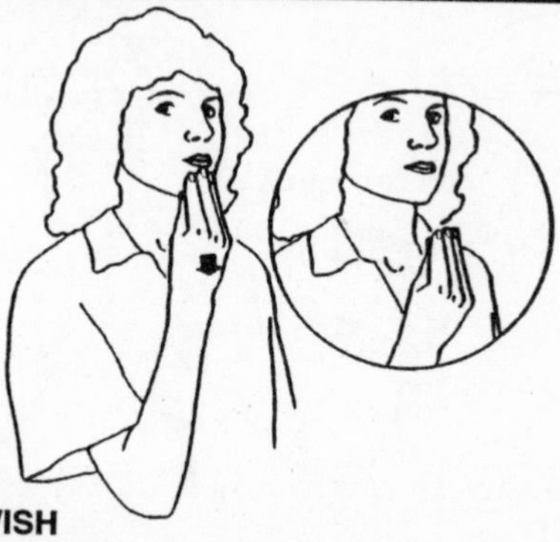

JEW, JEWISH
Bring the fingers of the right "5" hand, palm facing in, from touching the chin downward while closing the fingers into a flattened "o" hand.
Hint: Shows the shape of the traditional Jewish beard.

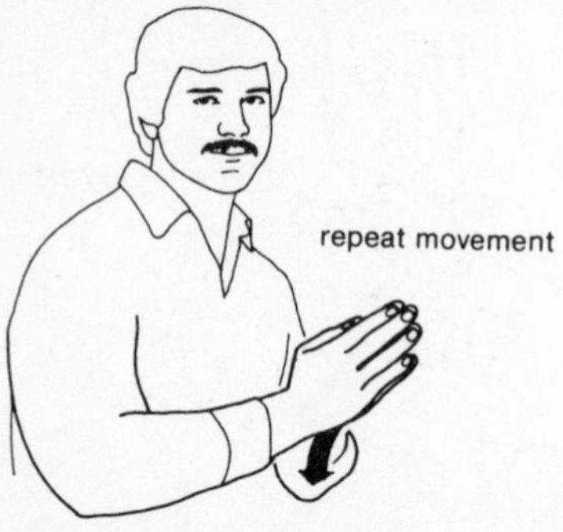

PRAY, PRAYER, AMEN
With the palms of both open hands together and fingers angled up, bring the hands downward toward the body.
Hint: Mime folding one's hands in prayer.

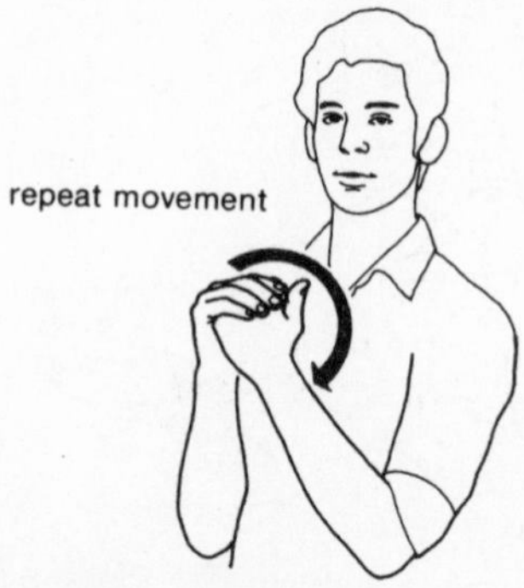

WORSHIP, ADORE, AMEN
With the fingers of the right hand cupped over the back of the fingers of the left "a" hand, palms facing each other, move the hands in a downward arc toward the chest.
Hint: Mime a worshipful pose.

GOD
Move the right open hand, palm facing left, from above the head downward in an arc toward the face.
Hint: The hand comes down from heaven.

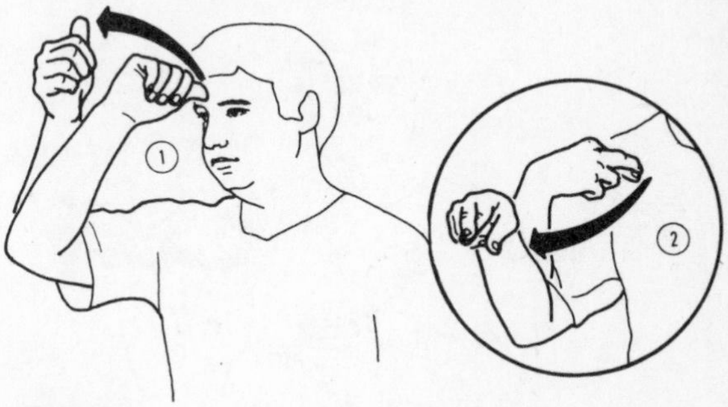

BUDDHA
Flick the thumb of the right "10" hand, palm facing left, forward from the center of the forward by twisting the wrist down. Then move the fingers of the right "r" hand forward from touching the right side of the chest, palm facing in, by twisting the wrist, ending with the fingers pointing forward.
Hint: An alternate form of "India" plus "religion."

CHRIST
Beginning with the index-finger side of the right "c" hand touching the left side of the chest, palm facing left, move the hand down to touch again near the right hip.
Hint: Initialized sign following the sash worn by royalty.

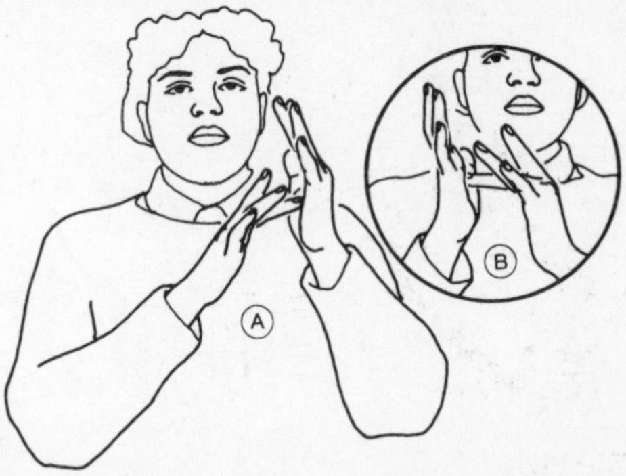

JESUS
Touch the bent middle finger of the right "5" hand to the open left palm; then touch the bent middle finger of the left "5" hand to the open right palm.
Hint: The fingers touch the location of the nail holes in Jesus' hands.

CHURCH
Tap the thumb side of the right "c" hand, palm facing forward, with a repeated movement on the back of the left "s" hand held across the body, palm facing down.
Hint: Initialized sign symbolizing that the church is build on a rock.

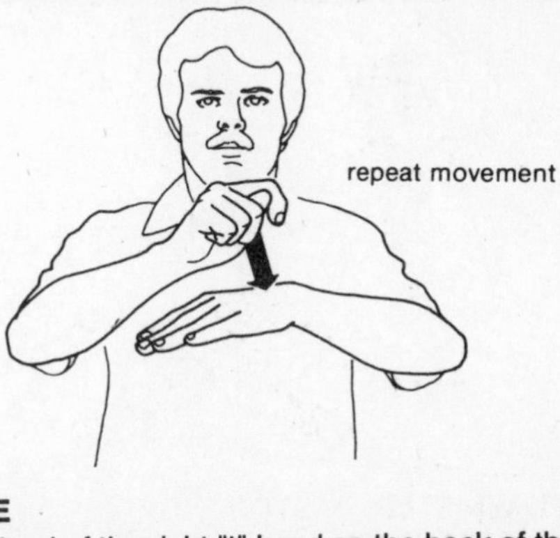

TEMPLE
Tap the heel of the right "t" hand on the back of the open left hand with a double movement, both palms facing down.
Hint: Initialized sign formed similar to the sign for "church."

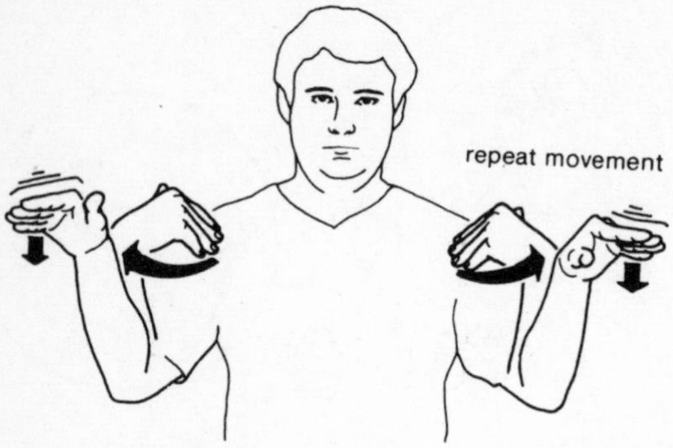

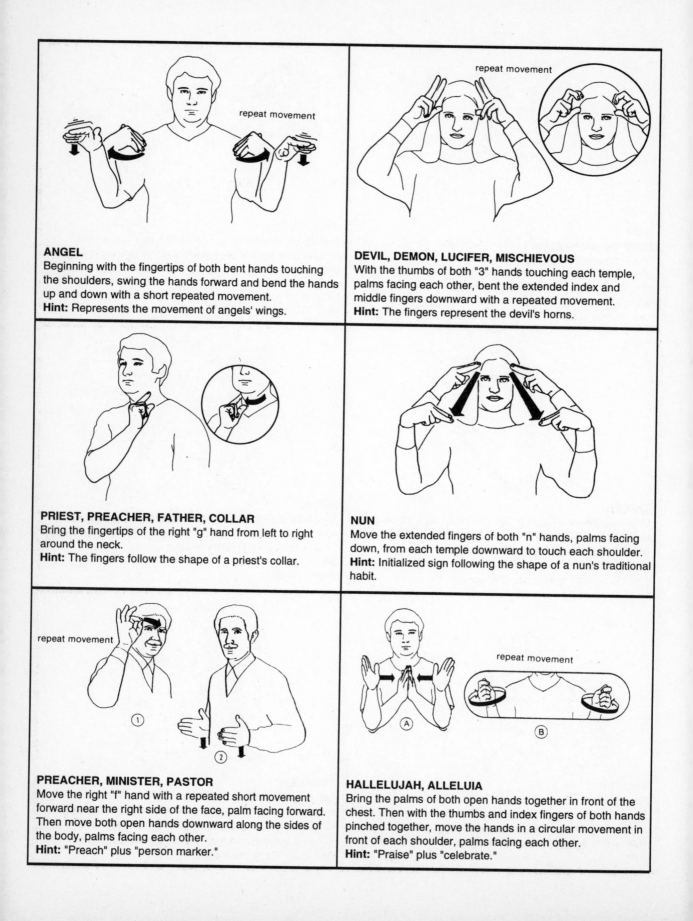

ANGEL
Beginning with the fingertips of both bent hands touching the shoulders, swing the hands forward and bend the hands up and down with a short repeated movement.
Hint: Represents the movement of angels' wings.

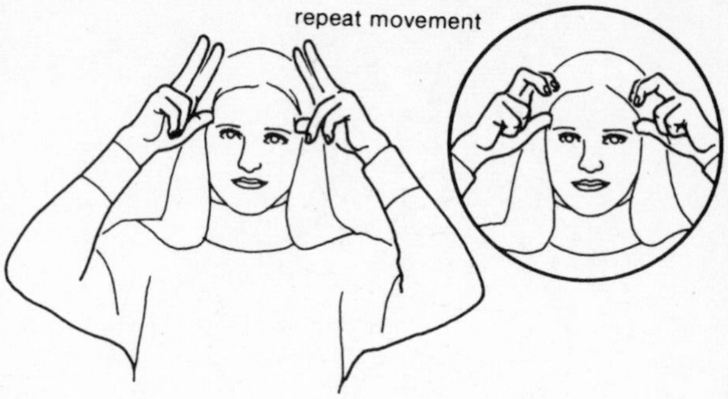

DEVIL, DEMON, LUCIFER, MISCHIEVOUS
With the thumbs of both "3" hands touching each temple, palms facing each other, bent the extended index and middle fingers downward with a repeated movement.
Hint: The fingers represent the devil's horns.

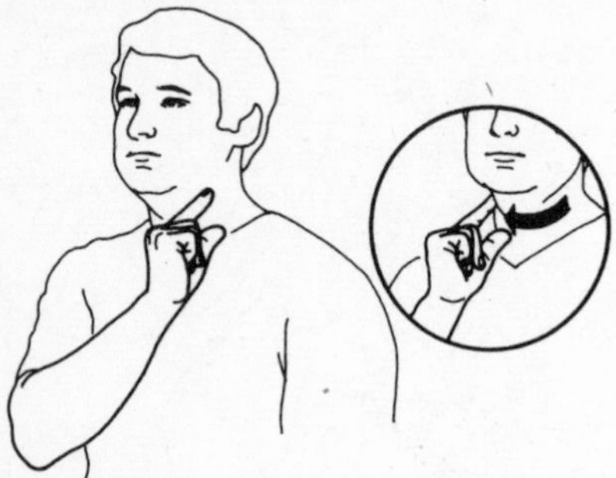

PRIEST, PREACHER, FATHER, COLLAR
Bring the fingertips of the right "g" hand from left to right around the neck.
Hint: The fingers follow the shape of a priest's collar.

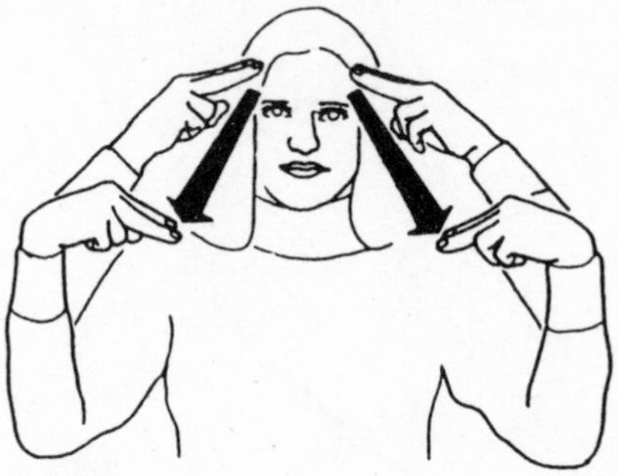

NUN
Move the extended fingers of both "n" hands, palms facing down, from each temple downward to touch each shoulder.
Hint: Initialized sign following the shape of a nun's traditional habit.

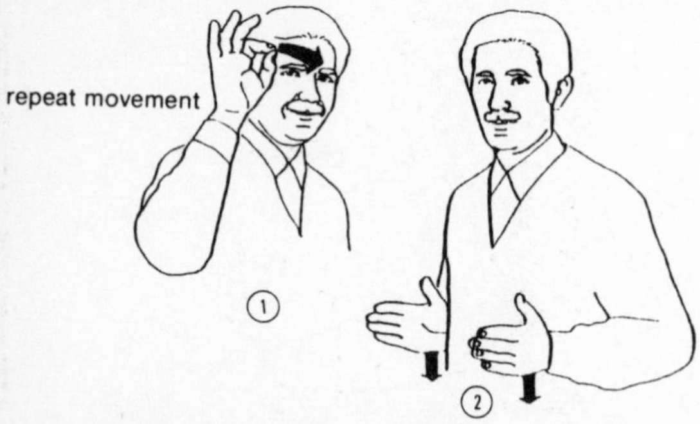

PREACHER, MINISTER, PASTOR
Move the right "f" hand with a repeated short movement forward near the right side of the face, palm facing forward. Then move both open hands downward along the sides of the body, palms facing each other.
Hint: "Preach" plus "person marker."

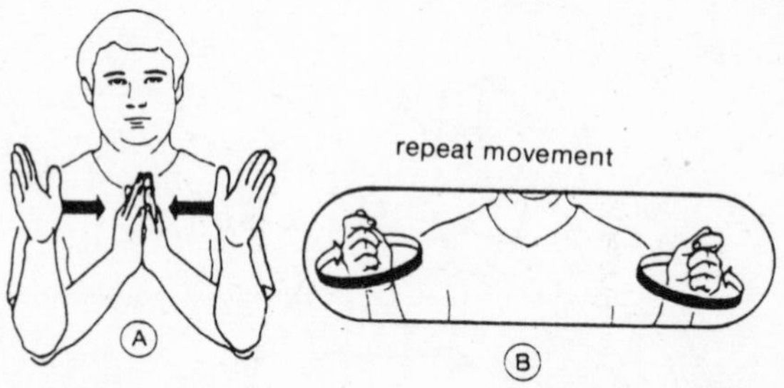

HALLELUJAH, ALLELUIA
Bring the palms of both open hands together in front of the chest. Then with the thumbs and index fingers of both hands pinched together, move the hands in a circular movement in front of each shoulder, palms facing each other.
Hint: "Praise" plus "celebrate."

COMMANDMENTS
Touch the index-finger side of the right "c" hand, palm facing forward, first to the fingers and then to the heel of the palm of the open left hand held in front of the chest, palm facing right.
Hint: Initialized sign formed similar to the sign for "law."

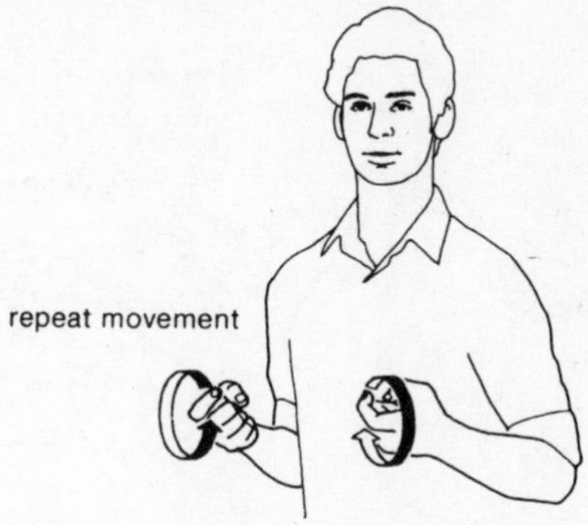

SIN, EVIL
Move both "x" hands, palms facing up, in repeated circular movements toward each other in front of each side of the body.

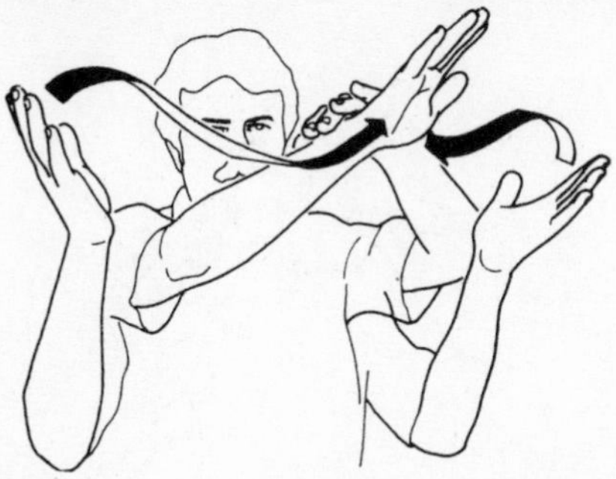

HEAVEN
Beginning with both open hands in front of each shoulder, palms angled up, turn the hands over and move them toward each other and upward, passing the right hand under the left.
Hint: Shows the spaciousness of the sky.

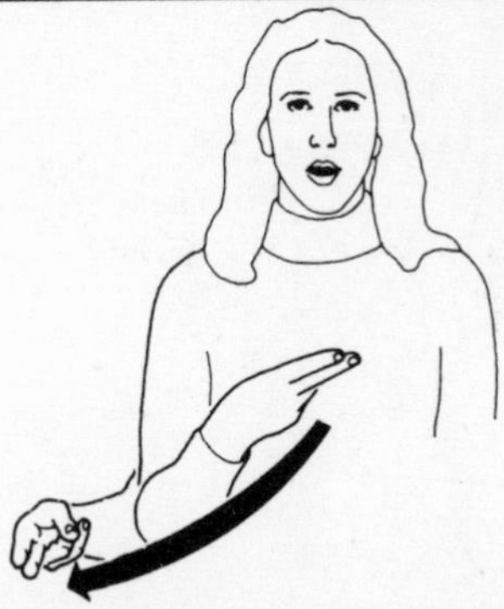

HELL
Thrust the right "h" hand from in front of the chest, palm facing in, downward to the right, ending with the palm facing left and the fingers pointing forward.
Hint: Initialized sign.

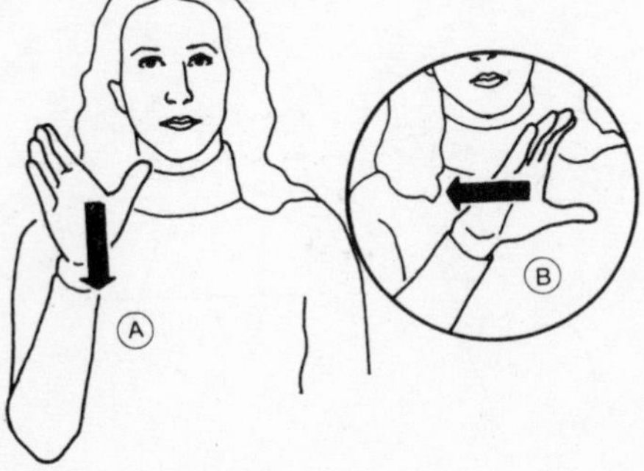

CROSS
Bring the right "c" hand, palm angled left, first downward and then from left to right in front of the chest.
Hint: Initialized sign showing the shape of a cross.

SPIRIT, HOLY GHOST
Beginning with the fingertips of both "9" hands touching, palms facing each other, bring the right hand up in front of the chest while the left hand moves slightly downward.
Hint: A thin thing, like a spirit.

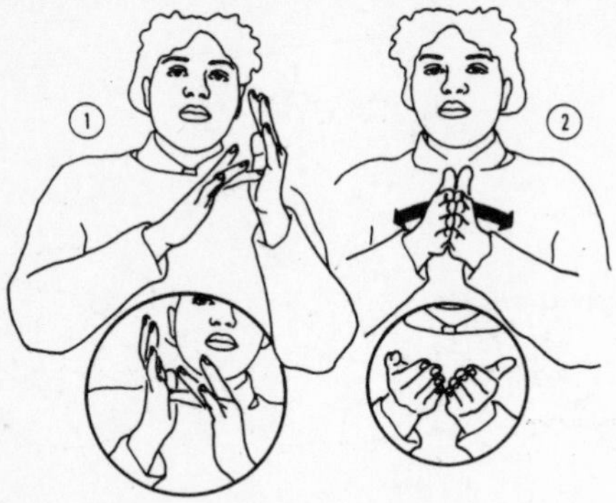

BIBLE
Touch the bent middle finger of the right "5" hand to the open left palm; then touch the bent middle finger of the left "5"hand to the open right palm. Then beginning with both open palms together, move the hands apart while keeping the little finger sides together.
Hint: "Jesus" plus "book."

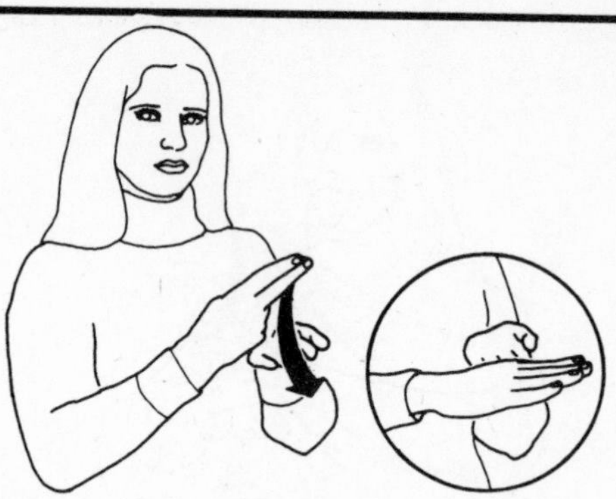

HOLY
Beginning with the right "h" hand, palm facing in, over the left open palm, move the right hand down while changing to an open hand, wiping the open right hand from the heel to the fingers of the open left hand.
Hint: Initialized sign formed similar to the sign for "clean."

PREACH
Move the right "f" hand forward with a short double movement near the right side of the head, palm facing forward.
Hint: Giving out information.

BLESS, BLESSING
Beginning with the thumbnails of both "a" hands from touching the lips, move the hands forward and downward while opening into "5" hands in front of each side of the chest, palms facing down.
Hint: Taking a blessing from the mouth and spreading it.

ALTAR
Beginning with both "a" hands in front of the chest, palms facing down, move the hands apart to the sides of the chest and then downward.
Hint: Initialized sign showing the shape of an altar.

FAST
Move the fingertips of the right "f" hand from left to right across the lips.
Hint: Initialized sign pointing to the closed lips that prevent eating.

Abstract Concepts

HABIT, CUSTOM
With the right "a" hand on the back of the left "a" hand, both palms facing down, move the hands downward in front of the chest.
Hint: The downward movement indicates a continued action.

INFLUENCE, COUNSEL, ADVISE, ADVICE
Beginning with the fingers of the right flattened "o" hand on the back of the open left hand, both palms facing down, move the right hand forward while opening into a "5" hand.
Hint: The distribution of advice.

HONOR
Move the right "h" hand, palm facing left and fingers pointing up, in a slight arc toward the face and then downward to in front of the chest.
Hint: Initialized sign.

RESPECT
Move the right "r" hand, palm facing left and fingers pointing up, in a slight arc toward the face and then downward to in front of the chest.
Hint: Initialized sign.

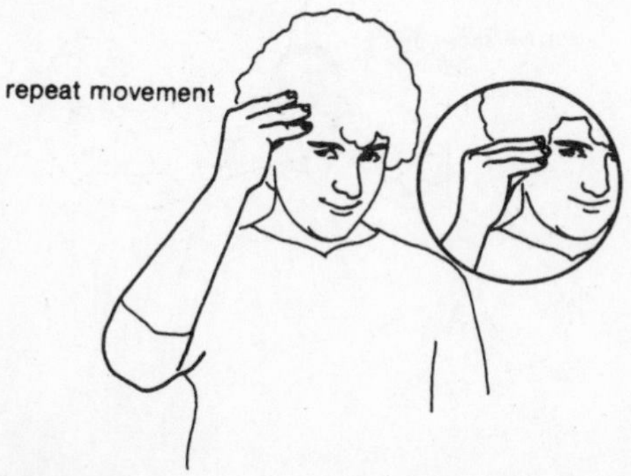

EXPERIENCE
Beginning with the fingertips of the right "c" hand on the right temple, close the fingers to the thumb with a double movement.
hint: Feeling the greying at the temples from experience.

RESPONSIBILITY, RESPONSIBLE, BURDEN
With the fingers of both bent hands on the right shoulder, palms facing down, roll the hands slightly forward on the fingertips.
Hint: Having a heavy burden on your shoulders.

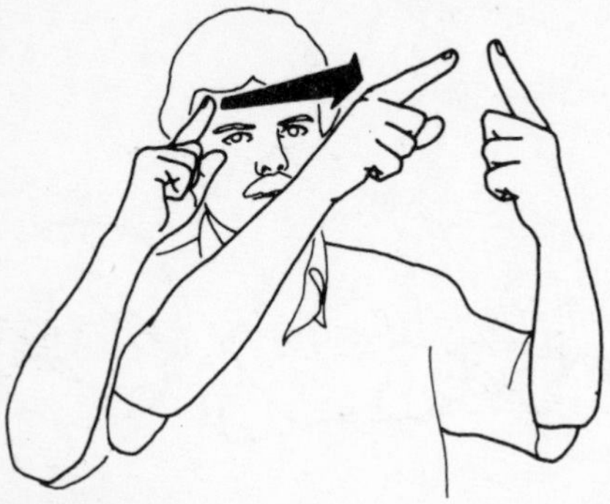

GOAL, OBJECTIVE
Bring the extended right index finger from near the right temple, palm angled down, forward to near the extended left index finger held in front of the head, palm facing in and finger pointing up.
Hint: Directing your mind to a specific point or goal.

CONCEPT
Move the right "c" hand, palm facing left, from near the right temple forward in a series of small arcs.
Hint: Initialized sign showing concepts coming out of the head.

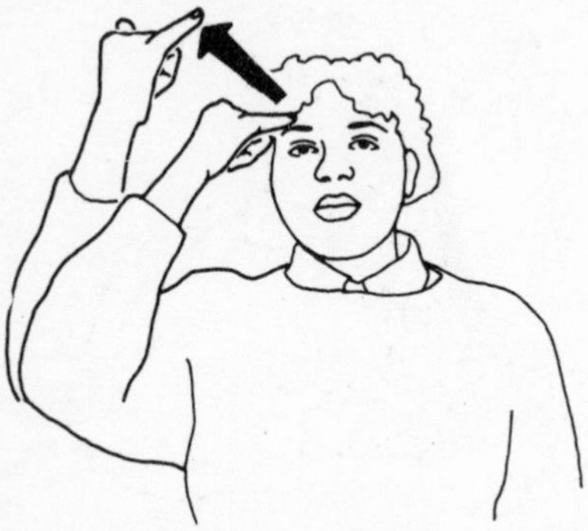

IDEA
Move the extended little finger of the right "i" hand from touching the right temple, palm facing down, upward and forward with a deliberate movement.
Hint: Initialized sign showing an idea coming from head.

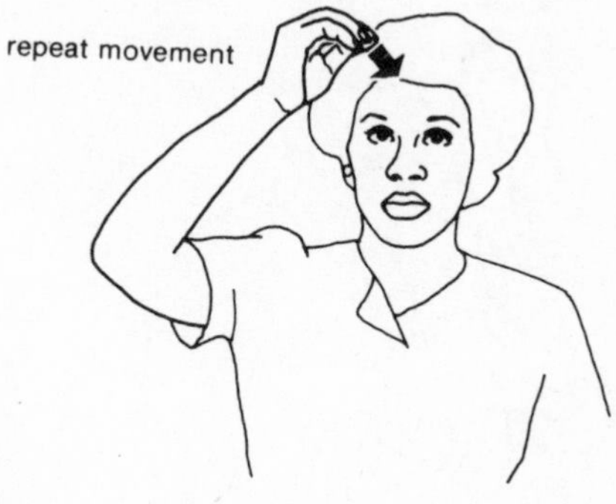

OPINION
Move the right "o" hand, palm facing down, up and down in front of the forehead with a small repeated movement.
Hint: Initialized sign near the head where opinions are formed.

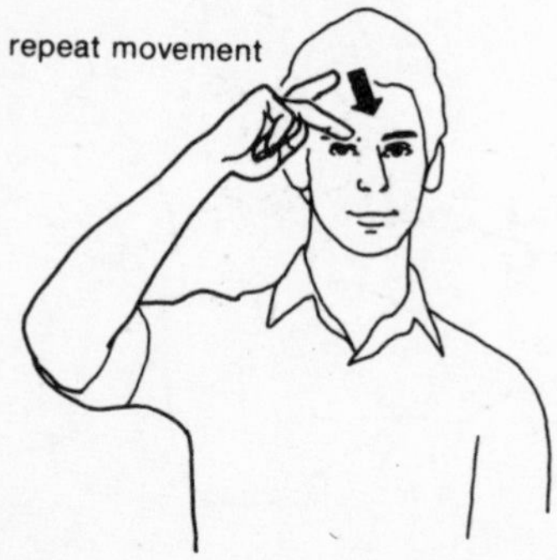

PHILOSOPHY
Move the right "p" hand, palm facing down, up and down in front of the forehead with a small repeated movement.
Hint: Initialized sign near the head where philosophies are formed.

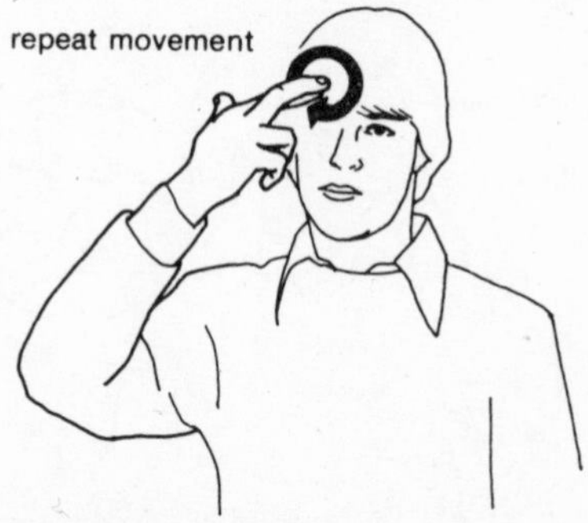

REASON
Move the extended fingers of the right "r" hand in a small repeated circle in front of the forehead, palm facing in.
Hint: Initialized sign near the head where reasons are formed.

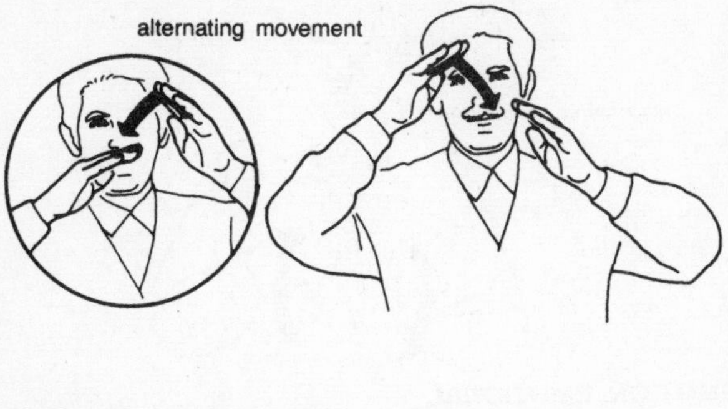

TROUBLE, WORRY, CARE
With an alternating movement, bring both "b" hands, palms angled down, from in front of the forehead downward across the face.
Hint: Things are coming at a person from all sides causing worry.

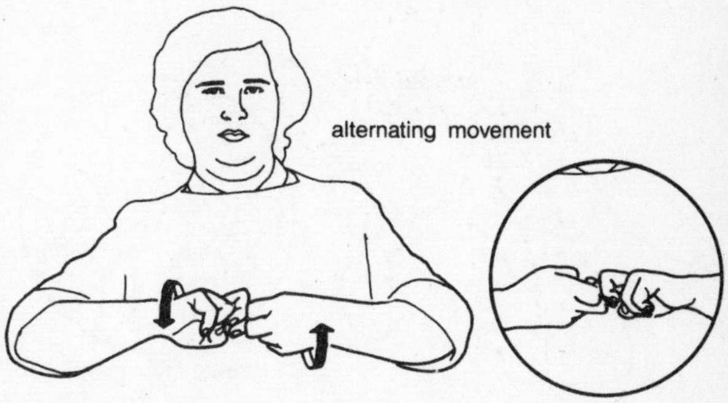

PROBLEM, DIFFICULT
With the knuckles of both bent "v" hands touching in front of the chest, right palm facing forward and left palm facing in, twist the hands in opposite directions with a double movement.
Hint: This handshape is typical of signs indicating "difficulty."

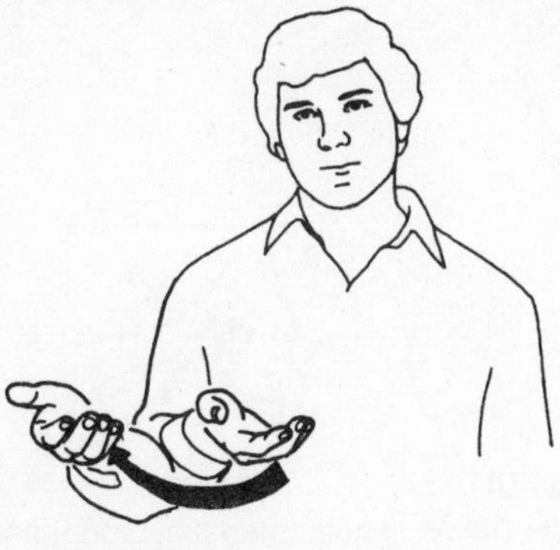

THING
Move the right curved hand, palm facing up, from in front of the body outward to the right.

FAULT
Bring the little-finger side of the right "10" hand, palm facing left, down on the back of the left "a" hand held across the chest, palm facing down.
Hint: The thumb is directing the blame toward another.

PRESSURE, STRESS
With the open right palm on the index-finger side of the left "s" hand held in front of the chest, palm facing right, push the left hand downward with a short double movement.
Hint: Demonstrates putting pressure on someone.

LIE, FIB
Push the extended right index finger, palm facing down and finger pointing left, from right to left across the chin.
Hint: Speaking out of the side of the mouth.

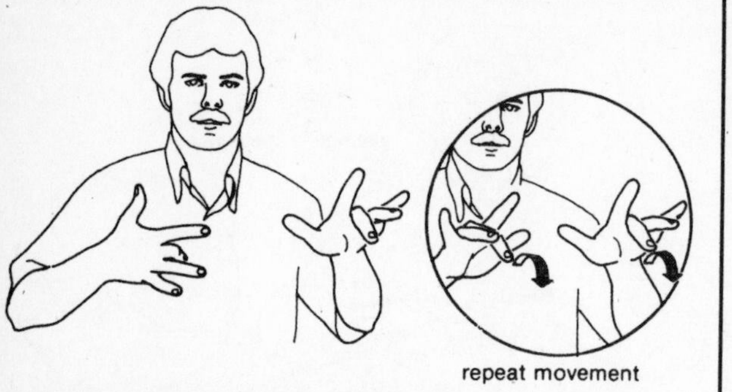

MERCY, PITY, SYMPATHY, EMPATHY
Beginning with the bent middle finger of the right "5" hand touching the chest and the bent middle finger of the left "5" hand pointing forward, twist the right hand forward and repeatedly stroke forward with both bent middle fingers.
Hint: Use the finger often used to express feelings to take feeling from your own hear and direct it to others.

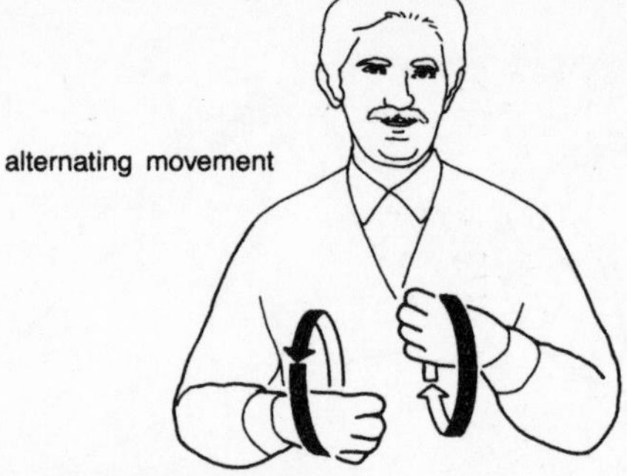

EMOTION, EMOTIONAL
Move both "e" hands, palms facing in, upward with alternating circular movement on each side of the chest.
Hint: Initialized sign showing feelings coming from the heart.

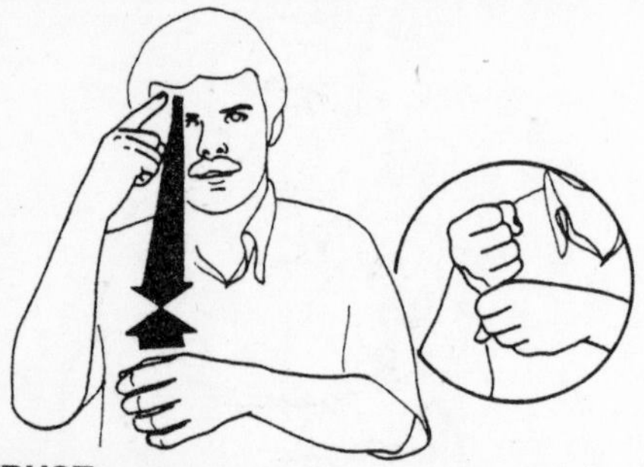

FAITH, TRUST
Move the extended right index finger from touching the right side of the forehead downward while changing into an "s" hand, ending with the little-finger side of the right "s" hand on the index-finger side of the left "s" hand in front of the chest, both palms facing in.
Hint: Taking information from the mind plus "trust."

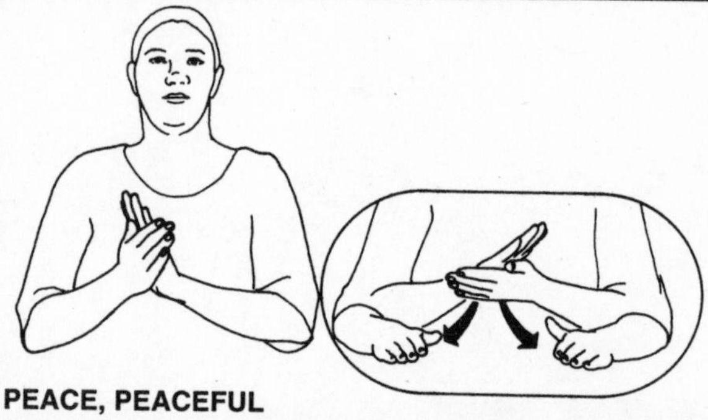

PEACE, PEACEFUL
Beginning with the palms of both open hands together at angles, left hand over the right hand in front of the chest, twist the wrists in opposite directions to reverse the positions. Then move the open hands, palms facing down, downward with a smooth movement to in front of each side of the body.
Hint: Shows a quieting effect over everything.

TRUTH, HONESTY, HONEST
Move the middle-finger side of the right "h" hand, palm facing up, from the heel to the fingers of the open left palm.
Hint: Initialized sign formed similar to the sign for "clean."

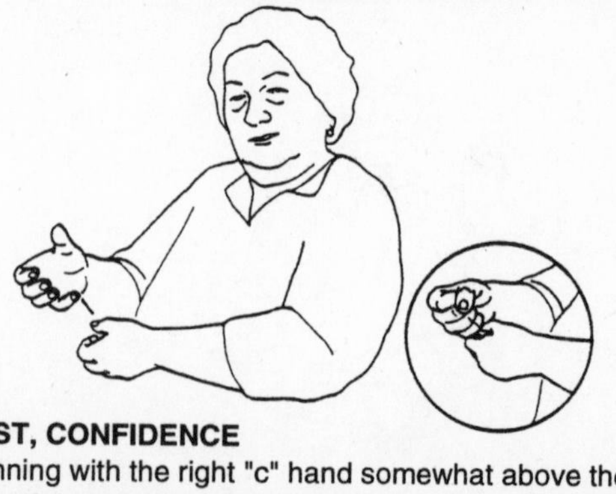

TRUST, CONFIDENCE
Beginning with the right "c" hand somewhat above the left "c" hand, palms facing in opposite directions, bring the hands downward toward the body while closing into "s" hands, ending with the little-finger side of the right "s" hand on the index-finger side of the left "s" hand.
Hint: Holding on to something with trust.

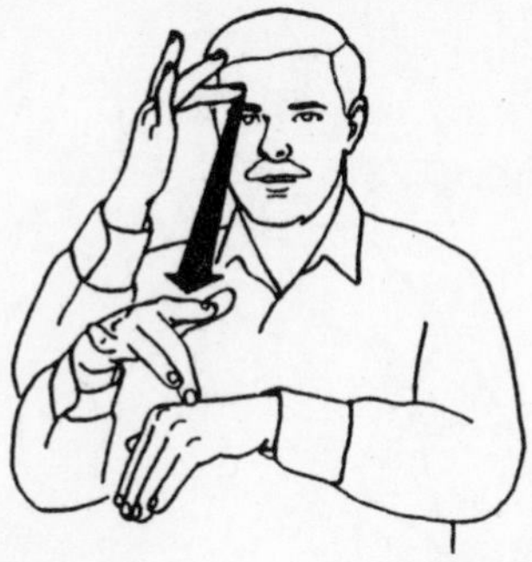

OBSESSION
Touch the bent middle finger of the right "5" hand first to the forehead and then on the back of the left hand held in front of the body, both palms facing down.
Hint: Something on one's mind moves to be seen all the time.

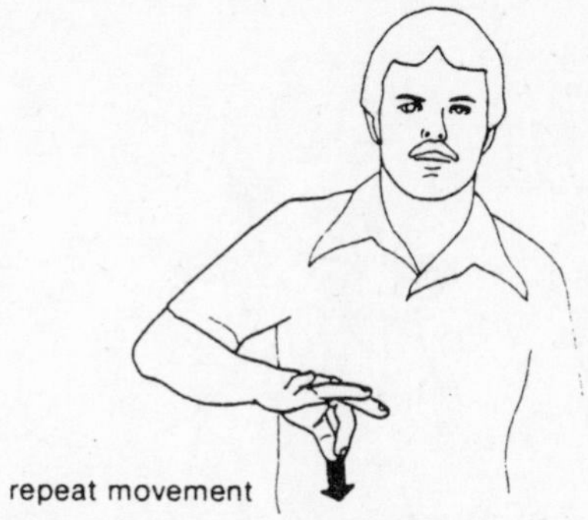

BENEFIT, PROFIT, ADVANTAGE
Tap the fingers of the right "9" hand downward with a small repeated movement in front of the right side of the body, palm facing down.
Hint: Putting money in an imaginary pocket.

NAME, TITLE
Tap the middle-finger side of the right "h" fingers across the index-finger side of the left "h" fingers with a repeated movement, palms angled in.

PROMISE, VOW
Beginning with the extended right index finger pointing up in front of the lips, palm facing left, move the right hand down while changing to an open hand, ending with palm of the open right hand on the index-finger side of the left "s" hand held in front of the chest, palm facing right.
Hint: Bringing words down to seal them in a contract.

ATTENTION, PAY ATTENTION, CONCENTRATE
Move both open hands, palms facing each other and fingers pointing up, forward from each side of the face.
Hint: Wearing blinkers to keep the eyes directed to the task at hand.

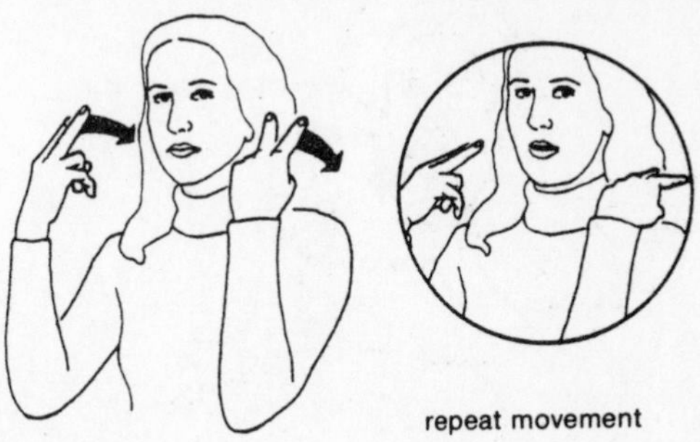

VANITY, VAIN
Move the fingers of both "v" hands, palms facing down and fingers pointing back, down toward the shoulders with a double movement.
Hint: Initialized sign representing that all eyes are on you.

Communication

SPEAK, TALK
Beginning with the index-finger side of the right "4" hand at the mouth, palm facing left and fingers pointing up, move the hand forward with a double movement.
Hint: Shows words coming from the mouth.

SAY
Move the extended right index finger forward in a repeated circular movement in front of the mouth, palm facing in and index finger pointing left.
Hint: Shows words coming out of the mouth.

TELL
Bring the extended right index finger from under the chin forward in a large arc, palm facing in and index finger pointing up.
Hint: Directing words from out of the mouth.

COMMAND, ORDER
Bring the extended right index finger from pointing up in front of the mouth forward with a deliberate movement, ending with the finger angled forward and palm facing left.
Hint: Directing words from the mouth.

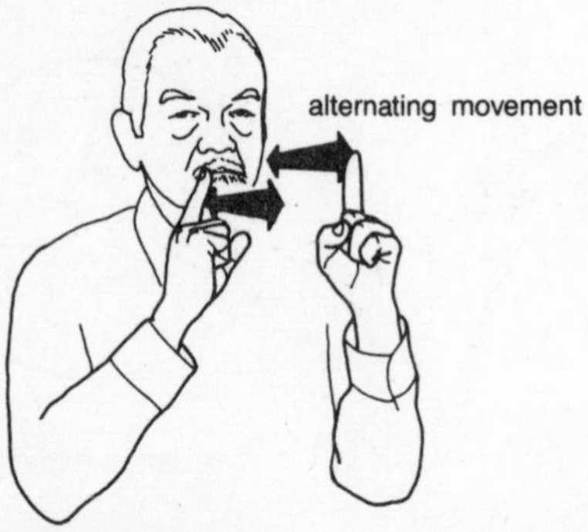

TALK, CONVERSATION
Move both extended index fingers, palms facing each other and fingers pointing up, forward and back with a repeated alternating movement from each side of the mouth by moving the entire forearm.
Hint: The exchange of conversation to and from the mouth.

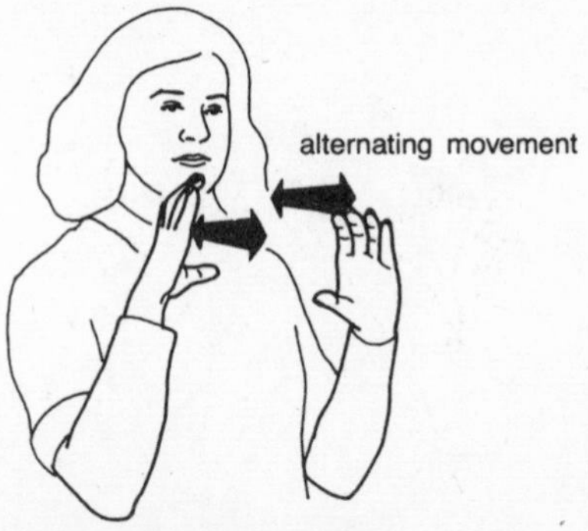

COMMUNICATE, COMMUNICATION
Move both "c" hands, palms facing each other, forward and back with a repeated alternating movement from each side of the mouth by moving the entire forearm.
Hint: Initialized sign showing the exchange of conversation to and from the mouth.

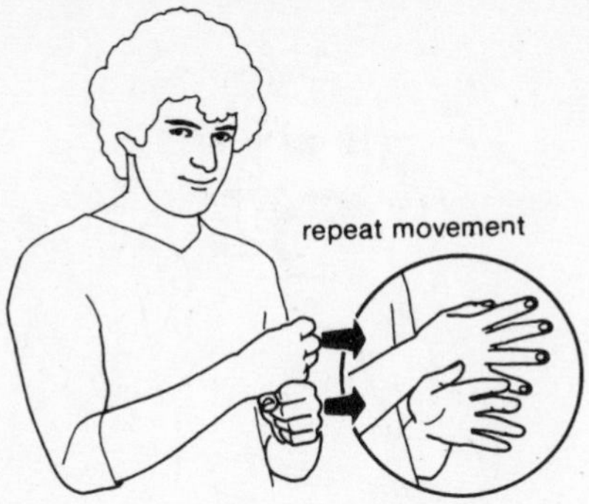

BAWL OUT
Beginning with the little-finger side of the right "s" hand on the index-finger side of the left "s" hand, palms facing in opposite directions, repeatedly open the hands into "5" hands.
Hint: Shows words coming at a person from all sides.

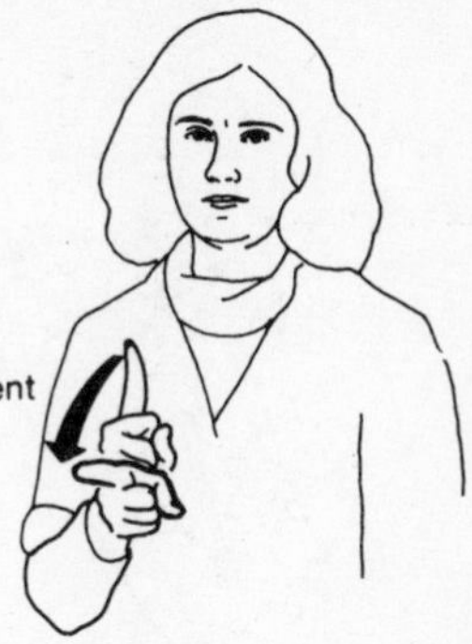

SCOLD, REBUKE
Shake the extended right index finger, palm facing left and finger pointing up, up and down with a repeated movement.
Hint: Mime scolding someone.

DISCUSS, DEBATE
Tap the inside of the extended right index finger, palm facing left, with a repeated movement across the open left palm held in front of the chest, palm facing up.
Hint: Presenting your point.

QUARREL, ARGUE, FIGHT
With both extended index fingers pointing toward each other in front of the chest, palms facing in, move the hands up and down with alternating movements past each other.
Hint: Two people giving opposing views.

ANNOUNCE, PROCLAIM, DECLARE
Beginning with both extended index fingers pointing toward the mouth, palms facing in, twist the wrists to bring the fingers outward to in front of each shoulder, ending with the palms facing forward.
Hint: Take words and tell them broadly.

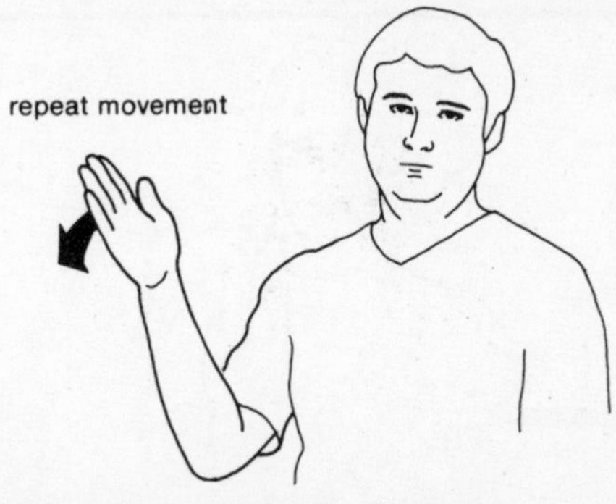

LECTURE, PRESENT, SPEECH, SPEAK
Shake the open right hand, palm angled left, up and down with a short repeated movement in front of the right shoulder.
Hint: Gesturing from a lectern.

VOICE, VOCAL
Bring the extended fingers of the right "v" hand, palm facing in, in an arc forward from under the chin.
Hint: Initialized sign showing where the voice comes through the throat.

SPEECHREADING, LIPREADING
Make a small circle around the mouth with the fingertips of the crooked "v" hand, palm facing in.
Hint: The fingers encircle the lips used for speechreading.

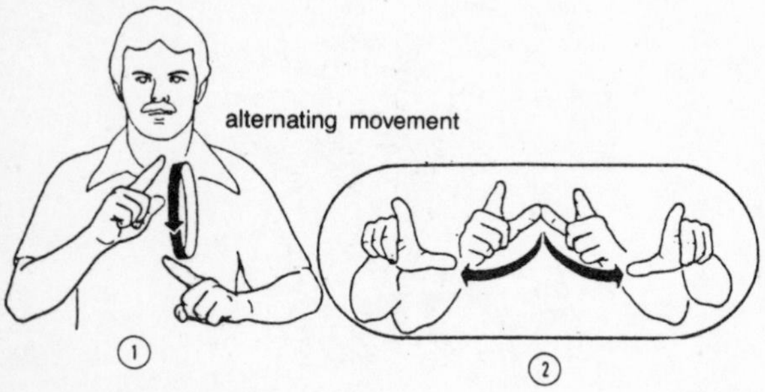

SIGN LANGUAGE
Move both extended index fingers forward in alternating circles around each other by moving the entire forearms, palms facing each other and index fingers pointing up. Then beginning with the thumbs of both "l" hands touching, palms facing down, bring the hands apart to the side.
Hint: "Sign" plus "language."

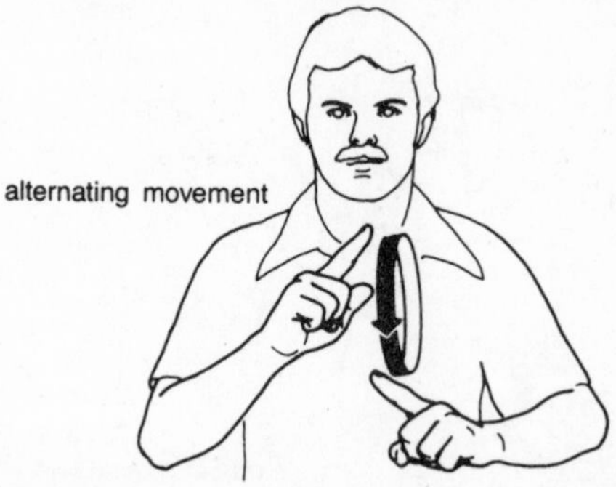

SIGN
Move both extended index fingers forward in alternating circles around each other by moving the entire forearms, palms facing each other and index fingers pointing up.
Hint: Shows the hands moving as when using sign language.

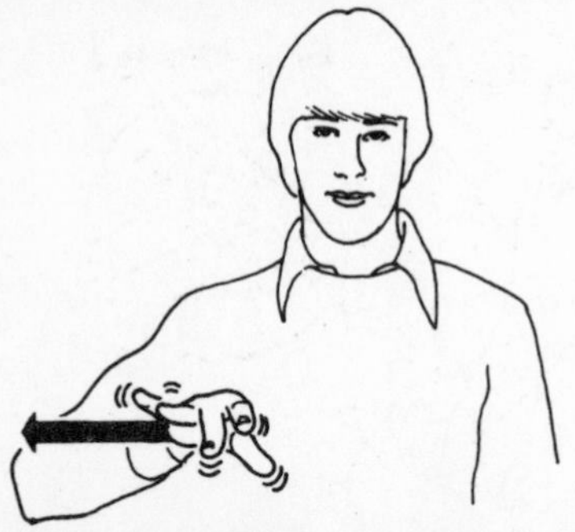

FINGERSPELLING, SPELL, ALPHABET
Wiggle the fingers of the right "5" hand, palm facing down and fingers pointing forward, as the hand moves from in front of the chest outward to the right.
Hint: Mime how the fingers move when fingerspelling quickly.

CHAT, TALK
Beginning with both "5" hands in front of each shoulder, palms angled up, move the hands downward by bending the wrists with a repeated movement.
Hint: Shows the gestures two people make when chatting with each other.

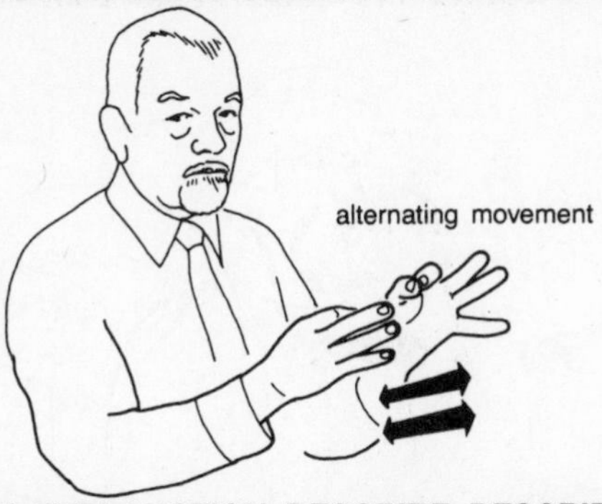

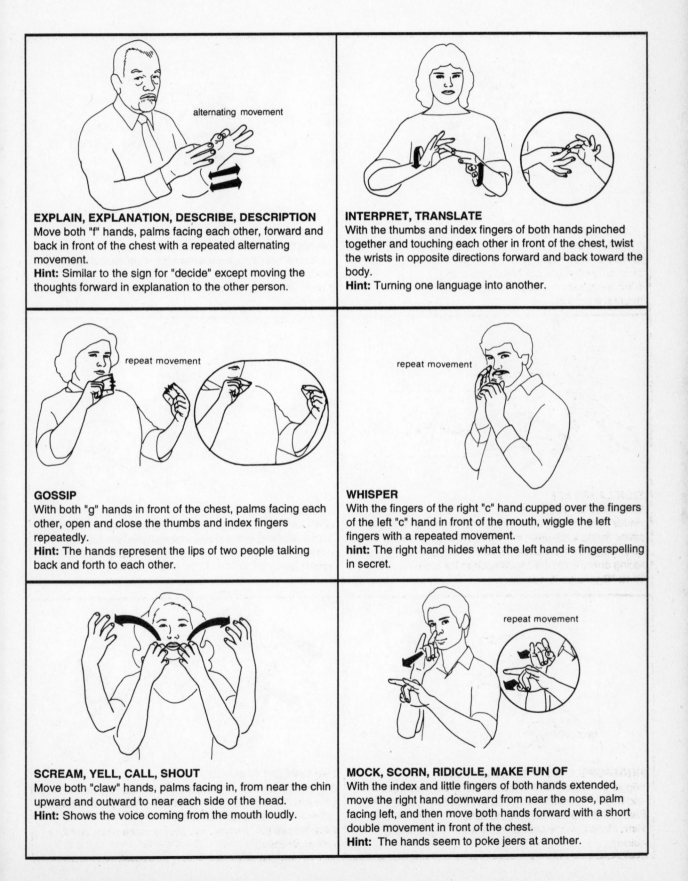

EXPLAIN, EXPLANATION, DESCRIBE, DESCRIPTION
Move both "f" hands, palms facing each other, forward and back in front of the chest with a repeated alternating movement.
Hint: Similar to the sign for "decide" except moving the thoughts forward in explanation to the other person.

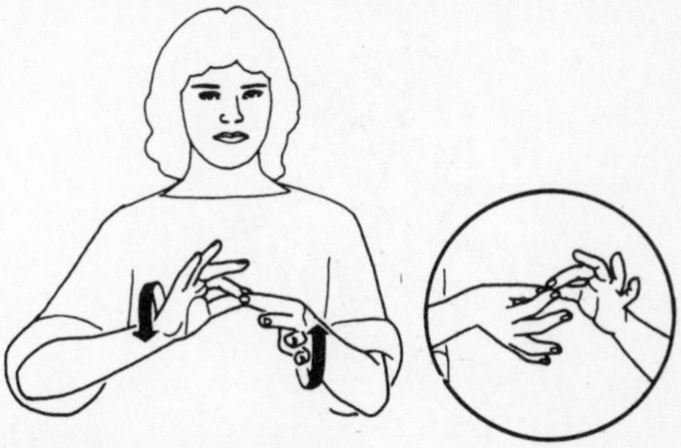

INTERPRET, TRANSLATE
With the thumbs and index fingers of both hands pinched together and touching each other in front of the chest, twist the wrists in opposite directions forward and back toward the body.
Hint: Turning one language into another.

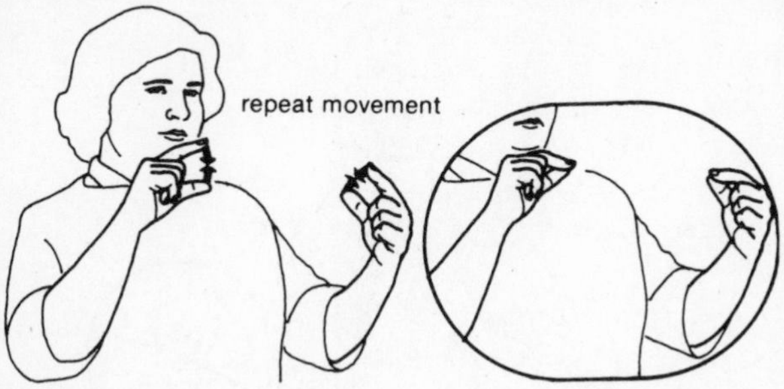

GOSSIP
With both "g" hands in front of the chest, palms facing each other, open and close the thumbs and index fingers repeatedly.
Hint: The hands represent the lips of two people talking back and forth to each other.

WHISPER
With the fingers of the right "c" hand cupped over the fingers of the left "c" hand in front of the mouth, wiggle the left fingers with a repeated movement.
hint: The right hand hides what the left hand is fingerspelling in secret.

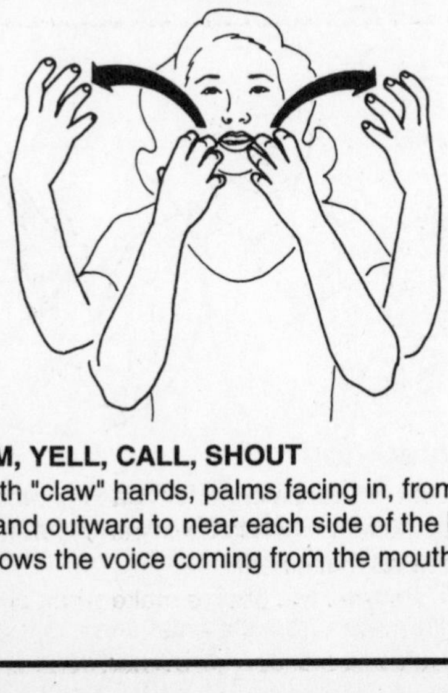

SCREAM, YELL, CALL, SHOUT
Move both "claw" hands, palms facing in, from near the chin upward and outward to near each side of the head.
Hint: Shows the voice coming from the mouth loudly.

MOCK, SCORN, RIDICULE, MAKE FUN OF
With the index and little fingers of both hands extended, move the right hand downward from near the nose, palm facing left, and then move both hands forward with a short double movement in front of the chest.
Hint: The hands seem to poke jeers at another.

COMPLAIN, PROTEST
Tap the fingertips of the right "claw" hand against the chest with a double movement.

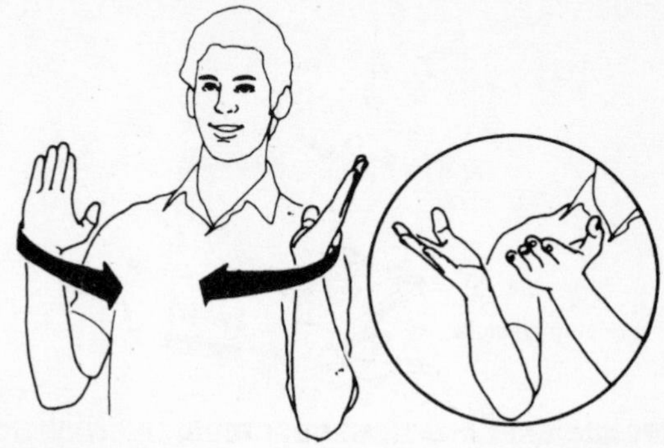

CONVINCE
Move both open hands, palms angled up, from near the shoulders deliberately downward toward each other in front of the chest.
Hint: Shoving your opinions forcibly on another person from all sides.

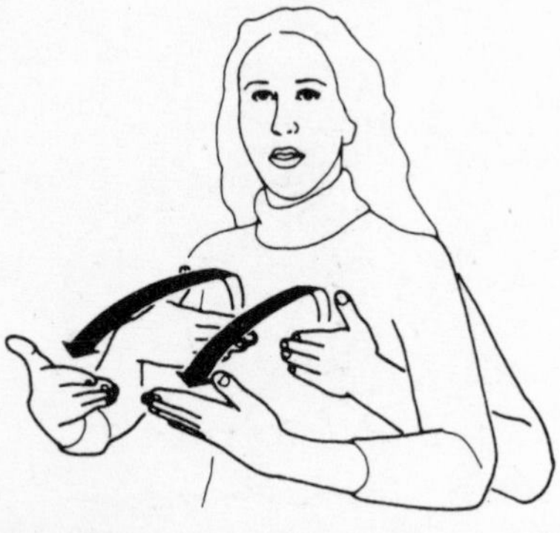

CONFESS, ADMIT
Beginning with the palms of both open hands on the chest, fingers pointing toward each other, move the hands upward and forward, ending with the palms facing up.
Hint: Revealing what's in one's heart.

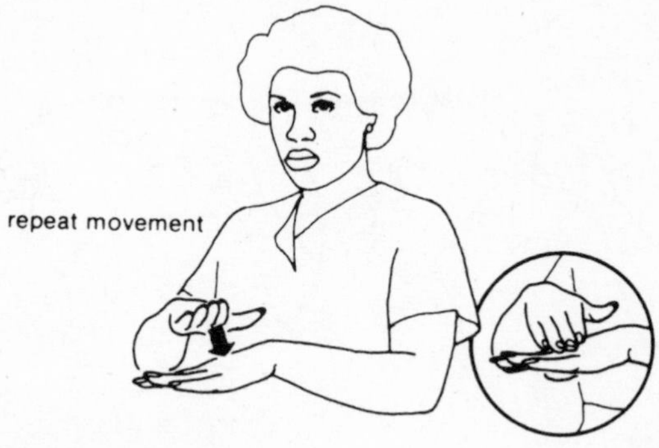

WARN, CAUTION
Tap the fingers of the open right hand across the back of the open left hand with a double movement, both palms facing down.
Hint: Tapping the hand to get one's attention.

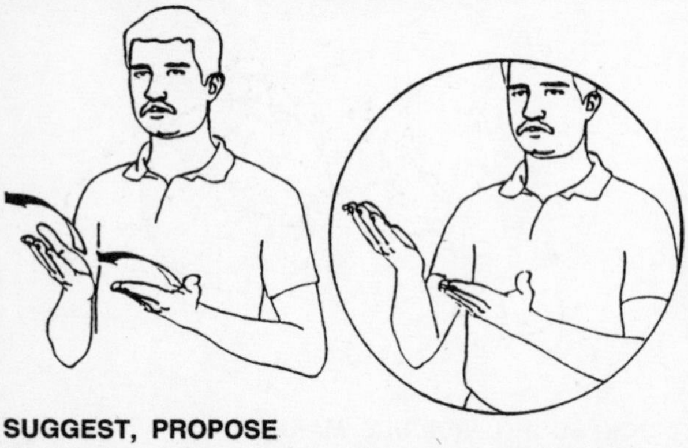

SUGGEST, PROPOSE
Move both open hands from in front of the chest upward and forward, palms facing up.
Hint: Offering a something to another for consideration.

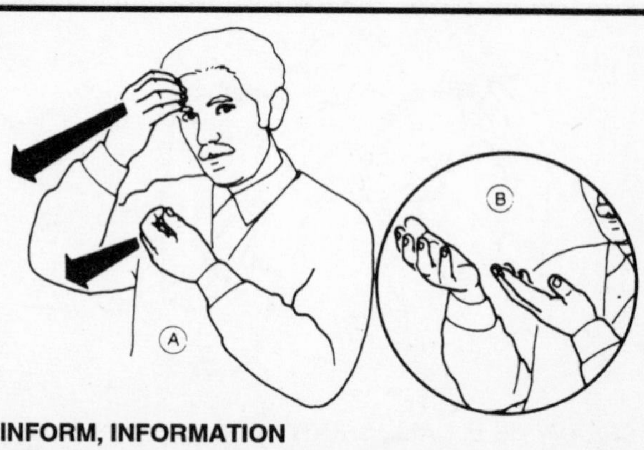

INFORM, INFORMATION
Beginning with the fingers of the right flattened "o" hand near the forehead and the left flattened "o" hand in front of the chest, palms facing up, move the hands forward while opening into "5" hands.
Hint: Taking information from the head and sharing it.

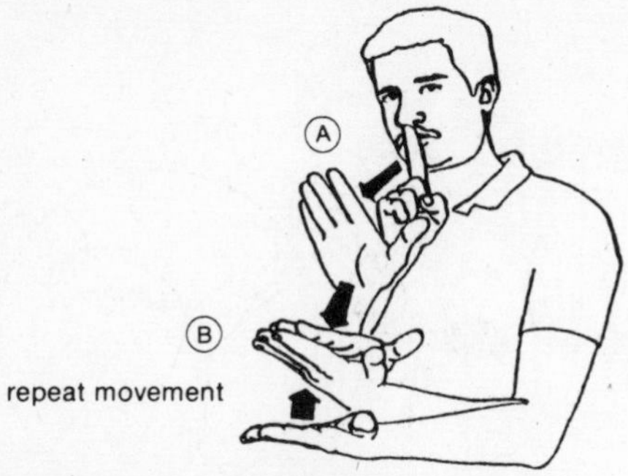

APPLAUD, CLAP, COMMEND, PRAISE
Beginning with the extended right index finger in front of the mouth, palm facing left, bring the right hand down while changing to an open hand. Then pat the fingers of the open right hand, palm facing down, with a repeated movement across the palm of the open left hand, palm facing up.
Hint: Mime applauding.

CALL, SUMMON
Tap the fingers of the open right hand across the back of the open left hand, both palms facing down. Then bring the right hand upward while bending fingers.
Hint: Tapping the hand to get one's attention.

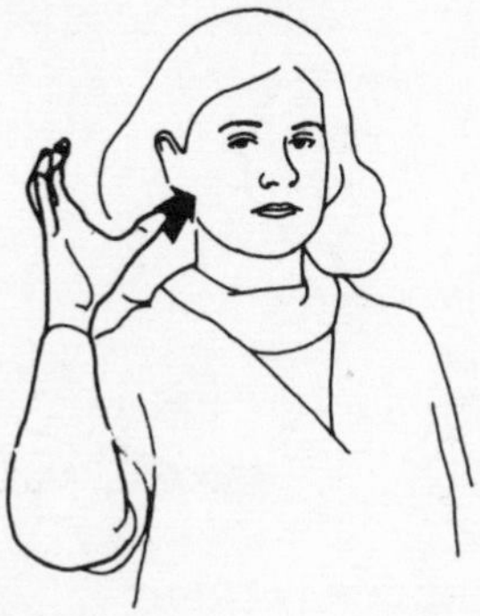

LISTEN, HEAR
Touch the thumb of the right "c" hand, palm facing left, to the right ear.
Hint: The hand cups the ear so you can hear better.

LETTER
Bring the thumb of the right "a" hand, palm facing left, from the lips downward to touch the thumb of the left "a" hand held in front of the chest, palm facing in.
Hint: Mime sticking a stamp on a letter.

INSULT
Move the extended right index finger from in front of the right side of the body forward and upward with a deliberate movement, palm facing left and finger pointing forward.

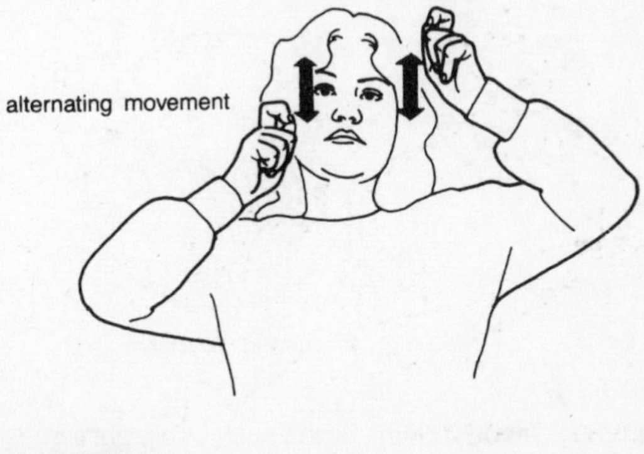

EXPRESSION
With a repeated alternating movement, move both "x" hands up and down in front of each side of the face, palms facing each other.
Hint: Showing how the face moves with expression.

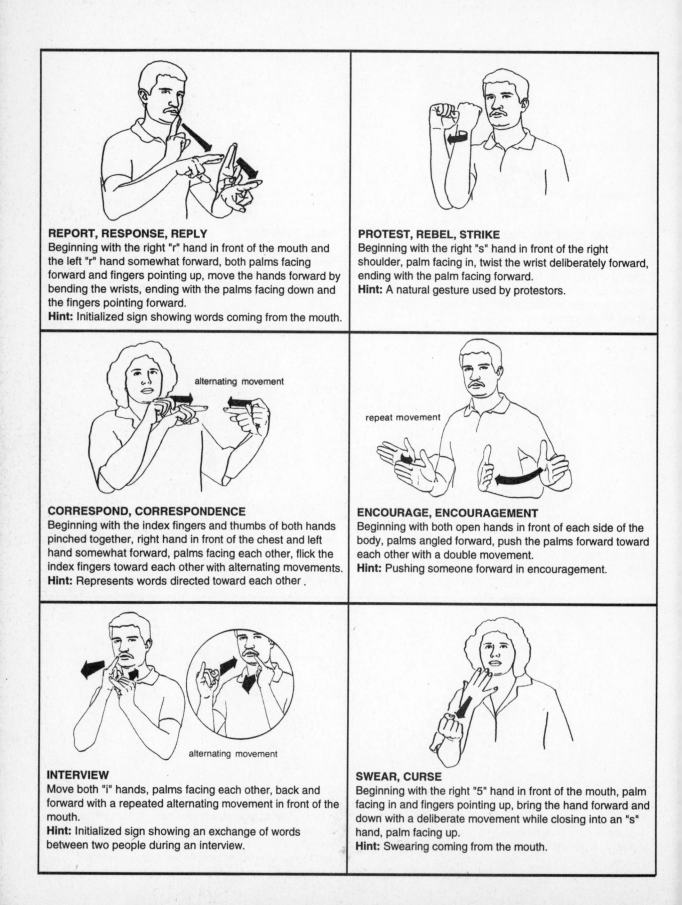

REPORT, RESPONSE, REPLY
Beginning with the right "r" hand in front of the mouth and the left "r" hand somewhat forward, both palms facing forward and fingers pointing up, move the hands forward by bending the wrists, ending with the palms facing down and the fingers pointing forward.
Hint: Initialized sign showing words coming from the mouth.

PROTEST, REBEL, STRIKE
Beginning with the right "s" hand in front of the right shoulder, palm facing in, twist the wrist deliberately forward, ending with the palm facing forward.
Hint: A natural gesture used by protestors.

CORRESPOND, CORRESPONDENCE
Beginning with the index fingers and thumbs of both hands pinched together, right hand in front of the chest and left hand somewhat forward, palms facing each other, flick the index fingers toward each other with alternating movements.
Hint: Represents words directed toward each other .

ENCOURAGE, ENCOURAGEMENT
Beginning with both open hands in front of each side of the body, palms angled forward, push the palms forward toward each other with a double movement.
Hint: Pushing someone forward in encouragement.

INTERVIEW
Move both "i" hands, palms facing each other, back and forward with a repeated alternating movement in front of the mouth.
Hint: Initialized sign showing an exchange of words between two people during an interview.

SWEAR, CURSE
Beginning with the right "5" hand in front of the mouth, palm facing in and fingers pointing up, bring the hand forward and down with a deliberate movement while closing into an "s" hand, palm facing up.
Hint: Swearing coming from the mouth.

fourteen

MISCELLANEOUS

Political
Education
Technology
Music

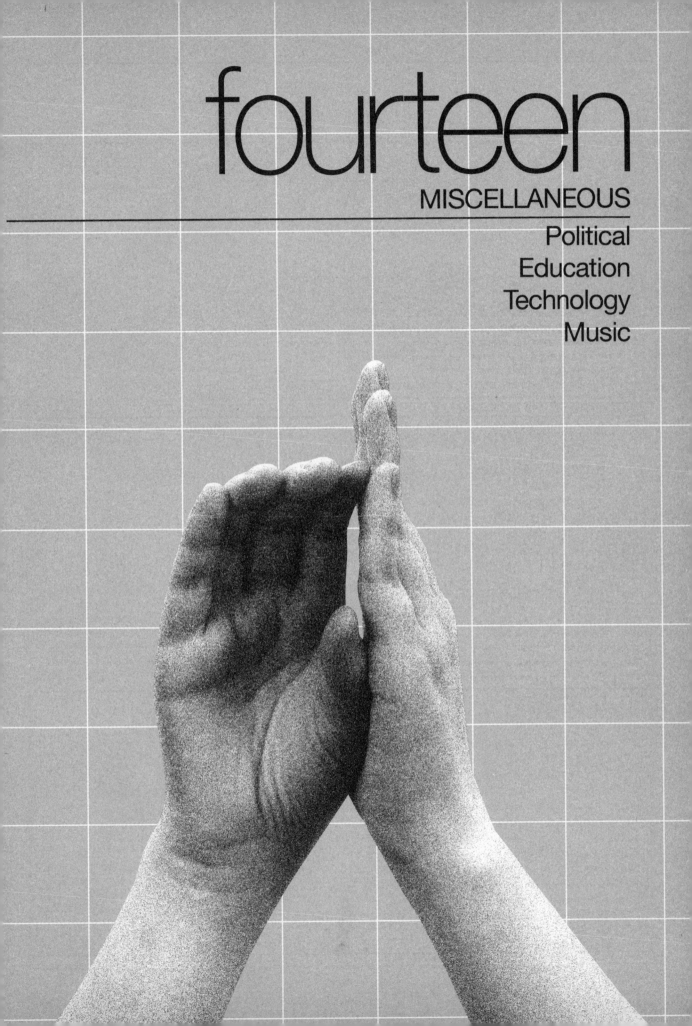

CONCEPTUALLY ACCURATE SIGNING

Signs do not stand for English words; signs stand for concepts. When signing a sentence it is important to think of the meaning or concept you are signing and not the English word. In English, many words sound alike but you get their meaning from the sentence. For example, "His *acts* show he doesn't care." and "He *acts* in the school play." In sign language there is a different sign for each of these concepts and you must choose which one to use by its meaning.

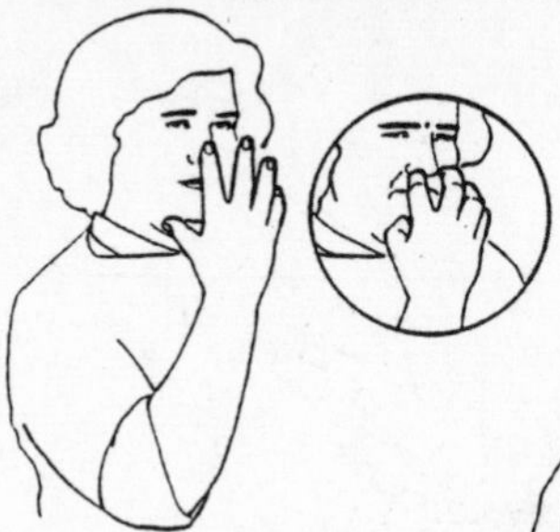

cross *(adj.)*

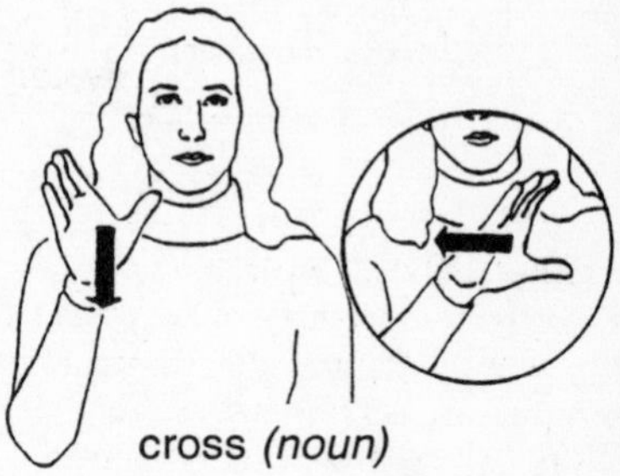

cross *(noun)*

CLASSIFIERS FOR SIZE, SHAPE, LOCATION

A classifier is a special kind of sign that gets its meaning from its location and use. Usually classifiers refer are used to refer to a noun. Classifiers contain information about size, shape, and type of object. There are approximately 10 classifiers used in American Sign Language. The classifier with an "f" handshape can show the location of spots, buttons, and other small, round objects. The classifier with a "g" handshape can show how thick something is, like carpet pile, a stack of papers, or a layer of icing.

Classifier: F

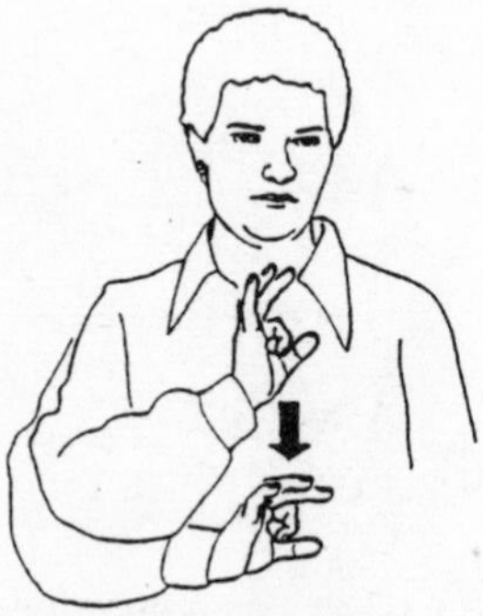

(Shows size and location of buttons.)

(Shows size and location of watch.)

NOUN/VERB PAIRS

Nouns and verbs are distinguished from each other in several ways in sign language. Often the sign for the noun is completely different than the verb, such as in "color." Sometimes the only difference between signing the noun and the verb relates to the movement. The differences in movement are not easily memorized by a single rule, but usually the noun has a repeated and restrained movement, and the verb is usually a single movement, but sometimes it is repeated, too. Sometimes, too, the verb is a continuous movement and sometimes a "hold" movement.

seat *(noun)*

sit *(verb)*

Music

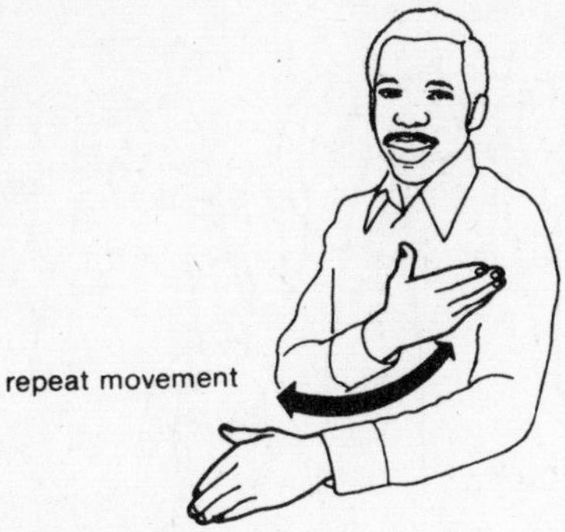

MUSIC, SONG, SING
Swing the open right hand, palm facing back, forward and back with a repeated movement from the wrist to the crook of the bent left arm held in front of the body.
Hint: Shows the rhythm of music.

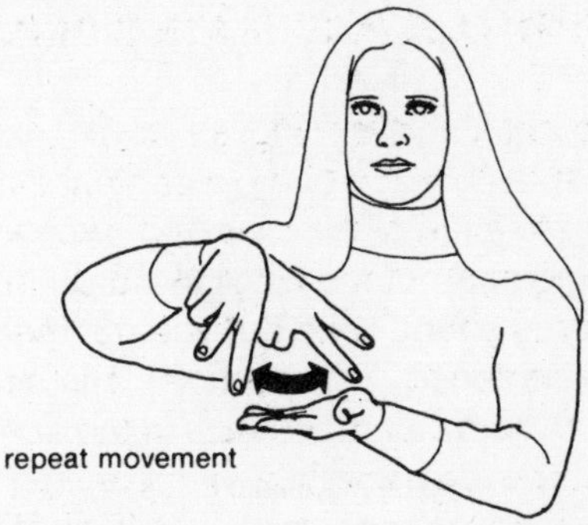

DANCE
Swing the fingers of the right "v" hand, palm facing in and fingers pointing down, back and forth across the palm of the open left hand held in front of the body, palm facing up.
Hint: The two fingers represent legs dancing.

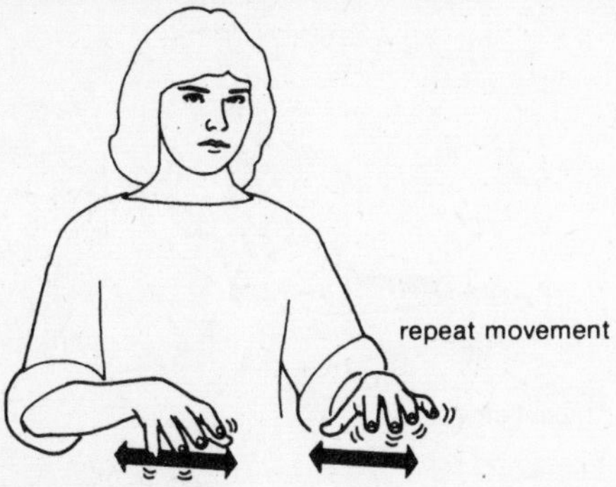

PIANO, PLAY PIANO
Move both "5" hands, palms facing down, back and forth in front of the body while wiggling the fingers.
Hint: Mime playing the piano.

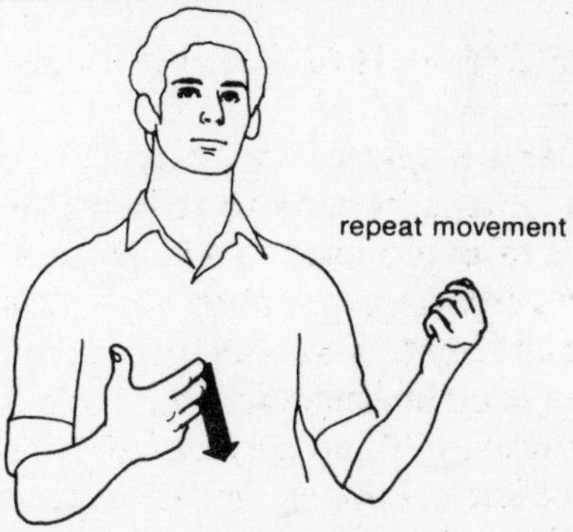

GUITAR
Move the fingers of the open right hand, palm facing in, up and down with a short repeated movement in front of the right side of the chest while holding the left "a"hand in front of the left side of the chest, palm facing in.
Hint: Mime strumming a guitar.

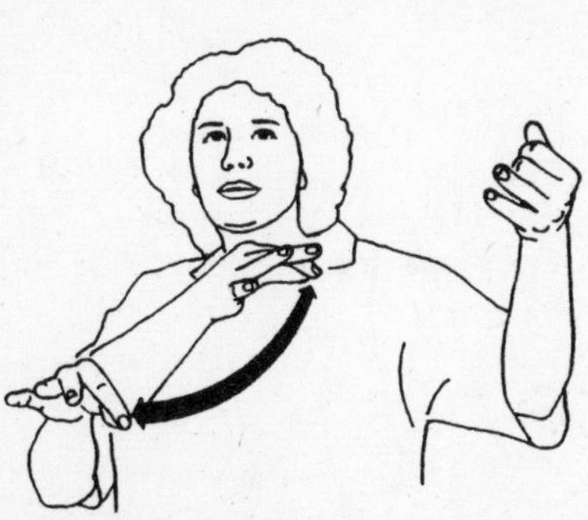

VIOLIN, FIDDLE
While holding the curved left hand in front of the left shoulder, move the right "9" hand in a swinging arc forward and back toward the left side of the chest.
Hint: Mime playing a violin.

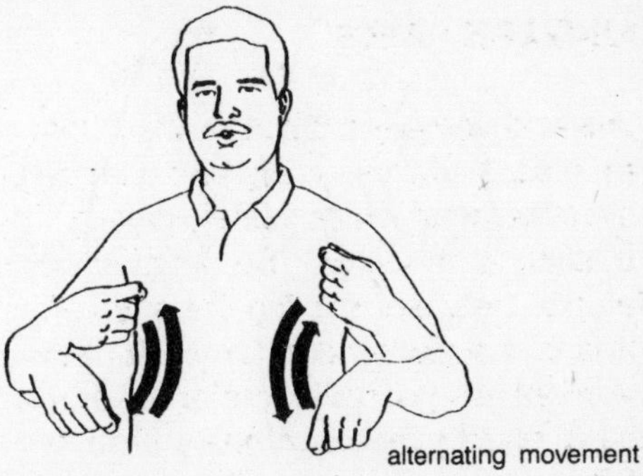

DRUM
With the thumbs and index fingers of both hands pinched together, palms facing the body, move the hands up and down with an alternating movement in front of each side of the chest.
Hint: Mime playing a drum.

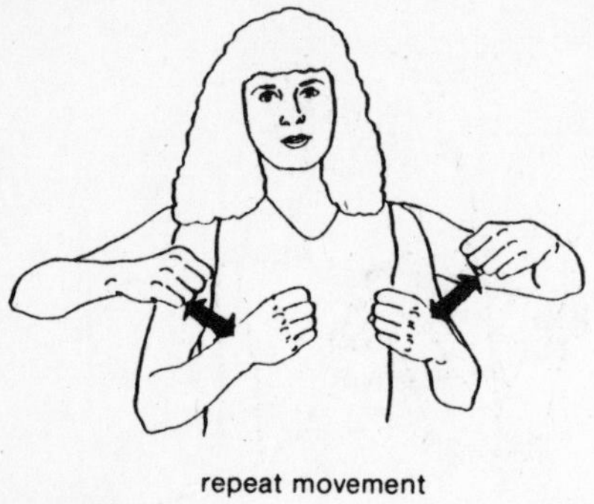

ACCORDION
Move both "s" hands, palms facing in, from in front of each side of the chest upward and outward with a repeated movement, raising the elbows each time.
Hint: Mime playing an accordion.

HARMONICA
Move both flattened "c" hands, palms facing each other from side to side in front of the mouth.
Hint: Mime playing a harmonica.

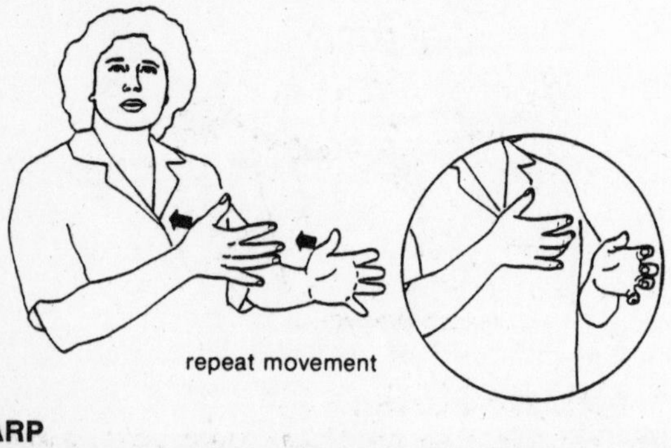

HARP
Beginning with both "5" hands in front of the left side of the body, right hand closer to the chest than the left and palms facing each other, bring the hands back toward the body with a double movement, constricting the fingers each time.
Hint: Mime playing a harp.

TROMBONE
While holding the thumb side of the right "s" hand at the mouth, palm facing left, move the left "s" hand forward and back in front of the left side of the body with a double movement, palm facing right.
Hint: Mime playing a trombone.

HORN
Hold the right "c" hand at the mouth, palm facing left, and the left "c" hand somewhat forward of the face, palm facing right.
Hint: Mime holding a horn to blow it.

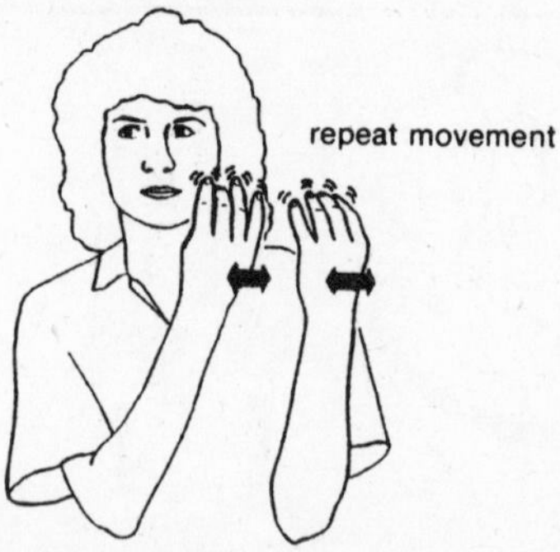

FLUTE
Move both "c" hands, palms facing in, from side to side in front of the mouth while wiggling the fingers.
Hint: Mime playing a flute.

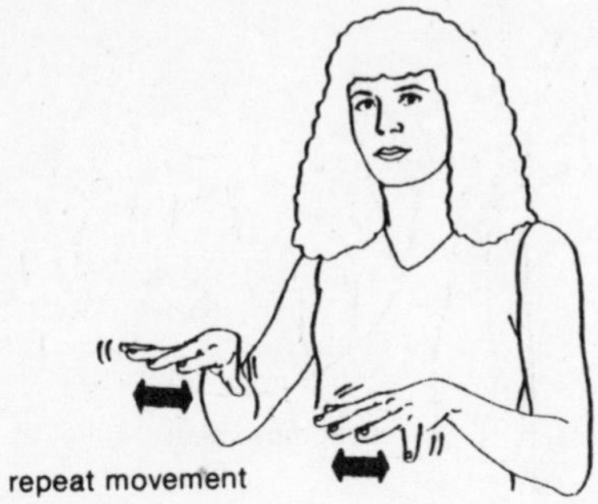

BEAT, VIBRATION
Shake both "5" hands, palms facing down, from side to side with a short repeated movement in front of the body.
Hint: As if feeling the vibration of music.

RHYTHM
Move the right "r" hand, palm facing down and fingers pointing forward, in a wavy movement from in front of the chest to the right.
Hint: Initialized sign showing the movement of a rhythm.

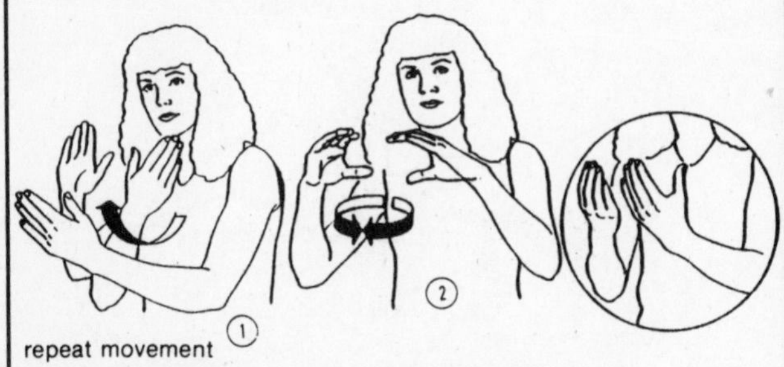

BAND, CHOIR
Swing the open right hand, palm facing back with a repeated movement from the wrist to the crook of the bent left arm held in front of the body. Then beginning with both "c" hands in front of the chest, palms facing forward, move the hands outward in a circle until the little fingers come near each other, ending with the palms facing in.
Hint: "Music" plus "class."

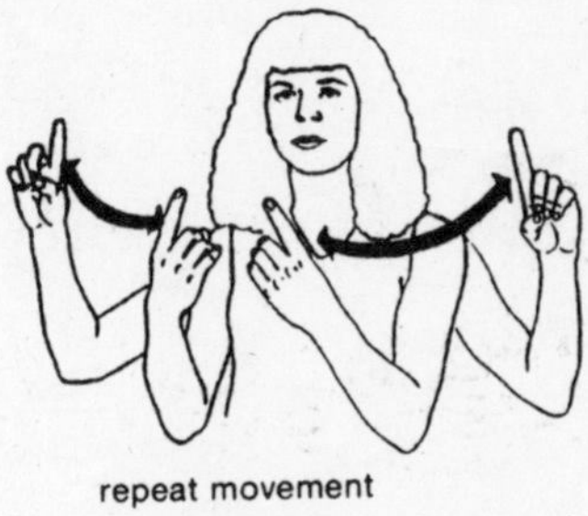

SYMPHONY, ORCHESTRA
Beginning with both extended index fingers pointing up in front of each side of the chest, palms facing each other, swing the hands outward with a repeated movement, turning the palms forward each time.
Hint: Mime conducting a symphony.

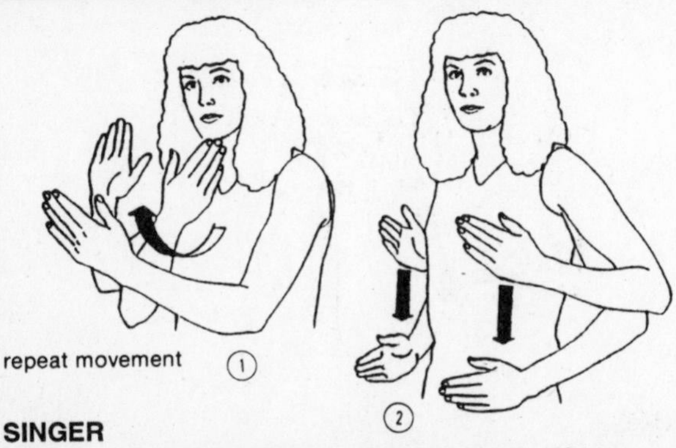

SINGER
Swing the open right hand, palm facing back, with a repeated movement from the wrist to the crook of the bent left arm. Then move both open hands downward along the sides of the body, palms facing each other.
Hint: "Music" plus "person marker."

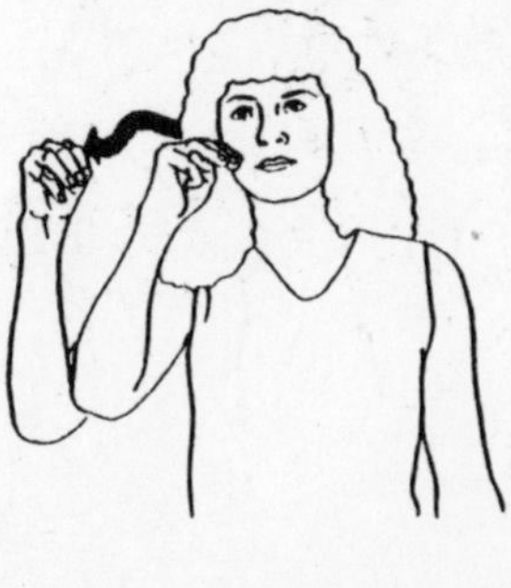

HUM
Move the right "m" hand, palm facing down, from near the right side of the mouth outward with a wavy movement.
Hint: Shows the rhythm of a hum.

Political

POLITICS, POLITICAL
Beginning with the right "p" hand near the right side of the head, palm facing forward, twist the wrist and touch the middle finger to the right temple, palm facing back.
Hint: Initialized sign formed similar to sign for "government."

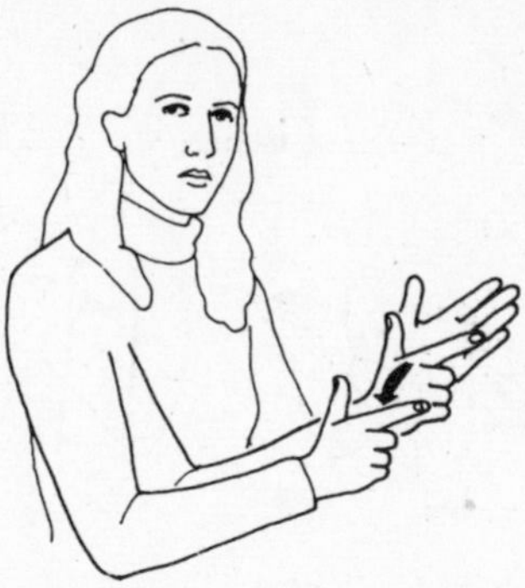

LAW, LEGAL
Move the right "l" hand across the left palm touching first at the fingers and then at the heel, palms facing each other.
Hint: Recording a law on the books.

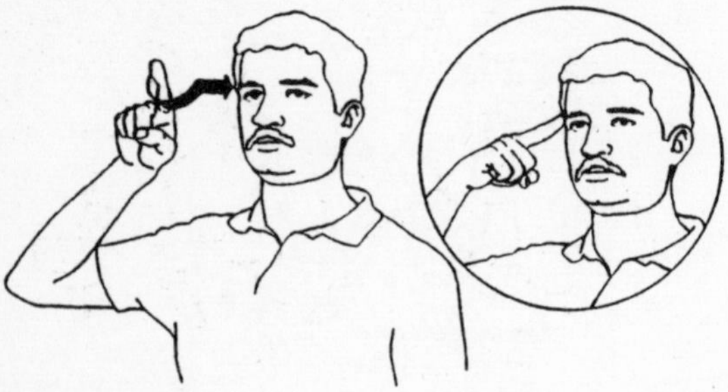

GOVERNMENT, CAPITOL
Beginning with the extended right index finger near the right side of the head, palm facing forward, twist the wrist and touch the index finger to the right temple, palm facing down.

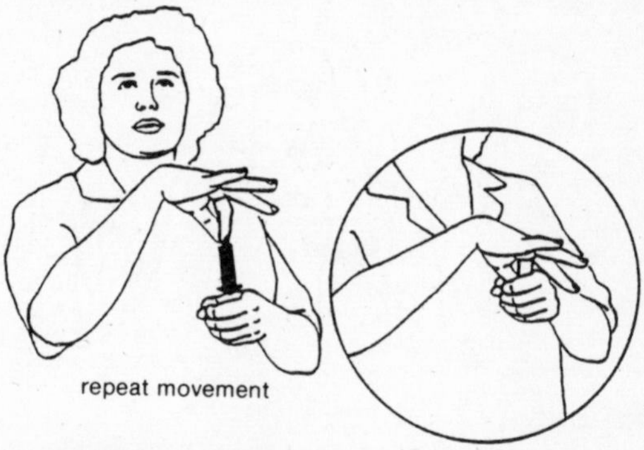

VOTE, ELECT, ELECTION
Insert the fingertips of the right "f" hand, palm facing down, with a double movement in the hole formed by the left "o" hand held in front of the chest, palm facing right.
Hint: Putting one's vote into the ballot box.

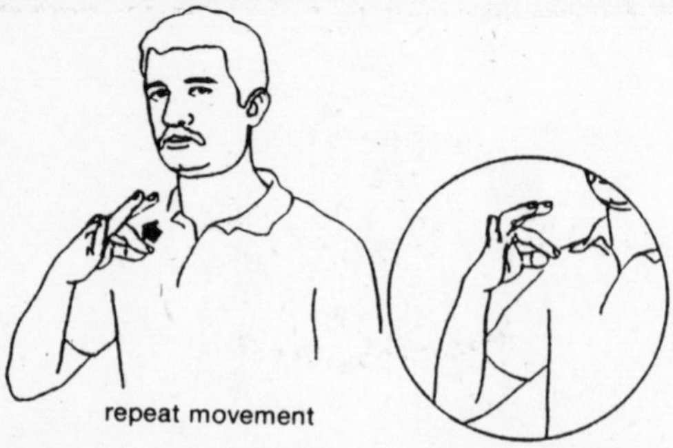

CANDIDATE, APPLY, ELIGIBLE, VOLUNTEER
Move the fingertips of the right "f", palm facing in, forward with a short double movement from the right side of the chest.
Hint: Pulling a candidate forward by pulling on the shirt.

APPOINT
Move the right "c" hand, palm facing left, from in front of the right side of the body to in front of the body with a deliberate movement while closing into an "s" hand.
Hint: Moving someone forcibly into a position.

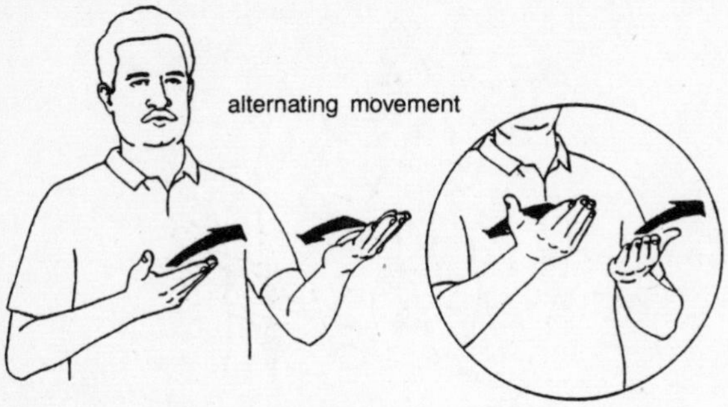

NOMINATE, NOMINATION
Beginning with both open hands in front of each side of the chest, one hand closer to the chest than the other and palms facing up, move the hands forward and back with a double alternating movement.
Hint: Presenting names in nomination.

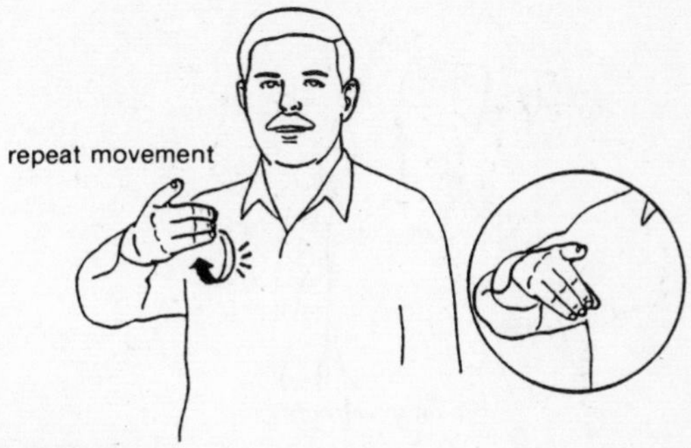

DELEGATE
Brush the fingers of the right "d" hand, palm facing in, downward on the right side of the chest with a repeated movement.
Hint: Initialized sign.

INAUGURATION, OATH
Hold the open right hand up in front of the right shoulder, palm facing forward, and the open left hand down in front of the left side of the body, palm facing down.
Hint: Holding one's hand on the Bible while taking an oath.

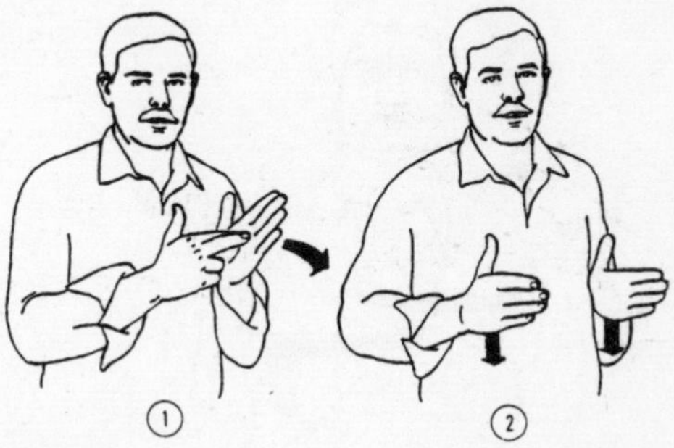

REPRESENTATIVE
With the fingertips of the right "r" hand touching the palm of the open left hand move both hands forward. Then move both open hands downward along the sides of the body, palms facing each other.
Hint: An initialized form of the sign for "show" plus the "person marker."

COMMITTEE, COUNCIL
Touch the fingertips of the right "claw" hand, palm facing in, first to the left side of the chest and then to the right side of the chest.
Hint: Initialized sign.

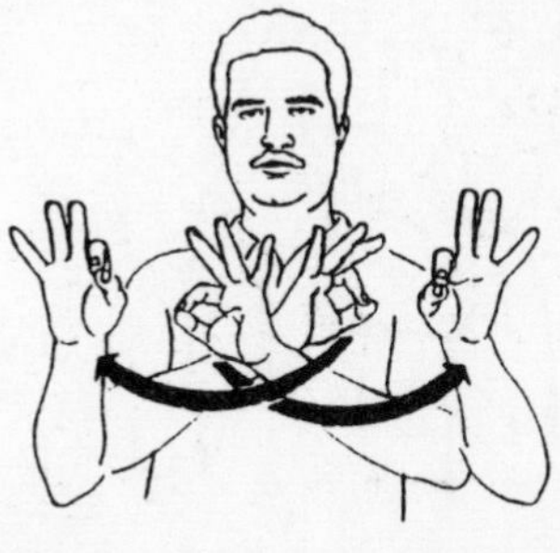

FREE, FREEDOM
Beginning with the wrists of both "f" hands crossed in front of the chest, palms facing in opposite directions, twist the wrists and bring the hands outward apart from each other, ending with the palms facing forward.
Hint: Initialized sign formed similar to sign for "save."

DEMOCRAT, DEMOCRATIC
Shake the right "d" hand, palm facing forward, from side to side with a short movement in front of the right side of the chest.
Hint: Initialized sign.

REPUBLICAN, REPUBLIC
Shake the right "r" hand, palm facing forward, from side to side with a short movement in front of the right side of the chest.
Hint: Initialized sign.

INDEPENDENT, INDEPENDENCE
Beginning with the wrists of both "i" hands crossed in front of the chest, palms facing in opposite directions, twist the wrists and bring the hands outward apart from each other, ending with the palms facing forward.
Hint: Initialized sign formed similar to sign for "save."

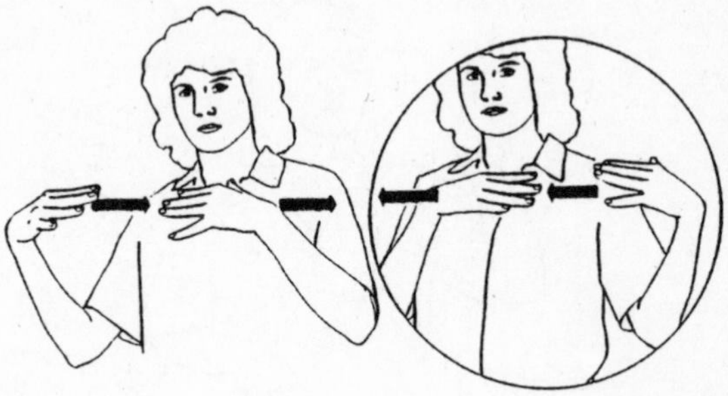

WAR, BATTLE
Beginning with both "5" hands in front of the right shoulder, palms facing down and fingers pointing toward each other, move the hands across the chest to the left and then back to the right.
Hint: Represents sparring opponents.

CONGRESS
Touch the thumb side of the right "c" hand, palm facing left, first to the left side of the chest and then to the right side.
Hint: Initialized sign.

SENATE, STAFF
Touch the thumb side of the right "s" hand, palm facing left, first to the left side of the chest and then to the right side.
Hint: Initialized sign.

Education

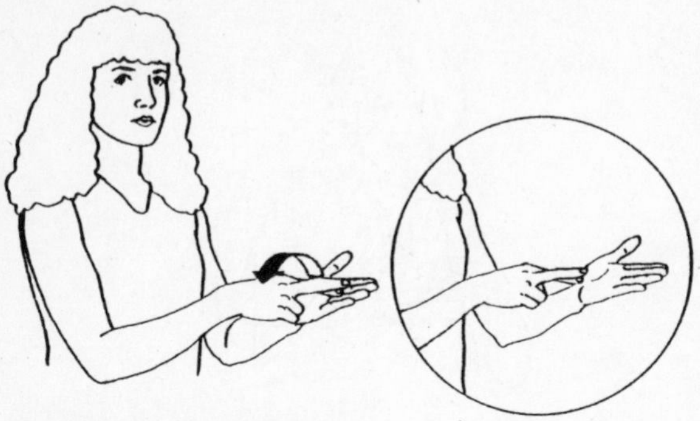

REGISTER, REGISTRATION
Touch the fingertips of the right "r" hand, palm facing down, on the left palm, first to the fingers and then the heel.
Hint: Initialized sign showing putting one's name on paper.

SEMESTER
Move the right "s" hand, palm facing forward, from in front of the right side of the chest outward to the right and then straight down.
Hint: Shows breaking up a page into lessons.

CURRICULUM
Move the thumb side of the right "c" hand, palm facing forward, from the heel upward on the palm of the open left hand, palm facing right and fingers pointing up. Then change to a right "m" hand and move back down the left palm from the fingers to the heel.
Hint: Abbreviation "c-m."

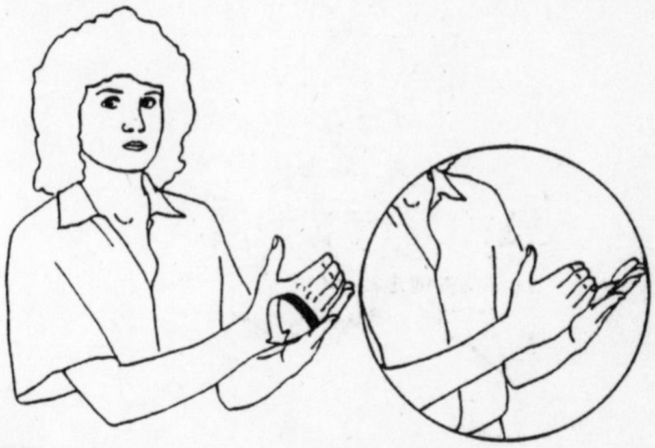

COURSE
Move the little-finger side of the right "c" hand, palm facing in, on the left palm, first to the fingers and then to the heel.
Hint: Initialized sign similar to sign for "lesson."

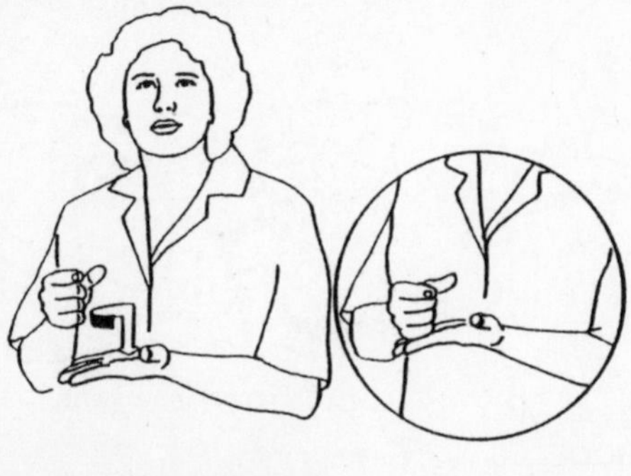

GRADUATION, GRADUATE
Move the right "g" hand, palm facing left, in a circular movement above the palm of the open left hand held in front of the face, and then straight down to land on the left palm.
Hint: Initialized sign.

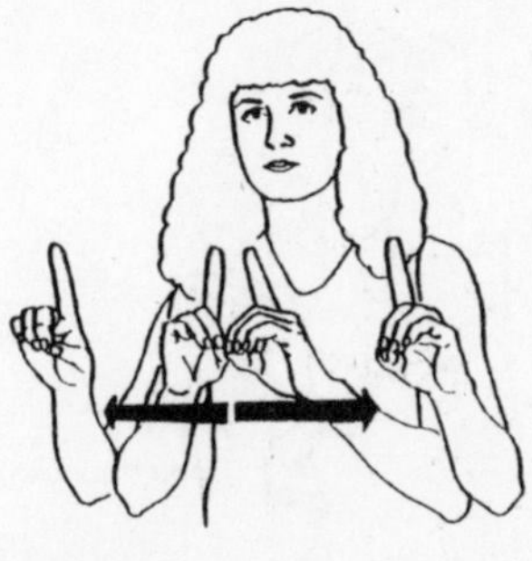

DEGREE, DIPLOMA
Beginning with both "d" hands together in front of the chest, palms angled forward, bring the hands apart to the each side.
Hint: Initialized sign showing the shape of a rolled diploma.

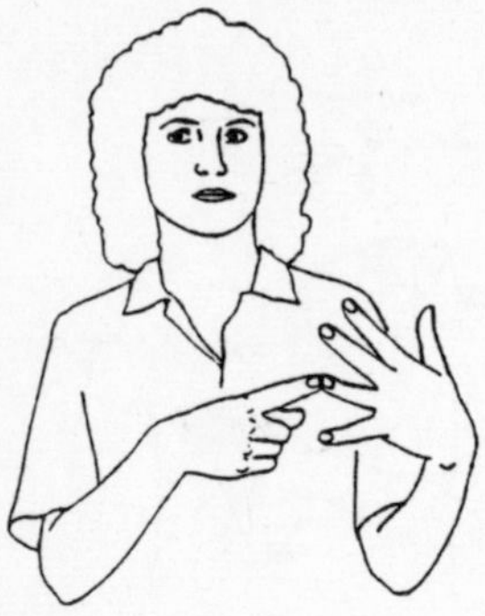

FRESHMAN
Touch the ring finger of the left "5" hand with the extended right index finger, both palms facing in.
Hint: Shows the second year in school including a preparatory year.

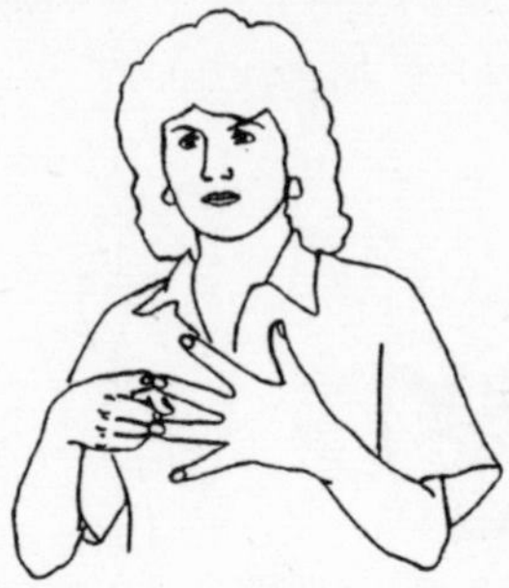

SOPHOMORE
Touch the middle finger of the left "5" hand with the extended right index finger, both palms facing in.
Hint: Shows the third year in school including a preparatory year.

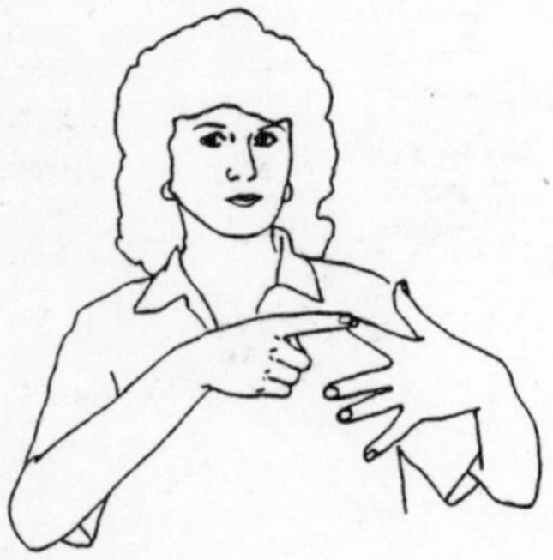

JUNIOR
Touch the index finger of the left "5" hand with the extended right index finger, both palms facing in.
Hint: Shows the fourth year including a preparatory year.

SENIOR
Touch the palm of the right "5" hand, palm facing down, on the thumb of the left "5" hand, palm facing in and fingers pointing left.
Hint: Shows the last year in school.

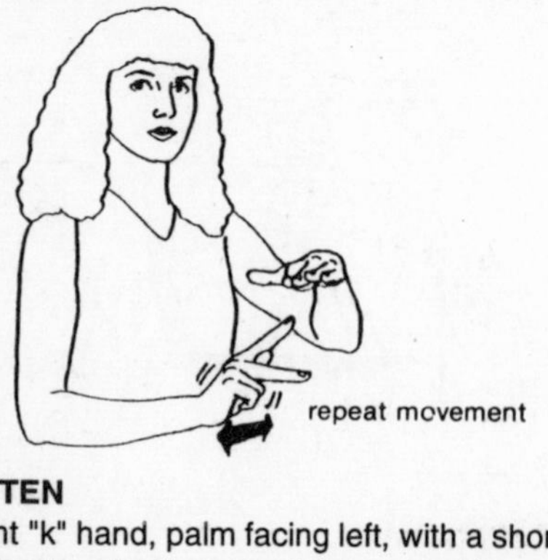

KINDERGARTEN
Shake the right "k" hand, palm facing left, with a short side to side movement under the open left hand held across the chest, palm facing down.
Hint: Initialized sign.

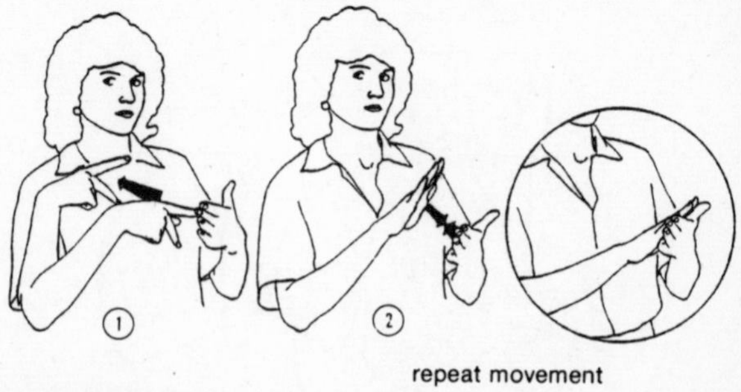

PRESCHOOL
Move the right "p" hand from the palm of the open left hand in toward the chest, both palms facing in. Then pat the palm of the open right hand with a double movement across the palm of the open left hand.
Hint: Initialized sign formed similar to sign for "before" plus "school."

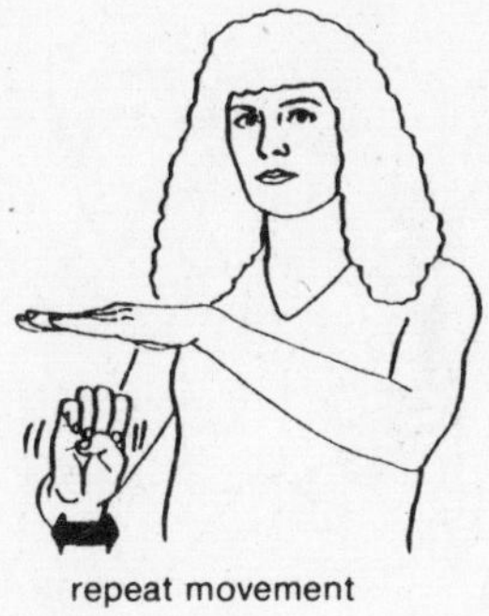

ELEMENTARY
Shake the right "e" hand, palm facing left, with a short side to side movement under the open left hand held across the chest, palm facing down.
Hint: Initialized sign.

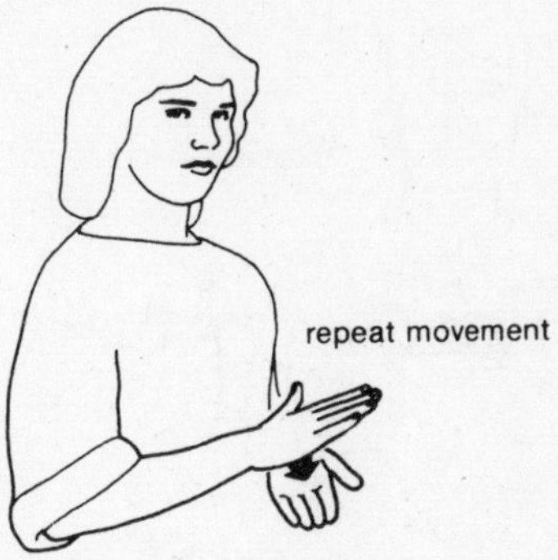

SCHOOL
Pat the palm of the open right hand with a double movement across the palm of the open left hand.
Hint: Clapping one's hands to get students' attention.

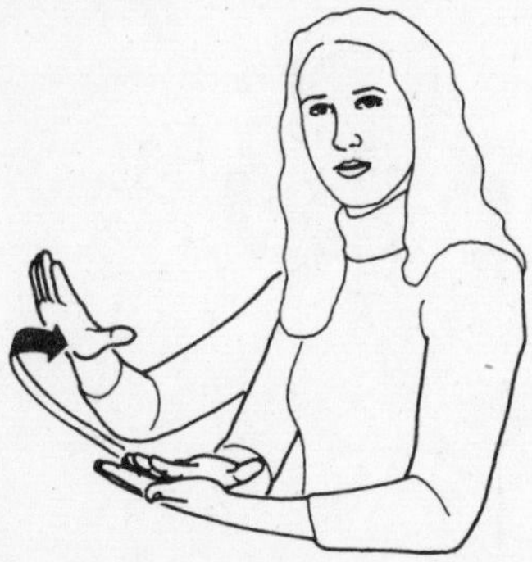

COLLEGE
Beginning with the palm of the open right hand on the palm of the open left hand, bring the right hand upward in a circular movement.
Hint: Begins similar to sign for "school" and moves upward to indicate higher education.

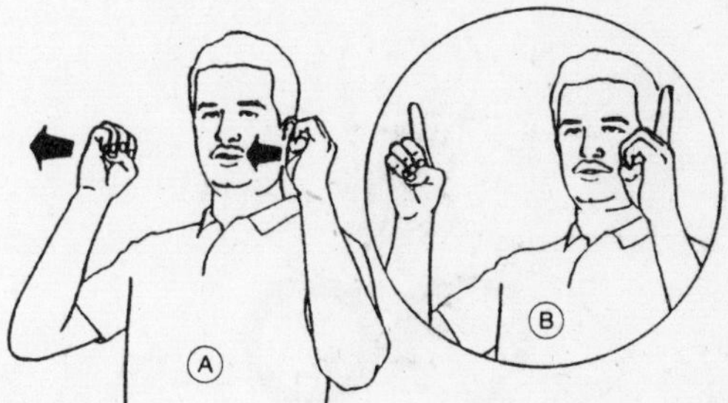

EDUCATION
Beginning with both "e" hands near each side of the head, palms facing each other, move the hands forward while changing into "d" hands.
Hint: Abbreviation "e-d."

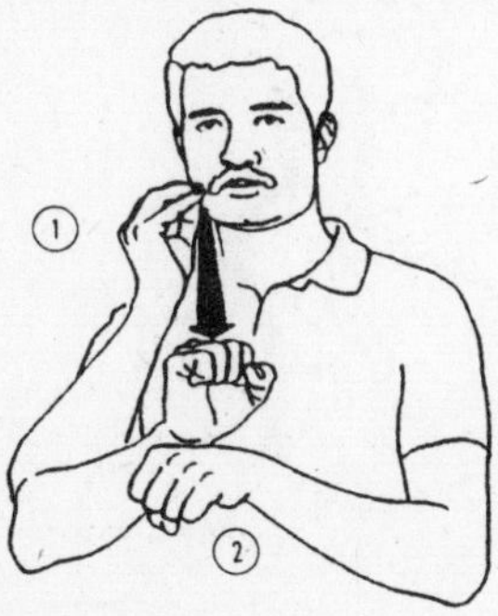

HOMEWORK
Beginning with the fingers of the right flattened "o" hand on the right cheek move the hand downward while changing to an "s" hand, ending with the heel of the right "s" hand across the back of the left "s" hand, palms facing down.
Hint: "Home" plus "work."

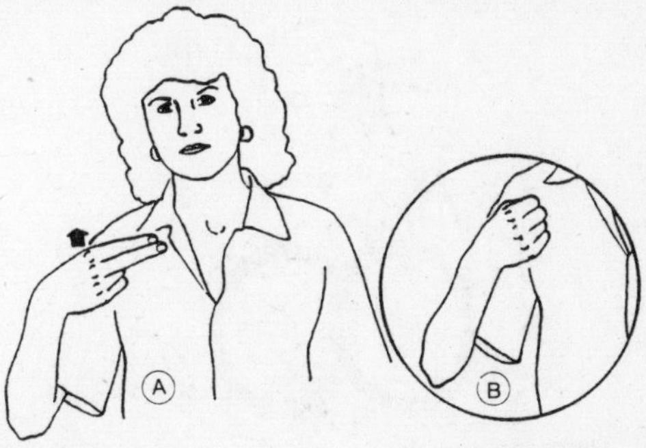

HIGH SCHOOL
Move the right "h" hand upward a short distance in front of the right side of the chest while changing into an "s" hand, palm facing in.
Hint: Abbreviation "h-s."

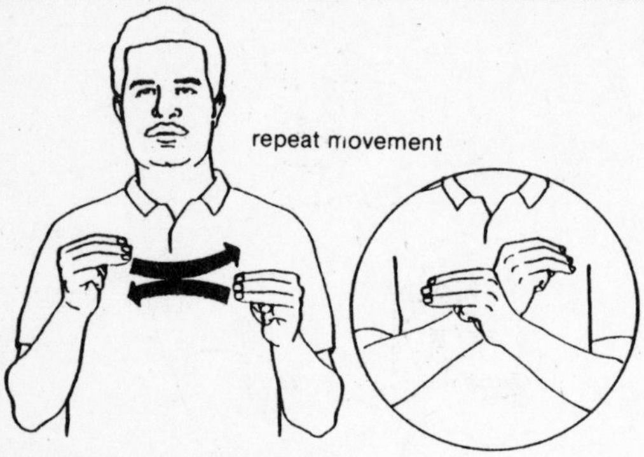

MATHEMATICS, MATH
Brush the little-finger side of the right "m" hand across the index-finger side of the left "m" hand with a double movement, both palms facing in.
Hint: Initialized sign.

HISTORY
Bring the fingers of the right "h" hand, palm facing left, downward with a double movement in front of the right side of the body.
Hint: Initialized sign.

SCIENCE
Move both "10" hands, palms facing forward, in large alternating circles in front of each side of the chest.
Hint: As if mixing chemicals.

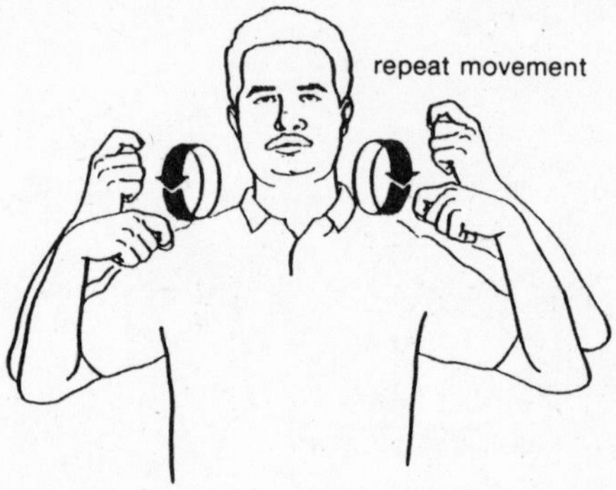

GYMNASIUM, GYM
With the index fingers and thumbs of both hands pinched together, palms facing each other, move the hands forward in repeated circles in front of each shoulder.
Hint: As if doing exercises in a gymnasium.

BIOLOGY
Move both "b" hands, palms facing forward, in large alternating circles in front of each side of the chest.
Hint: Initialized sign formed similar to sign for "science."

TEST, EXAMINATION, EXAM, QUIZ
Beginning with both extended index fingers pointing up in front of the chest, palms facing forward, bring the hands downward while bending the index fingers and then opening into "5" hands, ending with the palms facing down.
Hint: Form question marks as on an test and distribute it.

Technology

COMPUTER
Touch the thumb of the right "c" hand, palm facing left, first to the forearm and then to the upper arm of the extended left arm.
Hint: Initialized sign.

DISKETTE, DISK
Move the fingertips of the right "d" hand, palm facing down, in a circle on the palm of the open left hand held in front of the body, palm facing up.
Hint: Initialized sign showing the movement of a diskette in the disk drive.

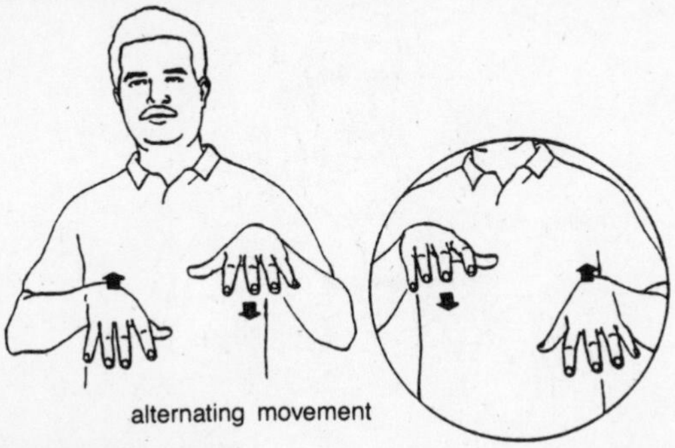

TYPEWRITER, TYPE
With both "5" hands in front of the body, palms facing down, move the hands up and down with a repeated alternating movement.
Hint: Mime typing.

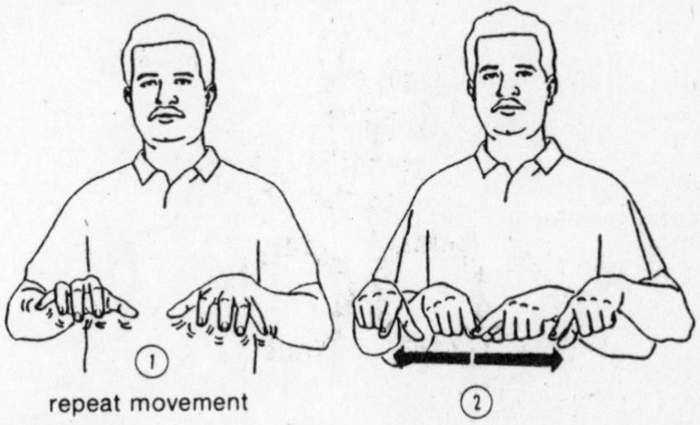

KEYBOARD
With both "5" hands in front of the body, palms facing down, wiggle the fingers up and down repeatedly. Then beginning with the extended index fingers and thumbs of both hands touching in front of the body, palms facing down, move the hands apart to each side.
Hint: The action of typing plus the shape of a keyboard.

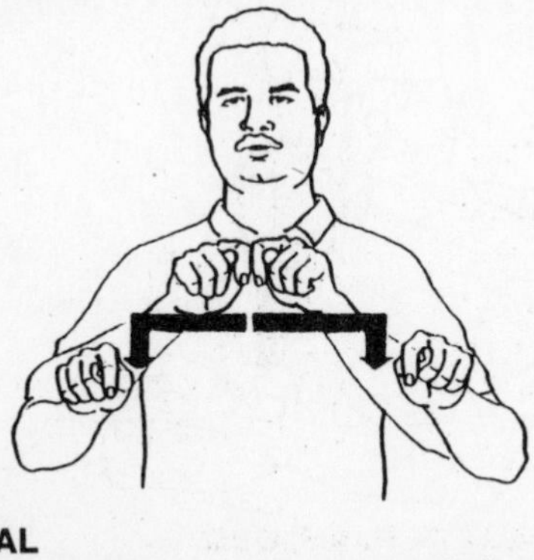

TERMINAL
Beginning with both "t" hands together in front of the chest, palms facing forward, move the hands apart to each side and then down a short distance.
Hint: Initialized sign showing the shape of a computer screen.

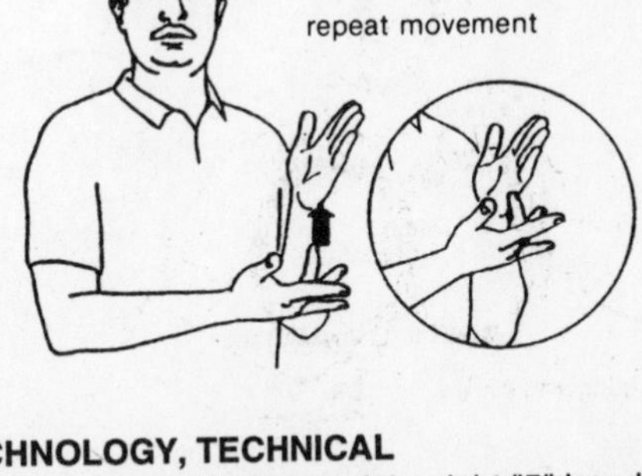

TECHNOLOGY, TECHNICAL
Tap the bent middle finger of the right "5" hand, palm facing up, with a double movement on the little-finger side of the open left hand, palm facing right.

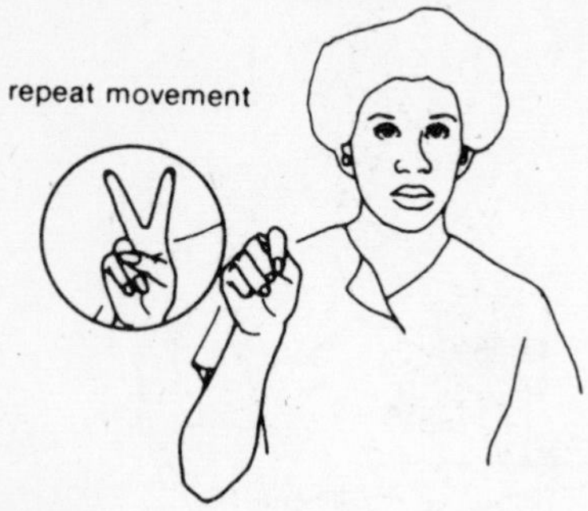

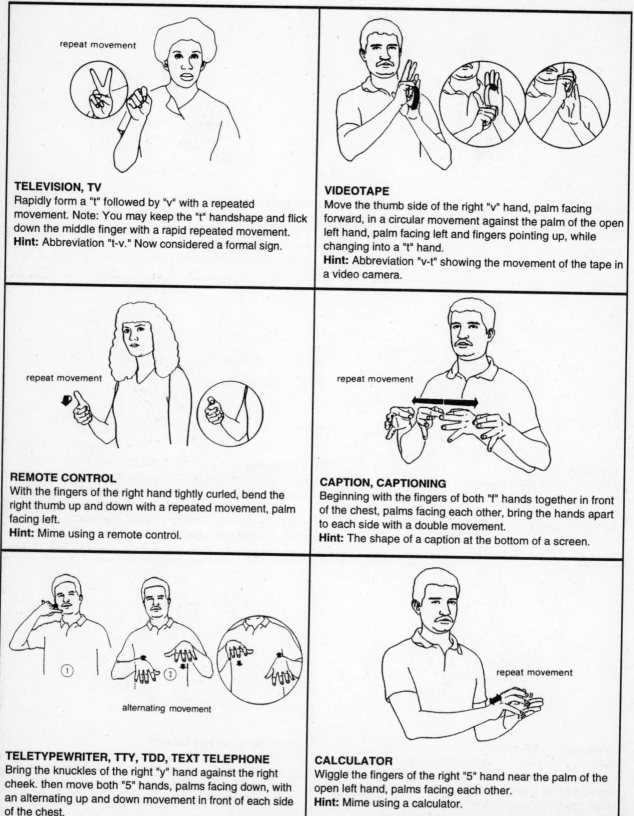

TELEVISION, TV
Rapidly form a "t" followed by "v" with a repeated movement. Note: You may keep the "t" handshape and flick down the middle finger with a rapid repeated movement.
Hint: Abbreviation "t-v." Now considered a formal sign.

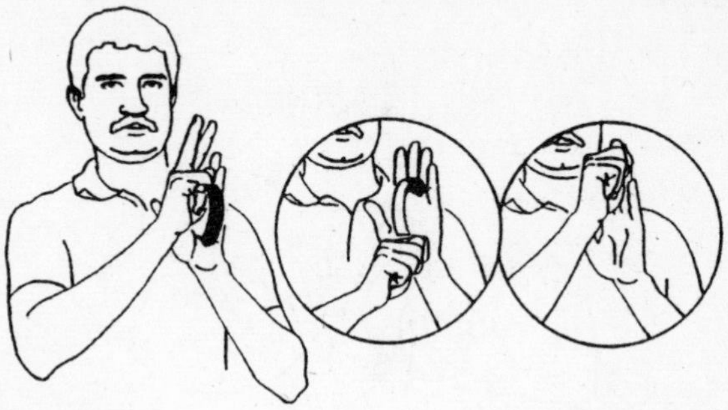

VIDEOTAPE
Move the thumb side of the right "v" hand, palm facing forward, in a circular movement against the palm of the open left hand, palm facing left and fingers pointing up, while changing into a "t" hand.
Hint: Abbreviation "v-t" showing the movement of the tape in a video camera.

REMOTE CONTROL
With the fingers of the right hand tightly curled, bend the right thumb up and down with a repeated movement, palm facing left.
Hint: Mime using a remote control.

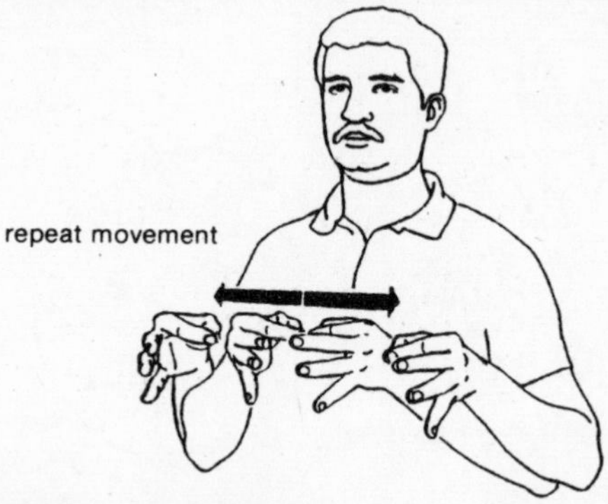

CAPTION, CAPTIONING
Beginning with the fingers of both "f" hands together in front of the chest, palms facing each other, bring the hands apart to each side with a double movement.
Hint: The shape of a caption at the bottom of a screen.

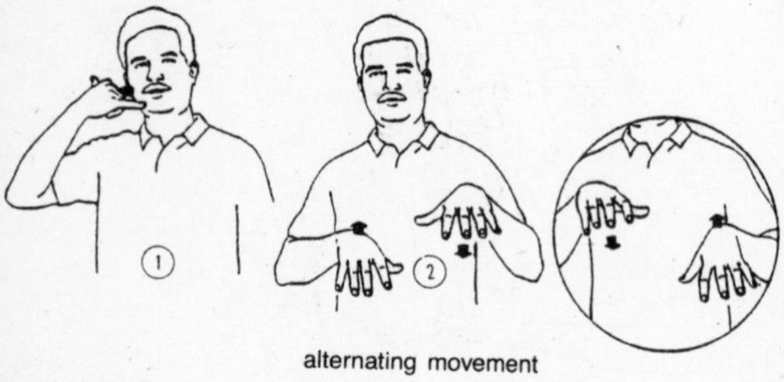

TELETYPEWRITER, TTY, TDD, TEXT TELEPHONE
Bring the knuckles of the right "y" hand against the right cheek. then move both "5" hands, palms facing down, with an alternating up and down movement in front of each side of the chest.

CALCULATOR
Wiggle the fingers of the right "5" hand near the palm of the open left hand, palms facing each other.
Hint: Mime using a calculator.

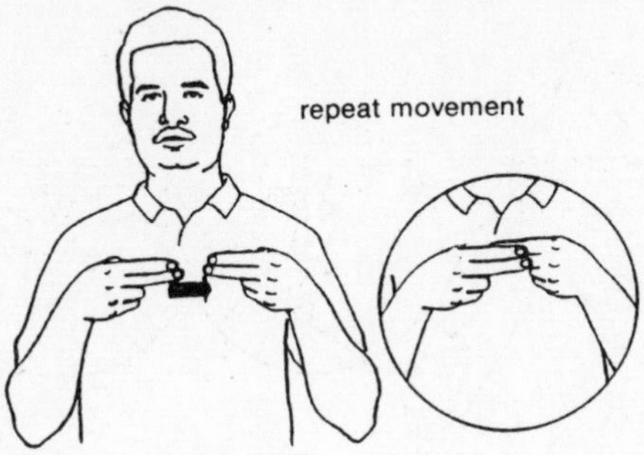

SLIDES
Slide the right "h" fingers with a double movement on the back of the left "h" fingers, palms facing in and fingers pointing toward each other.

COPIER, PHOTOCOPY, COPY
Move the right "x" hand, palm facing forward, from side to side under the open left hand, palm facing down.
Hint: The movement of the copier when making photocopies.

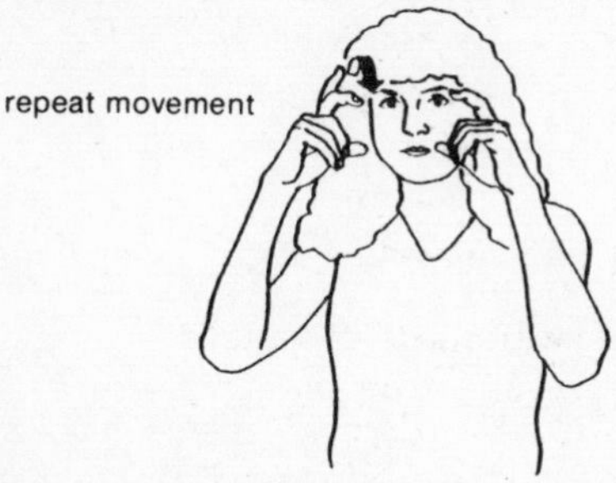

CAMERA
With the curved index fingers and thumbs of both hands near the outside of each eye, palms facing each other, bend the right index finger up and down with a double movement.
Hint: Mime snapping pictures.

MOVIE, MOTION PICTURES, FILM, SHOW
With the heel of the right "5" hand, palm facing forward and fingers pointing up, on the heel of the open left hand, palm facing the body and fingers pointing right, twist the right hand from side to side while keeping the heel in place.
Hint: The flickering of pictures on a motion picture screen.

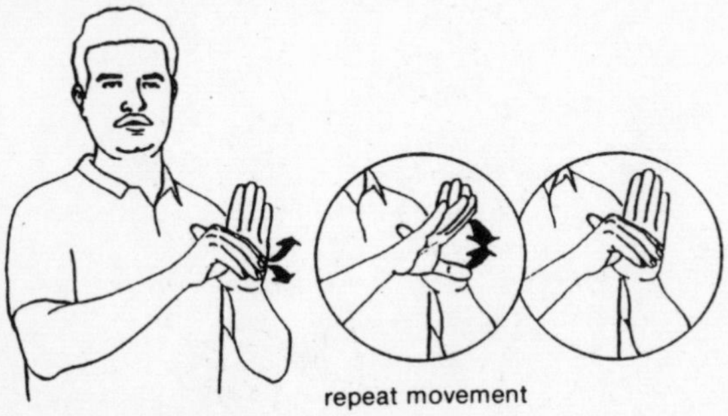

TAKE PICTURES, PHOTOGRAPH
With the thumb side of the right flattened "o" hand, palm facing down, against the palm of the open left hand, palm facing left and fingers pointing up, open and close the right fingers with a repeated movement.
Hint: The opening closing of a camera's shutter.

VIDEOTAPE, SHOOT MOVIES
With the right index finger and thumb pinched together move the right hand in a repeated forward circle near the palm of the open left hand, palm facing right and fingers pointing up.
Hint: The movement of the videotape in the camera.

index